Facing the Shadow, Embracing the Light

A Journey of Spirit Retrieval and Awakening

By Niara Terela Isley

ISBN-13: 978-1493556847
ISBN-10: 1493556843

Graphic Design by David Robison
Arvada, Colorado

Printed in the United States

Disclaimers:

I am an advisory board member of the Exopolitics Institute, since 2009. However, the views and opinions in my book are my own and do not necessarily reflect all the positions and viewpoints of that organization.

With deep gratitude and respect for the individuals whose quotes I've used in this book I state here that they are used for educational purposes and emphasis, and to support their work by generating more interest in what they offer. However, the use of such quotes in my book is not meant to imply in any way that these individuals support my book's content in part or as a whole.

Sustainability and Agenda 21

My use of the words *sustainable* and *sustainability* in this book are in no way whatsoever supporting Agenda 21. Agenda 21 tramples individual rights and freedom and would attempt to homogenize and pasteurize humanity and our planet in a way that would make us all subject to a fascist empire that wealthy elite factions on this world are working to implement.

Sustainability as defined at Dictionary.com:

1. the ability to be sustained, supported, upheld, or confirmed.

2. Environmental Science. the quality of not being harmful to the environment or depleting natural resources, and thereby supporting long-term ecological balance: The committee is developing sustainability standards for products that use energy.

Sustainability, to me, simply means that we cannot comsume, consume, consume natural resources without managing that consumption in a way that provides for whatever valuable resource to continue to be used in a way that is symbiotic, or mutually-beneficial to each organism and system. Contrast this with a host-parasite relationship where eventually the parasite kills its host because too much was taken, destroying the life of the host forever. Example: ongoing drilling for oil. It's removed from it's pocket in the Earth's crust, over and over again around the globe and burned into the atmosphere. Much like our bodies ecapsulate toxins in our fat cells, to keep them from harming other bodily systems, oil is a toxic byproduct of the breakdown of living organisms that was meant to be encapsulated and kept out of the way of living ecosystems. Drilling for oil, ravaging the environment to search for it and extract it, then burning it for fuel is not sustainable or representative of a mutually-beneficial symbiotic relationship. It is destructive to the ecosystem and living beings. Re: Agenda 21: So who decides what is sustainable or not? Sustainability is a good word and its meaning in #1 is more or less a neutral one. But when the elites use this word, THEY decide what IS or IS NOT sustainable, and the means they will implement to create a sustainable world that leaves the people of this world out in the cold. If the elites wanted true sustainability, free energy technology would be released to the whole world and they would stop their divide and conquer games with the population. They just want a version of sustainability that supports their empire, keeping the majority of humanity under their thumbs. THIS IS NOT NECESSARY. A humanity that is willing to choose love and connection over power and control can learn to steward our Earth, while adapting to living in harmony with her various ecosystems.

Love, especially the practice of unselfish and as much as possible, unconditional love, is an all-inclusive state of being where love directs one's course and all considerations for caring for ourselves, our families and our communities. Love will cause us to take as many thoughtful considerations into account as can be thought of or imagined to protect what we love and what enhances our survival and our ability to thrive. The practice of love for all life, and all living beings will bring us a meaningful version of sustainability, stewarding this planet for ourselves and the next seven generations to come.

Forward by Mary Rodwell

Part One: The Experiences

Prologue

Chapter 1: The Shadow and The Light

Chapter 2: Strange, Different, Other... Star Child

Chapter 3: Rights of Passage into Womanhood

Chapter 4: Part of my Life is Missing

Chapter 5: The Ground Jerked from Beneath My Feet

Chapter 13: Confronting Political, Societal and Cultural Demons

Chapter 14: Going Public

Part Three: Awakening

Chapter 15: Awakening

Chapter 16: A Precious Visit "Home"

Chapter 17: Quickening

Chapter 22: Anatomy of the Human Psyche: Spirit, Mind, Emotions

Chapter 23: Resonance, Dissonance and Discernment

Chapter 24: Energy and Vibration, Flow and Healing

Chapter 25: Spiritual Evolution Through the The Quantum Mirror

Dedications:

This book is lovingly dedicated to my friend and star brother, Robert O. Dean;

To any friends or family I may have hurt or injured in my earlier years of living in fear, emotional pain and insecurity;

To those souls who have been harmed by trauma-based mind control, perhaps also further suffering due to the subsequent challenges of trying to heal in a culture that does not want to acknowledge you out of fear of the darker side of our society that you and your trauma represent;

And finally, I dedicate this book to my grown-up children here on Earth, and to any of my star children who may yet live... May your own awakenings find you all, and light your way.

And to all of humanity... may you discover who you truly are and realize your fullest potential.

Dr. Michael Salla

Niara Isley has travelled a remarkable journey. While working with the US Air Force as a radar specialist she saw things that many would scarcely believe possible. Her experiences confirm that there is an extraterrestrial presence and that elements of the US Government cooperate closely with aliens. Her experiences have been far from positive, in fact they have been traumatic and left deep scars. Yet Niara has chosen to speak out about her experiences in a way that promotes her healing, spiritual growth and life journey. She has indeed chosen to embrace the light, and face the shadow as the title of this book so nicely encapsulates. For doing so we owe Niara Isley a great debt of gratitude.

~ Michael E. Salla, Ph.D., Founder, Exopolitics Institute and author of several books including *Exposing U.S. Government Policies on Extraterrestrial Life: The Challenge of Exopolitics and Kennedy's Last Stand: Roots of JFK Assassination Lie in What He Saw in 1945*

Gratitudes and Acknowledgments:

There is quite a list of people I am grateful to for their wonderful help and support during the grueling process of writing down the pages of my book, more than I can list here, and the list I'm putting down here is in no way full or comprehensive. I want to thank, from my heart, Janet Sailor for her invaluable assistance in proofing and editing, and for having me speak at the 2009 Paranormal Symposium; Galaxy Dancer for her additional help with proofing and editing; Mary Rodwell of Australia, founder of the Australian Close Encounter Resource Network (ACERN) for her wonderful support and for writing the foreward for my book; Chris Loomis for his 2011 photos and allowing me to use one for the cover of my book; David Robison for his beautiful book cover design, and his patience with me as we tweaked it as well as for formatting this book for publication. Other friends who provided wonderful support to me: Gloria Hawker for her kindness and understanding, inspiring the trust I needed to explore my memories further; Richard Dolan, Rebecca Hardcastle-Wright, Terje Toftenes, Michael Salla and Mark Kimmel for their kind endorsements of my book; and my friend Fred Burks, one of the brilliant and compassionate minds behind an absolute web-based encyclopedia of information, http://wanttoknow.info/ – things we all NEED TO KNOW about the world we live in – and for his friendship and support in helping me to more fully understand and come to terms with the trauma I experienced. I also want to thank loving and supportive friends Miesha Johnston, Betsy Allen, Crystal Andasola – an extraordinary psychic, Donna Chadwick, Michael Salla, Lakshmi Van Atta, the late Budd Hopkins, Aamann DeGarth, Dee Gragg, Katee McClure, Stacey Wright and Jim Mann of Phoenix MUFON, Generessa Rose, author, shaman, intuitive healer for her work with me in spirit retrieval, Michelle Emerson, Jovita Wallace, Cynthia Crawford, Jujuoli Kuita, Ann Ulrich Miller, who helped me with my hypnosis session transcriptions, and healer and fellow Earth-bound Lyran, Steve Anderson. I also thank friends and associates Kim Carlsburg, Tom Ascher, Annie DeRiso, Kevin Smith, Mark Snider, Melinda Leslie, Jocelyn Buckner, Mel Fabrigas, John Rhodes for our talk at the Las Vegas, NV restaurant that day years ago, as well as John Lear and George Knapp, Dr. Cynthia Miller, Nancy DeYoung, modern shaman; Bob Brown of the International UFO Congress for having me speak at the Congress in 2010 in Laughlin, NV and my friend "Kathy" from Australia for introducing me to him; and last, but absolutely not least, I want to thank John Hughes for his love and support and the irrepressible light, joy and fun he has brought into my life.

My sincere and heartfelt gratitude goes out into the ethers to Dana Redfield. I read her book, The ET-Human Link in 2007 and felt such a kinship with her, that I immediately searched her out on the internet. She had passed away just months earlier. I'm sure we could have been fast friends, maybe even would have recognized each other from adventures together out in astral space. The manner in which she wrote her book, painstakingly exploring her inner life, gave me the courage to also write down my inner explorations in book form.

Forward
Facing the Shadow, Embracing the Light

Mary Rodwell

'Apocalypse': a time of revelation or disclosure.

~ *Chambers dictionary*

There is no question that our beautiful planet Earth is in crisis. The effects of ecological disasters, global warming, wars and famine are reported daily. Many people believe this heralds the Apocalypse, a time of revelation or disclosure. And the most profound disclosure, in my opinion, has to be the revelation we are not alone, that our planet has been visited, and is still being visited by non-human intelligences. This information is apparent to anyone who sincerely seeks the truth, and yet the majority of humanity is still unaware this is so.

Scientific data confirms there are billions of potentially habitable planetary systems in our Universe. Logic dictates some of these planets must nurture intelligent life. The possibility that some of these extraterrestrial civilizations are sufficiently advanced to become space faring species is quite obvious. After all, we are close to this event ourselves. But the most compelling evidence we are not alone and never have been is clearly documented in prehistoric cave drawings and medieval art. They provide graphic examples which clearly show we have been visited for millennia. Many ancient manuscript texts, from Sumeria onwards, tell of human interaction with non-human intelligences. Religious manuscripts and mythology abound with tales of the "Gods" visiting earth. Gods who have demonstrated advanced technologies and accounts of interbreeding with humans. Indigenous cultures speak openly of their encounters with the "star visitors," and have been told by them of their biological connections to them, evidenced in our human DNA, which also suggest we are a hybrid species of intelligent design.

The recent release of thousands of government files of UFO sightings, from over a dozen countries, contains more compelling visual data and human testimony that craft of "unknown origin" are seen and photographed daily, across the globe. The most compelling of all has to be that hundreds of thousands of credible people have admitted to encounters with extraterrestrial intelligences. It is strange that despite this huge body of evidence, the general public, and media, remain skeptical. Why is this?

The answer in part at least, lies in western sociological, educational, scientific and societal programming which discriminates against any human experience which does not comply with agreed consensus reality. Experiences of a multidimensional nature, whether it be via intuition, psychic abilities or other states of consciousness, are still regarded as abnormal, or suspect. Therefore any person who experiences realities outside of the third dimensional paradigm such as sighting of UFOs or seeing extraterrestrial beings, will struggle to have their experiences accepted as real. However, what is not generally known is that one of the prime reasons for this skepticism is primarily due to a deliberate program of disinformation, and denial orchestrated by powerful covert government agencies who know the truth. Agencies who deliberately invalidate the visual evidence and witness testimony, for a number of self-serving reasons. A well-orchestrated covert agenda uses both propaganda and disinformation, coupled with ridicule, which is designed to negate the evidence we have been in Contact with these intelligences for well over 60 years.

The majority of the public are not so naive as to believe governments tell them the truth. Thanks to such mediums as the internet we are a more informed society, and have found that we are mostly given edited and sanitized information. But, despite this it still strains public credulity to believe that any government could lie about something so profound as extraterrestrial visitation. Especially a cover up of such magnitude and one that has lasted over 60 years! I have to say that I, like most people, would not have questioned it either, if it was not until literally hundreds of people have shared with me their extraterrestrial encounters. Their stories were so convincing, I had good reason to seek the evidence for the UFO reality. Since that time I met many individuals involved in the cover-up, such as former intelligence operatives, pilots and military personnel, even some who had seen crashed space craft and the occupants. All of them told me they were silenced under the official secrets act. There was genuine and deep fear for their lives or for the lives of their family if they revealed what they had seen. This fact alone makes it easier to understand how the cover-up has been maintained.

I certainly understand that most people, without being exposed to this information, could remain incredulous. But, if you genuinely wish to seek the truth, and if you can keep your incredulity at bay for a time, and be open to what you don't know, then this book is for you. *Facing the Shadow, Embracing the Light: A Journey of Spirit Retrieval and Awakening* will stretch your paradigm to its limits, but exposes a huge cover-up of Contact reality and how it has been maintained. It qualifies the phrase that truth is stranger than fiction. This book encompasses not only profound details of extraterrestrial contact, physical and non-physical, as well as information about agendas and complex programs by these extraterrestrials to encourage the progression and evolution of humanity.

For me the most disturbing and troubling is the awareness that a small group of self-serving humans have managed to keep this secret from the rest of humanity. The orchestrated cover-up is of such magnitude it is hard to accept it is even possible; a cover-up that can only be understood when one is aware of the profound implications of disclosure. The enormity of the possible changes is encapsulated in a statement from the late Colonel Philip J. Corso (formerly of the U.S. Military) recalling a meeting with an extraterrestrial outside a military base in the U.S.A. Col. Corso asked this extraterrestrial being:

So what's in it for us?

The extraterrestrial replied: A new world, if you can take it.

A new world, if we can take it! It was clear that by admitting to the reality of Contact, life as we know it would change forever, economically, sociologically and spiritually. The economic structure alone would be challenged by advanced technologies as to liken our technology to stone axes in comparison to present day computers. Technologies which could provide limitless clean energy, without reliance on fossil fuels. Technologies to control the weather and make deserts fertile. If we were to make use of such technologies, the present financial and economic structure based on dependence of fossil fuels, would be obsolete overnight. It doesn't take a genius to realize what this would mean to the power brokers on this planet who control the world's economy and political systems through our dependence on these resources. It creates a scenario that understandably would not be welcomed by those with a stake in the present status quo. When people ask me why is there a cover-up, it is not until people explore the implications and how the structure of our society operates, and how the distribution of wealth and power is held and controlled by a very small percentage of our species, that the reasons become clear. You only have to ask who has the most to lose if new technologies were introduced. Sadly the benefit of the few, has become the loss for the rest of humanity. And progress to a cleaner, more sustainable future and a healthy environment became a very poor second to self-interest and greed. A decision, that once made, was devastating not only for our planet, but those in our society who have been denied their reality.

There are many complex reasons why the cover up was deemed preferable to disclosure, apart from economic. The impacts on our present consensus reality and belief systems, for example, profound implications for religion and science. I believe the cover-up was understandable, at least at the beginning, because those in authority certainly needed more information as to the agendas of these intelligences apart from the psychological shock to our human psyche. The social, political and economic ramifications are huge; everything we believe about ourselves and our world would be irretrievably changed.

The outcome of this cover-up is that the biggest secret in human history has been kept from the public, enabled by a select few with the power, wealth, and resources to maintain it. Sixty years later, the impact of that decision has been catastrophic, not only because it continued our dependence on fossil fuels, which has left us with a planet in crisis ecologically. But the toll in human suffering is incalculable, as millions of people have their encounter experiences ridiculed. Humiliated, or alternatively perceived as mentally ill, these individuals will continually question their sanity. The cover-up has also meant that any individuals who spoke too openly about their encounters, were intimidated by secret intelligence operatives. Many had their phones tapped and were told to keep silent about their encounters! For some this was taken to new, disturbing, levels of trauma. They have been terrorized with physical abduction by covert military agencies, and taken to underground facilities to be drugged, bullied, interrogated and re-programmed to ensure silence. These programs are called MILAB [military and pseudo extraterrestrial abductions perpetrated by military and intelligence agencies] and they operate under the guise of protecting national security. Such strategies ensured the individual is not only disbelieved but their story is unbelievable. The truth is stranger than any fiction, and Niara's story is one of these.

I was drawn into this phenomenon, with little knowledge of its reality other than my eclectic taste in reading, and later witness testimony from my clients. This highlighted for me that an enormous number of people have a broad range of multidimensional experiences outside of accepted consensus reality. These experiences range from non-ordinary states of being, an ability to perceive beyond the normal visual range, such as seeing spirits, energies around people (auras) and out-of-body events. My first client with extraterrestrial encounters came to see me because he had heard that I was open-minded to anomalous experiences. I have never forgotten his first words, "There are support groups for everything, but with this there is nothing, people just think you are a loony!" Articulate and intelligent, he showed me the strange physical markers on his body such as shaved areas after encounters, and extraterrestrial images imprinted on his body, such as finger marks, and small unexplained implants. Later he went to find a rational explanation from Oxford University professors. They couldn't offer him any understanding and certainly not why these experiences also involved his partner and her children.

My eclectic reading had led me to Professor of Psychiatry at Harvard University, the late Dr. John E. Mack and his book, *Abduction: Human Encounters with Aliens*. This scholarly work explored the Contact phenomenon in great depth and in a therapeutic language. He had performed a battery of psychological tests and was left with little doubt these individuals were quite sane and that their encounters were real. To obtain more information and support locally, I took my client's case to counseling supervision in which many professionals from a number of disciplines were involved. It was interesting to note that it was never suggested he was psychiatrically unwell. But, ironically, it allowed the supervision group the freedom to share their own multidimensional experiences. A revelation which demonstrated to me how many of us have experiences outside of consensus reality. Soon after this I found that my first client had become the catalyst to opening a Pandora's box, and within a few weeks I was contacted by individuals with similar accounts. My first support group attracted 12 people. I discovered that the more I understood the patterns of encounters I realized what we have is a phenomenon that involved numbers beyond belief.

Since my first client with encounters, over nineteen hundred people have resourced the Australian Close Encounters Research Network (ACERN). Research has shown this experience to be inter-generational. Families, parents and children share encounters. It also affects all cultures and belief systems and does not rely on beliefs of aliens and UFOs to experience it. And like Niara, they did not have to believe in UFOs and extraterrestrials to see them, the encounters led them to KNOW what they have experienced is real. Sadly many of those that have sought traditional help received psychiatric labels, such as dysfunctional, fantasy-prone or schizophrenic. It is for good reason the majority keep their experiences secret, apart from sharing with a few trusted family members or close friends. The burden of isolation and trauma can become too difficult to bear. It is pot luck if they stumble on a open-minded and aware professional. In fact I suggest to my clients that a few well placed questions can provide answers to whether they are going to receive real open-minded support from professionals. It can be invaluable to check whether the person from whom they seek understanding accepts the limits of traditional psychology, or recognizes the validity of out-of-body states (OBE), astral travel, psi multidimensional abilities, or alternate states of consciousness. If not, it's pot luck as to interpretation, and many have had unfortunate outcomes from traditional psychological support because of this.

Although my former training in nursing and midwifery offered me a good understanding of the human body and how it functioned, it also demonstrated limits to our understanding regarding the role that emotions play in disease, such as how stress and emotional trauma weakens the immune system. My training in counseling provided a broader understanding of the source of illness and offered a more holistic approach to health. The skill of hypnosis became a tool of choice when seeking answers from the subconscious. This approach not only offered the conscious mind new data as to the cause of illnesses, but also an understanding of multidimensional experiences and explained some fears or phobias, including those related to non-human encounters.

The process of emotional support for any difficult human experience or trauma doesn't vary, the traumatized person asks to be heard without judgment. Trauma from the classic "abduction" scenario when the individual has encounters with small "grey" beings, and is escorted onto space craft stems not only from the "other-worldliness" of the experience, but often the lack of control in the encounter. What compounds this is a denial of their reality and experience by society, which brings in further isolation. A non-judgmental acceptance of their experience brings release from isolation and new feelings of empowerment and integration. Of course questions such as "why me?" and "what's it all about?" create for some the desire to explore their encounters from a deeper level. Hypnosis can offer information that can be both transformative and revelatory. This deeper process offers explanations as to "why" them, what happens on the craft and why. This may show medical and healing procedures or educational teaching elements for example, that they had been totally unaware of before this exploration. It also helps them understand their intuitive abilities, the awareness of other realms, and why they felt so different to everyone else. This kind of exploration often proved to be totally transformative in their outlook on their world as it totally changed their paradigm.

I discovered that there are many forms of encounter. My research brought data that suggested that they did not so much fear the extraterrestrials, but feared humans. Conversely they also felt more connected to extraterrestrials than their own species. I use the term "star seeds" for this group. They tell me that they "feel" very different, and disconnected from their biological family. They can exhibit psychic abilities such as telepathy, healing and awareness of other realms. They have a strong sense of mission or purpose, and feel they are here to help humanity in some way. Many of them tell me that they struggle with the density of Earth, and the primitive nature of humans. Their trauma stems from living in a human body with other humans. The late Dana Redfield, a friend and fellow author, described her feelings this way in my book *Awakening*:

> How do you tackle the fear of humans aspect? Maybe it surfaces as the consciousness expands and we realize how dangerous humans can be. It's all arms length until you have reason to protect yourself from the dangerous human. This is not the threat with a gun or terrorist kidnap, but ridicule, deceit, and ostracism, which can be just as harmful. This is alienation in the extreme, because who can we trust to talk to about it?
>
> Dana Redfield, experiencer, author of *Summoned and The Human-ET Link*.

This statement echoes Niara's experience. She has suffered the same sense of alienation, ridicule and ostracism when she was seeking support. But, in Niara's case, her trauma is compounded by the realization she was also abducted by humans. Abducted and terrorized in such a way as to make her story so far from accepted reality as to be unbelievable to most people. It was so unbelievable she struggled to accept it actually happened. She was fully aware that, extraterrestrial experiences aside, her accounts of human abduction would be easier to believe if perpetrated by a third world country or dictatorship. But, to have her own countrymen believe this happens in a nation which promises to protect human rights and defend individual freedom? To believe what she experienced was real and that her own countrymen could get away with such dreadful abuses of human rights without suffering any legal consequences, under the cover of protecting national security? To believe such covert programs kept profound secrets from the elected governments, even their own presidents as well as the public? It is not a picture that the patriot wants to believe or accept. Niara was a patriot, until she experienced MILAB abductions and betrayal by her very own countrymen. It was deeply traumatic to accept such betrayal occurred, and far easier to deny. But having said that, when Niara tried to heal from her pain she knew the body does not lie, and her body wasn't lying when it was triggered, re-awakening these buried traumas. To heal, Niara had to accept the truth. It is so much easier to accept non-humans are the bad guys, than to believe the bad guys are your own people. This realization takes Niara to the edge of life.

To seek the truth, one needs dedication and focus. It seems Niara and others such as her have this quality in abundance, an absolute tenacity in seeking the truth. Niara discovered her MILAB experiences are a recognized phenomenon, and a percentage of individuals with extraterrestrial encounters also suffer MILAB abductions. Although some Ufological researchers are still uninformed of this, many are understandably reluctant to explore this dark but human aspect of the phenomenon. After all, exposing such covert programs can prove damaging to one's health, as a number of researchers have discovered, and not all have lived to tell the tale.

My first exposure to MILAB abductions was when I was facilitating a workshop for a large group of experiencers, as part of the support offered by the International UFO Congress, Laughlin, Nevada U.S.A. I discovered that the most traumatized were those with MILAB abduction experiences. I also found similar accounts of MILAB covert operations in other countries, such as the UK, Europe and Australia. MILAB and other agencies do their best to cover their tracks, to prevent anyone exposing their operations. This is helped by the very "unbelievable" content of the story itself. Unless one has experienced it, most would struggle to believe it exists. This is coupled with intimidation and debunking of encounters. One organization that is alleged to be part of this is the Central Intelligence Agency (CIA), which came into being in 1947 after the Roswell cover-up. Part of its mandate was to continue the secrecy, and one way was to produce plausible explanations for anyone recalling military abductions. The label "false memory syndrome" was successfully employed to debunk any recall that could lead people to researching the MILAB operations and provide an answer to anyone retrieving such data.

In the many years of my counseling and hypnotherapy practice I have never encountered the false memory syndrome as described by the CIA. If the information is unusual or strange it is generally because it can conflict with present consensus reality. This doesn't make the data invalid because we can't quantify it through the present third dimensional lens. Naturally we struggle with data we cannot corroborate in the normal way. But the subconscious has no such dilemma, and has no need to filter the data as the conscious mind does, to edit out what is unacceptable. The subconscious has the freedom to multidimensional experience. It can be uncomfortable and challenging, but that doesn't mean it lacks validity or integrity, only that it conflicts with our dimensional programming. The parameters for its integrity are a deep resonance to the data by the individual, and an inner knowing of its truth, no matter how it may challenge their conscious beliefs.

This open subconscious exploration has offered valuable insights for many other issues, such as strange phobias and hidden trauma. And it may lead to data that can suggest a "past life" or non-human soul experience in another dimension. The more general use of these techniques has shown that, despite some extraordinary data revealed this way, it demonstrates a broader understanding as to the multidimensional nature of human experience. It is now being explored by the more open-minded psychiatrists and psychologists, resorting to hypnosis to seek the origins of traumas, even if it suggests past life experiences. Some of these professionals have since authored books demonstrating the validity and remarkable healing following this process. To quell some misconceptions of hypnosis in relation to extraterrestrial encounters the late Dr. John Mack stated that, in his opinion, "subconscious recall is likely to be far more accurate than conscious recall, because the conscious mind 'filters out' what conflicts with consensus reality."

Although Niara's extensive recall of her star seed origins is not possible to verify, other than it has a deep resonance for her, it does offer similarities to other experiencers recalling past lives as non-humans. I have heard many accounts where individuals have been shown their home planet, and feel a deep emotional connection to what they have seen and their "star family." Logically, given the richness, complexity and detail of Niara's accounts, I find it very compelling, and far beyond what I would deem as imagination. For those more skeptical of such accounts, it is interesting to note that this is not coming from the person's beliefs, but from both spontaneous emergence in memory throughout her life and recall in deep hypnosis. Regardless of whether there is a belief in reincarnation or extraterrestrials or not, the data will often conflict with their conscious beliefs. And furthermore, it seems that no matter how confronting the material is to their conscious beliefs, it will often have great meaning and will resonate at a deep level, evoking a tangible emotional and spiritual experience. In my opinion it is unlikely that such huge emotional reactions would stem from a fantasy or imagination. It is important to note that some of my clients do not believe in UFOs or aliens, but in hypnosis will find themselves on board a space craft. This has happened on numerous occasions where a client has come to see me to explore the origin of some trauma, nothing related to this phenomenon, but found themselves on board a space craft.

Hypnosis is a valid and effective tool, a useful tool that allows us a real window into the encounter phenomenon. It offers understanding that can create conditions for a spiritual awakening and transformational process. An understanding of the bigger picture, and the soul journey. Despite the complexity and variety, and sometimes trauma, of contact, it appears that the outcome will often become transformative. It is perceived by individuals as a 'wake up" call to their multidimensional nature. With integration and acceptance, coupled with new understanding, they will often lose their fear. Communication with the star visitors, expansion of their reality, healing skills, precognition, and clairvoyance emerge. These have been previously hidden or denied due to their fear of the unknown. The deeper exploration offers explanations that make sense, such as the reason for medical and healing procedures. It offers understanding of educational programs on the craft and the downloads of complex information. Their spiritual awakening seems to parallel a shamanic journey, with similar outcomes, such as an ability to perceive a multidimensional reality, with similar intuitive gifts as the shaman, such as healing and psychic abilities. They, like the shaman, learn to transcend human fears, and can operate in a multidimensional reality.

Niara knows her story will stretch the bounds of credibility. But for the more informed, and those with similar experiences, it will resonate. She makes no concessions for those of limited beliefs or judgments as she openly and honestly shares her human journey. Niara writes: "... if people can be induced to believe that all they are is skin and meat wrapped around a skeletal structure, (not that they are a soul inhabiting a body) they can be frightened into compliance with any number of institutional agendas." As she continued her healing and integration process, inquiring more deeply into her experiences and why they happened, the resonant understanding emerged that the events of her lifetime were a pre-birth agreement. When Niara asked her spirit guides what her personal path of service could be, they said, "Tell your story." Niara's heart-felt intention in sharing her difficult experiences and process; "I just hope that my contribution in some small way helps others, and helps our world become a better place, and shows others what is possible when you move beyond your fears."

Niara's multidimensional experiences shattered much of her reality programming in the same way the shamanic journey does. But like the shaman, they became the catalyst that facilitated for her new freedoms to explore and make sense of her experiences, as she expanded her new awareness of the non-physical realms. This also provided her with the comfort of on-going communication with her non- human family, which continues to support and nurture her. Niara's insights from her past lives, her perspective of the soul journey, are profound. One cannot but be moved by her courageous journey to healing. It will resonate with many who have undertaken a healing journey and offers understanding of the power of the healer within.

Niara's non-physical explorations have given her a new perspective to her life, and expanded her awareness of both her human and soul journey on this planet. She learns that she is a wanderer, an extraterrestrial soul who chose to incarnate as human. Her mission is to act as a conduit for us to learn about ourselves, and to report her experiences to her star family so that they can better understand humanity. I have met a number of star seeds who admit to similar roles —that they are recorders of human behavior and regularly and astrally report this data to their star family. Certainly, if this is the case, it would give our extraterrestrials insight from a human perspective which must be very valuable as a tool to understanding us.

I feel a deep gratitude to Niara and those like her who have the courage to share their story without apology. It is a story the public needs to hear, whether they want to hear it or not. How Niara survived to write her story is extraordinary in itself. The healing journey she undertook, although it exposed the abuse she suffered, also offered her the understanding of her star seed origins and soul mission. She learned that through her experiences with MILAB, she would be a voice for real disclosure, and her mission is to reveal the truth of the lies and deceit by these covert groups. In her transformative, healing journey, traumatic yet revealing, it offered her new understanding and the reason for her experiences. Coupled with recall of her star family she discovered, difficult as it has been, the purpose of her soul mandate – to expose the truth of our human shadow, and to stand up to the powerful and corrupt few who are denying our right to our true heritage, the heritage of all of humanity.

I finally met Niara in person at the19th International UFO Congress, in Laughlin, Nevada, 2010. Her presentation was both uplifting and inspiring. She demonstrated her deep understanding of the human journey, and her brave warrior spirit. The star seed was fully evident. It is a privilege to support her. I know her story will help many who have been too traumatized to disclose their own experiences, and I hope it will give them courage to do the same. This is not a story of a victim, but of a true warrior spirit, a courageous spirit who is helping humanity to evolve, and encourages us to be all we can be! With truth and revelation comes understanding. Niara has the courage to share her truth, and through that revelation inspires us to do the same, to speak our truth and be all we can be, and this will bring light to the darkness.

Bravo, Niara for bringing us your light!

Part One: The Experiences

Prologue

Light the story fires.
Light the sacred sage and cedar,
Smell the sweetgrass.
Be at peace.

Join this circle with full hearts.
Come with open hearts.
Sit with clear hearts.
Listen with strong hearts.

See me.
I am tying my ankle to a stake in the earth
That I may make my stand with courage.
I am taking back my power
From those who stole it long ago.

Hear me.
This is my medicine story
For the healing of my spirit.
This is stone medicine, of memory,
And water medicine, of hidden depths.

Hear me.
This is my prayer to Sky Father, to Earth Mother.
This is what happened long ago.
This is what has been forgotten,
And must now be remembered.
This is what has been hidden,
And must now be revealed.

Hear me.
This is for all people everywhere.

Medicine Story
~ Niara Terela Isley

This is my medicine story. In some Native American tribes, a warrior would stake himself to the ground, an act meaning he would not run from battle, but stay until he was victorious or until he stepped onto the Blue road of Spirit, of the Ancestors. In a way, I feel I am doing this by writing this all down for others to read.

This book a chronicle of my experiences from early childhood up to today, to help me examine the threads of light and dark that are woven throughout my life, to help me better understand them. Pouring my experiences out here, how I felt about them, tried to cope with them, and at last how I had to face up to all of them, is very much a catharsis that I hope will bring yet a new level of healing. Finally, this book is also meant to educate others about the kinds of things that go on in our country, as a warning to pay attention. At the same time it's also a call to a collective spiritual awakening that can empower us all to remake the world as we would have it; peaceful, abundant, caring and cooperative at every level.

This book should be considered as two books in one. Pseudonyms have been substituted for the names of some people so they can retain their privacy. The first two parts cover my experiences, trying to comprehend them and how they could happen, and to begin to heal from them. In Part Three I share the insights and awakenings from my years of healing and continued study in what I hope is a practical, useful and empowering way for my readers. I do my best to connect intersecting points and make sense of a world filled with hypocrisies and contradictions that present such thorny challenges for those of us who long for a better world, yet are daily forced to confront the power of controlling elite factions that threaten us all. How do we reconcile "what is" with what we would like to envision? I hope I can present a few ways in which to work with "what is" in ways that can actually inform and create the kind of world we would love to have for ourselves, our children and our future generations.

Several pieces of writing appear here and there in this book that I call *Entr'actes;* intervals between the telling of my story in the here and now. These are "memories" that have flowed from deep within me in a spontaneous way, different times throughout this lifetime from my early 20s. I have written them down as best as I could. I don't know if I have gotten them all in absolute accuracy as a record of a distant Earth past, or a history that predates Earth. But the writing of these words often moved me to poignant tears of joy and pain, at times actually weeping for losses I felt as deeply as any in my present life. Emotions stirred by a deep love of the Earth and all life that resides here. Whatever the accuracy of the actual words, I feel there is some thread of truth running through them. If you can, simply open to wonder about possibilities that extraterrestrials or extra-dimensionals could be walking among us. How better to get a true grasp of what life on Earth is like for humanity? Without upsetting society, culture or economics? If I truly am a Lyran ET wearing a human form on this planet today, and my memories are in any way a reflection of a true past, then I have a deep and heart-felt interest in things unfolding in the best possible way for humanity.

There are many footnotes with website links throughout this book referencing the myriad subjects I discuss in these pages. Please look to these footnotes as a springboard for beginning your own investigations of what I've written here.

Throughout the book, I capitalize the words Universe, Conscious Loving Universe, Source, Creator and so on, as I take the view that the whole Universe is itself a conscious, living being within which we all have our existence and live out the endless facets of our lives, contributing to the knowing of the Whole.

From my own healing, discovery and awakening process, profound insights have come forth. So, this book is also to educate others about Extraterrestrial Contact – and the common energetic ground in which it can take place. In one sense contact has been ongoing throughout the ages on this planet. In another sense, it is something we are moving towards in a fuller way, a more open way for all. We need to stand ready to meet our star neighbors as a newly mature species, not as a backward race of children still emotionally out of control. To meet them as equals, not projecting any mistaken godhood upon them.

Retired Sergeant Major Robert O. Dean[1], who I had the privilege and honor of meeting in February 2009, said in a little video I watched online that he feels "they" will be coming soon and the people are not ready. This book is my gift to help people become ready, stepping fully into my role as an emissary for the Star Nations of the Light, as I believe Robert Dean is as well. He, like myself, was a member of the military. He brings a wide spectrum viewpoint to this phenomenon, a spectrum that includes everything from military/government cover-ups to humanity's spiritual awakening and expansion of consciousness as a collective.

This book will help illuminate the kinds of human rights abuses that go on behind the wall of National Security Act of 1947 secrecy. One more voice joining others to reveal the horrific things that go on under this proverbial big black rock – and many of these others have been subjected to much worse treatment than I was. You can take "under" almost literally if you consider that so much occurs in underground bases. Once these things are revealed in a way that can no longer be ignored, then – and only then – can true change have a chance of happening. Truth does set us free and the gift of that freedom is true choice... if we have the courage to act.

Government cover-ups and disinformation campaigns have been the deliberate shaping of public opinion on UFOs and extraterrestrials to be one of ridicule and denial. If people saw something that the military/government hierarchy did not want them to see, they would disbelieve their own eyes and dismiss it, or at the very least, keep it quiet and to themselves. This has had

[1]Robert O. Dean served 27 years in the U.S. Army, retiring in 1978. He is a highly decorated combat veteran. He served at the Supreme Headquarters Allied Powers Europe (SHAPE), North Atlantic Treaty Organization (NATO). He held a cosmic top secret security clearance, the highest available in NATO. As part of his work there, he read a study called *An Assessment* that contained data from a years-long study by the military of the UFO and extraterrestrial phenomenon, and the conclusions drawn from that study. A kind and gentle man, deeply spiritual and with exceptional insider knowledge and insight into the extraterrestrial phenomenon, today Robert Dean is a highly-sought speaker at UFO conferences around the world.

tragic consequences for those who have experienced abductions, whether by the Greys, Reptilians or other ET groups. This is especially true for "MILABs" – those abducted by military or quasi-military covert ops groups in ways peripheral or parallel to the extraterrestrial phenomenon. Such terrible trauma, even if buried deeply in the subconscious, is stored in the body and the body suffers as a result, even if unknowingly. If memories emerge, the very strangeness of them, so far outside normal everyday human experience makes them hard enough to cope with. In the face of official government denial and subsequent ridicule of the public, such remembered experiences are very nearly impossible to deal with or heal from. It takes a brave soul – one determined or driven to plumb those depths by something more powerful than a fear of disapproval, censure or ridicule – to approach, touch, remember, heal, and create a new context for such memories and for life from that point forward.

Facing the Shadow, Embracing the Light

Facing the Shadow, Embracing the Light is my own such journey, the journey of a sensitive Earth female. It seems to me that I carried within me a process, a purpose agreed to before birth; of unfolding into awakening as a "wanderer" – the realization that I was/am an extraterrestrial soul in a human body. In processing the trauma I experienced in the military I was shaken or shocked awake to this realization, a shock that I now strongly feel I agreed to in my soul contract before entering this life. In facing the shadow, I've had to look at some of the deepest, darkest parts of the human psyche that are acted out on this planet as one caught in that web and subjected to things, by other human beings, that most people can't even bear to contemplate might really happen. I didn't want to believe in them myself, but the level of terror I felt in my body about those memories when they burst forth had its own truth to tell. As I began my journey to explore those memories, to research, to try to understand and find a context for what had happened and how it could be possible, I would find person after person, story after story, where points intersected with my own story's details, and I would feel a sinking-in-quicksand-feeling as my own deniability of these experiences slipped further and further away until I was left with the stark truth that this had really happened.

Being a spiritual (rather than religious) person my entire life from the cradle onward, I was in recoil from my memories and what I was learning. I had always believed in the basic goodness of people. However my memories were showing me such a dark side of humanity. I wanted to reject it. I fought it in myself. In my searching I met so many "conspiracy theory" types who were grimly sure of the government hiding things and doing things in secrecy that were harming the public without the public's knowledge. Many of these people were and are deeply angry and resentful at something that loomed far too large for them to exert any control over. There seemed no way to get a larger public, mired down in denial and ridiculing conspiracy theories, to wake up and pay attention to things sometimes right in front of them.

The bombshell of my experiences in the military shook me awake enough to take a good hard look and I didn't like what I saw. I got my memories back in a hypnosis session in October of 1994 and went into some level of shock. I spent the next couple of years managing a certain low level of terror, keeping it pressed down so I could still function in my daily life and job, but it was always there. It seemed to say, "Don't you dare talk about this, don't you dare question, or search." For a while, it was almost as if my throat and mouth didn't even want to form the words of telling the memories to someone. As I pushed through that, it got easier to tell it when circumstances required it. Much later, I found the fear to be a certain type of conditioning, like placing a phantom security guard in my own head to keep me quiet. However, I had to question, to search, because the implications of what I had experienced were even more terrifying than the experiences themselves. Some dark and secret force was at work within our government and military. From that secret place it seemed to have "carte blanche" to do whatever it wanted outside and beyond the law. Every time I opened my mouth to talk with someone about this stuff, I was scared and looking over my shoulder because somewhere, these people were still at large. If what I might remember was such a threat to be spoken openly of, I felt they might have some way of monitoring me. But speak and question I did anyway. I HAD to find out what the hell this was all about.

Two years later, with much more information, half of it deeply disturbing and the other half wondrous, relating to extraterrestrial contact (not just abduction) hinting at some amazing process unfolding for humanity, I just couldn't take any more. I didn't feel any closer to answers, only more and more questions. The government sure wasn't talking, nor were the extraterrestrials. I couldn't accept some awakening psychic experiences I was having, such as seeing things with my "third eye" rather than my physical eyes. I didn't want to join the ranks of the grim and resentful conspiracy theorists, though I couldn't help but see much of the truth they presented, forced to accept it by my own memories and research. My life had always been about spirituality, connection to nature and looking for the best in people. Not this. In my own anger and resentment I determined that my life was going to return to being about spirituality, connection to nature and finding the best in myself and others. I locked up all my experiences, memories, searching and questioning in a little mental black box and shoved it into a corner in the back of my mind.

Obviously, now that I'm writing this book, I've opened that little black box and allowed all the stuff in it to fly forth and be processed thoroughly – and that process may continue for the rest of my life in some respects, especially if I undergo more hypnosis. The challenge has been to face the shadow in there and choose to embrace the Light. Because everything in this universe of duality exists in relation to its opposite. So, I reasoned, if there is this big, looming dark shadow, it is only there because there is an equally huge corresponding Light.

There are those in Service to the One through service to the many, and there are those who serve only themselves at the expense of the many. Service to the

One through service to the many is a far more stable place to operate from. If one of us falls, the rest are there to give a hand back up to the path. With those who serve themselves at the expense of others, if one falls, others will rush to take the place of power that one who fell once occupied. When this process gathers enough momentum to run completely amok, we see what we are now seeing in our society, things falling apart at the seams. They say there is no honor among thieves and in the end, through their own fear of lack, they will turn on each other. Love for one's fellows and joint cooperation build and expand for all.

I've often wondered what the lure is of having power over others. The only answer I've been able to come up with from my own inner searching is that when one does not perceive or feel their connection to the larger All-That-Is, Source Creator and Creation, they will try to get that vital energy from other living beings by having power over them. Instead of an interconnected conscious living symbiosis, where relationships are mutually beneficial to all cooperating organisms, there exists a host-parasite relationship, where those driven by their own inner fear and emptiness must make themselves parasites, controlling and feeding off a host or a host population.

So many people, individually and collectively, don't want to face the shadow. They fear it. They cover over their own inner shadow, over the collective shadow of all humanity with mental drywall and the pretty paint of positive affirmations. But avoidance of the shadow will never deal constructively with the fears of the individual or collective that lurk in parallel with the shadows themselves. I know this. I know it because as I've talked about my experiences to various people, and there are those who are able to listen and those who shy away or ask me to please keep them to myself. They don't even want such things dropped into their conscious thought to sit there and torment or frighten them. But how will denial of the shadow dwelling in the collective Id of humanity serve those who refuse to hear about it if some experience befalls them that traumatizes them to such a paralyzing degree that they can't make good choices or decisions in that moment?

Think of the tragedy and horror of September 11, 2001. A nation and a Congress in shock and trauma from such an event was preyed upon by an administration who presented them with a most UN-Patriot Act. It was signed into law without even being read through by most congressmen. It gave this administration unprecedented power and began the erosion and dismantling of our constitutional rights, and the curtailing of our freedoms in the interest of "security". At best, the Bush-Cheney administration capitalized upon a horrible event to seize an opportunity to advance their own agenda of power and control. At worst, they engineered the entire horror for their own ends, and that agenda grew ever-more apparent during the eight years of that administration.

Growing numbers of Americans and others around the globe who look at the circumstances of this terrible event are drawing the same conclusions – 9/11 was an inside job done by an administration who wanted to grab power and begin to remove any legal means by which they could be opposed. Any who opposed them could be accused of aiding and abetting terrorists, by simply standing up and refusing to give up their constitutional rights to question, dissent or oppose something they found wrong.

Unfortunately, with all the promise held out by Obama and his campaign platform based on "Change," little seems to have changed in Washington D.C. A push for health care reform ran neck and neck with a manufactured swine flu/H1N1 pandemic crisis. The vaccines were shown to be dangerous and unsafe on a variety of levels, and many people rejected them. Economic crisis looms, and Obama's bailouts to Wall Street have been unwise and reckless. The Supreme Court voted to allow unregulated corporate campaign financing, an outrageous attack on any semblance of what remains of the U.S.A. and her government as a place where the voice of the people will have any real say. The collective voice of the people has been displaced by corporate interests with the money to buy off politicians to set policy in accord with their own profiteering agendas.

So far, the Bush-Cheney administration has gotten away with their crimes and Bush pardoned his questionable or criminal cronies, even himself, as he prepared to leave office. There must be accountability for such crimes or we send a message as a people and a collective that this is somehow okay to do. That as long as you hold the highest offices in the land, you can get away with murder, and on a mass scale. Obama has allowed the crimes committed by the last administration to go unanswered. We can never have a country that is the land of the free and the home of the brave without accountability for committing murderous criminal acts. Since each member of the U.S. Armed Forces, each member of Congress and the President take an oath to defend the United States and its Constitution against all enemies, foreign and domestic, then the Patriot Act and all subsequent legislation abridging the constitutional rights of U.S. citizens has been an act of treason, and should be so named and soberly considered. Those who instigated and supported such measures need to be held accountable for such treason. Constitutional rights and law still wait to be restored to their former strength and integrity under Obama, however no redress has been forthcoming.

I think sometimes that what holds us back as a nation from enacting the rigorous investigations and prosecutions for crimes committed at the highest echelons of government is that same denial of the human collective shadow, that part of the U.S. citizenry that cannot even contemplate – labeling as unspeakable and unthinkable – that our own leaders could coldly kill so many of its own citizens in such a terrible way for the completely selfish motive of seizing control of the most powerful nation on the planet for their own self-aggrandizement.

I was once a person who believed I lived in a world where such things were unthinkable and unspeakable. And when I suffered the trauma I did, my mind broke that part of my experience away from the rest of my conscious mind and buried it. It emerged years later, when I discovered, with a wave of nausea, three months of missing time while serving in the Air Force and underwent hypnosis to get pieces of it back. I'm going to tell you that part of my story here as well as much more that will eclipse the dark and help you to stand more firmly in the Light than perhaps ever before. I invite you to come with me as I share my story of facing the Shadow, embracing the Light.

Chapter 1: The Shadow and The Light

A Personal Parable: People of the Bubble

Once upon a time, there was a whole civilization that lived in a bubble. In this bubble there pervaded throughout the bubble world a particular reality that operated within a certain set of laws, rules and morals. Children were born into this reality, and this entire set of information began being transmitted to them almost immediately by their parents and the rest of society in the bubble world. People rarely questioned things about these laws, rules and morals. If asked about them, they would have just said; "That's just the way it is! That is life. Laws, rules and morals are here for everyone's safety and protection." Those miscreants who broke the laws, rules or morals could be prosecuted, put in jail, or shunned or ostracized from the rest of society in the bubble. They would be made to understand that, "you are to do things as they are done here," or suffer the consequences.

But, one day, one of the bubble people, a young woman who had signed up for a term of service in the military, all unknowing, was taken to a location OUTSIDE the boundaries of the bubble world. It didn't look all that different, but there was a different feel to the location – it felt dangerous. Somehow, she could feel that the usual laws, rules and morals didn't apply here. Even the solid-seeming ground under her feet felt unstable somehow. Her superiors, who had put her there, were clearly not operating by the usual laws, rules and morals.

Things went from bad to worse. She saw things she had been told by voices of authority from the bubble world that couldn't, that shouldn't exist. Yet there they were, right before her eyes. Each order from one of her superiors placed her in greater and greater danger – this from the very people she would have looked to for protection from such things. Her mind and heart beat like the wings of a frightened bird in a cage as she was ordered from place to place, each more frightening than the last. She was injected with a substance – she didn't know what it was – done against her will, without her permission. How could this be happening to her? How? She was thrown into an observation room and locked in, barely aware that behind a mirrored glass, these others watched as she went through the effects of the injection. Afterward, she was dragged out of that room and raped by two security guards while others watched. She was both terrified and enraged.

Horrific things were done to her until... her eyes glazed over, her mind fractured away the splinters of memory of this terrible, traumatic series of events that just couldn't – just shouldn't – have been able to ever happen to anyone... who lived in a bubble world where such unthinkable, unspeakable things just didn't happen... because there were laws and rules and morals in this world...

She was placed back in the bubble world, those fractured splinters of memory buried in the deep dark of her subconscious, so she could still function within her normal, daytime bubble world life. But they were still in there, building up pressure from within.

For all living beings, at the deepest core, their nature is wholeness, a seamless, flowing wholeness of being, interconnected with all life everywhere. Like a splinter of glass or wood buried deep in living tissue, that is worked to the surface to be expelled, the body works energetic blocks to the surface for release also. Living beings cannot live or function well in any kind of fractured state, physically, mentally, emotionally or spiritually. The drive towards wholeness is always there. Dis-ease of the body, disquiet of the mind and emotional distress are interventions from the body, mind and spirit; this inner chorus working to bring back into being the seamless integrated wholeness of consciousness and form.

Years passed for this young woman of the bubble world. Pressure built up more and more from within, seeking wholeness, re-integration. Unable to deal with the internal pressure at one point, and unable or unwilling uncover those terrible memories, she nearly took her own life. But there was a deep spiritual realization that she was not her body, and that the most essential part of her would not die, but would have to move into another form to complete what this one did not. This stayed her hand from pulling the gun's trigger that day. Instead, she made a 500% commitment to her healing and wholeness, no matter what it took, no matter where the journey led her.

One thing led to another, and another, and another –
synchronicities from the Conscious Loving Universe –
honoring her commitment to healing and wholeness. Each
synchronicity led her step by step to each place she needed
to go to confront the buried past. Finally she discovered
three months of missing time and underwent hypnosis to
recover the memories from that time. A portion of those
memories came tumbling out.

For her, the bubble world burst. It was a fiction. There was
grief and rage to deal with, and terror. But she kept putting
one foot in front of the other, her commitment to healing and
wholeness keeping her on course.

When she tried to talk to other people in the bubble world,
her experiences were so far outside the laws, rules and
morals that everyone accepted, were so unthinkable, so
unspeakable, many did not believe her. Yet she knew this
other reality existed, underneath the illusory reality of the
bubble world. She did find others who knew the same kinds
of things that she knew, but they were a minority. They
were regarded by others in the bubble world as conspiracy
theorists, spinning out fantastic tales only fit for movies and
fiction writing. It was nearly impossible to get anyone to
listen, to wake up. What would it take?

~ Niara Terela Isley

Caution: You are reading a book that will be taking you on a journey far
outside of "the bubble." After this journey, you might not ever see our world
in the same way again

The Shadow

Since recovering some of my memories from the missing time I discovered
from my time in the Air Force, and the subsequent quest I undertook to find
some understanding and context regarding what happened to me, I have often
felt like Cassandra of Troy in Greek myth, gifted with a special prophecy or
vision, and cursed that no one would believe her. What would it take to get
people to really peel back the layers and see?

Apparently, it has taken eight years of the Bush-Cheney administration to
get people to listen at least by half. Stolen elections, years of flagrant disregard
for the environment, wars of aggression in Iraq and Afghanistan. Open,

corporate war profiteering sanctioned by this past administration was peopled with individuals who committed brutal rapes on their own female employees. The existence of detention and torture facilities such as Guantanamo Bay and Abu Ghraib was revealed, disgusting and horrifying huge numbers of the American population. When I consider what happened to me, I have to wonder if any facilities may have been constructed and designated for worse forms of torture than waterboarding that never reached the light of any public attention or scrutiny. However, this is only my personal speculation.

The tragedy of September 11, 2001[1] was used as an excuse to go to war, and the huge stack of incongruities that surround that event point to facts that, at best, this administration knew about this "terrorist threat" and didn't lift a finger to stop it so they could use it for their own agenda. At worst, they planned it and executed it down to the last detail, having hundreds of pages of the Patriot Act legislation ready and waiting to railroad through Congress just days after the tragedy. It would be the beginning of them being able to pursue their own greed-driven agendas of personal power and have anyone who opposed them labeled a "terrorist." It was a domestic attack from within on our constitutional rights in this country, attempting to end personal privacy and freedom. It was accomplished through shock. A nation, and perhaps a Congress, shocked and traumatized, looked to government leaders to "do something." And do something they did – ramrodding the UN-Patriot Act through Congress; and we, as a nation, woke up too late, sadder but wiser. People who had lived comfortably and complacently in the great bubble nation of the U.S.A. began to wake up.

I remember watching the twin towers fall on TV, watching how they fell down neatly on their foundations just like controlled demolitions I watched in Las Vegas, NV, when an old obsolete casino was brought down to make way for a new one. I knew it was impossible for a jet to fly into a skyscraper, made of tons of concrete and rebar, and do that kind of damage. Possibly fires, explosions of jet fuel and extensive damage to the floors hit I could accept, but not a controlled demolition-type fall of the buildings straight down on their foundations. I remember feeling in my gut, at that moment I watched it on TV, that it was an inside job, never mind all the suspicions surrounding the events of 9/11 that came later. And so many "bubble world" people still refused to look, to see, even in the face of mounting evidence and scores of unanswered questions.

Why? Because it was unthinkable and unspeakable for the presidential administration of the United States of America, Land of the Free, and Home of the Brave, to commit such a crime against its own citizens. We did not want to face our collective shadow, a collective shadow that, in the form of the Bush-Cheney administration, had seized power and began wielding it like a club on the rest of the world and the American people. With their actions, they held up

[1] See documentaries Loose Change 9/11: An American Coop (website: loosechange911.com) and a more recent film offering from Architects and Engineers for 9/11 Truth (website:www.ae911truth.org), *9/11: Explosive Evidence – Experts Speak Out.*

a mirror for the rest of us to look into, and we didn't like what we saw.

Such a planned "terrorist" false flag operation has at least one known, well-documented precedent in our own country. Operation Northwoods[2] was conceived in 1962 for Central Intelligence Agency (CIA) operatives to kill American citizens and commit other acts of terrorism, then blame them on, and incite a war against, Castro and Cuba, using fake "evidence" to implicate Cuba in these terrorist acts. Fortunately it was never acted upon. Almost sounds like the Bush-Cheney administration's cries of Iraq having "weapons of mass destruction" to take us into war with Iraq, using 9/11 "terrorism" as an excuse even though there were no clear ties between Al Qaeda and Saddam Hussein. Of course, as we all now know, no weapons of mass destruction were ever found, but not until hundreds of thousands of deaths later, of Iraqi men, women and children, as well as thousands of our own U.S. troops.

Unthinkable. Unspeakable. Words we apply to acts so heinous that we shy away from believing they can even happen, from our indoctrinated, carefully-programmed world view. This world view is built from traditional religion and what it teaches us is right and wrong, from nationalism-patriotism, from cultural-societal norms. These become entrenched in our minds over time, breeding an "us-versus-them" mentality, otherwise used as "divide and conquer" of one human race in all its diversity. Far too often we don't question these ideas or norms, we think they are "just the way it is." Those who look or think differently than "us" are suspect. They are "other." From differences in color of skin to different beliefs, religions, countries, even from individual to individual, we judge each other by the yardstick of what we have been indoctrinated to believe is the "right way."

The real danger of being a bubble person, living in a bubble world, is that when something happens so far outside your religious-national-societal-cultural frame of reference, you are at risk of shock so traumatizing, that in that traumatized state you can be manipulated, coerced, even programmed, into any manner of outcomes not in your best interest, looking to corrupt governmental "father" figures to do something, anything, to keep you safe. The real question is, how much of your real personal freedom and autonomy are you willing to bargain for an illusion of safety and security?

I know this first-hand. I know because of what happened to me at the very hands of people I should have been able to count on to responsibly look out for those under their command, not to "unspeakably" abuse that authority and control. It was the very context and structure of the bubble world – its laws, rules and morals – that set me up to be so deeply traumatized by the abuse I suffered, that my own mind fractured, sending the splinters of memories too terrible to acknowledge in the conscious mental realm into the dark nether-reaches of my mind. On one hand, it was protection – my mind's mechanism

---

[2] Operation Northwoods entailed a series of 1962 proposals by the Central Intelligence Agency (CIA) in which operatives within the organization would commit acts of terrorism in United States cities and blame them on Cuba. These proposals were rejected by the Kennedy administration.

shielding me until I could handle looking at the truth. On the other hand, if the pressure of those unremembered traumas were behind my near-brush with suicide, it also could have just as easily destroyed me.

The Light

The stolen election of 2000[3] that landed Bush and Cheney in the White House brought about for me deep anxiety and refreshed symptoms of post-traumatic stress disorder – PTSD. With the things that were occurring, particularly the Patriot Act legislation and its implications, I was afraid that the whole of American society was being placed in a position where their constitutional rights could be systematically stripped away, piece by piece, just as my own rights had become non-existent in 1980, out in the middle of the Nevada desert. Through the Patriot Act and other legislation that followed, giving this executive branch of government unprecedented power, various forms of abuse could be visited on the whole population in some form or other, increasingly making any disagreement with the current administration's policies to be seen as "aiding and abetting terrorists."

I finally sought the services of a trusted and gifted healer to help me resolve much of the emotional fallout of my traumas, and while the Bush-Cheney administration continued in office for eight years due to a second stolen election in 2004, I managed to find some relief and some peace. I was on my way to more profound healing, wholeness and integration than ever before.

Love, Light and Truth are the true nature of the universe, of which we are all a part – interconnected and inextricably woven together. No matter what traumas are visited upon us, that drive towards understanding, wholeness and integration guides our steps, placing opportunity after opportunity in our path for us to see, to hear, to heal, to awaken.

A human being, and any other life form, is made up of a chakra system, little vortices of energy that, when healthy, spin in such a way as to take in the always-present, conscious, living energy from the Universal Energy Field, beautifully illustrated in the book *Hands of Light: A Guide to Healing Through the Human Energy Field*[4].

As I feel it and see it with my inner eye, our bodies are actually spun into our third-dimensional forms in a continually-dynamic dance and flow of energy from the Universal Energy Field. In some small way it looks like a magical-seeming "coming-out-of-nothing-into-form" that vendors of cotton

[3] See the film, *Unprecedented – The 2000 Presidential Election: A documentary about the battle for the Presidency in Florida and the undermining of Democracy in America*. Website: http://unprecedented.org.

[4] An excellent resource book on the Universal Energy Field is *Hands of Light: A Guide to Healing Through the Human Energy Field* by Barbara Brennan, energy healer and former physicist for the National Aeronautics and Space Administration (NASA). Brennan is a world-known energy healer and teacher. As a former research scientist, she takes a scientific approach to energy healing. She established the Barbara Brennan School of Healing and has devoted the last 30 years to research and exploration of the human energy field. She is also author of *Light Emerging: The Journey of Personal Healing*. Her website: www.barbarabrennan.com.

candy perform at carnivals, when the cotton candy seems to form around the cone, "spun" into being from something invisible. This is similar to how we are formed, though we have at least seven major chakras/vortices (more are now being discussed, particularly an eighth) all spinning to bring our body into form and sustain it. Each correspond to a glandular and/or nerve-plexus point in the human body. Our bodies also have corresponding subtler energy bodies that exist at higher octaves of vibration/dimensions on the emotional, mental, astral and etheric planes, while at higher and higher levels or octaves of vibration, we begin to blend again into the Great Oneness from which we are all formed.

The natural flow of this energy is to beauty, balance, harmony and wholeness. When we have an accident, become ill or experience a trauma, our energy-chakra system becomes compromised; and if it continues without being addressed, over time the compromised energy system will create a physical manifestation of disease – the inner cellular intelligence of the body's systems trying in a last ditch effort to get us to pay attention and correct the imbalance creating the disease. This is true from microcosmic systems to macrocosmic ones, even on a planetary scale, as our besieged and compromised environment is showing us.

And while we fight against death on our world – very literally at all cost – there are times when death and release from the physical body is its own healing, when the higher consciousness of that person cannot establish a meaningful dialogue with the 3D form's operating mind to facilitate healing. At an even deeper level, the higher consciousness may simply "know" that it is time for this soul's 3D life to come to a close, and that a higher purpose will be served by passing into the next realm than to stay in third-dimensional form.

Is it any wonder that at least some visionaries are catching on to the fact that there is an inexhaustible source of free energy to be tapped, waiting in this Universal Energy Field potential that exists all around us? Like "The Force" described by Obi Wan Kenobi in the movie *Star Wars*, it surrounds us, it flows through us, it binds the universe together – or, to my inner sense, it is the ever-present Creator-Love-Light in which we are all held and come into being as an individual light of the Great Light.

Beauty, balance, harmony and wholeness is the natural state of energy, of mind, body and spirit. When our energy or chakra system is in some way compromised through an accident or trauma affecting mind and body, the flow of energy into the body is damaged. But it continually seeks wholeness again, bringing those intersecting synchronicities of meetings with people, places or situations that will be messages or guides leading back to healing, reintegration and wholeness. Some people are able to pay attention to these synchronicities; others dismiss them as coincidence until a crisis point is reached and the soul decision at the highest level of consciousness is made, to embrace healing in life, or embrace healing as death and examine the immediately preceding life from the higher perspective. The whole dance of life – every thread, every intersecting life of every individual – is served in some way by the life-dance unfolding, no matter where the threads of our lives lead us.

In my own case, conscious crisis was reached in an inner angst, an anxiety that drove and drove from within until I decided I couldn't live with it any more. I decided to end my life at the age of 33. I came very close. I ended up not doing it, and the path from that choice led to where I am today.

I tried for a long time to fathom the reasons for the free-floating anxiety and depression that brought me to that particular point. I feel now that the internal pressure of then-unremembered trauma was driving the urge to end my life. But this kind of inner mental-emotional-spiritual friction was its own call to scrutiny and healing, to smooth out the friction and return my body's energy systems to flow and harmony.

This world has always been challenging for me to live in, and I'm sure that applies to many, many others around the world. For me, I couldn't understand, from my early teen years on, why human beings could have so little foresight or vision that they would allow the continuing destruction of the Earth's capital, non-renewable resources. Even to the girl I was in the 1970s, this was happening at a rate that I clearly saw could lead to humanity's extinction. I also couldn't really understand humanity's inhumanity to others of their own kind, as well as to other living creatures. It was an inner heartbreak to see and witness this kind of behavior from the tenderest young age onward. Growing up in a dysfunctional family with my father's alcoholism and violence and my mother's severe codependency issues complicated my life further and gave me more from which to heal and recover.

Thus far, I have only had a few hypnosis sessions to recover memories around these experiences. They are not easy to undergo. I relived the events and trauma that happened and the emotional fallout took many, many years to begin to deal with and heal from. On one side, I lived secretly managing an inner terror level that someone would come and kill me or take me away somewhere and I'd never be seen or heard from again, because I was remembering things and events that someone, or some group, didn't want me remembering, and most certainly did not want me talking about. On the other side, friends I tried talking to about this kept asking, could it be something else, could I be mistaken? They quite obviously did not want to hear about memories that were so frightening and so far outside everyday reality that they couldn't accept them.

It seemed to me that I was stuck between the devil and the deep blue sea. I didn't want to believe these memories either. I didn't want to believe that people could so brutally treat another human being as I was treated. I actually had an easier time with the alien abduction memories. But the terror I was feeling was very real, and the memories were very real. I fought against it. I didn't want this to be part of my life. My life was about spirituality and good people who helped each other, not people who inflicted pain and took pleasure in it. Not about strange episodes that no one wanted me to remember or talk about. I tried for years to shove it all away and live a life that my friends and family would approve of. Looking back, it seems like I ended up living half a life, a life in which I couldn't make anything work, not my marriages or really being the kind of mom I wanted to be – and tremendous time and energy poured into other career endeavors in more recent years came to nothing. It takes a huge amount of life energy to keep such a chunk of your life shoved into a box someplace in your consciousness, constantly guarding it to make sure it doesn't get out and wreak havoc with your life. The thing is, it was wreaking havoc with my life from the shadows. The years I lived before I recovered the memories were not a great deal different from the years after my hypnosis sessions. Knowing those experiences were there and that society would not approve continually undercut my self-esteem and self-confidence. Everywhere I went, I felt like I was coming in from some back door, hat in my hand, feeling like I was damaged goods, allowed to be part of things only on others' good graces – as long as I kept my mouth shut about things they didn't want to hear.

I covered this up of course, as best I could and I often felt like I was living some kind of real life. I do have a loving nature and a genuineness and sincerity that has made me some wonderful friends through the years that I'm deeply grateful for – friends who have stood by me while I worked all this strangeness through, even though they were not familiar with the kinds of circumstances or even the existence of things under the surface of our world, the secret context in which these things happened to me.

Not an easy life at all, from the beginning, from childhood. But, as philosopher Friedrich Nietzsche once wrote, "That which does not kill us makes us stronger." The trials of my childhood set my feet on the warrior's path I would need to navigate my life.

Entr'acte I
A Wanderer Remembers: Fragments from Other Lives

Lyra, Homeworld

As best as I can remember, I first came into form – what on Terra is called humanoid form – on Lyra. I came in as a baby... the beings living on this world were enjoying a procreation project, seeing how various vibratory energies attracted to each other, creating families. I was "born" to two loving parents on Lyra around the star of the same name. I was not born of my mother's body. My parents decided to energetically form a child of their love. I remember them stretching their hands out to each other, short of actually touching. They

9

*brought me into being from the interaction of their energy
fields between the two of them. This was for them like a long,
sensitive, creative meditation, each co-creatively adding their
best attributes to my formation, each making fun and loving
suggestions to the other on their shared qualities. As my baby
form came into being, I was held cradled and suspended
between my two parents within the gestation field. This was
nothing so long as a human pregnancy on Terra. The process
may have been complete in a few hours or perhaps a day. I'm
not sure, but I know it wasn't long in Terran human terms. And
time passed differently there any way.*

*I grew up knowing only love and living in complete harmony
with my parents, our society and our Planetary Being and her
environment. Lyra was a world existing in the energetic and
vibrational border of the fourth and fifth dimensions. We lived
lightly in our forms, going and coming from them easily and
consciously, refreshing ourselves in the Oneness of the All-
That-Is.*

*We did not own land or hold deeds. We belonged to Lyra in a
special sense through our vibrational relationship with her. We
had a conscious relationship with her and she cared for us.
When we had needs, for shelter, for food, for travel... bringing
these things into being, beautifully and naturally, was a co-
creative process between ourselves, our home planet and
the Conscious Living Universe. We created in thought what
we desired, and between us, Lyra and the Living Universe,
it was brought into being, our thought creating a matrix for
the rarified matter that Lyra was made up of to form upon.
Everything was alive, conscious in some manner, and had
organic, living components.*

*So we lived in structures created out of our own desire and
thought through the co-creative loving energies of ourselves,
our planet and the Living Universe. They were beautiful and
were natural extensions of the planet herself. Some homes
and other structures were formed of living crystal domes.
Others were formed of different types of rock with clear,
bubble-like crystal windows. Our family's home was of this
type. Some were grown from the trees and other plants
that abounded on Lyra. There were those of us who lived in
structures under the oceans, living closely with the cetacean
people, swimming with them, communing with them, sharing
and learning with each other.*

There were no roads on Lyra. Travel any place on our world could be accomplished instantaneously at the speed of thought, and yet, there were times when the travel itself was a matter of exploration and discovery. For this, for the wonder of travel for its own sake, to see and explore, we co-created gigantic, beautiful, spherical living mothership craft that would take us through deep space, within or between galaxies. We created smaller saucer-shaped scout craft to move as individuals or in smaller groups, as high above or as close to a planet as our thought would take us.

You might wonder why people who can travel at the speed of thought would need craft for travel. But there is a joy, and at times a necessity, to travel within a living craft, that craft handling the journey, sometimes with a pilot and others to attend to its needs. The rest of the beings on board can then turn their creative thought energy to other tasks that are appropriate and in alignment with their desires and intentions.

I had my own individual saucer craft that I navigated around the planet. It was like a natural extension of my own body, like using an arm or leg. It was also conscious and organic. My craft and I had a special telepathic-empathic link, we were tuned to each other. She never collided with any of the flying birds or insects of Lyra. She emanated a field while flying that they could detect and they would swerve, gliding up or down to avoid her. She also responded to the thoughts of my parents, taking me home when they called.

My life on Lyra with my parents and extended family was one of learning and exploration between my created form and my travel to the other realms, marveling at the energetic connections we could see, hear and feel woven throughout the Conscious Living Universe/Multiverses. We could see the special energies or forces at play in spinning the seen and expressed worlds from the unseen worlds of pure energy and spirit. The spinning into form was rich and vibrant in colors that delighted us. We delighted in being part of that creative process. One could not separate being alive from being an artist in some form. Art and science were interwoven, and I learned much interacting with my uncle about this, the brother of my father. Like a second father to me, he and I were very close. Our sciences flowed from the spiritual understandings of the Oneness, the All-That-Is of which we were all a part, manifesting in various practical applications of that understanding that we would design and create.

None of us were attached to our bodies in the way people are on Terra. We could come and go from them to higher realms, different octaves of vibration or density, whenever we wished. If you saw someone's body in a meditative posture, either sitting or lying down, you knew they were traveling to other realms. As a matter of etiquette and empathy, you did nothing to disturb their form while they were so engaged.

We didn't use names. Everyone had a unique energy signature that was telepathically and empathically sensed and recognized. I think this is why some people on Terra say they remember faces but have trouble remembering names, it is an ancient echo of unconscious memory from the time when vocalized names to reference a particular person were unnecessary. Once upon that long-ago time we just didn't use names. The indigenous peoples on Terra probably had the best ways of "naming" children, or changing those names upon adulthood, names that reflected the energetic qualities of the individual as they relate to the world and other living beings around them.

Telepathy/empathy is a rather cumbersome way of describing a form of communication that is as natural and graceful as breathing. At one level we are always sensing it. It is part of a field of energy we dwell within. It is never not-present. Yet it is so much a part of us and our experience we think no more of it than a fish thinks of swimming through water. The slightest disturbance within one of us would be instantly felt throughout all of us and immediately attended to with help or aid if necessary. Yet any need for this was extremely rare. In fact, I never encountered it in my life – until the strangers came to our world.

Chapter 2: Strange, Different, Other...
Star Child

To be Touched by Spirit,
To feel the fire,
Like food for the hungry,
It feeds your desires.

But what It asks in return
Is to take you by the hand,
And lead you through Life
At one with It's Plan.

It won't let you rest,
It won't let you sleep,
'Cause you know in your heart
That the Truth runs too deep.

If you try to pull away
Because the going gets rough,
You experience the anguish
Of losing the Touch.

To sever the tie
That brought you awake,
Say the Truth is a lie,
Is just too hard to take.

Touched By Spirit
~ Niara Terela Isley

The Quest to Know "the Really REAL Truth"

I was born Janet Marie Isley in southern California to a family that looked like a *Leave It to Beaver* 1950s family to the world, at least on the surface. My father was a successful assistant manager of a major food canning plant, working up to the position the hard way by starting out as a youngster at the company, stacking cans. My mother seemed a wonderful hostess when giving company parties and they had two nice-looking children, my brother and myself. Peel

13

back this acceptable social veneer however, and there were severe problems of violent alcoholism and codependency.

I, the daughter, was different than most kids I knew and grew up with, different than most of my blood relations, stepping to an inner rhythm that only I seemed to hear. I had a deep feeling and appreciation for nature, even what little I could connect with in our backyard in the suburb of Los Angeles where I grew up. One of my teachers in grade school sat me down one time and told me he didn't see me playing much or having much to do with the other children. He was concerned about this. Seeking to allay his concern, I told him that I had friends in the animals, birds, insects and plants I spent so much time observing and communing with in nature. The look he gave me told me that he definitely considered me "other." I felt his disapproval, but I couldn't exchange the love and connection I felt with the natural world. I could not bring myself to conform in order to attempt to get the capricious and unreliable approval of other human beings.

In spite of my father's alcoholism, Dad and I were kindred spirits. He was interested in many things and always learning. I remember some very precious times with my father, though unfortunately far too few. I was always longing for more time with him on that special level. One rainy day he sat with me and my dinosaur book on the sofa and taught me to sound out all the long names of each of these creatures, proud that I was so interested in learning things. Some evenings when he was home he and I would watch the fireworks from Disneyland over in Anaheim that we could see from our backyard. He would sometimes take us on drives in the deserts or mountains of California, where we lived, and he and I shared the same deep regard for nature. It was an unspoken bond between us. That sharing allowed me to fall ever more deeply in love with the natural world and all the creatures and growing things in it. I know now, what I only sensed then, along with the pain of feeling like an outsider on this world as a small child, that I am a starseed, a wanderer – an extraterrestrial soul who chose this human incarnation for a multitude of reasons.

My relationship with my mother was far more difficult. I did not seem to be the kind of daughter she wanted. I often felt like a dress-up doll with her, not valued in the least for having a mind and interests of my own. She wanted me to be a proper little girl, dressed up just so and behaving just so. She once permed my hair and I hated it, the stench, and the coiffed Shirley-Temple-curls it tortured my hair into. She wanted me to conform to some ever-elusive unspoken standard of what little girls were "supposed" to be. Rebelling against her and perhaps in some way seeking approval from my father, I became a tomboy. This was natural for me with my intense interest in Nature, and my private science and history studies that went far and away beyond what school required of me.

When very young, and having no help to deal with or understand the kinds of things that drive parents to do what they do, I did what many children do. I found my own ways to cope. Where matters of family were concerned, with the violence, unhappiness, malice and bitterness, I put my emotions under lockdown and became stoic in most situations, time in nature being the exception to that rule. And I would escape as often as I could into the world of my imagination – another of my coping tools. Now I have to wonder – was it really only my imagination taking me a million miles away? …to somewhere? Or were my loving spirit guides taking me on astral journeys in those moments to protect me from indoctrination into Terran institutional systems that they knew would not serve me and the life I was growing into?

My animal companions were also everything to me, giving me the unconditional love I didn't find anywhere else. I had a kitten that disappeared one day and I carried the grief of that into adulthood. We had dogs, two dachshunds that both came to bad ends. Though I struggled to hold onto her, pleading with my little brother to roll up the car window, Auggie pulled free and swiftly jumped through the car window to go after my dad into a very busy street. In almost the same instant she was killed in traffic while I watched helpless from our car. Cindy got into some kind of weed poison and died of it. Another little dog we had, Gidget, a toy poodle that even my mom – who barely tolerated animals – liked. But she also had to go because of a doctor's ruling that I, and particularly my younger brother, were allergic. We were both prone to asthma that, in a few cases, developed into life-threatening pneumonia. I had pneumonia a couple of times. My brother had life-threatening pneumonia nine times before he was five years old. Likely it was my father's smoking that was the worst cause, but dog dander was blamed for the respiratory problems of us kids. On a deeper holistic level, maybe it's because we lived in a home where we were afraid to even breathe. Whatever the cause, losing my animals was devastating for me; a huge grief in an already difficult life.

Other coping tools arose from an inner drive that is still a part of me to this very day. As a small child, I would tell it to myself this way; "I want to know the really REAL Truth." About God, the universe and everything in it, and what my place might be in it all.

So, I set out to find out with the academic resources at my disposal. As soon as I could read, the library was one of my favorite places and I checked out and read book after book on sciences of many disciplines. My favorites were the earth sciences like geology. As a small child I knew many words that a child my age would never normally know, like paleontology – both the vertebrate and invertebrate branches. I knew words from archeology and anthropology for the ancient, supposed forerunners of modern man, such as *homo habilis* and *australopithecine*. I learned of the archeological puzzle of the "missing link."

I studied volcanology and the different types of volcanic eruptions. There were the visually stunning flows that happen in the Hawaiian islands. Then the much more violent pyroclastic cloud types responsible for the destruction of the ancient Roman cities Pompeii and Herculaneum by Mount Vesuvius. There was the 1883 monster eruption of Krakatoa in the Sunda Strait between Java and Sumatra that was heard in Hawaii hours later and gave the whole world red sunsets for two years after. And more modern disasters like Mount Saint Helens. And yet, as long as you weren't in the path of destruction, volcanic eruptions brought about change and circumstances for the development of new life.

History fascinated me as well, ancient to modern. I loved reading biographies, about early American explorers and presidents and well-documented historical fiction. I tried my own hand at writing historical fiction in my teens, doing my own careful research and chronologies of events leading up to and through the Revolutionary War for independence of the American colonies from England.

I lost myself in the stories of the gods and goddesses of Greek and Roman mythology. I studied various mythologies to understand how ancient civilizations viewed the cosmic forces at work in their lives. And I attended my family's Lutheran church services and Sunday school to try to understand the concept of "God" in my own century.

The Loving Presence Versus "The Church"

I felt a special Loving Presence when communing with Nature. Everything seemed to have a place and a design. In Sunday school we learned about God – a being all-knowing and all-seeing. I felt this must be the Being, one-in-the-same, with the one I was experiencing out in Nature. But some of the other ideas taught there clashed for me, from a very early age. Such as to "love and fear the Lord your God?" The use of love and fear in this way in the same sentence felt wrong. I felt in Nature only the Loving Presence that seemed to pervade everything, everywhere. I began, young as I was, to question that people's interpretation of God might be a bit skewed.

The other difficulty with religion was the hypocrisy. In the teachings about Jesus, the son of God, he seemed so loving. He taught in stories or parables and his whole message seemed one of love – loving your neighbor as yourself, become as a little child – and the story of the good Samaritan who rose above petty rivalries to help one injured by the roadside, not of his own people, when others who seemed more likely to help could not be bothered. In our own church lived this same "us and them" mentality, which the Samaritan set aside to help to one in need. If you were different – in the intangible way I was different – you were, in some secret way, labeled outcast or defective. And treated as such. The same children I attended Sunday school and regular school with teased and made fun of me over and over about anything and everything they could pick on.

Though being different was the cause of deep pain, I was not about to compromise who I was by trying to comply with some vague, undefined "norm." I developed a mistrust of people in general. The cruelty I experienced with the other children in school, the complete opposite of what was taught in Sunday school or church, I saw reflected in their parents and in society in an "us versus them" mentality. So I became a loner. I spent my time alone communing with nature or studying about it in my science books. While I was a child, and did play with toys sometimes, I was far too fascinated with what I could learn about the world, and spent hours and hours reading, then off in my imagination (or astral travel) to contemplate it all.

I did stay with the Lutheran church and its teachings until adolescence, going through catechism and taking first communion to see if some mystery hitherto hidden would be revealed. It was valuable, as some of my metaphysical leanings were taking me into books like Kahlil Gibran's *The Prophet* (still a favorite) and into looking at astrology and reincarnation. I was able to ask the ministers teaching catechism some of my questions about these things. The answers I got were far from satisfactory. I was told, "there are some things just beyond our human understanding" concerning God and the universe, or more accurately, the church's interpretation of God's word. I came to the frustrating conclusion that, according to the church, God had given me this fine and questioning mind that loved learning, then commanded that I should keep it fenced in a pasture, not to wander outside the cultivated green dictates of Lutheran religious doctrine.

No great mystery was revealed in finishing catechism, or taking first communion. It all seemed to be rituals performed in a rote fashion, long devoid of any living energy or truth. I separated myself from the Lutheran church. I didn't know about Unity or Science of Mind, Religious Science or Unitarian Universalist churches back then. But because I wanted a belief that encompassed the infinity of the entire universe, and still feeling the Loving Presence in Nature, I began calling myself a Universalist.

Warrior Training

I reflect now that the Spartans sent their male children to warrior training school at the age of seven. I wasn't sent to any such "school" and I was female, but my warrior training started much earlier – in the home.

My half-sister, twelve years older than me, had lived with us up until I was four years old. She shielded me during that time from the full effects of my father's violence. She tried to run away at one point; when she was brought home, my father beat her with a belt while I stood by feeling helpless, hurting inside for her. It was intolerable for me to see such pain inflicted. She was sent shortly after that back to live with her real father. From that time on, I was on my own with two dysfunctional adults far more occupied with their ongoing alcoholic-codependent drama than really being parents.

In many ways, Nature herself parented me. She was a good parent, loving, instructing, *present*. Many years later I found a natural affinity for Native American spirituality because of my early connection to Nature, and replaced the word "God" in my vocabulary with "Great Spirit." I came to think of Nature as "Earth Mother." It may also have been in my blood; my father confided to me in my teen years that we carried Cherokee blood from an early relative. I feel my connection with Nature, and the Loving Presence, saved my life many times over. It continues to be a vital, life-giving, life-affirming and very real, connection.

The consequences of being left alone with two such parents, both of whom I loved as most children love their parents, was having to grow up in some ways far too quickly. I couldn't bear the helpless feeling of watching yelling and shouting erupting into violence. I had to do *something*. So one night as the violence escalated, still just four years old, I went to the phone and dialed "O" for operator. I asked her to send the police over "right away," because my dad was really going to hurt my mom. In actuality, he already had. He had thrown her out of the house by her hair.

My father caught me in this act, grabbed the telephone receiver away from me and slammed it back down on the hook, glaring at me. I was terrified, but he didn't touch me and in all the long years and more confrontations of one kind or another, he never did. I think it was because of the unspoken bond we shared. In that instance, the operator managed to trace the call and sent the police to our home that night anyway, so the violence was stopped for that night, to my great relief.

I was learning to put my fear on the back burner and act in defense of my mother against a large, angry, drunk and violent father. Becoming a tomboy was also natural for me as a young warrior-in-training. Later on, in the neighborhood and at school, I applied this in different ways. Though small for my age, when bullies would pick on those smaller, younger or different, I would step in and stop it. I did not allow my small size to stop me, and I made up for it with determination and tenacity, and carefully watching for my opportunities and advantages and taking them. I knew how bad it felt to be treated with scorn and derision, and I couldn't tolerate seeing others hurting or crying from the same kind of treatment. I backed up my protective challenges with physical force when necessary and then, often on reputation and due to the intensely-determined angry gleam in my eye, I was able to warn the bullies off without having to wrestle them down and pin them to the ground.

Throughout my entire life, I have never liked seeing the strong victimize those weaker or different. I became a warrior, ready to stand in defense of those who couldn't defend themselves.

Nights in a Different World

There was this terrifying dream from my childhood, again at age four. My sister was in it, with two of her "friends" but I couldn't see who they were. They took me to a place out on a very, very dark street with a single street lamp. They left me under the light of that lamp and told me to stay there and they'd be back for me later. I waited alone in the circle of light under that street light – everywhere that the light wasn't shining was black and impenetrable as pitch. My sister and her friends didn't come and didn't come. I got more and more scared. I woke up screaming and my mother rushed in, scolding me, "Be quiet! You'll wake your father." My child's self took this in as a message that I was not to trouble my parents with any of my own problems – they had enough of their own. More toughening up, more warrior training.

Retrospective Discoveries and Theories of MemoryRepression

Recounting this dream many years later to Budd Hopkins[1] as one of a string of strange anomalies throughout my life that had me wondering about extraterrestrial abduction, he found the dream of being isolated and alone under a light an abduction flag he was familiar with. More on that part of the actual session later as it was covered again in detail in a later hypnosis with Gloria Hawker[2], a wonderful woman I came to trust and allow to hypnotize me in 2003, to fill in more information about my ET and military abductions.

This is a difficult sharing, but one I feel is necessary: one other part of the Budd Hopkins hypnosis session that did not get put on tape due to the sensitive nature of the experience. But I definitely remember it. It began to explain things I'd had issues with much of my life up to then – and it was a memory of some kind of sexual touching that the Zeta Reticulan ETs did to me as a small child. They were covering my genital area with a clear gel-like substance that had some agent in it that was very arousing on the skin there. While under hypnosis I recalled it in my small child way of thinking and the feelings were powerful and also very frightening. I didn't really have words as a child to explain what I was experiencing, nor did I understand what they were about at the time.

The timing of having this session with Budd Hopkins was one of many synchronicities on my path to healing. At the time of the Budd Hopkins hypnosis session I was in therapy for sex addiction and also attending a 12-step group for the same. Now I began to understand what early conditioning might have led to it. My therapist told me that I had many of the signs of having been molested as a child, but I couldn't remember any instance of it. My father may have been many things, but he was not a child molester. There was a near-miss episode with a teenage neighbor boy; and while that was frightening to recall, I also remember clearly asserting my small self and saying no and leaving the scene. But here was a memory that began to shed some light on things that happened to me early on, that set in motion behaviors that caused me much trouble and heartache later.

[1] Budd Hopkins, June 1931 – August 2011, was one of the first and foremost researchers of the alien abduction phenomenon. He authored several books on the subject including *Intruders: The Incredible Visitations at Copley Woods* upon which a 1992 television miniseries of the same name was based. His website:http://www. intrudersfoundation.org/budd_hopkins.html

[2] Gloria Hawker is a clinical hypnotherapist, social worker who works with others who have had experiences of extraterrestrial and military abductions. She has a great deal of understanding, compassion and empathy for those dealing with such experiences. She is author of *Morning Glory: Diary of an Alien Abductee* in which she shares her own story of abductions with aliens and the military.

By way of honoring the human feelings – whether brought on by human or non-human beings – I feel that each child's sexuality should ideally belong only to him or her self. They should be left to have their childhood, to play and laugh; and one day when they discover, *all on their own*, the pleasure their bodies are capable of, they should be able to go to loving parents with the excitement of that discovery. They should be able to have their parents celebrate that discovery with them, without intrusion, without shaming or laying guilt on them because of it. Sexual intrusion by adults or beings of any kind steals that sexuality from the person it belongs to. It would be wonderful to see what kind of world we could create if children were raised in such a loving supportive way. We have such a sexually repressed society out of which arise all kinds of perversions; pornography exploiting women and children, pedophilia, rape and many more ways in which people are objectified, used, shamed and injured from the physical to the spiritual around sexuality. All manner of harm arises when sex is completely removed from the context of love in which it belongs.

There is a significant difference however between molestation by human beings versus the Zetas. Human beings who molest children in our modern technological culture know they are doing something wrong, yet such people do the acts anyway, and in fear of being caught and being prosecuted. They are afraid and their fear creates anger and threat directed at the child. So molestation done to children is overlaid with a sense of malevolence – dire threats and coercion on the child to keep silent about the abuse, "or else." With the Zeta's there was no such sense of threat, endangerment or malevolence. Just a detached and dispassionate curiosity. It is quite a marked difference in energy and intent, even while the experience itself remains difficult, strange and scary.

Stepping back and looking this issue from the cosmic viewpoint, most of us know we live in a far-from-ideal world. As I've learned over the years, the above paragraph looks at the experience from the third-dimensional human level, at what, in hindsight, would be ideal. I have learned that we must allow ourselves to feel and honor our human feelings before we can step to a higher level and begin to appreciate our lives, individually and collectively, from a higher perspective. As I have searched for understanding, inclusive of all my experiences and how I feel about them from a human level, and observed that we do indeed live in a world that is far from perfect or ideal, I also must acknowledge that if we rise to meet the challenges that life presents to us, we have the opportunities to learn tremendously. So on a soul level, I've come to feel strongly that I made a contract to come into this life, be born to my particular parents and have all the experiences I have had. And if what I have managed to learn from my experiences has shaped me into the person I am today, then I have deep gratitude for ALL of my life, and would not change any of it. If I were to imagine a me going through life without the difficult experiences that have challenged me to stretch myself, to grow, to reach and to overcome, I see a pale shadow of myself who never fully awakened, moving through life in a more automatic fashion, not nearly so alive. One of my favorite spiritual teachers, Ram Dass, aka Richard Alpert, taught us that *life is perfect as it is… and it stinks*. It's one of the strange paradoxes of life on this planet. It's about our E-V-O-L-U-T-I-O-N.

Some of my "dreams" were far more vivid than others, and later years of physical strangenesses around my reproductive functions were also flags of something going on. I know that the people and professionals who would like to stay in comfortable denial about the reality of extraterrestrial abduction can raise any number of arguments about my experiences and those of others being "something else." But the huge numbers of people who have recovered memories of abduction under hypnosis, added to those who have conscious recall of their abduction experiences – with no hypnosis necessary – and the array of similarities connecting all of them are too extensive to dismiss or ignore. Dr. John E. Mack – Harvard tenured professor and, to the chagrin of his peers, abduction and contactee researcher – did much serious work in this field and found abductee/contactees to have no particular forms of mental illness. His own research led him to accept the phenomenon as real and to delve into deeper aspects of it, such as looking at inter-dimensional communication before his untimely death. This esteemed advocate for those of us whose lives have been affected by this phenomenon is sorely missed.

I'm not sure why so many people don't remember their abductions or contacts consciously. I am one of them. I surmise several reasons for this. Perhaps the daytime dramas of some families take up so much conscious energy in the minds of the people entangled in them, that the strange, otherworldly, dreamlike sequences of abductions – so far outside the mind's conditioning of normal everyday reality – are easily pushed into a back closet of forgotten memory. Joe Montaldo[3] of Paranormal Radio Network suggested during an interview I did with him that the problems of alcoholism, domestic violence and other family dysfunctions are actually brought about or aggravated by the ongoing abductions and the internal pressure they create. This internal pressure can lead to the kinds of substance abuse and codependency that breed family dysfunction. I think both scenarios are valid and it becomes question of which came first; "the chicken or the egg," the abductions or the dysfunctions. If family dysfunction is in some way fueled by abductions of family members, then the dysfunction itself makes for an effective camouflage to fill the families' minds with other concerns, resulting in less time and energy to remember strange nocturnal experiences. Smoke and mirrors, bait and switch.

The extraterrestrials themselves are very likely using some method to block memory. The very nature of experiences that pull you out of an accepted reality into one completely outside of "normal" is often traumatic at some level, and the human mind may repress it for this reason. Human beings have different

[3] Joe Montaldo is the co-founder, international director and spokesperson for ICAR – International Community for Alien Research. Starting as a grassroots movement, ICAR is now well established with members in 11 countries. Montaldo and ICAR have investigated over 5,000 cases of alien contact and abduction. Weblink: http://icar1.com/Joe_Montaldo.html.

brainwave states for daytime functioning (beta), daydreaming and creativity (alpha), falling asleep (theta) and deep sleep (delta). If brainwaves are altered in particular ways during abduction or contact, then the experiences can seem dreamlike, except regular dreams don't leave the physical traces that many ET experiencers find on their bodies. They don't leave implants that have been removed and extensively studied, notably by Dr. Roger Leir[4]. Nor do dreams make pregnancies disappear.

Physical Signs

Many times I would wake up with blood running freely from my nose, a large red stain on the pillow. These were no small nosebleeds. I remember one in particular at my grandparents house in Minnesota, waking up with a nosebleed and more adults around remarking on it than usual.

Around age nine I woke up one morning with a pain behind my right ear. I reached up to feel behind it and was startled when my fingers found a small, but pronounced bump there. This frightened me. I wondered if if it was a tumor, if I had cancer and if I was I going to die. The real strangeness of this came later in the day, when I went from worrying that I might be going to die (a serious and intense concern) to completely forgetting about the bump, all my worries about it, and just went on with my life as usual. Staying true to my earlier learned "code", even through I had found this frightening bump upon awakening, I did not tell my parents, did not bother them with my problems. I simply – after being afraid I was going to die – forgot all about it. If I did feel the bump and thought about it later, it seemed that I then remembered it as always being there, that it was just part of my natural bone of the skull. It was like two memories co-existed around this bump, the surface memory of it always being there and being part of me, and the other one running hidden underneath, remembering the pain and the bump suddenly being there. This memory would partially surface from time to time, but having not died, having no explanation for it and not wanting to go to my parents with it, I dismissed it.

It was years later when seeing "Fire in the Sky" at the theater with a couple of friends, the flash of an owl's face on the screen brought the full memory of the bump rushing back in as well as how it had just appeared that morning bringing on the fear of the tumor and of dying. I sat in the movie theater feeling like all the breath had been squeezed out of my body.

Growing up with the Bad and the Good

The life of a child can be a strange thing. Your parents, your life as you move

---

[4] Dr. Roger Leir, author of *Aliens and the Scalpel* is a doctor of podiatry who became interested in and subsequently deeply involved in research of physical traces of abductions: implants. The objects he and his team have removed have been extensively studied by some of the most prestigious laboratories, including the University of California at San Diego and Los Alamos National Labs. His website: http://www.alienscalpel.com.

through it, with no life experience to measure by is all "just how it is" and you really don't have much basis for comparison to other people's lives to know how bad or good your own life is. It's just "your life." I knew my life was not good, that I was unhappy a lot of the time. A lot of time was spent waiting for the other shoe to drop, mostly in the wee hours of the morning when my dad would come crashing in, drunk and raging about something. So, so much upset in that home. My warrior training ground. I did my very best to get up out of bed, to be present for every drunken, enraged confrontation to insure that the violence did not go too far; and if it did, I would step in, calling the police, or standing up to my father with a yardstick or a piece of firewood. He would usually always back down, some still-rational part of him realizing that if his daughter was taking this kind of action, that he was getting out of control. I guess me taking up the warrior stance was his behavior barometer. My parents finally divorced when I was thirteen, but my childhood was already a loss by then; and it was just a shift from one kind of hell to another, one with less extreme drama, but still difficult to live through. My mother was not an easy woman to live with. She was not at all happy about the way her life had turned out.

I was happiest when I was able to be off exploring. We had moved to Ohio when I was eleven and I could cross the farm fields to a little patch of woods and that became my sanctuary. My other happiest times were when I was buried deep in my books, learning and exploring there, or at my maternal grandparents' home in Minnesota. My grandparents were wonderful, like storybook grandparents. Grandma always had the best home-baked cinnamon rolls, cookies and pies, and always the stainless steel pitcher of black cherry or grape Koolaid in the fridge – the old-fashioned kind made with a cup of sugar. She dearly loved every one of her many grandchildren and let us know it with her baked goods, hugs and kisses, and she always could make us laugh with her stories, antics and dancing, sparkling eyes. My Grandpa knew of my love of the outdoors and would take me fishing on Big Lake, Lake Ida, even once on the Mississippi River. I learned to play one of his harmonicas one summer and he gave it to me as a reward.

I loved the idea of space travel and watched with excitement, sitting with my dad, while we both viewed the first manned mission to the moon on TV. We watched Neil Armstrong take his first historic step on our small Earth satellite, the "giant leap for mankind." I was sure Mars was next and I was fascinated with the red planet and read all I could on it. I, at one time, hoped to go, but then it seemed our space program fizzled out.

Later on I discovered inner space – the world of spirit – and started walking the path of a different sort of explorer.

11s, Visions, Wonderings

At 17, because of my singing talent, I auditioned and was chosen for a youth ambassador chorus that would be touring Greece for ten days. I had to get a passport and my mother ordered my birth certificate.

I was born on November 11 and had always wondered about the eleventh day and eleventh month lining up. There on my birth certificate, I saw clearly that I was born at 11am – another eleven. Now I had more to ponder on "11" and what its significance might be to my life. What kind of coincidence brought that about? Born on the 11ᵗʰ month, 11ᵗʰ day, at 11am? It seemed more than just chance to me, even then. Later on in my metaphysical studies I looked into numerology and found 11 to be a master number, along with 22 and 33. I didn't feel like a master of anything! I was too busy still learning.

I had an experience at about 18 years of age that, looking back, seems now was a sign of things to come. By this time I had pretty much concluded that organized religion had nothing to offer me, but I still felt that powerful connection to nature. Some undefinable "something" connected me to nature and nature to me in a way that I definitely felt, but could not qualify or quantify in any manner that made sense to my thinking self.

One early evening, sitting in the family room of our home, alone in the house, I had a vision. The room melted away in front of me and I saw a pure brilliant white light, like a white hole or tunnel. An intense longing to go into that light, to melt into it, swept over me. To the right of the light was something that looked like a pile of refuse, junk, trash, clutter – ugly and unsightly. To me, in that moment, it symbolized aspects of the earthly life.

I could not move into the white light at that time, as much as I wanted to. Somehow I also knew I needed to stay where I was – on Earth.

***

My father passed away at 58 years of age from a catastrophic health collapse involving his heart and alcohol-related diabetes, brought about by a life of workaholism, alcoholism and smoking cigarettes. I miss him to this day. As I've remembered more of my own abductions and contact experiences, I wonder if there was some special purpose or message, to me from him, in handing me all three of Erich von Daniken's *Chariots of the Gods* books to read when I was 17. I devoured them – and wondered about what kinds of beings dwelt out in the stars. Later on, I also began to wonder, since abductions run in families, if my father had stayed out in public bars around people until they closed trying to avoid being "taken."

Von Daniken's books left quite an impression. In my reading, as I grew into young adulthood, I had heard of alien abductions and the subject fascinated me. I read a couple of books about it. I began to wonder if I was an abductee and to wonder about experiences as a young adult in a new light.

Chapter 3: Rights of Passage into Womanhood

This is a hard chapter to write. It deals with much that is very personal to me. We live in such a sexually repressed culture. Out of that repression arise many prurient and perverse sexual behaviors and exploitation of women and children – huge symptoms of just how unhealthy our culture is regarding sexuality. It's very difficult to tell about some of the experiences I'm sharing here. But I also know the difficulties that have arisen in my own life are due to a kind of sexual conditioning I seem to have had from my contacts with the Greys, or Zetas. If others are out there struggling with sexual issues in their personal lives arising from their abductions or contacts with extraterrestrials, and this helps them, it will be worth it. Such issues can manifest as promiscuity and sex addiction, or the reverse, frigidity or sexual shut down. I've experienced both.

***

"Are you sure you were a virgin?"

This question came from the first man I was with at nineteen years of age. During lovemaking, there had been no blood, no pain, nothing to indicate that this had been my first time with a man.

I insisted with absolute sincerity that I had never been with another man, that this WAS my first time. I was telling the truth. I had no memory of being with another man… I had not been with anyone else. Closing my eyes now, remembering that special "first" time with that man some years older than myself, to whom I had been so incredibly attracted, it seems to me that there was some hidden memory running far under the surface, like an subconscious subterranean stream, of a nocturnally-lived life in an entirely different place, part of an entirely different culture. There seemed the tiniest bit of uncertainty in my sincerity, a wondering, a questioning in my own mind, searching for some answer.

My lover of that day and time however seemed convinced. He took me in his arms again and kissed me, murmuring, "You could have lost it riding a bicycle."

Alien Lover?... Strange Pregnancy

I got married about a year later in July of 1974 to a young man my own age. I'll call him Chris. He was in the army and stationed in West Germany, and that's where we lived for about two and a half years.

There was a very strange episode that happened shortly after coming to live overseas. Chris worked some distance away from where we lived, out in a small German town called Gorxheim, so he would have to get up at 4am to get ready and go into his unit for a day's work. As early as that was, I would go back to sleep. But one such morning I woke up having an intense orgasm, all alone in the bed. I had been "dreaming" of a romantic interlude in a tent with a Rudolph Valentino sheik sort of character. Never, before or since, has *a dream* had such an effect on me physically. All by myself in the bed, awakened in such a manner, I flushed with embarrassment, looking around, but all alone.

Later as I learned about being an abductee and I started having suspicions, I told Gloria Hawker I wanted to look at this incident under hypnosis, and we did. More on this later.

In September I went to stay in Heigheim with a German girl friend named Anna, while Chris and Anna's boyfriend Carl were "in the field," meaning out on wartime training maneuvers.

Much of the small population in Heigheim came down with some kind of food poisoning, including my friend and I. It seemed that the little *fleischerei* (German for "butcher shop") in Heigheim had gotten hold of some bad wurst, or sausage. The abdominal pains were excruciating. An old German doctor came around seeing to everyone and gave them opium for the pain. It sure worked. Anna and I were flying higher than a kite, and feeling no more pain. After a couple of days, I was feeling better and started to get up and move around. I got up to go to the kitchen – and once there, I fainted. Anna, still in bed, heard me fall and called to me frantically. I came to a few minutes later on the floor, disoriented.

When I got back to let her know I was okay, but that I had fainted, I also told her about discovering some milky fluid coming from my breasts. Anna, alarmed, said I might be pregnant, or maybe had miscarried. I didn't see how that could be. I had been taking the pill because I didn't want a baby yet. The only thing to do at that point was find a military medical facility where I could be checked out. As an army wife, that was where I had to go. It took a taxi, a bus and the strassenbahn (a German electric cable or street car) to get to the nearest U.S. military medical facility because Heigheim was so far out in rural Germany. Once there, I told them what had happened. They took a pregnancy test and it came up negative. I was getting ready to leave the clinic when one of the medical aids, taking a second look at the test, came rushing out to tell me it was actually positive, not negative. I was sent off with prenatal vitamins and instructions to visit the U.S. Army medical facility in Mannheim, where Chris was stationed, for prenatal care. Since the pill had somehow seemed to fail, I now had to stop taking it due to the "pregnancy." Though the pregnancy was unplanned, I did want my baby.

From the pregnancy test results, I was given a delivery date in May 1975. As the pregnancy progressed, the Army doctors told me that the baby was too small and likely would not come to term or would not live. It was a very stressful time, wondering if I was going to lose my baby, month after month. On top of it all, I had morning sickness the entire nine months. I could feel the baby growing and moving, so I took what comfort I could from that.

May came and went and no delivery. The good news was, about the end of March, the doctor told me the baby's size had normalized and we didn't have to worry about a stillbirth or it being too small. When June arrived with no sign of labor, the doctor ordered an ultrasound, which had to be done in a German hospital. There they found that my baby was not yet full term, but would be in July and gave me a new delivery date of July 13. By this time I was pretty aggravated. It was like feeling eleven months pregnant instead of nine. When July 13 came and went, they brought me to the hospital to induce labor. I think they were as tired of my pregnancy as I was. The labor took two days and had to be induced all the way through. The afternoon of the 17th my daughter, Karly, was born, eight pounds, one ounce, nineteen inches long and as beautiful as a little china doll. She was nicely filled out, not red and wrinkled as some newborns are. I loved her immediately. She was active, happy and even started sleeping all night at three weeks, so she was pretty easy on her mom and dad.

But what caused such a strange teetering-on-the-edge pregnancy test before I was even pregnant? I had been on the pill, had had a regular period (though very light) and Chris had been gone on maneuvers for over a month. I suppose that the food poisoning might have caused some irregularity with this, and that's what I assumed in trying to make sense of it. Now I think what really may have happened is there was some "other" pregnancy that was either harvested or miscarried before or after the food poisoning episode. Because I thought I was pregnant, and stopped taking the pill because of it, I did actually become pregnant with my husband when he returned from the training maneuvers. Beyond surmising that, it's still a mystery of many unanswered questions.

After Karly was born, we made a visit back home to Ohio to see our families. My father was the proudest grandpa I ever saw and my mother was delighted with her as well. Karly was a fun baby, with a wonderful, sunny disposition. Dad showed Karly off to all his friends. I was really happy he got to see her because it was only months later that he suddenly passed away from the heart attack brought about by the years of alcohol and nicotine abuse.

I was growing extremely unhappy in my marriage. My husband was always feeling like he had to prove his masculinity from some deficiency he felt about being so short and slight of build. I felt like kind of a "trophy wife." I was an attractive woman and it seemed to boost his male ego to have a pretty wife. He did not seem interested in me as a person in the least however, or in just the two of us spending time together. When the news came of my father's passing, I had already announced my intention to get a divorce.

Chris tried to convince me not to do this, but I had been far too unhappy in the marriage to reconsider. But with the news about my father, I went home to the states to deal with that loss and grief. I wasn't surprised by the news, but saddened. When visiting with my father before getting married, I found he was often throwing up blood from an ulcerated stomach. He was in the final stage of his alcoholism. He needed a morning "hair of the dog" to steady his hands upon arising. He knew at that point his problem was severe, but did not know how to stop drinking. I pleaded with him to stop. I didn't want to lose my dad.

I remember seeing him in the casket when I got back home to the states. He looked like a waxen figure. My real father was not in there, that was clear. He was a lingering presence that I silently felt alongside me during the funeral, having our last communion, soul to soul, before he moved on.

I followed through with the divorce.

A Brush with Spirit Guidance

After breaking with the Lutheran church at sixteen and calling myself a Universalist (a name I felt might be big enough to express the kind of spirituality I was in tune with inside myself) I was excited to find the Unity Church of Toledo, Ohio. Once I found it I couldn't wait to attend and see what it was like.

It was a complete breath of fresh air. I was delighted to have found a place where people seemed to be looking for truth in similar ways to myself – seeking, questioning, looking in places that were outside the mainstream and the hypocrisy of orthodox religion – which, by that time, I had heartily had enough of.

I wandered through the church's book store after service, fascinated by all the books filled with subjects I hungered to learn more about. I wondered which book would be the best for me to read at this time to tell me more of how to live a spiritual, as opposed to religious, life.

Before I even finished forming this hint of an internal question, a gentle answer rang softly through my mind:

> Just decide what you believe is the best way to live your life
> for yourself, then live according to your own beliefs. Life itself
> will show you anything out of harmony within those beliefs
> and you can adjust and fine-tune them as necessary.

What an answer! I was very impressed with the quality of it, the wisdom of it. I did not buy a book that day.

I met Tim Northrup there, who would become a metaphysical mentor and friend. He played piano for Unity Toledo. I also met a wonderful woman, Martha Monahan, who became an immediate friend. I came to think of her as my metaphysical mom. She was so unlike my own mother – I could talk with her about anything and everything.

Later, in the parking lot, conversing with some people, I heard a young man mention "Eckankar" and that word stood out for me. His name was Keven.

Later in life, for several years, I became a student, or chela, of Eckankar. I learned a great deal of value there. In my second marriage, to a man I'll call Matt, I had a son. When I first became pregnant, I was doing my morning contemplation practice. A vision of the Eckankar inner master brought me a little blonde-headed boy of about three years old, leading him by the hand. He said, "This is going to be your son." I replied that I had been hoping for another girl. He smiled, and answered, "For many reasons we won't go into right now, you need to have a son."

I went back to bed and told Matt that I thought we would be having a boy. Eight months later, Travis was born. He was born with a head of black hair, but later it came in all light blonde. Travis took his first toddering steps in the Eckankar Center in Las Vegas, NV, and he was born on October 23, the day of the Eckankar new year.

Eckankar is called the Ancient Science of Soul Travel. Oftentimes, this would happen in the dream state. One night I had such an experience. The inner master came into my dream to take me to the higher dimensional realms. However, in passing through the astral plane, I kept getting lost in thought creations made of my own undisciplined thoughts. It was as if I would think of something and it would jump to life around me like a mock movie set and I would find myself involved in it like an actor in a scene. The master would come and tap me on the shoulder, gently telling me that this was not our destination. When this happened to me a third time, he smiled gently and told me we would try it again once I learned more discipline over my thoughts.

I have remembered this experience vividly down through the years. It was to have a profound impact on my life at a pivotal moment in the future.

I left Eckankar later on, when their spiritual leadership underwent a schism. My heart was pulling towards the former head of the organization. He had been the one who brought Travis to me in the vision so early in my pregnancy. He had been the one who had tried to guide me through the higher dimensions in my dream, so gentle and so kind. My mind however was pulling me to stay with the organization's new leader. I also thought a great deal of him. However, I could not find a way to resolve the split this created in me, except to go back to keeping my own counsel and following my own unique spiritual path.

A Difficult But Valuable Lesson

In those early days of attending the Toledo Unity Church, I became briefly involved with Keven. It was a relationship that taught me many hard lessons, but extremely valuable ones.

Mainly I came to see how manipulative he was, to a degree that for me, almost seemed to cross into the realm of black magic. It seemed so premeditated and precise. He would purposely do something that I would get very angry about, very afraid of, or very sad about. Then when I was in that emotional state, he seemed to know just how to push the right buttons to get me to do what he wanted me to do.

This game finally came to an end when he began working on me to give up my daughter Karly to a foster home! My love for and care of my daughter was an interference to his control. I talked with Martha about it, that I was feeling worried that he would keep pushing my buttons, manipulating my emotions until I started thinking it would be a good idea to give up Karly. Martha was really alarmed. She told me to put him out of my life immediately. It took very little convincing. I was pretty much at that point myself.

He left many of his possessions at my place, and after I ended the relationship, I came down with a strange ailment. My solar plexus region became tender and swollen. This happened to several people in my circle of friends, including Martha, who also knew Keven. Tim Northrup told us to go through our things and get rid of anything we had that Keven had given us or that we had that was connected to him or his energy. We did so and the distended soreness in the solar plexus left us.

I had the most stuff to get out of my home. I piled it all in the back of my truck and took it to his place and started pitching it out of the truck onto the lawn. All his manipulations were clear to me and I was not happy about it. Keven came out of the house as I was doing this and looked enraged, but he had not responded to my requests to come and get his things out of my home, leaving me no other alternative. As I looked at him, his face looked twisted to me, like a satanic goat's face. It was startling. I was glad to drive off and leave him and all of that experience behind.

This relationship did provide me with a good learning experience about how being emotionally off-balance leaves one open to all kinds of manipulation not in one's best interest. It left me with an ability to spot it in all kinds of places – especially the media – as the years passed.

I later wrote a letter to Eckankar about this person asking about him and his connection with the organization. Before even finishing the letter, I got a clear inner answer that this "troubled person" was in no way representative of the philosophy or teachings of Eckankar.

Dreaming of Extraterrestrial Craft

One of few the good things that happened in this relationship, was a camping trip where Keven took me to a place called Warren Light Center outside of Franklin, in northwestern Pennsylvania. It was a magical time in a lot of ways, being out in nature that I loved so much. And one of the nights there I had a remarkable... dream.

I dreamed of an extraterrestrial space craft and was shown its basic design and operating principles.

It was saucer-shaped and in the design, which was very simple and elegant, around the inside of the base of the craft were six donut or torus-shaped electromagnetic "coils" – meaning they functioned like electromagnetic coils, but were just smooth metal tori. These six tori were evenly positioned around the inside of the base of the saucer. I don't remember there being any wiring that connected them to anything. But in the center of the craft where a pilot would sit, there was a console that I knew was activated by the thought energy of the pilot, like a neural interface without any wires or connections to the pilot other than a hand or maybe even the body sitting in the seat connected to/touching the craft. He or she would just think, or intend where they wanted to go and the console would transmit this by field energetics as coordinates. These thought-energetic field coordinates then activated the magnetic field in the tori and generated the correct field in them to interface with the magnetic field at the location on or above the planet. Basically the craft and its technology operated like the extended body of the pilot, neurologically. The interface between pilot, craft, console and tori would make the speed-of-thought corrections to the magnetic field generated by the tori to move the craft in any direction, at whatever speed the pilot wanted to move.

I woke up from this "dream" amazed and excited by the details I remembered and by the idea of such a propulsion system, which I understood from being such a good science student, could work, at least in theory – though it was extremely advanced in comparison to our clunky, pollution-spewing automobiles, planes, or even our space shuttles. Here is a picture I drew of it:

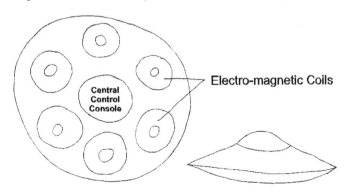

Central Control Console

Electro-magnetic Coils

Postscript to this dream: Over nine years later a friend fixed me up a blind date with a man. There were no romantic sparks, but we did have an interesting conversation about UFOs. I told him I had a dream about how they worked and that I could draw a picture and he excitedly said, "Wait, wait, wait!" He had me draw the picture while he went to another room. He came back out with his own diagram. Years ago for him, he had also had the same dream, coming back to his waking life with the same basic diagram! In a way, I wish we had stayed in touch.

***

Out of the Body

Another experience I had in my early 20s after my divorce and before joining the Air Force, was an out-of-body experience. My interest in metaphysics was taking hold.

In Tim's metaphysical class and discussion group, I learned about meditation, about the third eye and pineal gland and much more. I became interested in astral travel. I had no idea I was already doing it while I slept at night.

I read Robert Monroe's *Journeys Out of the Body*. One day I sat on the edge of my sofa and made up my own mantra for this: "I can, I will, I am..." meaning, astrally projecting. I closed my eyes and repeated it over and over.

Suddenly I felt a sensation as if a vacuum cleaner hose sucked me out of my body through the top of my head and a popping... noise? Sensation? I wasn't sure which. But there I was, out of my body.

It was nothing like I had imagined, which actually completely validated the experience for me. I had imagined a "ghost me" like my own form would step out of my earthly body. Not even! I could see 360 degrees, very hard to imagine in a body that sees out of two eyes that have a general range of 180 degrees plus some peripheral vision. It was as if I became a spherical being, or an orb, endowed with vision, auditory and other multi-sensory abilities without the human organs these faculties would normally would operate through. I felt incredibly free – there was no tug of emotional energies on this "body" that are always present to a greater or lesser degree in the human body.

I decided to look down at my human body, sitting on the edge of the sofa. When the intention to do this was formed, it was as if a thousand tiny points of light all gathered together and coalesced and shot a "vision beam" down towards my body. I had a general impression of floating at the point where the ceiling and the wall met, opposite my body on the sofa, at the same time feeling much more distant from it than this would suggest. In my attention moving along that beam to look at my body, my body looked very tiny and crystalline down there, like looking through the wrong end of a small telescope.

I realized with elation that I was really, truly out of my body – and wham! Suddenly I was back in my body. I have since wondered if I had to come back into my body to experience the emotion of elation or excitement I felt about successfully projecting out of it.

I wrote a poem to try and capture the experiential essence of what I had sensed.

Suspended...
On a sea of velvet night sensing a fine sparkle about me, not unlike stars.

I floated...
An atom of consciousness, a spark of awareness at once both minute and as vast as that nightime sea itself, endless in its splendor.

A being...
Complete, with a knowing beyond the complex realm of thought and reason, freed of the constrains of my human self.

I turned...
Noticing that my awareness moved out from my center like perfect vision in every direction.

I focused...
Down on my human-self, seen as through the wrong end of a 'glass, tiny and crystalline, the realization coming only then – I was no longer within my shell of flesh and blood.

Suddenly...
In that same micro-second as that revelation of freedom I was slammed back into my human sheath...

Trying...
Through my sense of wonder to translate the joy and magnitude of my experience of the Infinite into terms my human-self could grasp.

What peace...
What joyous adventure awaits me once my duties to this Earth world are complete!

~ Niara Terela Isley

This experience was a true gift. And the profound, total realization that I was more than simply a human body was a real lifeline to me in the years ahead of me.

***

As the years of my young adulthood went on, more strange things happened. I was continually frustrated by my figure – there seemed to be a little roundness to my belly much of the time that no amount of exercise or dieting would get rid of.

I didn't like doctors, didn't like their instruments, didn't like being poked and prodded and examined. But I did go to them when it felt absolutely necessary, for exams our medical system insists women get on a regular basis. Even still, I was delinquent in making appointments for these check-ups more often than not. And when I did show up for these exams, I almost always would be asked:

"Are you pregnant?"

This was not just a routine question in many cases, from the tone of the doctors' voices. There was something about the exams they did that made them ask.

I would say no – I was on the pill, or I hadn't been with anyone for however long. A couple of times, unconvinced, doctors did pregnancy tests, which came out negative.

I do remember that, in all the years of taking "the pill" I had only token, barely-there periods.

The "Are you pregnant?" question happened so often year to year that finally I asked the doctor why he thought I was pregnant. He told me my uterus was enlarged. I didn't know what to make of that and felt confused and frustrated. It didn't make sense to me. And I just wanted to get out of the doctor's office in each case as quickly as I could.

The rest of my life was still taking up a great deal of my attention. Growing up in a dysfunctional family often leaves the children with an addiction to drama and adrenalin. My first husband was also alcoholic, but not a violent one. My second husband Matt was a violent alcoholic like my father. I was playing out the family pattern as grown children of alcoholic and dysfunctional families often do. But I was questioning it. Why had I ended up in such marriages? In the first one, I had really wanted to get away from my own dysfunctional family. I wanted some peace. But that's not what I got. In the second marriage, it was such a confused period of my life, with a big chunk of missing time while I was active duty Air Force, it was hard to know what got me into that marriage. It was an intense love-hate kind of relationship. I look back now, scratch my head and wonder, why did I marry this man? More on the strangeness and wonderings about this in the next chapter covering my four years in the Air Force, when Matt and I met and became involved during that part of my life where so much memory is missing.

Another strange pregnancy happened in June of 1980, a tubal pregnancy. It ruptured and the pain was the most excruciating I have ever experienced. I lay doubled over, moaning and crying with it, and as a warrior woman who didn't moan or cry about much of anything back then, that's saying a lot about the shape I was in. I had excessive and profuse bleeding along with the pain. Matt took me to the Nellis AFB hospital emergency room. They told me I was just having severe menstrual cramps and sent me home with over-the-counter aspirin.

Actually, I was hemorrhaging to death inside from the rupture.

The next day on my own initiative I called a civilian OB/GYN doctor, Dr. Taylor, to whom the military had referred me for some care that couldn't be handled at the base hospital. When I explained what had been happening, the office staff had me come in immediately. The excruciating pain had subsided, but I was utterly exhausted and very weak. Once in his office, Dr. Taylor took one look at me and without even examining me, had me immediately hospitalized. My pallor had taken on a greyish cast because of the severe amount of blood loss.

Dr. Taylor operated on me later that afternoon and found the ruptured tubal pregnancy. He cleaned that out of me along with the destroyed right fallopian tube and ovary. I came within a hair's breadth of having to have a blood transfusion due to how much blood I had lost. Dr. Taylor saved my life. If I had relied only on the military doctors, I would have died.

This pregnancy happened because of Matt getting some conservative religious chaplain to gang up on me with him and convince me that if I really loved and trusted my husband, I would consent to getting pregnant and having a child with him. This was total craziness in actuality. When a marriage is in trouble, bringing a child into it is the last thing that should be done, but Matt had a way of wearing away at me verbally until I gave in. I had an IUD device at that time and had to go to Dr. Taylor off the base to have it removed. Then the tubal pregnancy happened soon after, nearly killing me. It was a life-threatening lesson in acting against my inner guidance. I didn't forget it.

I wasn't the greatest at being a good, enabling codependent wife, especially in my second marriage. I left the messes Matt made while drunk, not cleaning them up, so he would have to confront them when he was sober. I didn't bail him out of jail after the first violent episode that took me by surprise, though his buddies did and I had to go stay with friends for protection that night. And after that first episode, I was ready for him, my earlier warrior training in childhood kicking into full gear. Several times I hit back, even with a doubled up fist, standing ready and quite able to defend myself against his attacks. He was bigger, but drunk and unsteady. It was easy to get the upper hand and press that advantage. After a while, I made my point and didn't need to take swings at him.

I asked myself what the hell had gotten me into this situation and began to really look at childhood patterning. I finally divorced Matt, and have had zero tolerance for drinking or alcoholism ever since. No more drunks in my life.

Consciously, I thought I wanted to experience what a true loving relationship would be like with all my heart and soul. But I think my desire for freedom and problems with anyone trying to exert any control over me whatsoever may have been working from the deep unconscious – seeing relationships or marriage as a signing away of my personal freedom, and always finding a way to sabotage any that came up. Even non-alcoholic men were controlling at times, and I found I had a controlling streak in my personality as a counter-measure. Since I consciously thought I wanted a loving relationship, I did an intense amount of reading, study and processing to try and create the right conditions within myself to attract a healthy relationship. Later, as a certified body-centered relationship and personal transformation life coach, I learned that when you can't seem to create what you think you want in your life, you need to discover what the unconscious counter-commitment is deep within you to having it. This requires some deep excavation of the psyche, using body-centered techniques. I discovered only in the last few years a deep, hitherto unconscious desire to remain free, and equating relationships with being controlled and with a loss of freedom. I spent a great deal of time in my life focused on this issue, not on things extraterrestrial. Since I didn't even have hypnosis to recover my lost memories until I was nearly 40, it's no wonder I left the extraterrestrial material alone for so long.

Let's return to my school years for a bit. My school years were an intensely difficult time for me. I was always different, always off in my studies about the sciences and beginning to move into metaphysical studies, beginning with astrology. I wore glasses, and my parents forced me to get braces on my teeth. The fact that I had a great rock collection on display in the school's science fair cabinet did nothing to enhance my popularity with the "in crowd" either. I was just different, and with the handicaps of the glasses and braces, I was a social outcast. In spite of my warrior training and my stoic attitude, it hurt to feel so isolated, though I kept this to myself, deep within. I felt lonely. I would sometimes watch boyfriends and girlfriends together and wonder what it might be like. I wondered what it would be like to be popular.

In my senior year, the braces came off and I got contact lenses and I was suddenly, instantly, attractive. And it was like being handed a loaded gun. It was too late to change my nerd reputation at school. However after graduation, with my new attractiveness, I started to see what kind of life I had been missing out on for so many years. As a young woman who really liked sex, and thought of herself as a "free spirit" like so many who came of age in the early 1970s, I discovered only in much later years that a kind of sexual programming or conditioning in early childhood had been done with me by the Greys or

Zetas. It seemed to be for their purposes of studying human sexuality. My first hypnosis session revealed some of this while I was concurrently in therapy and a 12-step group for sex addiction, and I don't think the timing of that was any accident. I look at this now as a synchronicity from my spirit guides to aid me in my overall healing journey. Learning and understanding this has brought a great deal of peace, and a cessation of any urge to continue acting out such behavior. One of the other things that has brought peace to me is the final deep realization that what I really wanted to experience was love, and sex addiction behavior was destroying any chance that I would ever find the kind of love I was really looking for.

To recount all my relationship misadventures and the sexual acting out during the years of my twenties and early thirties is beyond the scope and purpose of this book. It did happen. Much of what happened was outside of my own value system, which is a sure sign of addiction. I definitely have some regrets. I did have extra-marital affairs, but in those cases, only when extreme unhappiness in the marriage drove me to find some comfort and solace elsewhere. Ironically, even though Matt, when drunk, always accused me of having an affair, I never did, not until nearly the very end of our marriage.

I've chosen to be open in sharing what was going on in my personal life around relationships and sexuality because I want to illustrate that there were issues I was dealing with that had their origins in the extraterrestrial abductions I had as a child – a kind of conditioning that I finally began to seriously question and examine in therapy after years of behavior that often made no sense and caused me a great deal of emotional pain. If you're reading this, and you are also an abductee or experiencer who has had to deal with similar issues, I hope at the very least it helps you to know you are not alone. You can overcome it if you have the courage to face everything you need to face to heal and recover.

Beginning the Journey to Inner Peace

I actually stopped the main acting out addiction behavior in my mid-thirties, though I still had to deal with the underlying issues. I concluded at that point that I was far happier when I was "the nerd" studying science, metaphysics and spirituality out of wondering what made this world tick at a deeper, unseen level than I was while acting out some role of an attractive woman playing the field. I got into a good relationship with a man named Rich Edwards. We were together for five years before trying to blend his kids and mine together, some money issues, and my own increasing episodes of depression (latent PTSD) caused us to part.

During that relationship, tension, depression and angst in me that I'd previously blamed on bad past relationships surfaced in a way that had me looking at myself more closely. It was hard to pin down to any current, conscious cause. When the intensity of it peaked at one point, I decided I just couldn't live with it any more and quietly decided to commit suicide. Obviously I didn't do it. But that episode did bring about a crisis in consciousness that took my life in a new direction. More about that in Part Two.

The journey to inner peace has not been an easy one, and I find it to be a continuing process. I returned afresh to spiritual studies and practices, taking up Buddhist Vipassana meditation and yoga. I found people in meditation and yoga communities that I could trust more and really connect with on much better levels than I previously had with people in general. My inner walls and stoicism began to break down.

***

This was the life I was living in young, then moving into middle, adulthood. A young ill-fated marriage and divorce, later a term of four years in the U.S. Air Force and a second failed marriage that ended once we were both out of the service. A good relationship for a span of several years, a near-suicide, then single again, beginning the years of self-inquiry, exploration and healing. If I thought about strange possible pregnancies and abductions at all, I shoved such thoughts to the back burner as too strange to deal with. There were no supportive people around me to talk about or explore such things, just an unspoken sense of disapproval that I somehow felt. I chose not to go there much in thought and almost never in word. If I mentioned my experiences to others, they would calmly explain that the people who believe such alien abductions happen must be mistaking such ideations for "something else." They weren't clear on what the "something else" might be. I didn't want to lose the support of new spiritual friends or community, so I kept away from the subject, at least ostensibly.

Other Physical Signs

Besides the strangeness around my female reproductive organs over the years with doctors asking me about pregnancies, there had been another physical sign. At age thirty-five, I decided I was done with childbearing, having had both my daughter by my first marriage and my son by my second marriage. So I saw Dr. Taylor who had saved my life during the tubal pregnancy incident in 1980 – he was one of the very few doctors I trusted – about having a tubal ligation. I didn't want to stay on the pill indefinitely. I don't like foreign substances or drugs in my body.

Dr. Taylor did the procedure in his office under general anesthesia, meaning I was awake for the procedure. When he had created the incision and opening to perform the procedure, he said with some consternation, "Your whole abdominal cavity is full of adhesions – have you had any other procedures?" Feeling concerned from the tone in his voice, I said, "No, I haven't. I kind of

38

tend to stay away from you doctors as much as I can!" I used a joking tone to ease the tension of the moment. He shook his head a little and made one more comment on the strangeness of it, and that was that. I was left wondering about this and what it could mean.

During my post-operative briefing, the doctor who did my hysterectomy in May of 2008 also made a point of remarking on the many adhesions in my abdominal cavity.

Years later when I had hypnosis to look at my abductions and learned of multiple pregnancies being harvested from me with a needle through my belly-button, there was a good explanation for such adhesions. I had been subjected to procedures that I didn't even remember happening.

***

The five-year failed relationship with Rich was almost a third marriage except there was no ceremony, we just lived together. We were great friends as well as lovers and remain close friends to this day. Trying to blend our different families – his kids with mine – was a challenge we couldn't seem to work out. Contributing factors were my episodes of depression and anxiety. I now know that I was suffering from post-traumatic stress disorder, PTSD. I just didn't know yet what was causing it or why.

Around this time I met a new male friend – I'll call him Nick – who was deeply involved in the field of UFO-extraterrestrial-government cover-ups. He was also well versed in matters of spirituality. I could talk to him about some of the things I had been wondering about for so long. It was Nick who noticed some inconsistencies in how I talked about certain things, particularly my military time in service. He noticed that while I was, in his terminology, "bright, detailed and articulate" in conversation about almost any other topic, I was often vague when talking about the time in my life spent in the Air Force. One afternoon he sat me down and asked me to tell him about my time in the Air Force, going through it chronologically. I agreed and we sat down to talk.

I was about to enter a realm where the world suddenly did a reversal, like the negative of an old film photograph, strange, frightening, surreal. Life would never be the same again.

Chapter 4: Part of my Life is Missing

Memory Works Just Fine... Up to a Point

"Tell me about your military time, starting from when you entered to when you got out."

Nick was asking me to remember as many details as I could. He had noticed a vagueness when I talked about this time of my life, a marked shift from what he called my usual articulate communication style. I'm actually sharing even more detail here than I did with him then, just to show that my memory works quite well the majority of the time.

I recounted my April 15, 1979 entry into the Air Force in Cleveland, Ohio, traveling from there to Lackland AFB, near San Antonio, Texas. I was in boot camp (basic training) for six weeks from mid-April to the end of May. I had a problem come up part of the way through with excruciating pain in my right foot, but if I reported it, I could have been set back to another flight, starting boot camp all over again from the beginning. I didn't want to stay at Lackland one minute longer than necessary – so I lived with the pain, running, marching and drilling until my flight (the group of women recruits I trained with at the 3703 squadron) graduated and we left for our various technical training schools. I must have done a great job of suppressing the pain (I was ever the warrior) because we were given the distinction of being an honor flight due to our exemplary performance on the drill pad.

I was also a quiet rebel. I remember one of our T.I.s (training instructors) seeing us girls rolling our eyes to one side at a flight of guys standing at parade rest alongside our flight, waiting to go into the chow hall, and he loudly told us to "Take a good look, 'cause that's what you're not getting any of for six weeks!" Nor were we allowed to have any alcoholic beverages during boot camp. As things turned out, that was not precisely the way it happened in my case. Because we were an honor flight, we got two town passes instead of one. The first one I spent with friends I'd made there at Lackland, doing the San Antonio tourist thing, seeing the Alamo and such. The second one I rode into San Antonio with an MP trainee I'd met on the base. We drank margaritas in the Plaza and then checked into the Davy Crockett Motel for the afternoon. Such was my respect for authority.

For my career field, technical training school was at Keesler AFB, in Biloxi, Mississippi. I was in the automatic tracking radar school, career field 33303.

Autotrack radar is a type of surface-to-air missile or anti-aircraft artillery radar. While there, I finally saw a doctor about my foot and found out my arch had collapsed! My foot was put in a semi-cast for six weeks. I marveled that I'd been able to endure the pain as I had at Lackland.

Keesler AFB was a time of schooling and lots of partying. I was still enjoying being an attractive adult woman after all the years of not being regarded so through school. But a serious fright sent me a wake-up call about all the partying.

Karly, my daughter, had come to live with me while at training school. We lived in a trailer park outside the back gate. One afternoon while partying and drinking with friends, the afternoon turned into evening and it started to get dark. I noticed that Karly was nowhere to be seen. I turned just about instantly sober with fear and went to look for her. After about a half hour search, I found her at a neighboring trailer with an old lady who was enjoying Karly's chatter and serving her cookies and milk. I was so grateful and so relieved! My inner spiritual perspective, which never really left me despite my detour into the party life, told me that this *was* a wake-up call, to clean up my act. I took it to heart, though partying was a habit at that point that took some time to break, since I had to shift or let go of some social connections. I was much more careful after that incident and resolved to really make a complete change in my lifestyle once I was at my new duty station – Nellis AFB.

Hurricane Frederick roared through Biloxi while I was there. We were called in to stay on the base for safety while it raged over the area. I had a bad sore throat and was home with Karly and had to pack us both in to the base. We stayed on the third floor of one of the squadron buildings, and I remember a foot of water even there on the third floor from the hurricane. Power was out for a few days after it passed. When Karly and I returned to our trailer, the sliding glass door had shattered into the livingroom and much was soaked. Quite a clean-up was required.

I was at Keesler AFB until November when, finished with training, I traveled to my mother's place in Ohio for Thanksgiving and Christmas before taking the bus with four-year-old Karly out to Nellis AFB in North Las Vegas, Nevada, my first duty station.

Once there, by way of orientation, I was introduced to Deb Jenkins who had been at Nellis for a while, and was in the same career field. We hit it off well and decided to rent an apartment together, since base housing was full. She had a strange but nice collection of friends, mostly all Air Force as well. There was Dan, who had a strange compulsion to massage the shoulders of any woman he happened to be close to. It creeped many of us girls out so we had to set boundaries. Basically he was a pretty nice guy outside of that and very much in his head, an intellectual. There was Marty and her girlfriend Barbara (not Air Force). And there was Barry Eastman, who I later became involved with for a several weeks.

Orientation around the base was fairly unremarkable. I was issued jungle camouflage fatigues and an O.D. (stands for olive drab) green Australian bush hat. It was a special uniform for the members of the 554th Range Group unit to which I was assigned. I remember an interview with a base officer, but only saw him the one time, so I don't remember his name. I remember that he needed a pen for some reason and reached out an took mine from my fatigue shirt pocket. I didn't like that at all. No strange man, officer or enlisted, had any right to place his hands that close to my person in the chest area. He could have asked me for it. This is the kind of thing that if a woman complained about back then, she was labeled too sensitive or something like that.

Many of us at Keesler had received our orders as we approached graduation from radar tech school. Almost all of the auto-track radar specialists had been sent to Nellis. There was a large pilot training facility there with a whole range of auto-track radar sites that were used in exercises to teach pilots to fly against radar threats in combat situations.

North Las Vegas, Nevada blended seamlessly into Las Vegas, the dream vacation destination for millions of people around the world. Many of my peers were excited to live in such a place where gambling was everywhere and magnificent shows with globally-known celebrities abounded.

I, turning over my "new leaf" and working on leaving the party life behind, was far less impressed with these aspects of Las Vegas than with the stunning natural beauty of the deserts that surrounded the city. I began to explore them, taking Karly on long drives out through the desert terrain. There were yucca plants, Joshua trees, short, brief little stands of cactus here and there, and piñon pine. There was juniper and graceful silvery-grey branching creosote, with its clusters of bright, waxy green leaves, that made the desert smell wonderful after a thunderstorm deluge. I fell in love with this glorious desert landscape and made frequent visits to Red Rock Canyon, Mount Charleston and Valley of Fire. It helped greatly to ease me back into my more spiritual and nature-connected lifestyle, out of and away from the party life. There are many other details from this time I remember, and could recount here – just to demonstrate that my memory works just fine – up to the next point.

Finally it was time to go to work up range, to Tonopah and the Tonopah Electronic Warfare Range.

When I got to this part of my story, I stared into space in dismay and a wave of nausea swept over me. I couldn't remember anything. The only thing I could tell Nick was that I worked at Tonopah Electronic Warfare Range, alternating weeks. One week up at Tonopah to work on the range, then one week down on at Nellis. I was shocked. Surely I could simply remember the just the name of the motel I stayed at in the town of Tonopah every other week, but that was a blank too. I felt scared and still slightly sick to my stomach.

"I can't remember anything... anything! All I can tell you is that I worked at Tonopah every other week."

Nick, with a straight face, told me that I had violated a security oath of some kind and was now under arrest. I looked at him, stricken, and he immediately dropped that facade, hard to keep up anyway with that hippie long hair of his and his decidedly anti-establishment attitudes. He could see that I was genuinely disturbed, frightened, shaken. He spent some time after that asking me gentle questions and trying to soothe the shake up I'd just experienced. He told me he was ever so sincerely sorry for cracking such a bad joke about the arrest. We are still friends, and he still apologizes periodically.

My memories seemed to pick up in more detail again once I had transferred from Tonopah Electronic Warfare Range to Tolicha Peak Electronic Warfare Range. The town we stayed at for work there was Beatty, Nevada, alternating weeks. It was a more rugged range unit there than in Tonopah, and in a mostly male-dominated career field, where putting up with various forms of sexual harassment were frequent and disgusting. Over a few months, and after making several complaints, I was moved to orderly room administrative duties down at Nellis.

The reason for the transfer to Tolicha Peak was because of my involvement with and marriage to, Matt, which occurred under strange enough circumstances. You'd think meeting a future husband would be memorable enough to stick in your memory, but I only retain a couple of memories of our time together in those early months, while I was still assigned to Tonopah. It was a marriage that quickly turned to a very dysfunctional love-hate relationship. The day we got married was not a happy one. Matt had nearly ended the relationship the night before due to him being drunk and calling me to break it off. He sobered up and came back in the wee hours of the morning and said he was sorry. In the morning, he wanted to get married. I didn't want to and we had another fight about that. I ended up giving in when I should have run like hell. To this day I have no idea why I gave in to something that was obviously, blaringly, a huge mistake. I resisted putting in my name change with the military for three months after the marriage because of our difficulties. Then there was the pressure and coercion he put on me to have a baby with him and the subsequent tubal pregnancy and near-brush with death. We nearly broke up several times in the first year. His violent alcoholism had me always on alert. If he had been drinking, I needed to be ready to physically defend myself. The marriage lasted five years – somehow – and we did have a son, Travis, together in 1982.

I've wondered in the years since then just what the hell was going on at that time that I landed myself in such a marriage and such a situation. Though I remember more from the time after leaving Tonopah and being assigned to Tolicha Peak, parts of my life are still vague and uncertain all the way through June of 1980 when the tubal pregnancy happened. I've uneasily wondered if Matt was either a knowing or unknowing participant in what happened to me at Tonopah, or not. Those questions remain unanswered.

My memories were much more normal during the time period covering the rest of my enlistment. I was at Nellis just over a year, then spent about a year at

44

Gila Bend Air Force Auxiliary Field in Arizona. After that we went to Mountain Home AFB in Idaho. Once again, I was tempted to re-up (re-enlist), stay in the Air Force and divorce Matt, who wanted to get out. Despite my issues with authority, there was an orderliness to military life that I felt comfortable with, and other opportunities within that structure that I would have liked to explore – such as getting more involved with working with people than electronics equipment. But I stayed married, and took my honorable discharge after serving my four years of enlistment. In hindsight, I'm very glad I got out of the military.

In Search of Memory

After this deeply disturbing discovery of a few months of life and experiences I couldn't remember, I set myself to probing into that area. For instance, I was sure I could at least remember the name of the motel the Air Force put us up at there. It took about a week but I finally did remember – it was the L & L Motel; and the motel that others were billeted at on the edge of town was the Sundowner.

I thought of people I had known before going to Tonopah who I knew had been at Tonopah the same time as I had. There was Deb Jenkins, whom I shared an apartment with, but she was on the other alternate week rotation and looked after my daughter when I was up range. Remembering her was not much of a problem. There was Susan Foster, a friend since tech school at Keesler AFB. I knew she had also been sent to Tonopah. I remembered another friend I'd known after Nellis at Gila Bend who had also been at Tonopah, Sherry Wentworth and her husband Steve. Working with my knowledge of these people, I tried to trace a path down into the abyss that my missing memories lay at the bottom of.

I didn't get very far. I was able to remember small things, and a few more people. I remembered a Tonopah celebration called Jim Butler days where Air Force personnel were given permission not to shave for a month for the beard-growing contest that was part of the celebration. There was one guy who won hands down, a Sgt. Boughman. He was the hairiest man I've ever seen. In remembering him, I then remembered a party I went to at Lake Mead with many of these other co-workers. Seeing him in swim trucks with so much hair was, let's say, memorable.

Because of my interest in astrology, I managed to remember another guy, a black guy, named Landon Hudson. He knew a lot about astrology, but used it to hit on girls so I kept my distance. Another couple of people drifted up into memory, but I could only recall faces, not names. One was a young man who was another radar operator at the radar site I worked at. He was really good at tracking the jets that flew overhead. Another was a man, likely in his 40s, who worked at the little one-room commissary at the Tonopah main facility on the range. It was a stop we all made before going out to the range to buy our lunches. He had wavy black hair and, I'm pretty sure, blue eyes. He was fit, tall and strong-looking and didn't seem to me to be a likely candidate for the job he held and I wondered if there was more to him than just a one-room commissary clerk.

Still working at recall, I also remembered a young man named Patrick Barnes to whom I felt strangely drawn, enough so that I broke off my several-weeks involvement with Barry Eastman, a fun relationship that I was really enjoying. In hindsight, I don't know why I did that in the least. Barry and I had fabulous chemistry and were having a great time together. Patrick was moody and kind of nervous and jittery seeming. Our time together was short-lived. In remembering him, I also managed to remember him driving us down from Tonopah in his car, which he had driven up range instead of taking the bus. In spite of me pointing out he only had a quarter tank of gas when we were passing the last gas station for over 90 miles, he chose to drive on thinking we'd make it. We did not and this caused me to be late getting home to my little girl after a week away. I was pretty annoyed and broke it off with Patrick at that point.

Tracking memory back through the people I remembered, I managed to remember Sherry Wentworth (the friend I remembered from Gila Bend) visiting the Tonopah radar site where I worked. She and I were standing on the deck of the radar van in the afternoon sunshine. She mentioned "Dreamland" and how much she'd like to know the kinds of things they kept out there. This was the very first reference I had ever heard to that area, so highly classified back then that it's very existence was denied by the military and the government.

I managed to remember a couple of nights out on the town in Tonopah, eating dinner at the Mitzpah, and shooting pool and having some drinks at a bar called the Joker with Susan Foster.

Extremely disturbing as I write this chapter is my effort to try and remember the "first date" when I became involved with Matt, which had to have happened during these three missing months. I remember becoming involved with Chris, my first husband. But with Matt I can't recall the process of becoming involved much at all. We did have a brief date towards the end of technical training school at Keesler AFB, but it didn't really go anywhere at that point.

After the unknown mystery of how Matt and I became involved in the first place, I do remember one totally crazy date together during what I think would have been the latter part of my time at Tonopah. I had driven my car up to Tonopah that week. One evening after getting back to Tonopah from the range I jumped in the car and drove at insane speed down to Beatty to spend a little time with him, then rocketed my car back to Tonopah afterward to grab a couple hours of sleep before having to get up and go to work the next morning.

But why can't I remember our first date at Nellis? Or remember what should have been some of our really best times together, of bonding and intimacy, the first flush of new romance?

This was about the extent of what I managed to remember, and it wasn't much considering I spent three months or so there. With the exception of the memory of the afternoon chat with Sherry and the young man who was a radar operator at our site, whose name I don't remember, there were no memories of "the work" I did up there at all.

Just What is Memory?

In trying to piece together memories, I realized that memory is associative and has what I call a fractal dispersion. It forms linking chains that have many associative connections, called "clustering," the organization of related information into specific and overlapping groups. I would add that these groups of related information are arranged in ways that have meaning to the individual, and that context and meaning vary from individual to individual.

In conversations with friends on any topic at all, I'd watch how the conversation would develop and the turns it would take to differing topics. One of us would mention something and that something would have a particular list of associations in the memory of the other of us and we would pick the most interesting or relevant association and share about it. Something in that sharing would create yet another association chain in memory and off we would go on that tangent or fractal iteration of the conversation. Thirty minutes to a couple hours – and many conversational iterations later – the conversation would be nowhere near where it had started.

Through these observations, I pondered over what it would take and how it could be accomplished to "erase" a person's memories. If you remember the earlier part of this book, I was always a good student of the sciences and still am. I wondered if "they" had a way to go into the brain and chemically or neurologically break the chains of memories to isolate a chunk from a particular time – removing it from the usual linkage or associative process of memory. I was both shocked and fascinated when, many years later, the movies *Paycheck* (2003) and *Eternal Sunshine of the Spotless Mind* (2004) came out. These movies demonstrated nearly the exact kind of technology I had envisioned back in the 90s while trying to figure out how my memories could have been taken from me. So exact was the movie imagery to my own surmising and deductions of nearly a decade earlier, I had to wonder if the movies were showing some actual technology that really existed, and had existed for quite some time that might have been used on me. Movies or television showing various scenarios using virtual reality also had a deep impact on me emotionally. *Vanilla Sky* (2001) starring Tom Cruise had me terrified and in tears. And I can't begin to tell you why.

Interested in adding an understanding of chaos theory to my knowledge, I read *The Turbulent Mirror: An Illustrated Guide to Chaos Theory and the Science of Wholeness* by John Briggs and F. David Peat. I got most of the way through it. I came upon a section of the book on chaos and the brain, and found an entry that mentioned Los Alamos National Labs experimenting with fractal dimensions of strange attractors associated with different levels of anesthesia. Los Alamos National Labs is a government contractor, also one of the significant presences out on the Nevada Test Site. I remember feeling like someone walked over my grave when I read that. I put the book aside at that point and never did get back to finishing it – yet another emotional red flag of something amiss in me.

Memory Recall: Stronger Methods

In 1991 the relationship I'd had for five years with Rich ended. I went back to government contract work for Computer Sciences Corporation, a contractor to the Environmental Protection Agency's facility in Las Vegas, NV. I was there just over a year when a flare-up of my chronic carpal tunnel syndrome in both hands caused me to be laid off.

The next job I applied for, with yet another government contractor, was again out at the Nevada Test Site, on the Yucca Mountain Project with Science Applications International Corporation (SAIC). I went for the interview out to the Sample Management Facility at Area 25, or Jackass Flats.

I later decided Jackass Flats was an apt name for such a place, since they were considering building a nuclear waste repository on the Nevada Test Site. The location is dotted with signs of ancient volcanic activity. A small cinder cone sits on an open plain to the west-northwest from the top of Yucca Mountain and Yucca "Mountain" itself is actually a huge layered ash-flow drift from a large volcanic caldera that had built up from many past eruptions. From my early studies and interest in volcanology I didn't think you could ever trust a volcano to be completely extinct. A better term is dormant, and even if the volcanic plug is hundreds of thousands of years old – cold and solid – magmas under pressure, rising again to the surface in the area will find the weakest spot in the earth's crust and do just that. One can only guess how drilling for core samples might have weakened the crust, or digging the tunnels for the underground nuclear waste repository. The nearby town of Beatty had Bailey Hot Springs just outside town. Hot springs are heated by still hot, active magma at some depth below the surface. The idea of a radioactive volcano erupting, spewing radioactive ash, lava or even a devastating pyroclastic cloud to poison an area of possibly hundreds of square miles depending on the violence of the eruption is a pretty ghastly thought.

SAIC sent me a job offer by mail, at a rate of pay I found completely unappealing. The job entailed four ten-hour work days per week, not including the two-hour drive on either side of that ten hour work day to get to work and then back to town. I sent a letter back declining the offer due to the low rate of pay. They came back with an offer of over a dollar an hour more from the previously-offered rate. I accepted the job at that point. I didn't think much of the raise in the offered rate until later on.

While working at the Nevada Test Site on the Yucca Mountain Project I had the opportunity to attend the 1994 Whole Life Expo in Las Vegas. It was there that I met Budd Hopkins, who did a lecture on alien abductions.

That connection, and the hypnosis session that happened as a result of it, caused my life to career off in a completely unexpected, and chilling, direction. My world was about to be turned inside out.

Chapter 5: The Ground Jerked from Beneath My Feet

Not making much money and short of cash at the time, I volunteered to help out at the Whole Life Expo that came to Las Vegas in 1994. This gave me the opportunity to attend some of the presentations, particularly the presentations that dealt with UFOs and abductions. I was planning a career change and had just graduated from a massage school in August a couple of months earlier, so massage was one of the skills I offered as a volunteer. One of the people I gave a neck and shoulder massage to was Alexander Collier. His plane had arrived late, creating a stressful situation for him. I later saw his presentation and from that time forward, I have been impressed with Alex's big heart, passion, sincerity and the depth of his caring for others, as well as the incredible information he imparts from his Andromedan contacts. I know his life has been far from easy.

I saw many fascinating speakers there but seeing Budd Hopkins was the most important for me. I'd seen him give a lecture in Las Vegas before, but did not approach him with questions at that time. This time, after his presentation on abductions, I raised my hand.

"I have three months of missing time from the Air Force; I saw a shadow-type of being you mentioned in another lecture I saw with you about a year ago; I have a childhood nightmare I woke up from about being under a streetlight and some other strange stuff I have always been wondering about – any ideas?"

"Please talk with me after this is over," was his reply. So I stayed until the question and answer session was over, along with another woman. Both of us had experiences that were rattling around in us unremembered and unresolved. She had a memory of seeing a praying mantis.

I accompanied Budd to where he did a hypnosis session with her. She had indeed had an experience where she encountered a mantis being, among other things. Later on, once her session was complete, it was my turn.

We did quite a long pre-session interview where I discussed the things that were bothering me, the wave of nausea that accompanied the fact that I could not remember months of my life, and the contrasts between what I could and couldn't remember. Budd remarked on how strange it was that I had hardly any memories of the early beginning days of my romance with my second husband, which also would have been taking place during the period of missing time from the Air Force."

Once he put me under hypnosis, we first looked at my childhood "dream" of being left alone under the street lamp. The suspicious thing about it was being "under a light." Many abductees are examined at length, and medical types of procedures are done on them under such a light.

The quality of the sounds and voices on tape from that session was very bad. There were lots of strange interference kinds of sounds that made the tape extremely hard to review or transcribe. A whole section of nearly twenty minutes was altogether missing, that section filled with only white noise. But here are the experiences that emerged, gleaned mostly from remembering the session and some attempts to review the tape. It's very hard to forget that material; it seared itself into my memory with some amazing and terrifying details.

That night I awakened at four years old – screaming and terrified from the "dream" – was indeed an abduction. I remember reporting that, "It's nighttime, but my room is filled with light!" I was lifted out of bed right through the ceiling and seemed to be with my older sister and two "unseen" friends. Much of this is reiterated later in more detail when I share my session with Gloria Hawker.

Me being examined with the stomach pressor.

The truly reality-shattering material came when we looked at the military missing time.

When we started this part of the session my breathing got more labored, more stressed. Even under hypnosis it was like the words to tell what was going on had to be forced out of my throat – I had to force them out through

52

my lips. The first thing I reported in this part of the hypnosis session, in answer to Budd's questions, was that I shouldn't be seeing what I was seeing and that my body felt strange; numbness and tingling running all through it. My head started to hurt, the pain becoming more and more severe as the session continued.

I found myself out on the deck of a radar van in the middle of the night with three men who were also radar operators. It was a type of radar that I was assigned to and that I operated – an auto-track radar.

Auto-track radar is a type of surface-to-air missile or anti-aircraft artillery radar. Because it tracks with a tiny pencil beam that paints a target on an aircraft, it gives that radar site, if fully operational, the ability to accurately target and bring down that aircraft with missiles or artillery fire. The radar van is like the back part of a semi-truck trailer, filled with radar equipment. Because of the height of the trailer from the ground, a wooden deck is usually built adjacent to it with steps for access. We taught pilots to fly against radar and use electronic countermeasures to break the radar locks on their aircraft when we would acquire them as a target. There was a big event once a year out there called Red Flag. A movie was actually made about it, more from the pilots' viewpoint, called *Red Flag* starring William Devane. We did other training the rest of the time with jets flying training missions, mostly out of Victorville in California.

Standing on that deck that night, I was watching lights in the sky – *saucer-shaped craft*. They would flash at times, lighting up the nighttime desert floor like heat lightning from a approaching thunderstorm. One was close enough to see in pretty good detail. Out just beyond the radar antenna array, perhaps a hundred feet or a bit less, away from the radar van, it was hanging in the sky, gently rocking. It was glowing orange on the bottom. The bottom seemed like a translucent metal skin from under which the orange glow was coming from. There was an appearance of a spin on the bottom, but it seemed to me to be the way the lights under that "skin" were rapidly lighting, round and round in sequence, rather than an actual spinning of the bottom of the craft. There was a round section in the center of the underside, making me think of the wheel within a wheel going on its side, mentioned in the book of Ezekiel in the bible. There were several craft in the sky that night, but this one was the closest. I think there may have been as many as twelve to fifteen, and I later heard Bob Lazar in a radio interview saying that there were nine craft out at the Groom Lake base in some of his testimony, so the numbers are close. My attention was focused on the one closest to me and the sheer amazement of seeing it.

I was also terribly scared. And not of the UFOs, or more correctly, the extraterrestrial craft. I only had a secret security clearance and what I was seeing had to be far more highly classified than "secret." The reason for the high level of fear was revealed in my subsequent hypnosis with Gloria Hawker. With her, I learned that myself and the others had been very harshly ordered and transported out there in Chevy or GMC Suburban vehicles in an intimidating and threatening manner. We were given our usual jungle fatigues to wear (this is what our unit wore out there on the range) but with no name tags, rank insignia or any identifying marks whatsoever. We were ordered in no uncertain terms not to speak to each other beyond what was necessary to run the radar and try to track these craft.

In this hypnosis sequence with Budd, that test was now over and there were some people I assumed to be officers inside the radar van talking about something, perhaps the results of the radar test. The radar was not able to track these craft at all. No clunky, mechanical, auto-track radar antenna device we operated out there could rotate around fast enough to track these things. They could move faster than the eye could follow. They could be in one place, then wink out of existence and reappear in another part of the sky. No way could a radar like the one I worked on maintain a lock on such a craft.

At one point I was asked what I thought I was seeing and I said, "Looks like UFOs to me." The answer I got was, "could be..." with a short chortle of unpleasant laughter. Not much of a straight answer.

I might have experienced wonder and awe at what I was seeing if I hadn't been so scared, so filled with apprehension. Next, we were loaded onto an old school bus painted Air Force blue, with painted over windows and taken "elsewhere." I don't know for sure if it was Area 51, but back then I couldn't imagine another base out there in the middle of the Nevada desert with so much in the way of buildings and various facilities. I have since heard William Pawelec's[1] posthumous interview with Steven Greer of the Disclosure Project about an underground facility at Tonopah. In light of this new information I now include that facility as a possibility of where we were taken.

About this time in the session I had a splitting, crescendo-ing headache. Budd gave me a suggestion to make it go away, and while it eased somewhat, it did not go away. My short, shallow, stressed breathing and tension level increased still higher.

We were unloaded in the destination location and herded into a large building with white walls and lots of light. From there we were taken to what seemed to be a waiting room in a medical dispensary or facility of some kind. The room was fairly square and had a row of chairs we were ordered to sit down on. These were arranged in the room running in a row, catty-cornered, the ends of the row pointing to opposite corners of the room, kind of bisecting it diagonally. Years later, a place I worked had some of the same types of chairs sitting in the offices, so I took a picture of one:

---

[1] Mr. William Pawelec was a U.S. Air Force computer operations and programming specialist with numerous credentials in security technologies and access control systems. He gave this interview with Dr. Greer prior to the 2001 National Press Club Disclosure event and asked that it not be released until after his death. Mr. William Pawelec passed away on May 22, 2007 and Dr. Greer received permission to release it in December 2010. A video of this interview is now available on YouTube. The following link is to an article about Pawelec featuring his wife, Annie DeRiso: http://www.skyshipsovercashiers.com/articles11.html#Pawelec.

The Chair

The lights were off in this waiting room, the only light coming in was from a hallway with closed double doors with windows, situated behind the chairs we were seated in. Again harshly ordered not to speak to each other, with an armed guard present to enforce this, we sat silently and waited, not knowing for what. Soon, one by one, our names were called to go into an adjoining room from that waiting area. People went in there, but didn't come out.

When it was my turn, I went in and was told to lay down, fully clothed, on a stainless steel examining table. There was another armed guard standing at parade rest next to the wall at the foot of the table. I asked what was going on, what was happening, but got no answers to my questions.

I waited some unknown time. It seemed very long because I was getting more and more terrified by the minute. Then a man in a white lab coat came in. He had dark hair, dark eyebrows, no glasses, and his face was covered by a surgical mask. He walked in the same door I had entered through, past the guard and up around the right side of the table, saying three times in a deadpan voice: "Stay calm, stay calm, stay calm."

When he got up beside the right side of my head, his hand came up in one smooth move, like he had done this many times before, and injected me with a syringe needle in the right side of the neck. Whatever the chemical was went straight to my brain. In the hypnosis session I felt more tingling and numbness, pins and needles, all over my scalp.

That was about when the session ended. I had had enough for one evening. Once back in normal waking consciousness from the hypnosis, the first words out of my mouth were; "God damn it." It came out more like a statement than an expletive.

Budd asked me why I was saying that and I answered, "Just... government shit. It's really aggravating the things... that people can just abuse your life as a human being."

The strange sensations and the pain in my head persisted once I was out of hypnosis. Budd suggested that I may have been given a directive that if I ever remembered any of this that my head would ache and/or feel strange, and I concur with that opinion.

We had a post-session discussion and Budd apprised me of what kind of process might unfold in the days ahead. He said some things would be vague or unclear but other things would become more clear and sharp. He said I might start remembering more details on my own and he actually gave me a suggestion while under hypnosis that this would happen. Although I didn't remember too much more than what I recalled in the session, the details of what I did get became sharper. I think I was afraid to remember more because what I had remembered was so frightening and disturbing. He warned me of physical shock reactions and going into denial – deciding it was too crazy, too nutty... never happened.

And yet this information did begin to connect with other parts of my life. It started making sense of things going on in my life that I had not understood fully up to this point. Budd also remarked on the deep authenticity of the feelings I had experienced under hypnosis when I was remembering/reliving the events I was telling about. He also tried to lead me in directions away from what I was reporting about to help add to the authenticity of what I remembered. He told me that if I was somehow "making it up" under hypnosis, I would have followed his leads and "imagined" something along the lines he tried to guide me into. I didn't go there – I was experiencing what I was experiencing and that was that – and that was what I told. He told me life would be kind of a roller-coaster for a while.

"Roller-coaster" didn't begin to cover it.

I had heard of abductions by beings with big, black eyes. I had never heard of the kind of things that came out of my military missing time. I had never heard the term "MILAB." Things done to me by the Greys paled in comparison to the kind of treatment I underwent while reliving the military experiences and the levels of fear they generated. I didn't want to believe this was possible, because if it was, then everything I had grown up believing about the United States of America being the land of the free and the home of the brave was a lie. There was the ideal of the U.S.A. that most people believed in, and then there was this other shadowy "thing" that did things to people under cover of some kind of highly-classified secrecy. No wonder it didn't matter if I had only a secret security clearance. *These people took me out there and exposed me to seeing extraterrestrial craft in action because they knew what was going to be done to me later would cause me not to remember it.*

I did exactly what Budd had warned me I might do, I *tried* to go into denial. This couldn't be true – could it? Denial held out some way to hang onto my current reality – to believe these memories and the potency of the feelings that went with them shattered it completely. The power of the sensations and heavy emotional charge I was experiencing had me in their grip despite the denial I tried to muster up. The headache after the session that had persisted for three days was real. I was caught between not wanting to believe it, and feeling a very real level of terror that I kept pushing down so I could function at my job.

And all this had happened out in the never-never land of the Nevada Test Site and here I was, working out there again at that time, on the Yucca Mountain Project. Getting on a bus to go out to work suddenly seemed like giving away too much control over myself to others. I started driving my own car to work. I wore a buck knife on my belt – the only thing I could get through the security gate that I could use to defend myself – if necessary. I started looking over my shoulder a lot. It seemed that someone had gone to a great deal of trouble to make me forget what I had gone through out there – surely they might be keeping some kinds of tabs on me to make sure I didn't remember. So I was terribly scared that "they" would find out that I was remembering – and then what might happen? I wondered what kind of other memories might emerge in more sessions, and I wasn't at all ready to find out. I both wondered about it and kept crashing some door inside me shut on even trying to find out more.

I needed more information. I started going to groups and lectures that were being done in Las Vegas at the time. I met a woman named Miesha Johnston who did contactee groups for kids and adults. She was the most helpful person, and had knowledge of the kinds of things I remembered. She was very supportive and tried to help me as best she could, with both the ET abduction memories and the military experiences. She introduced me to James Bartley at one point, telling me he had had experiences similar to mine, but at the time I shied away from really talking to him. I was afraid of hearing too much confirmation, and yet I needed to hear it and understand it. Just what the hell had really happened to me out there? And why? How could such things happen in this country? What was recovered was such a small piece of over three months of missing time. What else might be remembered?

It was a time of strange pushing away from hearing too much that would confirm my experiences, and at the same time desperately needing to understand more of what had happened. I read, I spoke with people, I attended talks on all subjects related to UFOs, some providing frighteningly similar testimony to my own experiences.

My race through dark places, my quest for information I was scared to even hear continued. If my memories were not true, I should not have found corroborating information out there. Instead, I found far more that confirmed my experiences than not. I talked with John Lear, Jr.[2] at his home in the Las Vegas area. I spoke with George Knapp once and I had a long talk with John

[2] John Lear, son of Lear jet inventor, Bill Lear, holds Federal Aviation Administration (FAA) certifications for all types of aircraft, including airplane transport rating, flight instructor, ground instructor, flight navigator, engineer, aircraft dispatcher, airframe powerplant mechanic, parachute rigger, and tower operator. During the late 1980s and early 1990s, John began coming forward with some startling revelations concerning the subject of aerial phenomena and UFOs.

Rhodes[3] at a local restaurant one day. All this, together with the level of fear I was feeling in my body, confirmed my experiences more and more each day. I knew intuitively then, and know now as a trained body-centered coach, that the body, and the feelings it feels, don't lie. And energetically, even when physical memory engrams in the brain might be disrupted or suppressed, everything that happens to us is stored in our human energy field, or aura, and cannot be erased. It is part of our energetic soul record.

I visited Rachel, Nevada and spent some time talking to Glenn Campbell, who had the Area 51 Research Center there at that time. It was Glenn who told Bruce Burgess about me, and this was how I ended up talking about my experiences in his 1996 documentary *Dreamland*. I was unhappy in the extreme with how that interview ended up being shown when the documentary aired.

While in Rachel, I also met a person there who had had a sex change operation so that the aliens would stop coming to take his sperm. This was kind of the last straw for me. Pursuing this kind of information from so many people who, like me, were trying to piece parts of an immense jigsaw puzzle together from their experiences and their own searches, began to feel like I was at the edge of a huge black hole event horizon, being sucked in to be spun off to who-knew-where. I met many grim conspiracy theorists who were angry (and quite justifiably so on one level). But it was kind of an impotent rage that I could not see doing anything to stop such human rights abuses from happening. It was, however, certainly negatively affecting the lives of those who harbored the anger.

Up to the point of the hypnosis session with Budd, my life had been mainly about spirituality, about trying to see and understand what was really true in the universe. I wanted it to be about that again. I did not want to be sucked down into this world of dark conspiracy, grim anger and paranoia of what this shadow government might be secretly perpetrating on an unsuspecting public. Experiencers and researchers seemed like a bunch of people running around endlessly trying to fit their pieces of the puzzle together and get some idea of what was going on. But the vital pieces, in the hands of the shadow government and the extraterrestrials themselves, were missing and out of reach. How could one ever get any real answers when so much was missing and inaccessible? Never, I decided resolutely. And I'm outta here.

I was making a move to California with another boyfriend who turned out to be very abusive. I ended the relationship with him. I focused on getting my social work degree, and went back to my meditation, a healthy lifestyle in a community with caring people. The memories of extraterrestrial abductions and especially the military experiences still haunted me, but I just kept shoving them away. Life felt more normal again and I was more or less content. I started working with people with the body-centered techniques I had been learning, helping them heal self-esteem issues and learn to be more transparent and

[3] John Rhodes is a researcher focusing on reptilian beings, underground bases, cattle mutilations, men-in-black and more. His website:http://www.reptoids.com.

authentic. This helped them to reclaim much of their life energy.

Yet it became more and more evident over time that my own life still had big holes in this area. When I looked into those holes, they became windows back into the dark memories of the terrible trauma I experienced while in the military. It became more and more clear that somehow I was going to have to deal with those disowned parts of myself to really reclaim my own authenticity and life energy. I was walking through life in a kind of apologetic fashion, trying to keep these memories and the terror that was connected to them from destroying my life. I saw my current friends as so very innocent of knowing the kinds of things I knew, and many of the people I tried to have a quiet conversation with about these things didn't want to hear about them. They were too scary, too paradigm-shattering for them to even contemplate. Some people were able to hear me, but I still felt at the outside edge of my circle of friends – looking in, but forever separate. My experiences set me apart, and no amount of spiritual practice from a place of avoidance was going to help me escape them. In fact, quite the opposite.

The essence of a spiritual journey through life is to know yourself deeply. And I could not forever run from the experiences that had such a hold on me from deep within. Energy medicine of various varieties shows us that when energy flow in the human body is blocked, the blockage creates problems in the body, in the mind and emotions, the heart and the spirit. It becomes a persistent itch, an irritant that commands our attention for resolution and healing. Ignored or suppressed for too long, such blocked energy turns to degenerative disease.

About the same time I was realizing that I needed to go more deeply into these memories from the past and find some way to deal with them, the presidential election in November 2000, through some kind of subterfuge, put Bush and Cheney in the White House. In another country of the world, it would be called a political coup. Here no one named it such. The future of our country hung by chads on recounted ballots. Finally it was declared over and the people of this country were presented with the *fait accompli*: a Bush-Cheney administration.

Right after graduation from California State University, Sacramento, spring of 2001, I moved to Durango, Colorado. It was a spiritually-directed move. I had wanted to go to Tucson, Arizona but my spirit guides within said southwestern Colorado or northwestern New Mexico. So I got out a map and looked at this Four Corners region, and Durango, Colorado seemed to light up. I "knew" that was the place. Amazingly, even on a tiny income, the money and circumstances seemed to fall into place and I was on my way just two weeks after graduation.

A few short months after settling into my new hometown, the horror of September 11, 2001, with the destruction of the World Trade Center, hit the country like a giant sledgehammer. I got a knot in my stomach watching the twin towers fall on television that day, seeing them fall like a controlled demolition. The level of total destruction was completely inconsistent with the damage of planes flying into the buildings.

Reeling in shock, a stunned population looked to Washington D.C. for help and our legislators passed the Patriot Act into law. Always paying attention because of my own memories of what people in the shadow government were capable of, I was angry and aghast at the Patriot Act, which was absolutely unconstitutional in my estimation. Then Bush-Cheney took us into war with Iraq on specious allegations of Iraq having developed "weapons of mass destruction." This war was not ratified by Congress. The situation in this country appeared to be spiraling out of control. The whole world was shocked at the behavior of the U.S., as a president and vice-president, not duly elected by the people, began to wield the vast military might of the U.S. like their personal arsenal. Drunk with power, they tried to pass into law anything and everything that would allow them to write themselves a blank check to do whatever they wanted, people and the environment be damned.

In this alarming political climate, the terror and the post-traumatic stress I had been living with – and trying to suppress – erupted into real fear again and nearly panic. It looked to me like all our constitutional rights could be stripped away, leaving people vulnerable to possibly similar kinds of abuse and trauma I had suffered out on the Nevada desert in 1980.

I needed more answers. I needed more of the blanks filled in. And in 2003, I finally found someone I trusted to look for it all with, Gloria Hawker.

Entr'acte II
The Fall of Lyra, the Flight to Terra

This is how I remember first experiencing fear and the contraction and limitation of consciousness. How learning through stark contrast started for us, for the people of Lyra.

The strangers who came to our world were reptilian humanoids. They were very courteous at first. They asked if they might mine our world for some needed ores and minerals to save their own world.

We, and especially our elders, were cautious of these strange beings. Their energy and vibration was very "alien" to us. We did not have any experience with such vibratory energy as they carried. We could not sense it in the way we were used to. In many ways, these beings were closed to us energetically.

It was in our nature to give aid however. Though mining was not a concept we were pleased with because of its disruption of Lyra's ecosystem, we gave permission for a particular area to be mined.

Over time, these visitors became more and more aggressive. In our travels over and around our world, we saw that they were not restricting their mining activities to the designated area. It was spreading, and devastating large tracts of the Lyran landscape.

A group of our people, some of them our elders, went out to speak with them about this. When a confronted, these strangers killed several of our people, including one of our elders. All around the entire planet, this act was sensed and felt. As a people, we experienced a terrible shock for the first time.

It was the beginning of truly knowing fear. The experience of it had terrible energetic consequences. The energy of fear contracted and densified our vibration. We could no longer access the higher planes and dimensions. We had difficulty in moving about at the speed of thought as we once had – it required a tremendous relaxed kind of focus that became very hard to achieve. We found ourselves locked within our forms. This increased our fear... we now knew how vulnerable our forms were. A survival mindset was swiftly born in us out of absolute necessity.

Once any pretense of amicable relations with the reptilians ended, they began more and more killing. Some of our people were enslaved, suffering unspeakably at the hands of their captors. We as Lyrans, always energetically connected, felt their agony, and some of us pulled our senses in from touching their minds and spirits for our own survival. It was a shame, yet a necessity. Some of us remained in contact to try to give the captured the solace of continued connection, but it took a terrible toll on those people to do so. Many of them did not survive, even though they remained "untouched."

My people came to know anger. Some of them wanted to strike back at these invaders, but my people did not know how to wage a war. Some tried to fight back but, completely inexperienced, they did were no match for the enemy. The engagements always ended in more of our people being slaughtered. My people fled, falling back more and more. Our planetary home was fast becoming a conquered world.

The reptilians were in no hurry to dominate everywhere. It was clear to them that we were no real threat.

Desperate to protect the younger Lyrans, a plan was conceived to save them. Several motherships that had been being prepared for colonizing and life-seeding missions to other worlds were selected to carry Lyra's younger generation away with them. Parents hurriedly instructed their children about the respective missions and their roles in them, getting their children and young people aboard these motherships as quickly as possible. The elders and advisory councils of each ship took charge of these young people.

My mother, father and and uncle got me passage on a ship that was headed out to seed a planet called Terra. At the cost of their own lives, they stayed behind to make sure I was safely away.

I arrived on the mothership in shock, taking my place among other young people as much in shock as myself. We were torn away from everything we'd ever known. From family. From our beautiful, living conscious planet. In one inner chorus of resounding grief, we wept for the the loss of a paradise we had been born into and loved with our whole being.

Chapter 6: The Extraterrestrial Experiences Transcript

During that weekend I stayed with Gloria, we did two long sessions, one on Saturday and one on Sunday. We looked at the extraterrestrial experiences first. On the session tapes Gloria spoke in a very soft voice much of the time so some of her words were undecipherable. Other insertions like (???) also indicate words that were too soft to be heard in transcribing the tape, and some words in brackets are more adult words that are better descriptors of what I was seeing and experiencing.

As I had worked on and cleared away any old material from childhood and adolescence I could remember that might have contributed to the sex addiction, stripping away any and all conscious causes for it, I was left with a troubling area I could not reach somehow. Though I was much more at peace around the issue, I was still wondering about factors that seemed hidden from me that might have a bearing on this.

In this session more answers began to emerge to fill in a more complete picture.

Thursday, March 27, 2003

GLORIA: You can speak anytime you need to speak. Any particular day... you're a brand new bride, August of 1974. What is your husband's name?

NIARA: Chris.

GLORIA: One night, both went to bed, knowing he had to get up real early, very early... the next morning. And which he does. What time does he get up?

NIARA: Four.

GLORIA: Four o'clock?

NIARA: Mm-hm.

GLORIA: I want to know how you're feeling.

NIARA: Sleepy... sleepy...

GLORIA: And what else?

NIARA: Just listening to him getting dressed and ready to go.

GLORIA: Where does he have to go?

NIARA: He has to go to the base in Mannheim.

GLORIA: And what kind of work does he do?

NIARA: He's a turret mechanic on tanks.

GLORIA: I want you now to take over. This is your memory, your story. And you tell me everything that happened before he left and after he left. You're there now. You're living that memory.

NIARA: He's gone. And I just want to go back to sleep, I feel so sleepy. I'm under a blanket with blue and white checks... the blanket has like blue gingham with checks... a big blanket. Hmmm... there's like somebody else here with me.

GLORIA: Who's this?

NIARA: It's hard to see. I'm feeling really... this... I just feel sexual in my whole body, from the tips of my fingers to the tips of my toes... and it's not right because my husband is not here.

GLORIA: Let's go back to you feeling something there. Where do you feel this presence?

NIARA: It's like there's someone floating over me.

GLORIA: Can you look at it?

NIARA: Yeah, I can look.

GLORIA: Your eyes open?

NIARA: It's... it keeps changing.

GLORIA: What is it?

NIARA: First I see these big eyes.

GLORIA: What color are the eyes?

NIARA: Black.

GLORIA: How big are they?

NIARA: They're really big.

GLORIA: The shape?

NIARA: Um... kind of oval... going up at the sides. And the face is really hard to see. I see mostly the eyes and there just doesn't seem to be much of a face.

GLORIA: Where are the eyes at right now? How close are they to you?

NIARA: They're right over my face. And then it changes and it starts to look more human.

GLORIA: What does it look like? Describe.

NIARA: It just kind of fades back and forth.

GLORIA: What does it look like?

NIARA: Um... it's a man with dark skin and dark hair. He has eyes that are really intense, hypnotic.

GLORIA: What color are the eyes?

NIARA: They're very dark, almost black or brown... very dark brown or black.

GLORIA: Can you see his face now?

NIARA: It feels like something touching my left breast, but it feels light and spidery feeling. And there's a feeling in the left nipple, like it's being touched very lightly.

GLORIA: What's your reaction?

NIARA: I feel scared and I feel really turned on at the same time.

GLORIA: Is it a human?

NIARA: It just seems to keep changing back and forth. I'll think it's this thing with big eyes. Then I'll start to feel scared and it kind of melts into this man's face, and it just goes back and forth, and...

GLORIA: Tell me what the other individual's like, or the other form...

NIARA: It's a pale grey skin, big eyes, and the body's very thin and white. (Pause.) I don't know why... I don't understand why I'm feeling so sexual with this person or this thing near me. I don't want to be feeling this, but I'm feeling it. It gets more scary, and then it goes back to the man.

GLORIA: Do you recognize the man?

NIARA: No, not really. He's somebody I don't know. He's very attractive.

GLORIA: Can you tell what he looks like?

NIARA: Big, very dark intense eyes,,, just looking into my eyes. Dark hair and he's touching me all over.

GLORIA: What does it feel like when he touches you?

NIARA: It doesn't feel like a healing touching me... it just really feels light, like spider webs.

GLORIA: And what do you do?

NIARA: The sexual feelings are so strong, I just want to go with them, even though it's scary. There's something in me... and it's just... I'm moving with it, just going with it... the sexual feelings are so powerful, I'm just going with it.

GLORIA: What happens after...

NIARA: I feel a little tight in my chest.

GLORIA: Do you feel another person lying on your body?

NIARA: It's strange. I feel something inside me, but I don't feel hardly any weight on me. And it's very erotic.

GLORIA: Do you still see the big eyes?

NIARA: No, mostly I just see the man, but it doesn't feel like he should feel. I don't feel the weight like it should feel. I just feel the moving in and out inside of me and feeling how erotic it feels, and just feeling myself floating closer and closer to having an orgasm. It just doesn't feel quite right.

GLORIA: Can you explain?

NIARA: Just... feels like what I'm seeing and what I'm feeling are two different experiences.

GLORIA: Okay, what happens next?

NIARA: Well, it's like... it moves away from me, but I'm still feeling a lot of erotic feeling.

GLORIA: (Undecipherable.)

NIARA: No, but it just feels like I'm still in the experience and so turned on that I'm still moving as though I'm being made love to.

GLORIA: What is this... doing?

NIARA: It's like moving away from me. It's just like floating away from me... It's strange... it's really strange. It feels like something still touching me somewhere, and...

GLORIA: Concentrate on it. Where is it touching you?

NIARA: It feels like right in my stomach, like right around my belly button or above it.

GLORIA: What's happening now? Describe it. Are your eyes still open so you can see?

NIARA: No, I think I've got my eyes closed.

GLORIA: Open your eyes and look at it. You're in a safe place.

NIARA: There's something, it's hard to tell if it's mechanical or organic, it's down attached to my stomach.

GLORIA: What does it feel like?

NIARA: It feels like it's inside my belly button. It feels almost like a thread.

GLORIA: What's it doing?

NIARA: It's hard to tell because the sexual feelings are so powerful, it's hard to feel anything else. Whatever it was it's not over me anymore. It's just that feeling of that string in my stomach, and all the sexual feelings are still there, very powerful.

GLORIA: I want you to concentrate now on the (???) smells... sounds...

67

NIARA: There's like a hum that I'm feeling in my body. I think it's part of what's arousing... it's this hum that is just vibrating in my body.

GLORIA: Make the sound of the hum that you hear.

NIARA: Hmmmmmmmmmmmm.... like that.

GLORIA: Do you feel like you're (???) out your body?

NIARA: Makes me tingle all over. This thing in my stomach feels like it's just kind of groping around inside of me, feeling here, in this way and that way.

GLORIA: Is there pain?

NIARA: No, I just like the sensation of it, seeking throughout my abdominal cavity.

GLORIA: Think of a noise of what you want to hear. Perhaps you hear something else...

NIARA: There's a hollow pitch noise like a... RRRROOOOOLLLL... like that.

GLORIA: Do you want to look around... where you might be?

NIARA: There was a little pain in my right hip, this little twinge. There's... I look around and there's like low light. I'm not in the bedroom anymore.

GLORIA: Where are you?

NIARA: It's hard to say because the lights are really low. It looks blueish, like blueish light. There's still this twinge in my right hip... right here. It's just a little pressure, like it's coming from outside, not inside.

GLORIA: Do you feel like you're in the bedroom anymore?

NIARA: No.

GLORIA: Can you move any part of your body?

NIARA: It's hard to move, I'm just kind of tingling all over. It feels like I'm restrained.

GLORIA: I want you to look at whoever's doing this to you.

NIARA: There's... one of those Grey people, and he's standing to my right and he's Grey, he's got big eyes... I can't make out a mouth. He's looking up and his hands are operating something over his head. There's some kind of machine up there. It's hard to see, but the thing coming out of it, it's like a wire... is going into my stomach. They must be really skillful with it because it's probing around and I don't feel too much pain, just discomfort. I can barely feel it, it's really thin. It's just like the sexual feelings are masking everything else.

GLORIA: Do you see anything else around?

NIARA: There's another one to my left... another Grey person with the big eyes. He's watching me, he's observing me. I feel like he's holding my right hand, like restraint... there's more tingling in my right hand.

GLORIA: What does his hand look like?

NIARA: It's very thin. three fingers across going across like this here... and it's like he's restraining my hand.

GLORIA: What does his touch feel like? I want you to use all your senses.

NIARA: I just feel this numb feeling coming from him... but it's stronger where his hand is.

GLORIA: Is his hand perhaps cold or warm?

NIARA: It's cold. Cool, not really cold. Cool. And he's really got me looking at his eyes. I think he was the one probing over me.

GLORIA: Look into his eyes and tell me about his eyes.

NIARA: They're just looking at me really intently, and something in them is just keeping me really sexually stimulated. I don't want to feel like this, but I can't seem to help it.

GLORIA: Is there any communication taking place?

NIARA: He's just telling me to relax and enjoy what I'm feeling.

GLORIA: How is he telling you this?

NIARA: He's thinking it at me. Just telling me to relax, and thinking at me to just keep relaxing and just enjoy the feelings and allow what's happening to happen... it's kind of calming.

GLORIA: What do you suppose they want you to feel this for?

NIARA: They don't want me to feel what's going on.

GLORIA: What do you think is going on?

NIARA: Well, it feels like they're poking around inside of me at my female organs, especially on the right. There's something going around the right, it feels like. It doesn't feel discomforting, it just feels like there's a tickle in there.

GLORIA: What do you think they're doing?

NIARA: I think they're taking an egg... or more than one.

GLORIA: What happened to the male that you saw?

NIARA: He's gone. He's not here, but there's something in the eyes of the person to my right... the black eyes of the being on my right... that remind me of the man... it's like the same eyes, only they just change from the man's eyes to these Grey's black eyes. But there's the same intensity.

GLORIA: Tell me more about what they're doing to your body.

NIARA: I feel like they've got what they wanted. It feels like I feel this wire just slowly pulling out of me... I feel like this little tickle, slowly pulling out, moving back out of the belly button.

GLORIA: Where do they put it?

NIARA: I'm watching it. It's just going up, back into the machine... the end of the wire rose almost back right up into the machine, and then it comes out again and it goes to this little pod that's floating up there. It seems like it's floating, maybe it's not. It's hard to see what exactly it's doing, but the wire goes into the pod. It's like a solar metallic pod. Then the wire's done. The person on my left is really holding my wrist, my left wrist. He wants me to keep looking at him and looking at his eyes. Now there's a sensation that I'm sinking... I'm sinking and sinking and sinking... Now it's like the whole scene has disappeared and I'm sinking... and everything is black. But I still feel the thing with me on my left... the person with me on my left, still holding my wrist. Now I feel like I'm back in my bed. And I feel like this thing is going back inside me. More sex happening... and all the arousal that I've been going through for so long.

GLORIA: Do you see that Grey's face again?

NIARA: I see the Grey being and the eyes... and this feeling of being penetrated again.

GLORIA: Do you think it's one of the Grey's that is penetrating you?

NIARA: That's what it feels like, that's what I'm seeing. It's like seeing two things at one time. Now I'm seeing the man again. It's like I can see both of them at one time. And I'm focusing on the man and then I feel myself... (SIGH)... having the orgasm, and feeling my body move... and waking up.

GLORIA: When you're awake, where's the Grey and where's the man?

NIARA: All gone.

GLORIA: I want you to see them leaving. They're finished with you. What happens? He's pulled himself out of you. And you look at him. Concentrate on him... on what he looks like.

NIARA: It's really strange, it's like seeing two beings. It's like a flash of one and a flash of the other, and a flash of one and a flash of the other. Almost like I can see both of them, overlaid over the other.

GLORIA: Well, look at him real good. Tell me where he goes. He walks out of the room...

NIARA: He doesn't walk away. He just disappears. Just like into thin air.

GLORIA: Okay, look at him real good before he disappears, and describe what you see. Are there any odors to be smelled that you can think of? How are you emotionally?

NIARA: A lot calmer than I feel like I ought to be.

GLORIA: Are you still looking at him?

NIARA: Yeah, I'm seeing more the man aspect of him now, those intense eyes, almost like the eyes are penetrating me with the look that they're giving me. and it's very erotic.

GLORIA: What color are the eyes?

NIARA: Dark brown.

GLORIA: And the other person that it changes into?

NIARA: I'm not seeing him any more, just the man.

GLORIA: Have you ever seen him before?

NIARA: Yeah.

GLORIA: Go back to that memory.

NIARA: I've seen him lots of times.

GLORIA: Go back to the last time you saw him. Where were you? How old were you?

NIARA: I'm thinking... fourteen.

GLORIA: What happened then?

NIARA: Lots of sexual feelings. It feels like somebody is massaging my stomach, just above the pubic bone.

GLORIA: Can you (undecipherable) ?

NIARA: Yeah, it's like they're looking at me, they're feeling this feeling right here.

GLORIA: Do they have hands?

NIARA: Long skinny hands, long fingers. There's a feeling here, like a full feeling.

GLORIA: Where are you?

NIARA: It still seems to be like a poorly lit, round room with blue light, it's not very well lit. I can sort of see things, but it's like shapes and shadows and it's not very brightly lit.

GLORIA: How do you think you got there?

NIARA: They just come and take me through the ceiling out of my bed.

GLORIA: How do they take you?

NIARA: It's like a float up in a light.

GLORIA: Can you see them?

NIARA: Mm-hm.

GLORIA: And what do you see as you're floating up?

NIARA: I see my room fall away and I see myself go through the roof. It's kind of strange, but...

GLORIA: Who's going with you?

NIARA: There's nobody with me until I get up in the ship.

GLORIA: Do you see the ship as you. floating over? What does it look like?

NIARA: It's a bright shiny metal, like aluminum. I just watch it get closer and then I just go through the wall of the ship, into the ship, and then I'm on this table and there are these beings around me, and they have these big eyes.

GLORIA: Can you tell me what these beings look like?

NIARA: They look pale grey with big eyes, and I can sort of make out a mouth sometimes, but the lighting is so low, and it's hard to see it.

GLORIA: Do you see any other beings around?

NIARA: It seems like there are some over, standing away, but... and they do seem different. I feel like I'm pregnant. It just feels like there's something in here.

GLORIA: Describe the feeling.

NIARA: There's just a small feeling of a... a small feeling of a knot under the skin here, and it's pressing against my bladder because I feel like I have to go to the bathroom now.

GLORIA: Tell me what happens during this time. And who these beings are that we can't see over there.

NIARA: They just seem to be observing.

GLORIA: Who is observing?

NIARA: Those other beings. They're just watching from way over on the other side. It's like they're over here, in that direction to the left and far off... but not too far off... maybe ten feet. They seem bigger than the two Greys near me.

GLORIA: Tell me more about them.

NIARA: Well, they have big eyes too. They look kind of like the Greys. But they just look taller and beefier, like they have a lot more substance to them.

GLORIA: So they could be Greys?

NIARA: Well, they have grey-looking eyes, those big eyes... big black eyes... but they look more human, I guess. I can't say they really look human either, but they're bigger and chunkier and taller.

GLORIA: How are you feeling right now? Lying on the table...

NIARA: Well, they're taking the baby out. They haven't done it yet, but I know that's what they're going to do. I think that's a good thing, because I'm not supposed to be pregnant at my age.

GLORIA: What's happening now?

NIARA: I'm trying to see how they're taking the baby. It's like they're trying to take it the same way they take me out of my house. With the light.

GLORIA: What does it feel like?

NIARA: It feels strange. It feels like strong magnets, all over, right here.

GLORIA: How does that area feel like?

NIARA: It feels pressure, like there's pressure, and tingling... and now it just feels lighter, like they just took it out. I don't feel like I have to go to the bathroom quite so bad any more.

GLORIA: Can you see the baby?

NIARA: It doesn't look like a baby.

GLORIA: What does it look like?

NIARA: It's tiny. It's just a little shape.

GLORIA: What do they do with it?

NIARA: Well, it's still in the light, and they're kind of taking it off over to the right, and it's going into a little container.

GLORIA: How large is it?

NIARA: How large is the container?

GLORIA: No, the baby.

NIARA: The baby? Oh, two inches... two and a half inches... very tiny. It doesn't look like a baby. It just looks like a little thing with some things sticking out. I feel funny about it. I feel like, you know, how can they be taking my baby out and how can I be feeling so calm about it? I don't understand that. I sure can feel those other beings on the other side of the room. They're kind of distracting.

GLORIA: What are they doing?

NIARA: They're just standing over there. It seems like they're moving a little closer, like they're just watching me.

GLORIA: Do you hear any noises?

NIARA: Just the humming sound. It hums here a lot. There's like this hum. And not much sound. It's pretty quiet except for the hum. Sometimes the hum gets louder and sometimes it's faint, but the hum is always there. It's always humming there.

GLORIA: What happens next?

NIARA: I am hearing voices, but they're faint, they're far away, and it's like they're in another room. They sound like other people talking.

GLORIA: Can you make out what they're saying?

NIARA: No, I can't really hear what they're saying. Just the voices. They don't sound distressed. They sound normal, which sounds really strange because it's so abnormal to be here. I feel like it's normal and abnormal at the same time. It's weird. And every time I'm with these things I feel so erotic. There's just this erotic feeling. Maybe that's why I wake up so many times feeling like this. I don't know. (Sighs.) I guess I just... they use it to distract me from other things.

GLORIA: Is anything else happening?

NIARA: Well, part of me feels a little sad that the baby is out of me. But they've done it before.

GLORIA: What do you mean they've done it before? Go back to that time.

NIARA: They started right after I started menstruating.

GLORIA: When was that?

NIARA: Thirteen.

GLORIA: Thirteen?

75

NIARA: I started at thirteen, and that's when they started this.

GLORIA: Did you have these experiences before you were thirteen?

NIARA: Yeah... oh, for a long time. They've been visiting me for a long time. They showed me other little kids that I can play with. Going back really early, I'm just a little girl... and maybe... three... and...

GLORIA: Are you there now?

NIARA: Yeah.

GLORIA: How old are you?

NIARA: Three. There's other little kids here to play with.

GLORIA: And what do the kids look like?

NIARA: There's two of them with me that look just like me.

GLORIA: What do they look like?

NIARA: They don't look exactly like me, they're just normal little kids. One little girl has blond hair, and she's a little bigger than me.

GLORIA: Are there any boys?

NIARA: No, well, not right with us, there are some little boys around but there aren't any little boys with us right now.

GLORIA: Where is your mommy and daddy?

NIARA: Oh, far away, I'm like in a whole different place. These other little girls, they're nice. They're nice to me.

GLORIA: Are you in a play room or what?

NIARA: We're playing. I don't know if it's a play room or not.

GLORIA: Tell me what's happening.

NIARA: Well, we're just looking at each other and we're thinking how strange this is and I'm whispering, "Where do you think we are?" And the other one says, "I don't know, but it feels OK." And she says, "You know, I'm bigger, I'll take care of you. I'll make sure that you're OK."

GLORIA: What is the girl wearing? What does she have on?

NIARA: Well, we have on some more things. She has a pair of pajamas with feet, and I have that on too. Just different colors. Not that different. One has more pink... I think hers has more pink in it and mine has some blue... some little blue flowers.

GLORIA: (Undecipherable.) Who has you there?

NIARA: Well, they're kind of scary looking, but they don't feel scary. They're grey and they have big space eyes, and they look scary but they don't feel scary. Most of the time they're nice, and then sometimes they're scary.

GLORIA: What makes them scary?

NIARA: Well, they get scary when they want to do something to me. They look at you and sometimes they put you on a table, or something like a table. It's just a flat thing and they float me up on it and lay down.

GLORIA: What kind of a table?

NIARA: Like a table, it sticks up out of the floor and it's flat so that I can lay on it. It's hard. There's really some pressure on my [sinuses] at this moment. The other little girls are watching.

GLORIA: Watching what?

NIARA: They're watching me on the table.

GLORIA: What's happening to you on the table?

NIARA: There's a lot of stuff overhead. I don't like it when they do that because it's usually uncomfortable. Sometimes it hurts. And I don't want to do it. And I get kind of mad and I want to go off the table, and that's when they get kind of scary and I just feel like... they look at me and they make me lay there, just by looking at me. Sometimes they put their hands on me. Sometimes on my chest, sometimes on my arms...

GLORIA: (Undecipherable.)

NIARA: They're doing something around my face right now and I don't like it.

GLORIA: What part of your face?

NIARA: I feel something. I feel a sensation in my left [nostril]... like it's going up inside my head.

GLORIA: What's going up?

NIARA: I don't know, it's just something... it's like filling up my left [nostril] and it's going up inside my head. It's going up right in here, right into this place right here...

GLORIA: Can you smell anything right now?

NIARA: No.

GLORIA: Are your eyes open?

NIARA: No, I close my eyes a lot when they do this because I don't like to see.

GLORIA: Tell me about the experience.

NIARA: Well, it's staying up there and it's like... we'll get around up there, and it's really uncomfortable. And I feel this feeling down between my legs, and it's distracting me from what's happening in my nose.

GLORIA: What's happening between your legs?

NIARA: It's just all warm down here... and wet. It's like something's rubbing me. It's one of those beings rubbing me. Except it's a different one, it's not like the Grey ones, it's different...

GLORIA: Okay...

NIARA: It's hard to look at him.

GLORIA: I want you to look at his eyes. What color are his eyes?

NIARA: His eyes are blue. It's funny looking because the other beings have such black eyes, big black eyes with nothing in there. But this is blue eyes and they're really bright, a pale bright blue...

GLORIA: What color skin?

NIARA: It's real pale... it looks like our skin, but there's a kind of yellowish tone to it.

GLORIA: Where's the yellow?

NIARA: It's all over. It's a little golden more than yellow maybe. It looks like normal skin but there's just a little golden [cast] or like a golden [tint] under the surface of the skin.

GLORIA: Like the Greys' skin?

NIARA: No, not like their skin. Their skin's kind of rough. It's a little sand-papery or scaly or something.

GLORIA: And does his skin feel smooth?

NIARA: His skin feels smooth, his hands feel smooth, and he just keeps rubbing this warm gel on me.

GLORIA: How tall is he?

NIARA: He's pretty tall, he's taller than the grey ones.

GLORIA: How tall are the Greys?

NIARA: They're little. They're a little taller than me. They're like... they're taller than me.

GLORIA: Okay.

NIARA: But this other one is big, not as big as my dad. Definitely, because my dad's pretty tall.

GLORIA: Is this yellow being the same shape as the Greys?

NIARA: Well, he has really big eyes... blue eyes, but they look normal... more like normal human eyes, but they're really big, and he has a really tiny nose. And I can see just a hint of lips in his mouth, but it really looks like a normal mouth but you can see sort of lips there...

GLORIA: (Undecipherable.)

NIARA: They're kind of just straight, it's like maybe just a touch of a smile.

GLORIA: Do the Greys have lips?

NIARA: No, they just have a straight line where the mouth is.

GLORIA: (Undecipherable.)

NIARA: Yeah, like two holes, and there's a little tiny [protuberance]... a little tiny thing that sticks out where that is... and it's just barely there.

GLORIA: And the yellow being?

79

NIARA: He's rubbing this stuff on me, and it feels good, but it's confusing... I don't understand what this feeling is.

GLORIA: Is it a good or a bad feeling?

NIARA: Well, it's just such a strong feeling. It feels good and it's scary at the same time.

GLORIA: What are the other little girls doing?

NIARA: Somebody took them away and they're playing somewhere else.

GLORIA: Do you suppose they are going through the same thing that you're going through right now?

NIARA: Yeah, they do.

GLORIA: Have you seen them?

NIARA: Not right now.

GLORIA: Do you think they are going through the same experience that you are going through?

NIARA: (Sigh.) I feel sorry for them when they're on the table.

GLORIA: Why?

NIARA: Because it's so uncomfortable... there are so many things going on at one time... it's confusing.

GLORIA: What do you want to tell me...?

NIARA: I'm just a little girl. They shouldn't be doing all these things to me.

GLORIA: Do you think they would respect your wishes?

NIARA: No.

GLORIA: From age three, when did you see them again?

NIARA: The time when they really scared me.

GLORIA: When was that? How old were you then?

NIARA: Four.

GLORIA: What happened?

NIARA: No, they took me out of my room the same way and I didn't get to play with anybody else. I didn't get to see any other little kids. I just went to the table and they started doing things. And nobody did anything down between my legs. Didn't stroke me this time. And it was just really uncomfortable. And they were looking at me and they were just scary this time.

GLORIA: Who were they?

NIARA: They're just these Grey beings, and they just are staring at me. There were six of them around me now, staring down very intently and it's like their stares make me lay still. And even still I'm not wanting to lay still, I'm wanting to move. And there's this one up on my left shoulder that's holding me, and he keeps poking me in a place that hurts, when I really get strong about wanting to move... and they put this thing on my stomach that's pressing on me really hard. It's really uncomfortable, it's starting to really hurt... and it just stays there for the longest time and I don't know...

GLORIA: Can you describe this thing on your stomach?

NIARA: Well, it comes down from the ceiling and it's got this round metal piece and it goes down on my stomach, right here, and it just keeps pressing and pressing and pressing... and it doesn't seem like it breaks the skin, but it just keeps pressing me. And it's really uncomfortable.
(Once out of hypnosis, I seemed to understand this was like ultrasound equipment.)

GLORIA: Do you know what they're doing?

NIARA: No, I don't know what they're doing, but it's like... I just want to get up. I'm scared and I'm angry, and they just keep looking at me with their eyes and making me lie still.

GLORIA: Can you tell them anything?

NIARA: I really don't like this. I'm really mad at you for doing this to me. I don't like you.

GLORIA: And what do they say then?

NIARA: They just say that they have to do this, and it will be over soon.

GLORIA: And what other questions do you tell them?

NIARA: I didn't say anything else. Or think anything else... I've just been feeling uncomfortable and just waiting for it to be over.

GLORIA: Do you ever try to hit them or kick them?

NIARA: No.

GLORIA: Or try to kick them?

NIARA: They just look really fragile.

GLORIA: Do you ever try to scratch them or fight them?

NIARA: No, I get really mad sometimes and really scared. I don't like to be scared, so I get mad.

GLORIA: What do you do when you get mad?

NIARA: I just think I'm mad, and I know that they know that I'm mad. And then they look at me and it's like I'm held down even tighter. It's like their eyes make me lay still. And then there's a couple that hold me, just in case. The eyes aren't enough to keep me still.

GLORIA: Are any of the yellow beings around?

NIARA: Not right now. The one yellow being with the blue eyes is nice. I see him sometimes a lot. He's always nice to me.

GLORIA: And?

NIARA: This is the same time I woke up and was screaming. (Pause.) I don't know where to go.

GLORIA: They came and got you when you were five years old as well... and six years old?

NIARA: Yeah.

GLORIA: And are they taller? Different? Stronger?

NIARA: Yeah.

GLORIA: And did you fight them?

NIARA: No, they look at me and keep me still with their eyes. And I just get mad.

GLORIA: What do you do when you get mad?

NIARA: Well, when they think to me, I think to them, and I think about hurting them. I don't really try to, because I'm afraid of what they might do, but I think it to them... just like they think their stuff to me... and then they just make sure that I can't move.

GLORIA: How do you get back home?

NIARA: It's hard to tell how I get home. I guess I go home it seems like the same way that I get out. They just kind of lower me back into my bed through the house.

GLORIA: When you were age three, describe your bed for me. What type of bed?

NIARA: Well, I see a double bed. It's pretty big, and...

GLORIA: Do you sleep alone in that big bed?

NIARA: Sometimes my sister sleeps with me. She's a lot older than me.

GLORIA: How old is your sister?

NIARA: She's... um... she's 12 years older than me.

GLORIA: Do you ever see her on the ship?

NIARA: No. (Pause.) I don't think she goes with me. I think sometimes I see her on the ship, but I don't think it's really her. It doesn't feel like it.

GLORIA: Go to a time when you think you might see her... are you there?

NIARA: Hm-hm.

GLORIA: How old are you?

NIARA: I'm six years old.

GLORIA: What kind of pajamas do you have on?

NIARA: I have pajamas on.

GLORIA: What color?

NIARA: They're kind of a yellow color.

GLORIA: What kind of fabric?

83

NIARA: Some kind of cotton.

GLORIA: Where are you?

NIARA: I'm on the ship and... I think I'm seeing my sister, but it's like seeing two things at one time.

GLORIA: Where is she?

NIARA: She's standing over at the foot of the table, to my left, and she's just looking at me and she's not saying anything.

GLORIA: How old is she?

NIARA: She looks like maybe... 15... 16... like the last time I really saw her.

GLORIA: What does she have on?

NIARA: She has on a sleeveless blouse... that's plaid...

GLORIA: What color?

NIARA: What color... it's kind of a plaid. It has different colors in it... mostly, I guess, kind of a blue and brown to it... and there's a little white... and she's wearing peddle-pusher pants.

GLORIA: What color are they?

NIARA: They're a light color... like a light tan color.

GLORIA: What color hair does she have?

NIARA: She has kind of [medium] brown hair.

GLORIA: How tall is she?

NIARA: And it's real short.

GLORIA: It's real short?

NIARA: Yeah, it looks short. And that's kind of strange.

GLORIA: Why?

NIARA: I didn't think she had short hair. When I look at her, it's like I see two things at one time. It's really confusing. I see her and then I see the big dark eyes and one of those Grey faces. It's like seeing both of these at the same time.

GLORIA: Can you separate them? Try separating them and see why you're looking at two separate things at one time.

NIARA: Well, it's one of those Grey things that wants me to see my sister. So it's just making me see [projecting] my sister.

GLORIA: You don't think your sister's there?

NIARA: I don't know. It doesn't feel like she's there. My sister feels a certain way to me, and this doesn't feel like her.

GLORIA: How does it feel to you?

NIARA: It just feels like one of them.

GLORIA: Have you ever touched her?

NIARA: No, no...

GLORIA: Can you look at him while she's standing there?

NIARA: He's just making me mad again because I know it's not really her. I don't know why they try to trick me all the time. I'm too smart for that. They can't trick me all the time.

GLORIA: Just look at your sister. Just concentrate on your sister.

NIARA: My sister's a lot more emotional than that. I'll tell you that for sure. She sure wouldn't be standing there totally calm in the middle of all this.

GLORIA: Tell me what you see.

NIARA: She's standing there and she's smiling at me. But she's like so calm...

GLORIA: You see two normal human looking eyes?

NIARA: Hm,hm, she's just smiling at me.

GLORIA: And a nose and a mouth... someone that you've known for 15 years... what's her reaction other than smiling?

NIARA: Nothing, she just stands there, looking down and smiling.

GLORIA: Does she move her hands?

NIARA: No, she has her hands behind her back.

GLORIA: Does she talk to you?

NIARA: Nope, she isn't saying anything.

GLORIA: Do they tell her to do anything?

NIARA: No. I don't think it's her. If I look at it really hard, I can see it's really one of them. And now the blue-eyed person is there, and he's down there putting stuff on me, between my legs again. I don't know why they keep doing this... it's strange. It feels good, but... it's weird.

GLORIA: Is it the same yellow person?

NIARA: Yeah.

GLORIA: Do they tell you anything?

NIARA: They're just telling me to enjoy how it feels, but it just... I'm starting to get an idea that it's a like grown-up thing, and I'm just a kid... and it's just... not my time for this.

GLORIA: Okay, let's take you back to August 1974. Do you think this yellow person with the big blue eyes might have been there that night after your husband left for work at four in the morning?

NIARA: Yeah. (Long pause.) So strange. Why do I see so many different things?

GLORIA: What do you see?

NIARA: Well, first I see a man with the dark hair and the really intense dark eyes.

GLORIA: (Undecipherable.)

NIARA: Mm-hm. And then I see the Grey with the big dark eyes, and then I see the blue eyes. (Pause.) I think he's the one that was inside me.

GLORIA: I want you to look at him. You're in a safe place, and you're just reliving your story. You're a new bride.

NIARA: I wish I could stay with that man with the blue eyes.

GLORIA: Why?

NIARA: He's always really nice to me. He makes me feel really good. My husband doesn't make me feel that good. My husband isn't really very good in bed. But it's not that way when I'm with the blue-eyed guy.

GLORIA: (Undecipherable.) ... blue eyes...?

NIARA: He's been touching me between the legs and doing things for so long that I just have a response every time I see him. I think he was inside me and then I saw the Grey over me, and then I saw the other man and... It just kept changing.

GLORIA: What is he there for?

NIARA: I don't think he's inside me, but I think he's trying to figure out what it is I'm feeling and responding to when I'm having sex. It's like he's studying it. He's just getting really close and looking right into my face while this other person is inside me. To try to get some idea of what it means to have sex, or how it feels. I don't know. That's what it seems like. It's irritating.

GLORIA: What would you like to tell them?

NIARA: Get the hell out of here. Leave me alone. Let me be happy.

GLORIA: Do you want to tell them that now? Tell them.

NIARA: Go away. Leave me alone and just let me be happy.

GLORIA: (Undecipherable.)

NIARA: Go away and leave me alone. I just want to feel happy when I feel happy. I don't want to look at you.

GLORIA: Now if you had the chance today, to tell them that...

NIARA: Yeah, that's what I would tell them.

GLORIA: Right now I want you to go back to your place in Sedona, to your very very special place... (*continues to bring her out of hypnosis.*

Deeply troubling, deeply disturbing – that was all I could feel about this session. Starting in childhood, it seemed like there was some kind of programming happening to create an increased sensitivity and inclination to sexual activity with the Greys, or as I call them now, the Zetas. This session went a long way in supplying the hidden impetus for much of my behavior during my young adult life. Behavior that caused me a great deal of emotional pain and anguish.

I felt very strongly that the device the Greys used to press into my stomach/ abdominal area was an ultrasound device and that they were examining my internal reproductive organs.

The understandings that came out of this session – over time and more study and research – exorcised the remaining vestiges of the addiction issues I'd been dealing with. Regarding those issues at least, I was finally able to set them to rest, and find *some* peace.

It was a good thing too, because I was to spend the majority of my time in the ensuing years dealing with the trauma in the wake of what the military hypnosis session revealed.

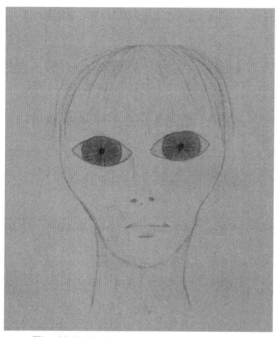

The Hybrid; his eyes were vivid blue.

Chapter 7: The Military Missing Time Transcript

Caution: The transcript that follows may be deeply disturbing to read. I decided to include it almost in its entirety, only trimming redundant sections to keep the length down. During the course of the session, the strange headache and sensations I felt when under hypnosis with Budd Hopkins came up again. As in the previous session, Gloria spoke in a very soft voice and some of her words were undecipherable this time as well. My breathing at times during the sessions became very labored and my voice filled with stress as I relived these experiences.

Some of this material will be remarkable and perhaps unbelievable to some. I don't require anyone to believe anything here. Just know that as I relived it under hypnosis, it felt very real. It may be that someone will read this some day who has other pieces of the puzzle of these experiences. I encourage people to take what they read here and start doing some study for themselves. Find out how many others there are who have had similar memories emerge, from hypnosis, or even without it.

Niara Terela Isley with Gloria Hawker
Session, March 28, 2003

GLORIA: A brand new job at Nellis AFB. How do you feel about this?

NIARA: I really like to look at Sunrise Mountain. It's beautiful here.

GLORIA: Are you anxious to begin this new job? What date are you supposed to report to work at Nellis AFB?

NIARA: The first week. The first week in January.

GLORIA: Did you find an apartment to live in or a house?

NIARA: Yeah... an apartment with a roommate... Deb Jenkins.

GLORIA: Now you've come upon the day that you report to work for the first day.

NIARA: It's morning. I'm at somebody's office. Someone's office on Nellis AFB.

GLORIA: Who's office?

NIARA: One of the officers...

GLORIA: How'd you know that you had to go there? Who told you to go there?

NIARA: I just went there with somebody else.

GLORIA: You're there right now. You can remember. You have the memory. You're just going to relive it.

NIARA: I don't remember his name. I only saw him the one time. I didn't like him because he reached over and grabbed a pen out of my shirt pocket. I don't like to have somebody's hands that close to my body.

GLORIA: What's your assignment there?

NIARA: They're telling me about orientation. We're going out to work... I have to go get jungle fatigues and uniforms for the outfitting part of... I'm glad to get outside the office again, to look up at the sky and the clouds... and Sunrise Mountain is so close to the base.

GLORIA: And what type of work are you supposed to do there again?

NIARA: I'm supposed to take care of radar, operate radar and fix it if it breaks.

GLORIA: And what does this radar do?

NIARA: It tracks aircraft. It's a special kind of tracking radar... with a really small radar beam, so the aircraft can be targeted and shot down.

GLORIA: What type of aircraft?

NIARA: Jets.

GLORIA: Tell me what a typical day is like.

NIARA: Well, we get on the bus and we go out to the radar sites. We usually stop at the compound and get food, and then we go out to the radar sites. And... we check and see if there's any periodic maintenance to do, turning things on and off, and just do that and then... if there's a call on the radio that we have aircraft flying in from the Victorville, then we turn on the radar and wait for instructions from the main radar area, to pick these planes up and try to track them.

GLORIA: You said bus. Where did you used to live that they had to bus you in, and how come did they had to bus you in?

NIARA: I live in Las Vegas. We have to get on a bus all the way up to Tonopah. It's four hours from Las Vegas.

GLORIA: Do you get to know people on the bus?

NIARA: Sort of. A lot of people sleep on the bus.

GLORIA: How many miles is it from your pick-up point to the base area?

NIARA: It's about 200 or so miles one way.

GLORIA: And it takes you how long?

NIARA: Four hours.

GLORIA: And you do this every day?

NIARA: No... we do this once a week. We go up on Sunday, so that we're ready for work on Monday. We stay at the motels.

GLORIA: Which motel?

NIARA: I stay at the L & L Motel, and some people stay at the Sundance. But I don't, I stay at the L & L. It's kind of an older place.

GLORIA: So it's mostly your routine every day?

NIARA: Yeah, I feel so sleepy…

GLORIA: Okay... after the long days' work… what's causing you to be feeling sleepy? What time of day is it?

NIARA: [Yawns.] It's late. We just got back from the site. We go out early in the morning from the motels to the radar site and do our day of work out there, and then we come back on the bus. And I fell asleep on the bus. I'm just tired. [Yawns again.]

GLORIA: Do you talk with anyone on the bus?

91

NIARA: Yeah, a little bit.

GLORIA: What do you talk about?

NIARA: Oh, just what we're going to do in town. What restaurant we're gonna go eat at, or what bar we're going to go to for a drink. Play pool... I like to play pool.

GLORIA: Are there other women on the bus?

NIARA: There's more men than women. There's this guy, [Landon Hudson]... he's a black guy, and he's always using astrology to try to hit on women. It's kind of disgusting.

GLORIA: Are you into astrology?

NIARA: Yeah, I know a lot about it. He can't really bullshit me.

GLORIA: And?

NIARA: [Yawns.] I'm kind of sleepy tonight...

GLORIA: What's causing the tiredness?

NIARA: I don't know. It's like I fell asleep on the bus and I couldn't wake up. I've got to have something to eat. And... I decide to go to bed early.

GLORIA: Is everybody tired like you were?

NIARA: Yeah, a lot of people sleep on the bus.

GLORIA: Is that unusual?

NIARA: It doesn't seem to be... I'm having a little pain in my head, up here.

GLORIA: On the top of your head?

NIARA: [Breathing starting to get a bit forced.] On the top right side... it was just kind of a little flare-up of something. Now it's diminished a lot.

GLORIA: What does it feel like?

NIARA: Pressure... like I bumped my head.

GLORIA: Did you bump your head during the day?

NIARA: No.

GLORIA: Go back and remember that day. How did that day go?

NIARA: It was just the usual day... I think I felt tired all day.

GLORIA: You mean from the morning time?

NIARA: Mm-hmm.

GLORIA: Did you get a good night's sleep?

NIARA: I don't think so.

GLORIA: With each outside noise, you'll relax deeper... and deeper...Why do you think you didn't get a good night's sleep?

NIARA: It just seems like... I'm busy at night. [Breath shortens.]

GLORIA: Doing what?

NIARA: I'm not supposed to remember.

GLORIA: Who says you're not supposed to remember?

NIARA: I don't know... Somebody just gave me an order not to think about it... or remember... I just remember sleeping...

GLORIA: Who gave you the order?

NIARA: [Long pause.] I don't remember.

GLORIA: Go back to that night, then. Perhaps you just got off the bus, maybe went to a bar... a restaurant to eat dinner...

NIARA: My head's feeling strange. [Breathing starts to get short, forced here.]

GLORIA: Tell me about it.

NIARA: Now I have a feeling of pressure on this side... [Moans softly, breathing short and stressed... several sighs.]

GLORIA: Top of your head and on the left side of your face... My hand is going to be on your right wrist. You are safe, and you're just remembering. It's okay. You came through it, and now you need to have the memory, so let it come through. It's okay.

NIARA: It's like I was hit... thrown against the wall.

GLORIA: Who threw you against the wall?

NIARA: The men... ahhmmm...

GLORIA: What men?

NIARA: [Long pause.] I don't know...

GLORIA: Have you seen them before?

NIARA: No, I haven't seen them before.

GLORIA: Where did this happen?

NORIA: It happened during the night. [Voice starts to be filled with stress, fear, apprehension, grief at this point.]

GLORIA: At the motel?

NIARA: No...

GLORIA: Where were you that this occurred?

NIARA: They didn't even wait for a first day of work. It was like... I got up there [to Tonopah] around Sunday night, before I even had a day of work... and they came and got me out of the motel that night.

GLORIA: Who did?

NIARA: Just some men... in uniform. One of them looks blond, kind of older maybe... forties... with a blond mustache. [Voice shaking.]

GLORIA: What was he wearing?

NIARA: He's wearing desert camouflage fatigues.

GLORIA: Okay. One or two men?

NIARA: At least two.

GLORIA: And the other man. How was he dressed? What does he look like?

NIARA: I'm feeling some kind of pressure on my groin too.

GLORIA: What's happening? [Pause.] It's okay…

NIARA: It's like they're holding onto me there and forcing me to move. It's really humiliating. They're telling me that I'd better not tell anybody. [Hard to even speak about what is happening… breathing short and shallow.]

GLORIA: Are you alone?

NIARA: No, they're putting me on a vehicle… like a Suburban that the military uses. It's painted military color, dark blue.

GLORIA: Where are they taking you?

NIARA: I'm not the only one. There's other people there.

GLORIA: How many others? Men? Women?

NIARA: There are just men… there's the driver, the blond guy… and the other one that came to get me, he had dark hair. They've got guns.

GLORIA: What kind of guns?

NIARA: Sidearms.

GLORIA: Who else is there?

NIARA: [Pause… more sighing.] They gave me special fatigues to wear, but there's nothing on them. There's no name tags, no nothing on them.

GLORIA: Where did you put them on at?

NIARA: I put them on in my room before I leave.

GLORIA: Do you know where you're being taken?

NIARA: I think the pressure was that somebody stuck a gun in my groin. [Voice distressed.]

GLORIA: What did you do?

NIARA: I just went with them.

GLORIA: Did you try to fight them?

NIARA: No.

GLORIA: Where did they take you?

NIARA: I got on the vehicle, the big Suburban… navy blue… and there's other people in fatigues sitting there. We were told, really sternly and in a really nasty voice, that we're absolutely not to talk to each other, not even look at each other.

GLORIA: Who is telling you that?

NIARA: The blond man in the desert camouflage.

GLORIA: Are there any other women on there? Do you ￳ee other any other women?

NIARA: I don't see any other women.

GLORIA: Okay, what other men? Count them, that are being taken.

NIARA: There's four of us, including me.

GLORIA: And where did they take you to?

NIARA: We drove out to Tonopah EW Range. [EW = Electronic Warfare.] It's night time. I'm tired. I just wish I didn't have to do this. I just want to go back to bed. And I'm scared.

GLORIA: I want you to look over the area, your environment. Tell me where you're going, what the road is like. Do the other men look like they're fearful or afraid?

NIARA: Yeah, nobody looks very happy.

GLORIA: What time of night is this?

NIARA: I think it's about midnight.

GLORIA: Do you see any other traffic?

NIARA: No… this is the only vehicle on the road.

GLORIA: What are you thinking?

NIARA: What the hell have I got myself into?

GLORIA: Go over your memory…

NIARA: I'm scared, but I'm also really mad. I wish there was something I could do about it. I wish I had a gun. I'd show 'em.

GLORIA: Keep going. Where did they take you to?

NIARA: I'm seeing this missile that's at the entrance of the electronic warfare range. And we're going through the gate, going past the guard... and we drive straight out. We don't stop at the compound. We just drive straight out to one of the radar sites – not the one I usually work at – but it's the same kind of radar.

GLORIA: I want you to hear ... what conversations might be taking place...

NIARA: No, they're just giving us instructions... that they're going to be watching us the whole time. They're going to have guns on us. We're not to talk to each other or even look at each other beyond what's necessary to run the radar. And there are going to be special aircraft out there, and we're going to be trying to track them with the radar.

GLORIA: Do you know what kind of special aircraft?

NIARA: They just say it's special aircraft. I don't know what kind...

GLORIA: Go forward in time... just a few more minutes... and then you're arriving at the site. You're there now.

NIARA: Well, we were there when they were giving us those instructions. We were just parked in the vehicle. Now they're letting us out so that we can go in the radar van... and so we're turning it on and getting it ready to go. [More sighing.]

GLORIA: Are there any conversations between you and the other men?

NIARA: No, absolutely not. I just don't even want to look at them. Those people have guns. They're scary.

GLORIA: Do you recognize anyone that you worked with?

NIARA: I think I've seen him some place, but I'm afraid to look at him very much. God, I think that one of them is Patrick...

GLORIA: Who's Patrick?

NIARA: Patrick Barnes. Young man that I was involved with real briefly.

GLORIA: Mmhmm... okay. Are you inside a building?

NIARA: It's inside the radar van. There's a wooden deck built onto it, and we go up the steps and we can walk around on the deck. We go inside the radar van. There's like inside of a semi-truck trailer kind of thing.

GLORIA: Do the semi-trucks or vans have numbers of them to identify them?

NIARA: Yeah, they have some numbers on them, but I can't see what they are because it's dark and we're just going inside.

GLORIA: And there's no other light at all?

NIARA: There's a little bit of light inside, but the lights are low. There's just enough light so that we can see what we're doing.

GLORIA: Are there any other vehicles around other than when you came in?

NIARA: Yeah, there's one other vehicle. It's the same kind of vehicle. There's two of them parked out there.

GLORIA: Who came in the other vehicle?

NIARA: Some other people who wanted to watch the tests… testing the radar to see if it will track these special aircraft. We get some calls from the big radar, the ATC radar... [Air Traffic Control radar] … and they tell us where these things are, and we're trying to track them. It's hard to get a lock on these things. They don't show up on the radar screen very well, they just… it's like they're there and then they're not. It's not a real good radar return. I think we tracked one because it was just sitting there. And that's really weird… I mean, jets just don't sit there. This thing is just sitting out there. We have a lock on it, and then it just disappears off the scope, and the lock is broken. Whatever they've got flying around out there… it's crazy… to expect these kind of clunky [radar] machines to move fast enough to keep on that thing. I don't really understand why we're doing this test. It seems useless. Kind of stupid. I don't understand it, but I'm not going to say anything.

GLORIA: How long do you think you're out there?

NIARA: Not too long. We just run the radar up, and try to track these weird things. I don't know what they are.

GLORIA: Did you ever get to see these weird things?

NIARA: Yeah, I got to see them all right. They told us to turn the radar off and go out and wait on the deck of the van. "Make sure you don't talk to each other. Just keep your mouth shut and wait out there until we're ready to take you back to town."

GLORIA: How many times have you been out there?

NIARA: Seems like I'm out there two or three times a week. Every week I'm out there.

GLORIA: And this was the first time you've seen these weird things?

NIARA: I think it was the second week I went out. Kind of like… the end of January.

GLORIA: Tell me what you see outside of the van.

NIARA: Yeah, that's when I see what's up there, and there's all these saucers up there, glowing orange on the bottom.

GLORIA: How many?

NIARA: It's hard to tell. I think nine.

GLORIA: What are they doing?

NIARA: They're just kind of hovering right now. They're not being tracked any more.

GLORIA: How big are they?

NIARA: It's kind of hard to tell, too. The one's that closest, it looks pretty big. Maybe 30 feet. Maybe 40, maybe 50 feet… it's kind of hard to tell. Uhmmm… it's out just beyond the radar antenna. So, the radar antenna's about a 100 feet from the van. It's out just beyond there. So it's pretty close.

GLORIA: Do you see any other lights around?

NIARA: No, it's all really dark out there. It's night time and stars… glittering. All these millions and millions of stars glittering, it's really pretty. The one nice thing about being out there. I'm scared about seeing these saucers. I don't think I'm supposed to be seeing them. I only have a secret clearance.

GLORIA: Did you see anything like this before?

NIARA: Well, I usually see it when I come out like this. Usually. Sometimes they make us just sit in the radar van and not go out until it's time to get on the truck.

GLORIA: Anybody at any time say who is piloting these saucers?

NIARA: [Softly.] No.

GLORIA: How high up do they go?

NIARA: They go really high, and they go really fast. They can sit still in the air and then they can take off like a bat out of hell. And they go up and down, and every which way.

GLORIA: What shape did you say they were?

NIARA: They're saucers... saucer shape.

GLORIA: And just a glowing orange?

NIARA: Glowing orange on the bottom. There's an effect that looks like spinning on the bottom, but I think it's just the lights.

GLORIA: When you're standing outside, can you feel any vibration, any noise?

NIARA: Yeah, I just felt a tickle on my face, like my hair's standing up on end, like static electricity in the air.

GLORIA: What's the noise they're making? Listen closely.

NIARA: There's kind of a faint hum. Kind of like hmmmmmmmmmmm. And it shifts in pitch a little now and then. It does feel funny on my face and my hair, it just kind of tickles. That thing must be generating one hell of a field from out there beyond the antenna to be affecting me all the way over here. Some of the other people I'm with look like they're itching... a little.

GLORIA: Are you itching?

NIARA: It feels more like tickling than itching. Like all my hair is standing on end.

GLORIA: Do you hear any other conversations?

NIARA: Some people are talking inside the radar van. That's why they sent us out, because they didn't want us to hear. But I can't really hear what they're saying. I'm just looking up and thinking why the heck am I seeing this? Why do I have to be seeing this? It's really cool to see this. It's like, you know there's people from another planet here. But the circumstances are scary. [Breathing continues to be short and shallow while relating this information.]

GLORIA: Was it the same men all the time that would come and get you from the motel?

NIARA: Yeah, the same men.

GLORIA: Could you identify these men today if you saw a picture of them?

NIARA: I could identify the blond one... I think. He was in pretty good physical condition, not overweight or anything, but just really an asshole. It scares me because I only have a secret security clearance. I don't even have a top secret security clearance. I shouldn't be even seeing this stuff. I'm thinking why in the hell am I allowed to see this when I only have a secret clearance? And that scares me, it really scares me.

GLORIA: These saucers are piloted by humans or, like you said earlier, other species from other planets?

NIARA: Well, there was a dream I had before I went into the Air Force. I was camping in Pennsylvania... and I had a dream about how these saucers work. Their technology is so sophisticated, there really aren't that many controls to touch... and in my dream these saucers were controlled telepathically by the operator and perhaps even tuned to the operator... and if real human beings flying these craft that can make them do these maneuvers, then I'm trying to put it together with my dream, it makes me think that they have to have aliens flying these things to make them do what they're doing... because if they fly on that principle... but maybe they don't. Maybe they're a different craft or they built them differently and people can make them operate that way. It just seems to me that it would be hard on human beings inside those things to have them do the maneuvers they're doing and have the people be okay inside. So, I'm thinking it's probably aliens flying them.

GLORIA: Did you ever see a man in or outside the craft?

NIARA: [Softly.] Yeah... [Getting much more scared in session now, more stressed, labored breathing.]

GLORIA: You did? When?

NIARA: Not this night. [Sounds of grief in voice.]

GLORIA: What night was it?

NIARA: It was a different night and we came out and we did the same thing. But they brought a bus out and they picked us up in the bus... [Heavy sigh.] and there were other people on the bus from other radar sites that had been out there. There were quite a few.

101

GLORIA: How many would you say? Men? Women?

NIARA: Eighteen to twenty people. Mostly men. I think it was mostly men. They kept us all in the dark, with not very much light. We're not allowed to talk to each other. We're not even allowed to look at each other. And they were watching us with guns all the time. [Sounding very scared.]

GLORIA: What kind of guns?

NIARA: Just side guns. Some people had rifles, but mostly just side guns. [Voice shaky.]

GLORIA: The same two men were there?

NIARA: Yeah, the same two. They're in charge of our group.

GLORIA: Did they rough you up again that night?

NIARA: I don't know... they just put us on this bus and we were going to this other place and it's further into the Test Site. And I'm wondering if it's this Area 51 or Dreamland... I don't know.

GLORIA: A different site?

NIARA: Yeah.

GLORIA: Tell me what you see out the bus.

NIARA: I can't because the windows of the bus are painted over.

GLORIA: And you can't look out the window. Is it a military bus that you're on?

NIARA: Yeah, it's an old school bus-looking thing that's painted blue. The windows are painted over. And we get to this one place. It's still the middle of the night or the early morning hours. We're getting off the bus.

GLORIA: Does the bus have numbers, like in front?

NIARA: Yeah, but I didn't look back at the bus. I was just looking where I was going.

GLORIA: You're there now.

NIARA: All the guards are making us go into this building... I hate this place...

GLORIA: You're safe... you're safe. Why do you hate this place?

NIARA: Because the people are so brutal here. [Voice shaking, almost a sob.] They just don't care about you. It's like... it's like all of us are a bunch of lab rats.

GLORIA: What do they do to you?

NIARA: Well, we have to go into the waiting room and sit there and wait. It's like the same thing over and over again. And there's these black chairs... there's a diagonal row of chairs. They keep all the lights off in this place, except for indirect lights, like from a different room shining in. The same waiting room with all these chairs.

GLORIA: Have you been here before?

NIARA: Mm-hm. And there's a diagonal row of chairs down the middle of the room, going from one corner, catty corner, to the other corner, and there are places to walk in between. And most everybody's sitting in those chairs and people are sitting in some other chairs next to the wall... and we're just supposed to sit there...

GLORIA: And then what?

NIARA: We just sit there and wait until it's our turn.

GLORIA: Our turn for what?

NIARA: To go in this little room. As we come into the room from the outside, the room is to the right.

GLORIA: What happened to you in there?

NIARA: You sit there and you wait your turn, and you wait and wait and wait... and then they put something in your neck when you go in there. They shoot you with something... with a needle... [Heavy sighing.]

GLORIA: Let's go back to when someone comes to get you to go in the little room.

NIARA: Nobody really comes and gets me. They just open the door and say, "Isley, get in here." And so I get up and go in there.

GLORIA: Who calls you? Is it a man or a woman?

103

NIARA: No, it's not a woman. There's a guard in there. He's the one that calls people in.

GLORIA: What is he dressed like?

NIARA: He's wearing desert camouflage fatigues and he's got a rifle, both a side arm and a rifle.

GLORIA: Can you see the color of his hair and his skin?

NIARA: It's kind of dark in there, there's just a little tiny lamp on. It's hard to see him. They did this all on purpose. They don't want us to see anything more than we need to see.

GLORIA: How are you feeling?

NIARA: Angry and really scared. [Voice shaking.]

GLORIA: Had you been through this procedure before?

NIARA: Yeah...

GLORIA: So you know what to expect...

NIARA: Yeah. They even say, "You know the drill, get on the table... and lay there and shut up." And so I lie down on the table, face up, and I'm just waiting... I'm just dreading it... holding onto the other table and just gripping it with my hands because I know what's coming.

GLORIA: What kind of table is it?

NIARA: It's an old... it looks like an old table. It's stainless steel on the top, real cold.

GLORIA: [Undecipherable.] on the table?

NIARA: Yeah... [Long pause.]

GLORIA: What is happening?

NIARA: The guard is putting straps on me, so that I won't move.

GLORIA: Why does he do that?

NIARA: Well, he lets me know that I know that they're going to give me another shot. [Short, shallow breathing.] Even when I'm scared, it's hard not to move away from that shot, it's so awful.

GLORIA: What's the shot for?

NIARA: [Softly.] I don't know.

GLORIA: Okay, continue on.

NIARA: I'm just waiting for the person in the lab coat to come in. He comes in and he's got kind of sparse hair on top of his head, it's dark, little touches of grey in the temples. He's wearing black-rimmed glasses this time.

GLORIA: How old is he?

NIARA: Early fifties. [Sniffling.]

GLORIA: Okay, go on.

NIARA: He doesn't hide the shot this time like the first time he hid it, and he didn't have me strapped down then. But this time I know it's coming, so they strapped me down. And he comes in. It's like he enjoys that I'm afraid because he just holds the syringe up and I can see it, and it's this green stuff. It looks like toxic waste or something.

GLORIA: How many cc's do you think they give to you?

NIARA: Not too many. Yeah, I can see that it's green in the faint light in there, because it's kind of fluorescent... I don't know what it is.

GLORIA: Where do they give you the shot?

NIARA: They put it in right here. [Touches right side of neck.] It goes into the artery right here on the side of my neck.

GLORIA: On your right side? Is it always the right side?

NIARA: Mm-hm.

GLORIA: Tell me the feeling that you get from the injection.

NIARA: It hurts... and then... The bloodstream just takes it right up into my head, and my head starts to hurt. [Shaking, feeling it now in session.] It just feels like it just immediately... just disperses all over the inside of my head.

GLORIA: Is it tingling... cold, hot?

NIARA: It feels kind of cold, and then I feel it start going all the way through my bloodstream. It seems to trigger an effect in my pituitary gland... and all of my glandular system starts doing some strange things. I start shaking... the effect gets worse and worse, and then I can feel little particles of this stuff getting through the rest of my bloodstream... and I just start shaking worse and worse and worse... I feel like I'm just going to shake apart. [Voice shaking now in session.] And they've taken the straps off, and they're taking me out of that room by a different door. And I'm going down some stairs... and they're dragging me because I can't walk... I'm shaking so bad... just violent... getting to be violent, violent shaking... and, ah... down this long flight of steps, and then they throw me in this room. It's the same room that they always put me in... it's like... there's a window that looks like a mirror on my side. I don't think it's a mirror. I think it's something where they're watching me. And I don't want to scream this time because I don't want them to get any pleasure out of that. So I'm trying to stay quiet.

GLORIA: What's the room like?

NIARA: It's just a little room... it's not that big.

GLORIA: Are there lights on?

NIARA: Yeah, there's one little light on. I guess so they can see me through the mirror. I don't think they're worried about me being able to see anything.

GLORIA: Where's the light coming from?

NIARA: A corner, in the ceiling. And so I just do what I always do when I lie down on the floor. I wrap myself up in a ball and just try to hold onto myself... And I just shake... and I'm clenching my teeth because I don't want to scream. It's not really painful... it's just this shaking, this terrible, terrible shaking... it's so scary. And I wonder what this stuff is doing to me. Is it like doing something terrible to me that it's never going to be right? I just don't know. Sometimes it feels like I'm going to die of shaking... or of exhaustion... one of the two.

GLORIA: What does your heart feel like, and your breathing?

NIARA: It's... my heartbeat is kind of irregular, and my breathing in coming in little gasps. It's hard to get breath in and out while I'm shaking like that. I really have to work at it.

GLORIA: [Undecipherable.]

NIARA: It just feels like I'm coming apart. It feels like... it feels like something is just trying to make me come apart... at the molecular level.

GLORIA: What happens next?

NIARA: Finally, the stuff dissipates. I guess… it's got a quality to it where it just dissipates out of your system after a while, and… I'm just so tired. I don't have to hold on any more… I let go of my knees and just kind of lay there on the floor, exhausted, and the shaking is subsiding. And then they come in.

GLORIA: Who comes in?

NIARA: The guards. That one blond guard is there. It's almost like he's assigned to me or something. And two of them drag me by the arms out of that room into another room. And then they start yelling at me.

GLORIA: What are they yelling?

NIARA: They're telling me that all the stuff that happened didn't happen… [long pause] that I better make sure that it didn't happen and that I don't ever remember that it happened, and I'd better think about my little girl… because she could sure get hurt or killed if I ever remember. And they… [short, shallow stressed breathing] they've torn off all my clothes… and I'm getting raped… by one, and then another.

GLORIA: Who's raping you?

NIARA: That blond guy, and then the other guy.

GLORIA: Right at this moment, what would you tell those men?

NIARA: If I had a gun, I'd blow both their heads off and laugh.

GLORIA: Will you tell them that now?

NIARA: Yes.

GLORIA: Tell them.

NIARA: If I had a gun in my hand, I would blow both your heads off and I would just laugh while you bled to death. I would laugh while your brains splattered on the wall.

GLORIA: [Undecipherable.]

NIARA: Yeah, I could. I don't want to do that.

GLORIA: You don't think you could do it?

NIARA: I don't want to. I don't want to be like them.

GLORIA: Okay, okay.

NIARA: I felt angry thoughts come up like that, but I don't really want to do it. I'm not a murderer.

GLORIA: What would make you feel at peace with the situation... [Undecipherable] what happened to you, to make you stronger. What would it be right now?

NIARA: It's just so bad... the rape is so ugly... and there's other people watching. [Sounding close to tears.]

GLORIA: What other people?

NIARA: Other people, like the one in the lab coat... he's more interested in the effects of the shot, but he's just sitting there watching while they...

GLORIA: Anybody ever say what was in the shot?

NIARA: No.

GLORIA: Do you have any idea what was in the substance?

NIARA: No, but it didn't feel like liquid.

GLORIA: What did it feel like?

NIARA: When it went in, it felt lighter than liquid... I'm not sure how to describe it. I don't know. Like soda pop... with carbonation.

GLORIA: Bubbly? With bubbles?

NIARA: Yeah.

GLORIA: You felt it... ?

NIARA: No, I felt it while I was getting the shot.

GLORIA: What else about it?

NIARA: It made heart palpitations. I'm wondering if that's why I had heart palpitations for so long [after getting out of the military]. They did say one thing one time that made me wonder if... I wondered why I didn't die from it... the violent reaction I was having.

GLORIA: Do you know of anyone that had died from it?

NIARA: I think people [might have] died.

GLORIA: Did you know of anybody?

NIARA: Not personally, but I just think that some people died, because they kept wondering... you know... they'd just say once in a while... she doesn't die from these.

GLORIA: Do you have any other men that originally began going to this area, were the same men always there with you as your group?

NIARA: The same guards, or the same crew?

GLORIA: The same crew. Were they always there all the time? Did you ever notice anyone missing?

NIARA: Well, there were changes sometimes. There were changes, but different crews. They didn't have very many women doing this. But they just said that they'd do something to my daughter, and that they could come and do whatever they wanted to do to me, anytime, if I ever remembered and if I ever talked about it.

GLORIA: And while you were lying on the floor, and they were raping you, and telling you all this. What happened next? You were lying on the cold floor?

NIARA: No, I'm not on the floor. I'm on some old couch.

GLORIA: What color is the couch?

NIARA: Dark green or black and it's vinyl. And then they tell me to get dressed.
[*Author note: I can describe this couch in exact detail. I memorized it to keep myself from focusing on the rapes.*]

GLORIA: Is there a lot of light around in this particular room?

NIARA: No, there's not much light. It's just like a single light bulb.

GLORIA: Where were all the other people standing who were watching you while all this was happening?

NIARA: Well, there was this couch over against the wall and they have me on that, and that's where they're doing all this stuff... and then there's other people sitting in chairs, including a man in a lab coat at the other end of the room, just watching what they're doing. And then they tell me to get dressed and throw my clothes at me. And... then, once my clothes are on, the guy in the white lab coat comes and gives me another shot in the arm.

109

GLORIA: Is it the same substance?

NIARA: No, it's different. It makes me really sleepy. [Heavy sigh.] They take me back to the bus, and then back to the radar site. I'm trying to stay awake. I don't want to be asleep. I want to know what the heck is happening. It's really hard. I'm feeling really drugged. It's really a lot of work to try to stay awake, especially how tired I am after all that stuff. So I think I stay awake long enough for part of the bus ride.

GLORIA: I wonder what kind of substance they gave you to make you sleepy.

NIARA: I don't know. I think... I don't know, just some sort of drug to make you sleepy or knock you out. They were afraid to give me too much because of the other shot, so they just gave me just enough to make me really sleepy. And then I would fall asleep or be drugged out. And then it's like, I'd wake up and it would be time to go to work, and I'd be in my motel room. And it would be time to wake up and go to work. Really, really early in the morning, still, and it was like I just barely got back.

GLORIA: What time would it be?

NIARA: Four o'clock in the morning. Time to wake up and get ready, have some breakfast and go. I just remember being so tired. It's like, gad, how am I going to do it? So I just work to try to get ready, eat some breakfast and then got on the bus to go out to work and go back to sleep... try to get some more sleep before I go back out there. Gad, no wonder I don't remember any of that stuff.

GLORIA: You said you had seen an alien at one time.

NIARA: Yeah.

GLORIA: Where?

NIARA: Sitting in that room, watching the rape.

GLORIA: Who were they, what type of aliens?

NIARA: The usual Grey type of alien.

GLORIA: Tall Greys or...?

NIARA: Not terribly tall.

GLORIA: The small Greys?

NIARA: Mm-hm, four or five feet.

GLORIA: Were there any hybrids there?

NIARA: No.

GLORIA: Just Greys?

NIARA: Mm-hm.

GLORIA: How many?

NIARA: I think two.

GLORIA: What were they doing?

NIARA: They were sitting there with that guy in the lab coat, and they were just watching.

GLORIA: Do you think they were studying you?

NIARA: Yeah.

GLORIA: And that's happening?

NIARA: Mm-hmm.

GLORIA: Did you see them any other time besides…

NIARA: I saw one outside one time.

GLORIA: Where?

NIARA: It was right after getting off the bus. I saw one… standing next to the building we were going into, which I think was a clinic or an infirmary or something.

GLORIA: And did you communicate with him?

NIARA: No.

GLORIA: Did you ever enter one of those saucer type looking ships when you were there?

NIARA: I don't know. [Deep sigh… long pause.] My whole body feels really heavy when you ask me that question.

GLORIA: Why? What does it feel like?

NIARA: [More sighs... long pause] I'm working to get at this. I'm trying to remember.

GLORIA: Any the memories there in your conscious mind?

NIARA: I think I was on the Moon.

GLORIA: How did you get there? Go with that memory… it's okay.

NIARA: [Long pause.] I did get on one of those craft.

GLORIA: Where? What craft?

NIARA: One of those... saucers.

GLORIA: Do you think you were in Area 51 or Dreamland? Is that when you got on the craft?

NIARA: Yeah, I think so. [Very long pause. Very reluctant to speak further.]

GLORIA: Where was it? Go to this memory. Be there. Take your fingers and peer through your conscious mind's file drawer, and go through the files. You know where it's at. And gently pull that file out, and it tells you exactly what happened.

NIARA: Well, I see an alien standing outside a craft. And they tell me to go on it.

GLORIA: Who told you?

NIARA: That same blond guard… tells me to go on board. He's not going to get on board, though. And I get on, and I think I felt heavy when the craft accelerated and went…

GLORIA: Where did you sit?

NIARA: I was on the floor.

GLORIA: What did it feel like?

NIARA: [Pause... hard to speak.] A little cushiony.

GLORIA: Did you feel some cushions?

NIARA: Oh, very little. Just a little bit. Like the floor was just slightly squishy.

GLORIA: How many people were there with you?

NIARA: There's three other people.

GLORIA: Men? Women?

NIARA: Men.

GLORIA: Do you recognize them?

NIARA: Just one.

GLORIA: What kind of clothing do you have on?

NIARA: [Swallowing.] I have a jumpsuit on. It's kind of weird not to have my fatigues on. But it's kind of a tight-fitting jumpsuit. Kind of a silvery grey color.

GLORIA: Can you feel the material?

NIARA: Yeah, it's a little rubbery.

GLORIA: Anything on your hands?

NIARA: Not right now, but there are gloves that go with it, and boots.

GLORIA: What color are they?

NIARA: They're all the same color.

GLORIA: Who put the boots on you?

NIARA: I put them on.

GLORIA: What do they feel like?

NIARA: They're pretty comfortable.

GLORIA: How high up your legs?

NIARA: Mid calf.

GLORIA: Laced boots, or what?

NIARA: No, they're kind of strange boots. You put them on and they kind of fit themselves to your leg, without ties. They slip on and then they just kind of vacuum onto your leg. Really strange. The same with the gloves, the gloves do the same thing. They're like regular gloves. You put them on and they just kind of vacuum onto your hand.

GLORIA: And you can put them on yourself?

NIARA: Mm-hmm.

GLORIA: Anything on your head?

NIARA: My head's bare... for the trip right now.

GLORIA: Have you been on this trip before?

NIARA: Yeah.

GLORIA: How many times, do you think?

NIARA: I'm thinking eight times... or maybe ten.

GLORIA: Who's piloting this craft?

NIARA: One of the Grey aliens.

GLORIA: Can you see him?

NIARA: Mm-hm.

GLORIA: What does it feel like to be on the ship?

NIARA: [Long pause.] Well, it could be really fun if only it wasn't so scary.

GLORIA: Tell me about it.

NIARA: They just have some work that they want us to do.

GLORIA: What kind of work?

NIARA: Just some work where we're going.

GLORIA: Do you know where you're going?

NIARA: Yeah, we're going to the Moon, but it doesn't take very long to get there.

GLORIA: Who told you you're going to the Moon?

NIARA: That guard told me before I got on the ship. He said, "Have fun on the Moon, sweetheart. See you when you get back." And... he's really unpleasant. I know what "See you when you get back" means... it means more rape, [Stressed breathing] more threats.

GLORIA: What's the environment like on the ship?

NIARA: There's low light. There's some windows, little round windows. You can see out here and there.

GLORIA: Can you look out the window?

NIARA: Mm-hm.

GLORIA: Have you ever looked out the window?

NIARA: Yeah, it's just I happen to lay on the floor, because there's not enough seats in there for everybody.

GLORIA: What do the seats look like?

NIARA: They're just real small little seats. They fit the Grey pretty good. The regular people are sitting in the other ones. There's like three other ones and they don't fit so good. But the unimportant people are told just to lay on the floor for the trip. So I'm laying on the floor.

GLORIA: Do you feel some pressure?

NIARA: Mm-hm.

GLORIA: How does the ship go up? What does it feel like when it goes up?

NIARA: It just feels like pressure. Like I'm pressed into the little cushion areas on the floor. And I can't move for a minute. I just feel really heavy. So I just lay there and I try to see what I can see out of this one little window that I can see from where my laying... but I can't see too much from it. It would be fun to get up and see if I could look back and see Earth, but I can't get up.

GLORIA: While this ship was still on the ground on Earth, where did they take you to? Let's just back up for to ask this question. Go back to that time. How did you get to the ship?

NIARA: Well, they took me out of the clinic.

GLORIA: Was this after they raped you? Where did they take you, and how did you get there?

NIARA: I'm trying to remember… [Very long pause.]

NIARA: Well, we were still underground. We went down that long flight of stairs to get to that room, and then we were still underground, and went through this hallway… or tunnel… and it opened up into a large area, and that's where there was a ship… a space ship… and that's where I saw the alien standing outside the space ship.

GLORIA: Was there a lot of light?

NIARA: No, there's not a lot of light, it's still pretty dark. And that's when we got told that…

GLORIA: That's sort of a hangar then?

NIARA: We were told to change into these other clothes, and so we did… and we had to change right there in front of everybody.

GLORIA: You removed your camouflage suit… [Undecipherable.]

NIARA: And we put on our other things… and then we climbed onto the ship and some people that… you know, I keep thinking officers, but I don't know if they were officers… were sitting in the chairs. And then the rest of us, me and three other people… guys… were on the floor. They just said, "Lay on the floor until we tell you to get up." And then when the craft started, it went up and the more it accelerated, the more I felt heavy and just pressed into the floor. It must have gone up and gone out a door on the surface of the earth.

GLORIA: After they finished raping you, then were you allowed to get dressed again, before you were taken to the ship? And did they give you back your clothes?

NIARA: Not right away.

GLORIA: Why?

NIARA: They wanted me to feel bad.

GLORIA: Then after?

NIARA: Yeah, after a few minutes. I think the guys, they took time putting their pants on. And then when they were all done, then they gave me my clothes.

GLORIA: And you weren't allowed to shower or anything like that?

NIARA: No.

GLORIA: And then who walked you to the ship?

NIARA: The guards. The guy in the white lab coat and one of the greys. [Pause.] And also some other people… the other three members of the crew that I went on the ship with. They joined us during our walk down the hallway, with their guards…

GLORIA: How were they reacting?

NIARA: They didn't look in much better shape than me, and I was wondering if they raped them, or what they do to men.

GLORIA: You never got to ask?

NIARA: No.

GLORIA: What was the air like?

NIARA: There was a musty smell, kind of close, a little humid.

GLORIA: How far did you have to walk to get to that ship?

NIARA: It was quite a ways. I think it took about ten or fifteen minutes to walk there.

GLORIA: How many stairs did you have to go down?

NIARA: I didn't have to go down any more stairs… from the stairs I went down after the shot.

GLORIA: It was all on the same level?

NIARA: Yeah, it was all on the same level down there.

GLORIA: And when you got into the large room, where the ship was at… [Undecipherable.]

NIARA: Well, I got to the ship. There was an alien standing under it… kind of… and I'm feeling that strange pressure in my groin again… it's right on the left side of it.

GLORIA: Look at it and see what's going on. Look down. What do you see?

NIARA: [Gulps.] It's like one of the guards is grabbing me there, and using that to humiliate me and pull me around.

GLORIA: Do you feel his hands?

NIARA: Yeah. I just move where he wants me to move… and I'm really, really angry, but I don't let anything out. I'm just really, really angry.

GLORIA: Where's the opening to the ship?

NIARA: Well, it's like it's sitting out there, and the alien is standing here. And the opening is underneath over here.

GLORIA: Underneath the ship?

NIARA: We have to climb a ladder to get inside.

GLORIA: How many steps is the ladder?

NIARA: Ten or twelve rungs.

GLORIA: Could you recognize any of the men watching you go into the ship?

NIARA: Just that one guard… that one blond guard.

GLORIA: Where were the men that you felt were officers?

NIARA: [Sigh.] Well, they were already on. They got on before me.

GLORIA: And then you climbed the ladder… what kind of ladder?

NIARA: I was like the third person on the crew to go in, and there was one behind me, and then we were told to lay on the floor… It was a metal ladder.

GLORIA: Was it a different kind of metal?

NIARA: Well, I don't know if it was a real different kind of metal. It looked like something they had specially welded together for that purpose, to get from that distance, from the floor to the ship.

GLORIA: How big was the opening that you went through?

NIARA: It was fairly large. It was like a large porthole. Two people could have gone through it if they'd had two ladders. And… [Sighs] I feel really hot.

GLORIA: Is it hot in there?

NIARA: Yeah, my palms are sweaty.

GLORIA: How hot is it in there?

NIARA: It's just kind of hot and feels kind of humid, I'm not sure why.

GLORIA: How big would you say it is inside this craft?

NIARA: It's pretty big, but I would sure call it a shuttle rather than some big mother ship or something.

GLORIA: Okay, I'm going to let you sit there for just a little bit, okay… Okay, you're sitting in the ship and… [undecipherable.]

NIARA: There's a Reptilian there.

GLORIA: Where is he at?

NIARA: He's sitting in one of the seats.

GLORIA: What does he look like?

NIARA: He's kind of a brownish color.

GLORIA: Has he always been there?

NIARA: He was there when I got on board. I just didn't see him right away.

GLORIA: Have you ever seen him before?

NIARA: I think so.

GLORIA: Do you know where?

NIARA: [Long pause.] In the lab.

GLORIA: What lab?

NIARA: [Pause.] A lab where they keep the green stuff.

GLORIA: And where do they keep this green stuff?

NIARA: [Pause.] It's not a room that I've been in very much, but there's just… like I've gone past it. But when I went by, there was an open refrigerator door and some of the green stuff was in there, in tubes with corks in them.

GLORIA: Was it in this clinic?

NIARA: It was underground.

GLORIA: Do you see anybody in the lab?

NIARA: The Reptilian's in there.

GLORIA: Doing what?

NIARA: He's just standing in there right now.

GLORIA: Any human beings in there?

NIARA: Mm-hm, yeah.

GLORIA: Who do you see in there? Men? Women?

NIARA: [Pause.] There's a couple of men... and a woman.

GLORIA: What do they look like?

NIARA: I didn't get to see very much. I was just passing by.

GLORIA: Who were you walking with?

NIARA: I was walking with the guards and... the grey and the man with the white lab coat, who gives me the shots.

GLORIA: How many times have you passed this lab?

NIARA: Just a few... maybe three times.

GLORIA: Do the men or women recognize you? Do they say anything to you?

NIARA: No, they don't.

GLORIA: What are they doing?

NIARA: Uhmmm... I don't know, their backs are to me. They're standing at a counter and I'm just walking by and... I can't stay and look.

GLORIA: What color hair do they have?

NIARA: The woman had dark hair.

GLORIA: How long?

NIARA: Long enough to pull back in a ponytail.

GLORIA: The men had dark hair?

NIARA: Mm-hm, they both had dark hair, and the one was bald on top. But I really didn't see much of what they were doing. I walked by, and I just kind of flashed on all of them standing in there, looking like they were working at something, and the Reptilian was watching me... and then I was walking by.

GLORIA: Was he in command?

NIARA: I think so, I think he was in charge.

GLORIA: [Undecipherable.]

NIARA: No... no...

GLORIA: Okay, you're back on the ship... you're lying on the floor... tell me what it looks like when you're on the ship...

NIARA: At first it's slow and it doesn't feel much like anything, it just... it starts to accelerate really fast and that's when I start just feeling really heavy. It has a strange emotional effect, too, it's very depressing emotionally. It's like feeling despair. [Voice heavy with saddness.]

GLORIA: Does anybody talk? Say anything?

NIARA: No. Everybody's just focused on the flight, and it doesn't take very long at all. It just feels like a few minutes, and then we're... landing.

GLORIA: Where are the Greys?

NIARA: Well, one of them was piloting the craft, and then the Reptilian was in one of the other seats, and then there were two other human beings in the other two seats. There were four seats.

GLORIA: Was there anything else happening?

NIARA: Not that I could tell. They were just being quiet during the time of the flight.

GLORIA: What is the energy like? Can you feel it?

NIARA: I just really don't like it. I don't like... how they're treating me and the other three guys.

GLORIA: How are they treating you?

NIARA: It's like… like these things that just don't matter… just things to be used. And it's so different from the regular world, where people have rights and everything. It's just I don't have any rights in this place, not the tiniest one… you have to do what you're told…

GLORIA: Tell me what you feel about the ship.

NIARA: Well. I see some stars out the porthole. You don't really get to see Earth or the Moon… just see stars from the angle that I'm at. But all the people that are sitting in the seats, and the Reptilian, they're all looking out at the port hole that they can see from where they're sitting. And I guess they have a good view of what's going on because they're just watching, and that's why I don't think they're saying much, because they're just watching the view from the port hole. So they're all really quiet.

GLORIA: Do you ever see the Earth as you're leaving?

NIARA: No, I can't see it from where I'm at... I'd sure like to see it, but I can't get up.

GLORIA: Perhaps there is a special feeling of excitement among all the members that on the ship?

NIARA: Yeah, kind of a sense of wonder.

GLORIA: Is there anybody else looking out the windows?

NIARA: Just the people in the seats are looking out the windows. I try to look out my window – but this little port hole that I can see – but I don't really see much from it. Except stars.

GLORIA: Why do you think you were chosen for this mission?

NIARA: I think it has something to do with the fact that… those injections… that I didn't die from them.

GLORIA: Is there anything covering your head?

NIARA: Not right now… not on the ship. There's something that I have to put on to go outside.

GLORIA: How long do you think you're in the ship?

NIARA: It doesn't feel like that long. Maybe thirty minutes.

GLORIA: That's quite fast... what do the stars look like?

NIARA: Maybe thirty or forty minutes. It's strange now because at one point we can see the stars. And then you look out the window and it's almost looks like we're in a tunnel... a light tunnel.

GLORIA: And what happens when you sense you're getting closer to the Moon?

NIARA: Well, we slow down really quick, and then the stars are out there again and... I feel the craft settle on the ground. I can feel it, but it's really a gentle... a gentle landing.

GLORIA: What do your ears feel like when you're traveling on the ship?

NIARA: [Gulps.] They're kind of uncomfortable. There's a lot of pressure changes.

GLORIA: What happens if you need the bathroom?

NIARA: [Long pause.] Well, I don't think there's a bathroom on the ship.

GLORIA: What do you do then?

NIARA: Well, it didn't come up for me because I didn't need to use the bathroom. But I think there's a bathroom on the planet... on the Moon... it seems like we're on the Moon. [Pause.] We're on the dark side of the Moon.

GLORIA: What does it look like? What do you see?

NIARA: Well... facilities with lights. And... we have to put a helmet on and walk over there.

GLORIA: Tell me what you see.

NIARA: [Yawns.] I'm sleepy again... I just walk over there.

GLORIA: Who gets off the craft first?

NIARA: The Reptilian is just kind of guarding us now. The grey, who was the pilot, and the Reptilian and the two men who were sitting in the seats, they got off first.

GLORIA: Do they have names?

NIARA: Not that I know of.

GLORIA: Do they ever call each other by a name?

NIARA: No, they're pretty careful. They don't want the crew to remember... me and the other three guys... they don't want us to remember anything extra. So they're like really careful. They're always really careful about how much we see, about how much light we're able to have to see by, and... they're really careful.

GLORIA: What's the [Undecipherable] like?

NIARA: Well, like I said, they all get off the ship first, and then... we get off. I'm the next to the last one off again, I think. We walk towards these buildings where there's some lights. [Yawns.] I think that maybe we use the bathroom when we're in there. Because they have a regular bathroom in there.

GLORIA: How are the buildings constructed? Who's there?

NIARA: There's a lot of people there working.

GLORIA: How'd they get there?

NIARA: Well, the same way we got there.

GLORIA: Are there other craft around?

NIARA: Yeah. Some coming, some going.

GLORIA: Is it cold outside or what?

NIARA: I think it's pretty cold outside. My suit's pretty insulated. They take us where we can use the bathroom, and then they give us some work to do.

GLORIA: What kind of work?

NIARA: Electronics. The funny thing is, the Reptilian is guarding us this time... and he's really scary.

GLORIA: Why?

NIARA: Um... he just looks really scary and mean.

GLORIA: Can you describe what he looks like?

NIARA: He definitely has scales, and he's kind of brownish, tannish looking. And his eyes are really horrible.

GLORIA: What do his eyes look like?

124

NIARA: [Long pause.] They're kind of yellowish with a vertical pupil.

GLORIA: Mm-hm…

NIARA: He's got sharp teeth. Kind of seems to like to roll his lips back away from his teeth a lot. He seems to do that a lot.

GLORIA: How tall is he?

NIARA: He's pretty tall. I think seven feet. Pretty tall.

GLORIA: Where are you taken after you use the bathroom?

NIARA: Taken back outside… we're supposed to operate some equipment for excavating. They're going to be like building more underground facilities on the Moon. And the equipment is electronic, so because of our radar experience with certain things, they just feel if you have the skills, they'll transfer to this work. So they give us a little explanation on what we're supposed to do. A couple of technicians that are there explain that. And then they turn on the equipment and just kind watch and monitor how it's working and… and it starts enlarging this whole area… creating sort of like this indentation down in the ground.

GLORIA: Do you hear any noise?

NIARA: It's not terribly noisy machinery, it's more magnetic. No, it's not that noisy. You can hear the ground being moved out of the way, and you can hear kind of a humming… that's about it.

GLORIA: How many people would you say are there? Human beings?

NIARA: There's a lot of people walking around different areas. We're just in that one area.

GLORIA: There's different buildings, you mean?

NIARA: There's different buildings and… different buildings and different people. And some of the buildings… it's like they don't put anything particularly beautiful there… or innovative… or anything else like that. It's like the same old ugly buildings that are back on the Test Site. They just put the same kinds of things up there.

GLORIA: Are they wearing uniforms?

NIARA: No, they're not in uniforms. They're wearing similar stuff to what I have on… a tight-fitting, grey suit.

GLORIA: Do you see other species there?

NIARA: I see Reptilians and Greys.

GLORIA: Tall greys or short Greys?

NIARA: Both.

GLORIA: What else are you doing there? What other kind of work?

NIARA: [Heavy sighing.] Entertainment.

GLORIA: Entertaining whom?

NIARA: The men that are there.

GLORIA: How are you entertaining them?

NIARA: More sex. [Dosen't want to talk about it.]

GLORIA: How long have some of those people been there?

NIARA: Some of them have been there for a long time. I'm only there for a week.

GLORIA: Does anybody down there on Earth know that you were going? How did you explain... or how did they explain that you were gone for a week?

NIARA: Well, I was supposed to be gone for a week, to work at the Test Site, to work at the electronic warfare range. So I was gone from Las Vegas for that week. And then the people at my work site were told that I was sick and back at Vegas... sent back to Vegas. So it was real convenient for me to be there for those few days.

GLORIA: So what did you do for that full week on the Moon?

NIARA: Well, what passed for day, I was just operating equipment.

GLORIA: What was the texture of the Moon like?

NIARA: Well, rocky... real rocky... and then there's powdery... powdery dust.

GLORIA: Were you [Undecipherable] the dust on the Moon?

NIARA: Yeah, I spent what time I could looking at it. We were being watched all the time.

GLORIA: By whom?

NIARA: By the Reptile.

GLORIA: Were you taken to eat? And sleep?

NIARA: They wanted him to watch us because he was scary. Yeah, we were taken to eat and sleep. Every once in a while we were given something to eat, but... you know it didn't taste very good, but, you know, when you're hungry you eat.

GLORIA: What kind of food?

NIARA: Some kind of soup and bread. And water to drink.

GLORIA: What did the soup taste like?

NIARA: It tasted kind of like a beef... sort of thing... a thick broth. No butter on the bread. It was the same thing for lunch and the same thing for dinner all the time.

GLORIA: Were you tired?

NIARA: I was allowed to sleep a little bit, but not a great deal.

GLORIA: Where?

NIARA: There was a barracks, but I had to stay in the same room as the three other guys that were with me, so...

GLORIA: Was the atmosphere cold at night?

NIARA: It was hard to tell because the temperature was controlled inside, but I think it was really cold outside. [Heavy sigh.] The Reptilian stayed with us pretty much the whole time.

GLORIA: What happened to the other men that went up there with you?

NIARA: Well, they kept us together. It's really funny, because I can't really focus on looking at them. Again, we were still supposed to stay pretty much isolated from each other, not talk to each other, and not have any interactions, and... there was always somebody there to make sure that we did what we were told. So I was pretty much focusing on what was directly in front of me. I was scared of that Reptilian. And at the end of the week, they put us back on the ship and we were taken back.

GLORIA: What was the trip like?

NIARA: It was similar to the trip there, not much different, just going in a different direction. They took us straight to Nellis AFB. They didn't return us to the Test Site. They took us straight to Nellis AFB. It was dark out and I was wondering about my stuff, because I had a suitcase that was left up at the motel in Tonopah. But when they told me to put my fatigues back on, they gave me my fatigues that had my name tags and everything, and all my regular uniforms, and they told me to put that back on. And my bag… my suitcase… was in the room. The Reptilian stayed on the Moon. And my bag was in there. And then… [Long pause] so I got dressed and… some guy I hadn't seen before came in and gave me another shot in the arm.

GLORIA: What was this one for?

NIARA: It was another one to put me to sleep. This one was really strong and I went to sleep right away. [Long pause.] It was strange… I woke up in my apartment, in my bed… and I kind of wondered how I got there. I thought I must have been really tired. I didn't remember how I was getting there.

GLORIA: Where was your daughter?

NIARA: I had to go pick her up from where she was staying.

GLORIA: And where was she staying?

NIARA: She was staying with… somebody on the base… on Nellis AFB.

GLORIA: Right now I want you to go back to Sedona… to your safe place… [Brings her out of hypnosis.]

Aftermath

After this session I was stunned and silent. Any awe or wonder at such information coming forth was completely overshadowed by the feeling of having been virtually a laboratory animal and slave in a variety of ways as these experiences flowed forth. While speaking under hypnosis many times it was a struggle to force the words out, lots of long pauses and a strong feeling of being afraid and not wanting to speak.

About three weeks after the sessions, I felt a intense rising tide of panic and shock well up in me about these military experiences. The extraterrestrial ones paled in comparison. And yet, my life was in another transition. I had to move at that time, from one apartment to another, packing, hauling, unpacking. There was little time to feel or address my feelings in any way. I did only what was absolutely necessary, unpacking only the essentials in the new place to make it livable. It stayed that way for nearly a year.

Though my memory loss was created by design through trauma, and also perhaps drugs, I knew it was created also by my own internal safety mechanism, shutting out what I could not handle until the day when I could. Had that day now arrived? I was not at all convinced it had, but here were the reclaimed memories from this session, all the same. I didn't know how I was going to deal with them.

I spent days sitting on my sofa, arms wrapped around my knees, hugging them to my chest while I stared off into empty space, fighting a panic inside me that threatened to engulf me. I was afraid to give in to it for that very reason. Post-traumatic stress set in more deeply, and circumstances in the U.S. were not helping. I knew from my past study and research that there were no real answers to address what had happened to me, or why or how. But somehow, some way, I had to deal with the emotional fallout.

I remembered the fairly extreme heart palpitations I had had to deal with after getting out of the military. They had come up while working for EG&G. My heart would take off at a mad gallop, pounding in my chest, and at the same time it would feel like I was being choked or suffocated. Very frightening, very confusing. I saw my family doctor for this problem, and he had me wear a heart monitor for three days to record the length and intensity of these spells. Under his care, I managed to avoid having medication to deal with them, using simple, calming yogic breathing when they occurred, lessening their impact and frequency greatly until I rarely had these spells anymore.

Was the cause of this intensely unpleasant heart arrhythmia rooted in a past where so much was still obscured? These spells had started to bother me while working at EG&G. What the trigger there may have been – what activated an unconscious memory that manifested as this arrhythmia, I am not sure. I feel now that at some unconscious level I was seeing some of my male co-workers as possible threats to my well-being. Again, I was working mainly around ex-military men, and I did not always feel safe. I had to put up with crass sexual remarks and innuendos, some of them general, some specifically directed at me. Always the warrior, I was still on hyper-alert back then, ready to pick up the nearest "equalizer" and give someone a good whack if necessary. I didn't go to my supervisors. I'd already experienced the opposing open and covert positions on sexual harassment from the military – ostensibly, they do not approve of it, but repercussions to offenders are generally the equivalent of a slap on the wrist. In making a complaint, I, as a woman, felt subjected to a veiled kind of disdain. I just wasn't tough enough to handle working out there in the field with the boys. And boys will be boys after all. My private, vigilant attitude had been this: if violence was all certain guys could understand, I could have dished out some violence of my own if I absolutely needed to. I could be as tough as I needed to be. Fortunately, at EG&G, the situation never did demand that extreme.

There was also another possible contributing cause of my arrhythmia; in more recent years, I have had flashbacks of being slowly strangled by the blond security guard until I lost consciousness, being allowed to revive back to being conscious, then having him do it again, perhaps three or four times in a row. It was terrifying. The flashback carries an incredibly similar feeling to those spells of arrhythmia – my heart racing while also feeling like my windpipe was being pinched closed at the same time. I didn't realize it at the time, but these heart episodes, the hyper-vigilance, and at times, suicidal ideations, were symptoms of PTSD – many that I experienced before really understanding what was going on with me or why.

I looked at the moon in a new way. How does one come to terms with such fantastic information? All I could do was wonder, and in my quest to try and understand what had happened I found some correlating testimony from others – such as Sgt. Karl Wolfe from the Disclosure Project who reported learning of a base on the back side of the moon, which, when I heard him, caused yet again that strange feeling of someone walking over my grave. And more recently, watching Jose Escamilla's[1] Moon Rising also caused feelings of tension, tightness in the throat.

In past interviews, I have said I only went to the moon one time that I knew of – here in this transcript, I mention that I went there eight or ten times. I also realize I made a mistake in saying that a Reptilian piloted the craft to the moon when in my session and transcript, it was actually a Grey. These errors may be picked out, debated and perhaps criticized. But all I can say about any discrepancies is that this hypnosis session was extremely difficult to go through and I remembered cruelty and abuse that was extreme. Going back and listening to it again and again was not something I wanted to do. I hardly ever listened to it at all until having to deal with it to put it in the book. After going through it to edit the transcription that someone else did for me, to make sure it was all correct, I spent an entire afternoon with it, listening to myself and Gloria, stopping and starting the recording to edit, all the while being impacted emotionally by remembering yet again, by having to listen to the stress in my voice reliving, in a way, what had happened. I stayed with it all that afternoon because I couldn't bear the idea of dragging editing this particular section out for three or four days – I wanted it over and done with. After I finished those hours of listening and editing I was shaking severely. I had to just go to bed and allow my body to shake until it stopped, since today I know that shaking is the body's natural trauma-release mechanism.

I suspected the injections in the arm, perhaps the ones in the side of my neck as well, had something to do with my memories being submerged as they had been. And with what I was recalling, once again, I had no desire to dig any more into my unconscious or even to listen to the session tapes, which I put away out of sight after my sessions with Gloria.

[1] Jose Escamilla is a producer and director of documentary films dealing with the UFO phenomenon. Among them are UFO: The Greatest Story Ever Denied and Moon Rising as well as Interstellar and a new project in the works; The Battle of Los Angeles. His website: http://tbinfilms.com/index.html

I needed help, but I had no idea where to go or what to do for myself after these sessions. Nor did I know who I could trust.

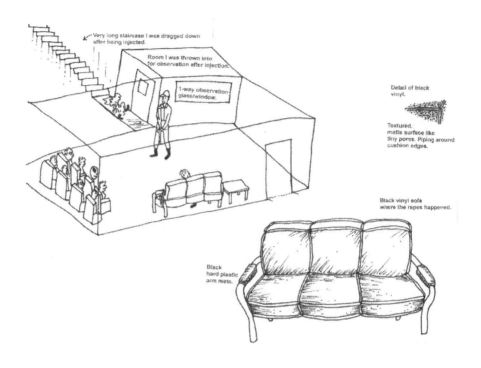

Very long staircase I was dragged down after being injected.

Room I was thrown into for observation after injection.

1-way observation glass/window.

Detail of black vinyl.

Textured, matte surface like tiny pores. Piping around cushion edges.

Black vinyl sofa where the rapes happened.

Black hard plastic arm rests.

Part Two: Healing...
The Path to Within

Chapter 8: Crisis... Hitting the Wall

wasteland

used up, worn out
given up, broken down
emptied out, beaten

i passively view the wasteland
with a fear so deep
it doesn't shake me

fingers pried away...
one clutching slender extremity
after another

so silent a despair
i never heard it

a malaise so transparent
i never saw it

a will so sedated
i never noticed i had given up...

a rage so deep
i forgot it was there

i sit at the edge of my past,
my face turned away...

there is grief so deep
the tears run far below the surface...
a subterranean torrent

~ Niara Terela Isley

When did I embark on a consciously undertaken journey to healing? Start the process that set up the synchronicities, one by one, that I would follow for years to come?

For that we need a short trip in my personal time machine, back to a point of confrontation with inner demons I could not identify. Back in time – noting symptoms and mentally excavating various patterns that snaped my life.

***

At age 33, my life was careening towards complete internal chaos, and I was not sure why.

I was in a relationship with Rich Edwards, a connection that was one of both lovers and best friends. We enjoyed so much together. We both loved the desert, the same television shows, and had endless fascinating discussions on widely varied topics.

My previous two marriages had been riddled with dysfunction, stress and emotional pain, so this one was wonderful in comparison. Even though Rich and I had some difficulties blending our respective children into a harmonious family, and some of the money difficulties that many relationships cope with, so much was truly satisfying, fun and very connected.

Why then this chaos inside of me that began to spill out and threaten a generally happy and contented picture? Why episodes of depression that were like being mired in quicksand, unable to escape?

I didn't really know about or understand post-traumatic stress back then, and even if I had, with memories as yet unknown, I would not have known where it was coming from.

At Rich's insistence, I tried an anti-depressant – Prozac – for a few months. Instead of helping, it seemed to generate more depression. I've always disliked drugs anyway. I didn't feel that I should have to take a pill to make me feel better. I felt like I should be able to help myself. But the downward spiral continued. Finally I decided I could not live like this any more. I was a wreck. I felt useless to both Rich and my kids the with my inner angst at such an intense pitch.

I decided to end my life.

I made my plan very quietly, so as not to arouse anyone's suspicions. I talked to ex-husband Matt, my son Travis' father, about taking in Karly, my daughter from my first marriage; that she should not become separated from her brother, should anything happen to me. Karly had had five years with Matt anyway, learning to call him "Dad" during that time. There had been no contact with Chris, her real father, for many years – he had abandoned her. Matt was fine with taking in Karly, said he would have done it in any case; and accepted that I was just trying to cover things in the event some accident or injury occurred. I knew our animal companions would be cared for. There was not much else I was concerned with. I knew people would be unhappy about me taking this way out, but I rationalized that I was causing them unhappiness in my current state any way.

The day arrived that I had planned to actually end my life. I had drugs in the medicine cabinet or a gun, and I was favoring the gun. I didn't want some pathetic, failed, "cry-for-help" attempted suicide. I wanted the done deal. I knew enough about human anatomy at this point to know where to point a gun to be effective. So, at any time in the next few minutes, I could be laying dead on the floor. No one was home. There was no one to interfere.

Since I was at the precipice on that day, at that moment, I decided to stop and think it over for five minutes. There were no obstacles to my plan. There was time to think and consider.

Spirituality came into sharp focus – my whole life journey up to that point, all my spiritual experiences. The one that came to the forefront was the time I'd managed to project out of my body when I was in my early 20s. That experience had made it irrefutably real for me that I was not my body, from that time forward. I inhabited this body. So, if I'm not my body, and I killed my body, where would I be?

The answers to that question crowded forward in other experiences. There was the soul-traveling dream experience from when I was in Eckankar, where I was passing through the different dimensions or vibratory levels of the multiverse. In that "dream" – more than a simple dream – I discovered, while traveling through the astral plane with the inner master, how my undisciplined thoughts caused me to manifest and find myself in a projected scene of my own creation. This happened as instantaneously as the stray thoughts arose. The master would gently extract me from my mental creations. After the third time this happened, he had returned me home with that gentle directive to learn to keep my focus better. Thought is instantaneously creative on the astral plane.

I remembered reading Raymond Moody's book, *Life After Life*, and other accounts of near-death experiences (NDEs). Often, though not always, NDEs from suicide attempts were very different from those whose NDEs happened accidentally through injury, medical procedure, or life-threatening illness. While suicide-precipitated NDEs could not all be called negative, they did impress a new knowledge on the experiencers that suicide is no escape. Experiencers saw the people they had harmed through their suicide. They saw the current lives they had agreed to take on from a higher perspective. They saw the things they were supposed to accomplish in their lives that they would not complete if they committed suicide. Some learned that if their body truly did die, they would be trapped somewhere on the other side.

It didn't sound at all pleasant. Nor did it sound like any kind of escape to "get away from it all."

It also did not sound pleasant to think that, if my body were dead on the floor and I was immediately transported to the astral plane, that I could simultaneously be confronted by negative thought-forms of my own creation in the same nanosecond of my arrival there. There would be no body to escape back to. I would be stuck there. How would it manifest? Would I suddenly be confronting monsters of my own subconscious, immediately mired in my own illusory astral creation? Would I have the consciousness and awareness to pull myself out of such a real-seeming frightening scenario? In my current state of mind, I decided, almost certainly not. And what if the negative mental state driving me to take my own life became self-reinforcing on the other side? I could seem stuck in such a place for what would seem like an eternity.

I thought about my children again from a now-more-clear mindset. My son was still so young. Did I want to leave him only to the influences of his father? That couldn't be the right thing to do. His father was still struggling with alcoholism and had no apparent inklings of any spirituality outside of traditional religion. This was also true for my daughter, for the same reasons and one more. Our current mother-daughter relationship was in the throes of her junior-high-school-age rebellions against all things parental. If I checked out of her life now, by my own hand, would she blame herself? I couldn't let that happen either.

As I contemplated these grave concerns, I mentally inched myself back from the edge of the suicidal precipice. I looked back at it longingly though, because the inner shadows haunting me, that had brought me to the edge of that abyss, still loomed large. How can even a warrior fight something they can't see, or hear? How does one swing at shadows with no form or substance? I was experiencing their effects – anxiety and depression. I felt helpless, powerless. I truly was at a loss to understand what was happening to me. When you understand what's going on with you, you can do something about it. I had no idea what was going on with me. I was just experiencing the results of... something. Those effects were what had brought me to the edge on that day.

Faced with knowing I couldn't go on living the way I had been, and now realizing that suicide was not "a way out" either, I was backed into a corner. Killing my body could make everything much, much worse, but I had not looked at it precisely in this way before coming to the suicidal point of crisis.

Whatever kind of healing it was I had to do seemed, at that time, to require a herculean kind of commitment. I didn't know how to start or where to begin. What I did do was to mentally square my shoulders, pull myself up by figurative bootstraps and make a huge, 500 % full body commitment to this process – no matter where I had to look or what I had to do to make it happen.

After a few more years with Rich, our blended family and money issues taking their toll, along with my personal emotional rollercoaster, our relationship came to an end. In hindsight, I don't think I could have truly undertaken the healing journey I needed to take with a partner in tow. Several more failed relationships in the years after underscored the point. Relationships were places I tried to hide from whatever goblins were there in the shadows, waiting to be confronted. Whatever was going on with me, I needed to walk alone to discover all the aspects of it, unfettered by the pressures, burdens and concerns of making a relationship work.

Later on, in my body-centered trainings, I learned that when you make a whole-body commitment, it goes out into the Conscious Loving Universe and begins aligning your path with all the right encounters of all kinds to bring about what you have committed to. With the intense commitment to healing I made that day I decided NOT to commit suicide, I didn't realize where it might take me at that time. I had no clear path before me as to how to proceed. But that huge commitment went out into the ethers at that moment, awakening energetic forces that would be my allies. The awakening process began to unfold. Synchronicities began to guide me through the ensuing years to where I needed to go to find healing – and the beginnings of peace.

Climbing the Wall

Not having recovered my ET experiences or military trauma memories at this point, I began digging into what I could, what was available to me in my accessible memory – looking at how my family history was affecting my present. I had developed a meditation practice by this time, and with it, a new degree of inner reflection – an "inner observer." I was scrutinizing some of my relationship and sexual behavior that just wasn't making any real sense to me any more. Trying to find "true love" had become a nightmare. My behavior in this area had violated my own personal and spiritual values several times over. It was much more difficult to excuse or rationalize away any more. Just what the hell was going on with me?

I started with what material I could recall in my conscious mind. Growing up in a dysfunctional alcoholic-codependent family had definitely taken a toll. I did a great deal of work in this area in the years that followed. One of the things I had always wanted in my life was a truly loving relationship – nothing like my parents' power-struggles-degenerating-into-violence that had stolen away my childhood. Yet I had taken mental-emotional "snapshots" of people and situations that, over time, became entrenched beliefs. Certain types of men were likely to be untrustworthy, unpredictable and violent; add in alcohol, and you could multiply that by a factor of 10. Women could be silly, spiteful, venomous, too concerned with outward appearances, and often filled with unkind gossip about others and manipulative with tears and emotions. I learned in childhood that people in general could not be trusted on a variety of levels. I had eased back on this mistrust a great deal in my spiritual seeking, finding a more kindred spiritual community of others who were also seekers. They were mainly a gentle, kind group of honest people in most cases. Trust began to grow back in me where people were concerned during my 30s and early 40s.

I grew up wanting to somehow control or stop the intolerable violence that went on in my childhood home. I was naturally a tomboy with a deep love of nature and all creatures in it. In trying to stop the violence in one way or another, I developed the warrior persona whose mandate was to protect – protect my mother from my father, and in some ways, protect my father from himself. Who knows how far the violence might have gone if I was not there as a barometer of his own behavior, letting him know somewhere deep down inside – in spite of being drunk – that he was about to cross a line he dare not cross? But it was still a role that, in a more ideal world, a child should never have had to take on.

My warrior persona carried over into other areas of my life. I protected the weaker kids at school, the ones who got picked on and made fun of. I protected myself too. As a tomboy, like many boys and men in our society and culture, I learned to see showing feelings and crying tears as weakness and even manipulation. So I became stoic, pulling a wall down over my feelings. Manipulation was as distasteful to me as violence, especially when I caught myself falling into doing it, being human after all.

From childhood on into adulthood, the only place it felt safe to open to my emotions was being alone in nature, or with my animal companions. With my dogs, or out in the woods, I could experience my feelings as I felt they were intended to be experienced, in a pure way, just for themselves. They were not interfered with, no one tried to judge or fix them. They could just "be."

As an adolescent moving into young adulthood, there was a longing for a special someone, another human being with whom I could be truly, deeply connected, with whom I could truly be myself.

I now feel that some of this longing is the wanderer's or starseed's loneliness on planet Earth, thinking if they could just find that one special person to love and be loved by, it might assuage the loneliness and the isolation they feel – cut off from their own people and culture in which they felt connected and in continual tel-empathic[1] communion with those around them. We can expand this metaphor to a larger spectrum. If all consciousness, energy and matter in the universe is truly One – as spiritual adepts, saints and sages throughout time have tried to teach us – then perhaps in the deepest recesses of our own consciousness we remember being part of that undifferentiated Oneness. Coming into a third-dimensional Earth life suddenly thrusts us into a realm of separation and limitation. This could be likened to being thrown into icy water. The shock of it may have us struggling to survive, to breathe, to discover what it is to truly live – and the memory of where we came from is lost in the struggle, perhaps only a tiny spark left that can become our guiding star if we

[1] "Tel-empathic" is a word I have borrowed from listening to Bashar, an extraterrestrial being channeled through Darryl Anka. While I do not follow much channeled information, I find the information from Bashar through Darryl to be very specific, insightful and valuable. Website link: http://bashar,org

seek it out and re-develop our connection with it.

Love is most often very dysfunctionally expressed on this planet because as humans, we feel so isolated. Cut off from our previously expanded senses, we fall into fearful survival attitudes and the mind-ego of the human form takes over. It constantly tries to out-think itself and everything around it that it perceives as a threat in some way. It mentally spins its wheels, trying incessantly to figure out everything, to control and manage everything, when it should just step aside and let the intuitive heart be the guide, taking a supporting role. We know we need love in our lives and our ego fears we won't get it and/or we don't deserve it, so we become codependent – conniving, scheming, cajoling, manipulating and threatening to get the love we need. What we get under such conditions is a pale counterfeit of love. Love cannot breathe and reach its full potential under such circumstances.

In spite of how badly I *consciously* wanted a loving relationship, it eluded me. I've learned that when you consciously want something that continually seems beyond your reach, there is an unconscious counter-commitment to having it. As I pressed into those unconscious places in myself, two answers to the riddle of why I hadn't found the relationship I *thought* I wanted presented themselves.

The first was that I wanted my freedom more than I wanted a relationship, because unconsciously I equated relationship with a loss of freedom. Loss of freedom in relationship had always been my experience, likely because I unconsciously expected, and therefore attracted it to be that way. Another part of the equation was how much freedom would I allow a partner to have when in the grip of my own mind-ego fear of abandonment?

The second answer to my riddle, realized more lately the past few years, was that in my pursuit of a "loving relationship" I was using that pursuit to run away, to use relationships and/or sexuality, as a way to avoid... something.

For several years, one of the things I was most critical of in prospective partners was any fixation they seemed to have with a sense of mission in life that eclipsed other areas of life, even relationship. How could they "know" with such conviction that the path they were following was not a delusion, one that would end up costing them dearly in the end? My criticism of this trait provided a clue that took considerable time for me to discover... that I was avoiding my own sense of purpose, right dharma or "mission" with all my might, and trying to put a relationship above everything else in my life to blot it out. No wonder I would expect a partner to do the same.

It was a hell of a bind. Consciously I wanted a relationship. Unconsciously I pursued relationship to wrap around me as a sweet blanket to shield myself from that "something" that loomed out there in the ethers somewhere. Then my inherent desire for unfettered freedom would assert itself and prevent relationships from working, or attract partners they couldn't work with – even when I added a strong requirement that a future partner be a compatible spiritual match.

Spirituality moved to the forefront of my life again as my relationship with Rich was ending. I was seriously questioning the dubious value of being an attractive woman. The shift from nerd to attractive young woman began when I got the braces off my teeth and gave up glasses for contact lenses in my senior year of high school. Suddenly I'd had the opportunity to find out what being attractive could mean. But it had fallen far short of expectations. I felt I was actually happier when I was on my own, learning and exploring all the things I was so passionate about.

My practice of vipassana meditation for several years was another step on my path to healing. Also called "insight meditation," it provided just that; much insight into myself, my fears, wishes, hopes and desires. When going truly deep enough into a meditative state, there were also glimpses into the true nature of the universe from the vantage point of inner space. Enough to grasp that time and space are illusory, and that these constructs were also convincing enough to take up most people's thought and energy for their entire waking lives.

I was at a four-day silent vipassana meditation retreat when I had my next big insight and synchronicity that led me to my next step in healing.

The retreat was totally silent, no talking by anyone. We rose at 5 am to the tingsha chiming. Meditation, simply called "sitting" at the retreat, began at the next ringing of the bell at 5:30 am. When the tingsha chimed again at 6:30 am, it was time for walking meditation. During sitting, the practice was about staying with the breath, flowing in, flowing out. We were to notice when thought, emotion or body sensation took our attention away from the breath, and then consciously return our focus to the breath. During walking meditation the focus on the breath was replaced with the lift, place and step of one foot, then the other. We would silently lay claim to whatever piece of floor, outside deck, or dirt road beyond the driveway we could claim for the hour of walking. Retreat days passed with the hours of sitting, alternated by the hours of walking, with two silent yoga practice sessions morning and afternoon, to keep the body fit for meditation practice. Breaking for mealtimes was also done in silence, eating with chopsticks, to make sure we took the time to be with the total experiential meditation of taking in our nourishment. Afterwards, retreat attendees silently cleared the table and did the dishes, moving away table and chairs to clear the room for sitting or walking again.

During sitting practice, I was having difficulty. I would close my eyes and focus on my breath but then my mind would wander to sexual thoughts – and with partners I knew to be most inappropriate. This was very upsetting. I had not been "acting out" sexually for a number of years now; my life was concerned with other priorities. I was not at a meditation retreat to sit and have my mind conjure up such thoughts. I was there to move as deeply into a

140

thought-free state as was possible. In my earlier years I had considered myself a "free spirit," coming of age in the 1970s, fresh after the sexual revolution of the 1960s. But I had been working in recent years to set such "free-spirited" behavior aside and work on other aspects of myself. I did not want more flings. I wanted a committed, loving, long-term relationship, or no relationship at all.

There was one opportunity to speak at this retreat, and that was to have a short interview with the meditation and yoga teacher who was running the retreat. I had gotten to know him and his wife enough over the last three years that I trusted him to talk with completely. I told him what was happening during my sitting practice. He listened thoughtfully. When I was done, he asked if I had ever looked at the possibility of having sex addiction.

I was startled. I had not considered that sex could be an addiction. But I was disturbed by the recurrent thoughts I was having. They were not welcome. Yet I couldn't seem to let them go or shut them off. I agreed to look into this possibility when the retreat was over and I was back home.

This retreat was an important part of my healing process. On the last day of the retreat, a special circle was created by our teacher to help us open back up to speaking and interacting with each other in preparation for going back out into the world again. A kind of reintegration back into a busy society.

Carefully-chosen music and gently-spoken suggestions by our teacher flowed through the space around us as we sat in this final circle. All around me people who had held their energy within during the days of shared silence were breaking into tears. I sat there completely stoic, my heart feeling like it was encased in stone. I wondered if something was wrong with me, or if something was wrong with all these people around me who were venting so much emotion. I began to feel irritated.

Then our teacher began to speak to how we felt as children, and to remember how much our parents loved us and wanted the very best for us.

Such words. Coming in now after the days of silence with no outlets, no escape from the parade of all kinds of thoughts – sometimes giving way to deep silence within. After feeling minutes stretch into timelessness, the flow of my breath ever slowing, slowing. After any boundaries between "me" and the Sea of One Consciousness began to dissolve, experiencing a suspendedness in the deep silence for unmeasured parcels of time...

Something in the silence had opened me, despite the struggle with unwanted thoughts and feelings. It was as if my journey through this retreat had worked away at my stoicism from the inside, eroding the barriers I had placed around my heart from within, leaving that barrier thin and fragile.

The words about parental love broke over me like a tidal wave. That now-thin shell of stone around my heart broke open. I began to sob as I never have, before or since. I was weeping desperately for the child I had been who had never truly experienced her parents putting her and her best interests first, being too mired down in their own entangled dysfunctions. I cried and cried for the loss of something I had never truly had or known.

The reintegration circle ended and people began to speak with each other again. Still I wept floods of tears with racking sobs, until I began to fear I could not stop. It took a huge effort to get this flood under control, and in hindsight now, I wish I hadn't even tried to. It would have been better to let it flow. I have never cried like that since though. Maybe that day with all those flooding tears, sobs and emotions was enough. A very significant crack had been made in my various learned warrior defenses. Also significant to me was being with loving and supportive people, no one trying to cajole or fix me, push me this way or that. They were simply there as heartfelt compassionate witnesses to a grieving event, years upon years overdue. If ever there was a safe place to feel such feelings this was it. My warrior persona, forged in childhood and further tempered with four years of U.S. Air Force active duty, who did not cry under nearly any circumstances, was completely disrupted.

This retreat was a huge step in the healing process that began at the moment I decided not to kill myself and completely committed to living life and healing. Looking back from where I am today, I know that we never heal by repressing and bottling up our emotions.

Later, I was in my car driving away from the safe space of the now-ended retreat, still shaken by the riptides of grief I'd experienced. But I felt cleaner, lighter. This had been a very important few days for me, a chance to confront things in myself that life in my busy outer world did not permit. I resolved to follow the meditation teacher's advice and look into the sex addition issue.

Origins of Issues... Looking for Answers

Within my spiritual circle I asked trusted friends about this issue, looking for a good counselor to work with. To my surprise, others I knew had also worked on this type of addiction. I found someone who was exactly what I needed. He did group work with both women and men, and had not only the education, degrees and certifications, but also had worked through his own challenges with sex addiction, as well as alcoholism, drug addiction and codependency. He was a seasoned veteran in the addictions arena.

He could tell I had a warrior attitude straight away, and during the three years I was in his group, we locked horns with fiery eyes more than once. But he was usually right. I learned a great deal from him including that codependency is the central addiction around which all the others revolve. Codependency feels so bad to do or be the recipient of, that it gives rise to all the other addictions as an unhealthy, dysfunctional form of temporary relief.

I also attended 12-step meetings for sex addiction and codependency during those years. I learned a great deal there as well, things that people don't as a rule learn in their nice little civilized spiritual gatherings. I learned that many people involved in various forms and practices of spirituality were nearly hopelessly entrenched in codependent behavior and justified it over and over again as being the right thing to do from their spiritual perspectives of service and self-sacrifice. They felt they had a right and obligation to interfere, confront or meddle in the lives of others, controlling them for their own good, very similar to the born-again Christians' self-anointed right to try and convert the world to their belief systems. I now noticed people who martyred themselves in various ways to try to "help" others – then secretly or not so secretly grinding their teeth in resentment when the object of their "help" was unresponsive or unappreciative. I recognized this pattern in myself to a degree, and how prevalent it was in both my parents. I read in one of my therapy books that "'Help' is the sunny side of 'Control'." It doesn't take too long to figure out various forms of control masquerading as "help." Controlling help in effect says to the recipient of the "help" that they are so ignorant, so defective, that the helper/controller has to control-rescue them in a way that the helper/controller decides is "best."

In contrast, Ram Dass' book, *How Can I Help? Stories of Reflection and Service*, co-authored with Paul Gorman, says a great deal simply in the title. When you ask someone, "How can I help?" you empower them to make a choice about what they need for themselves. Then your help becomes a true act of service to another.

In 12-step groups for sex addiction, I found that the addiction takes different forms in different people. For some, mainly men, it was running up uncontrollable debt for phone sex, cyber-sex or frequenting prostitutes. For most everyone, sex addiction was a combination of sex and the adrenalin rush that came from indulging in something forbidden or risky, equaling high adrenalin-producing drama.

Sexuality and adrenalin are a potent and addictive mix. Like all substances that are abused, such behaviors become a problem when people cannot say no to them. And sex addiction is not like drugs or alcohol that you can lock away, not buy, or otherwise avoid. Your own body makes the drug. So recovery presents some huge challenges, and an intense scrutiny of what you are doing and why – a "20 questions" game every time you feel like you want to get close to someone, with a flurry of what's, why's, and how's to sift through. Your choice is to become peacefully celibate, or to learn to determine what constitutes a *healthy* sexual expression, based in non-controlling expressions of love for yourself and your partner. Loving expression is also based in good communication, in an understanding of emotional states in yourself and others, and dealing with such states with empathy and compassionate witnessing for each other, without trying to "fix" the other person. Once you establish the parameters for yourself about what you feel constitutes a healthy personal sexual expression, you do your best to adhere to them. If you've made a mistake in your parameters, it will become evident over time. You can adjust and tweak the parameters according to what you learn as needed. What constitutes healthy sexual expression can vary for different individuals also.

My definition of addiction became any use of substances or behavior that a person could not control – that person also violating his or her own value system, morally and/or economically, to indulge in the substances or behavior.

Facing the fact that you have somehow, in your journey through life, lost control over your ability to choose is quite a disturbing truth to face. In my case, one that demanded action to take back control over my own life. "Action" was more meditation from a new understanding and deeper place in myself. I made stark changes in my lifestyle to bring about a deeper sense of inner calm. From my meditation practice I was very familiar with Buddhist teachings about "dramas of the mind," the mind being the field in which all dramas ultimately play out. They are filtered, shaped and magnified by our own past experiences which have formed our perspectives, beliefs, opinions and judgments. When you are hooked on drama to any degree, creating calm in your life and refusing to indulge in drama can seem like a boredom that will drive you mad. Your adrenalin-addicted body whispers in your ear to do something – anything – to bring on an adrenalin rush to get the fix. You have to stay with the process of non-drama until you realize that what you are internally screaming about as being BOREDOM!!! is actually peace, or the beginnings of peace. To make such changes for your own good often means you let go of some friendships and cultivate new ones with people who are supportive of the new way of living.

The most healing realization I had during the years of working with the counseling and 12-step groups was a full, whole-body, cellular realization, in a huge momentary flash of insight, that my addiction was destroying any chance that I would ever experience the kind of love or relationship I was wanting. This cellular realization was profound, touching me at every level. It was a pivotal moment that defused my sex addiction – I no longer had the desire to act out any form of the addiction, though I still realized that I would have to walk consciously and mindfully in this area of my life henceforth.

The ET Factor in this Equation

My years in these programs also left me with a big question. My counselor told me that given my behavior and symptoms, he was sure I had been molested as a child.

I had no memory of any such abuse. Male relatives lived out of state and were poor candidates even to be considered for such abuse of a child. This was also true of my father. He was many things from saint to sinner, but he was not a child molester. So when and/or how had any molest occurred? I decided that my counselor must be mistaken. It was the session with Budd Hopkins, where I found that I had been tampered with in this way by the Greys that finally shed light on where the original molestations had occurred. In addition, the origin of the connection between fear-generated adrenalin and sexuality became clear.

I was in a couple of informal womens' groups during these years as well. I found a lot of joy and comfort in being part of them. I came to really value my feminine friendships. We could understand each other and be ourselves with each other, as women. It was in one of these groups that I was introduced to body-centered therapy. We learned and used the methods in our interactions with each other. This is a process of examining, working with and processing issues and feelings in various ways, not just talk therapy. Body-centered therapy works with what is felt and sensed in the body through the interplay of the mind and emotions. Breathing, movement and other techniques are used to assist in "feeling feelings to completion" to clear personal issues. The results were profound for me. I was inspired to do some professional trainings in this work and obtained certifications in body-centered therapy and life coaching.

In spite of all the progress I was making in some areas, I was learning that I had to keep the extraterrestrial and military-covert ops experiences I was trying to understand and integrate in their own little mind-compartment, away from the rest of my life. If I brought them up, very few people in my usual circle of friends seemed to want to hear about them. They would ask if I could be mistaken somehow, especially in the case of the military experiences, which they found too disturbing and frightening to spend any time considering. Many of them could not believe such things could even happen. I knew how they felt! If I had not undergone the hypnosis and had to deal with re-experiencing these events and feeling their aftermath, I would not want to believe they could happen either. But I no longer had the luxury of ignorance about such things. I had to find a way to live with this new reality and some of the truly ugly things contained in it.

In 1996, during the certification training for body-centered transformation therapy and clearing birth issues, another little signpost emerged, pointing to more experiences to uncover. I had had my first hypnosis session with Budd Hopkins by then, in October 1994, so I was aware of some of my early experiences with the Greys and the military experiences up to the point of the first injection. At the training, we were having an afternoon question and answer session with our trainers. I had been troubled with horrendous, crippling menstral cramps accompanied by very heavy bleeding monthly for years. Since we were examining the body-centered concepts around health of mind and body, I asked what this might be an indicator of. The reply was that it usually indicated severe sexual trauma. Again, just like with my addiction counselor, I was puzzled. No such conscious memories were there for me. It was only in my March 2003 sessions with Gloria Hawker that the severe sexual trauma that happened after the injections was revealed. Another dot connected.

Also during that training session, someone asked about alien abductions. The trainer said that since experiencers described the aliens as having thin, spindly bodies with oversized heads and large dark eyes, and there was a resemblance to humans in fetal form, that experiences of alien abduction could just be a kind of imagery associated with some form of birth trauma. However, he did not elaborate on this.

My heart sank. I would have loved to accept such a hypothesis for my experiences, and gratefully distanced myself from the strange world of abductions, alien or military. But I simply could not and did not believe this explanation. What I had re-experienced under hypnosis was too real.

I completed this training and actually took more with these trainers because I found what they had to teach very valuable on both a personal and professional level. But it was also one more place where I did not feel I could bring up some of the deepest issues affecting my life. One more place where I felt I had to stand on the outside of a social group looking in, separate because of my experiences. The trauma rattling around inside of me continued – undiscussed, unprocessed and unresolved.

My hypnosis session of 1994 had answered a few questions; given me some insights into why I might have some of the issues I was currently working on. However, it raised many, many more. The childhood molestation my counselor was certain had occurred, that gave rise to the issues I wanted to resolve in counseling, had not happened by way of a human victimizing me. One of the memories that came forth was having one of the Greys spreading a clear liquid on my genital area when I was a small child of four or five years old. Why would they do such a thing? What the hell was going on? Had someone or something else been running my sex life all these years? If so, why? I needed more answers and understanding, but was not sure where to go to get them. The idea of undergoing more hypnosis filled me with trepidation. Finding a hypnotherapist I felt I could trust was a huge issue, as well as having the financial resources to pay for the sessions.

I remembered the nausea and fear that swept over me when I recounted my military history to Nick and found that big gap of missing time. Missing time within which I could not remember anything, except the location where I worked and other broad general points, with no finer detail whatsoever. It was truly terrifying to find out I had participated in a radar test on extraterrestrial craft, watching them in the night sky out on the remote Nevada desert; and then – like a prisoner with no basic rights whatsoever – had been put through the horror of an injection that induced trauma. It was no wonder I felt fear when I discovered the three months of missing time. I began to wonder if it was the pressure of these buried memories that caused the angst and depression that nearly made me take my own life years earlier.

In my body-centered certification training, I learned that the body does not lie. Could I feel this terrified if my mind was somehow fabricating these stories under hypnosis? I absolutely did not think it could. Yet accepting my memories meant leaving behind a world I'd believed in my whole life, of the good old U.S.A., democratic champion of the world, defender and liberator of the oppressed. A country with laws to protect people, a country that was supposed to hold the U.S. Constitution and Bill of Rights as a sacred trust of, by and for The People. I didn't want to give up that illusion; but illusion it was, and I could do nothing but accept it, especially as more and more corroborating information came to me.

How does one heal from such horror? When your conscious mind doesn't remember what happened – or if it does remember, doesn't want to accept what happened – and your heart and soul and body are screaming that it did happen – you end up dwelling in an in-between shadowy netherworld, caught between the darkness that invaded you and the light that could set you free. It's hard not having support, and yet to reach out for support is to acknowledge that what you are afraid happened to you did indeed happen.

Warrior's Requiem

Am I going to feel afraid
     for the rest of my life?
Is this the price of wearing
     a warrior's armor

Until it became a second skin
     I had to peel
From my body in pain, drawing
     my own blood?

Mixing it with my own few tears
     that grudgingly fall
From eyes too long kept dry,
     Never allowed to weaken,

And cry.

~ Niara Terela Isley

My warrior-self, used to being so tough, going it alone, maintaining as much invulnerability as possible, was getting in the way. I'd made some progress chipping away at her armor, but apparently not enough. The mandate from my mind-ego was to protect the sensitive soul I truly was inside. Trying to get help felt like a huge risk. The world I thought I knew had been jerked out from under me. I was living in my own private paranoia. Whom could I truly trust? My warrior-self didn't want to need anything or anyone – for anything.

A spontaneous prayer wafted to the surface of thought from deep within me...

> Dearest Great Spirit, Conscious Loving Universe,
> Let me let go of being strong.
> Let me melt and dissolve away
> Into your Infinite Love and Light,
> And be completely restored,
> Washed sparkling clean,
> Any need for healing a forgotten memory.
>
> ~ Niara Terela Isley

The old childhood feelings of feeling like a stranger in a strange land, never far from the surface, came back into the open. Feeling a part of things in this world had been difficult enough in my life. I had played the role of an attractive woman for several years, trying to find out what I might be missing in regular society. I found out that I hadn't been missing much, and that sacrificing who I really was to have a social life was just not really worth it. I'd found a belonging of sorts in spiritual circles with others who had a high affinity for deep personal inquiry into themselves and the universe. But now that was hard to be a part of too, trying to come to terms with my recovered memories. There seemed to be no one in these circles who could really deal with hearing about them.

Because of my glimpses into a covert reality, I had a sense of foreboding I could not shake off. Secrecy gave far too much power to the secret keepers. Where would it go? How would it end? I didn't like to even contemplate it, but I sensed that something, some grab for power by this shadowy government, was going to happen some day in the future. A game of power chess was going on in the dark, moves and counter-moves building to some checkmate. I still felt a little like Kassandra of Troy, gifted by one god with a sense of prophecy, cursed by another that no one would believe her. Hence, in spite of her warnings, Troy fell.

I watched my friends and acquaintances living in the old reality I had once occupied, longing to return to it and knowing I never, never could. I felt incredibly lonely. I was out on the edge of things, a fringe-dweller, hat in my hand, knowing I better keep certain things to myself or I would no longer be welcome. It did nothing for my self-esteem, nor did it help me to deal with the inner fear that swelled up at times and became terror. I kept it under lock and key inside. I couldn't let it out to lay waste to my life.

Chapter 9: Outsider in Most Places, Insider in New Ones

If in one realm of my life I was a fringe-dweller, in a new one I was now an insider. In my search to find answers, I was meeting other people who had had some similar experiences, with whom I could share and discuss. However, after my associations with the meditation and yoga communities, which I loved, much of it still seemed a race through dark places.

I met a wonderful woman, Miesha Johnston, at a lecture in Las Vegas. Miesha held groups for abductees and contactees called Star Family Contactee groups. Through her friendship, I did get some help and support, finding I was not alone in having such strange and frightening military experiences. I was far less disturbed by my memories of experiences with the Greys, or Zetas, as I later came to call them.

In the beginning of my post-hypnosis quest, I had somehow hoped I would find no correlating testimony. It was a futile hope. The more I searched, spoke with people, attended various talks and lectures, the more testimony I encountered in support of what I had experienced in the military. With every confirming bit of information I gathered, I would get this sinking-in-quicksand feeling. I felt more and more mired in a new and strange reality that consciously I would never have chosen to be a part of. A someone-just-walked-over-my-grave feeling. It was dark, it was unnerving, it was frightening. A very ominous picture of the world I lived in was emerging, as though suddenly I was seeing things in a surreal kind of way – like the negative of a photograph. One view of the reality photograph was sunny and bright, people smiling. The other was reversed, dark and strange, people's smiles turned inside out.

Mind Control and the False Memory Syndrome Foundation

The only thing offered up to counter hypnosis memories was something called False Memory Syndrome. I just couldn't buy into it, and later found out that the False Memory Syndrome Foundation had ties to the CIA, with untrustworthy agendas around government and military secrecy. It seemed to me that they had an agenda to keep secrets and discredit those recovering memories of various forms of sexual or other trauma or alien abduction through hypnosis.

Information about mind control programs has been leaking out into the mainstream for some time. In 1975, a mind control project called MK Ultra was publicly exposed. 20,000 pages of documentation on MK Ultra was found under the Freedom of Information Act (FOIA) and congressional hearings were convened in 1977 to examine this information. It was found that the CIA had used as many as eighty "front organizations" (organizations set up and controlled covertly by a parent organization, allowing the parent organization to avoid blame or culpability for wrong-doing). Through such agencies, the CIA was able to conduct their mind control research. Such "research" was usually tantamount to torture. Many of the individuals in these front organizations were not aware of the covert CIA involvement. The False Memory Syndrome Foundation is just such a front organization whose agendas are highly suspect and as such, their research and conclusions patently unreliable and flawed.

Other mind control project names came to light; Monarch, Bluebird and Artichoke. Most of the documentation was ordered destroyed by then CIA director Richard Helms, but the MK Ultra documentation was somehow overlooked in that sweep. This fraction of surviving documentation is damning in the kinds of information it contains about mind control experimentation done on prison inmates and unsuspecting citizens.[1] Children – the younger the better – were often used in these programs due to their personalities still being in the formative stages.

How did this happen in the land of the free and the home of the brave? In part, through Operation or Project Paperclip[2]. After World War II, under the auspices of Project Paperclip, German scientists from Hitler's Third Reich were brought to the U.S.A., many given American-sounding names and put to work for our own government and military. Some of these scientists were the very ones who had conducted horrific experiments in mind control on Jews and others detained in the Nazi concentration camps. People in secret programs here in the U.S.A. wanted to know what they knew. Why? To apply that ill-gotten knowledge for their own purposes and worse, to continue such research.

The U.S.A. won World War II. But then, tragically, our leadership imported such Nazi individuals, with their Third Reich ideologies. How much subversion took place from within after such a coup we can only speculate. But one only needs to look around at the world we live in today to make a guess about where such agendas of power and control could have come from, finding support from the corruptible within our own ranks.

And how are such secrets kept in what is supposed to be a free and democratic society? Through the National Security Act of 1947. Signed into law

[1] MK Ultra and much other well-documented data, testimony and video on mind control can be seen online at www.wanttoknow.info/mindcontrolinformation

[2] Operation Project Paperclip was a program initiated by the U.S. Office of Strategic Services after WWII to recruit Nazi scientists for employment after the war. One rationale for this action was to keep them out of the then Soviet Union (U.S.S.R.) in the emerging cold war between the U.S.S.R. and the U.S.A. The other was to gain control of their knowledge and continue their various forms of research.

and implemented by President Truman just two months after the Roswell UFO crash, it was dream-come-true legislation for those wanting to do things behind closed and impenetrable doors concerning the study of alien technology and all manner of other unsavory "research." It made them untouchable for any heinous acts they might commit, even in courts of law, due to "REASONS OF NATIONAL SECURITY."

All of these things I learned while searching for answers about what had happened to me – why had it happened, just what could possibly be going on, and in what context such things could even happen in this country. Don't believe me and my testimony solely. Do some digging and research for yourselves. A knowledgeable citizenry is an empowered citizenry; empowered to demand positive change. The countless mind control victims out there, deceased or still alive, deserve no less.

With learning about mind control, and ritual abuse victims coming forward with terrifyingly similar stories of absolutely horrific abuse – much of it starting out in early childhood – this whole idea of False Memory Syndrome was to me highly suspect. It seemed put in place to protect the perpetrators, ultimately perpetrators at high state levels. It also fit too neatly that if our government, or shadowy factions within our government or military, are so resolute in their denial of UFOs and extraterrestrials, then having some fabricated way to discredit those remembering alien abductions is far too convenient. This is especially so if research in recent years uncovering the probability of a pact made between a particular group of aliens and our own military is true. This possibility is explored in Michael E. Salla's[3] book, *Exposing Government Policies on Extraterrestrial Life: The Challenge of Exopolitics*. In it, there may likely have been a deal made between this group of extraterrestrials and top secret military members, a deal of alien technology given in exchange for a license to run their own abduction program among unsuspecting human citizens for genetic experimentation.

This correlates with information I found in *Above Black: Project Preserve Destiny*, by Dan Sherman[4]. Dan Sherman served in the United States Air Force for 12 years. His career field was Electronic Intelligence Specialist. He was decorated with the following distinctions: Air Force Commendation Medal, Air Force Achievement Medal and the Air Force Outstanding Unit award. Sherman was also honored for his service in the Persian Gulf War.

While serving in the USAF, he was trained by the National Security Agency as an "intuitive communicator" to gather communication telepathically from

[3] Dr. Michael E. Salla is an author and one of the pioneering founders of Exopolitics, the scholarly study of the individuals, political processes, organizations and institutions involved with extraterrestrial civilizations involved with our world, though not disclosed to politicians, the media or the public. His websites include http://www. exopolitics.org, http://www.exopoliticsjournal.com and he is also the founder of the Exopolitics Institute, http://www.exopoliticsinstitute.org, offering study programs and certifications in exopolitics.

[4] Dan Sherman's website is http://www.aboveblack.com and his book, *Above Black: Project Preserve Destiny*, is available for sale there, and on Amazon.com. He has also been interviewed by Project Camelot. This video is available on their website archive at http://projectcamelot.org/dan_sherman.

extraterrestrials and enter it cryptically into a computer, to be whisked away to an undisclosed location for unknown purposes. While in this program, Sherman became disillusioned with the secrecy involved with his work. His growing suspicion that some of the data he was collecting referred to human beings being subjected to some kind of experimentation by extraterrestrials resulted in his taking action to separate himself from military service, even though the Air Force had intended to keep him in that position indefinitely.

In reading his book, I found some of the same personally-triggering kinds of correlations between Sherman's story and my own.

Sherman wrote that he was chosen for this special duty because he was an abductee and had been "adjusted" by extraterrestrials while in the womb. He got this shocking news from a superior officer who "recruited" him for the intuitive communicator training. Sherman himself had no knowledge whatsoever of his special "adjustment." This was how his superiors knew he would be able to do intuitive communication.

I have strongly felt that my military superiors knew that I was an abductee, and I have also strongly felt that that I was picked for the radar exercise and other experiences because I was "adjusted" or hybridized – a child of both my parents, but with something "extra." Coincidentally, the researched time frame of February 20-21, 1954 – when then President Eisenhower was alleged to have met with extraterrestrials – took place the same year I was born, later that year in November. Another April 1954 meeting, said to have taken place at Holloman AFB in New Mexico, is where the alleged deal or treaty was struck that allowed Grey extraterrestrials to pick up humans for their own experimentation and hybridization program. Some researchers have maintained that three meetings with extraterrestrials took place; one with a group called "Nordics" who look more like human beings. This group warned Eisenhower about going down the nuclear weapons path. And subsequent shutdowns of nuclear weapons in the U.S. by ET craft down through the years are now well-documented – though in no way officially endorsed by our government.

Whistleblower Milton William Cooper,[5] stated that the extraterrestrial treaty terms – with a group of grey extraterrestrials – were as follows:

> The treaty stated that the aliens would not interfere in our affairs and we would not interfere in theirs. We would keep their presence on earth a secret. They would furnish us with advanced technology and would help us in our technological development.
>
> They would not make any treaty with any other Earth nation.

---

[5] Milton William Cooper served in both the USAF and the United States Navy. He was a government whistle-blower who published a book, *Behold a Pale Horse*, available on Amazon.com. In his lifetime and in this book, he provided extensive information on secret programs with the U.S. government and military, the Illuminati network and more. He was killed in 2001.

They could abduct humans on a limited and periodic basis for the purpose of medical examination and monitoring of our development, with the stipulation that the humans would not be harmed, would be returned to their point of abduction, would have no memory of the event, and that the alien nation would furnish Majesty Twelve (MJ-12) with a list of all human contacts and abductees on a regularly scheduled basis.[6]

If you look at any one of these sources of information alone and isolated from other data, they look like they could simply be sensationalistic nonsense. When you start collecting testimony and documentation, even when circumstantial, and start piecing it together, you begin to get the feeling that there is enough proverbial "smoke" to indicate a "fire" somewhere. Especially when one's life time began right in the middle of it all, and that life has been impacted by extraterrestrials and military and/or covert-ops black projects. And incidently, Dan Sherman states in his book that behind many black projects are "grey projects" relating directly to extraterrestrials themselves.

While in training, Sherman was forbidden to talk to his "classmate" in intuitive communicator school. While out on the Nevada desert for the nighttime radar tests on the extraterrestrial space craft, the radar crew members, of which I was one, were also forbidden under threat by firearms to speak to each other.

Sherman mentions that he has a little bit of Cherokee in his bloodline. When I was a teen, my father told me of our Cherokee heritage from his side of the family. In my own research I've found that a high number of abductees seem to have Native American lineage. I'm not sure why.

Dan Sherman's story is one of many pieces of the extraterrestrial puzzle I've encountered over the years that has shaken me more than a little.

Abduction study and research over many years have revealed that some kind of genetic hybridization program is going on due to the nature of what occurs during extraterrestrial encounters. My case is no exception; in fact, it underscores this fact.

With regards to secret programs using mind control methods of various types – including using physical, mental and emotional trauma to create human automatons that would carry out orders without question – secretive agencies would certainly want to cover their tracks. Such methods have been explored in film and television, starting with the 1962 movie, *The Manchurian Candidate*. Such drugged and programmed individuals are very likely responsible for theater and school mass shootings, especially in the last decade to shock and outrage people into accepting unconstitutional gun control measures, paving the way for possible seizure of personal firearms in the future.

[6] The information on this treaty with Grey extraterrestrials is taken from Milton William Cooper's book, *Behold, A Pale Horse*, under a heading of *The Secret Government: Origin, Identity and Purpose of MJ-12*. Link: http://www.bibliotecapleyades.net/sociopolitica/esp_sociopol_mj12_1.htm.

The CIA or other agencies didn't count on the natural human being's inner drive for freedom of expression that would subconsciously guide people to recovering themselves, even when traumatized in the worst ways imaginable. This inner drive is why survivors of this type of abuse find ways to recover their memories and knowledge of what has happened to them and become free of programming. If human beings were truly mere bio-chemical machines, then such undoing such programming might not be possible. The fact that people do remember and recover is a testament to the intangible, freedom-seeking human spirit. More on this later, in Part Three of this book.

As I explored this strange and disturbing realm of military abductions, or MILABS, I simply could not grasp at the straw of "false memory" to escape from the implications of my recovered memories. If what I was remembering was false memory, then how could it be that I found others who had such similar memories, some of them remembering such events *without* hypnosis? I remembered my session with Budd Hopkins. He had not "led" me anywhere. If anything, he tried to lead me away from some of what I was remembering. He inserted other suggestions that I countered while under hypnosis, staying true to my emerging memories as they flowed forth.

And what reputable hypnotherapist or researcher would try to lead a client into remembering something that was not true? If discovered, such disreputable acts would discredit their work and research and they could be barred from their practice. I would suspect any hypnotherapist or researcher who did lead a client into some contrivance of false memory as being part of the False Memory Syndrome Foundation connected to the CIA, purposely misleading and subverting the client-subject in order to cast aspersions on the entire field of legitimate hypnotherapy.

Once upon a time, testimony from hypnosis was considered to be so accurate as to be allowed as evidence in a court of law. And if the body does not lie, as I had learned and experienced in my body-centered trainings, then why would I feel so afraid, so terrified during my hypnosis session and after? Why did I have such vivid recall and re-experiencing the events, complete with body-flags like shortened or labored breathing, body tension, and other signs of obvious distress? I trusted my body's reactions as truth.

It seemed to me that the truth, the actuality of events, places, situations stood on their own. Untruth usually seeks to hide or obscure truth in some way, twisting truth this way and that to cover up, or lying outright to draw attention away from truth. Even in childhood, when I had done something I shouldn't have, I would find myself afraid of my parents finding out I'd done something they didn't want me to do. I would look at the ways I could somehow cover it up. But telling a lie felt terrible too, and it made fear of being found out go on and on, until I would come clean.

I wonder how many people involved with secret programs at various levels feel dirty with the secrets they must keep, with the lies they must tell? I wonder what means are used to force them to keep secrets? In Steven Greer's Disclosure Project, we hear testimony of people who were afraid for their lives and their families' lives. I wonder just how afraid, and therefore desperate, some of the people at the top feel about keeping their secrets at any cost, especially in today's world when so much that was once secret is finding its way out into the open? As countries around the world release their previously-classified UFO files to the public domain, the U.S.A. has not. It is more than likely that the secret agencies operating in the U.S.A. have some of the worst and most heinous secrets to hide and they fear severe public outrage and dire consequences. Some kind of amnesty program will be needed for any type of full or meaningful disclosure.

In my race through these dark places for answers, I attended a particular group in Las Vegas in Commercial Center off of Sahara. I was nervous, anxious, sitting in that circle of people in that room, that evening. I listened carefully to the experiences of others. Finally it was my turn to share.

I didn't want to give any details of my experiences to muddy things in any way. I was looking for details that would confirm my own. So I shared in general:

> "Well, I had a hypnosis session with Budd Hopkins about a time when I was in the Air Force back in 1980, where I was taken out in the middle of the night to test the radar on UFOs, then afterward they took us to what I think was Area 51 and they did some kind of mind-wipe procedure on us."

> A man sitting across the room spoke up. "Did they inject you in the side of the neck too?"

The anxiety swiftly raced past fear, welled up into terror. The now-familiar goblin danced over my grave... I felt myself sink deeper into the quicksand. I could only nod. I forced myself to sit in my chair, the terror zipping around in my body. I desperately wanted to just get out of there, to run like hell – but where to? I didn't know. When the group was over I immediately left, got in my car and drove home. My last shred of denial about my experiences died that night.

In hindsight, I should have talked with that man, but that night, I just couldn't face the thought. I was severely rattled. That had been the most confirming data-byte collected up to then.

More Strange Experiences: In the Past, and in the Now of Back Then

Participating in Miesha's groups, meeting other ET experiencers was an amazing experience, and far less dark than the MILAB stuff I encountered.

I was thinking back about strange experiences I had had throughout my life. Certainly that childhood nightmare of being left under the street lamp, waking up screaming had been more than a mere dream. I looked again at waking up with the bump behind my right ear, the many nosebleeds I'd had as a child, and still had at times.

I attended another of Budd Hopkins' lectures in Las Vegas. He did a presentation with slides about these beings people were encountering that were simply called "Shadows." A descriptive term for the drawings people had done of these beings, some of them reptilian-looking. They were frightening apparitions. And what's more, I had had such an encounter back in the years before joining into the Air Force.

I had not thought of this experience for some time, which was a wonder in itself, as thinking of it now I remembered the indelible impression it left on me. It had happened after my first divorce, when I was a single mom of my toddler daughter, Karly.

I was studying metaphysics with my friend, Tim Northrup. We had been friends for quite a while by now, right up until I went into the Air Force, which he tried hard to talk me out of. (I should have listened to him!)

In studying metaphysics with Tim, I joined an esoteric mystery school that operated out of Sedalia, Colorado; Brotherhood of the White Temple. It centered around the spiritual and mystery teachings of Dr. Doreal. I was learning some fascinating things about spiritual forces in the Universe, about the play of energies and increasing my sensitivity to the unseen world around me. I had developed a healthy respect for the world of empirical science during my childhood, so inching my way into these energetic realms was just that, inching my way. Yet I also knew there were things I was experiencing – had always experienced from an early age on – that could not be explained by empirical science. So finding and meeting Tim in those earlier years was very important for me, a way that provided some insight into those experiences.

One night, I laid down to sleep and dreamed an extremely vivid dream, recounted here:

> I was being chased by some unseen, non-corporeal entity.
> It was terrifying. I could feel it wanted to possess me. I ran
> and ran in the dream, going all kinds of places trying to avoid
> being captured by this thing. One of the places I found was
> some kind of bible study group. When I went in, the group
> was just breaking up for the evening and I waited for everyone
> to depart so I could talk to the leader and see if he could help.

> I explained what was happening to me and he said yes, he
> could help me. I was starting to have a bad feeling about him.
> He was thin, with a pale, pasty complexion and eyes rather
> sunken in his head that fastened on mine with an almost

hypnotic quality. He spoke in strange tones that were meant to reassure me as he held my gaze with his eyes and moved closer and closer. When he was standing right in front of me, he opened his mouth and bent down to put his mouth over mine, but not as a kiss, just an open mouth over my mouth. For what purpose or why I don't know. The bad feeling about him I was experiencing became so intense I bolted and ran out the door before he could touch me. I felt like he was in league with the invisible entity that was chasing me, which I could feel like an energy sticking to my back, close and terrible. The only place I could think of to go now was to Tim's place, to see if he could help me somehow. Getting there was very difficult, the entity was gaining control over me. Fighting my way up the stairs to Tim's doorway was like fighting a hurricane. I pounded on the door and Tim opened it. Immediately the feeling of the entity was gone when my eyes met Tim's.

At that same second I awoke in my bed. The terrible feeling I had felt with the entity in the dream was all around me in my room. I glanced at my bedside clock. It was 3 am. The feeling in the room was hideous energetically, vibrationally, as though someone was crashing their hands down on a piano or organ keyboard, every chord they struck a discord, causing a screaming, terrible noise in my body. The feeling was coming from my window, where I saw a dark and shadowy form standing in front of it, huge head and shoulders and a torso that faded out below the waist. I could see the window and curtains *through* this entity. My bedroom was deathly silent; just that terrible energy clashing around the room. I kept my eyes on the figure, afraid to look, afraid to look away.

I lay silent and, either paralyzed with fear/afraid to move, or perhaps truly partially paralyzed, I don't know which. Finally some reason entered into my mind and I remembered that I had some booklets from the Brotherhood of the White Temple in my living room with words to send away negative energies. I forced myself out of bed to go and get them. I came back into my bedroom with them and found the words and said them. Immediately, the shadow entity and its horrible energy were gone, just like that. I was relieved. Then I noticed, on the opposite side of the room in front of and over the doorway to the little room where my daughter was sleeping, three white luminescent figures. The feeling coming from them was as wonderful and loving as the other energy had been horrible. I was "seeing" them energetically, not with my physical eyes. I knew they had been watching over me thoughout "the dream" and through the whole waking episode with the shadow entity. I felt from them that they were very pleased with me that I had gotten a hold of myself enough to get what I needed to send the dark energy away. I felt very connected to them, love flowing between myself and them like a gentle current.

Later that day I told the dream and the whole experience to Tim. He shared with me that he had awoken at 3 am himself with a strong feeling he should call me on the phone, but didn't because it was 3 am, after all. We just shared a look after that admission. Undeniably, something had happened which had profoundly impacted me, and had reached out and touched him too, as my earthly teacher and guide.

And, I didn't realize it at that time, but the three luminous beings I saw that night had always been with me, my whole life. I was being watched over from a higher dimension. This was not the last time I would encounter them.

The black figure by the window

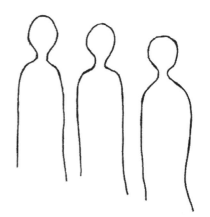

White luminous figures on the other side of the room

Other things were happening in the "now" back then as I was exploring my experiences with Miesha's support, living in Las Vegas, Nevada, out in the Summerlin area. It was like some extra-sensory perception was coming online for me. It had always been there of course, but now I suppose I was paying more attention to it. I was also paying more attention to dreams and anything strange I noticed about my body; marks, sensations – anything out of the ordinary – that cropped up.

Strange things did crop up. I jerked awake one morning finding myself laying on my stomach in bed, unusual for me, a dedicated side-sleeper. The dream-image that caused me to jerk awake: the distinct feeling of being held down while something was being inserted under the skin over my sacrum. Jesus H. Christ... what the hell...?

One day on my way to the pool at the apartment complex with my son

Travis, I noticed a strange scooped depression on the top and right side of my right wrist. A scoop mark. I pointed it out to Travis as we continued on to the pool. Within a couple of weeks it filled itself in, but the outline of it still remained on my right wrist for a long time. Whatever made it fill in, tissue growing back, it was not like the surrounding skin and tissue. It formed a little raised place there instead of a scoop, firmer than the normal skin on my arm. Go figure.

I woke up one morning, got in the shower to get ready for work and noticed to my dismay that my genital area was swollen. I'd gone to bed alone and woke up alone. Very disturbing. What could I "do" about it? Nothing. I was just left wondering, with a feeling of disquiet inside.

Another morning as I was getting dressed, I noticed three little bruises on my inner left thigh almost midway down to the knee. The looked like they might have been made by childlike fingers pressing into my flesh. Sigh. What the hell was going on with my life while I was sleeping?

One morning I woke up and somehow, the usual, normal physical world around me in my bedroom and out the window felt extremely fragile and ethereal, as though all I needed to do was move or blink, and I would be "somewhere else," – some other plane of existence who-knew-where. Concerned about leaving the usual, normal world behind for something unknown, I laid there and took deep breaths, feeling myself anchor into my body until the fragility faded and the 3D physical world resolidified and felt "real" again. It didn't feel at all "bad"... just strange. What was up with that?

Then there was a time I had a bad cold. Inspite of congestion, I managed to fall asleep only to awaken in the wee hours of the morning sometime (I didn't look at the clock). It was still dark out. But oddly enough, I could see around my room pretty well, including a little golden luminescent being watching me with large dark liquid eyes, floating with his/her/its head stuck through my bedroom wall from outside in. I was not seeing this with my physical eyes either, I was seeing it with my – for lack of a better term – third eye; energetically, with this expanded sense that was increasingly becoming active. As soon as the little golden being seemed to notice me seeing him, like lightning, he shot away, withdrawing his head back through the wall in a flash.

I "saw" one of these beings again as I got up one morning to go into the bathroom. I entered and before turning on the light switch (there were no windows in the bathroom) there was the distinct visual impression of one of the little golden luminescent beings floating in there. I was startled and he also became startled, shooting away through the ceiling, gone.

This was all too strange at that time. I had a talk with Spirit. "I don't want to be seeing or experiencing this stuff," I pleaded. "If I can't see it with my physical eyes, I don't want to see it. I need to know what I'm seeing is r-e-a-l." Whatever "real" meant. Things I could touch, see, hear and feel through my physical body was what "real" meant to me back then. I had been aware of my expanded senses for most of my life, but what was happening then was too much, too fast.

Too many questions... no real answers. The need to figure it all out with the mind and mental facilities was a very real need back then. I needed to learn that to open to and access one's expanded senses, one most often needed to drop the mind and mental processing and simply feel and experience. I just wasn't there yet. It was all too strange. But it did seem that the strange happenings decreased in frequency after my plea for them to stop.

For Every Answer, More and More Questions

Miesha continued to connect me with many people, books and resources to help me in my search for answers to what had happened to me, especially with the military. These people were very different from the spiritual people I'd been keeping company with for almost a decade. Some of them were deep into conspiracy theory, and many seemed grim, angry and overshadowed by the dark. I was struggling not to allow the dark to overcome me, yet I needed some of this information; so I stayed with the process, talking with these people, attending the groups and lectures, collecting and correlating data.

Driven though I was to find answers, I felt dragged into all of this kicking and screaming inside.

How was I ever going to have any kind of normal life now? It was becoming more and more impossible to imagine it. Would I ever be able to find the relationship I had hoped for? How could I keep such experiences from a partner, and if I did share, would it be too much for him to handle? Could I even trust any man I might meet to be in a relationship with? Just what the hell was going on out in the Nevada desert? What kind of agenda was playing itself out? Why were there ETs here, what were they doing and why? If they were creating hybrid ET-humans, why? Why were people being picked up and used in such a fashion, without their consent? What role were they playing with the military? I could rationalize that ETs might be picking people up and doing studies with us the way we did with animals, examining us, taking samples, tagging us with implants for some reason. I could not, however, rationalize such excuses for what had happened to me at the hands of other human beings.

Deep inside of me, right alongside the inner terror, was rage. I think it was the rage that kept me going on my quest for information when the terror might have stopped me. How could human beings do such things to other human beings – to me? Why? Why? Why? Why me, goddamit? Why did I have to carry this around? Why did I have to not only carry this around, but because of it be an outcast with the friends and people I cared most about being close to? The rage and terror were both symptoms of PTSD, along with constantly looking over my shoulder, obsessively locking doors and sitting in public places with my back to the walls so I had a clear field of vision over the whole room or venue.

Every question had a litter of "kittens," splitting into more and more questions. They blended together in my head into a big, screaming "WHY?!!!" When I re-watched the movie, *Close Encounters of the Third Kind*, I completely understood the motivations and obsession of Richard Dreyfuss' character, Roy Neary. I understood it in spades.

I supposed I could go public. I contemplated it briefly. I would need more hypnosis to fill in some big blanks, and there was no way I was ready to look there. The very thought made me shudder. And if I went public, got labeled a crazy-UFO-conspiracy-theory-person, what kinds of employment, friends, personal life or relationships might I be restricted to? I thought angrily, "I'll be damned if the only career opportunity available to me is going to be speaking at UFO conferences. The hell with that." No fucking way.

Rage was my safe place to hide from a deep grief that was rippling through me as well, kept deep, even under the fear. Grief at losing the world I thought I had known. Grief that human beings were capable of such horrible acts against other human beings. Anger and rage helped me to feel somewhat in control of myself. Giving into fear or terror, even though it was there – and especially giving into grief – felt far, far too vulnerable. I had to avoid such vulnerability at all cost. I had to hang on; I had to stay hyper-alert. Who knew what could be waiting for me "out there?" There was a big personal cost to me, keeping all these roiling emotions inside. But the pressure they built up over time created further steps to healing along this strange and dark path, and ultimately, led me out of it later on.

My inner rage kicked my fear and grief into the background, and continued to fuel that driven race through dark places to find answers, or at least more information.

Mentioned previously, I had that long talk one afternoon with John Rhodes, reptilian and underground base researcher, at a local Las Vegas restaurant. I spent a good chunk of time vigilantly scrutinizing people at the nearby tables. I found yet more affirmation of my experiences from John. More of the sinking-in-quicksand feeling.

I sent two similar letters to John Lear, and to George Knapp of KLAS TV in Las Vegas, who had done the UFO series on the evening news back in the late 80s that had so riveted me to the television night after night.

The letters are included here, with the differences in the opening paragraphs for each individual included at the top:

February 9, 1995

George Knapp
KLAS-TV
(Address removed for privacy reasons)
LasVegas, NV 891xx

Dear Mr. Knapp,

We met briefly at your recent presentation at Garside Junior Highschool on February 1. I am writing this letter to you in hopes that you might be able to meet with me to clear up some issues that have arisen in my life relating to secret government agencies concerning alien spacecraft.

February 9, 1995

John Lear
(Address removed for privacy reasons)
Las Vegas, NV 891xx

Dear Mr. Lear,

We met briefly at your recent presentation at Eldorado High School on January 25. I am writing this letter to you in hopes that you might be able to meet with me to clear up some issues that have arisen in my life relating to secret government agencies concerning alien spacecraft.

I have followed UFO information in the media for some years now, open to the possibility that we were/are being visited and even interacted with. Several anomalies have occurred in my life that I have always wondered about, whether or not they actually had something directly to do with aliens and alien intervention in my life. As time has gone on more has come to light and I have become increasingly apprehensive about this, but I hesitated to enter into the field of UFOlogy directly because of an obsessive hysteria I observed in individuals associated with this phenomena.

I prefer calm, rational objectivity, and though I am open to many areas of new thought, such as psychic phenomena and higher states of consciousness, I have devoted myself to personal study of scientific theories that provide support for such phenomena, such as quantum mechanics, and most recently, chaos theory. I have been a good student of the sciences since early childhood and have an admiration and respect for scientific objectivity, while, again, remaining open to possibilities that may exist beyond our present knowledge and capability to study.

I had discovered in 1991, through conversation and questions asked of me by a close friend about my U.S. Air Force enlistment (April 15, 1979 through April 15, 1983) that in 1980, while stationed at Nellis AFB and working at Tonopah Electronic Warfare (Combat) Range, that my memory of this period of my life basically wasn't there, a period of approximately two to three months. After the shocking realization that I could remember almost nothing of that time and very few of the people I knew then or worked with on a daily basis, I of course worked my brain overtime trying to remember some details but could only recall sparse amounts of detail or incidents, such as a couple of men I dated briefly, and two women friends that I knew either before or after I had worked up there. I can promise you that for the most part, I have an excellent memory.

162

At the Whole Life Expo here in Las Vegas last October, I attended Bud Hopkins workshop on Alien Abductions. When the question and answer session came up I raised my hand and started to speak about the many anomalies in my life, including the missing time from the Air Force. He asked me to meet with him afterwards. To make a long story short, he did a hypnosis session with me and some of the lost memory came back. What came out was pretty fantastic by the average person's reckoning. I would rather not go into more details in this letter, because what I am hoping is to meet and talk with you to see if in all the people you have talked to about this entire phenomena you have run across anything similar, then share with you what I experienced under the hypnosis. These memories that have apparently surfaced, which I fear are true because of the emotions that also surfaced around the events remembered, seem so "far out there" in the realm of the believable that I have been conducting my own private inquiry with various individuals to check out the information. So far, it has for the most part been corroborated. This has led me to form some opinions based upon my direct experiences that tend to force me to conclude that the government cover-up is very real, a fact that I had probably accepted intellectually before the hypnosis, but has become more frighteningly real and personal since the hypnosis.

So I hope that you can help me continue my inquiry into this matter. The more light I can shed on it helps to give me some peace in some regards, and stirs me up about what is going on in the "secret government" in others. I hope to find the means to undergo more hypnosis in the future by qualified and objective persons.

Thank you for your time in reading this letter and for returning my recent phone call. If you could meet with me it would be most appreciated. The best times to reach me by phone are mornings on Saturday, Sunday, and Monday, after 8:00am and before 11:00am. My phone number and address are listed below.

Sincerely,

Niara T. Isley

(Address removed for privacy reasons)
Las Vegas, NV 891xx

I talked with George Knapp at least briefly, but there were no revelations to be had there, at least not for me personally; there was little information that I had not already uncovered.

I met and talked with John Lear Jr. at his home on the east side of Las Vegas, looking for information and answers. Some years back I'd seen him give a talk at Eldorado High School in Vegas about UFOs and ETs and the Dulce war[7]. That was the first time I had heard of Dulce. Digging into Dulce was a horror

---

[7] The Dulce War is a reference to an alleged military confrontation between aliens and humans at an alleged alien base underground at Archuleta Mesa. The Dulce base is named after the nearby town of Dulce, New Mexico on the Apache reservation in Rio Arriba County.

story in itself. With the memories I was living with, it was far less difficult to believe in the stories of what might be happening there.

I also met Bill Uhouse once, listening to the information he had to offer.

I was becoming disenchanted with the whole UFO investigative and research field. There were no real answers to most of my questions. The people who could really supply answers – the extraterrestrials themselves and the government, or the shadow factions within the government – weren't talking. I was afraid I was becoming too enmeshed in this phenomenon.

I had gathered enough correlating data from others relating to my own MILAB experiences that I no longer doubted them. Living in a reality paradigm outside the mainstream one, looking at it as the sham it was, was very, very hard. I wondered about others out there like me, trying to find answers because they had gone through similar military-type experiences. There seemed to be far more support for ET abductees and contactees than there was for MILABs. Thank heaven for Miesha, who, from her own experiences and research, into both ETs and MILABs, understood and was there for me during that time. I felt compassion for others who might be out there struggling with the same things I was struggling with – wanting to find a way to reach out to them. A way did come along, but it was badly mishandled.

I wrote earlier about speaking with Glen Campbell of the Area 51 Research Center in Rachel, Nevada. He was collecting stories coming out of the Nevada Test Site and Area 51. He was impressed enough with my story and sincerity that he put me in touch with a couple of television productions.

One was a man from a TV news station out of Texas somewhere, doing a segment for some evening news show. We did a short interview with me silhouetted against the setting sun to hide my identity. I was promised a copy of the interview on tape. The man never delivered on that promise; no video tape ever showed up in the mail.

The other I mentioned briefly earlier was the UFO documentary, *Dreamland*, being filmed and produced by Bruce Burgess. The condition of doing the interview was that my identity be concealed. I was interviewed for about an hour about various aspects of my experiences. It was condensed into a segment of just minutes for the film. I did get a tape of the full interview this time, and one of the documentary itself.

When I saw the documentary I was launched into a new wave of fear and rage. It was like being re-traumatized all over again. My identity was very poorly hidden. My face a was shown in a shadow profile against a lamp in the room where I was interviewed, and my voice was not disguised. My voice and profile were fully recognizable to anyone who knew me. In later years later when this documentary re-aired on television, people who knew me would come up to me and ask, "Was that you on that UFO show?" There was little point in denying it, it was so obviously me. It was a testament to how much people did not want to know more about such experiences that very few of them inquired any further into my experiences once I affirmed that it was indeed, me.

I had agreed to do this interview as a way of reaching out to any unfortunate others out there, not to have my identity revealed nationwide to any people watching who already knew me. I was scared again, and furious. Any fear I had felt before – and there was a lot of it – was now amplified further.

This seems to be typical of how experiencers are treated by the media – as fodder to be used for the filmmakers' own sensationalism and self-aggrandizement. Experiencers' stories are gleaned and exploited for sound-bytes that suit the agenda of the filmmakers. It's all about profit at the expense of the experiencers. No regard or consideration given to how difficult it is for people to come forward and share their experiences. Such people are used, then thrown out onto some metaphorical trash heap. Possible consequences to their lives are not considered.

I was afraid that those who had inflicted such severe trauma on me, causing my subconscious to bury my memories, were likely keeping covert surveillance on me to make sure the memories stayed buried. The fact that I had a chunk of my memory back was terrifying in and of itself. Now I was nearly certain that if I was being watched, "they" knew I was talking, to other people and on camera. Everywhere I went, I was looking over my shoulder.

This was kind of the final straw for me. There were too many unanswered questions I had no hope of getting answers to. Too much strangeness. Too vulnerable. I felt at risk of becoming completely obsessed with a field of endeavor from which I might never, ever find any satisfactory resolution.

I had finally become involved with a new relationship and we were going to move away from Las Vegas, NV to Roseville, CA, in autumn of 1997. I decided that once moved, I was going to put this UFO business behind me, unanswered questions and all, locking it all up tight in a little black box in the back of my mind. My life was not going to be about this dark and ugly MILAB stuff. I was going to go back to vipassana meditation, spiritual communities, and a healthy lifestyle, mentally, emotionally, physically and spiritually.

I was done with all this UFO, ET and MILAB crap.

Or so I thought.

Entr'acte III
Destination Terra: Lemuria

I made the passage to Terra feeling my energy fluttering, unanchored, like living tissue which had been torn away from an entire living system... looking to find something to bond with that would restore my vital life-energy-consciousness flow. This was the state of everyone else on the ship.

We were, most of us, very young compared to our parents and other mature Lyrans. We were a race of beings who had enjoyed virtual immortality on our world. There had been a timelessness to the passage of years on Lyra, with no rush towards maturity. Suddenly bereft, despite our ages (some of us at actual ages in years that would rival the elderly of modern day Earth), we felt even more young than some of us had been when we fled our world.

There had been one elder assigned per mothership, to guide the advisory councils that would in turn guide the Lyran youths in their coming tasks. We knew our mission – to seed the new planet Terra in such a way as to create humanoid life. We would guide their evolution towards greater and greater freedom of expression. Towards the development of expanded spiritual faculties and a consciousness that would grow to reach out and touch the All-That-Is Oneness of which we were all a part.

We hoped to recover something of what we had lost. This was very important to us all.

We arrived on Terra, landing on a pristine continent that we named Lemuria. When I disembarked the ship, I threw myself on the ground, in a way trying to hug Terra for just being there in all of its sparkling and primal beauty. It was different than our Lyran planet, but conscious just the same. We felt welcomed.

The first sense of peace I had felt since leaving home began to enter into me. I thought of my parents and uncle with longing. I could still touch their minds and spirits with my own. I knew they were no longer in form. Yet they held themselves at the edge of the great ocean of the All-That-Is to continue to reach out to me. The touch of their spirits brought me comfort on this new world. In a way, they had never left me.

We set to work, gathering organic samples and testing which would be the most likely to work with to create a new race of beings.

In the fullness of time, we were successful in our creation. Undertaken with a deep sense of love and honoring of all life, we taught these Lyran philosophies to them. We loved them deeply. It was pure joy to watch their growth and development.

Our new "children" lived in harmony with Terra for many millennia. The original ancients who had made the crossing from Lyra after its fall retired to remote mountain valleys to live out their lives, leaving the emerging new human cultures to find their own way. The ancients were satisfied that they had given them all they needed to do so.

Some of us elected to let go of our old bodies and be born into some of the new bodies of our Terran children. I myself chose to do this. It was then that a tide turned in the affairs of Terran human beings.

Incarnated into the new forms, we still carried the now-ancient memories of how we had fled from Lyra, and why. Concerned about the possibility of such an incursion happening on Terra, some began to develop technology with which to "protect" our new civilization. Technology that would not fail in the face of some threat to our survival. Living beings could become paralyzed with fear, but a machine would not.

Some of us opposed this, trying to persuade these new-thought groups to keep to the old ways of living in complete harmony with the land. A few of the ancients came down from their mountain valleys to add their voices to their original teachings and directives to live in harmony with Terra and each other.

Finally, the new-thought people led an exodus of themselves and those who believed in their ideas and philosophies, out of Lemuria.

Tugged in both directions, I was one of those who left for this new land. If all of us who dissented stayed behind, how could we hope to bring a guiding voice to this new and unknown branch of humanity? I was not alone. There were a number of us who went along as watchers, and hopefully guiders, of this new human experiment.

We settled in a new land far to the south and east, across the vast sea.

We called that new land Atlantis.

Chapter 10: Trying to Run Away...
and Guided Back to the Path

The relationship for which I moved from Las Vegas to Roseville, California did not work out either. I missed my beautiful deserts around Las Vegas, but Las Vegas itself was a city I knew I could not live in or near again. My expanded sensitivity was increasing – Las Vegas just didn't feel good. It never had, but I had become more susceptible to the vibrations as time passed. I moved from Roseville up to Auburn. I went back to college, pursuing a degree in social work there, at California State University, Sacramento (CSU).

I became involved in new spiritual and vipassana meditation communities in Auburn. I worked at a local women's center running a supervised visitation program. I also shared an office space with other holistic practitioners where I did body-centered work with people. I attended my university classes.

I stayed the hell away from the UFO subject in any open manner. Privately I kept up with at least some of my UFO studies, kept a weather eye on any current events through TV or the internet. I met a couple of people who were interested in such things, and I shared with them my journey up to then about what had happened to me and the kinds of information I had gathered. Wanting to stay somewhat connected to any new information coming out, I joined an email group in 1998 called the Andromeda Council, started by Alexander Collier, whom I had previously heard speak in Las Vegas. I was impressed with his information, his candor and his sincerity; and his information resonated strongly with me. I made some online friends in the group who I later met in person, including Alex Collier. I was with the group until it was disbanded in 2001 after the 9/11 event shocked and traumatized the whole country.

Meeting one of my online friends who lived in northern New Mexico, was a revelation. We both seemed to "know" each other and meeting in person there was strong recognition and an instant connection. It was like we knew we had met on an ET craft somehow, astral traveling out there at night while our bodies slept. This was a powerful feeling, not just something that happened in passing. It was as if just meeting her opened up a little bit of memory impressions for both of us. She remains in my thoughts. I wish her the best and hope she is well and happy. This type of recognition and instant connection was something that would happen more and more in meeting new people as time passed.

I finally began to wake up to some kind of guidance at work in my life. The year 2000 was an election year. Al Gore ran against George W. Bush. We all know what happened. For weeks, our country's future hung by a chad as vote recounting was done down in Florida. Finally the Supreme Court ruled, effectively ending the process and we wound up with Bush and Cheney installed in the White House.

I felt like the world was coming to an end. At a time when our Earth needed all the legislative support possible to heal our environment, we got the worst administration possible in our country's capitol. Bad as it seemed, I didn't realize how "worst" worst could get.

The morning after it was clear we were stuck with Bush and Cheney, I sat down to meditate as usual. I was so angry, I could do little but sit there and fume, thoughts racing around my head about where this might go. So it was a little startling to hear a clear, calm voice cut through the angry chatter in my mind:

> *Bush is exactly the right person, in exactly the right place, at exactly the right time. Because he is president, many people are going to wake up.*

This was not the first time I had heard this voice. Immediately my thoughts calmed as I considered this statement. I knew that people in our country, even our world had definitely fallen into complacency. My own path since 1994 and the things I'd had to consider – clearly things most people didn't want to look at – underscored the point. Could an administration like Bush-Cheney in the White House be the catalyst for a vast awakening of humanity?

I didn't know at that moment, but I did calm down, and settled in to watch as the months passed. I had no idea how right this voice would be. From a perspective of a few years later, they were absolutely right. People around the world began to wake up in droves.

Spirit Guidance... Star Family

march winds, spring rains

a home, carefully chosen.
things picked with love,
carefully placed, thoughtfully hung.

i created a sanctuary
wrapped it around myself
like a cocoon.

if i wanted to be outside,
but wasn't...
my eyes could reach out,

touch the saguaro branch,

the dried yucca stalk...
carried home from hikes.

books, furniture, music,
sacred stones and pieces of wood,
artwork and a square of starry night sky.

now change...

like march winds,
and spring rains.

i stir in my cocoon,
untried new wings ache
to be unfurled...

i want to fly...
i cannot bring
my cocoon with me.

restless... a desire to let go
walks uneasily, holding hands
with loss and grief.

in opening to something new
  ...still unknown,
something old is dying...

even as i walk with joy
and open arms
into the something being born.

~ Niara Terela Isley

In my meditation practice, I kept mentally and emotionally bumping up against the little black box in my mind where I had locked away all the mental and emotional turmoil concerning my Air Force experiences. That same calm voice that had given me the insight about Bush-Cheney was also urging me to open up that black box and begin dealing with what was in there. I knew I was not going to find "answers" at this point. But could I begin at least to deal with the emotional fallout of the experiences?

As nice a place as Auburn, California was, I was longing to move back to the desert southwest. I did not want to go back to Las Vegas. I had always loved the Arizona Sonora desert down around Tucson and I began to think of living there, making a plan to move there after I graduated from CSU.

I was studying a map to see what small towns nearby Tucson were down in that area. The clear calm voice spoke in my mind again, a voice I felt as much as heard, like a kind of telepathy.

Tucson is not the right place. Look at northwestern New Mexico or southwestern Colorado.

Curious about this new direction from within, I moved my gaze on the map to that area. Durango, Colorado kind of seemed to light up briefly. I "knew" that was the place. It was like dominoes falling into place somehow. I began to plan my move there.

I had become aware of a Native American spirit guide about a year earlier. The local Unity Church had shamanic practitioner and author Hank Wesselman come and do a workshop that included a shamanic drumming journey. I encountered a Native American guide during that drumming journey that I came to call Sky Walker. He was always on my right and had the appearance of a Native American Indian with shoulder length jet black hair, a large eagle feather fastened in it at the back. He always wore buckskin leggings and a breechclout, and rarely did I see him wear a shirt, but when he did, it was beaded and fringed, also buckskin. I realized that he had been with me my whole life.

No wonder I had felt so loved when on my own, out in Nature. In addition to the energy of nature and all the life around me, I'd had this invisible guide and protector around me, nurturing me, and in a sense, parenting me when my own earthly parents were not. My love of animals and the natural world that I shared with my earthly father were further shared with Sky Walker, in silent communion. This inner sense of communion later blossomed into a love of the nature-centered spirituality of the Native Americans. This connection was a lifeline as well, sustaining me and supporting me at those times when life looked dark and bleak. And it was through my connection to nature, there my whole life since early childhood, that this expansion of my finer intuitive senses was happening.

I knew, however, that the voice I had been hearing, regarding the Bush-Cheney administration, regarding moving to Durango instead of Tucson, was not Sky Walker. This voice, or combination of voices I was hearing/sensing was different, *felt* different. A different energy, a different vibrational signature than what I had come to feel from Sky Walker.

I now became aware that there were also some other spirit beings guiding me. All of these spirit guides I had sensed here and there for some time, dismissing them as some kind of adult version of imaginary friends, like a little kid might have. But it was time to acknowledge that they were indeed there. I had acknowledged Sky Walker. Now it was time to acknowledge these others.

I went down to the trails by the American River Confluence near Auburn and sat on the rocks where the two forks meet in a thundering rush of water and energy and sat down to talk with "them."

"So who are you?" I thought to them.

172

The answer was there in the same instant I formed the question, before my mind could finish expressing the words.

We are your inter-dimensional teachers.

I sat quietly with this new information, feeling a little awed. Inter-dimensional teachers. I watched the river rushing by. What might be the implications of this? I thought to myself; 'maybe now I don't have to make a lot of stupid human mistakes... I can just ask my inter-dimensional teachers before I decide to do something...'

Interrupting these thoughts, more words flowed into my mind.

We are not here to replace your own life's process, nor to change who you are by our presence. You still have the ultimate responsibility for walking your own life's path. We are here to teach you, in ways you will come to recognize over time.

Sigh. Oh well. I still have to be me – flawed, human, limited-in-my-prescient-vision me. Still, I felt a new awareness of being cared for, watched over. It was different somehow from the way Sky Walker watched over me. The only way to describe the difference is as a finer, higher vibration. Sky Walker was closer to the Earth plane in his vibration. He felt more like someone I might know in a human body, though he was in spirit. These inter-dimensional teachers seemed from some higher plane. I felt happy to have become aware of them.

Somehow, I knew there were three of them and that they were stationed always on my left. They confirmed this. And as I was listening, I caught something else. Trained through meditation and body-centered techniques to tune in deeply to what was occurring in my body, I felt this communication come in the subtlest wave of vibration that ever-so-gently touched my left arm, and the left side of my body. It was a feeling even less than the whisper of a breeze that barely touches the hairs on your arm. The instant I felt it, the vibration translated to the words I was comprehending. This had to be telepathy, or what I would now rather call "tel-empathy." I thought, with a touch of humor, it was like having my own biological or energetic Star Trek universal translator.

I began to realize ways in which these beings had been touching my consciousness over the past years of my life, though I was not aware enough back then to notice it. These were the same beings who had watched over me when I had the nightmare experience with the shadow being – the one I woke up to find still in my room. How did I know that? The energy or vibrational feel was the same in every case, unique to these beings and unmistakable.

Like the special time I had sensed my father, deceased since 1976, moving into my presence during a service at the Auburn Unity church, next to me where I sat in the back row. Like a fragrance not smelled for many years, but instantly recognized, his energy was unmistakable to me. I can only say that I felt feelings, a vibrational energy in my body that I had ever only felt in my father's presence. I sat there quietly sharing those moments with him, a chance to say goodbye I had not had when he died. A chance to say how sorry I was for some insensitive things I had done and said to him that I knew had hurt his feelings, and to hear from him how sorry he was for all his drinking and violence in my childhood.

***

There was another earlier contact with my inter-dimensional teachers from the unconscious. While stationed at Gila Bend Air Force Auxiliary Field, my duty station after leaving Nellis AFB, I played around in the ceramics studio for base personnel. I've always loved creating art. I decided to create a sculpture in clay, of three flowing, graceful, abstract forms, standing together, rising from a single base. Very pleased with it, I left it to dry on a shelf. The person who was in charge of the studio, familiar only with ceramics and not with the longer drying time needed for clay sculpture, fired it too soon and it exploded in the kiln. I was devastated. I had so wanted that sculpture!

This piece I had so wanted to bring into form has stayed with me in mind and heart in all the years since. I kept the sketch I had made of it. It was many years later, after I had become acquainted with my inter-dimensional teachers, that I realized in a flash of insight that I had been trying to create a three-dimensional representation of them.

***

I remembered a solo trip down through Arizona in July of 1991. It was a trip of magic, synchronicity and spirit guidance. I visited Tucson and Sedona. I moved through Sedona on impulses, consciously watching for, and following, synchronicities. I was discovering the guiding power of such seemingly coincidental events.

In a local spiritual newsletter, I found a sweat lodge was happening on July 11 and decided to attend. I was recognizing even back then that 11 was a special number for me. The people doing the sweat lodge were participating in an upcoming event called "11:11 Opening the Gateway" under a woman called Solara.

It was my first time experiencing the cleansing and calming effect of being smudged with sage and cedar. We entered the sweat lodge; there were prayer rounds. After the sweat lodge there were refreshments, and the people there explained a little about Solara and this 11:11 event. Knowing as I did about the three 11s that lined up at the moment of my birth, I realized that connecting with this sweat lodge and the people running it was no accident. I was still kind of a lone wolf, go-my-own-way, keep-my-own-council kind of person, definitely not a joiner-follower. But following a strong inner impulse in this case, I decided I would participate in this 11:11 event over the coming months.

A Native American woman who arrived after the sweat lodge gave each of us a brief intuitive reading. She told me that I had been connected to the Boynton Canyon vortex area in the distant past, in a previous life.

Of course, I knew then that Boynton Canyon would be my next stop. As soon as the sweat lodge gathering broke up, I headed out to Boynton Canyon.

Traveling to Sedona was a "crossover" trip for me. Before this trip, I was still standing with most of my weight in the arena of needing hard empirical evidence for things, one tentative foot stepping gingerly forward into the metaphysical extrasensory realm of energy and vibration. Yet, through a lifetime of my own personal experiences, I *knew* there was "something more" going on in my life that I needed to investigate. Studying Native American spirituality gave me a framework for paying attention to what was happening around me and following "medicine signs," – things that seemed to happen at significant times that led me to significant events or insights. So, on this trip, I followed each medicine sign and the impulses that accompanied them, suspending my usual need for hard evidence that the mind demanded, listening first and foremost to my own intuitive heart, and possibly, without recognizing it at the time, the whispers of my spirit guides.

Boynton Canyon was a beautiful place, especially in that late afternoon sunshine. The vivid red rock of the Sedona area was filled with the kind of high desert foliage I had come to love in all my years of living in the desert and mountain southwest. Pine and juniper were scattered among the red rocks and hilly terrain, with an incredible blue sky overhead and rock bluffs all around me as well as in the distance.

I thought; I'd really like to stand right in this "vortex" whatever that was or meant. So I tried an experiment. Feeling a little silly, I raised both my hands in front of me, palms facing out, kind of like a radar dish. I wanted to see if I could feel the energy and let it guide me. I shushed the mental voice and its judgment that this whole procedure was stupid.

Amazingly, I did feel a slight tingling in the palms of my hands in one particular direction. So I hiked in that direction. I would stop to check with my hands again every so often, then would again strike out in the direction I felt the tingling the strongest. Following this "energy trail" led me up a small hill and around a little juniper tree at the top. There in front of me on top of that hill was a small medicine wheel that someone had laid out there. I was awestruck. I had found it by following the tingle of energy in the palms of my hands.

Photos I took of the Sedona-Boynton Canyon medicine
wheel and adjacent area, 1990

What confirmation! This was the first real evidence I had that I could more solidly trust my inner guidance, trust my subtler feelings and senses. I sat down at the east of the medicine wheel and faced west, where the sun was now getting low in the sky. I stayed until it dipped below the horizon, then started back to my car.

The hike back was a tricky process. All the landmarks I had passed on my way to finding the medicine wheel had now changed in the early twilight. I had my general direction okay, but found I was picking my way back through different trails. I turned on my flashlight, and immediately in my head I heard:

Turn your flashlight off. Let your eyes adjust to the dark and you'll find your way better.

Well, I really wanted the comfort of that flashlight in the darkening wilderness, but I decided to trust again what this voice was telling me. I turned it off. My eyes adjusted to the dark and didn't have to try to adjust back and forth between the dark and the little flood of light from the flashlight. I *could* see my way, and much better. I found my way back to the car, and drove back to my campsite.

***

Years later, living in Durango, I had a stubborn bladder infection crop up. It did not yield to my usual ways of dealing with bladder infections, like lots of water, teas, and cranberry juice. I knew I was going to have to get an antibiotic, which I hated taking because it disrupted the healthy bacteria balance in my body and often caused other problems. To make matters worse, I was allergic by this time to so many antibiotics, I had no idea what I'd be able to take. I made an appointment at the Veteran's Administration (VA) clinic, where I went – rarely – when I needed something from the traditional medical establishment.

A day or so before the appointment, a word came into my head, playing over and over. The word was "Cipro." Like someone playing the same single piano key at spaced intervals, I kept hearing it. Cipro, Cipro, Cipro. What the heck was Cipro?

The day of my appointment came and I was sitting with the nurse. She looked up from my file and said, "Do you have any idea what you might be able to take? You're allergic to so much..."

Plunk. There was the Cipro "piano key" again, in my mind.

"Cipro?" I asked, kind of uncertain. I didn't know if it was a drug or not. To me it was just a word.

"Cipro it is," she said, and got me the prescription.

I was amazed! This prescription was really from my inter-dimensional teachers.

Once I got the bottle of Cipro home, the next inner guidance from them had me energize a tiny quartz crystal in my hand with the intention that the Cipro eradicate the bladder infection, but leave the rest of my body still in balance, and put it in the bottle with the pills. I did this. It worked. The bladder infection left, and I experienced none of the previous unpleasant side effects of taking an antibiotic.

***

My interdimensional teachers taught me another valuable lesson much later on. It underscored just how codependent we human beings are, in contrast to how they, my my spirit guides, were not.

I was living in Durango by that time, some years later. I had been moving through my PTSD recovery, working with my healer, Helen. I was finding out just how much I could not afford to harbor fear in my body. Fear can hide in a lot of places in the mind and body. We just have to move through our process, and as we bump into those places, we take what time we need to let go of the fears or anxieties that are attached to the various parts of our lives.

I resolved that I would never again allow fear to keep me from looking anywhere.

Someone had given me a video about their encounters with fourth-dimensional Reptilians. It was a scary video. I didn't really want to look at it, but the fact that it scared me demanded it. I needed to know what was actually in it, rather than just imagining, which was worse.

The part of the video that was most disturbing was hearing that all spirit guides were actually manipulating fourth-dimensional reptilians masquerading as nice spirit guides. I wondered if this was true. What if it was? Was I somehow being fooled?

In the moments I contemplated these fears, I felt my guides, Sky Walker and my inter-dimensional teachers, pull away from me. It was as if, energetically, they removed themselves from my immediate presence. No words, no counsel, no guidance about what I'd just watched... nothing at all. Just gone, or far, far away.

That felt worse than contemplating the fear that they were Reptilians; yet I felt frozen in my own fear, considering such information.

I wandered through this energy swamp for several weeks, wondering and uncertain. Then one day, in a quiet moment of my own insight, I *knew* that my guides were not Reptilians. It can't be explained in terms of reasoning, logic, analysis or mind.

There is a process of knowing by direct perception that is energetic and vibrational. It bypasses the mind. It is felt on multiple levels in the body in a way that can't be faked. Or if it can be, then there is little point in going on living or trying to navigate life on any level. If our bodies and what we sense with them can be so completely fooled, then we are living a pointless existence, nothing but targets for evil entities that milk our energy for their own purposes, trapped in a hell from which there can be no escape.

My entire life is a testament that this is not the case. I can go on trusting my feelings or cave in to a world of the mind-ego reacting to everything in my environment from fear and suspicion. A way of living that is no life at all.

Through that flash of insight, I resolved my fear. Everything I was as a person up to that point, all I had felt and experienced in my life's journey again became more real to me than any fears of the mind.

In the same instant I *knew* that my guides were truly the beings I had come to know and trust, they were back. We shared a reunion of quiet inner joy together with the dawning of my own new understanding. That feeling of continuous communion, like silent celestial music both felt and heard in the cells of my body was a relief to have back again.

I discerned their lesson in this way. When I first felt afraid of my guides, wondering if they might be Reptilian entities, what they *did not do* was the most important part of the lesson. If they had been regular human beings, they might have tried to reason with me that they were not such creatures. They might have presented convincing arguments, trying to comfort or cajole me into a kind of nest of their own making. A nest that they would then have to continue to reinforce and maintain to "take care of me," since I would have surrendered my own ability to know and perceive in this particular regard.

This is the essence of codependency, that I learned about in 12-step groups. To be codependent is to control through wheedling, cajoling. If these cloying control attempts fail, the next ones become threats – of abandonment, of limitation, even of violence. To be codependent is to perform dis-empowering rescues of others, because we see them as too weak, too stupid or too incompetent to take care of themselves. To be codependent is to do martyr-like deeds of self-sacrifice on behalf of others, making sure they know just how much they "owe" the martyr for such sacrifices, burdening the recipients with controlling guilt. Human beings are all codependent with each other to a degree, from minor ways to severely dysfunctional ones.

But my guides were not codependent. They noted my fear. They knew I had to resolve it on my own to recover my inner balance, to empower myself as a sovereign individual. Without working this through on my own, my entire intuitive ability and sensory landscape could be undermined. So they "withdrew" and allowed me to work it out for myself.

Maybe some reading these words might think it could have been a clever, reverse-psychology way to get me to welcome back such negative entities in disguise. One always has to admit to possibilities such as this, in a logical fashion. But I don't feel this is so. And someday, when I exit this body to pass into the next realm, I'll know just how wise or how foolish I may have been in following my own heart and feelings. Until then, I'm content as I am.

***

I'm glad I was able to resolve that dilemma with my guides, because about a year later, I faced a much greater health challenge. Sky Walker and my inter-dimensional teachers were instrumental in how the healing unfolded.

I had been plagued with female problems most of my adult life with extremely heavy periods, including severe bleeding in between at times. The latest incident of this was the worst so far. I was very weary of this issue and trying to find solutions to it. In talks with Helen, she suggested that since I had suffered such violent attacks on my femininity with the rapes, that my most feminine body part, my womb, was weeping in its grief. Though I had made much progress in learning to cry, I still was not a person all that given to tears. So my womb was doing it for me the only way she could. Helen's insight fit with the answer I'd gotten years before at my body-centered training as well, that severe female problems of this nature bespoke of some intense sexual abuse.

Once again, I had to go back to the VA clinic, which I dreaded; but this time, there seemed a special guidance at work in the process. When I had gone in about a year earlier with the same complaint, one of the staff there had put me in for a referral to a local OB/GYN consult with a doctor of my choice. I was both grateful and frustrated by this – grateful to have this unexpected boon, but frustrated that in a year, no one at the office had called to let me know that I had this referral available. Oh well.

I could go to a doctor of my choice. I checked on OB/GYN practitioners that my women friends trusted and found one. From there, everything seemed to fall into place almost effortlessly. As I left the initial appointment, I wondered if having a hysterectomy was the right thing to do – excising a part of my own body like that. I had always been against such a procedure.

But now, it seemed like my womb had her own quiet voice within. I felt from her, with some surprise, that she was tired and was ready to go. Better to let her go than have her go and take me with her. I felt the necessity of it, and the tiredness of this part of my body that had taken on the burden of carrying my emotional pain for so many years. I let the doctor know I decided to go ahead with the hysterectomy.

Things continued to flow. A pre-op appointment was coming up. I turned to my guides with some of my concerns. Healing from a hysterectomy was said to take six weeks or more. I was very concerned about not being able to be up and around sooner than that – my back could get into pretty bad shape with weeks of laying around. Even more importantly, I was not a trusting soul when it came to hospitals and medical personnel. I felt good about my woman doctor. She came highly recommended and my appointments had engendered a good sense of trust in her. It made the whole process easier for me. But still, being in a hospital, surrendering to anesthesia for this procedure was a leap that was very difficult for me.

As usual, I only got a few words of my request formed before they were there with a response. My full request was something like: "Could you guys help me heal more quickly for the sake of my back, so I can be up and around? And please watch over me in there so nothing happens that I would not want to happen?" Their reply:

Already taken care of. We've gone forward in time to the operating room and taken care of everything. All will be as you wish. You need only move into the space we have created for you.

This reply was so swift and so sure, I could not help but relax. I got an image of what they had done. It was like they folded time somehow. I got a fleeting image of the operating room and could see the doctor doing the surgery, her support staff assisting. And my inter-dimensional guides, along with others called in specially for this event, were there as well, one guiding each person in the operating room, all of them holding me in their energy as my hysterectomy was being performed.

The day of the surgery three weeks later had the amazing feel of just what my guides had told me, that the me in that moment was moving into sync with the situation that had been prepared those same weeks in the past.

The roughest part of the recuperation was in the hospital itself. Once discharged, I made an amazingly speedy recovery. I needed no more pain medication once I was home. I was up and around and doing well in four weeks. My energy level was amazing. I had a great summer, bike riding and floating the Animas River and enjoying all kinds of activities.

I am very grateful to my higher-dimensional helpers.

***

Out beside the rushing rivers near Auburn that day I had finally made real, conscious contact with my guides. Recalling all the ways my inter-dimensional teachers had touched my life, I recognized now that nearly all of this guidance, and certainly the voice that had told me to turn off my flashlight that night, was the same voice, the same energy signature of these inter-dimensional teachers. They are also watching over me, always.

They have never told me any of their names, they don't seem to have names as we use them here on Earth. I later came to sense one as female, and the other two as male. And some years still later, reading an email excerpt of information about Lyra, I was flooded with a flash of insight, accompanied by a flood of tears and emotion – emotional resonance – that my inter-dimensional teachers were in fact my parents and uncle from Lyra, in another lifetime.

These kinds of things have been my experiences with energy and vibration. They may not be enough to convince some people of the reality of this kind of subtle sensory perception, and that is okay. This is something each individual must gain personal experience of in his or her own way.

***

181

Following the direction of my guides to move to Durango, I, at first, planned a very sensible strategy for my move. I would graduate from CSU in the spring, get a job, and work and visit Durango several times to get the lay of the land and complete my move there within two to three years.

In actuality, the move happened much more swiftly than that. Synchronicities lined up swiftly as I was moving towards graduation, and money for the move, a place to live and a job to move to all fell into place like dominoes. I graduated in May 2001. By June I had loaded my belongings on a U-haul and was headed for the southwest. I made a stop in Henderson, Nevada to see my son Travis graduate from high school, visiting briefly with him and my daughter Karly. Then I was off to Durango, Colorado, as yet sight unseen.

Driving across the deserts of northern Arizona on my way was in itself healing. I could feel knots in my body that were years old beginning to loosen and unwind. I was back in my beloved Southwest. The increase in my sensitivity that had begun back in Las Vegas was continuing. One of the things prompting the move away from California was being able to feel the density of the population in that state. As though somehow the minds of all the people there were creating a background noise like psychic static. The less I could shut it out and the more aware of it I became, the more tiring it was to be in proximity to millions of minds broadcasting busy-thought beta brainwaves. Whatever process of "becoming" was happening within me, I did not want to shut it down and try to endure such an environment. I wanted to open up to this sensitivity and see where it might take me. I needed more open spaces with far less population.

I had barely gotten settled in Durango when the "terrorist attack" of September 11, 2001 occurred. I watched in shock on nationwide television with millions of other Americans as World Trade Center structures fell neatly onto their foundations like controlled demolitions. I knew that no planes crashing into these buildings could cause that. The official explanation of a terrorist attack was a lie; lies covering lies, covering lies. My sense of foreboding about the machinations of a shadow government appeared fully validated on that day. And with the swift introduction and passage of the Patriot Act legislation, my post-traumatic stress grew in intensity. It could not be ignored any more.

Post-traumatic stress, together with my insights, showed me that if I was truly going to "know myself" through any spiritual practice, I had to know ALL of myself. It became crystal clear that this healing journey now had to be consciously undertaken. I needed to open up the little black box I'd locked away in a far corner of my mind, full of tangled-up memories and emotions. I needed to begin to clear the emotional fallout and continue my life from a new and stronger place. I could no longer squelch myself, my memories, my feelings, nor the years I had spent gathering all the corroborating information to ensure the comfort of my family, friends, acquaintances, or community. I had to step up and find the courage to heal.

Amazingly, it seemed like there were a few more of my friends at that time open to hearing about my experiences and supportive of me finding healing. Looking back now, I feel my spirit guides were in part responsible, bringing me into connection with these people.

However, this was no headlong launch back into reading, study and investigation of the UFO and ET phenomenon, though some of that was included. It was more an opening to my feelings around my experiences, and feeling them as much as possible to completion. I realized that I needed more hypnosis, more answers about what happened after the injection, but the right person and opportunity did not present itself for a while. Still, allowing my feelings the space to be acknowledged and contemplated was a relief. I was deeply grateful for those few friends who were part of my spiritual community who were willing to simply listen.

Chapter 11: Wrestling Personal Demons

memories...
like scars from fires...
worn on the inside,
mishapen and taut,
          pulling on my mind

memories...
a silent cacophony...
clamoring, haunting,
surreal tones felt,
          not heard

memories...
shards from pieces
of different lives
combine, then float apart
          looking for completion

memories...
shadows grafted into
my very flesh,
insistent tendrils woven
          throughout my soul

memories...
if i could find and eat
the lotus of blessed forgetting...
wipe them all away...
          would i still be me

Memories
~ Niara Terela Isley

The mind-ego, its primary function being to protect us from any pain or discomfort from any source, has a million tricks to shoot our attention away from being present and staying with painful emotions. This is actually a mind-mechanism that works to the advantage of those nefarious individuals who inflict trauma-based mind control abuses on their victims. I found staying present while confronting my feelings about what had happened to me very, very difficult. Yet staying present with the emotional pain and fear, the rattles and tremors it created in my body, allowing it to be fully experienced and discharged was precisely what I needed to do.

In the early days of recovering the lost memories and recounting them to people like Miesha and others, trying to piece together some kind of coherent picture of the UFO and ET phenomenon, it was actually physically difficult at times to get my mouth and vocal cords to form the words. And, like playing an old, scratched vinyl record, the "music" would play only so far, then hit the "scratch" and go skittering off to an entirely different, not-related place or some memory-less void. In addition, I was sure there was some kind of programming done to keep my mind veering sharply away from any memories that lay within the months of missing time from 1980, while in the Air Force.

As written about previously, I met Gloria Hawker in 2003 at the Aztec UFO Symposium. With her, I finally felt the trust I needed to have more hypnosis. Gloria has a beautiful heart. She is a very special soul whose research and work flows from a desire to help others. I spent a weekend with her and had those two long hypnosis sessions, one on Saturday – the ET experiences – and one on Sunday – the military experiences. A great deal of information came out of those two sessions that did address at least some of my questions – in particular, some of what happened to me after the injections during the military experiences. The ET session also answered at least a few of the whys, particularly regarding my experiences with the Zetas. In recovering these chunks of memories, I was continually working to get into them more, without too much success, at least on a mental "figure-it-out" analytical level.

Just What Is Memory? How Do We "Remember?"

I examined thoroughly what I knew experientially about thought and memory. I had learned a good deal about human biology throughout my life, most recently during 100 hours of anatomy and physiology while taking massage certification training. In meditation, I had experienced realms of inner space which pointed to a different reality where there was no space and no time, or at least where space and time were so different as to be completely outside human experience of them here in this "reality" on Earth. Inner space could be experienced while in the body, but it seemed to be a dimension neither encompassed within, nor beyond the body, but rather a space, place or point where consciousness was projected from into the body. In my metaphysical studies, I had learned that the pineal gland in the center of the brain is the point where the soul/consciousness joins with the body, at the chakra point known as the third eye. If our chakra system is made of little vortexes, spinning our bodies into form from the Universal Energy Field, perhaps individuated consciousness is the origin of and the focal point around which the spin revolves, creating and remaining connected to the human form. If this is true, then consciousness could be the origin of all spin in the Universe. The Native American belief that all things, animate and inanimate, have an intangible spirit and are alive in some way would be very literally true if this could ever be proven.

In other metaphysical texts related to energy healing, I learned that everything that happens to us is recorded in our human energy field. This is evidenced by those sensitives who can see the human energy field, or aura, in full colors and detail, such as Barbara Brennan, former National Aeronautics and Space Administration (NASA) physicist and Rosalyn Bruyere[1], a clairvoyant who participated in the "Rolf Study" done by Dr. Valerie Hunt[2]. This study is also reproduced in Bruyere's book, *Wheels of Light: A Study of the Chakras, Vol. 1.*

To me, thought and memory are a product of our linear and experiential journey through the Earth plane of existence. Richard Bach had a wonderful way of putting it in his book, *Illusions: The Adventures of a Reluctant Messiah,* where he said something to the effect that our lives are like a movie reel of film. The whole movie exists on the reel all in the same instant as you hold it in your hands, but it requires time and space to experience it, to move through it. That is the simple explanation. Somehow I also felt that while this "movie" of our lives needed time and space to be experienced, our reactions and responses to life events are not fixed, but are, in a sense, fluid. When we decide to go one way at a certain crossroad in our lives, perhaps others of "us" take other paths and explore those other choices. The concepts of alternate realities have been explored in many movies and television shows. We can't know whether or not alternate realities exist with absolute certainty, not from within our earthly incarnations. Or at least, not yet.

If all our experiences are recorded energetically, not only in our brain tissues, but in our human energy fields, then while one might be able to tamper with the tissues of the brain, thereby damaging the "hardware" to prevent access to the storage field of memory in the human aura, the memories are still there. According to spiritual and metaphysical teachings, all memories and knowledge also reside in the larger, other-dimensional fields of what are known as the Akashic records, also called soul and oversoul records. If souls incarnate on Earth to gain experience, then it only makes sense that the Universal Consciousness of which we are all a part would have some way of keeping the memories of experiences intact to glean the value from the learning-through-contrast process. I now feel that hypnosis and perhaps other forms of deep relaxation help our body-mind to access these other-dimensional sources of our memories, bypassing the brain's accessing hardware.

---

[1] Rosalyn L. Bruyere is an internationally known healer and clairvoyant. Her collaborations with physicians and scientists reflect her belief that healing and health should be a cooperative effort between patient, physician and healer. Her scientific and spiritual focus is evident in her teaching and writing and serves to bridge the gap between concept and reality. She was an instrumental part of the Rolf Study with Dr. Valerie Hunt, and is author of *Wheels of Light: A Study of the Chakras, Vol. 1.* Her website: http://www.rosalynlbruyere.org.

[2] See Dr. Valerie Hunt's, *A Study of Structural Integration from Neuromuscular, Energy Field and Emotional Approaches,* http://www.somatics.de/huntStudy.html.

In looking at memory and how it works, I also simply observed normal, everyday conversations with friends. I watched all the twists and turns the conversations would take. The twists and turns were all made through *associations* or *relationships between subjects* in the minds of each of us. A conversation that went on an hour or more would almost always end up far from where it started, as the most relevant associations for each person came up in the discussion related to the subject. The subject itself would shift over time, more associations for each person applied to each new subject until the subject itself changed yet again – and on and on. Yet in trying to use this associative process to get at my lost memories, outside of a hypnosis session, I just could not get there.

In trying to recall my own memories, the ones that seemed blanked out, and knowing that memory is associative, I had tried to remember friends I'd had that I had known before going to work at the Tonopah Electronic Warfare Range, and after. Working with those memories, I tried to remember as many associations as I could regarding those friends during my time at Nellis AFB, 1980, during the three to four months in question. I just didn't get very far. With some effort, I had managed to remember the name of the motel where I was billeted in the town of Tonopah, The L & L Motel. Then through that association, I remembered the Sundowner Motel on the edge of town where others were billeted. I remembered the Mitzpah Hotel where we ate sometimes. I remembered Tonopah's Jim Butler Days where military guys were allowed to not shave for the beard-growing contest and I remembered Sgt. Boughman in our unit who won hands down – he was so hairy. In remembering that, I then remembered a party at Lake Mead where he was in attendance with others from Tonopah, my friend from technical training school before Nellis, Susan Foster, included. Oddly, the rest of that party and it's attendees was a blur. I remembered a Tonopah bar called The Joker where I shot pool with friends, but the only friend I could really remember from that time was Susan Foster. The others were unclear. I got into a few work memories, about riding the bus out to work at the range, and the guy that tried to hit on me with astrology, Landon Hudson. Associated with arriving at the main facility I remembered rows of tan buildings and dirt drives between them. I remembered a small one-room commissary where we all went to buy food for our day out on the range at the radar sites. The guy that worked there was tall, fit, strong-looking with black hair and piercing blue eyes and seemed to be in his forties. I remembered wondering why he was working such a nothing job. I also wondered if he was keeping an eye on all of us as we passed through his little store.

That was it, that was all I could get at. Trying to get at any other memories was like traveling a path and suddenly coming up on a place where the path had been bombed to oblivion, leaving only a huge, deep crater – a dead end.

I wondered just how one's memories could be so effectively blocked. Was it chemical? Technological? I tried to imagine just what kind of technology could do this. Brain surgery was out of the question because it would leave a lot of obvious physical traces behind. But could there be a way to examine memories technologically somehow, and then disconnect or disrupt the neurological pathways in the brain, effectively isolating that block of memory? Giving the usual associative process of memory, in effect, no place to go? I wondered about all of this during the first couple of years post-hypnosis with Budd Hopkins, 1995-96.

So imagine how seriously startling it was for me in 2003 and 2004, when the movies *Paycheck* and *Eternal Sunshine of the Spotless Mind* came out. In these films the same technology was being used on people that I had "imagined" might have been used on me in 1980. Again, there was that someone-just-walked-over-my-grave, sinking-in-quicksand feeling. I have no way of knowing if this is simply a coincidence or not, but it seemed very odd to me that I could have imagined – so accurately, back in 1995-96 – technology that was now shown in two science fiction films nearly a decade later. I have heard many times, that accurate details of secret projects get "leaked out" and appear in movies and television. I've come to suspect that this is likely very true.

Other movies that have had an impact on me were *Total Recall*, set mostly on Mars and *Vanilla Sky*. I didn't see *Total Recall* at the theater when it came out, I saw it later on cable, after I'd had my hypnosis. Seeing Arnold Schwarzenegger's character get that injection in the side of the neck left me rubbing the side of my neck where I had gotten the injections. In addition, I've had a complete fascination with Mars since childhood and have had dreams of living and working on Mars.

I had a totally unfathomable reaction to *Vanilla Sky*, about a man living in a virtual reality while his body was undergoing a long healing process. I came out of that movie shaken and sobbing, completely clueless as to why. After going through 12-step and counseling, I had worked on letting go of my stoicism and allowing myself to cry more easily. I learned that people need their tears to be healthy. So I was able to be with this emotional reaction, and there was a friend there with me who was very supportive as well.

I haven't the slightest idea why that movie caused such a reaction, unless, perhaps, I had been put in some kind of virtual reality net at times back during those lost months of 1980. I have since wondered if I learned that being wired up to a virtual reality net was a prelude to terrible experiences such as life-threatening interrogations and other physical abuse I remembered in my flashbacks. Abuse inflicted in a virtual reality could feel real, but might not leave actual physical traces. It could also be a way of manipulating time, making a few hours seem like many. If that was my experience with virtual reality, then no wonder the movie created such a reaction. I don't think all my traumatic experiences were from virtual reality. I think the injections and rapes really happened – there was no experience, memory or any felt sense of being hooked up to virtual reality equipment during any of my hypnosis sessions. I think going to the moon really happened because a new hypnosis session in 2010 brought information out relating to the moon experiences that, if it had been a

189

virtual reality experience, should not have been part of those experiences. But perhaps some of the other experiences I remembered as flashbacks were from a virtual reality. Who knows?

This virtual-reality theory may really open a can of worms with some people, but to relate my experiences and all their associations, I must honestly include it with everything else. I've found a kind of peace considering all of these things, because I know that someday, either in this lifetime or once I've transitioned out of this dimension through the death of the body, I will at last know what was true and what was not. Until then, I'm doing the best I can. And even if all my experiences were part of being wired into a virtual reality net, they are no less abusive or traumatic, nor are the people in charge of such virtual abuse any less culpable.

I can only wonder about such things, and try to piece together what I can. To do it responsibly for yourself and those around you, you keep your feet on the ground in the day-to-day world you live in. You can only construct hypothetical possibilities from the fragments of emotions that certain imagery evokes in you. Then you file them away, knowing you may never be able to test any of the hypotheses to upgrade them to working theories or established facts. But the associations these movies brought up in my body were at the very least something to pay attention to and note for the future. And I can also say from experience that when certain imagery or other stimuli such as music or fragrances brings up feelings, such stimuli also brings with it the memory of the time I experienced those stimuli, when memory has not been tampered with or subverted in some way.

Flashbacks

I have had, and still have, flashbacks. They come through my body; feeling sensations and experiencing mind's eye imagery with them. *Association* and *context* are important and sensitive features of memory recall. The flashback imagery would actually originate simultaneously with body sensations. I'd feel a sensation somewhere in my body in *association* with some situation or event – providing *context* – happening in present time. The sensation was usually felt in the stomach and/or chest, or neck and shoulders. The memory would squeeze itself out of the sensation – through association – in images that would spring spontaneously into the mind. Where did they come from – some wild imagination? All my training and experience as a body-centered therapist said no. Body sensations, emotions, visual images – sometimes even sounds, smells or tastes – that arise in association with whatever current contextual stimuli are occurring are to be paid attention to – that our body-minds can be trusted to select the most relevant associations. Emotional reactions can then be worked with or cleared with various types of processes.

In my years of working with body-centered therapy I find this associative principle to be reliable in nearly every instance, as long as the client is staying present with what is experienced in the body and not drifting into trying to analyze through the mind. The body-mind picks the most congruent association that relates to whatever is being experienced, wondered about or discussed in the present moment, and puts it to the forefront of one's thoughts. If the image or memory is painful in some way, the mind-ego will also try to shunt it away in the same moment with some kind of mental subterfuge. It usually takes a skilled body-centered therapist to be there, encouraging the client to speak moment by moment about what is being experienced. The therapist-coach creates a safe space to explore experiences and feelings through being sensitive, compassionate and demonstrating trustworthiness as much as possible. Encouraging clients to stay present with painful or frightening emotions and the sensations in their bodies is part of the process. This helps to identify and short-circuit the usual mind-ego tricks, like thinking of a task that needs doing at the crucial moment that sensation, emotion or memory is just emerging. Other subconscious mind-ego tricks can be having an accident, or any number of mental-physical distractions to take one away from the emotional pain or fright. There is much data in the fields of holistic, vibrational and energy psychology and medicine pointing to the fact that the mind-ego considers the creation of physical pain an acceptable way to provide distraction from emotional pain. This also can make such physical pain, often ongoing and chronic, extremely difficult to treat because of all the mental and emotional factors involved.

Most often, my flashbacks would come in instances when I was experiencing something in some way similar to what I had experienced during the months of missing time while in the Air Force. A man I was involved with for a several months was very critical; his style was like a courtroom prosecution attorney, moving swiftly from one point to the next. It wasn't pleasant, but my reaction to it was out of proportion to what he was actually doing. He and I did not have enough history together for me to have such a programmed reaction to his tactics. In the face of his barrage of prosecution-type criticism, I would become like a deer paralyzed in a car's headlights. Later I would feel angry and wonder why I didn't just speak up and give him a good piece of my mind.

Synchronistically, I was actually at a training for certification as a body-centered coach when this issue emerged during a training session. We had paired off in groups of two for practice. I said I wanted to work on this "deer-in-the-headlights" issue. It was very current for me, having had this prosecution-attorney experience on the phone the night before with the soon-to-be-jettisoned boyfriend. I wanted an end to the paralysis, and to be able to speak up for myself.

As I worked with my partner and she encouraged me to stay with my feelings, I suddenly started shaking and crying. The images that flooded my mind were of being in an interrogation-type of setting, sitting in a chair, light preventing me from seeing my tormentors while they hammered away at me verbally, threatening me not to remember things I had seen or things they had put me through. They threatened me with more rape, even death. They also made these threats against my daughter, who, back in 1980, was only four years old. As a mother, I was terrified for my little girl. I could not "speak up" and say anything confrontational or in my own defense in such a situation.

I stayed with my feelings with my training partner as much as I could, and was grateful to her for her compassionate encouragement and witnessing. Later on, it was easier for me to speak up for myself and not go into deer-in-the-headlights mode.

Other body-centered flashbacks emerged over time. There was a pain that arose in my right shoulder that brought an image of being shoved or thrown hard against a wall, hitting it with that right shoulder. Repeated pain and tingling in my shoulders brought an image flash of being hit between the neck and shoulders with some kind of electro-shock stick, like a cattle prod, but sized for human beings. And once while getting a neck and shoulder massage, the man giving the massage placed his hands gently around my neck for a few moments and instantly my whole body went on hyper-alert, going rigid. The memory that spontaneously popped out of that little gesture, meant to be nurturing, was of being slowly strangled, hands very gradually squeezing, tightening around my neck until I lost consciousness. Then I would be allowed to revive. I had the distinct impression that this strangulation was done repeatedly during one certain space of time. The face of the blonde security guard loomed as the perpetrator of this cruelty.

I mentioned earlier reading *The Turbulent Mirror: An Illustrated Guide to Chaos Theory and the Science of Wholeness* by John Briggs and F. David Peat, because I wanted a better understanding of chaos theory. When I got to the section on "Chaos and the Brain," it mentioned experimentation being done in this area by Los Alamos National Labs (LANL). LANL had a facility based out at the Nevada Test Site. I remembered the injections I had gotten in the side of my neck, how experimental they had seemed to be. The sinking-in-quicksand feeling; feeling tight, tense – a knot in my stomach – all of these were body flags indicating events initiating fearful situations and trauma. No wonder due to this disturbing internal shake, I set this book aside and never finished it.

Processing my Experiences with the Zetas

Standing back and looking at my experiences with the Zetas and the military or covert/black ops experiences, the very different nature of how they were carried out stood in stark contrast to each other.

I suppose this is why I don't feel much anger any more at the Zetas. Human beings – even outside of covert ops or black projects – are capable of such horrible actions, and for far less good reasons than trying to save their species from extinction, which is what I've come to believe about the Zetas. What would humanity do if it was faced with extinction, and knew that blending the genetics of another species would make it possible to save themselves? Would they ask permission if their need was overwhelmingly great? From all I've seen that humanity is capable of, I would guess, no. Humans would likely carry out their agenda without mercy and with considerable brutality to the species they were using for their own purposes. When certain people want something that other people have, they justify taking it by demonizing those others in some way, making them less than human. Look at the way the Native Americans have been treated in the Americas, or the Aborigines in Australia. Sometimes people are demonized just to rally allegiance to a particular ideology, such as the ways the Jews were treated in Hitler Germany.

I realize you could apply what I've just said to the Zetas, that they carry out their agenda without mercy and considerable brutality to the species they are using for their purpose. I know there are people who would largely concur with this position. I don't. And I don't because I have the military or black ops experiences and how they were carried out to compare them to. For me there is a big difference in painful abuse intentionally inflicted with great emphasis on instilling terror, as in the black/covert ops experiences; and fear or pain unintentionally created out of not understanding what kind of procedure or examination is being performed on you, feeling no control over what is happening to you, or for what purpose, as was the case with the Zetas.

What the Zetas did was certainly very strange and greatly uncomfortable, both physically and emotionally for me. The setting in which these extraterrestrial experiences happened was very clinical and the beings themselves very dispassionate. There was no love-making in any normal human sense. The closest thing to concern or affection I experienced was from the hybrid that had sex with me. It seemed he could sense my emotional discomfort, because he would sometimes put his hand out to touch my hip or stomach during the act. He did not seem entirely devoid of emotions, though they were the palest impressions of emotions compared to humans. The gesture seemed meant to be comforting. I was grateful for any shred of empathy that he demonstrated under such circumstances, even though everything inside of me was screaming that I should not be with such a being, so different from human. It was very hard to endure, painfully embarrassing and evoked great feelings of shame, because I could not force my body to shut down and stop responding. Sex naturally feels good to human beings, so on one level, when you are experiencing it, you want to go with those feelings. I came to describe this as having one foot pushing the accelerator to the floor of the "sensation-car" of this experience, and my other foot pushing the brake into the floor at the same time. I was feeling the powerful euphoric feelings sexuality can bring on, and at the same time I couldn't let myself feel good, couldn't allow myself to "go with it", not with someone who wasn't human in the usual sense. And because of the fear, the embarrassment and shame, I was also getting a good drenching in my own adrenalin. Sexual feelings and high adrenalin – an essential recipe for sex addiction. At least until I got enough insight into the issue to begin to heal it.

With the rapes in my military experiences, I don't remember feeling anything – it was as though I left my body and sensed the rapes as an observer, and collected details about the setting in which the rapes occurred to keep myself from experiencing what was happening to my body. But with the Zeta hybrid, I either was prevented from dissociating by the ETs somehow, or, because of my contact with these beings since I was a small child, I no longer perceived them as a frightening enough threat to dissociate from. The conditioning for sexual feelings had started in childhood with these beings.

I was left with some serious issues around my own sexuality which caused me a great deal of personal emotional pain, from sex addiction behaviors, to other times when I shut down completely and couldn't endure even the thought of being close to anyone.

During my recovery and therapy process, I saw people who were far worse off than I was. I was grateful to have a spiritual foundation in my life that assisted my understanding and recovery. I was glad of my propensity for questioning, to look outside the usual frameworks of traditional religion and the morals and rules it projected onto society about what "correct" behavior should be. From a cross-cultural perspective, there are many different ways in which sexuality is regarded and practiced in the world. Western society's ways are far and away not the most enlightened, nor at all healthy. In many ways, they actually help to set people up for sexual dysfunction and the more perverted and twisted sexual acts that plague our society.

The Zetas likely did what they did perhaps not understanding the way human beings in Western culture regard sexuality – as extremely personal and private and usually in the context of intimate personal relationships. It was obvious they had some agenda, but it never seemed as if that agenda was to purposefully cause me embarrassment, shame or emotional pain. My feelings and reactions were just incidental to the situations. I don't believe we can apply Western civilization's human standards of sexuality and sexual conduct to the Zeta or hold them accountable to such. To do so sets up an embattled position with regard to these extraterrestrials from the start, when some allowance and understanding of differences and needs should be taken into account. They are not us, they are not humans. People are so inculcated to our Western culture they are like fish swimming in water – if you were to point out to them that they are swimming in water, their reaction would be: "Water? What do you mean, water?" People all too often just accept the cultural rules, values and morals they are raised with, and move through life thinking "this is just the way life is," never questioning much, never thinking outside their particular belief system's box. Questioning and dialogue will be absolutely necessary in this case to achieve any mutual understanding with the Zetas, should we ever have such an opportunity afforded by open public contact with them in the future.

My reactions to the Zetas and development of emotional and sexual issues that arose in relation to their study of me I now feel were simply unfortunate side effects. I was an Earth human female steeped in my own particular Western Earth culture who was suddenly removed from that culture and made a participant in one that was very, different, very alien. No pun intended. Very different rules applied there.

In the interest of staying as objective as might be possible for an experiencer, I realize that my feelings, thoughts and explanations about the Zetas could be seen as rationalizations for a person suffering from Stockholm's Syndrome – a kind of capture-bonding where a person abducted and subjected to these types of experiences begins to identify with their captors-abusers, expressing sympathy and empathy towards them. While I admit this could be a possibility, I don't feel this is the case, at least with me. There was a general progression of coming to awareness of what had happened, being angry about it for some time. As the healing process unfolded, so too did an exploration of possibilities for understanding what had happened from both sides, mine and the Zetas. And I feel no such identification, sympathy or empathy for what was done to me in the military covert-ops experiences – quite the opposite in fact.

***

I encountered many on the sex addiction recovery path (with no abduction experiences that I knew of) who did not have a conscious connection with spirituality or nature, and it seemed they continually could not establish any lasting recovery or inner peace in their process. Traditional religious concepts often left them with a belief in a harsh and punishing God. Whenever something bad happened to them, they felt it was payment for their sinful nature. They often had had harsh and punishing parents, and it looked for all the world like they were projecting an image of such parents onto their idea of God, helped along by biblical Old Testament descriptions of the Almighty. At 12-step meetings, when religious people spoke of the Father, Son and Holy Ghost, I would, in the silent privacy of my own heart, replace these words with Sky Father, Earth Mother, and Great Spirit. I had not had the greatest parents in the world either, not by a long shot. But my experience of a Conscious Loving Universe was undeniably and inextricably woven throughout the fabric of my life. I could not give in to any belief in a punishing, vengeful god. Though I saw many people in 12-step groups achieve great serenity, there were others who felt bereft of any nurture or comfort from their "God." They could not forgive themselves, often because their behavior was out of their control, so neither could they conceive of their God forgiving them. They often felt desperately alone, abandoned, isolated.

When you think you are all alone in the world, it seems a very, very hard road to walk. I have often felt very alone on this world myself, but from the sense of being so different from other people for the most part and on a variety of levels. I felt set apart and it has been painful. I was deeply grateful for the connection I felt to the invisible, energetic Conscious Loving Universe. Trying to fit in here on Earth didn't work. I had to abandon who I really was to try and do it, and later on, I had to come back home to myself to begin to find peace. But

I always felt, and still feel connected to something very loving and far larger than myself through my lifelong affinity to nature and spirituality. Sometimes I would go out to the desert when in need of comfort and find a place to simply lay on the ground, imagining myself cradled by the Great Earth Mother. She was like a loving sponge... I could feel my emotional pain and inner turmoil drawn out of me while I smelled the warm ground, the creosote and sage, and listened to the songs of the birds around me, feeling at one with all of it. This energetic connection continues to sustain me.

With years to contemplate all of this, from a well-rounded life experience and cross-disciplinary studies in various sciences, philosophies and spiritual perspectives, I now believe that it may be our fractured and compartmentalized human consciousness that in part causes the Zetas to look upon us the same way we humans regard animals. Humans dwell almost entirely in the realm of their conscious minds, while our subconscious/unconscious, and our super-conscious or higher-self consciousness remains mostly inaccessible. A telepathic or a tel-empathic being could see into all of those compartments of a human being's psyche, and this may account for reports of how those big dark Zeta eyes seem to peer into the depths of one's soul, stripping it bare. This is often reported as a terrifying experience. Could it be terrifying because in those moments, the things we hide from ourselves are revealed to our resisting conscious minds? Very possibly. If true, then the Zetas, and perhaps other ET species interacting with humans, may not see us as a fully sentient race, just as humans who experiment upon animals do not see them as sentient or having any kind of soul or consciousness. Humans have traditionally seen animals as beneath them, subject to them and their uses. As an animal lover, I am certain that animals have souls and hearts that love and experience joy and sorrow in their own ways. I find a kind of sideways irony in the fact that certain groups of ET beings may regard us as subject to them and their uses. With our individual compartmentalized consciousness, we very likely may not appear fully sentient to them. And while I might regard this issue with a wry, reluctant humor on a cultural level, on a very personal one I certainly don't wish the physical or emotional pain of going through difficult extraterrestrial experiences on anyone.

I remember reading in Whitley Strieber's *Communion* that he confronted these beings about not having the right to do what they were doing to him. The beings told him that they *did* have the right. This is a recurring theme in abduction literature. Why? I think the answer can be found in looking at the idea of soul contracts, agreements we make before incarnation in our present bodies and lives on Earth. It's an esoteric concept, but it was one I finally opened up to exploring. More on this later.

On an even broader scale, if quantum fields build the reality we see around us from what we hold in our own consciousness – subconscious-unconscious, super-higher consciousness included – then shadow factions within governments and corporate power structures of this world are very likely our own creation within our whole collective human consciousness. Our reality becomes an outer observance of compartmentalization within government, military and corporate structures, that "need-to-know" basis which so frustrates those of us trying to get to the truth, generating activist movements for disclosure about the UFO and ET phenomenon. The realms of shadow governments, black projects, covert-ops and all the horrible things done under their control more than qualifies as the subconscious/unconscious Freudian Id of the human collective. True to this Freudian model, most of humanity has denied a shadow government existence for a very long time, not wanting to confront the reality – or the fear – of being visited by beings from other worlds or other dimensions. The majority of humanity has not at all wanted to crack open the mind's door to peer into the horrors of intentionally inflicted trauma and mind-control abuses. Or to look at the fact that society as a whole has been subject to subtler forms of mind control as well.

And as humanity approaches a shift in consciousness within the corridor of transformation represented by years leading up to and after 2012, it could be that the disclosure happening at the grassroots level is evidence of the collective human consciousness breaking down the barriers between the different realms of our own human psyches.

In Contrast: The Military Experiences

As members of human society, we all know the darker expressions of human sexuality – including torture, rape and murder, generated by the perpetrator's need for power and control over another person.

My experiences with the military or covert ops types definitely fell under that category. When I recovered the memories of the rapes and other things done to me over which I had no control, I was enraged and outraged in equal measure to the fear and terror I felt. These "people" had no excuse for inflicting such harm. They were other human beings who knew exactly what they were doing and what the effects would be. They were in fact doing these things to me *to generate* fear and terror. And some of them, that one blonde security guard in particular, enjoyed and took a great deal of satisfaction in exercising such control. He would often gloat and lord that control over me, knowing I could do nothing about it. He seemed to so revel in his control over me and in inflicting abuse that I feel he must have been a sociopath, hired because of his ability to wreak pain and suffering on people without any pangs of conscience.

If any moment had arisen where someone dropped their guard, allowing me get a hold of a gun, I would have emptied the clip into everyone around me until they were all dead several times over, especially that blonde security guard. Realizing this brought up more internal conflict inside of me. At the core of who I am, I abhor violence and consider life sacred. My hypnosis brought me squarely into confrontation with a part of myself that emerged from these experiences, someone who was capable of picking up a gun and methodically killing people around her. Yes, it would have been self-defense, an ultimately defensible position. But for me, it was still terrible to know that I could have done such a thing.

I was angry about what happened to me and I was angry that it had happened to a woman. After seeing my dad's violence against my mother, being married for a time to Matt, a violent alcoholic, and then working at a womens' center and seeing the kinds of violence perpetrated on women, up to and including murder-suicide, I saw my experiences as yet more acts committed on women. This was not just about violence to me, but to my gender.

Later on I realized that similar acts of violence are also perpetrated on men in these kind of black ops situations. They also have their lives and their families lives threatened. And if they are being sexually assaulted in some way as well, how much worse that must be for them? According to the male myths in our society, men should be able to prevent – somehow – such things happening to them. But under such circumstances as I experienced, there was nothing I could do, nor could a man in my position have been expected to do more. I suppose I could have made some foolhardy attempt to try and get the upper hand. I'm certain it would have resulted in worse abuse or maybe my death. I could really do nothing more than I did in the situation. I was just trying to survive.

Excavating Through the Rubble of Emotional Fallout

Layers upon layers of difficult feelings had been piling up inside of me for a long time. From the experiences themselves, from mentally tracking back into my past, I was discovering ways that PTSD had been affecting me even before having hypnosis or any memory recall. So much emotional turmoil and anguish had built up over the years. I had carried all of this around with little to no support for so long, not knowing where to turn for help.

I was deeply grateful to *finally* find a healer I could work with in Durango who had the heart and capacity within herself to listen to what I had remembered under hypnosis and to the volumes of corroborating data I had found. Helen Janssen had the skills and empathy to sense all the emotions tangled up inside of me around this. At first unremembered from 1980, then remembered through hypnosis in 1994 and 2003, these events had hung over my entire adult life.

We began our work together. Session by session, Helen encouraged me to stay present with my feelings, to allow them to move through my body as sensations of energy, unwinding, discharging.

One particular session was a real turning point in the process.

Helen suggested that I visualize a scene to act out, in which I would turn the tables on my abusers and attack, even kill all of them. I resisted. Wouldn't that make me as bad as them? I knew this rage was still inside of me, and I was afraid to touch it. After some more discussion however, acknowledging the emotions I was still carrying around about all of the abuse, I agreed to try it.

I stood in the center of the healing room and closed my eyes. I first visualized myself standing holding a long, black metal pipe, like a staff weapon – that was what first came to mind and it seemed to fit. Then I visualized a lineup around me of all the people who had hurt me – with injections, with threatening me at gunpoint, with sexual assault, with witnessing and doing nothing. Keeping my eyes closed to maintain the visualization, I let myself feel all the rage. Physically, violently acting this out in the open space of the room, one by one, I beat each of them to death, finally breaking their skulls with the metal pipe. The blond security guard I beat the longest, to a bloody pulp.

When I opened my eyes, the room of was of course empty, except for me, Helen and the few pieces of furniture in there and the sunlight streaming through the windows. But I felt very different.

This was definitely a catharsis. Though I would never have done such a thing in real life, by doing this visualization exercise, I felt an actual kind of heavy and viscous energy had been squeezed out of my body's cells, leaving me lighter and cleaner somehow. Just moving my body felt lighter and easier. I felt a kind of awe. Helen said I did a great job with this exercise. Just tuning into me she could feel the difference too.

With whatever energy I expelled that day, I was changed. Fear no longer had the grip on me it once did. All human beings feel afraid at times, but now, at least in some ways that were very meaningful to me, fear no longer "had me." If I did feel it, the difference was that I "had the fear" rather than the fear "having" me, which had been like a kind of paralysis. It was far easier to turn to some of the next healing tasks, like forgiveness.

One of the key elements to healing is forgiveness. But how in hell does one forgive such extreme abuse? A key for me was in my friend Fred Burks'[3] way of saying that inside every single person, every living being, is a heart that wants to love and be loved. Some people, hell-bent on following a path of power and control over others, may tie up their heart, gag it and toss it in a proverbial dungeon to languish and ache, but it's still there. In reaching for that heart-part of the people responsible for, or party to the ways in which I was brutalized, forgiveness was a game of one-step-forward and two-steps-back for quite a while. It was a long time coming and I'm sure there are still hidden pockets of tangled up feelings inside of myself that will continue coming to light for

---

[3] Fred Burks served for years as a language interpreter to U.S. presidents and dignitaries before resigning in 2004 due to excessive secrecy demands. Having inside information and contacts as well as receiving a great deal of eye-opening information regarding various government cover-ups from respected friends and colleagues, Fred and his friends were inspired to create the Public Education and Empowerment Resource Service (PEERS); a family of websites which includes the www.wanttoknow.info and other websites dedicated to a vision of global community founded upon love and cooperation. What sets the PEERS group of websites apart from many others is their commitment to not only educate about cover-ups and wrongs committed in this world with carefully documented material, but also their commitment to tempering deeply disturbing and frightening data by also providing an equal measure inspiring, beautiful and loving information to balance the darker material.

resolution and integration through forgiveness. Just when you feel like you've got it completely handled, you can run into another area of your life where a tendril of unforgiving, justifiable anger is wound tightly around some issue, and again, you need to work the process through. When anger and rage is completely justified, it can be very difficult to let go of. Emotional excavation is a continuing process.

It's important to point out that forgiveness does not excuse wrongs done, or criminal acts committed. Forgiveness is as much about letting go of the energetic poison of hatred and rage we carry inside – so that inner peace can begin – as it is about forgiving any who have harmed us, however undeserving of forgiveness they may seem. To carry around rage, anger and hatred year after year, refusing to forgive because we see the perpetrators as absolutely unforgivable, only sets us up for some kind of degenerative disease to set in later on. These unprocessed emotions become pockets of stagnant energy in the body. They can cause blockages over time that can bring about physical illness. Energy wants to flow freely in our bodies for health and well-being. True forgiveness frees up that energy once again for ourselves. And it sets free the one who is forgiven, creating a possibility to transform into a better human being because you have let go of the energy deadlock that existed between you.

Another process that helped me greatly was a gestalt-type of exercise. It involved setting out two chairs in my livingroom. I had a list ready of the "people" I wanted to dialogue with from the instances of the injections and the rapes. I sat in one chair while imagining – one at a time – each of the people who either inflicted abuse on me or who were simply witness-participants in the other chair. I also switched and took a turn in "their" chair, imagining myself as each of them, having to confront an imaginary "me" in the other chair.

It was a process that, again, allowed me to address my anger at what happened and at everyone who did things to me or allowed them to happen. Some amazing insights came from this exercise.

Of the ten people I "interviewed" in this exercise, most of them seemed very sorry for what had happened to me. They said they were powerless to stop it out of fear for their own lives or the lives of their families. Some of them had surreptitiously turned their eyes down, not really being able to stomach what they were being forced to observe. From the grey ET was the same puzzlement as I had sensed from him during the whole happening – he wondered why people would commit such brutality on one of their own kind. The man who had given me the injections seemed almost like an automaton. When I asked him "Why?" it was as if his eyes went blank, emotionless, expressionless except for something that seemed like a touch of sarcasm or ridicule. He shrugged off my question with some kind of mumble about needing human subjects. The dark-haired younger security guard who had done the second sexual assault came across in this exercise as filled with terrible remorse. He said he didn't know what came over him at the time that even caused him to be able to do such a thing. He could barely look at me. The blonde security guard was – as in my memories – gloating and remorseless. Even in this visualized re-creation, it was as if he was looking straight into my eyes, trying to further intimidate me. My suspicion that these projects actually seek out and employ sociopaths who can carry out brutality untroubled by conscience or regret was further affirmed. I don't know for certain if this is the case, but I strongly suspect it is.

Taking a turn sitting in the other chair, doing my best to take on the energy of each of these people was quite an experience. I was left with an impression, with only a couple exceptions, of these people as lost souls in some kind of covert-ops hell. In different ways, they were as much victims of the situation as I was. Within me, a kind of deep, energetic in-breath occurred, with a stronger sense of forgiveness on the exhale.

I began thinking just how needed a well-thought out amnesty program would be if these types of black projects were ever to be brought out into the public. Review panels comprised of lawyers, psychiatrists and social workers would need to be carefully developed from those practicing around the country, themselves scrutinized and investigated for no connections to any covert ops projects of any kind. These review panels would have to hear many individual cases and make a determination on how much criminal behavior they had actually done and whether it was done freely or under coercion. Polygraphs would need to be used as the questioning proceeded to try and measure truthfulness in the kind and quality of information these people were willing to offer in exchange for amnesty. And what to do with unrepentant sociopaths? So far as I know, there is no cure for sociopathology. I'm not sure what kind of meaningful amnesty could be offered to them. They would have no place in a truly post-disclosure world. Unless a way can be found to rehabilitate them, they could be a continuing danger to society.

How does one forgive a sociopath? I'm still working on it, but my current process includes the idea that such people take on incarnations in bodies that are simply not wired properly to allow their hearts to hold the reins on their humanity. They take on a lifetime where they become an instrument of spiritual growth for others. It can seem very "either-or." Either these people are monsters and deserve to be punished terribly – or forgive?! such individuals and off they go, scott-free, to hurt someone again?! "Never in a million years!" when we think like that.

What really needs to be cultivated is a "both-and" approach. "This person did terrible things to me and he may never, ever show any remorse for it – AND – I choose to feel my rage, my fear, my grief about it because those are natural feelings to feel about such horrible personal violations. I choose to feel all these feelings, give them their season within me, like personal thunderstorms, then let them go." Forgiveness is for my own best and highest good. It's when we hold onto those emotions, not letting them go that they become problematic.

And when we try to be a "nice person" and forgive, without honoring and allowing the very real human emotions that are a natural consequence of being terribly wronged, we do "a spiritual bypass."

It was Helen who introduced me to this great descriptor; spiritual bypass. Lots of "nice" spiritual folks don't want to deal with the very real human feelings they have about having been used and abused. They are afraid of getting entangled in the darker, violent "not nice" emotions. They avoid looking at and feeling them except momentarily, like sticking a toe into icy water and jerking it back out. They often adopt a placid appearance of acceptance with the attitude, often stated aloud, of things like:

"Wouldn't that make me as bad as them?" (This was my own spiritual bypass attempt. It was rather half-hearted because I knew better from my own body-centered training.)

Other examples: "It must have been my karma." "Just think of how the soul felt who had to take on doing such a thing to me." "It must have been part of my soul's agreement for this lifetime." And more similar such "spiritual bypass" rationalizations.

From a spiritual perspective, all of these statements likely have some real basis in truth. I have come to feel very strongly that I agreed to a soul contract for my experiences in this lifetime, to shed karma and for my soul's expansion of awareness. But I didn't leap to this understanding at the beginning, clinging to it as an avoidance strategy to keep myself from experiencing my own emotional sludge. It came after a great deal of difficult processing had already been done. It came as a rather inescapable conclusion to lots of inquiry and soul searching. It came especially through looking at my life as a quantum mirror, showing me what I might be carrying deep in my psyche, hidden from my conscious mind.

But using such spiritual bypass statements as band-aids to avoid dealing with the very human, very messy, unpleasant, scary emotions allows the emotional pain and trauma to sit and fester inside. Just like hard, armored holding-onto-rage-unforgiveness, these emotional hurts can, through the energy they knot up in different areas of the body, create actual physical illness. A spiritual bypass allows such nice people to avoid facing their own inner shadow – emotions of anger, rage, hatred and fear they harbor deep inside about the ways in which they've been hurt. Emotions they've labeled as negative, bad or evil... emotions that frighten them into thinking they are not nice people after all. So, as a cop out, some people do a spiritual bypass.

Grief is another very difficult emotion to deal with. If given in to fully, we can fear being washed away on a tsunami of heartache and anguish. It feels incredibly vulnerable to give into grief. For me, that was the big tough one to cope with. After spending much of my life working to forge my personal armor against people who might hurt me, emotionally or physically in childhood, I

202

became as stoic and invulnerable as I could. No crying or showing any sign of being hurt, that people around me could see as a weakness and further attack, ridicule or make fun of.

If Sky Walker or my inter-dimensional teachers were watching over me in childhood, as I'm sure they were, they may well have stood back and watched this process of girl-child turning warrior, knowing just how much I would need that armor for what was to come in my life. And need it I did.

In recalling the injections, the multiple rapes, and other ways I was humiliated and abused over the period of missing time I worked on reclaiming, it seemed that I needed that invulnerability more than ever. I went stoic and statue-like, leaving my body and observing at a distance. I would not give any of those abusers – especially that blond security guard – any extra pleasure by unduly crying out, or giving into tears. This was sheer survival for me, not just physically but emotionally. In my hypnosis sessions I have no memory of giving into grief or fear in front of those who hurt me. I hope I never did.

Opening to grieving in the healing process was a different story. In feeling my feelings, allowing the emotions to move over and through me, I knew from all my own body-centered training and experience that a spiritual bypass was not an option. I needed to honor, through allowing myself to feel fully, the very human feelings of rage and anger inside of me, and work my way through them to the grief underneath it all.

Experiencing grief, opening to it from such cruel abuse, is like allowing yourself to experience your psyche fractured into pieces, or allowing at least as much as you can handle in given spaces of time. As a person who cares for people, for life and all living things, who considers life a sacred gift from the Creator, confronting this kind of horror, confronting the fact that there were people in the world who could inflict this kind of intense suffering on other human beings was enough to shatter my heart into a million pieces. This awful truth that I resisted and fought and plastered over with busyness and a pretense at "living" had torn away every last shred of innocence I possessed. I was left with an inner me broken and totally bereft in some imaginary wasteland, while the me in the outer world tried to carry on some kind of day to day life.

The part of me avoiding grieving, afraid of the vulnerability of grief, was trapped there in that place, still in pieces. Another part of me, the angry part, had stood guard over the part of me that was in avoidance, protecting the part of me in pieces. I was trapped between pushing away the reality of what had happened to me because it was just too terrible, and accepting it fully at last, that such things do in fact happen in this world and allowing the grief of it to wash over me. I was actually holding off the grieving process by still struggling to avoid accepting that such cruelties do happen. To me, and to many others. Intellectually, in my mind I had accepted it in the face of all the corroborating material I had gathered, but in my heart and deeper being, I was still struggling to avoid accepting it. Grief is about loss and I did not want to lose my belief in a world of beauty, truth and essentially good people. The human collective Id reflected in my memories was hideous to me. In accepting the truth, it felt like a loss of all innocence. It felt like the loss of a vision of a world I had believed in my whole life. But giving up that vision was necessary to begin the grieving process.

Acceptance and forgiveness was not a catharsis that happened for me all at once. I had to take it in manageable chunks. Even as I write this, I still feel autumn leaves of grief stirring around me in a moving breeze of emotion, and my eyes moisten. Writing this book is another part of the process of acceptance, though I am well down the road of acceptance and healing today.

In the last few years, a good friend shared an article with me via the internet by healer Paul Levy[4], that appears in the articles section of his website, www. awakeninthedream.com. Here is an excerpt from that article:

> Trauma is a normal, healthy response to an insane and intolerable situation. There is an intimate correlation between being traumatized, abused, and wounded, and having a shamanic initiation/spiritual awakening. Trauma is an experience that is overwhelming to the ego, in that it can't be assimilated by the ego in the typical way. The trauma initiates and catalyzes the deeper process of the archetype of the shaman to begin to form-ulate and crystallize itself in the unconscious of the future shaman. This precipitates a deeper part of the psyche to become mobilized, as the shaman journeys deep inside themselves, flying on the wings of their creative imagination to address and become acquainted with what has gotten activated within them.

> "The shaman's descent into the darkness can be agonizing, a veritable crucifixion. Part of the (arche)typical shamanic experience is to become dis-membered, which is a cooking and smelting of psychic contents that have become rigidified, ossified, and have outlived their usefulness. To quote [Carl] Jung[5], "The shaman's experience of sickness, torture, death and regeneration implies, at a higher level, the idea of being made whole through sacrifice... The goal of the shaman's death and dismemberment experience is to "re-member" themselves, which like true soul retrieval, brings all of their dissociated parts back together into a more integrated synthesis.

[4] Paul Levy is a pioneer in the field of spiritual emergence. He has studied with some of the greatest spiritual masters of Tibet and Burma and is an innovator in the field of dreaming – both night dreams and waking, day-time dreams. He is the author of *The Madness of George Bush: A Reflection of Our Collective Psychosis* and *Wetiko: The Greatest Epidemic Sickness Known to Humanity.* His website is www.awakeninthedream.com.
[5] Carl Gustav Jung, a contemporary of Sigmund Freud, developed the process of analytical psychology and individuation as integrating opposites in human psychological development as well as developing the concepts of archetypes and the collective unconscious.

We Are All Shamans-In-Training, by Paul Levy, 2010.
Reprinted with permission of the author.

Levy's words describe very accurately the process I myself had to move through, a shamanic process of putting myself back together in a larger way that could include the new realities that had become part of my life's experience. And he also explores in-depth in his books an idea that I have come to share; that all of humanity is dreaming into existence the world's reality we see around us and that we are complicit in it at a deep, unconscious level.

It took time to realize I had not completely lost my sense of wonder at the world, or all of my innocence. I had not completely lost my vision of humanity's essential beauty and goodness. It was only obscured by dark clouds as I came to terms with my experiences. Because of society's denial of this part of our world's reality, it had taken me years longer than it might have otherwise.

But in recent years, as my own understanding of my process has expanded, unfolding in the larger universe I live within, I finally had to claim responsibility for that version of denial-reality. Perhaps the people around me for so many years who could not accept what I had to tell them were just mirroring back to me my own deeper resistance to accepting it myself. The quantum energetic field was faithfully mirroring my own inner reality back to me so that I could uncover it, recognize it and learn from it.

And today, staying out of coulda, woulda, shoulda – most of the time – I often turn to the Four Immutable Laws of Spirit that I learned in an audio program, *Power and Love in Relationships,* from Angeles Arrien, cultural anthropologist and educator, which she in turn got from her friend, Harrison Owen:

1. When something begins is exactly the right time.
2. Who shows up are exactly the right people.
3. What happens is the only thing that could have happened.
4. When it's over, it's over.

We spend so much time in our lives trying to change what is or what has been, wishing "if only." There is such deep wisdom in the Serenity Prayer from my 12-step days. Here is my version:

Great Spirit, grant me the serenity
To accept the things I cannot change,
The courage to change the things I can,
And the wisdom to know the difference.

I couldn't change what happened to me. But I could choose to heal. And out of "The courage to change the things I can," has come this book. I often think back on the huge commitment to healing I made when backing away from suicide. That commitment definitely set my feet on the path to today, even though navigating that path had seemed very random while walking it at times. Yet there were those moments of synchronicity when it was crystal clear that a higher guidance was at work. If I had taken on a difficult soul contract to experience in this lifetime, then those higher dimensional teachers around me were also there to minister to me, guiding me through the healing process.

Another shamanic metaphor that seemed most appropriate came from the movie, *The Trial of Billy Jack*. In training with a Native American elder, Billy Jack undergoes a rite of initiation where he allows himself to be bitten by a rattlesnake; and he then must, through his consciousness, transmute the poison within his body before it kills him.

This felt incredibly similar to me – I had had experiences that were like poison to me, to the essence of who I felt myself to be. I had to transmute those experiences through a conscious and strong desire and commitment to heal. It was a good thing I had had the earlier confrontation with suicide before this all came to light, giving me the inner knowing that suicide is no escape from yourself. Even if you commit suicide, wherever you go, there you are. It was a good thing because many times, especially after the sessions with Gloria filled in the picture so much more, I wondered just how I could go on living with such memories. I knew I had to find a way. And year by year, step by step, as I was ready, synchronicities occurred to lead me exactly where I needed to be to actualize each step of my healing process.

Another good friend and shaman-person in Durango, named Aamann, suggested we do a "soul regression" for me to look at the events that transpired from a soul level. It was similar to hypnosis, but guided from a different place. As I watched myself go through the difficult experiences again, the torture of the injection and its effects, from this soul perspective I could see Sky Walker and my three inter-dimensional teachers around me, like a circle of light, pouring their love out to me as I passed through that injection nightmare and the hell of the rapes that followed. For whatever reason, they could not prevent the trauma, but they were there providing unseen support and deep compassion.

So even then, I had never been alone. I came out of that session, my face wet with tears of gratitude, relief and love for the support of my unseen "family."

When something begins, it is exactly the right time, who shows up are exactly the right people, what happens is the only thing that could have happened; and when one part of the process is over, it's over.

Chapter 12: Comprehending the Incomprehensible

"In the first place, good people are rarely suspicious; they cannot imagine others doing the things they themselves are incapable of doing; usually they accept the undramatic conclusion as the correct one, and let matters rest there. Then, too, the normal are inclined to view the multiple killer as the one who's as monstrous in appearance as he is in mind, which is about as far from the truth as one could well get." He paused and then said that these monsters of real life usually looked and behaved in a more normal manner than their actually normal brothers and sisters: they presented a more convincing picture of virtue than virtue presented of itself—just as the wax rosebud or the plastic peach seemed more perfect to the eye, more what the mind thought a rosebud or a peach should be than the imperfect original from which it had been modeled.

~ *The Bad Seed*, William March, 1954, Harper Collins.

Human societies around the world are experiencing a battle of paradigms; between those who seek power and control over others versus individual personal empowerment. These fundamentally different paradigms affect us both in deeply personal ways and at global societal and cultural levels.

In the *The Verbally Abusive Relationship: How to Recognize It and How to Respond* by Patricia Evans[1], she discusses these two types of power, identifying them as Reality I and Reality II. Reality I is about power over others; Reality II is about personal power. Those who live in Reality I operate from control and dominance; those who live in Reality II relate from mutuality and co-creation.

The frightening clash that occurs between these two differing paradigms happens when a person from Reality II tries to resolve a conflict with the person living in Reality I. Using the qualities and skills of empathy and listening; coming from a willingness to acknowledge their shared role in whatever

---

[1] Patricia Evans is an interpersonal communication specialist working specifically in the area of verbally abusive relationships. She has published four books. Her websites are www.verbalabuse.com and www.patriciaevans.com.

207

conflict has arisen, the Reality II person tries to appeal to such qualities in the Reality I person. They assume that all people share an ability for empathy and a desire to understand. The Reality II person does not comprehend that if these human faculties exist in the Reality I person at all, they may be so deeply buried as to be effectively non-existent. This can stem from one of the psychopathic personality disorders such as narcissistic or anti-social personality disorder, in which case there is little recourse for the partner of such a person other than to just leave and cut off all contact as much as possible. If the problems originate from family, religious or cultural conditioning about some need for males to be dominant and in control of their female partners and children, then it may be possible for some type of intervention to improve mutual communication, empathy and understanding. From the Reality I person's operating paradigm, the actions of the Reality II person are a ploy, designed to try and maneuver power and control away from them and subjugate them. They only see the Reality II person as trying to control and dominate them as they regularly do to others. The Reality II person is shocked, confused and frightened at the often-vehement rage that their understanding and empathy causes to come boiling forth from the Reality I person. Usually paralyzed with shock, there is little they can do in that moment except mumble an apology for whatever offense they gave, often not even understanding what the "offense" was. If they are smart, and care for themselves enough, they will come to see the inability for compassionate reciprocity in the Reality I person. Sooner or later, in the face of the Reality I person's unreasonable resistance and eruptions of rage and verbal abuse, the Reality II person will leave them, especially if counseling or other types of interventions are unsuccessful.

Such acrimonious and abusive behavior is traumatizing and devastating for the Reality II person. It can take a great deal of time and effort to heal from such a relationship, depending on how long it went on and available resources for support. They are at risk of never healing, never understanding what has happened to them unless they are educated about and come to accept that the paradigm the Reality I person operates from is usually absolute; a black and white world where one is either in the supreme seat of power and control, or being subjugated and dominated. Mutuality and co-creation are seen as threats to such power and control, diminishing or eliminating it. Empathy and compassion are seen as flaws and weakness, and even worse, traits to be exploited.

This clash of paradigms is not restricted to the realm of personal relationships. It plays itself out on the world stage every day in politics, government, military and religions through the media. With the media controlled as it is, we see only what those who have control of the media want us to see. Whole populations can be traumatized and at risk for more trauma when a preponderance of Reality I people have seized control of the institutions that govern our lives.

What kind of people populate a Reality I paradigm? What makes them tick? How can we understand just what kind of people we are dealing with?

How can we comprehend the sheer scope of political, corporate, economic and environmental problems they have manufactured from sheer pathological selfishness, problems now confronting humanity on a global scale?

Personality Disordered Individuals Giving Rise to Disordered Societies

> Psychopaths are not disoriented or out of touch with reality, nor do they experience the delusions, hallucinations, or intense subjective distress that characterize most other mental disorders. Unlike psychotic individuals, psychopaths are rational and aware of what they are doing and why. Their behavior is the result of choice, freely exercised.
>
> ~ from *Without Conscience: The Disturbing World of the Psychopaths Among Us* by Robert D. Hare, PhD[2], 1993. Reprinted with permission of The Guilford Press

A deeper look at this is necessary to truly understand further, and there is a set of personality disorders that need to be looked at to bring about that understanding. In the *Diagnostic and Statistical Manual of Mental Disorders, fourth edition, text revision*[3] (*DSM-IV-TR*) they are found under Axis II, called Cluster B personality disorders. These are characterized as dramatic, emotional or erratic disorders. They include anti-social (also known as sociopathic), narcissistic, histrionic and borderline personality disorders.

These disorders are often lumped into one term: psychopaths. They have the following traits in common: a lack of empathy or remorse, superficial emotions, egocentricity and deceptiveness. Psychopaths are often antisocial and abusive of others. They comprise a large segment of the general population responsible for violent criminal behavior. Although they lack empathy and emotional depth, they can be skilled at pretending to be normal people by feigning emotions – often exceedingly well – and putting out dishonest representations of their pasts.

The two that are most problematic, especially in our society, government and corporate empires are the narcissistic and anti-social or sociopathic personality disorders.

---

[2] Robert D. Hare, PhD is a criminal psychology researcher and author of several excellent books about psychopathy. He developed *The Psychopathy Checklist-Revised* (PCL-R) which is fast becoming an assessment standard world-wide for its validity and reliability. His website: http://www.hare.org.

[3] *The Diagnostic and Statistical Manual of Mental Disorders, fourth edition, text revision* (*DSM-IV-TR*) is used by mental health institutions and professionals as a tool for assessing the magnitude or severity of people whose behavior brings them repeatedly into conflict with other people and society. A newer version, the *DSM-V*, is due out in spring of 2013.

The narcissist can be one of the most dangerous. Often superficially charming, magnetic, even charismatic, the narcissist is a ruthless predator who uses his or her charm to get to the "top." With a keen and uncanny ability to "read" people or situations, they idealize and flatter to gain trust and ingratiate themselves with others. They are consummate actors. Under the charm boils a cauldron of narcissistic rage that spills over at any real or imagined slight by another. Narcissists have an inflated, grandiose self-importance. They exaggerate their achievements and feel entitled to be treated as superior, whether reality warrants it or not. They are fixated upon ideations of unlimited success, power, intellectual brilliance and/or physical attractiveness. They feel they are special and unique and can only be understood by or associate with special, high-status people. They are inter-personally exploitive, manipulative and arrogant. The take no personal responsibility for their actions – things that go wrong are always blamed on others. They require constant and excessive expressions of admiration and praise from others or public adulation, called "narcissistic supply." If they don't get it, they go into a fury. They lack any ability for empathy or compassion.

All of these characteristics, combined with ruthless selfishness, makes them dangerous in any arena, from personal relationships to positions of authority in government, military, corporations or religious hierarchies – the very arenas of power to which they are most attracted. They have the charm and magnetism to attract public attention, thereby maneuvering or manipulating their way into positions of control. Once there, holding the reins of power in government or corporations, the damage they can do to common people's rights or the environment is devastating. If people try to enact legislation that attempts to overturn their agendas of control, they use their money and power to "buy" politicians and lobby for overriding legislation that will subvert or circumvent it. They must maintain control at any cost. Knowing what they themselves are capable of, they most likely harbor a deep, well-hidden terror of anyone else gaining control over them or making them accountable for their actions.

The evidence that this has become a pervasive problem in government are the steady streams of executive decisions and legislation that are proposed or signed into law that seem to have little to no regard for the well-being of the people they will affect, or the good of the environment. Corporations headed by such ruthless individuals have used money and influence to turn our democracy into a corporatocracy. Their agendas are self-serving in the extreme, without regard for Constitutional rights, basic human rights or severe damage to our environment.

Just as dangerous, but without the surface charm of the narcissist, are individuals with anti-social personality disorder. Again, there is no capacity for empathy. There is no remorse for lying, stealing, injuring or even murdering others. These people are irritable, aggressive and violent and show a reckless disregard for their own or others' safety. They are irresponsible and blame others when things go wrong. Such people deceive, lie, or con others for profit and personal pleasure, exploiting people of empathy, conscience and compassion, at the same time holding them in contempt for such weaknesses, even justifying their actions on such a basis with a Machiavellian[4] attitude.

Several books on narcissism point out in detail that our entire society has become contaminated by such disordered influences. Though Lisa E. Scott wrote *It's All About Him: How to Identify and Avoid the Narcissist Male Before You Get Hurt* as a guide for individuals, she also addresses our current societal propensity for rewarding extremes of grandiose and egocentric behavior:

> Sadly, today's culture rewards selfish and arrogant behavior. Narcissism is validated and reinforced everywhere you look. We have celebrities who have become famous for being rude, insensitive and arrogant. We have shock jocks and women like Ann Coulter, who say cruel and mean things about the widows of 9/11 to get attention. American culture rewards this behavior by putting them in the spotlight. The media caters to them.

The "spotlight" – the ultimate form of narcissistic supply – is exactly what these individuals desire above all else. As long as we pander to such people by watching them on television, in movies and buying glossy magazines with celebrity gossip strewn over the covers, we feed such monsters; narcissists who are driven to seek center stage for the attention they single-mindedly crave. Whether in entertainment, politics, the corporate world or any place where public attention and power beckons, narcissists and their anti-social associates and henchmen will be attracted to such positions like moths to flame. Political power gives them the frightening ability to put themselves in control of their own "supply." Since their need for it is bottomless, and many are in competition with each other for the limelight, they can become more and more extreme to command such supply, like an addict who needs more and larger doses of a drug to feel "the rush."

While women can also be narcissists, statistics show a higher percentage of men to women with this disorder. Men are most prone to childhood conditioning to bury their empathy and emotions. Messages such as: If you cry you're a sissy; Show no weakness (empathy); Be successful at (school, sports, college, career)" condition men to the necessity of ruthlessness in order to have success, control, and supremacy in all areas of their lives. In a more equal opportunity world, women who have taken on this previously-male drive for success can adopt these succeed-at-any-cost traits as well. When women were still primarily confined to the home, there were, and still are, females ruthless in their competition with other women for male attention.

[4] "Machiavellian" is a descriptor deriving from a book called The Prince, by Niccolò di Bernardo dei Machiavelli in the early 1500s. In the pursuit of political power, The Prince advocates the calculated application, as tools of "statecraft," that include deceit, brute force and violence, embodying the saying that the end justifies the means.

We have created an entire culture that rewards ruthless behavior, such as Rush Limbaugh's steady stream of outrageously insulting attacks on women, gays and lesbians, African Americans, etc., with statements like the following:

> A Georgetown coed told Nancy Pelosi's hearing that the women in her law school program are having so much sex they're going broke, so you and I should have to pay for their birth control. So what would you call that? I called it what it is [i.e., slut and prostitute.]. So, I'm offering a compromise today: I will buy all of the women at Georgetown University as much aspirin to put between their knees as they want. ... So Miss Fluke and the rest of you feminazis, here's the deal. If we are going to pay for your contraceptives and thus pay for you to have sex, we want something. We want you to post the videos online so we can all watch.

~ Rush Limbaugh, March, 2012

I sincerely doubt that Rush Limbaugh is concerned at all about bad press from his blatant crassness (except possibly for the loss of advertisers and their dollars for his "show" – squeezing a most-likely hugely insincere apology from him). But the attention from all his extreme and insulting remarks remains and continues to generate the attention he craves. Even if it relegates him to the halls of infamy forevermore, it's still massive public ATTENTION. I don't even like putting his quote or name in here, in some ways giving him more, but I needed an example and he provides so many highly pertinent examples of overt, public verbal narcissistic abuse.

If drama, grandiosity or arrogance gets attention, and attention is the goal, then we ourselves are responsible for unwittingly giving such people the attention that is their drug. In such a culture it is much easier for individuals to justify heartless and cruel actions in the relentless quest to "get ahead." In the current narcissistic culture, one of increasing extremism, this conditioned tendency has taken on a pathological intensity.

Appealing to psychopaths' "humanity" to get them to see reason is a lost cause. We must find other ways to deal with such people, concrete, material ways. If such people are motivated only by their own interests, their own greed, and avoidance of consequences for shameful, immoral or illegal actions, then these are the means we need to apply to deal with them. A renaissance of adherence to the Constitution and Bill of Rights is the place to start. It's no wonder current political and corporate influences are working to subvert and destroy the Constitution – well-defined and legally-upheld human rights are a threat to absolute power and control.

An understanding of these personality disorders and their characteristics – so they can be recognized and prevented from gaining power in the first place – is another. With this kind of knowledge and a return to the laws of the land that were instituted to protect us all against tyranny, we can hold such people legally accountable for their behavior. With such leverage, we can remove them from any positions of power and influence. By knowing what to look for in the behavior and character of those seeking office, we can prevent other such social predators from taking their place.

Not all abusers are narcissists or sociopaths. Male modes of conditioning and healing from such conditioning are addressed in other books. Distinguishing a personality-disordered individual from someone who has developed a pattern of abusive behavior from childhood or other conditioning is defined by their ability – or not – to come to understand their abusive behavior, seek help and change it. Narcisissts and sociopaths do not feel anything is wrong with them, they notoriously blame and find fault with their victims. Very rarely do they ever seek counseling for their disorders.

People of Empathy, People of Conscience

Yet you cannot lay remorse upon the innocent nor lift it
from the heart of the guilty. Unbidden shall it call in the night,
that men may wake and gaze upon themselves.

~ Kahlil Gibran, from "On Crime and Punishment"
in *The Prophet*[5]

Gibran's words apply to the majority of us with heart, empathy and conscience. As people who experience the full emotional spectrum of what most of us call "human," we fall into the trap of thinking that all human beings experience that same full spectrum of emotion and empathy for others. But this is not the case.

The question of nature (genetics) or nurture (environment) comes to mind here in considering narcissistic and other personality disorders. On the "nurture" side of the coin, current popular theory states that people with such personality disorders were severely abused and/or idealized to an unrealistic degree by their parents or caregivers. The true needs of the child to simply be and be accepted as he or she was were ignored. The parents' agenda for their child ran how they interacted with their child. The child's true self or personality was excised by such pain to a nether region of their subconscious nevermore to be heard from. Who they truly were was unacceptable to their parents. Still having needs like all human beings, they set out to learn how to get their needs met in whatever ways would work for them, through putting on an act, through deceptions or manipulations. Through doing what was expected and basking in the praise. Conditional love conditions the child craving some

<hr>

[5] *The Prophet* is the best-known and best-loved literary work of Gibran Kahlil Gibran (1883 - 1931), a Lebanese artist and writer. The Prophet has never been out of print since its publication by Alfred A. Knopf/Doubleday in 1923 and has been translated into over 40 different languages. The wisdom and beauty of its prose transcends religious ideologies, opening its readers to the depths that lie within them.

semblance of "love" into a creature that loses touch with their innate feelings and humanity, trading them in for what they learn works with their caregivers in their home of origin.

Yet there may also be a physically inherited or genetic component to such personality disorders as well. More recent research, as in the Equinox documentary *Psychopath*, released in 2000, discusses malfunctions in the brain that are very likely genetic in nature – observing that psychopaths are born that way, not created by bad parenting, though dysfunctional parenting could make these types of personality disorders much worse.

However, there are also people who are raised in dysfunctional environments who still retain their total human spectrum of emotions and empathy, who are in fact inspired by their dysfunctional upbringing to become something better. They go on to become people of deep empathy and compassion, even healers of individuals and societies.

Most of us would feel sympathy and compassion for such people whose problems arise from a bad childhood home, and we would be right to do so. But that should not stop us from holding these individuals strictly accountable for their wrongs. In their minds, this is the only coin that will count with them, the only stimulus that will hold any weight. If they still possess any humanity at all, it is so deeply buried as to be non-existent. There is a story of the scorpion and the fox that teaches us to be wary of creatures whose ingrained nature is to harm or kill:

> There was a scorpion who wanted to cross a river. It asked a fox preparing to swim across to carry it to the other side on his back. The fox said he could not do that, that if he allowed the scorpion on his back, the scorpion would sting him and he would die. The scorpion replied that if he did that while the fox was in the river, they would both die. This made sense to the fox, so he agreed to carry the scorpion across on his back. Halfway across the river, the fox swimming, the scorpion stung the fox.

> The fox cried out, "Why did you do that? Now we will both die!"

> "I couldn't help it," replied the scorpion. "It is my nature."

We must understand that it is the nature of psychopaths to do what they do. Trying to cure them of their psychopathy is unsuccessful – at least so far in our society. These people on the whole do not want to change, they see no need to change – they like themselves just fine as they are. If life impresses upon them enough cumulative consequences from their behavior that they come to see a need for change, the best that can be hoped for therapeutically is training

214

to modify behavior. There is always a risk that they could revert to their old patterns.

From an esoteric perspective, it's possible that a soul itself may select such a personality-disordered lifetime for whatever reason, to learn, and perhaps also be an instrument of learning for others. However, this is little to no comfort to those whose lives have been devastated by a blindsided encounter with a narcissist or sociopath. Nor does it help those of us that watch with consternation, fear or anger at the ongoing encroachment of a "big brother" society, or the destruction being wreaked on the environment we all depend upon for life.

Spiritually-oriented people live in the Reality II mutuality and co-creation paradigm. We are loving, empathetic, compassionate and do our best not to judge others too harshly. We feel we should be accepting of others as they are. Yes, we also get angry and afraid, but accept these as normal emotional responses to various situations and events in life. True emotions serve valid purposes in our lives in many ways.

> Psychopaths' lack of remorse or guilt is associated with a remarkable ability to rationalize their behavior and to shrug off personal responsibility for actions that cause shock and disappointment to family, friends, associates, and others who have played by the rules. Usually they have handy excuses for their behavior, and in some cases they deny that it happened at all.
>
> ~ from *Without Conscience: The Disturbing World of the Psychopaths Among Us* by Dr. Robert D. Hare, PhD, 1993. Reprinted with permission of The Guilford Press.

Our assumption that all human beings share the same modes of feeling and emotion is a risky, dangerous set-up when we encounter individuals who do not experience empathy, compassion or remorse. Such people see our capacity for empathy as a weakness they can exploit and manipulate. The only defense we can create against such people is knowledge; to learn to recognize the characteristics of their disordered personalities and cognitions, and neutrally applying natural, logical, and if necessary, legal consequences for their actions and behaviors.

The Other Side of the Coin Regarding "Mental Health"

While soberly acknowledging true personality disorders which are well-established with soundly-researched criteria, we should be very wary of trusting the *DSM-IV-TR* or other such manuals as any absolute authority. The book, *Making Us Crazy: DSM: The Psychiatric Bible and the Creation of Mental*

Disorders by Herb Kutchins and Stuart A. Kirk, challenges the DSM manuals and points out the proliferation of new personality disorders being defined in it. Some kind of mental health diagnosis could be applied to almost everyone in the world at this point, with an accompanying mandate to prescribe drugs for concocted, made-up conditions. Pharmaceutical companies are quick to supply – for a price – any number of designer drugs to "help" whatever particular condition, making a profit at our expense and very likely undermining our health in the process. So by following the money and the ability to exploit for wealth and power, we must hold suspect and be cautious of the many voices and texts of "authority" produced in the last few decades. We are reaping serious consequences as a society heavily influenced by psychopathic individuals in the corridors of power. This includes those who guide or influence the text that goes into such manuals. Reshaping and redefining mental illness and disorders could give those in power the means to stigmatize, as mentally unstable, those who would legitimately speak out against them regarding abuses of power. There are disorders listed in the *DSM-IV-TR* called "oppositional defiant disorder" in children that shifts to "conduct disorder" in adolescents and adults. Are those in the "Occupy" movements suffering from a conduct disorder? Or are they simply people fed up with abuses of economic power that have left them homeless and jobless? Mental health diagnoses could be used to justify locking up and perpetually-drugging government whistleblowers or others who appear to be "politically inconvenient."

The newest version of the DSM, the DSM-V, is due out in spring of 2013, and it seems that my wariness is well-justified. Articles are appearing online from those in the psychiatric and counseling professions protesting at the creation of yet more fallacious mental health diagnoses. From 106 mental disorders listed in the DSM-I, published in 1952, that number has metasasized into over 300 disorders in the DSM-IV. How many more will be introduced in the upcoming DSM-V is not yet known, but drafts of the document are inciting waves of concerns and complaints. The following is from an online article titled *Therapists revolt against psychiatry's bible*, by Rob Waters, published in December, 2011:

> The latest rebellion against the DSM-5 began with a salvo from across the Atlantic. In June, a special committee of the British Psychological Society complained in a letter to the APA [American Psychiatric Association] that "clients and the general public are negatively affected by the continued and continuous medicalisation of their natural and normal responses to their experiences." The committee criticized the proposed creation of an "attenuated psychosis syndrome" – a sort of poor-man's psychosis with less severe symptoms – "as an opportunity to stigmatize eccentric people." They also objected to a proposed reduction in the number of symptoms needed to diagnose adolescents with attention

deficit disorder (ADD) because it might increase diagnoses and the use of meds.

Then David Elkins, professor emeritus at Pepperdine University and president of the Society for Humanistic Psychology, a division of the American Psychological Association, formed a committee to discuss similar objections and draft a petition enumerating them. In October, he posted the petition online. "I figured we'd get a couple hundred signatures," Elkins said.

The response stunned him and his colleagues. The petition attracted more than 6,000 signatures in three weeks; as of mid-December it had topped 9,300 signatories and garnered the endorsement of 35 organizations. On Nov. 8, American Counseling Association president Don Locke jumped in with a letter to the APA objecting to the "incomplete or insufficient empirical evidence" underlying the proposed revisions and expressing "uncertainty about the quality and credibility" of the DSM-5.

"This has become a grassroots movement among mental health professionals, who are saying we already have a national problem with overmedication of children and the elderly, and we don't want to exacerbate that," says Elkins.[6]

As we can see, there are serious problems with the new DSM-V underscored by the very people who could be compelled to use it once it's published.

What of the differences in each of us that make us unique, and potentially valuable for such uniqueness? New perceptions, new visions, new innovations? In our inner quest for life's meaning, for self-fulfillment or even simple happiness, are we to be pasteurized and homogenized through a fear of being labelled with a mental disorder and drugged or worse? Hand-in-hand with a national healthcare system that would favor traditional pharmaceutical-based medicine and then could declare you mentally-unfit and drug or institutionalize you for wanting to choose another alternative, this would be a tragedy and an outrage.

> If a man does not keep pace with his companions, perhaps it is because he hears a different drummer. Let him step to the music which he hears, however measured or far away.
>
> ~ Walden, Henry David Thoreau, 1854

With a possible new and erroneous diagnosis of "attenuated psychosis syndrome" that could "stigmatize eccentric people," all kinds of individuals

---

[6] Link to the Rob Waters article: http://www.salon.com/2011/12/27/therapists_revolt_against_psychiatrys_bible.

with various, non-mainstream personal philosophies, beliefs or creeds could be targeted for pharmaceutical control or worse. For those of us who've had experiences outside the mainstream, who've had to look "elsewhere" for answers, healing and try to make sense of what has happened to us in a society which refuses to look at or acknowledge such experiences, we are a population at odds with much of society already. In a new DSM-V regulated world, if its framers, writers and revisors have their way, we could be even more at risk.

Waters' article ends with an allusion to the infiltration of psychiatric organizations by narcissists, referring to the "greatest minds" and the "biggest egos" as a battle within the ranks of the "301.81s" – the DSM-IV's numerical designation for narcissistic personality disorder. This is yet one more way that the clash of paradigms is manifesting between the insane, bizarre, "big brother" world that government and corporate narcissists would make for us and a healthy, clean and properly-stewarded world those of us with heart and conscience would create for ourselves and our descendents.

***

The fabrication of new personality disorders will almost certainly springboard to yet more prescriptions (more $$$ for pharmaceutical corporations – follow the money) for anti-psychotic drugs with side-effects such as weight gain, diabetes and disruptions to the body's metabolic processes. Various drugs work differently in different people. Anti-depressants, anti-psychotic medications can have serious side-effects that can worsen the very conditions they are prescribed to control. This can have deadly consequences in many instances, such as in senseless mass-shootings.

A firestorm of controversy erupted across the country in the wake of the December 2012 Sandy Hook school shooting in Newtown, Conneticutt over our second amendment constitutional right to bear arms, activating intense debate on both sides of this volatile issue as the president and Congress work hard to enact more stringent and unreasonable gun controls, despicably using this tragedy for their own gun-control agendas.

As the sobering reality that many of these mass shootings are reportedly done by individuals under the influence of prescription anti-psychotic medications is scrutinized, diagnoses and mandates to drug more people under the guise of made-up, fantasy mental disorders could be a recipe for more massacres. If people are bent on killing, they will find other means to accomplish it even if guns are taken away. Our only real defense against bad or disturbed people with guns, or other means of doing serious harm, are responsible people with guns – with caring hearts and consciences.

My heart is filled with sorrow over the Sandy Hook killings and the devasted hearts of the parents who lost small children. I consider myself a strongly non-violent pacifist. But surrendering our right to bear arms in the face of an encroaching fascist regime in the U.S. – as evidenced by attack after legislative attack on the constitutional protections of people against tyranny – is sheer stupidity. If we could appeal to the "humanity" of those in charge of our government, perhaps we might have a chance to turn things in a positive direction for us all. However, the evidence of serious government and corporate infiltration by narcissists and other psychopaths can be assessed by observing the types of already-enacted and proposed unconstitutional, or other corporate-lobbied legislation. This evidence suggests that we may have to find other ways to make our rights and needs known and addressed. Political narcissists and other psychopaths have no humanity to appeal to, other than the charade they play out at election time. The issue of violent crimes is about *people* and getting them *true* and *real* help – not specious mental disorder diagnoses and drugs that could make things worse. How people can be helped in ways that self-empower them needs to be addressed, not in managing and controlling them with drugs, or institionalizing them. And we have nothing to fear at all from a humane, educated, responsible *armed* civilian population in a world where people see the value of working together and caring for each other.

Defining "Mental Health"

So how do we, ourselves, determine if we are "sane" in a meaningful way? We have an ability to self-reflect in a way grounded in reality. We have the facility to look at the facts of things around us and of our interactions with others. We are able to separate our beliefs, opinions and judgments about people, events and situations from the reality of the facts themselves. We have the capacity to recognize both our faults and our good qualities and not overindulge in fixation about either. We have the emotional depth to empathize with others, to vicariously feel what they feel, to understand and respond appropriately from that true empathy. We have the ability to anchor ourselves in the present, distinguishing what is happening in the present from what has happened in the past. We can differentiate the people we are interacting with in our present from how people acted in our past. We understand that the past can have an impact, that we can react without thinking from past hurts, but we return to an understanding of the separation of past from present in people, events and situations.

We can ask if what we have to say is true, necessary or kind. If what we wish to communicate meets at least two of these criteria, it needs saying. Through empathy, we understand when and how to interact with others, what to say at various moments. We understand the timing and placement of our communication – though emergency circumstances can make saying certain things necessary out of a situation's urgency. But in our current world, with all the emotions that simmer and move through us, both the pleasant and the dreaded, there is a need at times to define what true emergency is. Emergency is rooted in what is happening around us externally, like heading for a lifeboat on a sinking ship. While the pressure of emotions can feel like an emergency for many of us, if external conditions are not dictating "emergency" then it can be wise at such times to pause, breathe, check within and calm ourselves before proceeding with any words or action.

In our current chaotic world, we can see just how much belief, opinion and judgment spin around and around and are generated, manipulated, exploited and abused by those in power. Belief, opinion and judgment are subjective, but they are treated as objective data by many people today. This is encouraged by the controlled media. Those in the grip of such subjective thoughts and emotions, treated as real and objective truths, are very easy to manipulate. Many people take on reflected narcissistic traits (not necessarily a true disorder) as a survival strategy in today's world. This is how the rise to power of people with true personality disorders affects those who must then try to somehow survive under their control in a society with political "leaders" that look more and more crazy to the rest of us.

As you read the next chapter detailing the problematic assaults on our liberties and basic human rights, understanding something about the mindsets of the kinds of people who have seized control of our governments can help you to understand the increasingly crazy-making and insane behavior of our legislators and corporations. You will appreciate why we must find ways to preserve our rights to any number of freedoms that should not even be in question at all. You will begin to comprehend why the very people who took office with an oath to protect and defend our Constitution are chipping away at its very heart and soul. The very freedoms and Bill of Rights the Constitution was meant to protect and preserve have become obstacles to those with an agenda of absolute power, control and profit at any cost.

We the People are the ones paying that cost.

Entr'acte IV
Atlantis: The Devolution

In many ways, it was wonderful to be present at the inception of the Atlantean civilization. Other Lyran offshoots who had settled in other star systems visited at times, though they no longer called themselves Lyrans. They had become new civilizations in their own right. Many of them added touches of themselves to the still-developing Terran humanity. Early Atlantis became a place of so much being blended into our original human experiment. Genetics, ideas, sciences, philosophies. Not all of it was successful, but much of it was.

The Arcturians in particular had taken the original Lyran philosophies and deepened them into a form of spiritual science. I found myself very attracted to them and their world. I spent some in-between lifetimes among them when the

Terran lives I had chosen to live ended. It was like visiting a monastery for a long retreat, deep in spiritual practice, communion with Source Consciousness. It was an immersion in peace and rest, while maintaining an inner view of things transpiring elsewhere in the galaxy.

Sadly, Lyra's original beauty had been completely destroyed by the reptilian incursion. But as the ages unfolded, the inner vision turned in that direction showed signs of new life. The planet and her ecology was restoring herself, eon by passing eon.

Ages, eons... time. How do we speak of such things when "time" is so relative to each world and its expression? When time is a creation of every individual planet in concert with all the life it nurtures within its fold of space within the Great Consciousness? I can only relate it to time as it appears to pass in its linear fashion on Terra, knowing that it is only a construct that allows life to exist and to learn through contrast on this world. The inhabitants of each world shape the nature of its reality and its destiny. The living and conscious planets themselves do their best to support and nurture the process of the life that dwells upon them, unfolding in all its various twists and turns.

Terra is such a world, a world filled with so much life and beauty, in which I have invested so very much of my heart.

As time marched forward in Atlantis, things began to go wrong.

There is a mindset that goes with an inner directive of "protect." Does the creation of weapons somehow predestine their use in the manner in which they were designed? Does it vibrationally attract the situation in which their use would be "justified?" This is the only way I can describe how things progressed on Atlantis, the steps that led to its destruction.

It seems now, in hindsight, that when we as Lyrans experienced the reptilian invasion of our world, fear became part of our experience as a race. Indeed, this invasion and destruction had to have been a seed of contrast planted deep within our psyche as a species; a contrast to our beautiful way of life on Lyra that we did not realize we carried inside of us. In the aftermath, it was as if we somehow ingested a fraction of the reptilian consciousness that had destroyed us. Fear split a part of us away from ourselves that became unconscious – something we could not face in ourselves. Yet it somehow crept into our development on Terra. It wove its way from us into our human children. As the original Lyrans, our conscious philosophies would never have permitted us to move in such a direction, to take such a path. But when we began to incarnate within Terran human forms, a shift in our consciousness began. We were, more than ever, of this world. Yet our souls still carried the seed of ancient memory of what had happened before on Lyra. We did not want it to happen again, here.

The mandate to "protect" shifted over time to "control." Our vibration as a people was no longer purely of love and connection. Others in the lower dimensions of the galaxy of like-vibration to that which we were shifting into found us, including more reptilian conquerors.

There was war. We drove them off. But the toll it took upon the Atlantean civilization was terrible.

We rebuilt. More and more we were exploiting the natural resources of Terra, in a sense taking parts of her and alienating them from her. We built more weapons, stronger, better, more powerful.

We abandoned our origins of being able to accomplish through thought anything that any machine could do. We wanted our machines. They could function in ways under pressure that we as biological beings could not. The use of our expanded abilities began to atrophy. In time they were forgotten by most, except in the spiritual orders, where those who retained their abilities served Atlantis in the priesthoods. Spirituality became religion. Whether religion became a tool of statecraft, or statecraft became a tool of religion, was difficult to tell.

Chapter 13: Confronting Political, Societal and Cultural Demons

To start out with at least a fractional understanding of the probable scope of the issues facing humanity, I offer the following essay by the late Don Harkins[1]. As my comprehension of the full spectrum of forces at work on our world has increased, my appreciation for his words has deepened.

Slavery and the Eight Veils *This article was inspired by a conversation Don Harkins had with his father soon after Sept. 11, 2001. His father was really upset that Don did not buy into the terrorist nonsense and told Don that he believed he was more patriotic than Don was as he stood next to "ring-nosed" hippies at candlelight vigils in memory of those who perished in New York on that day. Don being an investigative reporter, on the other hand, noticed that the alleged perpetrators were named in the media immediately without any investigation. The following essay was Don's insight into why many of us are unable to communicate newly discovered truths to family and longtime friends.*

Reprinted from the *December 2001 Idaho Observer:*
by Don Harkins (1963 – 2009)

Over the last several years I have evolved and discarded several theories in an attempt to explain why it is that most people cannot see truth -- even when it smacks them in the face. Those of us who can see "the conspiracy" have participated in countless conversations amongst ourselves that address the frustration of most people's inability to comprehend the extremely well-documented arguments which we use to describe the process of our collective enslavement and exploitation. The most common

---

[1] Don Harkins, 1963 – 2009, was founder and editor-in-chief of the *Idaho Observer* in Spirit Lake, Idaho. His essay, found online: http://www.proliberty.com/observer/20091134.html. published in the *Idaho Observer* in December 2001, has been shared widely online, explaining why some people cannot begin to comprehend the darker, covert forces at work in our world. A webpage dedicated to Don Harkins by his widow, Ingri Cassel-Harkins, regarding the strange mycoplasmic illness that claimed his life: http://www.proliberty.com/observer/20090902.html.

explanation to be arrived at is that most people just "don't want to see" what is really going on.

Extremely evil men and women who make up the world's power-elite have cleverly cultivated a virtual pasture so grass green that few people seldom, if ever, bother to look up from where they are grazing long enough to notice the brightly colored tags stapled to their ears.

The same people who cannot see their enslavement for the pasture grass have a tendency to view as insane "conspiracy theorists" those of us who can see past the farm and into the parlor of his feudal lordship's castle.

Finally, I understand why.

It's not that those who don't see that their freedom is vanishing under the leadership of the power-elite "don't want to see it" -- they simply can't see what is happening to them because of the unpierced veils blocking their view.

All human endeavors are a filtration process. Sports is one of the best examples. We play specific sports until we get kicked off the playground. The professional athletes we pay big bucks to watch just never got kicked off the playground. Where millions of kids play little league each spring, they are filtered out until there are about 50 guys who go to the World Series in October.

Behind the first veil: There are over six billion people on the planet. Most of them live and die without having seriously contemplated anything other than what it takes to keep their lives together. Ninety percent of all humanity will live and die without having pierced the first veil.

The first veil: Ten percent of us will pierce the first veil and find the world of politics. We will vote, be active and have an opinion. Our opinions are shaped by the physical world around us. We have a tendency to accept that government officials, network media personalities and other "experts" are voices of authority. Ninety percent of the people in this group will live and die without having pierced the second veil.

The second veil: Ten percent of us will pierce the second veil to explore the world of history, the relationship between man and government and the meaning of self-government through constitutional and common law. Ninety percent of the people in this group will live and die without having pierced the third veil.

The third veil: Ten percent of us will pierce the third veil to find that the resources of the world, including people, are controlled by extremely wealthy and powerful families whose incorporated old world assets have, with modern extortion strategies, become the foundation upon which the world's economy is currently indebted. Ninety percent of the people in this group will live and die without having pierced the fourth veil.

The fourth veil: Ten percent of us will pierce the fourth veil to discover the Illuminati, Freemasonry and the other secret societies. These societies use symbols and perform ceremonies that perpetuate the generational transfers of arcane knowledge that is used to keep the ordinary people in political, economic and spiritual bondage to the oldest bloodlines on earth. Ninety percent of the people in this group will live and die without having pierced the fifth veil.

The fifth veil: Ten percent of us will pierce the fifth veil to learn that the secret societies are so far advanced technologically that time travel and interstellar communications have no boundaries and controlling the actions of people is what their members do as offhandedly as we tell our children when they must go to bed. Ninety percent of the people in this group will live and die without having pierced the sixth veil.

The sixth veil: Ten percent of us will pierce the sixth veil where the dragons and lizards and aliens we thought were the fictional monsters of childhood literature are real and are the controlling forces behind the secret societies. Ninety percent of the people in this group will live and die without piercing the seventh veil.

The seventh veil: I do not know what is behind the seventh veil. I think it is where your soul is evolved to the point you can exist on earth and be the man Ghandi was, or the woman Peace Pilgrim was - people so enlightened they brighten the world around them no matter what.

225

The eighth veil? Piercing the eighth veil probably reveals God and the pure energy that is the life force in all living things - which are, I think, one and the same.

If my math is accurate, there are only about 60,000 people on the planet who have pierced the sixth veil. The irony here is too incredible: Those who are stuck behind veils one through five have little choice but to view the people who have pierced the veils beyond them as insane. With each veil pierced, exponentially shrinking numbers of increasingly enlightened people are deemed insane by exponentially increasing masses of decreasingly enlightened people.

Adding to the irony, the harder a "sixth or better veiler" tries to explain what he is able to see to those who can't, the more insane he appears to them.

Our enemy, the state
Behind the first two veils we find the great majority of people on the planet. They are tools of the state: Second veilers are the gullible voters whose ignorance justifies the actions of politicians who send first veilers off to die in foreign lands as cannon fodder -- their combined stations in life are to believe that the self-serving machinations of the power-elite are matters of national security worth dying for.

Third, fourth, fifth and sixth veilers are of increasing liability to the state because of their decreasing ability to be used as tools to consolidate the power and wealth of the many into the hands of the power-elite. It is common for these people to sacrifice more of their relationships with friends and family, their professional careers and personal freedom with each veil they pierce.

Albert Jay Nock (1870-1945), author of "Our Enemy, the State" (1935), explained what happens to those who find the seventh and eighth veils: "What was the best that the state could find to do with an actual Socrates and an actual Jesus when it had them? Merely to poison one and crucify the other, for no reason but that they were too intolerably embarrassing to be allowed to live any longer."

Conclusions
Now we know that it's not that our countrymen are so committed to their lives that "they don't want to see" the

mechanisms of their enslavement and exploitation. They simply "can't see" it as surely as I cannot see what's on the other side of a closed curtain.

The purpose of this essay is threefold: 1. To help the handful of people in the latter veils to understand why the masses have little choice but to interpret their clarity as insanity; 2. To help people behind the first two veils understand that living, breathing and thinking are just the beginning, and; 3. Show people that the greatest adventure of our life is behind the next veil because that is just one less veil between ourselves and God.

~ Reprinted with permission from Don Harkins' widow, Ingri Cassel-Harkins

There are layers or levels to working through the information in this book and in this chapter. This is a long chapter; the reader may want to take it in parts, a sub-section or two at a time. As we come into awareness of how we've been lied to and what has been and is being done to us, you may feel very human fear, anger and grief. Feeling these emotions is a natural reaction, and a first step on the path to greater awareness.

When we have fully honored our human feelings, forgiveness becomes a necessary bridge to personal peace. Remember that forgiveness does not eliminate the necessity of holding criminals accounable for their crimes, but it does help to ensure that actions taken will be done from a cooler and more objective space within us. In the expansiveness of peace, we move beyond fear, anger and grief, grasping the understanding that the essence of who we are is indestructible and forgiveness is within our purview.

Finally, it becomes possible to take flight in a desire to see our lives and our world from an even higher perspective, from a cosmic perspective, understanding that all is One, and seeking out the ways in which our world unfolds and what our individual roles are in that unfolding.

All these layers are woven together. We move around and between them because we still live here on Earth, in a human body, and that human body is still subject to having to deal with the day-to-day ways in which much of what I will share in this chapter affects our lives. We can experience sublime moments of spiritual insight – then, in the next moment, be angry again about injustice, lies, and abuses that rack our world, even when a part of us knows that at the highest level, events may be proceeding exactly as they are meant to. This is certainly true for me.

***

227

My earliest confrontations with the way things play out on this planet were pretty grim. At around age seventeen, it was clear to me that the rape of the planet's capital, non-renewable resources would likely continue until this world could be rendered uninhabitable; and the march of years from then to now has not proven me wrong. Corporations have jockeyed for and won much of the political power to give them freer and freer rein to do whatever they please. Yet I had no idea in my youth just how deep the corruption ran. Once my military experiences came to light, the facts I had to face became more diabolical and more malevolent to try and cope with.

Resolute as I was for so many years to keep my experiences to myself, feeling that there were enough people out there publicly keeping the UFO issue current and in discussion, I privately kept up as much as I could with UFO/ET current events. I knew this was a real phenomenon. I was angry and frustrated that so many years were marching by and still no announcement by Dan Rather on the evening news that extraterrestrials were indeed real and our government had in its possession extraterrestrial technology that was going to change our world for the better.

Time continued to pass; Dan Rather retired. The political-societal media machine creaked and clanked on. However, within it were warning flags of trouble. What passed for "news" was shifting. From the calmly – albeit often gravely – stated evening news stories from the Walter Cronkite and Dan Rather years, more emotionalism, sensationalism and a creeping extremism began to appear in news reporting. Looking back now, it seemed like the first wave of rising winds that warn of a coming hurricane.

I felt disgusted. Feeling like a person out of place and time had become a chronic condition by then. As much as I participated in my communities and with friends, there was still the feeling of standing on the outside looking in. Some of my closest friends were there for me to discuss these issues with, and I'm deeply grateful to them for that. But still, mostly, I felt I had to keep quiet, caught between the military-black ops "devils" from whom I feared repercussions, and the "deep blue sea" of a mainstream public fed too many years on the pablum of propaganda to see the socio-political forest for the individual symptomatic trees. Mainstream, out-in-the-open trees of politics, damage to the environment and shifting ecomomies. Trees of denial and ridicule of anything that stood outside the accepted reality paradigm. Trees of government, military and corporate institutions that were determined to keep control of the flow of information for their own survival and accumulation of power.

More whistleblowers began to step forward with incredible stories to share. Many dedicated UFO researchers kept the subject alive and well. Instead of the UFO phenomenon fading, the trickle of whistleblowers into the public arena began to increase.

To the mainstream public, these people looked like crackpots. The campaign of denial and ridicule instituted by the factions within the government-military-corporate complex, that I first heard outlined by John Lear in 1989 in George Knapp's[2] *UFOs: The Best Evidence*, was still working quite well. However, the shifting political landscape of the U.S.A. was catalyzing change in how such information was regarded that would become more pronounced over time.

The growing number of whistleblowers emerging seemed a symptom of this fomenting change in our world. There was a change in how various political and military institutions were regarded; the ones that seemed to hold the reins on how the world was run. From the tumultuous 1960s / Vietnam War era onwards, people were less-accepting of government propaganda and more questioning of the status quo. Lobbying and corporate money flowing into the U.S. political process were more apparent, and the results were increasingly problematic for the well-being of ordinary citizens. Just who was our government working for? The citizens who elected them to office, or the corporations that poured on campaign money and back room bonuses to manipulate the law to suit their own ends?

Some of the worst pieces of legislation, in my opinion, were the legalized encroachments that designated corporations as "persons," endowing them with the same rights as individual citizens. This set up our society in an unending struggle where the rights of individuals will always be in conflict with the rights of the "person-corporation." Corporations have have entirely different, wealth-driven agendas quite clearly not in the best interest of the billions of common individuals who make up the citizenry of the U.S.A. and the world. Over and over again corporations have shown themselves to exploit both natural resources and people with little to no regard for either. Profit is their sole agenda. And when their money buys the best lawyers and cuts secret backroom deals, the common people of this world can often come up on the losing end.

Health Care or Human Herd Management?

Cover-ups extend far beyond the UFO subject. As I've watched the unfolding of current events throughout my life, I could tell that change was occurring on many fronts. UFOs and extraterrestrials aside, I watched a variety of other areas of personal interest. I had been involved in communities for many years that educated themselves about the healthiest lifestyles, from spiritual practices to exercise, food, and the ecosystem we all live in. Supporting healthy practices for the environment was a natural extension of healthy personal living. I find it significant that in recent years, the focus in new age circles, spiritual and personal growth-oriented organizations and individuals have increasingly

---

[2] Since 1995, George Knapp has been the chief reporter on Channel 8's I-Team investigative unit. In that capacity, he has earned two Edward R. Murrow awards along with other honors. His *Street Talk* commentaries have captured five Emmy Awards. Seven times, he has won the Mark Twain Award for best news writing from the Associated Press. And in 1990, his series *UFOs: The Best Evidence* was selected by United Press International as best in the nation for Individual Achievement by a Journalist. It was later compiled into a documentary film, see: http://www.ufoevidence.org/researchers/detail88.htm.

begun looking at things that once would have smacked of conspiracy theory to them. For people with a high awareness of the health benefits of clean, organic food and healthy supplementation, encroachments on our rights to continued access to such items began to capture their attention. Related to this is watching out for the rights of small family farms to continue growing organic and local produce, free of harassment from huge agri-corporations like Monsanto. Growing our own gardens is also a right that apparently needs vigilance and protection. On personal health fronts, dangers of vaccines, the avian flu, and more recently the swine flu/H1N1 vaccine and it's horrific side-effects alerted people to begin to begin scrutinizing the pharmaceutical corporations much more closely as well as the medical profession that dispenses medications and vaccines. Vaccines have long been implicated in creating autism in children.[3]

And since the onset of severe economic problems in the U.S., affecting the majority of the population, people on all levels have begun to ask "why?" Wall Street bailouts granted by the current administration have angered people struggling to make ends meet. Hit people in their pocketbooks, and they start paying attention. There is a lot more willingness to look for answers underneath surface of the mainstream media's usual rationalizations and spin.

What the hell has happened to this country? Here is how I've observed it.

In the late 1980s in Las Vegas, NV, there were raids by agents of the Food and Drug Administration (FDA) on health food stores, seizing an herbal supplement, chaparral. Citizens organized about this and I attended some of the meetings. This was of great concern to us, that somehow we were not allowed the right to take a supplement that we educated ourselves about and deemed a benefit to us. Chaparral was said to cure cancer. It was this claim that caused it to be pulled from store shelves by the FDA. This was quite an education for me, alerting me that something was wrong in our government – and this was years before my first hypnosis session plunged me into the dark world of conspiracy "theory."

I had read a magazine article around that same time; it stated that Americans over the past year had spent over $8 million dollars out of their own pockets for alternative health care – care not covered by health insurance. Back then, $8 million was a very significant amount. And how did corporate America respond? In any way a free enterprise system should – by competing fairly with better preventative health care and better, safer pharmaceuticals? No.

I look back now and realize that, for me, reading that article seemed the point at which I began to see more and more corporate interference in our political processes. Attempts to restrict and limit our choices with regard to vitamins, supplements and alternative health care are ongoing to this day.

---

[3] The Vaccine Liberation Organization has an excellent website online providing books, information from scientific studies and activist campaigns to legal help about avoiding vaccines; especially pertinent for parents of small children who could be forced to have their children vaccinated or have them taken away. There are also links for taking part in activism about the dangers of vaccines maintained by Indri Cassel: http://www.vaclib.org/index.htm.

You can take everything I just wrote above and apply it also to our rights to grow organic food for ourselves or buy it from organic or small local farmers, or even maintain supplies of heirloom seeds – original and unaltered in any way and free of toxic chemicals.

It has become increasingly clear that pharmaceutical corporations, whose regular drug pushers are the "traditional" allopathic medical profession, will do their utmost through the national legislative process to try and limit or restrict our health care choices to what they want to sell us.

The same is true for huge agribusiness. Through meddling in our hallowed congressional halls they are trying to make heirloom or organic seeds illegal to even possess on grounds that they will contaminate their genetically-modified crops – which a significant amount of the population want no part of eating. Corporations like Monsanto would like to restrict our food choices exclusively to what they offer – they don't want to lose money on the patented seeds they've spent tremendous amounts of money developing. How dare people not want to eat their "frankenfoods!" So they lobby to make it illegal to grow our own food and by trying to manipulate food production regulations in such a way that it could put smaller organic and local family farms out of business.

When independent studies present their results on pharmaceuticals and of food either contaminated with pesticides, genetically modified or both – we find that, as human beings, we appear to be under assault. Not in such a way that kills us quickly. Efficient parasites – in this case, corporations – don't kill quickly. They have learned to take "just enough," as killing their hosts too quickly can exterminate themselves as well. They negatively affect the health of the lifeform they are feeding on, but that lifeform can continue to function at least for a while, though at increasingly diminished capacities over time.

Corporations, with very few exceptions, are parasitic on humanity. They won't get wealthy from a lot of dead people. But as long as we can continue working for wages and paying them for their tainted products, they can reap their wealth. If they are allowed to restrict our choices to only what they have to offer, they will do just that.

They will do it in ways that undermine our health on multiple levels and diminish our well-being. When we feel less-than-well, or truly ill from substandard food, the pharmaceutical industry waves their designer drugs before our eyes to "fix" the problems created by tainted food. It seems that while we no longer have truly good health as a people, we are able to struggle along for the most part, continuing to work our jobs, only to fork over hard-earned cash for more tainted food and drugs that perpetuate the cycle of less-than-optimal health. If people educate themselves about these food and drug traps and reject them, then corporate pressure on our political process intensifies to restrict and limit our food and health choices even more.

Human bodies respond to many food additives and toxins by packing on the pounds, as fat is one way our bodies take toxins out of the way of our

231

biological processes so they can do the least harm. Everyone who has tried and tried to lose weight, trying many different approaches, can attest to all the high-priced diet gimmicks out there that promise to help people lose weight. Almost none of them work, either because they are chemically-based and not healthy to begin with and/or because we are still living in a toxic environment and consuming the problematic foods that are responsible for the weight problems in the first place.

In recent decades we have had to become hypervigilant as a society. Multitudes of increasingly-educated consumers-turned-political-activists have organized through the internet. They pounce upon every piece of offensive legislation introduced in Congress that threatens the health of ourselves and our ecosystem. They work to beat back assaults on our most basic freedoms to *choose* for ourselves. They fight to protect our freedoms to think and speak for ourselves, to eat and care for our own health as we see fit, to protect Earth's environment, her wildlife, and much more.

Fight, fight, fight. If you care about all of this, you can find your email inbox filled with activist emails poised to pounce on scores of freedom-limiting legislation. Read between the lines of "fight, fight, fight," see the polarization. The opposing opposites. "Us" against the latest and most threatening version of "them." And that fight-energy creates yet more problems. We risk becoming warped and exhausted by the stress of living in a world gone so far and away wrong – politically, socially, economically and environmentally. "Fight" is a buzzword of politics. Political parties fight each other for supremacy. We fight to hang onto our rights to life, liberty and pursuit of happiness as we see fit, when such "inalienable" rights are supposed to be guaranteed us by our Constitution.

Fight, fight, fight. Stress. Exhaustion. Succumbing. Fight energy gets a downgrade to resentment. And according to alternative holistic practitioners, stress and resentment are some of the key emotional elements in the creation of cancer, very likely in conjunction with tainted food and water.

It's become very clear that cancer treatment has become a huge industry in this country. With that seizure of chaparral back in the late 1980s to the suppression of all kinds of alternative breakthroughs in treatments of cancer – without toxic radiation or chemotherapy – one has to begin questioning just what is going on. Billions of donated-dollars pour into "cure-for-cancer" research, by well-meaning people, many in the grip of bereavement at losing someone to cancer. The billion-dollar cancer-cure research machine has quite likely become counter-productive to ever actually finding a cure for cancer. If a drug that unequivocally cured all cancer was ever found, a whole billion-dollar industry would collapse. Would those who are profiting from all that revenue ever permit that? Hardly. Those in charge, lurking in the shadows, will never allow any cancer cure found to see the light of day, just as they make sure that alternative treatments for cancer are ridiculed, marginalized and suppressed – or outright destroyed.

I'm sure many people could convince themselves that this is just the worst kind of opportunistic capitalism run amok; that there is no real design or nefarious purpose to all of this. It's just evil corporations manipulating the system, trying to make billions, with no heart or conscience as to who they hurt or kill. And that is certainly bad enough.

But you can't get a full picture of what's going on unless you stand back far enough, looking at the whole tapestry and all its various parts. Observing how they fit together and how they have all traveled through the years, and where they are heading. And of course, follow the money.

When you look at the parts of the human body – largely the human brain – that seem to be targeted with chemical additives in foods, drinking water and various pharmaceuticals, an even deeper, darker purpose lurks in the shadows. This purpose is obscured through a variety of smoke and mirror tricks trying to convince people that certain drugs are good for them, or that various food and water additives or artificial sweeteners are harmless. The crux of the design of food, water and sweetener toxins, and certain pharmaceuticals, may be an attack upon human consciousness itself. Specifically, attacking the human ability to actualize the next evolutionary leap in conscious awareness.

And what do you know? "Coincidentally," all this is taking place at a time in human history and evolution when a huge consciousness shift seems underway in the whole human collective.

The human brain – our neurological, glandular control unit – seems the most targeted area of the body by most food and water additives, and drugs or drug side effects. The rise of elderly people diagnosed with Alzheimer's can be linked to food and water additives, according to other independent studies, revealing that certain excitotoxins cause an accumulation of metals, such as aluminum, in the brain. The accumulation of aluminum in the brain is implicated in Alzheimer's. This disease is on an alarming rise, striking people at much earlier ages – before age 65 – than in previous decades. In addition, more metal particulates get into our food and water supply through chemtrails, also called aerosol spraying. Fluoride, added to most of our water supplies across the U.S., has been shown to interact with aluminum in the body allowing it to cross the blood-brain barrier – which it could not do without fluoride, as was found in a 1998 study administering fluoride to lab rats by Julie A. Varner and her co-workers at the State University of New York at Binghamton. In one of his articles *Study Proves: This Everyday Drink Lowers Your IQ*, Dr. Joseph Mercola (www.mercola.com) cites 24 studies, including the Varner study, linking fluoride to lower IQ and neurological impairment. Add this data to the information in the next section on chemtrails, and we have to wonder just how close – and how deliberate – the connections really are, with implications that some powerful groups operating covertly in this world have a specific agenda to actually create ill health in the general population. Why? Read on, and do some of your own research, and draw your own conclusions.

The bottom line here is that the more blatant and obvious that human herd management becomes, it ceases to pass for "health care." And people interested enough in truly caring for their health get ultimately get wise and find ways to circumvent such "management." And then they educate others.

A Brief but Relevant Detour: Chemtrails

I often wonder about a possible connection between the High-frequency Active Auroral Research Program, (HAARP) and chemtrails and all the substances in our food and water supply causing an accumulation of metal particulates in the human brain. Lots of questions come to mind.

Does the grid-like layout of chemtrails in our skies have any relation to the grid-like layout of the HAARP array? When the HAARP array is energized, is its range extended by the almost microscopic metal particles in chemtrails to regions on our planet overlaid with chemtrails? If so, why and for what purpose? Is the chemtrail spraying of metal particulates one more way to taint our crops, causing people to ingest more metals – could this be related in any way to the accumulation of metals in the human brain? I have to wonder if, when the HAARP array is active, does it somehow affect the metal particulates in human brains through electromagnetic fields? Does the fact that chemtrails drop a variety of metal particulates that get into our food and water supply also have a connection to HAARP, or to some covert attack on expanding human consciousness through damaging the pineal gland?

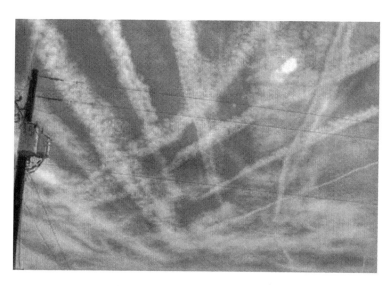

Above, a grid-like chemtrail pattern in the sky.

The HAARP array.
Photos used with permission from the Carnicom Institute[4], dedicated to the study of chemtrails and their effects. (http://carnicominstitute.org)

To date, I have no real, hard data on any of these possibilities, nor have I had time to research them in depth, but I do feel wary about possible connections. The data may be out there, intensely scrutinized, studied and theorized by other researchers in the chemtrails field, but it has not been my primary area of focus. However, I do give this issue at least a portion of my peripheral attention. Because of the food and water toxins issue to which chemtrails may be related, I think it pays to stay aware and cautious. Enough to keep myself drinking the cleanest water possible, and fixing a good deal of my food – local and/or organic – from scratch, so, as much as possible, I know what I'm consuming.

For those who have not been exposed to the term "chemtrails," (and I hope this book is not just preaching to the choir) chemtrails are etched in our skies by specially-outfitted aircraft that spray some kind of unknown aerosol trails across the blue overhead; very often in grid-like designs. No one is positive of the complete content or full purpose of this spraying though much independent research is being done. No official admission or explanation of chemtrails has been forthcoming and so it's not possible to know for certain their chemical content. Different than normal jet contrails, which dissipate quickly once the jet has passed, these chemtrails leave crisscrossed streaks across the entire sky that, several hours after being sprayed, puff out, spreading into an ugly milky haze across otherwise beautiful blue skies. Tests of ground and water under heavily sprayed areas reveals particulates of barium, aluminum and other substances. Chemtrails have been implicated in a parasitic disease called Morgellons[5], and

---

[4] The Carnicom Institute, founded by Clifford Carnicom, is a non-profit educational and research organization brought into being to serve the public welfare. The institute is extensively active in conducting scientific research and public education relating to the consequences of chemtrails implicated in geoengineering and bioengineering. Website: http://www.carnicominstitute.org/. The Carnicom Institute is one of many such organizations researching chemtrails and their effects on the environment and humanity.

[5] Definition of Morgellons from the Center for Disease Control and Prevention (CDC): "Morgellons is an unexplained and debilitating condition that has emerged as a public health concern. Recently, the CDC

are also suspect in other public health issues. Symptoms of Morgellons can be so severe as to cause suicidal thoughts in the sufferers as an escape from the torment of skin-crawling, itching and stinging sensations.

In 2001, a legislative measure to stop chemtrail spraying was introduced by Ohio Congressman Dennis Kucinich (HR 2977, the Space Preservation Act of 2001)[6]. In it are mentioned a list of "exotic" weapons including chemtrails:

> High altitude extremely low frequency (ELF) or ultra low frequency (ULF) energy radiation weapons systems; land, sea or space-based systems using radiation, electromagnetic, psychotronic, sonic, laser, or other energies directed at individual persons or targeted populations for the purpose of information war, mood management, or mind control of such persons or population; expelling chemical or biological agents in the vicinity of a person; chemtrails; plasma, electromagnetic, sonic, or ultrasonic weapons; laser weapons systems; strategic, theater, tactical, or extraterrestrial weapons; and chemical, biological, environmental, climate, or tectonic weapons.

> The term 'exotic weapons systems' includes weapons designed to damage space or natural ecosystems (such as the ionosphere and upper atmosphere) or climate, weather, and tectonic systems with the purpose of inducing damage or destruction upon a target population or region on earth or in space.

There are many scary terms in this document such as "psychotronic," "mood management" and "mind control," among others. If a U.S. Congressman drafted such a document, it's reasonable to assume he had done some research and/or had some well-founded idea that such technology does in fact exist. Dennis Kucinich is a well-known champion of the common people as well as an outspoken advocate of peace. Was he attempting to safeguard the public against misuse of exotic technology? He raises other technological specters in the language of this document; technologies that can change weather or climate, and tectonic weapons that can affect the ground beneath our feet through earthquakes or volcanoes.

has received an increased number of inquiries from the public, health care providers, public health officials, Congress, and the media regarding this condition. Persons who suffer from this condition report a range of cutaneous symptoms including crawling, biting and stinging sensations; granules, threads or black speck-like materials on or beneath the skin; and/or lesions (e.g., rashes or sores) and some sufferers also report systemic manifestations such as fatigue, mental confusion, short term memory loss, joint pain, and changes in vision. Moreover, some who suffer from this condition appear to have substantial morbidity and social dysfunction, which can include decreased work productivity or job loss, total disability, familial estrangement, divorce, loss of child custody, home abandonment, and suicidal ideation."

[6] Kucinich's *H.R. 2977 – Space Preservation Act of 2001* from October 2001 appears on this government website with the full text here: http://www.govtrack.us/congress/bills/107/hr2977/text#.

There is a great deal of information available online that mentions scalar[7] energy and scalar weaponry that could induce earthquakes or hurricanes. Scalar energy is also known as over-unity or zero-point energy. Basically, weaponized scalar energy devices utilize longitudinal waves (LW) that are directed using at least two devices to focus the tremendous energy potential that exists in the vacuum of space to a particular point on the surface of the Earth. Essentially, this energy is transferred from another dimension – the fourth; the dimension of time – that occupies the same space as our own but at a higher vibrational frequency. The transfer of energy is focused through the interplay of the two focusing devices (such as HAARP in interplay with a chemtrail aerosol grid over a particular area) in a way similar to the way sunlight can be focused through a magnifying glass to start a fire.

This is the same energy that, properly harnessed, is used as the power source for extraterrestrial craft, allowing them to perform feats of flying that break our Newtonian laws of physics. It is the same energy that, sanely and humanely utilized, could power the entire human civilization on this planet. No more nuclear power plants; no more oil, gas or coal need ever be extracted from the Earth or burned as fuel, thereby ending forever these devastating forms of environmental destruction. Costs of producing and transporting goods and services would drop dramatically. World poverty and hunger could come to an end. We would essentially enter a new age on Earth, the age of free energy. The only people with a great deal to lose from a new age of free energy are those making billions from dirty and damaging energy sources and their associates in other industries.

Therein lies one of the huge remaining reasons for UFO secrecy – UFO secrecy is free energy secrecy. Hard on the heels of UFO and extraterrestrial disclosure will come knowledge of the type of energy that ET civilizations use and the demand for such energy – and an end to oil, gas, coal and nuclear power – will be immediate. Once out of the bottle, there will be no way for the free energy genie to ever be put back in. With free energy knowledge will also come the human awareness that the Earth and her people have been needlessly exploited for many decades, with direct and indirect loss of lives numbering in the billions; with environmental damage that will take generations to reverse – if it can be reversed at all. While there are justifiable military reasons for secrecy, National Security Act of 1947 secrecy has given power-mongers many organizations in which to hide, strengthening and refining their power over this planet and its people. Originally put in place "FOR REASONS OF NATIONAL SECURITY," such secrecy has almost utterly destroyed the "national security" of the people it is supposed to be protecting.

From the vast array of subjects that UFO secrecy touches upon and from what other areas of leaked information I have studied in more detail, I am quite

---

[7] A basic study of scalar energy can be found in the online material of retired Lieutenant Colonel Thomas E. Bearden, PhD, director of the Association of Distinguished American Scientists. Bearden's studies include theoretical concepts in the active study of scalar electromagnetics, advanced electrodynamics, unified field theory, free energy systems, healing and more. His websites: http://www.cheniere.org/index.html and http://www.prahlad.org/pub/bearden/index.htm.

sure that such scalar weapon technologies could indeed exist. Unfortunately, I also must concede that there are powerful agencies out there that are definitely capable of covertly abusing such technologies for their own profit or gain, with no regard for human life or environmental harm. Especially if it appears to be a natural disaster and can't be tracked back to them. It's important to understand and consider the possibilities and probabilities of the use of such exotic technologies. If one looks at each of the issues mentioned in this chapter separately they are easy to dismiss, especially for those of us that are enlightened and caring individuals. Taken all together as part of a larger tapestry of all kinds of apparent assaults on humanity and the environment is the only way to really fully comprehend that some force is bent on controlling us all, even wiping out large numbers of us. This is being carried out as covertly as possible by psychopathic individuals incapable of compassion or empathy. Such psychopaths think that everyone else exists to be used, abused or exterminated as they deem fit. If you just write all of this off to "conspiracy theory" without taking the trouble to truly look into these issues, you are at risk. Education and continually evolving information being revealed empowers you to make the choices in your daily life to enhance, not harm, your health and well-being.

There is a documentary video available on chemtrails for viewing online called *What in the World are They Spraying?*[8] Its sequel, *Why in the World are They Spraying?* has just become available to view online as well. There are other films on this topic available via an internet search on YouTube – a good one to watch that doesn't really mention chemtrails by such a name, but still reveals the climatic and environmental implications of aerosol spraying is a British Broadcasting Corporation (BBC) documentary called *Global Dimming*. With local TV stories on chemtrails beginning to creep into the evening news, this phenomenon is getting more and more widespread attention, even in our controlled mainstream media.

Attacks on the Expansion of Human Awareness

Back to personal and public health. Let's look at some of the evidence that has appeared in more recent years damning a common additive to water; fluoride. If you use a fluoride toothpaste, on the tube you will see a warning on the label like this one:

> Keep out of reach of children. If more than used for brushing is accidentally swallowed, get medical help or contact a poison control center right away.

This is because fluoride is a neurological poison when ingested, right up there with arsenic and lead. Yet we were sold on the idea years ago that adding fluoride to our drinking water would improve our dental health, helping us to

---

[8] The film, *What in the World Are They Spraying?* was created and co-produced by Michael J. Murphy, journalist and political activist. The film explores the chemtrail phenomenon and all independent research into this phenomenon. This group recently completed a new, companion film to the first; Why in the World are They Spraying?. Both films can be seen for free online on YouTube, however, purchasing the film will help this research continue. Website: http://www.whatintheworldaretheyspraying.info.

get fewer cavities. We were even prescribed fluoride drops to give to our babies if we lived in an area where the water was not fluoridated. Surely the Food and Drug Administration (FDA) would not approve something for human consumption that was dangerous, would they? In our innocence and trust of years past and our faith in a government entity like the FDA, we accepted the fluoridation of our public water supplies. Fluoride is still added to water supplies in many areas of the U.S.A. We had no idea that we might be giving our children some kind of slow poison, or something that would lower their IQ, affecting their ability to learn, and/or create hyperactivity, a problem that has been a widespread diagnosis in children over the last few decades, complete with a pharmaceutical prescription "fix" – ritalin.[9]

In addition to being a neurotoxin, the most recent effects of fluoride now cite that its effect over time is the calcification of the pineal gland in our brains. Melotonin, responsible for us getting a good night's sleep is one of the substances manufactured in the pineal gland. Many people suffer from a variety of sleep problems and disorders today.

If we look at the research implicating the interaction of fluoride with aluminum along with chemtrails/aerosol spraying and a phenomenon called "electromagnetic sensitivity[10]," caused by accumulation of metals causing heavy metal toxicity in human bodies, this connection raises even more suspicion about the consequences to public health from chemtrail fallout. Toxic metals saturating our water sources and farm fields are creating not only diseases of dementia from aluminum accumulating in our brains, but also possible electromagnetic manipulation of people's minds, moods and health through directed electromagnetics from HAARP and chemtrails.

Recent discoveries show that Dimethyltryptamine (DMT), called "the spirit molecule," is also made by the pineal gland and seems to be linked to experiences of a spiritual nature in human beings. If DMT is somehow linked to spiritual experiences and the expansion of human consciousness, are we somehow being disabled from accessing a part of ourselves that we were uniquely designed to be able to activate for our own spiritual evolution? If we are being disabled in this way, then why?

When we also consider the vibration of the emotion of fear and its related emotional states of anger and stress along with their effects on human biology, on human DNA codes[11], we must begin to question a media machine that,

---

[9] See Vigilant Citizen's well-referenced website article, *Dumbing Down Society Part 1: Foods, Beverages and Meds*. This article cites the studies that point to the real dangers of many substances that are now added to food, water and drugs. http://vigilantcitizen.com/?p=4051 and http://www.holisticmed.com/fluoride/.

[10] Electromagnetic Health, and organization online has listed quotes from various doctors and researchers at this link: http://electromagnetichealth.org/quotes-from-experts/ and an Electromagnetic Sensitivity Primer with hundreds of scientific references for physicians on biological effects of electromagnetic fields on human health can be purchased at this link for a small fee: http://electromagnetichealth.org/electromagnetic-health-blog/electrosensitivity-primer/. Their primary area of concern is electromagnetic fields and their detrimental effects on human health.

[11] See article, DNA Report by Gregg Braden, in which he cites three experiments that were done showing the effects, including non-locality, of emotions on DNA. Link: http://www.bibliotecapleyades.net/mistic/esp_greggbraden_11.htm.

through news and entertainment, dishes up tons of high adrenalin intensity and fear imagery. When we consider all of the above, together with the combined effects of food/water additives and pharmaceuticals, including vaccines which commonly contain thimerosal, a mercury (read: "poison") preservative, it begins to look very bad indeed for those government agencies that are supposed to be looking out for the welfare of the public. Many of us paying attention realize that the FDA has become susceptible to payoffs from pharmaceutical corporations and big agribusinesses. It begins to strain credulity that all of this could have transpired solely out of woefully misguided accident. It does look as though there is an agenda playing out in which humanity is being controlled and managed in some way, especially to limit the expansion of human awareness into extra-dimensional realms.

Why, indeed. Because the expansion of human awareness into extra-dimensional realms will also be an expansion of personal and collective human freedom that will not be able to be controlled or contained by the various elite power organizations on this world. Powerful groups that hide behind the governmental, military or corporate structures on this planet have deemed themselves to be humanity's handlers and controllers. They have enjoyed lives of privilege that they have created for themselves through Machiavellian statecraft and control of populations, resources and information for a very long time, possibly for thousands of years.

The expansion of human extra-dimensional awareness signals "game over" for such handlers and controllers. When humanity evolves to a full understanding of their individual and collective place in the grand design of the Conscious Living Universe, including a full comprehension of what quantum science's "observer effect" truly means, we will become the masters of how to create and shape the world we live in not just with our hands and imaginations, but with the directed energy of our consciousness itself.

Secrecy: The Real Danger to Our Freedom

[There exists]... a shadowy Government with its own Air Force, its own Navy, its own fund-raising mechanism, and the ability to pursue its own ideas of the national interest, free from all checks and balances, and free from the law itself.

~ Senator Daniel K. Inouye, Hawaii[12]

So, are government whistleblowers nothing but a lot of kooks with crazy stories?

[12] Senator Daniel K. Inouye, Democrat, made this statement in May of 1987 when he served as Chairman of the Iran-Contra Committee, investigating the Iran-Contra affair. It was revealed that senior government officials had operated covertly, using deception and exhibiting disdain for the law; the U.S. had contradicting foreign policies – one public and one secret; and there were serious flaws in the policy-making mechanism of the U.S. government, and more. See website: http://www.brown.edu/Research/Understanding_the_Iran_Contra_Affair/h-themajorityreport.php.

No. Most whom I know personally, or know of, are people with little to nothing to gain and a great deal to lose by coming forward with what they know. Ex-career military members risk their retirement pensions and much more, if they or their families were threatened in any way in relation to keeping secrets. Many of these people are highly decorated. Retired Major George Filer stated, while giving his testimony for the Disclosure Project, that he was considered competent to carry or work with nuclear weapons while in the military, but not competent if he reports seeing UFOs. The ridiculous incongruity of this should be clear.

Our astronauts in the NASA space program are thought of as our very brightest and best. They are thought of as American heroes. Do American heroes keep secrets from U.S. citizens, especially if it becomes clear such secrets are not in the public's best interest? Apparently not, as over fourteen astronauts have come forward revealing their sightings of UFOs/extraterrestrial spacecraft while on space missions, or under other situations. Several of them, such as Gordon Cooper, were some of the original Mercury astronauts.

Why would these decorated and celebrated people do this? Here is how I've come to think of it.

During World War II and the following cold war era, we were told that the Union of Soviet Socialist Republics (U.S.S.R.) was the great enemy of free peoples everywhere. President Ronald Reagan called U.S.S.R. the "evil empire." As good patriots, we were sold the idea that our good old U.S.A. needed its military personnel and citizenry to understand that certain secrets had to be kept for reasons of national security. It was a more innocent time for U.S. citizens. We trusted our republic, our democratic form of government, and as good patriots, we wanted to cooperate to help keep our country "safe." We counted on those in charge to keep that trust and parcel information out on a "need-to-know" basis. We believed in the righteousness of our country.

Yet even back then, right after WWII, a malignant cancer within our government had formed various covert agency "tumors," created under and protected by the secrecy of the National Security Act of 1947. These organizations had their own own agendas of power and control, likely being seduced and guided by the Nazi scientists brought into the U.S. under Project Paperclip and put to work for our government. The National Security Act of 1947 was signed into law a short two months after the Roswell UFO crash in July of 1947. The Roswell incident clearly demonstrated that some kind of secret-keeping, emergency management/damage control of such situations was absolutely necessary to keep such sensational and potentially panic-causing information from the public.

The problem was, and still is, that such need-to-know-basis secrecy – beyond any real or effective public or congressional oversight – is a fertile breeding ground for those seeking money and power to twist to their own nefarious purposes. Too much power and control went to appointed, non-elected officials who positioned themselves to be put in charge or on the boards or panels of such secret agencies and organizations. And once there, they often stayed in place for many, many years, likely passing their positions of power to specially-chosen cronies and proteges, grooming them to be selected for successive or new appointments.

As the decades marched by, those good patriots, whether military or civilian, who had been touched by or involved with such military or government secrets – told they must be kept for reasons of national security – watched the country they had sworn an oath to protect, slip away, little by little. At least some of those privy to the reality of extraterrestrial technology knew it could create a world no longer dependent on oil. These ex-military and ex-government civilian employees with secret knowledge of extraterrestrial contact and technology, watched the unfolding of current events, year after year. They knew what was being sequestered away from public knowledge. And they had to be increasingly more often asking themselves – why? What was the purpose of the secrecy today? Was our country benefiting? Were her citizens? No. And their oaths of non-disclosure kept them largely isolated from each other. It kept them from talking as a group and comparing notes to piece together any larger picture.

It was a very tough proposition for ex-military and/or ex-government employees to come forward and break their oaths of non-disclosure. Revealing secrets could mean prosecution and prison.

However, a platform for disclosure was developed by Dr. Steven Greer.[13] In May of 2001, Greer's Disclosure Project broke out publicly with a press conference at the National Press Club in Washington, D.C. This extraordinary press conference along with Dr. Greer's documentary, *The Disclosure Project: Witness Testimonies* (a two-hour and a four-hour version) provided that vital platform and safety in numbers. Over 400 former military members and ex-government employees were able to come forward and share their testimony of what they had seen and experienced, regarding which they had previously been threatened into years of silence.

To me, these whistleblowers coming forward en masse was an ultimate act of patriotism, a return to keeping faith with the oath of service about protecting the United States of America and her Constitution from all enemies, foreign *and domestic.*

As I listened to and watched such government whistleblowers, especially the many who came forward and told their stories in the *Disclosure Project: Witness Testimonies* video, I could hear the emotion and stress in some of their voices. I could see how disturbed some of their countenances were, and in some

---

[13] Dr. Steven Greer, creator of *The Disclosure Project*, which organized and brought together over 400 witnesses who gave testimonies in his book, *The Disclosure Project: Military and Government Witnesses Reveal the Greatest Secrets in Modern History.* Many of these witnesses appeared at the May 2001 press conference at the National Press Club in Washington, D.C., and their testimonies were also chronicled in the Disclosure Project Witness Testimony DVD in 2-hour and 4-hour versions. Website: http://www.disclosureproject.org/.

of them, could even see little beads of sweat breaking out on their foreheads. The personal emotional cost of what they had had to carry around was clear. And I certainly felt great empathy and understanding for them, and lots of compassion. I knew how they were feeling. The old childhood addage, "It takes one to know one," applies.

Those out there who attempt to discredit this project by picking out one or more of its participants to try and ridicule or debunk should try living through what these men and women have lived through. It's easy enough to resort to armchair quarterbacking and intellectual smugness to protect your cherished version of reality when you haven't walked a few hard and scary miles in someone else's shoes. Could there be a few in the lot who were disinformation agents, planted there to cast aspersions on the whole project? Certainly, though I doubt this myself. But not possibly enough to discredit the whole project.

A few months later, September 11, 2001 a "terrorist" attack occurred that brought down the World Trade Center towers, including Building 7, which was not struck by a plane.

Suddenly eclipsed by a nation in shock and grief, the importance of The Disclosure Project National Press Club event, with its vital information about extraterrestrial technology, contact and other related issues, was abruptly diminished.

September 11, 2001: Unanswered Questions, Controversy and Suspicion

We are all familiar with what happened on September 11, 2001. So many questions around this event exist, still unanswered after ten years. There are many websites with members demanding a truly independent investigation of what really happened.

Here is my personal experience of what happened on September 11, 2001.

I was still getting settled in Durango and had just rented a room from a friend. On September 11, in the morning, I was reading my email. Many messages filled my inbox about what had happened, especially a very telling one that read; "It's started folks."

I joined my friend and others in her living room. We were all gathered around the television watching in shock as the twin towers of the World Trade Center in New York City – one, then the other, went crashing straight down on their foundations. At that very moment I noted the incredible similarity to controlled demolitions, which I'd observed in the past. My heart sank. I knew inside that the buildings did not fall due to planes hitting them, as was being reported on the air. And if the reason we were being given for the collapse of these buildings was not true, then this was not a Muslim extremist terrorist attack – this was something else. I began to suspect that very day that the terrible events of 9/11/2001 were some kind of inside job.

Durango being the great and supportive community that it is, a few individuals stepped forward and organized meditation gatherings for everyone else. I attended two of them that day, one in the afternoon and one in the evening. We were all in shock. I kept my "inside job" feelings to myself. It was not the time or place to voice them that day. It was a time for all of us to support each other in our shock and grief, and to send loving support and sympathy from our hearts to the hearts of all those much closer to this disaster, and also to those who had just crossed over, losing their lives.

All the contorted information that spilled out as the days went by, ominously juxtaposed itself with outraged questioning of the official 9/11 story. I read a great deal of it. I was not alone in my suspicions, not by a long shot.

People who were paying close attention started asking some very pointed and well-thought out questions. Building 7 was not struck by a plane, why did it fall down? Why did the twin towers and Building 7 fall just like controlled demolitions? The questions kept flowing. Exactly who were the terrorists? Muslim extremists hijacking planes? Or some faction much deeper, much darker and much more powerful, operating from a well-established foothold somewhere within our own country?

Unthinkable. Unspeakable. Good people of heart and conscience, conditioned to a particular version of reality, can't believe powerful people within our own government are capable of such things. I understand all too well why they can't wrap their heads around such human evil. Their whole reality could collapse, leaving them suddenly adrift on a nightmarish sea of treacherous uncertainty, with no solid ground to stand on anywhere. And as long as such good people are too terrified or revolted to even consider the unthinkable and unspeakable, those capable of such heinous acts can continue to perpetrate them.

On an entire cultural level, society did not want to face the truth about the kind of atrocities people and organizations within our own nation were capable of, right on our own country's soil. It seemed that the perpetrators of such atrocities counted upon and relied upon that denial.

The denial was fed by our religious indoctrination and conditioned ideas of right and wrong. It was fed through the education of our youth about our fight for freedom from tyranny at the inception of our country. We learned about our U.S. Constitution, our Bill of Rights, and the legal and political system of checks and balances set up as our government – a form of government that is supposed to work FOR the people. Later, as adults, the conditioning continued through written, broadcast and televised media, both news and entertainment, about how great our country is, about the honor of serving in the Armed Forces as a patriot and defender of our land of the free and home of the brave. For Mom, baseball and apple pie. Whatever political squalls sprang up between party factions, our system of government, with its checks and balances, could not go too far wrong, or so we thought.

Religion, nationalism, patriotism and even racism have been used over and over to create endless divide-and-conquer scenarios, pitting humanity against one another, diverting our attention away from the instigators. Indoctrination ensured that people believed in their government and elected officials to hold the reins on what is decent, lawful and in the public's best interest. Even as it began to become evident, years before the Bush-Cheney administration, that things were beginning to go awry with our country and government, people still clung to the idealized image of a United States of America they were conditioned from childhood to believe in.

Me included. Right up until my recovered memories – and all the corroborating information I collected to try and grasp the political and social context of how such horrible abuse could happen – destroyed the mythological U.S.A. for me forever.

I think it's entirely possible that 9/11 was done – from inside our own government – as some kind of mass trauma-based mind control maneuver on the population of the U.S. It plunged us as a people into shock, trauma, grief and rage. It made possible the passage of the Patriot Act, a most unpatriotic piece of legislation designed to erode our basic constitutional rights. It was 342 pages long and available suspiciously fast after 9/11. The nationwide shock and trauma that followed 9/11 caused the Patriot Act to be voted into law. Most of our elected representatives did not even read this document before voting to enact it. 9/11 was used to initiate a "war on terror," justifying war with Iraq, and war in Afghanistan.

Inflict shock and trauma, then while people are under that paralyzing emotional influence, present them with something that looks like it will make them safe again, more secure, and they will, under the influence of that shock, seize upon it. They will put up little to no resistance to a constructed (by whom, and for what real reasons?) war on terror, legitimizing the preemptive invasions of Iraq and Afghanistan.

Many of us woke up later, sadder but wiser.

The Reality of Mind Control: From the Collective to the Individual

One of the biggest human collective shadow demons we must face is mind control abuse. Yet it must be faced in order to stop it. We need to face it on all the levels it appears, from the abuse to individuals, to the ways it is perpetrated on entire populations. At the scale of populations, it appears as indoctrination through early education, various forms of media information dissemination, some of it using subliminal messaging. While on the surface, subliminal messaging is against the law, I don't feel we can count on such laws to protect us as individuals against subliminal manipulation in advertising or in other forms of media. If our constitutional rights are subject to violation through phone taps and other forms of surveillance without our knowledge, then being subjected to subliminal messages without our knowledge could very well be happening also. Other forms of mind control include coercion through threats and fear, and even through highly-emotional states of bliss created by specific words, sounds and imagery, manufactured and delivered by very charismatic speakers. Not all such speakers are covertly and/or selfishly manipulative, but if a person has a special charisma or magnetism, then that ability can also be misused.

Some emotions feel bad to horrible, some feel good to ecstatic. But extremes of emotion on either end of the negative-positive scale make us very susceptible to manipulation. It is only when we personally cultivate a calm center in our being, a strong relationship with our inner observer or inner witness, that we can also develop a relationship with our own inner knowing or intuition. Strong emotion of any kind can jam our intuitional radar, putting us off-balance and easier to push in a particular direction. These truths have been part of my own personal life experiences, learning through the school of hard knocks. One learns through experience about the many voices we all carry within. Voices of all the emotions, our desires, our worries, our fears, even voices in our physical bodies borne of aches and pains. And underneath all of these is the still small voice of our core self, the part of us that is closest to Spirit. When we learn to quiet all the other voices, finding our inner balance, we can then hear that one still, small voice within – the one we most need to hear.

With individuals, for specific purposes, mind control is far more invasive and traumatic, using the protective psychological processes of a person against him or her. This occurs when traumatic abuse is so diabolically-calculated and severe that the victim's ego is completely overwhelmed. The ego then breaks away the memories of, and/or around the trauma and places them in the subconscious mind, there to stay, lost and unknown, until such time that the person can handle their re-emergence. For those inflicting the abuse, the emotional overwhelm produces a person who then becomes programmable to a greater or lesser degree, or the memory suppression becomes a cloak hiding the abuser from legal consequences. However, the trauma is still within the victim at the level of the body as well as the mind – unresolved, and seeking resolution to return the person to a state of full health in body, mind and spirit. Trauma can make itself felt in the body when any familiar or familiar-seeming places are visited, or circumstances arise that rattle those suppressed memories. Enough encounters with familiar situations can finally bring the suppressed memories to the surface.

Religion of Fear, or Religion of Love?

Mind control of populations appears in religious indoctrination where ecclesiastical authorities command blind faith and obedience to their interpretations of what they proclaim to be "sacred scriptures." I'm not saying all religions are bad or that they should be abolished. Religions have provided a foundation upon which human behavior has been shaped through deep love and compassion, often bringing out the very best in us all. But they have also been responsible for wars rooted in absolute intolerance of the belief systems of others. Horrible atrocities have been committed in the name of religion with movements such as the Spanish Inquisition. Accusations of heresy and the ensuing tribunals were designed to terrify common people into complete subjugation to ideologies devised by people who were at best misguided, at worst, drunk with the power of their high offices.

An entire book, referencing nearly countless historical, religious and spiritual texts, and including many interviews with religious and spiritual leaders alive today could be written to explore this topic.

Suffice it to say, I don't advocate anyone dumping their religion if it is truly adding to their quality of life. But I do think it's healthy to question anything that comes into conflict with the values and inner counsel of your own conscience. Jesus, upon whom Christianity is founded, came primarily to teach us to love one another. He abhorred intolerance, as so many of his parables taught us with love and inspiration, not fear. I can't imagine him condoning any of the many wars or persecutions that have been responsible for so much death and destruction in his name. I've included this topic due to the fact that blind faith often discounts and denies all other areas of evidence, proof and fact. Because of this, where religion is concerned, there is a dangerous inclination to act solely from woeful misguidance, misjudgment and fatally-flawed reasoning.

Ask yourself how you are practicing love and tolerance. If you need a guideline for yourself, remember how you may have felt when someone was kind to you, when you were kind to someone else, or how you felt when you witnessed someone being kind to another. Remember stories that inspire you, either read about or seen in a movie. There is nothing so moving as those moments when two adversaries in a movie or story discover a common ground or a common element between them, realizing they share a unity that helps them to overcome their differences. It's what we feel at moments like these that shows us the luminous thread within our inner path. We must grasp hold of this thread and follow it to a true connection with the largest vision possible of the Creator of us all, whatever name we might give to such a being. No ecclesiastical intermediary should ever supercede this private and personal relationship between you and the Infinite.

Education or Indoctrination?

Indoctrination as a form of mind control also winds its way into our psyche through the educational system. The ways that we are educated in the sciences can be as restrictive as religions in some cases. The sciences are cloaked in more open and tolerant attire such as scientific methodology; hypothesizing, testing, then developing a theory based on the test results. This looks good and works well in many cases. But we run up against the same kinds of limitations we see in religion when those in the sciences become so wedded to established theories that they simply cannot tolerate any questioning of those theories. These attitudes discount new evidence coming to light which call for a reexamination of newly-discovered artifacts. For instance, Michael Cremo[14] has encountered vehement opposition to his presentation of evidence that man is far, far older than science has originally supposed. His findings call into serious question the entire theory of humanity's evolution as it is popularly taught.

Even worse is that science has become a marketplace commodity. Getting funding for true and unbiased science has very nearly become a thing of the past. Grants and funding now direct science and desired outcomes are placed before impartial results, causing flawed research to provide the outcomes that the funding organization wants to see established as pseudo "facts" to get people to believe in, and buy their products.

There is an intellectual pride in the science fields, though perhaps mostly covert, which assumes that what we human beings "know" from our own studies down through the ages is that humanity is the crowning achievement of evolution. So much so, that if our human sciences have not been able to conceive of something, it must not or cannot exist. This is at least one reason I feel that the UFO field is so reviled by traditional science. UFOs demonstrate properties that they feel are impossible. Therefore, they cannot exist.

Retired Sergeant Major Robert O. Dean, who held a Cosmic Top Secret security clearance, reviewed a document while on active duty called *An Assessment* – a comprehensive military study of the UFO and extraterrestrial phenomenon, far beyond anything done in Project Blue Book[15]. In this assessment it was concluded that there were four primary extraterrestrial races involved in observing humanity, one of them being as human-looking as any of us; that their spacecraft demonstrated abilities that defy our current laws of Newtonian physics; that they are able to manipulate space and time; and that some UFOs were multi-dimensional in their origins. They were far beyond any technology that we have, or at least that we had at one time. It's difficult to speculate just how far back-engineering projects involving extraterrestrial technology have gone by now.

For traditional scientists, this is a slap in the face to their intellectual pride and assumptions that humanity is at the top of some evolutionary pinnacle. Since they cannot conceive of a craft at our level of scientific knowledge and technological expertise which can fold space or travel beyond light speed, it is therefore judged impossible. And no other hypothetical beings in the universe

---

[14] Michael Cremo is an author-researcher who looks at archeological evidence that many call anomalies – artifacts in fossil records that do not conform to the usual theories of evolution. His theories and book *Forbidden Archeology: The Hidden History of the Human Race*, co-authored by Richard L. Thompson, have been criticized for this by his peers and for investigating sacred Hindu texts for clues to human origins. His website: http://www.mcremo.com.

[15] *Project Blue Book*, considered by many to be a cover to debunk UFO sightings, was begun in 1952 and terminated in 1969. Blue Book's conclusions were that most people reporting UFOs were suffering from mass hysteria, were after publicity for themselves, were mentally unstable, or simply mis-identified conventional aircraft. However it was later determined that psychological or hoaxed cases represented less than 10% of all cases, and 22% of all the sightings remained unresolved.

could do it either, by extension of the term "impossible" projected onto other such possible intelligent life.

It's also frightening to contemplate life from other worlds visiting Earth, as was publicly demonstrated in a recent statement by physicist Stephen Hawking, in which he said that if "ET" calls, humanity should not answer the "phone." Historically on our world, the stronger, smarter, more technologically advanced civilizations have always conquered and subjugated the weaker and less advanced. So, since our government and military assure us that such things as UFOs and aliens don't exist – and are ready to supply grant monies to projects whose scientists fall in line with this propaganda – well, such things as UFOs and aliens just "don't exist," and it's ridiculous to even spend any time, money, energy or thought upon such a premise.

Francis Crick, who co-won the Nobel Prize with James Watson for discovery of the double helix structure of deoxyribonucleic acid (DNA), discovered in his later research that humanity had 223 extra genes which he concluded had to have come from "elsewhere." He came up with the idea of "directed panspermia" in which he theorized that an extraterrestrial civilization deliberately transmitted microorganisms to seed life here and likely on other worlds. Like most good scientists, he postulated an unmanned or multi-generational ship traversing the parsecs of space between worlds, never exceeding the limitations that science puts upon space flight at our current public knowledge of how this could be done. Yet if ETs truly can move through dimensions, manipulate space and time, it's entirely possible that they could have come here and overseen such a life-seeding project in person and guided it's development over the ages.

None of this material is taught in public schools. If one encounters it in one's journey through life, particularly as an experiencer of the ET phenomenon in some way, one is left struggling to make sense of experiences that mainstream culture in a variety of areas denies are even possible.

Our schools have become a battleground of two diametrically-opposed camps: science, its established disciplines traditionally taught in schools; and religion, whose proponents demand that creationism as laid out in the Bible be taught alongside science as an alternative to evolution.

For those of us whose experiences drive us into investigations outside mainstream religious or intellectual approval, we are confronted with alternative sources of information that call into question the established orders of traditional science and religion. Various parcels of new evidence point out that modern man as we know him today is far older than archeological science has theorized, and far and away older than the 6,000 years suggested by some biblical scholars as the point in time of God's creation of man.

Current experiences and research show us that humanity has been and is being visited by extraterrestrials, from ancient times to the present. From the plains of Nazca and the Piri Reis maps to the extraterrestrial abduction phenomenon – which is filled with significant testimony of ETs creating hybrids between ourselves and them; from the failure of science to find any compelling "missing link" between apes and man to Crick's discovery of the 223 extra genes in humanity, distinguishing humans from other life forms on Earth; support builds for the idea of extraterrestrials having a definitive connection to the inception and existence of humanity.

As we continue turning over the various archeological stones that fall outside both the established sciences and traditional religious texts, we find much that raises serious questions. While religion can always claim faith in the Almighty as its final authority, and accuse evidence to the contrary to be clever tricks manufactured by Satan to mislead us, science cannot continue to ignore data that is inconvenient or undermining to its cherished theories and continue to call itself "science."

For those of us who cannot simply dismiss new evidence on either traditional religious or traditional scientific grounds, who must seriously consider such new evidence of modern man's true age and possible origins and wonder about it, that consideration begs the question "Why is such evidence so summarily dismissed and ridiculed without a major study undertaken to investigate it?"

When people are taught information in school that is dogmatic in any regard, they are being programmed to join the ridiculers and naysayers later on in life, without giving new data and evidence a fair hearing. If authority figures in such matters tell people these ideas are preposterous, then that is what indoctrinated people accept.

For those of us who do give new information a fair hearing and some real consideration, we have to pass through an uncomfortable period of cognitive dissonance – the internal intellectual conflict between what we've been conditioned to believe and accept and what new evidence and knowledge we are presented with that we can no longer ignore – information we have to factor into a new reality paradigm for ourselves.

When we come to realize that what we are traditionally taught in school is flawed or incomplete, then we must begin to question the whole educational process. Is it more indoctrination than education? If so, then why?

News and Entertainment Media: Manipulation of Our Minds and Emotions

Those mysterious groups orchestrating all of the indoctrination, propaganda and manipulation remain invisible within the web they have created to trap people's very ways of thinking and feeling. This is what keeps such groups powerful and in control. As illustrated in the sections of this chapter discussing health, many people in the mainstream have been carefully dumbed-down over the passing decades.

Conditioning and indoctrination are reinforced in adulthood through mainstream media. A few truly good movies still leak out of Hollywood once in a while; however there is less and less difference between material tagged as "entertainment" and material tagged as "news." Painted garishly loud with lots of drama and extreme, intense action, the media adrenalin-ride – whether news, movies or TV shows – is more and more geared to manipulate minds and emotions. People who have been raised taking prescription drugs, eating chemical-ridden food and getting a poor education may have little truly independent thought left with which to navigate their lives. What they have instead is us-versus-them (take your pick of what group constitutes "us" or "them") adversarial media rhetoric and religious dogma. In some ways, the divide-and-conquer game has never been easier to foist on the population than in this electronic age.

I'm quite sure that the powerful elites, Illuminati or shadow governments – whatever you want to call them – are well aware that if they can keep our mental attention and emotionalism riveted on whatever programming they spin out to capture it, we will continue to unconsciously direct the quantum field that underlies our reality to keep spinning out a world in which they remain in charge, and we remain subjugated. The term "television programming" has a double meaning for sure; beneath all the schedules and descriptions of movies, TV shows and other material, people are being programmed mentally and emotionally to play right into the hands of those who wish to subjugate them.

On a more positive note, much of what is seen in the media these days bespeaks a high level of angst on the part of those who have deemed themselves humanity's handlers and controllers. The kinds of material coming out, from extreme, high-adrenalin movies that pass for "entertainment," to the "news" itself, with its high drama and immoderate emotionalism are blatant symptoms of desperation. We would never have seen such extreme behavior from the era of Walter Cronkite and his contemporaries. Such behavior back then (compared to what we see now) would have been considered absolutely unprofessional. That we are seeing it now, and have in fact been habituated to it, shows a crazy desperation in the spin-meisters, that they resort to more and more extreme measures to keep people's attention on all there is to fear in this world. And as alternative healing and holistic medicine are now showing us, fear and adrenalin as regular operating mechanisms in our lives lead to stress, suffering and disease. Fear, anger and adrenalin hijack our biological functions right down to our DNA, keeping us limited and shut down.

The good news is that the propaganda and human management system becomes so stressful over time that more and more people are reaching maximum overload with it and opting out, through one means or another. Caring for your health is one means, especially when traditional health care falls short, having little to offer beyond drugs and surgery that only treat symptoms. The underlying causes of chronic health issues remain, and resurface unless deeper healing approaches are found. Caring for your children and coming to see that the current systems are not serving them, either health-wise or educationally, prompts parents to seek changes in their families' lifestyles from embracing organic foods and holistic health practices to home schooling. Environmental destruction and how it affects human and other life on Earth is yet another. Just as individuals get stressed and ill, so does our planet's ecosystem, needing healing that responsible, holistic sustainable practices can provide.

So for every desperate, extreme story that is spun out in the media, generating more fear and adrenalin in its audiences, perhaps more and more individuals decide to shut off or do away with TV altogether. They then turn to changes in lifestyle to create a better quality of life for themselves, personally and environmentally. With every person who does this, another measure of mental and emotional energy is taken from the quantum field that is contrived to generate a world of fear, anger, misery and war, perhaps shifting that energy to creating a new paradigm of peace, caring and sustainability for ourselves and each other. For every human being who opts out of the propaganda machine and begins to educate themselves and make positive changes, the expansion of human consciousness is served, and all of humanity benefits.

Any spiritual path includes multiple confrontations with one's self, facing demons that hide within our subconscious minds, controlling us from its shadows without our conscious knowledge. Through spiritual practice and mindful observation of ourselves moving through our own lives, those demons can be revealed and can then be integrated into the wholeness of ourselves in an ongoing process of becoming. We take the subconscious/unconscious and make it conscious. In so doing, we can consciously choose where we will stand, on what principles and with what values. And we are all on a spiritual path through life. It's just that some of us participate with that journey, and others of us are unaware of it, ignore it or fight it.

As each individual human being is on his or her own spiritual path, that path is mirrored in the human collective of Planet Earth on a planetary scale. All around us secrets are emerging that we react to or respond to according to which angels of our natures we listen to the most. It boils down to choosing love or fear. If you choose fear, then acting from that fear may torment you and exhaust you until you re-evalutate your course and choose to live from love.

Trauma-based Mind Control on Individuals

Institutional indoctrination and media propaganda are the generalized societal and cultural forms of mind control. Severe trauma-based abuse inflicted on individual children and adults is an institutional practice as well – it's just that the institutions that perpetrate it are well-masked. They don't want their atrocities exposed because the total fury of public outrage would destroy them. They hide behind public denial of such extreme abuses. This is because what they do is so unthinkable and unspeakable in the minds of most people with values and behavior guided by their hearts and by their innate sense of right and wrong – it couldn't possibly be really happening – could it?

252

If (or more likely, when) people's memories of horrific abuse begin to emerge and they start speaking about them, they are seen as troubled individuals who must be remembering incorrectly. How could they make such horrible accusations? When they began to recover memories under hypnosis as started happening in the latter part of the 20th century, a conveniently-timed organization sprang to life to discredit them – The False Memory Syndrome Foundation, with it's claims that these poor souls have been misguided by their hypnotherapists, through error or by design. It might have been a more credible organization had some of its board members not been discovered to have ties to the Central Intelligence Agency (CIA).

One of the founding board members of the False Memory Syndrome Foundation was Martin Orne, a psychiatrist. He is one of the leading experts on hypnosis of the 20th century and for 30 years, he was the editor of *The International Journal of Clinical and Experimental Hypnosis*. Orne is one of two professional psychiatrists and documented CIA mind control contractors that were active into the late 1990's. The other was Dr. Louis Jolyon West. Dr. Ewen Cameron, psychiatrist and CIA MKULTRA researcher/abuser, has been written about more extensively in various books, one by one of his former childhood victims, Carol Rutz. A mind control victim from childhood who managed to find a way to heal and recover, she writes of her experiences in her book, *A Nation Betrayed: The Chilling True Story of Secret Cold War Experiments Performed on Our Children and Other Innocent People*.

Who should know better than operatives in the CIA about what extremes of abuse are needed to program people for whatever purposes? The CIA has done the studies, research and experimentation, building on what was learned from the Nazi scientists brought to the U.S.A. under Project Paperclip. Using trauma to create dissociative identity disorder (previously known as multiple personality disorder) such fragmented personalities are programmed through trauma; trauma causing the mind of the subject to photographically record what is being programmed.

Yet such programming breaks down over time and memories of abuse do reemerge. Carol Rutz, mentioned above, is one such individual. Another book of healing from mind control abuse is *Rattlesnake Fire: A Memoir of Extra-Dimensional Experience* by Jean Eisenhower. Other chronicles of mind control abuse are *Thanks for the Memories* by Brice Taylor, and *Trance-formation of America* by Cathy O'Brien and Mark Phillips. Not reading for the faint of heart.

The CIA as an organization is documented in several sources as being prominently involved in trauma-based mind control abuse. In my opinion, no wonder they would create an organization regarding "false memory syndrome" to refute claims of abuse that could be tracked back to them.

In addition to mind control abuses, the false memory hypothesis has also been used to debunk extraterrestrial experiences recalled under hypnosis, thereby attempting to explain that phenomenon away as well – except some experiencers remember their encounters without hypnosis. Such conscious recollections line up with incredible similarity to what those under hypnosis remember. This type of debunking is yet one more attempt to silence any people trying to tell the public truths that need to be heard, or at the very least, seek help for themselves.

Fortunately, through organizations trying to help with mind control and ritual abuse, like the North American Freedom Foundation (NAFF – http://naffoundation.org), Stop Mind Control and Ritual Abuse Today (SMART – http://ritualabuse.us/) and Survivorship (http://www.survivorship.org/), society is being educated about this problem, and victims are getting help. But since abuse often happens through institutions and organizations, trust in any organizations with a mandate to help may come very hard to people who have been abused.

There is a paper trail on mind control abuse in the U.S.A. starting with Operation/Project Paperclip, mentioned earlier in this book. Under Paperclip, German scientists who served in Hitler Germany were recruited and imported to the U.S.A. to keep them from being "acquired" by the U.S.S.R. or the United Kingdom. Most such scientists had their Nazi backgrounds expunged from their records so that they could be brought to the the U.S.A. and put to work here.

In a summary of the book *Mind Controllers* by Dr. Armen Victorian on the wanttoknow.info website appears this paragraph from the book:

> The Nuremberg trials revealed the extent of Nazi Germany's mind control experimentation on Jewish concentration camp prisoners, as well as prisoners of war. As a result of the trials, 23 German doctors were convicted, and an injunction was brought to the effect that humans should never be used in such a fashion again. On the contrary, such trials only served to attract the interest of the Western intelligence agencies, inspiring them to research and develop methods of controlling and altering the human mind.
>
> ~ From *Mind Controllers*, by Armen Victorian, Lewis International Inc., September 2000, P.67[16]

It is astonishing and sickening that, after all the money and lives sacrificed by the U.S.A. to defeat Nazi Germany and the kinds of atrocities that went on in the concentration camps, our own U.S. intelligence organizations invited the perpetrators of those horrors to live in the U.S.A. and work for them.

Credible documentation linking the importation of Nazi scientists to the U.S.A. under Paperclip appears in multiple sources, including this next excerpt

[16] Summary from webpage, http://www.wanttoknow.info/mindcontrollers10pg. Dr. Victorian's book is considered an excellent introduction to the subject of mind control. The website, http://wanttoknow.info, contains volumes of excellent and well-documented information on mind control and many other subjects for public education.

taken from a *Mind Control Summary: The Secrets of Mind Control Based on Three Books by Top Mind Control Researchers*. The reference links in this excerpt were removed for inclusion in this book – they can be seen and accessed through their hyperlinks on the webpage where the original article appears.[17]

> After the end of World War II, German scientists were being held in a variety of detainment camps by the allies. In 1946, President Truman authorized Project Paperclip to exploit German scientists for American research, and to deny these intellectual resources to the Soviet Union. Some reports bluntly pointed out that they were "ardent Nazis." They were considered so vital to the "Cold War" effort, that they would be brought into the U.S. and Canada. Some of these experts participated in murderous medical experiments on human subjects at concentration camps. A 1999 report to the Senate and the House said "between 1945 and 1955, 765 scientists, engineers, and technicians were brought to the U.S. under Paperclip and similar programs.
>
> According to the Central Intelligence Agency's Fact Book, the NSC (National Security Council) and the CIA were established under the provisions of the National Security Act of 1947. In December 1947, the NSC held its first meeting. James Forrestal, the Secretary of Defense, pushed for the CIA to begin a 'secret war' against the Soviets. Forrestal's initiative led to the execution of psychological warfare operations (psy-ops) in Europe. CIA personnel were not opposed to working with Nazi doctors who had proven to be proficient in breaking the mind and rebuilding it. In some cases military bases were used to hide these covert activities. It was decided that the communist threat was an issue that took priority over constitutional rights.
>
> The concept of running a secret 'black' project was no longer novel. In 1941, Roosevelt had decided, without consulting Congress, that the U.S. should proceed with the utmost secrecy to develop an atomic bomb. Secrecy shrouded the Manhattan Project (the atomic bomb program) to the extent that Vice President Harry Truman knew nothing about it. The project meant that by 1947, the U.S. Government had already gained vast experience in the initiation of secret operations. The existence of 'black projects' funded by 'black budgets' was withheld not only from the public, but also from Congress for "REASONS OF NATIONAL SECURITY."
>
> ~ Used with permission from the www.wanttoknow.info website from their section on *Mind Control*.

[17] For the entire summary with reference links, see webpage, http://www.wanttoknow.info/mindcontrol10pg.

Because the CIA engages in its studies and experimentation under the auspices of protecting national security on a "need-to-know" basis, protection for this type of heinous abuse falls under the National Security Act of 1947, under which the CIA was formed.

Known names of mind control projects include: BLUEBIRD, ARTICHOKE, MONARCH, and MKULTRA. There are likely other names not listed here. CIA director Richard Helms ordered all documents pertaining to MKULTRA to be destroyed in 1973. However they overlooked some 20,000 MKULTRA documents that were revealed publicly through a Freedom of Information Act request in 1977. Senate hearings were held on this scandal the same year.

It has been reported that all materials on MKULTRA have been declassified, and the CIA states that mind control experimentation has been halted. I don't trust that we can count on that to be true. Not from an agency that has gone to incredible lengths to keep its activities secret and protected from public scrutiny. It is very likely that the CIA is just taking better and more extreme measures to keep its secrets.

On the Discovery Channel a documentary on mind control, John DeCamp's *Conspiracy of Silence,* was scheduled to air on May 3, 1994. It was pulled from programming at the very last minute through the powerful influence of the Federal Bureau of Investigation (FBI), police, and members of Congress, who also had all copies of the documentary destroyed. A surviving pre-production copy now in circulation tells why. This documentary exposes a huge child prostitution circle that leads into the hallowed halls of Congress and even to the White House. The surviving copy of this documentary is available for viewing online.[18]

Mind control abuse must be stopped, but as long as the mainstream public remains in denial under a barrier of terms like "unthinkable" and "unspeakable" it will not truly stop.

Trauma-based mind control is most often perpetrated against children. Why? Because they are so impressionable and malleable. If you start with a child, the younger the better, you will have a person completely indoctrinated and subjugated into a controlled existence in which they know nothing else, have little to no basis within their programmed reality for comparison to a happy, healthy life and childhood. The control is more complete and harder to break out of. It may be less likely to be spoken of or reported to others when children are normalized to this kind of treatment early on.

As I've worked through my own healing process on a personal level, a microcosm to macrocosm metaphor has emerged.

Decades ago, before the horrible reality of children being molested by adults began leaking out through those who could no longer keep silent, sexual

---

[18] *Conspiracy of Silence* (length: 55 minutes) by investigator John DeCamp, a decorated Vietnam war veteran and 16-year Nebraska state senator can be viewed for online at: http://www.personalgrowthcourses.net/video/conspiracy_of_silence.

molestation and abuse of children was considered unthinkable and unspeakable. Family members, friends of family, even clergy members were implicated in such sexual misconduct as the stories began to be told by recovering adults. We heard stories of these people, as children, being spanked or having their mouths washed out with soap for making such unthinkable, unspeakable accusations about a family member, adult friend, pastor or priest. Yet finally it became accepted that children were and are targets of such formerly unthinkable and unspeakable abuses. Measures began to be taken to protect children.

Child abuses happened at the microcosmic levels of families and communities. Trauma-based mind control practices – many of which include sexual abuse of children as well as adults – are instituted and carried out at the larger macrocosmic societal and national levels, and not only in the U.S.A. They could very well include events engineered and staged to affect whole populations, reinforced by media propaganda selecting the specific words, sounds and imagery to keep people emotionally and mentally off-balance and subject to manipulation.

For every person that asked me from their own disbelief, "Are you sure?" "Could you be mistaken?" or, going into denial; "I just can't believe that," I knew what kind of indoctrination – a method of mind control in itself – had been instilled in them. I had done too much study, too much research, correlated too much other testimony fitting with my own. I knew these abuses went on and they went on within our own country, sanctioned by secret organizations now drunk with the power and protection secrecy gives them.

In the face of such denial-based questions, I felt like the child who had been spanked, who had her mouth washed out with soap for trying to say what unthinkable and unspeakable things go on in our own dear and exalted U.S.A.

I know personally at least some of the kinds of terror and cruelty inflicted on people under the control of individuals and organizations operating under highly secretive programs. What happened to me could never have happened if we truly lived in a country where our constitutional rights and the letter of law was in full effect everywhere; not "exempted" out in the middle of the Nevada desert, some lawless nether-zone where people could be enslaved, experimented on and abused with no help, no hope, no legal recourse whatsoever under the auspices of the National Security Act of 1947. I was harmed by the very people that, in a world where all the usual rules and morals apply, I might have gone to for help.

When one really begins to dig into this secrecy-creating legislation that essentially legitimizes any program or project which falls under the umbrella of "National Security" and we begin a systematic search through research writings and testimony of people – citizens – who have been abused under such projects, we must begin to question just whose national security is this legislation protecting? We as U.S. citizens? Or the security of those who treat citizens as a usable and disposable commodity?

It is quite simply time for such secrets to come into the open. When forces of tyranny and oppression put pressure on the common people, those common people – who love freedom and will not stand for their freedom to be more and more severely limited or curtailed – must stand forth and speak.

***

Even the terms "unthinkable" and "unspeakable" scream of thoughts, images or acts so ugly, we fight to hide them away from ourselves deep in our subconscious/unconscious. Why? Because we cannot bear to think of them as even being possible, as being a part of ourselves. Such acts seem a stain on the entire collective soul of humankind.

In this passage, "On Crime and Punishment" by Kahlil Gibran, he speaks to the idea of humanity as a collective:

> And as a single leaf turns not yellow but with the silent
> knowledge of the whole tree, so the wrong-doer cannot do
> wrong without the hidden will of you all.

From the underlying unity found in teachings of eastern philosophies and spiritual paths throughout the world, to Carl Jung's collective unconscious, to modern quantum science demonstrating interconnectedness through the quantum field, the concept of a unified energy of which we are all a part reveals the ways in which we are all connected at the most fundamental level with everything that exists everywhere.

This knowledge is also experiential for those who dedicate their lives to spiritual practices that set aside the various clamoring voices all people carry within, voices of mind, emotions and body, allowing their consciousness to expand. In states of nirvana, such adepts touch the Infinite and rest in the experience of the Oneness of which we are all a part.

I count upon Oneness as the basic truth of our existence. Applying a practical understanding to how this oneness manifests and governs our physical reality through the collective consciousness of humanity is the next step to creating conscious shift in our world. This is a process by which we – humanity – as a collective are empowered to change our reality, if we can free ourselves from the mindspell cast by the powerful elite groups that currently control the flow of information through the media.

If this world is a quantum mirror to us for all that we hold in our individual and collective consciousness, with all the compartments we have in our psyches that contain things we hide even from ourselves, then could not the coming to light of such dreadful information be a spiritual process of the human collective facing its collective shadow? Could it not be a shocking, disturbing, but necessary step in the expansion of human awareness on our planet, at this particular time in our history? A time in which we bring ALL of who we are as a species into the light for healing and integration as we move into the next great iteration of discovery about who we human beings truly are?

The High Cost of Human Awakening: Will We Choose to Make it Count?

Now, with a change of administration in the White House, we are still feeling the backlash of those Bush-Cheney years when so much of who we are as a people has been seriously undermined, if not almost completely usurped. The U.S. flag still waves over our cities. The platitudes and chants of freedom and democracy still echo in our ears. But it is as if our precious Statue of Liberty, standing tall and proud in New York Harbor, has been eaten away from inside by parasites. Only a fragile shell remains, a shell that would break into pieces under any real, serious scutiny. There has been no real action as yet to restore full constitutionality to our government.

Some of the richest oil fields on the planet are, or were, controlled by Middle Eastern countries. After the shock of 9/11 and the passage of the Patriot Act, the Bush-Cheney administration constructed their new platform, the "war on terror" from which to initiate "justifiable" aggression at their chosen targets throughout the world. They took us to war with Iraq under false allegations of "weapons of mass destruction." None were ever found. The basis for this war turned out to be a lie, but it didn't stop the war. Troops were sent into Iraq under a banner of "Operation Iraqi Freedom." Free them from what? Being alive? Having homes to shelter their families and children? To any thinking, reasoning person with two brain cells to rub together, it was transparently obvious that powerful corporate interests in the U.S. wanted to gain control of those rich oil fields. And corporate war profiteering has never been so blatantly evident.

Under the title "Operation Enduring Freedom," the invasion of Afghanistan was launched. Initiated ostensibly to ferret out Osama bin Laden, Al Qaeda, and the Taliban, I imagine a lot of U.S. citizens are scratching their heads and wondering why we are still over there. Years ago, a cop once explained to me that the best way to win the "war on drugs" would be to legalize them. Then society could actually help users instead of locking them up, and put pushers out of business, ending huge crime syndicates that thrive on illicit drugs. In all that I've learned over the years, I've come to know that black budget projects cost obscene amounts of money. That money cannot afford to be tracked through regular government budget ledgers. Opium production has been on the rise again since the U.S. invaded Afghanistan in 2001. Before that, the Taliban had limited its production. Since the CIA gets a lion's share of opium from Afghanistan and the Taliban had put a ban on opium production, it's quite likely that the true reason the U.S. is in Afghanistan is to keep the opium flowing, and the illegal, therefore lucrative, sales of it pouring money into the coffers of those black budget projects that still need those obscene amounts of money. Even that has not been enough for the 1% at the top of the money pyramid, as the crumbling economic situation in the U.S.A. makes crystal clear to everyone.

This chapter is long enough and I'm not going to get too far into the criminal economics of the elites that are robbing people across the country of their livelihoods and homes. But I will say that it appears to me that those elite and powerful groups in the world are like spoiled children who have never had to hear the word "No." Their lavish lifestyles have outstripped even their billions of dollars in annual incomes. They have gone after money they have no right to. On 9/10/2001, Secretary of Defense Donald Rumsfeld announced that $2.3 trillion had gone "missing." We all know what happened the next day to take our attention away from such a staggering amount of missing federal money. Incoming President Barack Obama was confronted with Wall Street corporations begging for bailouts, apparently so they could keep living and operating in the manner to which they had become accustomed. I think the economic chickens of decades of unrestrained greed and spending at the most privileged echelons of society are coming home to roost. The debt-based, fractional currency system[19] of the Federal Reserve is running up against its own game.

Yet for people living on the most meager incomes imaginable, such as social security and disability, there was no cost of living allowance (COLA) increase in 2010 or 2011, (usually only a $9 to $13 per month increase over the previous year). The reason for this? A statement issued by Social Security that there has been no change in the Consumer Price Index, i.e., "no observable rise in the cost of living," therefore, no COLA for all the people subsisting on tiny social security incomes. Yet Wall Street gets bailouts of billions of dollars. Hmmmm.

***

A recent, devastating environmental disaster, the 2010 Gulf oil spill, (more like an oil volcano) which has ravaged the livelihoods and health of people living along the Gulf of Mexico, as well as marine and other life, need never have happened if oil had been abandoned as an energy source when others were readily available. The Exxon-Valdez oil spill in Alaska in 1989 is still impacting that area all these years later, and it was not even close to the scale of the Gulf oil spill. It does appear that the Gulf Stream has been affected or even stalled, as severe winter cold descends on the United Kingdom and other European countries in that area of the world. These areas have relied upon the flow of the warmer Gulf Stream to provide their more moderate winter weather for thousands of years.

---

[19] For a thorough description of the Federal Reserve's debt-based fractional, fiat currency system, see the movie *Zeitgeist Addendum* at this website link: http://www.zeitgeistaddendum.com/. The movie also suggests some uplifting alternatives to creating a new money-less and free-energy society.

Hard on the heels of the Gulf oil catastrophe came the 2011 Fukushima nuclear disaster, caused by the Tohoku earthquake and tsunami, severely damaging the nuclear power plant there. The radioactive fallout is currently being carried through the Earth's weather system around the world.

We still have yet to fully comprehend or experience the total fallout from these twin disasters of involving oil and nuclear energy. What people's reaction will be to this when they someday find out that these disasters need never have happened if free energy alternatives had not been suppressed for decades I can only guess, but I know how I feel today, knowing how unnecessary it all was, and is. I feel angry. Horrified. I feel deep grief and heartache for the suffering of the people and wildlife affected – which could include many of us at some point as the repercussions from these catastrophes continue to make themselves felt.

***

Imagine if all the billions of dollars spent on the Iraqi war, the Afghanistan war and the "war on terror" were turned instead to the release, development and implementation of of clean, free zero-point energy devices for this world. If there was truly a concern about the countries in the Middle East gaining too much power from the richness of their oil fields, their economic teeth would be virtually removed by such a shift to free, clean, alternative energy. People crushed under the weight of so much poverty around the globe, exploited by corporate interests increasingly allowed to rampage worldwide, would be given a much-needed reprieve as the cost of energy needed to transport goods and services fell to nearly nothing. The costs of the human labor to make needed products, to gather and prepare harvests of food, to provide care and services would drop very dramatically. A whole new economy would be birthed from an entirely different foundation than oil, which has been at the root of every type of industry on this planet for both production and transport.

But wait – this means that the powerful network of multi-national corporations might have to completely reshuffle themselves and their ways of doing business, not to mention learning to deal with a new economy. What could possibly serve their interests as well as having the cost of oil regulate the world's economy?

What if the mass majority of people didn't need them any longer, their energy needs taken care of without having to pay anyone for it? What if, through free energy, people could become self-sufficient and sustainable in a chain of networked and sharing communities worldwide? We might not need those multi-national oil corporations and related industries anymore. We might design lifestyles, livelihoods, even entertainment that suits us best instead of having them forced upon us by those who decide what we will see, hear and do from their own agendas for our lives.

261

The Big Picture: Observing Shift Happening

Government, military and corporate cover-ups extend far beyond the UFO and ET phenomenon. I've only scratched the barest surface in this chapter. In the last few decades such shadowy operations on our world have become more and more obvious. I have watched the awareness of "something wrong" in our government begin to cross various societal lines and areas of interest that have little to nothing to do with UFOs. From questions about glaring incongruencies around the events surrounding 9/11, to assaults on people's freedoms on multiple levels, across our society, across the planet herself, people are raising their heads, paying more attention, and getting wise. Whatever group has been trying to dumb us down as a world population, they did not dumb us down soon enough or effectively enough. They are running out of time and their desperation is becoming quite apparent. As players at the world's poker table, they tipped their hand a bit too soon, and enough of us have spotted it to make a difference.

This long, mondo chapter is my attempt to give my personal observations of how life on Earth and in the U.S.A. has been unfolding as I've sought understanding about the larger social and political context in which we've all been living out our lives. This quest began as an effort to understand how what happened to me in the Nevada desert could happen in a world where such things are not supposed to happen, not in the U.S.A. The quest led me to these conclusions, which are still in development today. Developments that ultimately are affecting us all.

It is beyond the scope of this book's purpose to do an in-depth exposé on all the risks and dangers in the many areas of concern to truthseekers, who care about their physical, mental, emotional and spiritual health, as well as the world we live in. But I would urge readers to do some research into these matters on their own. The footnotes I've provided are a start.

It would seem that my inter-dimensional teachers were correct: Bush was the right man, in the right place, at the right time. Because he was president, and because of all the extreme measures instituted under his administration, multitudes of people have awakened. It is not a pleasant process for us as a people, but it is a very necessary one. Humanity's collective shadow is being dragged into the light so that the integration process can begin. So we can move forward with more collective self-knowledge that will bring more momentum to the expansion of human awareness. We are taking our next evolutionary steps as a species.

One of the quiet actions I've always taken in my life is to look at samplings of a broad spectrum of material in many areas – including current events, the sciences, the spiritual practices of the world, and all the various aspects of the UFO and extraterrestrial phenomenon. I think it's important to cast our nets wide in our search for knowledge and truth, and to look at what we catch, observing similarities and differences, noting correlating and non-correlating information. I feel that if we restrict our attention to only a few subjects, we can never hope to get a fully-cognizant view of events happening in the world or assess the meaningful context of those events unfolding in the particular melting pot of national and global society.

Today I see that melting pot as a crucible, in which chaotic political and social forces are fiercely clashing, blending and differentiating. Earth-Gaia herself is adding to the turmoil geologically and environmentally, helped along with human-caused disasters like the Fukushima nuclear disaster and the Gulf oil spill. While many groups cry "global warming" on Planet Earth, there is evidence that all the planets in our solar system are warming up, not just our Earth. Earth changes are upon us, but they may be part of a larger cosmic design. In any case, all we can do is ride them out as best we can, with love and support for each other.

Polarization of society is occurring on many levels, with lines being drawn in the proverbial sand. People are choosing, either consciously or by unconscious default, where they stand in the energetic maelstrom that is life on Earth today.

My heart hurts for the loss of human, animal and plant life, and the people that must live with the aftermath of the tragic occurrences on our world. However, I'm gratified when I see so many hearts around the world responding with so much compassion to environmental disasters like the 2004 tsunami that hit the coastlines of India, Sri Lanka, Indonesia and other countries; like the devastating hurricanes Katrina and Rita that decimated the Gulf coastal areas; like the Haiti earthquake and many other natural and man-made catastrophes.

While those of us with heart and conscience would never wish such events to happen to any one, the outpouring of love to those affected by them – much of it in very tangible forms – is a wonderful thing to behold. And when we begin to know that there truly is no death, then we can perhaps wonder if those multitudes of souls who chose mass exodus from our world at those times may have, at a level of higher knowing, chosen such a transition so that those left behind would find in their hearts a deeper opening as they consider the human loss of life, and the travail of those left behind. I think that none of us, especially from relatively safer vantage points on the planet, can contemplate such devastation and the suffering without some deep, silent part of us touched with the knowing that there – but for the grace of the Conscious Loving Universe – go I.

Could it be that such environmental tragedies, happening today in a world on the brink of a great Shift, are helping to guide the living human souls left behind to the path that will take us to that shift in awareness, energy and vibration that could usher in a "golden age?" A transformation that will move us into the next great human adventure? We can only wait and see just what this all means and how it will unfold. But I believe each of us is instrumental in the unfolding of this "Shift of the Ages."

Just so my readers know, the darker nature of these observations are not conclusions that I *wanted* to draw from my years studying the largely unseen subterranean forces of this world. But after all these years, driven my my own need to know and understand, I have learned to keep a weather eye, a kind of peripheral attention, on the darker elements at work in this world. I give them just enough of my attention to do what I can to stay one step ahead; to discern what I can't do anything about, and take action where I can make a difference.

There is a verse from the Bible, Ephesians 6:12, and while I have no affiliation to any organized religion, I find truth in these words:

> For we wrestle not against flesh and blood, but against
> principalities, against powers, against the rulers of the
> darkness of this world, against spiritual wickedness in high
> places.

I know many in the conspiracy theory circles who dwell almost completely on the dark, filled with impotent rage and anger at each new manifestation of "evil." If you only dwell on "the Dark," it looks as through when we decided to incarnate on Earth we must have all passed under a sign that said, "Abandon Hope, All Ye Who Enter Here." But I know that "the Dark" is not the only game on the planet. It is in fact evidence, in and of itself, of The Light.

In a world of duality, everything exists in relation to it's opposite. But there are a couple of vital differences between them.

The Dark is subject to entropy, a winding down to a dead halt over time as it exhausts its resources while trying to keep the dense heaviness of its vibratory nature going. The Dark is divisive and adversarial within itself. The Dark is an energy thief, and is made up of dens of thieves. There is no honor among thieves, and the lesser thieves always bide their time waiting for the greater thieves to topple so they can rush in and seize their power. The Dark and its minions are energy thieves because they shun connection to the infinite Source energy of the Conscious Living Universe. They've opted instead for a vampire-like hunger addiction to stealing the energy of others, gloating in their "we-have-power-over-others" supremacy. They make themselves "illuminati – illumined ones;" those of the secret societies, with the hidden, esoteric knowledge of this world. They reduce everyone else to expendable creatures to be used for their purposes.

The Light is made of Love. It is self-creative. Because Light/Love nurtures and supports, It is Source Itself, a well-spring that is ever-expansive. Love reaches out to give and receive in equal measure, so like a good community, living in harmony with the Earth, Love is ultimately self-sustaining. This is why Light/Love, in the end, will always triumph.

I learned a great deal about the differing energies and vibrations of fear, anger, grief, and also love, joy and peace when I used to facilitate drumming and dance workshops. In working with people, I would have them dance or drum out the fear, anger, or grief energy within them. Such emotional energy would move up, through and out very quickly. It simply exhausted itself, ran down, hit entropy – and this would always happen in three to seven minutes or so. Then the movements and beats would always shift into the lighter, joyful rhythms that kept bodies dancing or hands drumming for much more extended periods of time.

To continue on the bright side, for every limitation "The Matrix" tries to throw our way, more of us awaken to the forces that try to control us. This is a game they cannot win. The very fact that they have become more open and extreme in the ways they try hard to dish up every kind of fear imaginable shows how desperate they're getting about losing control. With each new extreme measure, they edge themselves out of the shadows and into the light for more and more of us to see. Wielding fear like a club, more often and more intensely, is ultimately self-defeating.

Fear is an energy that becomes exhausting over time. It exhausts our adrenal glands. It compromises our immune systems. Because of this, individual by individual, at some point, it pushes us into choosing a new path. I know this as personally and completely as anyone, because of the fear I lived with for years.

You get to a point you just can't live that way any more. You decide to let go of it and do what your highest self is calling you to do, to live and speak your highest truth, no matter the consequences. Even if it means you feel like you're falling off a figurative cliff into some imagined abyss. Yet as you fall into that surrender, you are caught by the arms of Grace. You are lifted up by the love and energy of the Conscious Living and Loving Universe Itself, with all the higher dimensional beings who accompanied you on your journey through this human lifetime watching over you and guiding you. You find you always were free, and no one can ever take that away from you.

You can only be seduced, coerced or threatened to give your freedom away, and this a choice that is yours to make, day by day.

Entr'acte V
Cataclysm

In my last incarnation on Atlantis, I found myself to be a young priestess initiate. I served within an order that interfaced with a huge crystal that in these latter times was primarily used to balance the energies of the Atlantean continent as they were assaulted by the political elites bent on building bigger and better weapons.

As a people, many of us could feel cataclysm coming, either through more war or natural disaster, or a combination of both.

There was much unrest in Atlantean societies. There were factions that were teaching a return to the old ways of living in harmony with the land, of dismantling our technologies and restoring the lands of Atlantis. But those in power, who had held its reins for so long, were loathe to give it up. Many of these dissenting groups packed up and left Atlantis by sea, just as those of us had left Lemuria so very long ago.

As a gifted initiate with strong inner sight, I was having terrifying visions of what was coming. I would awaken at night in a cold sweat from nightmares of a huge tidal wave suspended far over my head as I stood on a beach. It paused only a moment before I could see it begin to crash down over me. I always awoke before it reached me, trembling.

In my contemplations, I traveled in my light body, spending time with the ancient Lyrans in their mountain valleys. They told me that events in Atlantis had to play out as the people there were creating them. I understood, though it brought me a kind of heavy-hearted comfort. I was part of Atlantis. I needed to be there and prepare myself for what was to come.

Prerequisites of being in our spiritual order were gifts of inner vision and telepathy. As my dreams of the tidal wave and other natural disasters increased, I was forbidden by the high priests' council to leave the temple grounds any longer. Any of my visions transmitted to others in Atlantean society, on purpose or inadvertently, would only serve to further foment the current volatile unrest and dissent within the population.

The political leadership of Atlantis had given the priesthood strict orders to maintain the status quo and continue balancing the energies of the continent through the huge temple crystal. Some from our priesthood had already joined many of the dissenting groups who had left Atlantis by sea in the last several years. This was no longer allowed to happen. The leaders of Atlantis saw that this kind of exodus was only making a bad situation worse.

The balancing of energies could only be maintained so long.

As our highest priests became corrupt, seduced by wealth and power offered by the Atlantean government, the system failed more and more.

I awakened one morning to no nightmare, no vision of the tidal wave. I was filled with a strange and deep peace. Today was the day.

I sought out a young priest initiate I was close to. We shared much, finding a way to do so privately through direct touch, holding hands. This morning when I found him I immediately took his hand. His eyes suddenly locked with mine, wide with understanding. We knew it was time for our plan.

A common cloak covering my temple garb, I slipped quietly and stealthily out of the temple and off the grounds. There was a strange calm over the city in the early morning, a stillness. Not even a bird's song stirred the morning air.

I made my way down to the beach. It would be chaotic in the city later. I wanted no part of that.

I walked along the beach. I had not been down there for a long time, not since I had been forbidden to leave the temple complex. I breathed the cool, still air as I walked along the beach. The air was crisp and clear and I was experiencing a perfect quiet clarity deep within my whole being. The high cliffs above to my right were lined with tall slender cypress trees, as still as the air around them. The morning looked crystalline somehow, as I viewed my world from that place of perfect clarity.

Down the beach ahead of me was my friend, the young priest. We loved each other, but initiates in our order were not permitted to marry. It was thought that marriage would dilute the gifts of expanded awareness that our order required of us. But today would be our time, however short, to be together.

As we met and embraced, the sea withdrew from the shore in the lowest tide we had ever seen. We continued to hold each other as we looked out to sea. It was not long before we saw the wave, sparkling in the morning light, huge, growing ever larger, ever swifter as it swelled towards the shore upon which we stood. We trembled at the sight of it and held each other more closely, fingers intertwined. As it began to tower over us we could look no more. We closed our eyes.

In the next instant, the wall of water crushed the life from our bodies. However, I barely felt it. I was immediately out of my body. So was my companion. Both of us were in a place of pure light, surrounded by welcoming beings in their light bodies all around us.

***

The fall of Atlantis opened the door for others to come to Earth with agendas of control. Humanity's genome, inherited from we Lyrans and other enlightened races contributing to the people of Terra, was tampered with. What we originally endowed them with was unlinked and disconnected, striking them energetically blind, deaf and dumb. From such limitation, more fear settled deep into the human collective psyche, passed from generation to generation. The human experiment seemed to go terribly wrong.

However, things are not always as they seem. The seeds of transformation were planted in the darkest dark during the ages of oppression. Only time would tell if they would grow, and growing, if they would wither or spring into full flower.

Chapter 14: Going Public

As much as I admired the whistleblowers who were stepping out and speaking up, I held out a little longer from coming forward. I still wanted to hang on to some semblance of my old life. I didn't want to become an open representative of a reality that I felt most of my friends and family wanted to live in denial of. I thought to myself, in light of all the other information coming out, my story is just not that important. There is enough coming out, I thought. I was still afraid of "going public."

I had been struggling with low back pain and carpal tunnel syndrome for years. My back issues began in 1993, when I began working for SAIC on the Yucca Mountain Project out on the Nevada Test Site. In the years after my hypnosis sessions I had an uneasy feeling that my body might have had a reaction to working again in an area adjacent to where I had been so badly traumatized.

In all the years since then, I've discovered almost as much confirmation of my experiences in the PTSD and chronic pain I've had to deal with as in all the research I've done in the UFO field, encountering all the testimony so similar to my own. The back pain came up conspicuously on the bus rides to and from work between 1993 and 1996 while working for SAIC at the Nevada Test Site. In 1980, it had been a bus that had taken me, terrified and trapped like an animal, to where I had been injected, raped and traumatized in other ways. The deep iliopsoas and piriformis muscles went into painful spasm and have more or less stayed that way. I have since learned in my studies of PTSD that the iliopsoas muscles are the fight-or-flight muscles of the body; the piriformis muscle spasms are characteristic of rape or sodomy victims. With the subconscious emotional involvement in keeping these muscles in spasm – due to an overall feeling of being in danger that has been very hard to shake off – I've had to deal with this pain for many years now. All the various forms of treatment and healing work I've tried have helped temporarily, but never eliminated the pain. The heart arrhythmia problems that came up while working for EG&G associated back to working once again in an ex-military male-dominated career field and feeling at risk again there. I had to deal with some ugly sexual harassment there as well – causing me to be always on my guard, feeling both threatened and angry. I had learned in the military that complaints of this generally went nowhere, and I didn't make complaints at EG&G since most of these people were ex-military. I couldn't afford to lose my job. My past depression and arrhythmia; the years where it seemed I had such a low flashpoint for getting disproportionately angry in certain situations where only minor annoyance was warranted; the current and continuing chronic back and carpal tunnel pain – all are symptoms of PTSD. Having PTSD shapes one's life when it goes on for years. It affects your ability to hold down a job, how you socialize, often choosing isolation over contact with others, and much more. The body has its own memory capacity and a way of reacting from those cellular memories when situations arise that have a familiar feel to earlier dangerous, traumatic experiences.

Over the years, my back seemed to almost fall apart. It was nearly impossible to work in such pain. I finally applied for disability. About a year after moving to Durango, I finally got it. It was a huge relief. Trying to keep the back pain manageable was almost a full time job in itself. Still I had hopes of developing some kind of work for myself that I could do from home. I tried hard to develop a coaching practice, then worked at my art. Back and hand pain continued to interfere however. And energetically, something was "off." The business coach I worked with for three years remarked on it as well. I followed all her recommendations, yet not much was happening. I had tried to talk with her initially about my military trauma and extraterrestrial experiences, but she just couldn't seem to hear about them. It was almost as if she had no information receptor sites to even be able to receive or process such information. It was yet another societal message to me that this stuff was just too tough for most people to deal with.

Finally, with no real results after three years, I stopped working with her. It was time for some serious introspection on my own.

From an energy perspective, what was holding me back? In much of my training, I had learned that when something you think you want just doesn't happen despite your best efforts, somewhere deep down there is an unconscious counter-commitment to having it. Down in my subconscious, did I really not want to be a coach or an artist? Was there something else I should be doing? Was I just dealing with too much pain and associated exhaustion? I had more functional times with my back, keeping some correct balance of exercise and rest; then there would be inexplicable pain flare-ups that resisted all attempts to alleviate or heal it. Drugs were no answer. The few I tried in times of desperation provided only limited pain relief while leaving me mentally fuzzy and physically hung over for twenty-four hours after taking them, hardly able to function. If there is one thing I've learned about my back in all these years, it reacts very badly to not getting walked and exercised.

Intuitively, I was getting closer to discovering reasons as to why developing some kind of right livelihood was not working. These experiences, especially the military trauma, had been with me my whole adult life, yet I'd been in one way or another recoiling from them the whole time. I did work on the trauma with Helen, and much progress was made and I had hoped that what we had done was enough – without going public.

But in every type of career I had tried to do, NOT talking about my experiences, trying to keep them to myself, was like trying to create some kind of life and livelihood with a 300 pound gorilla on my back – and I'm well aware of what that statement has to say about my back problems. I hope that writing this book will bring healing, or at least some significant relief.

In writing this book I find there is yet another level of acceptance of the things that happened to me, another step in acknowledging it all so I can finally let it go. Writing this book is a very necessary catharsis. With such terrible things that happened to me, it's been very hard to approach them in my thoughts and feelings. Some of the worst of them are the memories of being on the moon.

In interviews, people always want to know what my moon experiences were like and I can certainly understand such avid curiosity. I can only state that it was terrible on multiple levels. I was terrified for my life the whole time. I was very poorly fed and worked hard during the day cycle, operating some kind of electronic equipment for excavation at times, and doing hard physical manual labor at others, such as lifting and stacking boxes. Worst of all, I was used for sex during what passed for night there, from man to man. I was allowed very little sleep, and I've since learned that this is another facet of mind control abuse. I shut down during all of this to the point that I didn't even feel alive anymore.

That's as much as I can tell. Do I remember more details from the sexual abuse? Yes. But I cannot bring myself to utter the words, or write them here. My mind still flees from those moon memories, and I only hope I've remembered enough for some understanding and to work on my healing process. I am not at all keen on having more hypnosis sessions to delve into the moon experiences. I did "return" there briefly in my 2010 hypnosis session with Mary Rodwell, for a specific purpose, to collect another essential piece of understanding about myself. More on that in a later chapter.

It's no wonder, in the face of such horrific abuse, the human mind dissociates, breaking away the pieces of experience and memory that contain such terror and burying them away in the subconscious. I have to wonder how many people are out there in the world who may have had such experiences, splintering them away in parts of their minds they can't reach and may never be able to open up to. But the experiences and memories are still down in there, stealing the life-force from such people to keep them suppressed, leaving them living half a life.

Why had I had these experiences in the first place? Why me?

That question, asked so many times in the years since I recovered some of my memories, was still there. In the past I had screamed this question inside, in anger and rage, and in anguish. But now, finally, it was just a quiet question, with the energy of some true curiosity. The answers were a process in themselves, peeling back layers, wondering over time... and being ready to accept the answers.

Contact

That sensitivity that had been increasing in me for many years kept progressing further. The last several years I had become aware that something was going on with me many nights while I slept, and it was not necessarily experiences with the Zetas. This was another group. There also was a connection I felt between this other group and my inter-dimensional teachers.

Whomever they were, they had the feel of family. I felt I was learning a great deal with them, but I didn't remember what. I called it attending "Cosmic University." I'd travel out to them in my astral body while my physical body slept. And every so often, like my woman friend down in New Mexico, I would encounter a person where we would have that flash of recognition and we would both know that we had met or were close friends from a place not of this world.

The most profoundly I've experienced this remembrance was with my friend Victoria Liljenquist. A friend loaned me his copy of her award-winning film, *Encounters with Angels, UFOs and Divine Messages*. As soon as I saw her in the film, I felt a connection and wanted to find a way to meet her. Then about a month later, low and behold, I found out she was moving to Pagosa Springs, an hour's drive east of Durango! I got in touch with her and she invited me to a gathering she was having there, on my birthday, November 11th, 2007. On the way to this first meeting in Pagosa, I had a daylight sighting of a saucer-shaped craft over one of Pagosa's plentiful lakes. When I arrived and we saw each other, Victoria stared at me and exclaimed, "I've dreamed about you!" Victoria is a beautiful contactee who films remarkable higher vibrational lightships and other multi-dimensional energies. She has an angelic energy. She is also a gifted healer and my close friend ever since our first meeting here on Earth, and I'm sure much longer from "out there."

I asked my inter-dimensional teachers about the Cosmic University, and learning in the astral body out on a ship somewhere. I wanted to know why I couldn't remember. They answered that I would remember when it was important. Well, I wanted to remember now! One night before going to sleep I set a strong intention in my head to R-E-M-E-M-B-E-R.

I woke up in the morning with one phrase hanging in my waking mind:

... and then you will see a fully representational Earth.

It was a phrase that filled me with wonder and hope.

This awareness expansion kept moving to new levels. I wanted to see the craft in the skies for myself. For the most part, I had not. The only extraterrestrial craft I had seen were the ones up close while in the military.

That turned out to be the problem. The ones I had seen then had been part of an experience of fear for my safety, for my life. A flash of insight told me that "they" were staying away because they didn't want me to feel afraid, and the association was still there that to see something in the night sky would relate back to that fearful time in the military. I spent some quiet time with myself going over that in my mind, and cleared and let go of my fear of seeing any craft now. I must have done it correctly, because after that the night skies lit up for me, often with multiple craft.

I've photographed many, but it soon became evident that I could take and collect hundreds of such pictures. I love my sightings. But today, I'm far more interested in "landings" and "meetings."

I often leave my bedroom blinds open at night to watch the sky before going to sleep. The brilliant pulsing, multi-colored lights would stand out from the regular stars, all the more dramatic to me because regular stars were little light blurs to my uncorrected near-sighted vision. I don't wear glasses or contact lenses to bed of course, but if something drew my gaze with my uncorrected vision, I would then put my glasses back on and get up and take a better look at it. If it still looked remarkable once my glasses were on, then I would get out my binoculars and take a look. So many nights these pulsing, multi-colored "lightships" would dance around in the sky through the binoculars, delighting my eyes, before I would get sleepy and have to close them for the night.

One particular night I noticed a very pronounced, pulsing multi-colored "lightship." It cycled through reds, ambers, greens, blues and violets, very quickly. I took a look from bed with my glasses on, but was sleepy and did not want to get up and look with the binoculars. I went to sleep.

I jerked awake later. It was still dark. I was still on my side facing the window. The pulsing light was still there, but had moved much closer, and the pulsing was even more dramatic and flashing at some very regular intervals. I checked the time, it was 3:30 am. I had the distinct feeling that I had just come abruptly back to my body from being astrally out there on that lightship. The shock of awakening as I had was from a sudden re-entry into my body. I remembered this sensation from my out-of-body experience while fully awake so many years before. It also had the feel of when we are in between sleep and awake, and we are sometimes astrally floating just above our bodies, and just enough awake to feel the floating... and our minds tell us our physical bodies can't float... then we have that falling sensation that causes us to jerk awake.

I lay there looking at the now-closer, pulsing-in-intervals "light" in the dark sky, feeling a sense of wonder and peace – no fear. I felt I was not only was visiting them in my sleep, but that they were watching over me also. I felt all kinds of feelings about this; very alive, very alert, some part of me long asleep beginning to stir to consciousness. It felt strange and different but at the same time very natural. I relaxed back into bed musing it over, falling back to sleep pretty quickly, considering how alive and alert I had felt the instant of waking up.

***

The process of wondering why I had chosen such a life, with such experiences, was ongoing.

I have always felt that spiritual learnings should have practical applications to improve the quality of our lives, that attaining some adeptness at working with the energies flowing in our lives should begin to produce some desired results.

The first step is in observing what the quantum mirror of our lives is reflecting back to us as our reality. The next is to assume 100% responsibility for how reality is showing up for us. I had learned this in various places, including my body-centered certification trainings. In regard to my traumatic experiences, this was a tough pill to swallow. It took time and a good stretch of my healing journey processed and behind me to get to enough inner calm to ask "Why me?" from a place of quiet curiosity rather than my previous emotional storms.

If we somehow attract all our experiences to us, then why would I attract such horrible ones? Was it because I was a Scorpio? Scorpios like delving into secrets, at least that's in the sun sign description. I did have a lifelong drive to delve into all kinds of things, trying to get at the core of what "the really real truth is," as I had framed it when I was a child. All the studies of the sciences beginning at an early age; my forced march through a Lutheran upbringing right up to confirmation and first communion, just to make sure I wasn't missing something there; my explorations of metaphysics, spiritual practices... I wanted to know, truly, why I was here and what my purpose might be.

When I traced my path through my memories of my military experiences, being a Scorpio seemed to have little to do with it. I was dragged into that terror, in the middle of the night at gunpoint. I had not landed there out of any fascination with military secrets. Hell, back then, I had no idea that such projects or people even existed. UFOs, little ETs with big black eyes, yes. The horrors of entrapment in black projects, no – not an inkling.

As time passed, my introspection continued. I dug deeper, looked back farther.

I knew I was not my body and I had a good understanding of reincarnation from a variety of perspectives. Finally, I wondered... surely before I incarnated into this lifetime I must have had some idea of what this life would entail... and there was my answer.

It was like feeling myself as energy and vibration, moving through all kinds of territory, searching, seeking. With that opening of wondering, "surely before I incarnated..." I experienced a feeling of coming into contact with and melting into a kindred energy and vibration, something in full resonance with my own energy, and with the vibration of my query. It was subtle, but discernible. It was like a key finding the lock into which it fit perfectly.

274

A soul contract. That was it. I knew it, felt it.

Yet the next question immediately sprang to mind: Why would I choose such a life?

The answers emerged in segments over time. Put together here and now, from all the insights that emerged, as well as the 2010 hypnosis session I had with Mary Rodwell, the information that came was all there in an instant, fully perceived. That is how tel-empathic communication works – communication instantly received and understood without need for the linearity of time and spoken words. To communicate it in written language, an interview that led me into this lifetime went something like this:

> The council had been observing Earth for many millennia. Interference by some other manipulative and opportunistic species, crossing the parsecs of space, had, down through the ages, sowed seeds of trouble that were keeping an operating principle of fear the foremost one on the planet.
>
> There was much to be learned from fear. Fear had a great capacity to be a catalyst for awakening. However, the interfering species were expert at wielding fear and finding ways to thwart its potential as a catalyst. When it seemed that human beings might be on the verge of a collective awakening, actions were taken to stamp it out, with far fewer humans escaping the net than there could have been. Fear had become a trap instead of an opportunity to expanded consciousness. As the ages flowed onwards on this world, a great cosmic cycle was coming to an end. It was to be a time of great expansion of awareness for humanity. Something had to be done. Something that would not be a direct interference in the way that the other species had interfered. A way had to be found to infuse a higher vibration into humanity's world without open contact.
>
> Eyes, attention and energy turned upon me. I had been involved with humanity from its inception. I had taken human incarnations in the distant past to experience the world they were creating, and here and there throughout the ages. It was quite an experience, and some of those times I had completely lost myself in my human lifetime. So had others. There was no shame in this. It was all too easy to lose oneself through immersion in the human experience. What was hard was to recover yourself from within that human form, operating in an entire societal and cultural structure that had been so cleverly designed to keep human beings from awakening to their true nature. Some managed to free

themselves, but many times they had to isolate themselves in monasteries or on mountaintops to do so. There were times in my past sojourns on Earth that I had failed to awaken, and had fallen into patterns of action that had accumulated some karma.

The directed communion occurring between all of us now sorted itself out into parcels of collectively designed direction. The council wanted me to be one of the ones to go. It was a tremendous opportunity for me, for my own spiritual progression. I felt both joy and a touch of trepidation at the thought of returning to a human form. Joy because of what I could learn through the experience of such limitation on my consciousness. In human terms, it could be like going for an upper graduate degree at a university. The wisp of trepidation arose because of those lifetimes in the past where I had lost myself so utterly. If I lost myself this time, could I find a way to recover myself from within the system?

Together, we devised ways to do this. The council needed an operative on Earth this time, someone more than a mere observer. This would be a very special, and difficult mission. So much was going on on Earth right now that looked like sheer insanity observed from our vibrational vantage point. We needed to understand more of what it was like to experience this from inside the system. I would provide this. And because I would provide this, my lifetime would be set up with various challenges that would bring me into direct confrontation with things going on on Earth that the majority of the population were told did not exist.

I would be born at a precisely chosen moment in time that would astrologically imprint me with the sensitivity, personality, will and drive I would need to navigate this lifetime. I would have a difficult childhood. But it would toughen up my sensitive nature for other challenges to come, forging and shaping a warrior will to survive, to overcome – as well as instilling a vibration in me to attract the other experiences that would be part of my soul contract. The investigative nature I would be born with would propel me into lifelong learning and inquiry into the very nature of the Universe Itself, and my place in it. I would seek answers wherever I needed to look, even outside the structures and institutions governed by human authority systems.

I would be born into a family involved with the Zeta

Reticulans, being covertly picked up from time to time for their purposes of developing Human-Zeta hybrids in their efforts to preserve their species and culture. The touches of their genetic material added to my human form in utero would make a better human vehicle for me to operate through. Since these early extraterrestrial experiences were some of those monitored by the human military, such contact would in turn would set up the later challenges of being part of situations within the hidden and secret human military hierarchy.

These experiences had the potential to completely destroy me. It was a huge risk in two important ways. If my human self died as a consequence of my experiences, my service as an operative for my people, for our council, would be cut short, its full purpose and potential unfulfilled. My higher dimensional energy would touch those in such hidden, secret areas and subtly exert an enlightening effect, that could, or not – depending on the free will of those influenced – bear fruit in other subtle change down the line. In any case, through the possibility of affecting subtle change, and having the karma from my past lives on Earth paid in full, some purpose for this lifetime would be served. If I committed suicide under the burden of what had happened to me, in addition to unfulfilled purpose, I could find myself trapped in a kind of personal astral hell. Such a hell would be created and reinforced by my own emotional state at the moment of taking my own life. It would take considerable time and effort to reach me in such a case, and extract me from such self-entrapment. There would also be additional karma accrued from an act such as suicide.

But given the imprinting of my personality, sensitivity, will and drive to learn, it was more likely that I would choose to survive and bring all my investigative aptitudes to bear on pressing into the inner core of my experiences, and choosing healing. And within my healing process would be trigger-keys to awakening to who I truly am, and to consciously fulfilling my purpose on Earth.

I would be watched over every step of the way by other higher-dimensionals remaining in their non-corporeal forms as ever-present teachers and guides. Those who had once been my closest family members on Lyra when humanity first came into being in this galaxy would watch over me, as well as one of the First Ones, the Founders... a great honor.

My Lyran uncle actually agreed to incarnate there for me as my earthly human father for a time. There would be one I had known from some of my other Earth lifetimes as well, also a member of the council. And others from the races within the Alliance, some at specific times, some throughout this whole lifetime.

I would live, in a sense, in both places, with my people in their ships of light, dreaming a dream of my life on Earth. When my human body slept, I would astral travel to rejoin with my star family, sharing with them what I learned of life on Earth and also learning through the imprinting of various specific information that I would need in my Earth life. I would know it in the moment it was needed. The information I was given evolved through the information I shared with my people. It was not only shared through our tel-empathic link. Once aboard the lightship, my astral body would enter a circular, tube-like chamber. Resonant sound and light frequencies would then be activated within it, signaling my higher vibrational astral implants to upload all the data from my human body and everything it experienced at every level, physical, mental and emotional. It was from this multi-layered experiential data that the information imparted to me in my visits "home" was evolved from and adjusted as needed.

Like all higher dimensionals who volunteered for Earth lifetimes, our souls carried the higher vibrations of our people into our Earth forms when we incarnated. This in itself raised the vibration on Earth. Just as crop circles in recent decades on Earth radiate a special energy and vibration, imprinting it upon humanity in various ways, those of us who volunteered for Earth incarnations also brought a special frequency to Earth, our energy and vibration seeded within the systems and structures of Earth societies and cultures. Even if we lost our ourselves in our earthly lives, at the very least, at our higher vibrational energy still touched many, making a difference at even subtle levels.

Under all this spiritual intention and guidance, I was overjoyed to take on this mission, despite any trepidation. Trepidation was only an energetic hangover from previous Earth lifetimes. I knew I was indestructible. I knew how constantly and lovingly I would be monitored. I waited with excitement for the special moment that I would make my entrance into my next Earth life.

That moment came in the Earth's 11th month, on the 11th day, at 11am, in its year 1954 on the south and west side of the North American continent. The line-up of all those 11s at the moment of my birth was in itself a master number message encoded for me to discover later on.

I had arrived.

Moving Through My Fears

My attitude about speaking out and going public underwent a change during the ominous oppression of the Bush-Cheney years. So much was simmering deep down inside of me and from broader perspectives than what I often saw being presented in material I read, listened to or watched. The value of being a spiritual person my entire life, my love of learning across a broad spectrum, my encounters with my own mental and emotional nature and learning more deeply about these aspects of self, AND having had the experiences I had were forming a viewpoint that increasingly, I knew needed to be expressed.

What kept me from speaking out for so long? Fear. What kinds of things was I afraid of? I was afraid for my life if I spoke out. I was afraid that if I went public I'd be thought of as yet another UFO crackpot. I was afraid of losing the respect and friendship of my personal social circles. I was afraid I could kiss the possibility of any special relationship goodbye forever. I was afraid of becoming even more isolated and alone. More fears crowded up.

For every fear that cropped up about speaking out, I sat quietly with that specific fear and imagined myself actually having it happen to me. I walked myself through the experience in my mind's eye, even if it meant dying in several different ways I could envision. One by one, I realized that no matter what, I could move through any of them, even dying. I knew I was not my body. The essence of who I truly am is energy and vibration, and indestructible. Through my own experiences of being out of the body and soul travel, I knew I was, and am, ultimately safe in the Universe. I remember my beloved teacher Ram Dass speaking about Emmanuel. Emmanuel was a being channeled through Pat Rodegast, whom Ram Dass humorously called his "spook friend." Ram Dass once asked him what it was like to die. Emmanuel replied, "Ram Dass, dying is absolutely safe. It's like taking off a tight shoe."

Reports of out-of-body-experiences, near-death-experiences, experiences in meditation, studies and evidence of reincarnation... my own experience and understanding of the true essence of myself, together with all the other experiential testimony and anecdotal evidence I'd encountered over the years... all of it greatly aided, at last, the process of coming to terms with fear. Fear of all the kinds of things, from the little anxieties to the really big terrors.

I'm not saying here that I never ever feel afraid any more. That would be a very foolish claim. On a very human level, I definitely do feel afraid at times.

It's part of being human. But the difference is that I now have ways of handling and dealing with fear so it no longer shuts me down. It does not prevent me from speaking out.

Fear does not block me from the continuing and unfolding process of "becoming." Becoming what, I'm not sure yet. It's a journey full of wonder. That wonder has helped me recapture the sense of innocence I thought had been ripped away from me. Innocence is a vital quality to the exploration of life, beyond any book or institutional learning. Innocence is wonder and openness to explorations of whatever kinds, inner life of mind and spirit, or out in the world. Life's journey is rich and magnificent. If passing through the tempering fires of trauma led to who I am today, then today I am grateful for every step on my life's path.

***

I had no idea when I went public just how many people would be interested in my story. I was not prepared that I would go public with my article in UFO Digest in December of 2008, and then just over a year later, be a speaker at the International UFO Congress in Laughlin, NV – and get a standing ovation alongside my co-speaker, Melinda Leslie[1], a fiercely dedicated covert-ops abduction researcher.

I never thought things would go where they have, and I never knew just how much was inside of me waiting to be written down, or spoken to audiences – live, or via radio interviews. I have been surprised and awestruck by a profound awakening process that going public has brought about in me. Was this what my guides had meant when they told me I "would remember when it was important?" That I would know what I needed to know in moments of necessity?

This was some faculty that seemed to operate beyond the linearity of the third dimension. I thought again about my experiences that I called "cosmic nanoseconds" where I seemed to be living both here in my earthly life and some other dimension at the same time, a place where time, if it existed there at all, seemed to stand still compared to here. If the present moment is the only true moment, if the action we actually take at that moment is the only action that counts, that moment's action becoming the catalyst creating the next moment, then I now understand the guidance from my inter-dimensional teachers about moving through life in these chaotic times.

With so many around me planning for what they might need through earth changes, solar flares, a possible third world war, the passage of Niburu, "the twelfth planet," I turned to my non-corporeal family about what I should do.

---

[1] Melinda Leslie is a researcher and lecturer in the field of UFOlogy. Rather than using the term "MILABs" she calls the military-type of abductions "re-abs" meaning ET experiencers' being re-abducted by military or quasi-military personnel investigating people who are picked up by extraterrestrials. Her research is extensive and ongoing for over 20 years. Her website: http://www.alienexperiences.com/MelindaLeslie.html.

I had no real resources to "stock up" or take such planning measures. Their answer was immediate and clear, ringing through my mind.

Simply stay as centered in the present moment as you can. As each moment unfolds into the next, you will know, or be shown, what to do. Invest as little of your energy in any future scenarios as is possible, even the good ones. Simply be present and trust your ability to respond to the moment.

This seemed to me to be very good counsel. I follow it as much as I can in the current maelstrom that is life on Earth. And I know, no matter what happens, I will be okay. I may continue in this body and I hope I do. I would like to see how things turn out here from this human perspective. But if I exit this body in some manner, I'll still be a part of this transformation unfolding from another realm.

In emerging from the fear-lockdown over my body and consciousness, I discovered for myself an expansion of awareness with limitless potential. I sensed I could go as far as I liked with this new awareness, limited only by my own Earthly upbringing, to life as I had grown up knowing it here, in this body. I'm still in the process of unlearning those limitations. But to continue living my life here on Earth together with this new expansion, it seems I need to take it in increments, a step at a time, so I don't lose myself in other-dimensional realms. So I can still live in this body, on this planet, and effectively bridge the gap, and find ways to communicate new perspectives in human language.

My healing process and moving beyond the fear to go public has brought about even more awakening to the energetic and vibrational universe of which we are all a part. Speaking out continues to be a powerful way of demonstrating the actuality of not allowing myself to be controlled by fear, of moving beyond fear. I found through experience that the energy of fear in the body causes more than tenseness, stress, shallow breathing, and contracted muscles ready for fight or flight. It shuts down the perception of, and the expansion of, extra-dimensional awareness.

***

As I began to go public, speaking and writing, my healer Helen told me – with a glow of warmth in her eyes – that I was moving into my final stage of healing, the process of confronting my abusers. With most of her clients, that meant confronting a father, step-father or other adult who had abused or molested them. For me, the only way I could do this was to go public.

I know that going public will somehow affect those individuals and organizations who perpetrate mind control abuse on people. It will be confrontational. But I am not doing this so much to be "against" the perpetrators as I am doing it to be "for" all of us – those of us who have been deliberately traumatized – and for the whole population in general. My most heartfelt reason to go public is to reach out to others like myself, who may have suffered in similar ways. You are not crazy, and you can recover. You can move beyond being a "survivor" and learn to *thrive*. You can find peace.

This book is part of my healing, and I hope a beginning map to recovery for others, especially if you are willing to go all the way with your own healing.

I'm still finding out what "all the way" means. Being a wanderer means journeying, taking on each trek that intrigues us, fascinates us, fills us with wonder or awe, from lifetime to lifetime, dimension to dimension. Wandering, journeying, is. When one journey is done, we often can't wait to begin the next one.

Part Three: Awakening

Chapter 15: Awakening

> The experiences of a person in a religious [spiritual] altered state of consciousness - that is, perceiving Alternate Reality - are different from the symptoms of a person with a psychotic thought disorder. In the religious [spiritual] trance, there is a predetermined beginning and ending to each experience, and the individual returns to the ordinary state of consciousness with an intact and self-aware ego. The person also emerges from trance with a sense of renewal and a message or other gift for the tribe or community, no matter how arduous the journey into the spirit realm has been. Psychosis, on the other hand, is unpredictable and unwanted, a madness that is both disorienting and lacking in meaning in ordinary reality. The ability to begin and end an altered state of consciousness on cue and the sense of meaning and fulfillment that follow the experience are the criteria used to distinguish madness from spiritual ecstasy.
>
> ~ *Ecstatic Body Postures: An Alternate Reality Workbook* by Belinda Gore, PhD, 1995, reprinted with permission of the author[1].

It was a years-long process to open up to my own direct experience of a larger reality. In spite of my inner experiences, I was pretty attached to 3D empirical, material evidence and data and being as resolutely objective as possible. I had even learned in some ways to compete in this world on intellectual terms. I was afraid that if I let go of my grip on this stance, no one would ever take me seriously. I had to learn to loosen my grip on that viewpoint, through unlearning what I thought I knew.

I was opening up to a larger awareness, an expanded energy universe. I had always had a special sensitivity even as a child – though no words to describe it

---

[1] Belinda Gore has a PhD in counseling from Ohio State University. Also a student of the late anthropologist Felicitas Goodman, Gore is involved in further development of working with ecstatic body postures. Goodman discovered that when the postures shown in ancient figurines are assumed and held in a statue-like state by a person also listening to rattle, drum or other consciousness-altering sounds for shamanic journeying, that person takes a spirit journey specific to the particular posture being held that will also have personal meaning to the person journeying in this way. Goodman's work is shared in her book, *Where the Spirits Ride the Wind: Trance Journeys and Other Ecstatic Experiences.* Goodman also founded the Cuyamungue Institute to further explore and research such trance states. Website: http://www.cuyamungueinstitute.com. Belinda Gore's website: http://www.belindagore.com/.

– feeling it somehow set me apart. Despite my immersion in the 3D sciences, it remained with me. This sensitivity had been increasing incrementally for years in periodic spurts or surges. When Ben Kenobi of *Star Wars* described "The Force," I knew what he was talking about. He called it an energy field created by all living things, though to me it was rather the reverse – it was all living things that drew their existence from a living, conscious universal energy field. I could feel this energy, especially out in nature, surrounded by living things, even the earth under my feet.

As this expanded sense developed, I had to develop some trust with it. This was quite a process. While I felt my immersion in the sciences was a very necessary endeavor, and a richly rewarding one on many levels, it described a physical universe governed by Newtonian laws of physics. What happened within those laws was predictable and therefore, "real." What happened outside of them seemed imaginary. At least until I discovered quantum mechanics. All kinds of studies were launched by visionary scientists to test and measure what was possible in the realm of psi abilities through various models that quantum science now provided. Obviously, I was not alone in my perception of an energy universe, or experiencing sensory phenomenon beyond what was circumscribed by the five physical senses. And in my private life quest "to know" over the years of my life, discrepancies in science were cropping up. More and more often, traditional science began to look almost as dogmatic as traditional religion.

Coping with the expansion of my intuitive, multi-dimensional senses and some of the things I was picking up on, even though I now had a model for what was happening, still felt like moving out into a void – sensed, but unknown. It was like trying to walk on quantum water. Trust it, see it, know it as "real," and it would support you. Waver in that trust and you might drown. I felt like a person who had been blind, deaf and dumb her whole life now being given new little parcels of sight and hearing – and a completely new mode of communication – wonderful, but overwhelming at times. I didn't know yet how to adapt to them or make full use of them. Granted, this awakening had been taking place gradually for a long time. But it was becoming a crescendo that I either needed to learn to trust and embrace, or walk away from forever. I couldn't walk away. This expanded intuitive sense was part of the essence of who I was, who I am. And everyone else too, I felt. It was just that some people could not open to it or trust it... too many mind-ego structures of indoctrination had become barriers to perceiving the energy universe.

I asked my inter-dimensional teachers if they could help me with learning to comprehend and use these new abilities more effectively.

> *We cannot help you. You already have too many voices of authority on your world trying to direct your lives. We cannot become one more. You will have to go on learning through trial and error, stumbling for a while until you learn the*

intricacies of perceiving the energy universe. Remember it is part of you and you are part of it... that is the key to a greater understanding of what you are learning to perceive.

I couldn't argue in the least with such a perspective. They were too right. Apparently, I was on my own in learning to understand and use these abilities in practical ways. So be it.

This learning was, and still is, a process of sensing and feeling, trusting enough to act on what I sensed and felt, and watching where it led me. I learned that it's easy to mistake this still small inner voice for the other voices that clamor inside, voices born of emotions, desire or fear, or even physical tiredness or pain.

There is nothing wrong with emotions, or feeling them. However, human emotions have been grossly manipulated on this world, until they have eclipsed the still small voice within. Some people learn to fear emotional excess through the pain it can bring. They then retreat into the world of the mind-ego, equally restricting from a different basis. The emotions don't really leave at that point either, they just move underground and push and pull on such mentally-engaged people from the shadow realm of the subconscious.

More and more I realized that in the moments I could go quiet inside, to a calm stillpoint, I could trust the intuitions and insights that flowed from that place where emotions were at rest and the mind ceased its endless analyses.

I Have Never Been Alone

I learned that I could trust the perceptions that came free from any emotional charge. I might have an emotional response to the perception, but the perception itself arose directly and spontaneously from the quiet place inside. Often my emotional responses to the perceptions, or insights, took me by complete surprise.

Like the time I was reading the email with the information about Lyra. I was suddenly flooded with the knowing – no logical analysis, no figuring it out through deduction – that my inter-dimensional teachers were my father, mother and uncle from my time on that world. With that realization in the next micro-second I was flooded with the joy of reunion, of relief. My face was instantly soaked with tears, and sobs shook my shoulders as the waves of emotion rippled through me.

In that moment I knew I had never truly been alone on this Earth... was never truly some isolated soul abandoned in a hostile environment. I was here for a purpose, I had volunteered to be here, and had come knowing from a higher perspective that I would not be alone here. It's just that once here, I had to recover the ability to sense, perceive and comprehend this from my new reference point within the 3D reality.

285

My inter-dimensional teachers are family from possibly my very first lifetime in a body, back on Lyra.

I never could get "names" for them. Finally I realized we never used names as such. We knew each other by our unique vibrational signatures. Recently I've started calling them Ada, Ama and Unca so I can have a more personal and human reference for them, in the human language I've become accustomed to. I feel they are pleased with these references to them.

My memories of my homeworld carry that same deep emotional resonance. The memories of my life and the events there that have seeped into my memory are as potent as any memories from this lifetime in this body.

I hope I can help many people to build bridges in their consciousness from 3D empirical limitations to their inherent multi-dimensionality and help free consciousness on this planet. With our consciousness free, we can transform this world – no more ugly secrets, no more abuse, no more destruction of lives and our environment.

None of us are alone here on Earth, nor have we ever been.

Synchronicities, Messages and Visions

More and more I was learning to pay attention to synchronicities and thoughts that sprang to mind in a spontaneous manner, and the quality of energy they came with. Synchronicities, and especially noticing them, seemed like little messages from Spirit, or my guides, that I had followed the proper intuition at a figurative fork in my path and had landed in the "right" spot. With spontaneous thoughts, oftentimes it seemed like in my head, a vibrational note was struck, like someone plunking a single key on a piano. Sometimes there were multiple notes struck when the message was longer, but they were mostly short, one or two words, or short phrases or sentences. When one is learning to receive this kind of communication, I suppose the sender keeps things short so that the message is not lost in complexity. I remembered the experience with the word "Cipro," which turned out to be the medicine I needed at the time. Contexts within which words or messages came were as important and synchronous as the message itself.

Often the "plunk" of vibration in my head translated immediately into the name of a person that I was supposed to reach out and call on the phone, or within minutes, that same person would call me. The more I paid attention to this, the more uncannily it could be relied upon to be the right thing to do in the moment that it happened.

I asked my guides why they were so fast with answers to my questions, so much so that the question often didn't even get completed.

The question exists first as energy and vibration which we directly perceive. Forming a question with the mind is your mind catching up with the vibration of your query. When we receive the vibration of the question, we then answer it as your mind forms the question in words.

"So why aren't you just talking to me more?" I asked.

You are moving through a different dimension than we; it takes most of your attention and energy. We often 'speak' with you at a higher vibrational level, but your conscious mind does not register it. When you have a question, your attention is on us and our response, and you become receptive enough most of the time to hear our reply.

Other times messages came in picture form. Many times the images of scenes from my favorite older movies or television shows would pop into my head, again spontaneously. They would keep popping into my mind until I paid attention to them and got the message. It was always important to pay attention to the context in which they presented themselves. Again, this was a learning process. There were many times I would impatiently brush repeating images popping into my mind away like an annoying fly, dismissing them as manufactured by my mind. I now wonder how many messages I may have missed due to dismissing recurring imagery happening at a contextually significant time.

This is a delicate process and one in which I always have to carefully assess the feel of the energy of the message or image. If a logical mind process of reasoning, analysis and deduction is involved, I may think of the process as valuable, but not necessarily truly insightful. The information that comes spontaneously, "out of the blue" as it were, and the energy it carries and how it feels is where I apply my discernment. If I can't be sure for some reason that it's truly a message, if it is, it will confirm itself in some other way over time, usually sooner rather than later.

Sometimes there seemed no apparent context for the images that would come. A very persistent vision of some board room meeting, perhaps in the Pentagon, kept arising in my mind. A top-brass officer, perhaps a full bird colonel, was heading the meeting and they were all going through and discussing files on people. My file came to the top of the pile. Someone said, "she's out there talking you know," and the top-brass officer stated emphatically, "She is to be left completely alone." He took my file and placed it next to him on the conference table. That was all I saw.

This was a disturbing image to me. Even aware of the fact that its energy signature and continuing recurrence seemed to indicate it was something to pay attention to, I kept trying to brush this one away. I fell into analyzing it, writing it off to a trick of the mind. Still it kept surfacing. I did not want to entertain any of the implications it suggested to me.

I finally realized that it had occurred in one particular context; I was wondering why I was being left alone. Beyond sensing that my phone was tapped and hearing noises on it during conversations sometimes, I did not detect any kind of surveillance going on, though I always remain cautious to this day. I had rationalized that, because I had recovered my memories through hypnosis, and with the canned "official" explanations of why hypnosis memories were not credible, maybe they didn't think they needed to pay attention to me or anything I was saying.

And that could certainly be true. I had actually tried to join the Disclosure Project during it's formation, but was told that they could not use anyone whose memories came from hypnosis, all memories had to be actual conscious recall. I understood and accepted that. Dr. Greer needed to hold to that standard for what he was hoping to accomplish, and with an organization like the False Memory Syndrome Foundation out there, people relating memories from hypnosis could tarnish his project in the eyes of the public.

Nellie Bly

There was another vibrational key that started to plunk into my thoughts on a regular basis; the name Nellie Bly.

I remembered her name from a short story I had read of her back in my grade school days. Born Elizabeth Jane Cochran, she was a young woman who, in the 1880s – dissatisfied with covering fashion and theater stories – wanted to do serious journalism. She approached Joseph Pulitzer of the *New York World* newspaper about her aspirations. He asked her to take on a story, undercover, of reporting on conditions in a women's insane asylum. She agreed. Nellie acted insane to get herself committed to the asylum. The food was rotten and spoiled, the drinking water filthy; bathing consisted of being doused with icy water, and inmates were often beaten if they did not keep quiet. There were rats everywhere.

The *New York World* secured her release after ten days. Of her experiences, Nellie wrote:

> What, excepting torture, would produce insanity quicker than this treatment? Here is a class of women sent to be cured. I would like the expert physicians who are condemning me for my action, which has proven their ability, to take a perfectly sane and healthy woman, shut her up and make her sit from 6 am until 8 pm on straight-back benches, do not allow her to talk or move during these hours, give her no reading and let her know nothing of the world or its doings, give her bad food and harsh treatment, and see how long it will take to make her insane. Two months would make her a mental and physical wreck.

When I read her story, I really admired her for taking on such an assignment, and through her exposé, Nellie Bly greatly improved the conditions for the women inmates at that asylum. Her story is one of those that remained with me, like an echo from the past. Now my inter-dimensional teachers were playing that note in my mind that was my remembrance of the story of Nellie Bly.

I wasn't sure why, but it was as persistently recurring as the images of the Pentagon board room with the colonel saying, "She is to be left completely alone." Was there a link? This was another area I would have preferred to dismiss. But if there is something my guides want me to get from the words or images they activate in my thoughts, they keep pressing the vibrational key until I pay attention and get the message.

Finally I wondered if recurrent thoughts of Nellie Bly were showing me an analogy for "wanderers" – extraterrestrial souls volunteering for a human incarnation to help out Earth and the human race in some way. I had first heard the term from David Wilcock,[2] and from listening to that interview, I then began reading the *Law of One*[3] series of books by Carla Rueckert, Don Elkins, and Jim McCarty and found the term "wanderer" in those books as well. In reading *From Elsewhere: Being ET in America* by Scott Mandelker,[4] it was pretty clear that I fit quite closely the profile for being a wanderer.

Nellie Bly had volunteered to go spend ten days in an insane asylum to report on the conditions there. Already in touch with the idea of a soul contract for this lifetime, I mused that as wanderer, I was like Nellie in volunteering to come to insane asylum Earth in human form for the same reasons. Life on Earth was violent and savage, a hostile environment. It looked completely insane to me. I watched wars waged without regard for astronomical numbers of lives lost. My entire life I'd watched environmental exploitation and destruction continue at a frightening pace with little to no concern for the devastation of the entire Earth's ecosystem, the foundation upon which all life on the planet depends. Insanity, definitely.

I thought I'd gotten the message, but the vibrational key continued to sound in my being. Finally, I looked up Nellie Bly on Wikipedia online. All the information I was aware of was there, but also some pictures. There was a startling resemblance between her and myself, especially in pictures of myself

[2] David Wilcock is a professional lecturer, filmmaker, author and researcher of ancient civilizations, consciousness science, and new paradigms of matter and energy. His film *Convergence* and book *The Source Field Investigations: The Hidden Science and Lost Civilizations Behind the 2012 Prophecies* unveil the proof that all life on Earth is united in a field of consciousness, which affects our minds in fascinating ways. His website: http://divinecosmos.com/.

[3] *The Law of One* books were channeled through Carla L. Rueckert and documented by Don Elkins and Jim McCarty between 1981 and 1984. This material was channeled by Ra through Carla as the other members of the group supported her and recorded the sessions. Ra identified itself as a "social memory complex" of beings, member of a "confederation" that had visited Earth and walked among human beings some eleven thousand years ago to learn/teach. This is a fascinating series of five books, beginning with *The Ra Material: An Ancient Astronaut Speaks* is book one of the series.

[4] Scott Mandelker completed a doctorate in East-West Psychology at the California Institute of Integral Studies (CIIS) and began his own investigations into ET identity based on his own experiences and explorations of related spiritual material. His website is http://www.scottmandelker.com/. Author of *From Elsewhere: Being ET in America*.

close to the age of Nellie in the pictures I found. The books and work of Walter Semkiw[5] demonstrate case studies of reincarnations of people where the physical facial characteristics of individuals carry over to other lifetimes.

Nellie Bly (Elizabeth Jane Cochran)   Niara while in the USAF

Private Life to Public Life

My very first venture into public speaking was a community talk I gave in Durango, CO in January 2008, where I spoke about my experiences and showed the *Disclosure Project Witness Testimony* video.

Later in March that year, I did an interview with a local internet radio program about my experiences. It was one more foot edged out into the public arena.

An article published in the Winter 2008/2009 issue of Institute of Noetic Sciences (IONS) *Shift* magazine opened things up for me further. Dean Radin[6] had written *The Enduring Enigma of the UFO* and when I read it, I was pleasantly surprised. The article was a far more thoughtful treatment of the subject than I was expecting, and Dr. Radin actually cited some very good references to the subject. He is to be commended for having the professional courage to write and publish such an article. I was inspired to write an editorial back to the magazine with a bit of my own experiences and also to thank Dr. Radin and IONS for putting the article out there. I even got a nice email response from Dr. Edgar Mitchell who was cited in the article and is the founder of IONS .

---

[5] Walter Semkiw, MD, began researching reincarnation in 1995. His books, Return of the Revolutionaries: The Case for Reincarnation and Soul Groups Reunited and Born Again: Reincarnation Cases Involving International Celebrities make a very compelling case for the idea that physical characteristics carry over from lifetime to lifetime. His website: http://www.iisis.net/.

[6] Appearing in the popular 2004 film, *What the Bleep Do We Know?*, Dr. Dean Radin is a senior research scientist at the Institute of Noetic Sciences exploring quantum models pertaining to consciousness. He is author of several books including *Entangled Minds: Extrasensory Experiences in a Quantum Reality* and *The Conscious Universe: The Scientific Truth of Psychic Phenomena*. His website: http://www.deanradin.com.

That editorial was a kind of tipping point for me. I decided I needed to get my story out there for whatever good it might do, especially for anyone with similar experiences. I published my first article online about my experiences at *UFO Digest* in December of 2008. Many people emailed me about that article, sharing their own experiences or just expressing sympathy. Some from the other side of the world! I was surprised at the volume of responses.

Through a gracious and enthusiastic invitation from Katee McClure, I did my first real public appearance in Aztec, NM in March 2009 at the Aztec UFO Symposium. One of the speakers I had suggested to Katee was also invited to speak, Dr. Michael Salla of the Exopolitics movement. I got to spend some time with him during that weekend in March, and he invited me to become part of the Exopolitics Institute as an advisory board member. I was happy and grateful to accept. I have met many great people in the exopolitics field through the Exopolitics Institute.

As a result of speaking in Aztec, Janet Sailor, Director for the Alliance Studying Paranormal Experiences (ASPE) invited me to speak at the 2009 ASPE Paranormal Symposium in Angel Fire, NM that same September.

I was very moved by people's responses to hearing about my experiences. One man came up to me afterward saying he came prepared to not believe a thing I said, but found himself doing a 180-degree turn on that position, because what I said about my own life touched on several areas of his own.

Others came up to me and shared how glad they were I had the courage to talk about some of the sexual issues the ET experiences had created, because they were struggling with the same themselves, and they now felt some new understanding for themselves, and above all, some very needed acknowledgment. When one has carried around such experiences in mental and emotional isolation for a long time, it's a relief to know you aren't the only one. It had not been easy to speak about such things from a stage, but I had felt inside myself that it was very necessary. Obviously, that intuition had been correct. One person's eyes glistened with tears simply from finally feeling validated, hearing about the issues stemming from this kind of experience and its aftermath from someone else.

***

When I saw Robert O. Dean had come out of retirement to speak at the International UFO Congress in February of 2009 I decided to attend. There were many other speakers there that year I wanted to see as well.

I enjoyed the UFO Congress experience tremendously. I made several new and good friends. A new friend from Australia I met through the December 2008 *UFO Digest* article was there, so I got to meet her in person. She introduced me to Bob Brown, who had been putting on the UFO Congress for years with his daughter Nicole and their board of directors. In talking with Bob, I met Melinda Leslie, MILAB/covert-ops experiencer and researcher – though Melinda has renamed MILABs as ReABS, pointing out that ET experiencers are often re-abducted by military or quasi-military agencies. Melinda and I became friends and I think she has done some truly amazing work in this very difficult area of study. Black projects, covert-ops and mind control are some of the darkest and ugliest parts of this whole phenomenon, and many people just don't want to touch it. I hope she will do a book on the subject someday.

Bob let us know he was interested in having Melinda and I speak at the next UFO Congress in 2010.

There was another wonderful benefit to becoming friends with Melinda, news of my former friend and support person, Miesha Johnston.

I had lost track of Miesha Johnston when I moved away from Las Vegas in 1997 and had tried to put any life to do with UFOs and shadow governments behind me. As I opened back up to my experiences, I had tried to find her again, doing extensive internet searches, emailing people. I really wanted to re-connect with her and share my appreciation and gratitude with her for being there for me during what were some of my most difficult times after my initial hypnosis session. After being unable to locate her, first and foremost, I wanted to know she was okay. I wanted to let her know about my healing process, that I was okay, and more recently, that I wasn't hiding any more.

It was as if she had disappeared from the face of the Earth. And she had been so vocal and so involved with people around this phenomenon when I knew her that I really feared for her, and what might have happened to her.

Through Melinda and her sharing of her experiences with me, I got news of Miesha. She was fine, but she had withdrawn from the field for personal reasons that Melinda explained to me. I completely understood and was happy to know she was safe. Miesha and I are now back in contact with each other, and she is back in action again, facilitating support groups for ET experiencers as well as groups for military abductees, super soldier and mind control abuse victims. Super soldiers are an outgrowth of trauma-based mind control programs, likely one of the primary reasons for such programs – to create a super soldier programmed to follow orders without any thought of ethics, morals or conscience; basically a human automaton.

At the 2009 UFO Congress I also met ET sculptor Cynthia Crawford. She is an incredible woman with her own amazing experiences from childhood onwards. She is a sculptor of busts, bas-relief and figures of extraterrestrials, of many varieties. I got one from her, called a Ka-Tsa-Hayan. It reminded me a great deal of the shy little beings I saw while still living in Las Vegas years ago, that I had seen with my third eye. The Ka-Tsa-Hayan was painted a pale green, but when I got him home I painted him golden to more closely resemble the being I had seen, in its luminous golden form. Another woman, Jujuolui Kuita, shared her table and I got to be friends with both of them. I put a short chapter of my experiences in Juju's compilation book, *We Are Among You Already: True Stories of Star Beings On Earth.*

Finding these women was like finding star family on Earth, similar to Victoria Liljenquist and a few others. I saw them both again in Angel Fire, NM in September of 2009 at the ASPE Paranormal Symposium. At that time, I became very attracted to another of Cynthia's statues, a Mantis Being.

I visited her at her home in the Phoenix area in October and picked up this new sculpture. Almost as soon as touched it, I realized energetically that I had a very tall Mantis Being spirit guardian who kept a regular position behind my right shoulder.

Confirmation of the presence of this spirit guardian (the term "guide" did not seem to be an accurate term for him) came about three weeks later. Back home in Colorado, I drove to a movie night over in Pagosa Springs with friends. We watched Jose Escamilla's *Moon Rising*. Afterwards, we were discussing the film and other things. One of the men in attendance at this event kept looking at me curiously. Finally he spoke up and said:

"I don't want to alarm you, but do you realize you have a tall praying mantis being, about eight foot, standing behind your right shoulder?"

All of us in the room had not been having any discussion of spirit guides or anything relating to them that evening. So this query came straight out of the blue. I started laughing, and told him that yes, I was aware of this being and shared about the statue I had gotten only a few weeks earlier that had brought this being into my conscious attention. It was an amazing confirmation.

I've gotten others as well. At a talk I did in Albuquerque, NM in the fall of 2010, a psychic sat and listened and sketched the spirit beings she saw around me. Her representations were very accurate, including my inter-dimensional teachers and the tall being behind my right shoulder. Again, I did not mention these guides or beings in any way during my presentation. My guides are a very important part of my life, but up to writing this book and discussing them in it, mostly a private one. When intuitive people noticed them and described them to me, it was always a delightful affirmation of their presence.

This Mantis Being guardian had been watching over me for a long time, maybe my whole life, from a "distance." It was only when I became attracted to the statue that I feel I became "ready" for a closer relationship with him and interaction with him. He did not replace any of my other energetic companions, but he did step forward as the most prominent of all of them, taking an even more active role in guiding me and helping me with deeper healing. His has been the most powerfully-sensed presence so far of all my extra-dimensional teachers and guides.

***

During the months after the 2009 UFO Congress, Bob Brown had been in contact with Melinda Leslie and offered us a joint speaker slot. Each of us would have an hour to talk. Melinda had worked out the details with Bob and Nicole. Melinda would present her research first, and then me, talking about my experiences. I was looking forward to it, and to seeing so many people in the UFO and expolitics fields.

It was a wonderful week and a very busy one. I renewed acquaintances with friends from the previous year as well as made new ones. Two events in particular really stood out.

One was my presentation with Melinda. Our presentation was very well received. I heard a great deal of wonderful feedback on it, so many people coming up and offering heartfelt thanks for my talk, saying how moving it was for them.

***

The other event was quiet and private, with new friend Mary Rodwell,[7] whom I had met through the Exopolitics Institute – another hypnosis session.

Meeting Mary in person was a wonderful experience. When she offered to do a session with me, I accepted with deep gratitude.

Mary was also a speaker at the 2010 UFO Congress. During her presentation a flood of impressions spontaneously flowed through me, shaking me with emotional earthquakes. I recorded them just after the conclusion of Mary's talk on my digital recorder. In the recording my voice was still shaking with the feelings that were sweeping through me.

> I've often had an image come into my mind of someone, a colonel, at the Pentagon, who, whenever my file comes across their conference table, he just sets it aside or tells people to set it aside, and says,
>
> "We are leaving her completely alone, she is not to be bothered."
>
> Now I had the distinct feeling during Mary's talk additional psychic information or whatever popped into my head... that they *know* something about who I really am. That I'm something extra than human... I was an early indigo, for lack of a better term, just one of those special kids... they did enough horrible stuff to me... when I was in the military,

[7] Mary Rodwell is is a researcher and hypnotherapist working with extraterrestrial experiencers, outstanding in her capacity to help people explore their experiences without projecting her own beliefs, prejudices or judgments on the various kinds of experiences that emerge from the sessions. As a result, truly amazing material has surfaced in her clients that has helped them to integrate well with who they are and what has happened to them. Her research was central to creating two award-winning documentaries, *Expressions of ET Contact: A Visual Blueprint?* and *Expressions of ET Contact: A Communication and Healing Blueprint?* She is the author of *Awakening: How ET Contact can Transform Your Life.* Her website: http://members.iinet.net.au/~starline/.

> I think they may have let me go because they learned that I
> was somebody special, not to be fiddled with... and ah, and
> I'm upset by the violence but had to have it to become part
> of who I was and all of that stuff... and I just sat in Mary's
> talk, the first part of it, in tears, wiping the tears away as they
> overflowed, because it was just such a profound, whole-body
> knowing emerging out of me...

So much that I had been sensing and feeling over the years, especially recently, was taking my life in a direction I had not imagined. I had willfully tried for years to construct my life in a way that would not bring me into conflict with the "bubble world" and it's contrived reality paradigm. Marriage, family, career... trying to belong and fit in, and not rocking the boat in a way that would land me in the deep blue sea while the boat sailed on without me.

Inside, I realized I had been clinging to an idyllic image of family and earth life from my childhood, of being at my maternal grandparents home, summers in Minnesota. The entire extended family of aunts, uncles and cousins would be at huge family barbeques. There was so much great food, plenty of Grandma's cookies and cinnamon rolls, plenty of ice-cold grape and black cherry Kool-Aid. I played softball, climbed trees, fed nuts to Grandpa's squirrels that lived in the trees in the backyard. I belonged there by virtue of being a blood relative. I still love all of them. But even in that actual setting, at the time I experienced it, the difference between who I was and the rest of my family was becoming evident, though back then I didn't fully understand why. Now when I looked back, the longing I felt about it all was an echo of what it used to be. That world was hardly real to me anymore. What's more, with what I knew now, it had never been truly real. It was pleasant illusion. Even though these memories were part of the experiences of this lifetime, it was like looking back at remembrances of a previous incarnation... so far had I traveled down my life's path to who I was becoming.

Other attachments I'd had to being part of the bubble world were also falling away. Concerns that I might not be taken seriously if I wandered too far into the world of intuition, energy and vibration were fading. I found I was far more comfortable with other kindred souls who were also becoming more aware of the multi-dimensionality of our universe.

Such concerns were replaced with a calm inner discernment. The intuitions that arose that I needed to act on in the moment continued to turn out well. It was when I didn't act on them that I encountered some aggravation or annoyance. Each perception I missed acting on taught me about listening more closely with my whole body the next time. Any insights that came that could not be acted on, proved or disproved in the moment, I accepted – or not – based on their inner resonance or dissonance I felt in my body. Even if my intuition turned out to be incorrect, time would reveal this and adjustments could be made at the moment needed.

I had looked enough into the darkest dark. In this session with Mary I wanted some insights into the ET contact tugging at the edge of my conscious awareness, with beings I sensed were far more benevolent and evolved.

Chapter 16: A Precious Visit "Home"

My session with Mary was like a visit in real time to my fifth-dimensional celestial family. When I say "real time" it's because I don't really know how to describe it in terms of third-dimensional time, except it seemed that a part of my consciousness or essence projected to the realm in which they dwell. I was both in my body in the room with Mary, and also simultaneously with "my people."

There were many long silences in this session. During those long silences, I was experiencing a kind of rapture, as if listening to a heavenly chorus, but listening with my entire being, every part of me engaged in that listening. It was at once auditory, visual, tactile; all five physical senses rolled into one expanded sensory mechanism. More than simple music, it was the experience of a vibrational harmony of thousands, maybe even millions of souls vibrating in resonance together, connected by that shared harmony of vibration.

When Mary mentioned finding and seeing a gateway to my cosmic family, I saw an opening that was like a ring of white light. I began to move through something that was like a white hole, rather than a black hole... a white vortex of energy, filled with light. I moved through it very swiftly.

I emerged in a place that had the feel of a large room. There was a sense of standing in an upright position, though very light, almost floating. I seemed to know it was a room on a ship. No wonder I call the ships I see in the night sky "lightships." This place could be called nothing else but a lightship. Everywhere there emanated a golden white light. Where the light was more golden was where I could see many other luminous beings moving around, forms similar to human forms, as though their forms gave off the golden light. They glided where they moved rather than a walking sort of gait.

Being there in that white-gold light, I was reminded of the times when I would close my eyes and see a protective light around me, as if I was inside a protective egg of energy. At such times the light I saw with my inner eye was white-gold, shot through with rays of iridescence, and the egg was made of one-way glass. I could see out and interact with whatever and whomever I chose, but any energies coming to me, if they were harmful or negative, were reflected back to the sender.

This place felt so incredibly like home! There was such a feeling of belonging that flooded me with joy. I could feel my eyes tearing up. I wanted to melt away into this place, this energy, this joy, yet I couldn't, not completely. Whatever was tethering me to my human form in the room with Mary would not allow a complete merging. Now was a time for visiting only.

Mary would ask me questions about what I was experiencing. There were long pauses before I found my voice and the words to frame a reply. In addition to the rapture I was experiencing, I was not sure how to explain everything I was experiencing in human terms. I described a moving, shimmering light all around me, as much sensation as as it was visual. I described an energy chorus, both heard and felt with my whole form. The only understanding I could come up with once the session had ended and I had time to reflect back on it was that the separation of senses we have on Earth did not occur there. On Earth, in my human form, seeing, hearing, touching, smelling and tasting seemed distinct from each other. Here with my people, on the lightship, all of these faculties blended together. To experience the place and the people there was all encompassing, an experience that flooded my entire being. Since my reference point was my human lifetime and experience, it was overwhelming at first and I could not describe it. I quickly learned that it was a matter of where I placed my attention, and I soon got help with that.

Mary asked me what was directly in front of me. I saw one of the luminous forms moving towards me. As this being moved towards me his face seemed to either materialize in the area of his form where a face would be, or it just became clear the closer he got. And yes, this being seemed distinctly to be a "he," though there was also a sense of androgyny. Luminosity continued to light his human countenance; it seemed from somewhere within.

Mary asked if I knew this being. I did indeed. I affirmed this, and tried to come up with an earth word for who this person was. The only word I could come up with was "commander." Yet commander brought up such thoughts of military, hierarchy, echelons, and this being's mission, purpose and designation was far more than the term "commander" implied. He was more like the father or the elder brother you go to for guidance or comfort. The one who loves you and directs you ever so gently from that love, for your highest and best good, and the good of the whole family. He never orders or forces anyone to do anything... you simply know what it is you are to do and why, from his heart to yours. He is the one who watches over you from a distance, and over countless others as well.

Mary asked if there was something I wanted to ask him... and I said yes.

"Am a doing a good job? ... down here?" I asked.

His reply: "Yes. And you should not worry that you took too long, or came into what you are doing too late, or that you fought it too long. Don't give that any more thought. You have done everything in its own perfect time. You are doing well." I finally understood perhaps one of the reasons why I carried back so little memory from my astral visits to the lightship and the cosmic university. The contrast between life there and the challenges of life on Earth was so dramatic that to maintain my primary orientation to my Earth life the higher super-conscious part of myself inhibited me from remembering too much. That primary orientation to my Earth life needed to continue until my journey here was complete.

I have never seen such tremendous love pouring from a pair of eyes or from any soul as what was touching my being from this commander-father-brother. Christ-like was the only term I could find for it; a divine, spiritual kind of love. In the moment it touched me, I felt complete. Nothing more to do, to say, to be... at least in that moment. On Earth apparently there was still much to do, to say and to be. What, I wasn't sure yet, but I did have a powerful sense that I was following the right path, even if it was revealed only one step at a time.

This session with Mary was a special and fully-conscious glimpse of my home and my people I was experiencing as incentive and inspiration for continuing my earthwalk. It could not be allowed to become a distraction or a block to my life on Earth.

There was a profound sense of a difference in time between "there" and on Earth. There was a timeless feel to being there with my people. Life was lived at such a rapid pace on Earth. It was very different and very hard to translate to Earth terms.

Mary asked if there was something they wanted to communicate to me that I needed for my life here on Earth, for extra support or understanding.

I held Mary's question in my thought... and I asked if there were any more severe difficulties ahead of me. I got that there would be some challenges ahead, but the worst was behind me.

There was a gentle wave of energy that came into my third eye point from this father-brother being. The energy formed words within my own head, that I could trust myself:

> *You can really just trust yourself. You can trust the the ringing of energy and information that goes through your body at times, don't fear that, just trust. You know the right way to put it out to other people. Just watch the energy, watch the spontaneous flows that happen in the mind and the heart and the spirit... and just know that over time you will get confirmation about what is right and true, and there will be vindication over time if you are gentle with what comes to you.*

I know that often I've judged or not trusted my own intuitions. I've doubted and chalked my perceptions off to imagination. This message to me now was saying to pay attention and trust. We get feelings and intuitions and we should hold them in our heart. Not push for immediate confirmation, just let time unfold and reveal the truth of inner messages and intuitions.

Mary then asked, "Is there anything that he would like to show you that he feels you need to see or understand in some way?"

At that question the first thing that sprang to mind was my Earth father from this lifetime, who had passed away so many years ago. The understanding flowed into my thought that my father was also part of this celestial family. He watches me also, but from a different place. He is more a friend and companion than a father here. He also, upon his death as my father, decided to turn around and go right back into an Earth lifetime. We are both of us are doing a kind of double duty, as I'm sure many are. This means that a part of us is always here with our star family, while another aspect of ourselves takes on an Earth lifetime for a specific purpose and mission.

This was a remarkable realization... realizing that I lived with my star family simultaneously while having my earth lifetime.

Later, re-listening to this session, I also remembered that one morning waking in my bed in my Las Vegas apartment... the world I saw in the sunshine outside my window seeming so fragile that the blink of an eye might fracture it into a billion pieces, me finding myself... elsewhere. There? That celestial, fifth-dimensional realm? Had I had some brush with human mortality all unknowing in that night? Or some experience that took me more "there" than here in my human form and its world? I could only wonder.

The session with Mary continued to bring forth insights about things I had wondered about.

The next subject to come up was Mars, a planet I'd been completely fascinated with since I was a child. I'd collected lots of material on Mars, including keeping the *Life Magazine* "Mars" issue from the 1960s. I had had dreams of Mars, some incredibly vivid that stayed with me ever since. Within the last four years, I've had a dream of driving some kind of all-terrain type of vehicle on Mars. I was driving it into some foothills and the foothills were peppered with trees that reminded me of junipers on Earth. Within two weeks of having that dream someone sent me a link to an online video showing trees on Mars that were startlingly similar to the ones in my dream. What do you do with coincidences – synchronicities – like that? All you can do is file them away in your mind under: "I don't know... need more data."

When the luminous being I was with tel-empathically suggested we look at my Mars connection and I affirmed my assent, we zipped away from the light-filled room through another light-filled "tunnel" that brought us out over the Mars landscape, high above, traveling in light bodies. We were moving quickly over the surface. I could see there was a great deal of activity there.

Mary asked me to describe what I was seeing. I saw what looked like settlements, above ground. I knew there were also city-like bases underground. I told Mary that some of them were extraterrestrial and some were Earth human settlements. At the area of Cydonia, where the "Face" of so much controversy was discovered, along with pyramids, I saw much work going on, like an archeological excavation. I "knew" that these were teams of Earth human beings conducting this dig. I said that I thought maybe this was why we did not get more photographs of that area, because such photos could reveal the extent of the work going on there.

Mary asked who the people were, where were they from, their origin. I replied that they were special scientists from all over the Earth, many different countries, picked for their areas of expertise.

There were other things going on on Mars, in the underground facilities, that were just as hidden from the general population on Mars as underground base activities are a hidden and secret area from people on Earth. As has been wondered about and discussed about the Dulce underground facility under Archuleta Mesa in New Mexico, there were bio-genetic experiments going on blending viable DNA remains found on Mars with human DNA to assess how similar or how different each was to the other. The differences were enough that the beings created from such blending were suffering a great deal. On one level, such experiments were forbidden, yet on Mars, as on Earth, certain agencies had little regard for laws forbidding such studies and did their work in secret. It appeared that the levels of secrecy and covert-ops agencies were as much at work on Mars as they were on Earth, perhaps even more so. Mars was a secret area to begin with. That the secrecy differentiated itself into various layers there, perhaps even more than here on Earth, was not really that surprising, once the revelation of what I was seeing with my companion settled in.

The humans were aware of the extraterrestrial settlements on Mars, but there was limited interaction. Since many ET races are telepathic or tel-empathic, contact was a problem for both sides. Humans felt stripped down to the soul by such contact. Such contact brings parts of the human psyche out and confronts that human with the hidden parts of themselves. It was an intensely uncomfortable experience for most. For the extraterrestrials, it was a bit confusing how their contact could create such turmoil in the humans, even though they understood how much humans hid from themselves. Still, there were some humans who could handle the contact and serve as intermediaries when needed.

Mary asked what the Martians looked like. I told her they were not Martians, they were from somewhere else, just having bases there on Mars. While I felt there were different races there, the ones I was seeing were very tall and very slender, like perhaps they had evolved and lived in a low gravity environment. They reminded me of the tall ET that came out of the mothership in the film, "Close Encounters of the Third Kind" only they were more human-looking than that entity. I could not get a sense of where these extraterrestrials were from. It seemed hidden from me, like a privacy energy shield, especially since all my communications during this session were so completely open.

I then mentioned that I knew I had a previous incarnation on Mars. Mary asked if there was anything more I needed to explore about that. Two things arose from that question. I called it a strange, fuzzy sort of remembrance, like two different images superimposed, one over the other. In one, I could see that I'd had a previous life on Mars as a Martian. My people had built some of the structures now being excavated on Mars.

In the other, a strange realm of experience emerged that I had no real reference point for. The only thing that springs to mind that might provide a reference is *The Mars Records* by Michael Relfe, which I had started to read years ago, but found it very difficult to read at the time. It brought up a lot of the "sinking-in-quicksand" feelings from the earlier years of my wanderings through meetings, books, testimony and other material related to the dark, dank swamp of covert-ops and mind control, trying to find answers. While reading it, I had taken notes on any parts of Michael Relfe's story that correlated with my own. Whether by accident or unconscious design, there was a point where I turned away from reading in it any further. Maybe it's time to get back to it, once this book is done.

In this strange realm of experience, as it emerged in this hypnosis session, it seemed that there was a woman who had lived and worked on Mars in the mid-twentieth century. I'm going to call her Grace. I think her name was actually something else, but I have come to think of her as Grace because over time, she came to embody the quality of grace to me.

Was I Grace? Was she me? As it came through in the session, it seemed neither. But there was a connection made between us, whereby I got a block of her memories as her consciousness was linked to mine. We shared consciousness, mind, memories, feelings, sensations and emotions. This was done with a process of – somehow – linking us together through some kind of electronic computer device. I've never heard of such a thing, so there is not a reference to it that I have any understanding of, but I'm reporting it here as another puzzle piece that may have a correlation for someone else, somewhere, at some time. Once the device connections were removed, the consciousness link remained. And for a few months, it was a strong, conscious link. If it's still there, it remains only as a mostly unconscious whisper in my psyche.

I have no idea of the true accuracy of this, or fully what it might mean. I can only share what came out of the hypnosis session and my own correlations that seemed to be connecting threads to this part of my session and other parts of my life experience. If I can trust the correlations my consciousness makes in relation to emerging memories and data, then there may be very well be something to this.

We were linked together for a variety of reasons. Part of it was scientific research, studying the process of linking human beings in this way and recording the process and the effects. Another part of it was punishment for her, which seemed ongoing.

I reported to Mary that she had seen some of the genetic experimentation she was not supposed to see in an underground facility on Mars. She had suffered greatly for her horrifying discovery. Perhaps some part of her tried to reach out to me about this, because I had an incredibly vivid nightmare about this incident sometime in the three to four months after moving from working at Tonopah Electronic Combat Range (where my memory was extremely limited) to Tolicha Peak Electronic Combat Range.

The details of this nightmare remain clear to this day. Here is a recounting of it.

"I" had wandered into a part of an underground facility on Mars where I knew I was not supposed to be. Nervous, but curious, I kept tentatively picking my way around. Suddenly I opened a door and saw a row of cages, like an indoor dog kennel. But in the kennel enclosures were naked creatures that looked completely miserable, with reddish-tan skin, large liquid eyes. Some of them did not move or get up, but stayed huddled on the floors, their faces hidden. Others, however, fastened their eyes on mine, and in them was an anguished appeal to be freed from the cages or killed – anything to put an end to their imprisonment and experimentation. I stood petrified in fear, not knowing what to do. In the next instant, someone grabbed me from behind and a rag was put over my face. I felt myself go limp as I lost consciousness.

When I awoke, I was adrift in space in a small pod... a space lifeboat. I recognized what it was as seeing these had been part of my orientation for living and working on Mars. The food and water had been removed. The clocks had been disabled.

Hours must have gone by... that likely stretched into days. I had no real way of knowing. At first I was terrified, and screamed and screamed. Then I huddled in a ball weeping uncontrollably. Then I became enraged. I did everything I could to smash my way out of the pod and end my life swiftly in the vacuum of space. Every extreme of emotion crashed over me in wave after wave. Then I just became completely still.
Oddly, the recording log was still intact. I decided to make use of it. I made a vocal record of what I'd discovered, what had happened to me. I recorded messages for family and friends, saying goodbye, telling them I loved them. I prepared to die.

> I was just about to lose consciousness for the last time
> from lack of air when the there was a clank as the pod was
> retrieved. The hatch was opened. There was a rush of
> fresh air.

At that moment, I woke up from this dream, on Earth, next to second husband Matt, still asleep. I felt just as shaken, lying there in my bed, as if I had really been in that pod, experiencing all those emotions, waiting to die.

As the images and information continued in the session with Mary, it seemed to me that the memories of Grace were the ones I was experiencing... of driving the vehicle into the foothills with a shrubby kind of forest of Martian trees dotting the hills. The space-lifeboat nightmare as well. So some clarity around this began to be revealed under the gentle direction of my father-brother-commander to look, and to see this part of my experience... if I could accept it. I felt calm and kind of enriched with more understanding. But the logical mind-ego was still standing back from the experience, questioning and doubting. I can only hope that time will reconcile these memories and experiences.

I got the sense from remembering Grace, in the session with Mary, that she had enjoyed living and working on Mars before her curiosity led her into a dark world from which there was no escape for her. They kept her on Earth as a prisoner in underground facilities, her status that of a non-person, no Earth identity or citizenship any longer. It was as if she did not exist in any way where she would be missed or searched for. There was no help for her. It was as if she had become one of the creatures she had discovered under the Martian surface. I wished I could help her.

I could get a sense, or feel of the consciousness link between us. I could almost get an image of how she looked – an aging woman, with a hairstyle that reminded me of the actresses of the 1940s or 50s. Dark hair, graying. Throughout her incarceration, she had come to accept her fate with a kind of inner strength and fortitude. At some point it was as if she realized that no matter what they did to her, they couldn't really touch her soul or her spirit unless she allowed it. She had actually come to a place of peace and equanimity. I think she tried to reach out to me and help me in some way as well when I was going through my black ops experiences. I think she tried to give me some of her strength and peace. If there was a purpose to showing me this connection between Grace and myself, it was to bring her more clearly and firmly into my conscious mind, so that wherever she is, I can send her my gratitude, my love and my support... to a life and heart with none of the simple joys we take for granted under the open sky, breathing the fresh air.

There was such a sense of my being in two places during this session. As I go back over this session, I have to wonder if this wondrous luminous being, that I had called "commander" for lack of a better term, was guiding Mary in the questions she was asking. And it was not over yet.

Mary's next question: "What is it that makes you special in terms of how that understanding is from the greater context? What is it that has been highlighted with you that you feel makes it more of a problem for those that have harmed you?"

There was that word, "special." I've always felt afraid of being special in any way. Yet I had felt special and different my whole life. It set me apart from most of society, even from my own family, from childhood on. And then even more with the strange experiences with the Zetas, the terrible experiences I'd had in the military – experiences that underscored my being different. Fighting this feeling, I had pushed it down and suppressed it my whole life. It felt like too much responsibility to be "special." It was this trepidation that got in the way of my own inner sense about these vibrational keys that had been playing in my consciousness. But with Mary's questions, a flood of information poured out of me, finally able to bypass my trepidations so I could clearly grasp the insights being offered in some of those vibrational keys that had kept repeatedly plunking in my thought during recent months.

Ringing confirmation of my hesitant earlier intuitions about Nellie Bly came out first. Emotion welled up as I spoke clearly and unfalteringly about Nellie's assignment to the insane asylum being connected as a metaphor for my coming to Earth in a similar way, as a volunteer. This was also confirmation for me about my sense of taking on a soul contract for this lifetime.

I felt like a musical instrument, one with strings, like a guitar or violin. The information coming up and out of me was like the strings being played, singly and in chords, and with feeling the vibration of this "music" came waves of emotion that shook my voice as the stream of words continued to flow.

More details emerged about how the data I collected was transmitted back to my people. I learned that my people had placed higher-dimensional implants into my subtler astral form in areas corresponding to the pineal and pituitary centers of my physical body as well as between some of the lower chakra centers of my body. These were not harmful implants, they were simply there to collect data. In one sense, I was transmitting data all the time between myself and my people. But on the nights that I would astral travel out to be with them one of my first stops would be to go into a "resonance chamber." This was a large clear cylindrical tube. Once inside, it would be activated with resonating sound and light waves. These waves would pass around me and through me. These waves would activate the implants and then upload their multi-dimensional data – physical, mental, emotional and spiritual – about my experiences on Earth into what I can only call an extremely sophisticated holographic computer system. Rather than just a journal of writing, this information told a far more comprehensive story of my life. From this data, my people could re-experience my life as I was living it, gaining knowledge, understanding and insights they needed in their larger mission of study regarding how best to guide humanity to a greater understanding of light and love without interfering with their free will. Yet a way needed to be found to accelerate the awakening process in the last few decades on Earth for souls to take full advantage of cosmic conditions in the process of actualization now. So, as Dolores Cannon has discovered in her years of work, there have been many volunteer souls, and I know now that I'm one of them.

My people work with a lot of human individuals, touching those places in many where spiritually, at their super-conscious level, they have given permission to have their consciousness opened, refined, and expanded. This is a growing phenomenon now happening on Earth. People have experiences while their bodies sleep, attending the cosmic university, and at some point they will run into certain places and information in their waking life that will activate these seeds of knowledge within them.

I volunteered to do this job here on Earth. I'm doing the undercover work and reporting back in a multi-dimensional way. There is nothing sinister about it in any way. It is more anthropological than anything else. Assuming a role to study and research and discover those ways in which assistance can be given.

Mary said that made sense. She then asked if there was anything more that would help me at that moment in time, during the session, with my understanding of my undercover mission here.

When she asked that question, the moon came into view. It was as if my commander/guide and I in our astral forms, were floating out in space, looking at the moon. I held back. I did not want to go back there. Mary asked what I was being shown there.

I mentioned the explosions that were done on the moon earlier in the year, that the main force of the explosions had been neutralized by extraterrestrials there. I mentioned that there were also ET bases and influence on the moon, more than there used to be. It seemed that the human beings that live and/or work on the moon are operating there on the good graces of the extraterrestrials that are also there. I got a sense of strong disapproval of a lot of what the humans are doing, that the ETs don't interfere too much but they do have limits. Like "you can do this and this and this, but we draw the line here and here and here."

Mary asked what the purpose or need of showing me this was.

I sighed a deep sigh. I said that the first thing that came into my mind was that it could have been much worse for me on the moon than it was, but it was not allowed to be worse. I felt like I didn't want to move, not a muscle, not a thought, not a feeling.

Mary gently queried further... "Is there anything that comes to mind with that?"

I sighed more deep sighs. My mind wanted to veer completely away. But what was emerging was this:

I was looking at the moon of the past, that terrible week I was there. When I was on the moon at that time, one of the extraterrestrials there told one of my superior officers that they should not be tampering with me, that I was somebody special; in the same way that the military will plant someone in an organization to learn about it, that I was planted in human civilization to learn about it and report back to my people... and the bad things they were doing to me because they thought I was just a Grey/Zeta abductee... I'm somebody a whole lot more than that and they should be treating me better.

This was how I explained my impressions in my session, on the recording. In addition, I actually heard this ET telepathically telling my superior:

> You have no idea who you have here. Do you realize that
> everything you do to her gets reported back to her people?

I now knew this was why I was getting the image of the officer in the pentagon saying that they were going to leave me alone. Maybe why I was put out of the black ops goings-on altogether. And this was also connected to the understanding of some link with Nellie Bly. If, as all the pieces of intuition and information seemed to indicate, I was indeed a wanderer here on Earth, I was here to be a conduit of information back to my people, a "reporter" in a sense, reporting from the "inside." There was no breach of intelligence. The levels of secrecy in shadow governments or secret societies were not impervious to telepathic races of extra-dimensional beings as they were to the people of Earth, with their limited awareness. There was a pure and simple need to give a completely holistic sense of empathy and understanding to my people about what individual human beings endure in living on this planet.

The session was coming to a close. One last time, Mary asked if there was anything else my companion wanted me to know. I answered:

> I'm getting an odd sense of him reaching out his hand and
> putting it on my heart, and putting energy into me... also at
> the same time, there is a feeling of his hands or the hands
> of others on my shoulders also giving me energy... that I can
> receive it consciously... they say they do this for me a lot and
> right now I'm sensing it consciously in this experience and
> that I can return my consciousness to this image and these
> feelings of being infused with all this beautiful energy any
> time I need it. I'm to know that it's always there for me and it's
> always being given to me.

I used the word "odd" because it was as much an extension of energy as a "hand."

Mary then asked if there was anything I could do physically for myself to enhance my own balance and healing. My answer:

> Stop resisting who I really am, stop fearing it. He is saying,

307

stop fearing you're going to lose your grip on your reality... you won't, you are quite well grounded and you can trust yourself. Let yourself write and explore... write down anything you feel that seems pertinent or appropriate, then set it aside for a while and give it time to digest so that your 3D self can integrate it over time. He says I don't have to understand it all at once, but to just allow the flow to happen so the information can come out of it. It's just like a process that already happens when someone asks me a question about something... or I get a sense inside myself that I want to write about a particular aspect of the extraterrestrial contact, there is a whole flood of things that come out of me at those times. I can trust that flow. I can trust that the knowledge is coming out from what I've learned in the cosmic university at the right time and place... even through some people on earth would say that's bonkers.

They tell me I'm on the right track and doing well. I'm really looking forward to going "home."

Mary... "Is there any last thing that would be helpful to be aware of...?" Me:

The cosmic nanosecond experience... when I'm both on Earth in this body in it's usual functioning, and at the same moment I'm in a place where time and space are either different or there is no time and space. When I have this experience it's a multi-dimensional awareness and window to where I also exist on this other level with these other beings... all the time. Part of me is there all the time, and part of me is functioning here. That's more real for me now, and I can trust that more now, and that's a really good feeling. It's a lot of peace.

I thought of those brief moments I experienced at times, where I seemed to exist in two places... here on Earth in this lifetime and someplace else where time seemed suspended. I called such moments "cosmic nanoseconds." Now I knew what those cosmic nanoseconds were about, what they connected me with. There was no separation really, though from the Earth perspective it looked and felt as though there was.

This is where Mary began to vocally and energetically conclude the session, gently suggesting that all trauma energy be released and let go, allowing healing to come in. Allowing all to be integrated. Becoming aware of myself back in 3D again... I opened my eyes.

There was still such a sense of being "there" with my star family. Mary said she felt them still there in the room with me.

Love and service... love and service... love and service... this was the last echo of the session, like a chant between myself and all those luminous beings on the lightship I had visited.

308

I was left with a profound feeling of acceptance that perhaps I truly was special somehow. Though not in a way that excluded others from specialness, for every being is unique in their experiences, their viewpoints and in their journey and process through life. It was just that among the billions of souls incarnate on Earth, my journey was more challenging than the norm. And less challenging than that of others who had been through even worse than myself. I sighed, thinking how "relative" all experiences really are, delineated by degree or contrast.

This "visit home" was the most powerful experience yet of understanding more deeply that I had not been simply cast adrift on Planet Earth. I felt a new and deeper sense of connection to something truly wonderful.

***

I have come to feel that I volunteered to do this job here on Earth. I chose the life I'm living here. I am doing it for my people so they can know more intimately how it is for all of us living on this planet, with all its beauty and love, and its challenges and difficulties. How could my people make any determination on how best to reach out to this planet and life here without an insider's understanding of just what human life can hold, at it's best and at its worst? And why would they?

Love. A love born out of the understanding that everything in the entire universe, throughout every dimension, is connected. And out of that understanding of connection is the knowledge that, joined together in cooperation and honoring life, we all expand in our awareness. Which is why we take form in the first place – to experience the intricacies of working our way back to full awareness while within form – human or extraterrestrial.

Light and love are terms that have become somewhat flippantly tossed around in recent years. But to sit with their deeper meaning is to understand, truly, that one is the other. One can begin to see that light/love, love/light, is woven into the very fabric of our being. It is spun into our forms from the universal energy field of which our bodies are all made. Our DNA is infused with it, like a transmitter/receiver for the Universal Consciousness, stepping that energy down into the various forms of life. It sustains our bodies through our chakra systems. And it is how we allow or block the flow of light/love, through our consciousness and what we hold in our thoughts and beliefs that determines the health or illness of the system of energy that is us in form. That in turn determines the health or illness of the larger system of energy that is the human collective.

I understand that love, even though I struggle with the day-to-day challenges of living here like everyone else. Some days the challenges are intense. Sometimes I fall short of my own aspirations in expressing that love, but I do return to it. This book is an expression of that love. Some may take issue with what I've expressed here, but I have done my best to share my experiences and my process of coming to understand my life's journey as best I can. My conclusions are not things I immediately leapt to embrace, but rather what I was left with as I peeled away layer after layer of belief and indoctrination, increasingly allowing my intuitive heart to guide me.

I care deeply about this world and all the living things here, including human beings. When one has even an inkling of what the potential can be for each and every living soul – especially in contrast to how living systems and individual lives on this world are managed and controlled in ways that short-circuit the process of awakening – then out of that love you want to do all you can to free that potential to blossom to full flower.

***

I pledge to remember Grace always...
From my heart to yours, I send you my love, and my gratitude and my support. If you can still see through my eyes, see the beautiful blue of the sky with the white fluffy clouds gliding along. See the the birds swoop and soar. If you can still hear through my ears, hear their songs. Hear the wind in the trees. Smell the sweetness of the wildflowers in spring. Whatever I can give to you, I hope you can still receive it, wherever you may be.

Chapter 17: Quickening

A Life Filled with 11s

In numerology, to determine the vibrational signature of a number, we add the individual integers together, i.e., 1954; $1 + 9 + 5 + 4 = 19$, then $1 + 9 = 10$, then $1 + 0 = 1$. Double digit numbers like 11, 22, 33, etc. are not reduced down in this way. They are considered master numbers, carrying a special vibration. Being born on 11/11/1954, at 11 am I have pondered what the full significance is of "11" or groups of 11s for a long time.

As the years of my life marched on, I often wondered if being born under the influence of such a number was more curse than blessing. It seemed that I had more than my share of trials and challenges. But I'm still here.

What I needed to learn, and have learned at least moderately well, is that there is a universal law at work in the cosmos that none of us can thwart. This law compels us to L-E-A-R-N from our lives, and sets up the learning from what we carry within us, conscious or unconscious, through a quantum mirror that tries to show us to ourselves. Refuse to learn the first time, or the second or third, and the Universe gets a progressively bigger hammer to get our attention, individually and collectively. Those who ignore or forget history – personal, societal or cultural – are doomed to repeat it. Life eases from struggle to more flow when we decide to participate with our learning. We came here into form to learn, even though we forget it the instant we arrive here. We cannot break universal law. We can break ourselves against it if we resist it or fight it long enough or hard enough.

Moving to Durango, a spirit-directed move, was filled with 11s for me, to the point that I wondered with humor whether the extra-dimensional guidance that I had come to recognize in my life wanted to make sure I didn't miss the point. I turned 47 the year of moving there, $4 + 7 = 11$. When I went to the DMV to register my car in Colorado, the license plate I received was 011 DVI. As if 011 wasn't enough, I later learned that DVI was the Roman numeral for 506 which also reduced down to 11. When I changed my driver's license I noticed it would be up for renewal in 2011. Moving to Durango was an important step in my life. I found more peace, and healing, in Durango.

In 2009 four 11s lined up for me, month, day, hour and year, as I turned 55, another double digit number. It was a big year for me, a year when going public brought me into contact with many people who are important in my life. I had heard that whistleblowers should go public as widely as possible for safety's sake. As a measure of safety, I had hoped to speak and share many places, and I have. I am deeply grateful to everyone who invited me to speak at their conferences or have me on their radio programs.

In the year 2012, I will have lived in Durango for 11 years. On my 2012 birthday, 11/11/2012 adds up numerologically this way; $11 + 11 + 2012 = 27; 2 + 7 = 10; 1 + 0 = 1$.

One. The number of new beginnings.

If there is any truth to the idea that 2012 is a time of significant shift for humanity and our world, then I hope I can make some contribution, from how my life has unfolded and what I have learned from it. In working so hard to educate myself to understand what happened to me, in what context it occurred and how I could best heal from it, I've accumulated a full spectrum background in all aspects of the phenomenon, from government cover-ups and mind control abuses to the spiritual indications rippling throughout our world of a process many call "ascension." All of these aspects of our reality have impacted or touched my life in one way or another. The process of understanding and healing I had to embark upon, in a sense to save my own life, might just be important to share to help others come to an understanding of the dance of energies playing out on our world right now. On how we might be able to turn the tide in our favor. I feel that ET contact that can liberate humanity on multiple levels. I feel that contact will be a huge step in humanity beginning to realize its full multi-dimensional potential.

11s, singly and in strings, continue to be the crumbs and clues sprinkled upon my path as guideposts to greater understanding.

***

In the audio program *The Path of Service: Here and Now in the 90s*, Ram Dass shared the process of expanding awareness in this way:

> I'm a mouth for a process that many of us are going through. I really don't assume that there's anything I know you don't know. And so what I've found over the years is that the more intimately I deal with how it is for me, the more intimately I'm sharing with you... what it is with you. Because there is something common in our experience of people that would come to hear Ram Dass. It's a certain kind of a network, it's a kind of a network of consciousness and... it's like the stage we're at, we're flickery. We know something... but we're not sure we know it. We don't trust it. But we know it and so when you come together, you find there are a lot of other people as crazy as you are. It allows a new kind of reality to come in. See, the interesting thing is that you and I have all of the data, in our experiential showcase, that we're all living in... all the data for you to realize who you fully are.

However; because of the cultural context in which we dwell, very often, you treat a lot of those data as either non-existent or irrelevant... or quaint.

Ram Dass was speaking of a process of expanding awareness; one that has been going on for individuals down through the millennia. Expanding awareness is spreading to increasingly larger groups of people through the last century. I never heard Ram Dass speak of extraterrestrials, though I sense from some of his talks that he is aware of secrecy in government that tried to pull the wool over the public's eyes. He did often speak affectionately of his "spook" friend, Emmanuel, channeled through Pat Rodegast. So it may not be a far reach to consider that he likely contemplated life on other worlds or dimensions from time to time.

I share his statement here because it says so eloquently what I feel, and what I am hoping to do in this book... share my own process of awakening in a way that may touch and spark those places within each of you, to stretch with your feelings and inner resources out into the vast wonder that is our multi-dimensional universe and all it might encompass.

From the many people I've talked with, connected with in person and through the internet, I feel this third part of my book shares a quickening process that many of us are going through that definitely includes an awareness of extraterrestrials, extra-dimensionals and celestial beings. If you have picked up this book and are reading these words, then you may be exploring these possibilities for yourself. You may have discovered them in an inexplicable fascination with UFOs and ETs. That fascination may have brought about an adjacent interest in government cover-ups and collecting puzzle pieces as many of us do to try and understand what might be going on. You may even be discovering that you too, are a "wanderer."

I realize fully that in telling my story, that my readers are not living these experiences as I have, and am. If I were any of you, I would not simply blindly accept what I am sharing here. You must use your own discernment and develop your own ability to read energy and vibration... or not, if you choose. Even still, you might not get the same energy read or draw the same conclusions from my words, sharing these experiences as I am, and that must be respected. Many reading this book may still live in the mind's realm of logic and analysis, working only with hard physical evidence or first-hand testimony, consciously remembered rather than recalled under hypnosis. They may feel that is the only way to responsibly assess any data. And that is just fine, and exactly as it should be for them. Such approaches serve an invaluable role in the unfolding process of uncovering the truth.

My only caveat is that in a world where scientists and scholars are discovering that there may be far more truth to ideas and concepts taught by sages and mystics; where we are learning that our bodies and everything in the physical world is made up of atoms – nuclei of protons and neutrons with electrons spinning around them – then our bodies, and all matter, are mostly empty space. And further, we are living in a world where those probing the mysteries of our existence, whether it be in a laboratory or a lamasery, are finding that what we hold in our thought, where we place our attention and intention, charged with our emotional energy, has an effect on the existence of those atoms and how they arrange themselves for us, day by day.

When our minds and bodies are still, sitting in deep quiet, when thought and emotion are suspended for moments or hours, then we may, at such times, experience the bliss of what we could call the quantum wave of pure potential... energy and consciousness in a state unmolded, un-particle-ized into our relative reality by the busy thought-impulses of minds and emotions completely engaged in the collective dream of life on Planet Earth.

Do I question myself... my feelings, my impressions, my conclusions? Constantly. It would be irresponsible not to. I was born on Planet Earth and have lived a lifetime here from the reference point of a human woman of various experiences, living in a particular timeline. Whether lived by accident or by design, this lifetime must be honored and considered from inside the framework of what I have learned and experienced within the context of current society and culture and their various organizational structures.

But now there is an inner acknowledgment from all the threads of my experiences that some larger benevolent Consciousness, of which I am an integral part, wants me to find my way Home, and has littered my path with clues. Far more often than not, when I follow my inner feelings and direction, when I heed any warning ringing through my body, life works out. The times I have ignored my intuition and gut feelings, I've lived to regret it. At least I did go on living. There were times when I was reckless and less in touch with my intuition. I feel I stayed in this life on this planet due to the direct participation, guidance and intervention of my extra-dimensional family, whether I recognized their hand in things or not.

I entered this life with an astrologically-imprinted personality that has a passionate, even fierce desire to learn and understand as much about myself and the universe as I possibly can. It was as if, as early as was possible in this incarnation, I hit the ground running; driven by a sense of mission I didn't consciously remember. I have a deep sensitivity that could have caused me to try and curl up and die several times over in the face of so much travail in this life, yet I somehow developed the strength to meet it.

What has changed over the years I've been on this life journey is the quality of heart I now bring to this earthwalk. The relational heart, the intuitive heart, the shattered and rebuilt heart... with so much more space now between its shards. In working to heal, those pieces simply would not fit together in the old way they once had.

The relational heart taught me that it is ourselves in relationship to everything around us, right down to the subtlest of our experiences, in a life-energy-dance with the larger tapestry of our world and all other life that fills it, that defines who we are to ourselves. Defining and redefining who we are with every new thing we learn, with every passing day, is a vital part of our life's journey. When you look into the mirror, into your own eyes, do you take a moment to truly gaze deeply into them, into yourself? Do you like who you see in there? In the end, each of us is our own reward.

My intuitive heart would not allow my mind to exile it to the fringe of my existence, thrown into some dungeon in my psyche. It stayed in the forefront, right alongside my mind, patiently, touching my being with a stirring resonance every time I encountered something I needed to pay attention to.

The shattered and rebuilt heart, though it/I would never have consciously stepped into such trauma, pain, fear or grief, was forced to re-evaluate, re-assess, stretch itself and look directly into the darkest dark in order to re-build itself in a way that would not only survive, but thrive. In the larger context of my life's journey, with all my learning, my metaphysical inquiry, and healing of mind, body and spirit, I have found a realm of uplifting possibility and potential that those trapped in webs of analysis and logic of the mind may be missing.

Quantum science is showing us that our physical reality is not what we once imagined it to be. I hope this book opens people up to just how much our consciousness has been manipulated and controlled, from mass mind control strategies to techniques of individual mind control. Not to scare the living daylights out of them. To give them the power of choice and to re-learn that questioning authority is the highest form of loving self-care. To give them knowledge that can begin to unlock their own awareness. Through awareness we can free our minds, our emotions, our hearts and our souls. We can all find our way Home.

Our world is screaming out from this place in our collective unconscious. It's crying out to every human being on Earth in the form of insane political posturing in the face of serious economic instability and eminent ecological collapse. Out of this global maelstrom more truthsayers emerge. Such whistleblowers can read between the lines, they can see the ever-growing risk to us as a species. They and their loved ones live on this planet right alongside the rest of us, subject to the same dangers, the same multi-layered toxicity interlaced throughout our lives. Through them, more and more of the collective human shadow comes into the light. The shadow's growing appearance on the scene now, at this moment in human history, brings us the gift of expanding awareness if we can learn to positively and productively deal with our fears and move past them.

To rise to this challenge is the pivotal opportunity of humanity's collective lifetime. How we work with this opportunity will determine whether we complete our journey into full sentience, allowing us to make the next great evolutionary leap forward. The success or failure of our ability to face our shadow and embrace the light we're truly made of will determine the path of our next iteration as a human species.

Desperate to survive, the collective human shadow exposes more and more of itself to us in the full light of day. It reveals itself in shadow governments, black ops projects and secret societies loathe to give up the power they've accumulated, knowing that as human awareness expands, it means the end of their reign. So they step forward ever more heavy-handedly, hoping to frighten us into subservient compliance. But the more openly they show themselves only serves to awaken humanity further, especially if we seize the courage to do so.

The next evolutionary leap for humanity cannot be one of more conquest or manipulation to gain yet more power or indulge bottomless greed. These negative attributes are like a cancer that threatens to consume all life. Shadow institutions seek to limit, repress, restrict and curtail energy. Energy in the form of people's lives, their livelihoods, the living planet Gaia and all the life she supports... all expendable to the wealthy and powerful as energy to be controlled and spent for their own self-serving agendas. Ultimately unsustainable, such actions lead to destruction and collapse, just as we are observing on our world today.

The next evolutionary leap for humanity and our world must be one of choosing love and cooperation at every level of our living world's ecosystem, of which we are a integral part. As Chief Seattle stated in his letter to the U.S. government in the 1800s:

> This we know: the earth does not belong to man, man
> belongs to the earth. All things are connected like the blood
> that unites us all. Man did not weave the web of life, he is
> merely a strand in it. Whatever he does to the web, he does
> to himself.

I feel firmly that this emergence and integration of our collective shadow is absolutely necessary for the spiritual unfoldment of humanity and the Earth. It's coming out into the open now for humanity's healing and integration. Used as a gift to expand our collective awareness, it can help us shift into a new expression of ourselves... more awake, more aware, with a clearer vision of who we truly are and what our potential could be. And freshly inspired to reach for it.

Love is the reason we exist... the reason we have life at all. Not the often-selfish and capricious love of interpersonal human relationships, though at their best, they mirror the greater expression of love. This "Love" is the essence of the powerful energy that brought forth all the worlds upon which living beings walk, setting itself free within each of us to experience countless facets of who we are as part of the All-That-Is.

316

What does love mean to us on a personal level, as we journey through life? When we truly love, love directs our steps on our path. Even though we may try to direct the course of love in our lives, when we live in harmony with love, love directs our course, not the other way around. Love changes us, it refines us, it cuts away parts of ourselves that are of no real use to us. We must be willing to give up who we are for what we could become. It takes courage to live a life of passion and love and watch for the "medicine" signs on our earthwalk, the synchronicities that have meaning for us and light our next steps in life. When we have become pliant enough, flexible enough walking in companionship with love, we are then fit for what the Conscious Living and Loving Universe would choose for us as our destiny.

When we shy away from what love would choose for us, we sacrifice our ability to live – and love – fully. We live in a grey world where we may laugh or cry, but never to completion. Fear of following love without reservation makes a person who fears death, yet out of that fear, keeps one foot in the grave. Living life fully, with love and passion requires total commitment. Without a full commitment to love and living, only a half-life can be maintained.

When we try to pick and choose what we will be aware of, choosing only from what is lovely and alluring, shunning what is unpleasant and frightening, we simply relegate those things we revile to our subconscious. There they sit and rule us from the Id, the hidden darkness of the disowned shadow-realm of our psyches, without our conscious awareness. Powered by the emotions of our secret hidden fears, they take form in the world around us in shadow governments, black ops and secret societies. We call these "other" than ourselves, but the distinct probability is that they are our own collective unconscious creation, manifest as a quantum mirror for us to look into, to see and to heal ourselves deep inside our own psyches.

What if we all began consciously cooperating with this collective evolutionary spiritual process? Imagine a human population that has moved beyond its collective fears. How might our consciousness expand? What kind of world could we build with so much energy freed from the lockdown of fear? How fun, how joyful it could be for us all to find out together!

**

On many levels, it takes a lot of courage to write a book such as this one. Will the organizations who perpetrated my abuse come after me? Will certain people twist and pervert what I've chosen to share about the sexual aspects of my ET encounters and their impact on my life into jokes to snicker about? Will the UFO community of researchers appreciate or criticize such a book? Will the community of people interested in spiritual and personal growth be turned off by so much delving into conspiracy material? Could I just piss everyone off?

Possibly. But I'm betting that this account, written with as much heart as I can pour into it, will touch many. For some, it will get them thinking about their own subtler experiences, paying more attention. For those already doing so, it will affirm them. I sincerely hope it provides some map to recovery for any whose lives have been impacted by black/covert-ops trauma or manipulation.

Above all, I intend this book to be a catalyst of awakening for everyone who reads it. Awakened humans are the hope and salvation of this world... a new race of shamans, healing, stewarding and shapeshifting ourselves and our reality into lives of sparkling vitality and vibrance for every living creature on Earth, and for Gaia Terra herself.

Entr'acte VI
Seeds of the Ancient Past

So, into forgotten history passed the great civilization of Atlantis.

On Terra, now known as Earth, there is a saying from chaos theory that a butterfly beating its wings in New York can be the original cause that creates a typhoon much later off the coast of Japan.

On Lyra, we had never known fear. When fear came to our world, it was a tremendous shock, a trauma to our whole race. That original seed of fear planted within us so very long ago on Lyra, despite the great love and spiritual understanding in the hearts of my people, ended up, through us, taking root in an entire new species on a new world. Through us, that unconscious seed grew into an ideology that destroyed the entire Atlantean civilization.

If everything is One, if all that exists comes forth from the Conscious Living Source itself, then where did the reptilians come from? What was their place in the grand design of the One Consciousness? What contrast does apparent evil have to show us? What does it have to teach us about ourselves? These are the questions for contemplation.

After the destruction of Atlantis, what remained behind was also destroyed with the passage of time. The great library of Alexandria in which some of the last Atlantean records were stored, was burned – by either accident, vendetta, ignorance or perhaps even by design. Other remnants of any records are either well protected, deliberately hidden, or both.

318

Atlantean stories became legends. Legends faded into myths. Lemuria, even more ancient, faded even deeper into unconscious human memory.

Those who forget their past, who are forbidden access to it or even knowledge of it, are all too often doomed to repeat it.

Or are they? Can not the wise and prescient among us today read the writings of the past in our own souls? Can we not feel, deep down in our bones, history trying to repeat itself all around us?

Chapter 18: Facing the Shadow

I will not fear.
Fear is the mind killer.
Fear is the little-death that brings total obliteration.
I will face my fear.
I will allow it to pass over me and through me.
And when it has gone past I will turn the inner eye
to see it's path.
Where the fear has gone there will be nothing.
Only I will remain.

~ Frank Herbert, from his 1965 book, *Dune*

Fear is the antithesis of love, and freedom which flows from love.

In a sense, to say "I will not fear" is an impossibility, at least for those of us born into the human condition on Planet Earth. Fear is part of our emotional toolkit for very specific reasons. Still, I like this litany against fear. It contains the important elements of facing our fear, allowing it to pass over us and through us, and learning that we are still here afterward.

The level of fear I felt about my experiences and even more, speaking out in any public way about them, had its own truth to tell about what I remembered under hypnosis. As a person trained in body-centered therapy, I learned that the body does not lie. It doesn't know how to lie. My body could not have experienced that level of terror regarding my experiences, and especially about speaking out about them if they were not real. I have learned to trust that my body sense, deep down inside on a visceral level, was reacting to real, remembered experiences. In the beginning, despite my body's feelings, I did not want to just automatically accept them – I had not even heard of military or covert-ops abductions at the time of my first hypnosis session. I also wanted to reject them because I didn't want to believe people were capable of such inhumanity right here in the U.S.A. I went through months and years of looking at the testimony and research of others to learn more about this, and I found more corroborating material than not. Much of it triggered further body-centered emotional reactions in me as it hit upon things specific to my own memories. Finally I was forced to intellectually acknowledge the reality of my experiences, as my body had already done. In accepting them at last, I could truly start seeking healing, and the gifts of awakening that healing brought to me.

As part of that process, I had to face the fact that, by staying silent out of any level of fear, I was giving my power away to the abusers and the organizations that perpetrated such abuse. I also realized that my silence could be considered complicit in any ongoing abuse that could be still happening to others unfortunate enough to be under the control of such people and organizations. I could not abide that thought.

The last straw was the world veering off into the surrealistic nightmare of the Bush-Cheney years, which have continued under President Obama. In a post-Patriot Act world, abuses of basic freedoms and human rights people have taken for granted for so long are at risk of being disintegrated. A regime bent on having no obstacles to their agendas continues to warp legislative and judicial powers to co-opt the vast arsenal of a global superpower. They wanted to be able to write themselves a blank check to do whatever they wanted, brooking no interference. All kinds of sacrifices of freedoms could be "justified" in the name of a perpetual "war on terror." All kinds of outcries against invasions of privacy and abridgments of rights could be interpreted as "aiding and abetting terrorists," subjecting dissenting citizens to legal repercussions.

At a time when I could have felt the most fear about speaking out, this kind of political climate made the need to speak out all the more immediate and necessary. With help from Helen, my healer, I had brought the PTSD I felt during the Bush-Cheney years to a much more manageable level. I returned to my meditation principles, bringing my awareness into the present moment, recognizing that the fear was rooted in trauma of the past, and anxiety that it could be repeated in the future. I began speaking locally first. Then I put my story out on the web. I took things one day at time.

In taking action by going public, I sent a clear message to my own subconscious that I was not going to be controlled by fear any more. No longer laboring under the constricted energy of fear, the awakening process that had been part of my life all along began to accelerate.

***

It is not my intent to share the material I've put in this book to frighten anyone. I can understand that the implications of what I've shared in this book can be very disturbing and frightening. The more I uncovered, the more I felt that disquiet and fear. Having to deal with experiences that confirmed what I was uncovering made the process all the more intense.

I am sharing this material, in this book and this chapter, as a crash course in what I've found out through investigating my experiences. My intent is to show you that no data, no event, no catastrophe need paralyze you with terror and trauma. Once we have faced and can accept the totality of all that exists in this world, in both its inspirational beauty and in its darkest corners, there is more space within us to breathe; to stand back, to reflect, to consider and to choose. Truth does have the capacity to set us free, if we can move beyond the fear of what confronts us. While many people live in a paradigm where they don't really bump up against some of this material, nevertheless, it is part of our world and our reality. Therefore, those whose lives are impacted by this other, covered-up reality are entangled at the level of consciousness with those whose lives appear not directly affected by the covert world. At the deepest levels, the covert reality affects us all and our entire world both energetically and materially.

This book holds an opportunity between its covers for you to face the kinds of things that go on in this world in a compressed way, a vicarious way. To comprehend all of this is to be empowered to make day-to-day life choices from a deeper understanding. Not just politically but personally. And whether you think spirituality has been part of your life on this planet or not, I hope you will begin to consider your choices from a new understanding that we are all interconnected at the most basic level of our existence.

***

The Greatest Threat to Freedom: The Cancer of Secrecy

The very word 'secrecy' is repugnant in a free and open society; and we are as a people inherently and historically opposed to secret societies, to secret oaths, and to secret proceedings.
~ John F. Kennedy

Power tends to corrupt, and absolute power corrupts absolutely. There is no worse heresy than that the office sanctifies the holder of it.
~ Lord John Dalberg-Acton, 19th Century British historian

Secrecy is power. When the National Security Act of 1947 was passed into law, it was the beginning of an erosion of the constitutional rights originally put in place to protect our freedom. I know there are many out there who could make very good arguments that this subversion goes back hundreds or thousands of years, rather than just decades. I think the evidence that supports their claims is definitely worth consideration. But for now, we will just look back over the years from 1947 to present.

During our school years in the U.S.A., we learned at least something about history. In civics classes we learned about our democratic form of government with its checks and balances between the executive, legislative and judicial branches. This system was supposed to safeguard our constitutionally-guaranteed freedoms through the passage of time. And if the people elected or appointed to positions within these three branches of government had stayed honorably true to their oaths of office, it might have worked.

The oaths of office for the President, Congressmen, Federal judges and the Armed Forces of the United States read as follows.

Presidential:

> I do solemnly swear (or affirm) that I will faithfully execute the Office of President of the United States, and will to the best of my ability, preserve, protect and defend the Constitution of the United States.

Congressional:

> I do solemnly swear (or affirm) that I will support and defend the Constitution of the United States against all enemies, foreign and domestic; that I will bear true faith and allegiance to the same; that I take this obligation freely, without any mental reservation or purpose of evasion; and that I will well and faithfully discharge the duties of the office on which I am about to enter. So help me God.

Judicial (two oaths are required):

> I, _____ , do solemnly swear (or affirm) that I will administer justice without respect to persons, and do equal right to the poor and to the rich, and that I will faithfully and impartially discharge and perform all the duties incumbent upon me as _____ under the Constitution and laws of the United States. So help me God.

> I, _____, do solemnly swear (or affirm) that I will support and defend the Constitution of the United States against all enemies, foreign and domestic; that I will bear true faith and allegiance to the same; that I take this obligation freely, without any mental reservation or purpose of evasion; and that I will well and faithfully discharge the duties of the office on which I am about to enter. So help me God.

Armed Forces:

> I, _____, do solemnly swear (or affirm) that I will support and defend the Constitution of the United States against all enemies, foreign and domestic; that I will bear true faith

and allegiance to the same; that I take this obligation freely, without any mental reservation or purpose of evasion; and that I will well and faithfully discharge the duties of the office on which I am about to enter. So help me God.

The fulfillment and execution of such oaths depends on the honesty, honor and integrity of the people taking them. A couple of questions that beg answering here are:

1. What happens when defending and protecting the Constitution of the United States, the supreme law of the land, put in place to protect individual freedom, comes into conflict with "special interests" that have the wealth and power to influence how the executive, legislative and judicial branches of government shape and interpret constitutional law?

2. What happens when such interpretations begin to threaten, undermine, and erode the very Constitution that the above oaths were put in place to protect?

"Foreign enemies" is a fairly clear term, it means enemies from outside the U.S.A. Domestic enemies are defined as enemies from within the U.S. citizenry or its political structure. "Domestic enemies," apparently, is a term subject to far more fuzzy and obscure interpretation – if we are trying to reconcile the actions of individuals occupying the presidency, Congress and the Supreme Court and still maintain a belief in our system of government. Yet what has been happening over the years to our constitutional rights and freedoms? Just how far is government legislation and regulation to be allowed to intrude upon our lives, our freedom to live as we choose?

People still have the right to vote in elections from the local to the national level to determine who will hold office to protect and preserve our constitutional rights and freedoms. But has this right become an illusion, meant to try and reassure us we still have the right and freedom to choose?

From the turn of this century onwards, how many of us have had good and just cause to question the voting systems of this country? The manufacturers of electronic voting machines have clear, conflict-of-interest political ties to the Republican party.

Do you understand the process of the "electoral college," which has the final decision on who lands in the White House if the votes are close to tied? How do you feel if a candidate wins the popular vote, yet does not become president due to the electoral vote?

I make no accusations here. I don't think I need to. I only ask my readers to reflect within on how they feel such oaths are truly being fulfilled by the elected, appointed or enlisted people who take them. I ask if you feel your vote truly "counts." I vote on an absentee paper ballot. What measures do you take to try and ensure that your vote is correctly counted?

And if you are someone who serves in the U.S. Armed Forces, you understand, as I do, the chain of command. I understand the necessity of following orders of superiors who have a broader grasp of situations than the lower ranks. But I feel the time is long overdue when we must ask ourselves if we – active duty or former military personnel – are or were being used to destroy the very heart and soul of a nation that was formed from its inception to ensure "liberty and justice for all."

How Did Things go Wrong?

David Icke[1] has written in his books and talked in his lectures about a formula that gets used on unaware populations of "problem-reaction-solution". Those with the power to do so create "a problem" that will bring about a calculated "reaction" in the mainstream public, to which they already have designed a "solution" that brings their agenda one step closer.

9/11 is a good example. The powerful elite want an excuse to go to war and have unrestricted control of their originating country's economic and military resources. An incident is needed to give a rationale that the population will accept and get troops to fall in line with their propaganda. The incident, such as 9/11, is executed, creating a specifically-designed "problem." Citizens across the country are shocked, traumatized and angry. Shock, trauma, anger is the expected "reaction." Their congressional representatives in D.C. vote in their "solution" – the Patriot Act (anything but patriotic) – on the excuse that people are willing to sacrifice their freedoms "temporarily" to be protected from "terrorists." This act gives those in power their goal – a foothold to begin a takeover of the U.S.A., periodically and systematically undermining and destroying its Constitution – an obstacle to their plans. People with too many rights and freedoms are dangerous to those elite with an agenda of complete control. A war on terror can be reinvented and perpetuated continuously, justifying more and more abridgments of constitutional rights and freedoms.

I have come to believe that it was the National Security Act of 1947 that created a secret and shadowy government within our ostensible government, or it attempted to legitimize one already there. I believe the Patriot Act was a ploy in a series of much earlier, more covert ploys designed to garner power. Here is my brief theory, based on my own search to understand how the kind

---

[1] David Icke is one of the most well-known researchers into the forces that truly control our world from the shadows. Some dismiss him due to his speaking about reptilians and their influence down through the ages of mankind's history, but through public speaking and authoring many books, including *The Biggest Secret: The Book That Will Change the World, Children of the Matrix: How an Interdimensional Race has Controlled the World for Thousands of Years – and Still Does* and many more, he has brought much very useful information to light about the forces that have shaped our world. His website: http://www.davidicke.com.

of abuse that happened to me could have ever happened in this country. How such dark elements could ever have gained foothold here.

After the National Security Act of 1947, appointed officials within this secret government gained great power due to the secrecy they were privy to. Such knowledge was compartmentalized on a need-to-know basis, with only a select few having access to all secret data or projects. The need-to-know basis was used, over time, to exclude more and more of our elected officials from any oversight or even knowledge of what was really going on.

With little to no congressional or public knowledge or oversight, such secrecy conferred immense power on such appointed individuals and groups. Mainly this is the power to withhold or reveal such secrets; therein the power to make or break financial empires. To obtain funding for their secret "black projects," they likely courted extremely wealthy groups, such as oil corporations, both within and outside of the U.S.A. Faced with possible disclosure of free energy technology and a collapse of their financial empire, oil magnates agreed to fund such research as long they were kept in the information loop on all developments. They were determined to maintain their empire. Free energy was free to be developed and likely only allowed to be used in specific, highly-classified military-industrial projects.

From the huge financial requirements of black projects, black budget operations came into being. However, skimming too much money from the national budget was too risky. It could leave a paper trail that risked exposure. Required funding could not show up on any government ledgers. All kinds of illicit activities attracted the attention of those operating behind the wall of secrecy. The activities of the alphabet agencies formed under the 1947 Act may have been charged with the implementation and oversight of programs involving illegal drugs, weapons trafficking, human slavery trafficking, child pornography and prostitution, and mind control research and implementation. Anything illegal would be a lucrative enterprise providing needed off-the-books money for black budget projects.

On the surface, such things were reviled as serious and terrible crimes – laws, and continually stimulating moral outrage over such activities kept them illegal. This keeps the price tags on such crimes far higher, due to the increased risk involved. The more illegal, the higher the risk, the more the black budget profits increased.

Let's look at illegal drugs. Those who control – through wealth – the flow of media information can manufacture whatever rationales they like to drum up the public's emotions to keep drugs illegal. The "war on drugs" is evidence on this. The wording is chosen to activate good people of conscience into rallying together, pressuring elected officials into keeping such a battle going. Drug addicts are criminalized instead of getting the medical and psychological help they truly need. The small-time street pushers are thrown in prison. Others take their places as the suppliers at obscure "top levels" recruit new pushers in the poorest places, where the seduction of quick and easy money, and lots of it, is often too irresistible to refuse.

Extraterrestrial back-engineered energy technology, or zero-point energy technology created by visionaries right here on Earth could change our world for the better on a huge economic scale, making a vast difference in the quality of living for the general population. It could make environmental tragedies like the Gulf oil spill or Fukushima catastrophes of the past, never to be repeated, allowing us to truly clean up our ecosystem and restore its balance.

Mind control programs operating in secrecy put all citizens at risk of mind control. Mind control programs target our children most of all. It chills the blood in my veins when I see more and more institutional intrusion into family lives. And mind control does not simply happen through inflicting trauma on individuals. It happens with indoctrination through education and control of information. It is all too likely coming at everyone who operates cable or satellite television in their homes. Food and water additives and designer prescription drugs add things to our bodies that make us more susceptible to electronic forms of mind control, very possibly through HAARP and chemtrails.

If whistleblowers or victims of these black budget, covert-ops organizations try to come forward, their evidence or testimony is often thrown out of court for "REASONS OF NATIONAL SECURITY." The mainstream populace, dumbed-down and conditioned to listen to and accept what government voices of authority tell them, summarily dismiss such testimony. Some may listen enough to question and look deeper, especially with the rising visibility of insanity operating in the "leadership" in the U.S.A. Most Democrats and Republicans have become nearly indistinguishable from each other – their posturing and rationalizations almost totally divorced from the day-to-day reality of most peoples' lives.

If you peel away the layers around some of the most illegal and heinous activities that go on in this world, you start to get a truly bad feeling in your gut that, at the very highest levels, the shadow government is playing both ends of such criminal scenarios against the middle. "We the People" are that "middle."

If the National Security Act of 1947 was instituted to protect our country and its citizens from hostile cold war threats, just who is it protecting today? Such secrecy perpetrates great harm on unknowing, unsuspecting individuals and entire populations. It allows unnecessary exploitation and environmental devastation to continue, conceivably to the point of mass extinction events. If this Act was ever meant to keep all of us "safe" or to protect our democracy it has utterly failed. Subverted from within, it has now become something else entirely. It has become a huge "unseen thing", an ugly shadow-spider trying to trap and control everything and everyone in its web.

***

328

Illusions of Freedom: The Complacency Trap

If you think you're free, there's no escape possible.

~ Ram Dass

Illusions of freedom are dangerous illusions, because they are granted us by those that keep secrets. Would we continue to allow our world to be ravaged and destroyed by drilling and ourselves to be economically exploited by oil corporations if we knew that free, clean energy was possible? No way. We would demand the release and implementation of such technologies.

Illusions of freedom keep us from seeking out, knowing and claiming the real thing. The wealthy and powerful elite place an array of choices before us and tell us we are free to pick from what they offer. They can do this because they keep the secrets. They make sure we don't have all the information. We mustn't be empowered to make good, educated decisions about our environmental, economic, nutritional or medical well-being. Distracted by the "choices" the elite wave before us, we are diverted from questioning what the true nature of freedom might be, and from what creative choices we might come up with on our own.

On the surface of our culture and society, our educational indoctrination within the system continues to reinforce an illusion of freedom. The illusion is maintained by the media in our adulthood. Since we are in our essence freedom-loving beings, this illusion of freedom serves to keep us complacent. Whatever kinds of shenanigans go on in Washington, D.C., we trust that the system is designed in such a way that it can't go too far wrong. We elected those people after all, because they impressed us with their positions on the issues that mattered to us, at least during the campaign process.

We allow ourselves to be distracted from the monotony of our own lives with the latest gossip about Hollywood movie stars sprawled across the glossy covers of magazines at the grocery checkout. With adrenalin-drenched TV shows and high drama news. We navigate our lives emotionally off-balance as a result, to one degree or another.

The equivalent of such continual and off-balance distraction at this time in human history could be likened to giving morphine to the thousand-plus people who did not get a seat in a lifeboat on the Titanic. Drugged, they may have been more complacent about drowning.

Complacency is aided and abetted by the fact that so many people's lives are filled with responsibilities to their families and careers. Economic hard times in recent years have worsened this situation for many. There is so much work and stress taking up people's time and energy that they may not have time to educate themselves politically about the dangers lurking in too much government intrusion into their lives and freedoms – unless some pressure is put on them to do so.

That pressure came under the societal and political trauma of the Bush-Cheney years. Despite campaign promises of "change," this pressure continues under the Obama administration. The onus falls on us to educate ourselves, to better understand what is occurring in our country and in the world. The need for more information came through the various areas of freedoms we individually care most about. From the freedom to eat clean, healthy foods and supplement our diets as we see fit, to the freedom to seek better health care and refuse dangerous vaccinations. From watching catastrophic environmental abuse and mismanagement, as in the case of the Gulf oil spill. From being impacted by precarious economic instability, looking for all the world as though it was brought on by flagrant fiscal irresponsibility and excesses at the very highest corporate and government levels.

The truth is that there have been signs of trouble brewing for a long time. It only became chillingly evident with obvious stolen elections in the year 2000 and forward, and the subsequent cascade of events and aggressive political actions.

We are still struggling under the political fallout of those stolen years. We have become a nation of people who, if we care about the quality of our lives at all and about our freedoms to eat, drink and care for ourselves as we see fit, must be hyper-vigilant against the many incursions on our freedoms thrust upon us by powerful corporate forces. We have been forced to examine more deeply what is truly going on. We have had to become our own advocates and activists. We can't trust the people in D.C. any more to look after us – if we ever could.

Complacency and Internet Activism

Even in the face of so much gone awry politically, complacency still persists in our society. Many people still cling to the idea that somehow, the system will fix itself if we just put enough activist pressure on it. Activist organizations of all kinds have sprung to life to counter the many threats to our various freedoms. We celebrate the legislative victories we achieve through them. But before the ink is dry on the particular paper we are cheering about, another ugly piece of legislation rears its head and we have to launch into action again.

For a long while, I was on the email lists of fifteen or more email activist groups. We have to say "NO!" to such things, I felt. We have to take a stand for what is right and good in this world. We have to preserve our environment. We have to take a stand for freedom.

After a while I had to question such widespread political activism in a particular way: I noticed it was keeping my attention riveted on what was wrong in this world and trying to fight it. I noticed that activist language is filled with "fight the good fight" rhetoric, just as political campaigning is. In addition, it seemed that these organizations – environmental, human rights, health, food, freedom and more – were doing little more than running around with activist fly swatters poised to try and kill every offending piece of legislation that hatched out. Yes, they killed some of them. But the "unseen thing" laying the eggs of such freedom-attacking regulatory measures remains in the shadows.

I finally decided to unsubscribe from these organizations and take a break. I felt tired out from activist hyper-vigilance, trying to stamp out every offending bill that was proposed by that unseen "thing" with an agenda of more and more control. I needed to consider where I truly wanted to put my thought, energy and intention.

So what is the balance? How do we take a stand for ourselves, yet not get so embroiled in the issues that we feed them with our more intangible energy? I pick and choose carefully. I still act on some of the petitions and letters to congressmen that come my way. I even share them with friends if I think it's really vital. But I do it as quickly and efficiently as possible and allowing the least amount of my thought or emotional energy as possible to get tangled up in it. I don't think we can afford to let our thought, energy and attention get too deeply enmeshed in what's wrong in this world.

We must begin to empower ourselves to create the world we want. We need to stop waiting for politicians to do something or for activist organizations to petition them successfully on our behalf. While activism may have some importance, the majority of our thought, energy and intention needs to go into creating unity. It needs to go into visioning our future and making it the best we can collectively imagine. We need to take the first action steps together to create it ourselves, and keep taking each step as it presents itself. We can't expect divisive and polarizing partisanism to end in politics as long as we fall into it ourselves. It doesn't matter if you are conservative or liberal, Republican or Democrat, or any other party affiliation. Whether you think Obama is a saint or the anti-christ is not important. The real power to remake our world is in our hands... if we unify.

We are all human beings who live on Planet Earth. Earth's ecosystem is in trouble, therefore we are in trouble. How long are we going to allow divide-and-conquer rhetoric to keep us posturing on opposite sides of some imaginary line? Until we choke out our last breath trying to prove who was right? They who die "with the most toys" are still just as dead as those with none. The only thing we take with us when our body dies is the quality of love, purpose, honesty and integrity with which we lived our lives. If we live that way now, while we are alive, it's our best chance to make a difference here and now.

Thinking globally and acting locally is still a great slogan. It's through doing this that we empower ourselves to remake our world. Yes, governments may still try to enact their controls. But what if all freedoms to live, breathe, eat and drink as we ourselves choose are finally subjugated? Will we accept it like a meek human herd of sheep? What quality or meaning will life have under such control?

By taking what actions we can locally, claiming for ourselves the freedoms we know are a part of who we are, we send a strong message to those in power. Such actions might force the huge ugly shadow-spider fully into the light, trying to exact consequences on us for claiming our right to exercise our freedoms as we see fit. But make no mistake about it, this shadow-spider thing fears the light of day where it can truly be seen. Once it crawls completely into the light at last, I don't think it can survive there for long. Not once people finally see it for what it really is.

If you fear the ugly shadow-spider crawling into the light to make its last attack, identify and define what specifically you fear and make peace with it. The time for complacency is past. Complacency has become one more place where we hide away our fears from ourselves. Consider that life without freedom of expression is life without richness or meaning. Seize the courage to claim your freedom.

***

Getting to the Conspiracy Theory Crowd

Because those of us who are aware of the world of extraterrestrials and government cover ups are not taken in by the mainstream media news hype and deceit, the shadow government needs to find some way to get at us, to keep us afraid too, so that our awareness cannot activate and expand. All manner of scary stories in circulation could be an attempt by them to keep us hyper-vigilant and contracted with fear and anger. So while I grant that these types of scenarios could be true and/or could happen, fixating on them certainly serves the purpose of tying up our mental and emotional energy, directing it into fear-based scenarios.

If the shadow government ever does take overt action to step out of the shadows and become an openly-tyrannical new world order, they will also activate the visible will of the people against them. Human beings have the innate need and desire to be free. Strip away the illusion of freedom they've been living with for so long, and revolt of some kind is a certainty. Shadow organizations have a lot invested to stay in the shadows and control through infiltration and subversion. They want to stay hidden, but it's becoming harder and harder for them to hide who and what they really are. So they try and seduce the population into accepting more and more control over their lives incrementally, over time.

Even if all the rumors we hear come to pass, we will find some way through it all. The kinds of things we hear or read in "the news" or over the web may just be trying to keep us afraid. They will happen, or they won't. People have, with love, cooperation, tenacity and fortitude, gotten through many trials and tribulations down through human history. And we will continue to do so, no matter what. Our choice is in how we will continue; through embracing love and caring for each other, or in dis-empowered fear-reactions with evermore divide-and-conquer. In a divide-and-conquer world, we – the 99% – all lose, while the tiniest sliver, the .001% wins, and wins big.

The situation as I've come to see it is this: Through the increasingly aggressive political and corporate actions that are clearly destructive of our rights and freedoms, intruding into every area of our lives, more and more people are waking up. The shadow government takes even more extreme actions to frighten us, to contract our expanding awareness and keep it in check. And the more extreme they get, the more they reveal their agendas and show their hand. The more they reveal who and what they really are, the more people keep waking up as a result.

A tipping point in this process has likely already been reached. The human spiritual process now unfolding may very well be the first stages of a cascade of expanding awareness stirring to life throughout all humanity.

The shadow factions of the world have actually become the evolutionary pressure upon all of us to awaken.

***

Fear and "New Age" Philosophies

In an interview I watched with David Icke, he talked about the fact that fear of what others think of us is one of the invisible prisons we all live in. The first step to real freedom is to give up that fear and be your authentic self, live your authentic life.

This really resonated for me since this was one of the other fears I myself had to overcome – being afraid of what others would think or feel, or how hearing about my experiences might impact them. My periodic attempts to share my experiences were more often than not met with skepticism, troubled looks, or a blanket denial-refusal to hear about it at all with statements like, "Way too much negativity! I just choose not to hear about such things." Such reactions to me saying anything about my experiences were a dead giveaway that the people who refused to hear it, who cut me off, *were afraid to hear it.*

How I wished I had had the luxury of being able to take such a position of denial! But as an experiencer of "such things" I couldn't. I was the one with the memories and the PTSD. I HAD to find a way to deal with it.

Many in the the "love and light" communities teach not to look at the darkness. Just focus on light, on joy, on that which raises your vibration. I completely agree with this in large part. But what do you do when you have had the darkest of the dark intrude upon your life in some of the worst ways imaginable?

I had to come to terms with my experiences and the trauma around them. I've had to take the journey through the volumes of data and testimony relating to my experiences to try and sort them out. And I should point out here that it was my own love and light nature, innocently wanting to believe in the very best angels of humanity's nature that set me up for such severe trauma. It's severe trauma to suddenly find yourself outside the realm of society, law and culture. It's severe trauma to be stripped of all human rights and made into a lab animal, and have no control over what is happening to you.

I had to work to resolve what happened on the human level, walking through many "dark nights of the soul" over the years to find my way to the larger, cosmic understanding. On the human level, feeling shunned by the love and light communities because they couldn't bear to hear what happened to me left me feeling like a leper. Unclean. I knew I wasn't. But I felt gagged and locked up in a virtual penalty box nonetheless.

On the cosmic level, taking on the soul contract that I did, everything unfolded as it was meant to. Today, from a more healed perspective, I see such behavior in a different light, and with far more compassion.

While there truly may be a few select individuals who focus completely on the positive without it being a defense mechanism against fears that lurk in the recesses of their minds, I think many more are using it as an animal flight-or-freeze reaction to a predator ("If I just run away/stay still/look away – i.e., think happy thoughts – 'IT' won't get me." This is a fear reaction. Especially if such people stick their fingers in their ears and sing "la-la-la-la-la" to drown out what they fear hearing.

The problem with this strategy is that none of us are separate from the many-layered system of energy that is life on Earth. Like it or not, we are part of the whole human collective. We are energetically entangled with each other on the quantum level of consciousness, at the unconscious and super-conscious levels as well as the conscious. We share in each others' dreams of beauty and nightmares of horror. There is no shame in being afraid. But not dealing productively with fear can create more problems.

If the essence of any spiritual path is to know ourselves, then facing our own inner demons is of paramount importance, individually and collectively. What we resist, persists. That which we refuse to look at in our lives, controls our lives. If new age groups who profess to be so positive, loving and light-filled can only manage it through avoiding or shunning that which frightens them, then that fright and negativity still dwells deep within them. They are afraid of touching it with a 100-foot pole. It would be better for them to open to what frightens them, what appears dark or negative to them, and examine it for what it really is, for what it is about it specifically that frightens them. Then they could move beyond it. It would never have to cast a shadow over their lives again.

***

Quantum science has discovered that all matter, energy and vibration in this universe, in every dimension, is interconnected. Nothing and no one is separate from or stands outside this fundamental system of unity. Therefore, denying any part of reality is a denial of how it may be touching or affecting us, whether we consciously realize it or not.

We are all entangled together at the level of consciousness, conceiving, shaping and manifesting our reality. For any single individual or group to look at a particular piece of this reality and proclaim it as the absolute totality of all reality is simply incorrect. To ignore or shun any part of reality that is expressing itself is a continuation of the human collective psychological compartmentalization that manifests shadow governments, black projects and covert-ops – and allows them to continue. Individually and collectively we must bring the unconscious to conscious awareness. We must expand ourselves into the super-conscious. Evolution and the continuation of our species depends upon successfully navigating this process of awakening.

Chapter 19: Reclaiming Freedom

> ... if it is a despot you would dethrone, see first that his throne erected within you is destroyed.
>
> For how can a tyrant rule the free and the proud, but for a tyranny in their own freedom and a shame in their own pride?
>
> And if it is a fear you would dispel, the seat of that fear is in your heart and not in the hand of the feared.
>
> ~ From *The Prophet* by Kahlil Gibran, on "Freedom"

It is fear that undermines and restricts the full exercise of our freedom.

So how do we deal with the darkest dark in our world? Hellish things that come straight out of humanity's worst nightmares? Head on. Into, through and out the other side.

If we know that terrible things go on in our world, if we know, as from all kinds of news reports, mainstream and alternative, that war goes on, that torture goes on and more, then these acts touch the collective human psyche of which we are all a part. We can try to ignore them, but ignoring them does not productively or effectively deal with them. Such ugliness can become things we secretly fear. They lurk in the dark corners of our minds. But so many of us do the animal thing and avoid looking at them, hoping that they won't "get" us. We plaster over such fears with happy thoughts and positive affirmations. Like black mold in a house, plastering over it does not get rid of it. It has to be exposed and cleaned out or it will sit there and continue growing, malignant and unseen, undermining our quality of life.

We must stretch ourselves to understand that we are more than flesh and blood. The evidence for this is coming to light all around us. Those who have achieved expanded awareness through spiritual practice know the spacious, energetic and vibrational reality "within." Quantum science has given us a model for consciousness at work in our world, birthing new research into consciousness and psychic phenomena. Near-death and out-of-body experiences and the profound changes in the consciousness of individuals who experience them also support this. We are made of light, energy and vibration.

It is our consciousness, collectively, that dreams into reality the solid-seeming world we see around us, right down to the bodies we inhabit.

Organized religions have failed us by not addressing these parts of us. We have been cut off from the true knowledge of who we are through religious indoctrination. Traditional religion puts human authoritarian intermediaries between us and the Infinite. Intermediaries who are as subject to human failings and the seven deadly sins as the rest of us. At their worst, religions have attempted to control their followers with fear. Fear of eternal damnation, word pictures they paint of realms they call hell and purgatory. Why? Because the church leadership fears the loss of the power and wealth their followers bestow on them.

Governments have failed us as well. We must fight and make war with whomever the powerful label as "other." This other may have something they want to possess. So this other is made into someone "not like us." Savages, barbarians, heretics, infidels, terrorists. "Other" is evil. They use noble-sounding rhetoric that plays on the indoctrination of populations into taking actions they want taken. Their aggression masquerades as religious crusades, patriotic defenses of ideology or preservation of racial purity. Preemptive wars are justified to make sure such "others" are dispatched before they have the chance to "get us." And, oh well, as long as we've conquered the evil others, we might as well lay claim to their land and other spoils and make use of them as we see fit.

Divide-and-conquer is the way the rich and powerful play the game. They fear us as a unified population. There are billions more of us than them. They know that if we ever all got together, particularly with spiritual knowledge of who we truly are – consciousness inhabiting form – our collective, directed desire, thought and intention could put a decisive stop to their power chess game with the world and its people. They have a vested interest in our not remembering our own multi-dimensional and spiritual wholeness. They have staged an all-out war on expanded consciousness, trying to mask it in every devious way they can so we don't catch on.

Nothing to Fear but Fear Itself

The power chess game going on in this world is all about who can most effectively wield fear and control over populations. Fear is the gross base-level weapon of the few but powerful over everyone else. Emotionally-based bliss and ecstasy can be another weapon. Both have the potential, as extreme emotional states, to block our intuition from functioning. From there, the control devices get more and more subtle.

The best way to control anyone is for them to not realize they are being controlled. So they do it through televised media. They do it overtly with packaged content. And although use of frequency manipulation, subliminals, and other subtly invasive electronic measures are deemed illegal, they are still very likely covertly used, because honestly, how are most ordinary people going to be able to detect it and report it? One of the healthiest things you can do for yourself is disconnect from the public mind control feed in your own home: cable or satellite television. I'd even get rid of the boxes that bring the signal in. If you want entertainment, rent movies or TV shows from a local or online video rental service. You'll enjoy them a lot more without constant commercial interruption, and you'll pay far less. But watch them in moderation. Get out and live real life.

The first step in escaping what traps our consciousness in this world is learning of the ways it steals and cages our energy. If we come to remember that we are more than the bodies we inhabit, that we are indestructible beings made of spirit, love and light, then we have a choice. Are we going to allow ourselves to be manipulated by fear or other emotional extremes? Or can we learn to simply relax into the knowledge that we are energy and vibration?

If we can relax into such knowledge, we discover that fear – especially as it is brandished about in our society by those using it to manipulate us – is really a phantom with no real substance. Fear doesn't have any real power over us. It only has the power over us that we allow it to have. It tries to look terrifying in its many masks. It tries to trick us into surrendering our sovereign beingness as free consciousness to its thrall. This is to keep us locked into the 3D "solid" reality paradigm. If we can be convinced we are just physical beings subject to pain and death, we can be frightened into compliance. We are controllable.

The reward of achieving and maintaining a higher vibration of love and inner peace is that our consciousness can begin to awaken to its true nature. Our awareness can begin to expand.

It is very true that our bodies can experience pain, suffering and death. We are especially susceptible to threats to loved ones. But if you surrender your sovereign beingness on some hollow promise of being protected from pain, suffering and death, you may later find out that the price of such "safety" was far too high.

The United States Constitution is not a document that grants us freedom. If we believe that, then we can also fall into believing it can be taken away. The Constitution is meant to reflect that that we are in essence free sovereign beings, endowed by the Creator with certain inalienable rights. Freedom is not given to us by the state, nor can it be revoked by the state. Freedom is inseparable from who we truly are. We, humanity, cannot be "set free." Freedom is our natural birthright as spiritual beings having a human experience – as pure energy and consciousness. And even if we have given our freedom away, we can reclaim it at any time we choose.

Why else would there be so much propaganda out there, be it religious, scientific or medical, funneling our beliefs into ourselves as limited and frail human beings? Even in the face of new evidence of life and consciousness beyond bodily death, the old conditioning dies hard. The mainstream public eyes such information with both hope and suspicion. In the face of threats or danger, most still fall into the old belief systems. Fear can then be used to manipulate them into trading their freedom for "help, safety, security" – the seductions of the controllers.

In assessing my own exercise of freedom I ask myself the following questions from time to time:

- ⋏ Is it worth it for me to surrender my freedom for a illusory "promise" of safety and security?
- ⋏ How might others I give control over me manage my life: my safety, my health, my well-being?
- ⋏ Could I live with the consequences of such a decision?
- ⋏ Would it be better to stay free, live free, act freely, speak freely? Even if someone tries to harm me in some way to stop me?

I was afraid of what had happened to me. I was afraid of speaking out. But the time finally came when none of those factors could any longer compel me to remain silent. The personal cost became too high. The energy of fear was locking down my consciousness and exacting a toll on my body and my health. I had to shed it.

So far, I continue to take a stand for my personal freedom, day by day. What might happen to me if I was ever truly tested on my commitment to freedom no matter what? I'm strongly resolved to stay true to my principles, but in all honesty and integrity, I must also admit that I'm as human as anyone else. But so far, the questions above keep my personal compass pointed to "Freedom."

The only honest limits on freedom dwell within conscience; not to infringe upon the freedom of others nor inflict harm by word or deed. Honor all life and live in mutually beneficial harmony with it.

***

I looked at the dark as deeply as I needed to to understand what actually existed out there and to understand in what context my own experiences happened. I looked at volumes of it. Today my approach is this; don't turn or run from anything because it's too scary to look at, but deal constructively and positively with the fear and move beyond it. Do this as often as necessary.

Finally you'll get to a place where you don't have to look at any scary stuff any more. There isn't much left that fear can throw at you that you haven't already faced. If there is a new fear, you've strengthened your confidence to deal with it productively. You can now move beyond fear.

Once fear loses its power over you, your awareness can begin to expand and awaken in ways you could not have imagined. Then you can become a light in the world. You become a space-holder with that light for this world's transformation. If you take action in the world to help in its transformation, that's icing on the cake. I see many inspired to do just that, and that is a joy.

Today I know there are elite groups out there who consider the masses of humanity as a herd to manage, control and use to serve their purposes. They consider us expendable. I accept the possibility, even the probability of technologies out there in the hands of the wealthy and powerful that the mainstream public can't begin to imagine. These could include scalar technology for control of weather, earthquakes and volcanoes. If such technologies do in fact exist, it's the secrecy they are concealed by that makes them most dangerous. They are most likely wielded by wealthy, powerful groups with a terrifying lack of empathy, conscience or morals. Since the general public is unaware, natural-seeming disasters are accepted as acts of God, not men. Yet I can't help but feel suspicious when, in the wake of tsunamis, earthquakes and hurricanes with thousands to millions of people killed or displaced, their devastated lands are taken over and developed by corporations for profit in some way. The displaced people left after the disaster remain displaced, unable to return to where they once lived.

If you are just becoming acquainted with the darker side of our world, then some time spent looking at the depth and breadth of it may be necessary to formulate a complete understanding of it. Having a good grasp of the contextual landscape in which we live is important so we can direct our lives in the best ways possible. I have to wonder today if I had had a full understanding of the kinds of dark and ugly things that go on, would I have been so traumatized by what happened? Certainly it would still have been truly terrible to experience. But if I had known that chances existed to encounter people capable of doing such things as part of my understanding of the world I lived in, the trauma might not have been so severe, perhaps not severe enough to cause the repression of my memories. In a society that recognizes that such things do occur, one would hope that some kind of support system would be set up to help people deal with the aftermath.

I often wonder if the bubble world we have lived in, this contrived, matrix-like reality, is in part constructed as it is to leave the people living within it susceptible to severe trauma. If those who have the arcane knowledge of the dark underworld they have constructed need to use an individual, innocent of such knowledge, then they have someone conditioned to be vulnerable to the kind of trauma they can inflict. Susceptibility to severe trauma would certainly be an asset to groups with an agenda of control.

This is a dark idea and may or may not be true. I would much prefer it wasn't true, that it is just darkly incidental to such structures and processes. But having learned all I have, I can't totally rule out that this is done by diabolical design. I admit the possibility and leave it at that. Just having an understanding of the kinds of dark that operate in the world is a protection from it creeping up on you and paralyzing you with trauma, at least to a degree. Understand it exists as a possibility, and then set it aside.

Understanding the kinds of things that go on or that can happen is not the same as continually wallowing in them and allowing yourself to get emotionally overwrought with anger or fear. Understanding is simply to keep you from being so severely impacted should such knowledge or experience come your way. I hope this book helps to create a structure of healing resources for those who have had to deal with extraordinary and severe trauma. I also feel that peer support – being in the company of others like yourself – is one of the most powerful methods of healing we can create.

I no longer feel any need to dig into every bit of information on such dark possibilities or probabilities. I don't need to examine in detail every new piece of disturbing data that gets thrown in my path, and believe me, plenty gets thrown in my path.

I look at them as briefly as I would eye the weather on the horizon, assessing whether I need to get my umbrella or take shelter in a root cellar... *in that moment.* I find it dangerous to project "doomsday" scenarios into the world from thoughts and emotions laced with fears of the future. The scary possibilities predicted by people who look almost exclusively at the darkest of the dark sets whole groups of mind-egos desperately spinning. They try to plan for every possible contingency, devising a reaction for every possible dire event that could befall them.

I've also learned that when I face and make peace with the really big fears, I no longer have to look closely at all the little ones that litter my path. When you've faced whatever your mind morbidly manufactures as the worst things that can happen to you, the other stuff becomes insignificant. Annoying or frustrating perhaps, but far more easily dismissed.

Once we acknowledge within ourselves the kinds of dark things that are possible or probable, that is enough. Understand it's there, then dismiss it and turn your full energy and attention to something positive, loving or joyful. We must build bridges of understanding with each other. We must cultivate joy in ourselves if we are to build a better world. We just can't use contrived joy as some kind of denial defense mechanism.

The truth is, all kinds of things could transpire or happen to any of us at any time. Events that have taken place in the past may indeed have set in motion things that will happen in the future. But what if our positive focus and action in the present could impact our future in a positive manner? I choose to believe it can. And the more of us that collectively sign on to such an endeavor, the better our chances of affecting a positive outcome.

The present moment is the moment of positive action. The present moment, and what we choose to hold in our desire, thought and conscious intention, creates all our subsequent moments.

From Fear to Freedom

Fear works us up, stresses us out and exhausts us. We become hyper-vigilant, trying to foresee or predict our future and plan for multiple contingencies. Adrenal exhaustion becomes a way of life, and our bodies become depleted of serotonin, running on too much cortisol until it becomes a chronic condition. Our immune systems suffer. We become run down. We even put on weight for "protection." And yet fear continues to barrage us in more and more areas of our lives.

Deepak Chopra[1] once cited a study done on neuropeptides generated in the body within groups of people who watched two specially-selected movies. The neuropeptide results were then measured in each group. One test movie was *The Sound of Music*; inspirational, showing people caring for each other, triumphing over adversity. On the negative side, the movie used was *The Omen*, a movie in which terrible things happen through an evil child who lives on at the end to go on wreaking more devastation. In each case, the different neuropeptides generated by each film stayed in the bodies of the movie watchers for about one month. But the effects were vastly different. For the frightening film, the neuropeptides were destructive within the body, lowering immune response, increasing the effects of free radicals on the various body systems, affecting moods adversely. With the inspirational film, the neuropeptides generated had the opposite effect, aiding in moods of hope, happiness, peace and contentment; immune systems were enhanced and strengthened, and other body systems functioned in a more optimal manner.

When we look at all the images, words and sounds we take in each day, including our own thoughts and feelings, even what we dream at night – all having an effect on our bodies biochemically, the importance of keeping our thoughts primarily on positive, inspiring and loving imagery the majority of the time becomes clear.

***

Facing Fear

Unformed or half-formed fears lurking in the back of our minds can tax our life energy day by day. These are often anxieties we make ourselves too busy to identify and deal with. It is hard to take effective action or tune into our intuition while in the grip of fear. So the first thing to do is identify exactly what you are afraid of, whether it's one thing or several. Write these things down and know exactly what it is that you're afraid of or worried about.

---

[1] Deepak Chopra is an physician who has been instrumental in bringing the Indian healing system, Ayerveda, to the West. He has been one of the most vocal and persuasive proponents of mind-body-spirit healing arts for many years. He has authored over 65 books, many appearing on the New York Times best-seller lists. His website: http://www.deepakchopra.com.

The next step is to close your eyes and face each fear on the mental visualization screen of your mind. If this thing that you are afraid of was to happen, just how would you deal with it? How would you respond to it the moment that it happens? How would you like to respond to it? Knowing that many terrible things have happened on this world and that people have moved through such events and lived to tell what they were like, how might you be able to muster up the courage to take a deep breath, respond to what is happening moment to moment, and move through it? Visualize the feared thing, and see yourself moving through the experience in a way that leaves you whole and intact. Do this with each fear you identify. If you can see yourself successfully moving through circumstances that you fear, those fears will begin to lose their power over you.

If it is death you fear, begin to understand that you are not your body; you dwell within your body. It is a sheath, it is not who you are in your essence. Do some reading on near-death experiences (NDEs) and out-of-body experiences (OOBEs) to help open your understanding of what realms of consciousness exist beyond the physical. While most all of us, including me, would like to stay alive in our bodies and would avoid dying in every way possible, if it comes it is not the end of us. Our essence, our soul, our spirit is never born, nor does it ever die. We are eternal.

Even suffering can be met and dealt with, because we only have to deal with it one moment at a time. It's when we become caught in a pattern of past impacts and future fears that suffering can seem overwhelmingly unbearable. There are stories of how people have dealt with suffering and lived, and have even been transformed by the experience. Survivors of the WWII Nazi concentration camps, Tibetans under the Chinese occupation and other stories of enduring courage and perseverance show us it can be done. Human beings can be amazingly resilient when faced with adversity. We would not wish it on ourselves or others, but we do find ways to move through it.

Meditation and Spiritual Practice

Meditation can help, and there are many systems of meditation. There are meditations that use mantras or phrases repeated over and over to still the mind. There are meditative techniques that guide you through visualizations. I feel one of the best is vipassana insight meditation. Through simply following the movement or inflow-outflow of our own breathing, vipassana allows us to develop a relationship with "the inner observer" we all have within; that part of our own consciousness connected to the universal consciousness which is experiencing life through each of us. We learn experientially about life's impermanence.

Vipassana empowers you to learn about the inner witness part of yourself by simply observing your relationship to your thoughts and feelings and building a connection with that calm inner strength we all possess. Simply make following

344

your breath the focus of your attention and watch all the thoughts and feelings that arise in the mind and body as you do so. Notice how much of the material is unreal, in that it is past memory and/or future imagination. Even when you can't keep the focus on your breath due to inner mental chatter, or twitches and pings in the body, the experience is equally valuable. You observe how the mind-ego mightily resists calming down. It fears losing control, surrendering to the greater reality of who you truly are. It will manufacture all kinds of thoughts and sensations to pull you away from your focus on the breath. If you simply observe and stay with the process, you come to realize that you are not your busy mind, and how much mind is tied to ego. Mind and ego have their places in our life. They are present to ensure our survival as individuals. It's just that they can get stuck in overdrive, overwhelming our access to the deeper reality of who we are. This is why it is said by spiritual teachers that the mind makes a good servant, but a bad master.

Learning to clear and sharpen the mind and body is a prerequisite to getting in touch with your innate intuitive gifts. Vipassana teachings tend to underplay this, teaching us not to get caught in anything that takes us out of our connection with the meditative state. However, our expanded senses are an important part of who and what we are. Developing them is important. These also function best in the present, helping us to respond optimally to life as it happens moment to moment.

One of the Four Noble Truths of Buddhism is that suffering exists, and it is rooted in replaying past memories and imaginings of the future. This is true whether we replay or imagine painful memories or pleasurable ones. Through vipassana practice, we often find we live much of our lives ruminating on the pain or the pleasure in our pasts, or in anticipation of future pleasures or avoidance of fear or future pain. Much of the time we miss out on the present moments of our lives altogether.

One of the pitfalls of vipassana, at least for me, was getting caught in "process" – endlessly processing the same emotional, mental or physical material in different ways. Joy is also a part of life and who we are. In times like the ones we live in now, joy must also be cultivated and strengthened.

Use whatever spiritual method you choose to practice as a tool for becoming quiet and developing the relationship with the inner observer. Once you realize that your mind and your emotions are not who you really are, you are truly empowered with CHOICE about how you will direct your spiritual, creative energy and attention. It's one more step to freedom.

Meditation practice helped me to see that almost all of what is spun out through the media actually plays upon the unmindful human tendency to dwell in the past or the future rather than being present. It captures our attention, suspending us between remembering/anticipating pleasure or reviewing/avoiding past pain, our fears causing us to plan endless strategies to elude it in an imagined future. My studies about my experiences and the context in which they occurred showed me that this kind of spin and presentation of material through the media is almost certainly deliberate and intentional. When you put it together with the quantum and spiritual principle that our thoughts and what we put our attention on create our reality, then it becomes clear that some group wants our attention focused on creating what suits them, and uses the media to do it.

Breathing

Breathing is one of the best ways to identify if you have been knocked out of your center and feel out of balance. Short shallow breathing or barely breathing at all usually accompanies feelings of fear and anger. Just as our breathing mirrors our emotional states, choosing to slow and deepen our breathing can alter our emotional states quickly for the better, as well as enhance optimal functioning of the body.

Breathing can alter our state of consciousness in profound ways, as has been found in practices such as holotropic breathwork developed by Stanislov Grof. Pranayama, meaning "extension of the breath or life force," has been used by yogis for thousands of years to achieve higher states of consciousness.

If you find yourself in a highly emotional state with your breathing short or shallow, your belly and solar plexus tense and tight, begin to choose to breathe more deeply and mindfully. Fill your lungs to capacity so that your belly and ribcage expand. Keep it going for three or more minutes until your physical, mental and emotional state shifts into more ease and clarity.

Exercise

Taking in so much information each day that our minds can perceive as threatening builds up a charge in our bodies, like a human capacitor. We can feel the fight or flight impulse, but intellectually we know there is nothing in front of us to swing at or run from. Still, the energy charge in the body is in there. To continue allowing that charge to accumulate without discharging it is harmful in the ways mentioned previously here. Exercise, from brisk walking, running, dancing to various kinds of music, to weight-lifting can discharge the build up of energy in our bodies. Make your exercise even more powerful by setting an intention to discharge all negative emotional energy as you do it. Exercise is as vital to our mental and emotional health as it is to our physical health.

Balance Every Negative with Five Positives

For every dark, negative thing you look at, seek out five beautiful, inspirational and uplifting things to counterbalance it. Our families and children can bring us joy. The unconditional love of our animal companions is always a light in our lives. We have books or films that always inspire us each time we see them. Visiting a special place in nature, watching a sunrise or sunset can recharge our inner batteries.

Shift your attention and perspective, seek out and revel in all the wonder and beauty life endlessly offers… in the present moment.

Truth, Freedom and Responsibility

Just what is freedom? What does it personally mean to you, the reader of this book? What does it mean on a physical level? On a mental or emotional level? What does freedom mean on a spiritual level?

These are not test questions with any definitive or rote answers. These are questions to muse over and wonder about every day. They are contemplative questions to make rich with meaning over the passage of time. When you encounter any way in which you are not free in your life, on whatever level, reclaim your freedom in that area of your life.

Don't look outside yourself for someone to "give" you freedom. Freedom is your sacred birthright. No one can take it from you. They can only try to compel you surrender it to them.

A sword has been used as a symbol of Truth. Its two edges could equally symbolize freedom and responsibility.

The truth, if we come to know and accept it, shall set us free. With ultimate freedom comes ultimate responsibility – responsibility for the choices we make and how they will affect ourselves, each other and future generations. At any moment of choice, we can turn one way or another… we choose our destinies as much as they choose us. What we choose to do with our lives is all the more precious *because* of free will. Being told only what the powers-that-be want us to know, mixing truths with lies, leaves us in a risky position of making life decisions without all the necessary information. Exercising our free will to be and to choose comes when we have the broadest possible spectrum of knowledge and understanding of our world. The true exercise of free will can come only when the mind, heart and spirit are free, when we live, move and breathe in a world of transparency and truth.

We choose incarnations in a human body to rediscover freedom through the "confidence course" of limitations and barriers to it that exist here on Earth. To gain, through all the contrasts of duality that we experience here, a fuller understanding of what freedom truly is. Ultimately, to discover that true freedom lies in rediscovering who we are at the level of consciousness and interconnectivity. We live our material lives on Earth within the unified quantum field of potential that underlies the reality that we have created from our desire, thought and intention – even though we also decided to forget who we are when we come here to more fully participate in our creation.

Keep stepping back in your consciousness. We come into human existence and it becomes our reference point for everything we experience. We become part of religious, political and societal structures and they are added to our reference points for how we view life through these various lenses of belief and judgment. What broader context can you step back and view? Can you honor your human feelings and existence while stepping back further into a cosmic perspective? Can you imagine how extraterrestrials might observe life on Earth, especially with the destruction humanity wreaks on the ecosystem our lives depend on?

Can you imagine how it might affect telepathic or tel-empathic beings to touch minds that hide so much from themselves? Can you go further and imagine yourself a drop of consciousness merging with the universal field of all consciousness, suspended in the quantum wave field of all potential, dreaming dreams of differentiated realities settling into various dimensional densities of energy and vibration and bringing them into "real" manifestation?

It's my heartfelt wish that all people everywhere can learn to move beyond fear and discover the wonderful and incredible potential that awaits them as free beings.

Chapter 20: Movies for Reflection and Insight

The Celestine Prophecy

From the book of the same title by James Redfield, this movie shows people learning to calm and center themselves in challenging circumstances and thereby being able to perceive an expanded reality all around them. It gives us some great visual representations of where the current shift and expansion in human consciousness could be taking us. It shows people staying present and being able to access and use their intuitive faculties in-the-moment to move through dangerous situations. The real ability to respond to any situation lies far less in planning and strategies; far more in the ability to stay calm and present, assess situations, open to our intuition and take appropriate action in the present moment as it arises. It even suggests that, by shifting and raising our own vibrational frequency, we can shift dimensionally beyond the third dimension, no longer even sharing the same reality with those who are still trapped in their own belief structures.

What Dreams May Come

Starring Robin Williams, this film shows us possibilities of our existence beyond death. While I don't think everything in the film is to be taken literally, this film startled me – in a good way – with its remarkable parallels to my own insights about life after death. Coming out years after my own brush with suicide, the reasons I chose *not* to take my own life were chronicled in this film. If I had not truly believed I could find myself in a hell of my own making after pulling the trigger, I would very likely not be here today. My experiences out-of-body, in dream states on the astral plane were that real, that tangible to me. I do not believe we stay in such a painful place after death forever, as the movie indicated. I do feel we stay there as long as our will can keep reinforcing and replaying the pain that caused us to want to die in the first place. Our spirit helpers are ever-present as we replay such pain, looking for a break in the focus, a relaxing of the will, that will allow them to lead us out of our self-constructed hell and back into the light. I recommend this film for exploring spiritual and afterlife concepts.

Star Wars: **The Original Trilogy of Films**

The original Star Wars trilogy, the first three movies from 1977 - 1983, are timeless classics. The three films that came later, while filling in necessary blanks about Anakin Skywalker, the Jedi and the Empire, were filled with some of the extreme adrenalin-generating over-the-top action I've come to find boringly predictable in more recent films.

I feel strongly that their popularity came from touching a deep, latent knowing in all of us. We all have the potential within to tap into the unified field in ways that will allow us to redefine ourselves and break through our apparent human limitations. I personally feel there is nothing that technology of metal, microchips and fiber-optics can do that we do not have the innate ability to do ourselves, through our own biotechnology. Bilocation, psycho-kinesis, levitation, remote viewing and other marvels have all been demonstrated on this planet by spiritual adepts or specially-trained individuals.

Sharpening our expanded intuitive senses to help guide us moment-to-moment is one of the best securities we can provide ourselves within this challenging, chaotic world on the edge of great change. Practice it. Learn how to use and trust it. Learn when true inner guidance is at work and to discern when other voices of desire, or emotions like fear are whispering in your ear. As Yoda told Luke, while training him to be a Jedi knight:

You will *know*... when you are calm, at peace... passive.

Yoda also told Luke that "always in motion" is the future. This is because the present moment and how we respond to it determines our future. We want to make the best present-moment choices we can, from clear, quiet centeredness, enhanced by calm, full, relaxed breathing.

The Matrix

This is another movie that stirred something deep within millions of viewers. In it, individuals were used as human batteries to create a vast virtual reality net in which they all lived out their lives in a mind-simulation. Their actual bodies existed in pods of fluid where their bio-electrical energy was tapped to power a world of artificial intelligence that had made captives of them. This film was a powerful metaphor for our own world and I feel it touched people at that level of the subconscious where we all sense we are living in similar construct. The difference is that our construct has to do with unconsciously directed thought and attention and quantum particles arranging themselves accordingly, rather than actual physical bodies wired into machinery. The "matrix" in our own world traps us in multiple ways through indoctrination, programming and fear. This is why it is so critical to learn how to cope with fear in a positive and constructive way so that we can move beyond it – no matter what gets thrown at us.

The Thirteenth Floor

The Thirteenth Floor was not a particularly good film in my opinion, other than another illustration of people living out their lives in a virtual reality. In between the lines, the film prompts interesting questions about the true nature of our reality, just as *The Matrix* did. Just what is our reality? Is it a construct of energy built from thought and intention? If we create a holographic reality we can enter into and interact with, do the people we create there have the capacity to become self aware? Do they have souls? I tended to ignore the plot, as contrived violence in film is becoming a bore to me. It did have me wondering about a larger possible allegory for humanity's awakening consciousness. Are we bumping up against a similar paradigm boundary as the virtual characters who learned that their world ended some distance beyond their city's limits? As we begin to explore the quantum relationship between our consciousness and how our world arranges itself – particle-izes itself according to our desires, thoughts and beliefs, are we not beginning to perceive the energetic edges of our 3D material realm? Will the adventurous and pioneering spirit of humanity inspire us to reach beyond this third dimension and explore the dimensions that lie beyond?

V for Vendetta

This film illustrated the fall of a fictional British society to totalitarian fascism by a powerful few who developed a deadly virus while also developing a medicine to cure it. They instigated hatred for elements of society like gays and lesbians – "the godless" – then rounded up these undesirables and detained them. These people became the fodder for testing and development of the deadly virus. This powerful group, bent on total control of the country, unleashed the virus on a segment of the population, including a children's school. Almost 100,000 people swiftly died. Religion was used to manipulate the situation, calling on the faithful to repent, and then – seemingly miraculously – the cure and/or vaccine was introduced.

Capitalizing on religious rhetoric, the figurehead, Adam Sutler, of the small group responsible for the disease in the first place, postulated that it was a return to faith that wrought this "miracle" cure. Coerced by religious dogma and fear into trading freedom for security, this fictional England became a dictatorship under martial law and harshly enforced curfews, with a controlled media to propagandize the people into perpetual compliance... until a vigilante, "V" appeared, appointing himself as a savior of the people, executioner of the group responsible for the deadly virus. He set about avenging the deaths of those human beings who died as test subjects, of which he was one who survived.

One does not have to look too far or too deeply at our society today to see the metaphor.

What the Bleep Do We Know? **and** *The Secret*

The next two films I recommend seeing are documentaries, but still wonderfully educational, inspirational and mind-stretching as well as entertaining.

What the Bleep Do We Know? was a sleeper hit that took the country by storm at the box office in 2004. It got many poor reviews by people who did not have the knowledge, imagination or insight to grasp this film's importance, sadly demonstrating the woeful inadequacy of our current educational system. The powerful significance of the information presented in this film and its implications for changing how we think about our reality – even our ability to influence or change it – did a complete fly-by for such critics. I had experienced much the same excitement that this film created in me years earlier in reading *The Holographic Universe: The Revolutionary Theory of Reality* by Michael Talbot. That book, and *What the Bleep Do We Know?* opened, at last, a new world of possibilities for me. With my years of science and metaphysical study, my spiritual practices and experiences, I instinctively knew that these all must find a common ground somewhere.

The Secret is an inspiring film about the "law of attraction." While it was not intended as a sequel, it took the principles illustrated in *What the Bleep Do We Know?* and gave powerful examples of how they could be practically applied in all the areas of our lives. It briefly mentioned the law of attraction as an arcane principle kept sequestered in secret chambers of the powerful and wealthy. Such groups kept the common populace on a treadmill tied to the belief that hard physical work and lots of it was required just to eke out a living. If you worked "extra hard" and were "clever enough," you might become really successful.

Towards the end, the filmmakers alluded to changing the world we live in through the law of attraction, but no truly powerful example of this yet exists for illustration. Since all of humanity is entangled together at the level of consciousness, we need much more unity to accomplish these large-scale shifts rather than the divisiveness currently reflected in our world. Restoring health and well-being, creating love and unity with spouses and children through the power of changing and directing our consciousness are incredibly important steps in the process of awakening. Having wealth and a jet-setter lifestyle to go with it, if that is what you want, is also a fine way to demonstrate proficiency at learning to use the quantum principles alluded to in the law of attraction.

But I would just add here to look a level or two deeper inside yourself. Are you choosing what you "think" you really want from an array of choices and an endless parade of "stuff" that has been flaunted as "desirable" for centuries by the wealthy and powerful ruling classes of this world? Are you working to manifest symbols of wealth, status and power that have been defined for you rather than by you? Have we, observing our own lack of "wealth" compared to the opulent lifestyles of the ultra-rich, traded away a forgotten, deeper longing for a world of simple beauty, peace and love where we live in harmony with all life?

Consider it. Perhaps a more spiritually-mature use of the law of attraction is to join together as unified consciousness and create a world that serves *all* life on Earth, human beings included. Maybe learning to use it to "get more stuff" is preparation for bringing into being a far grander vision of how our world could be.

In *What the Bleep Do We Know?* there is an example given of crime rates dropping in cities where groups of people in meditation with a specific intent had a definite effect. It seemed they created a kind of energetic "peace quotient." They could not measure that energy, but they could measure its effects. This experiment, repeated in various cities, kept producing statistically-significant results. So we have learned that groups of people can have an impact on shifting reality. Dr. Dean Radin, in his studies of psychic phenomenon and quantum entanglement, has found evidence that the power of intention is increased when groups – the larger the better – all focus on a particular outcome. To a single soul pouring out a ton of desire, thought and intention on winning the lottery, it might tip the odds in his or her favor by a degree or two. But since the rest of the human collective doesn't really care if he/she wins the lottery or not, there is significant consciousness "weight" keeping that person's odds in the random category.

I have come to see the law of attraction presented in *The Secret* as wonderful play for consciousness becoming more and more aware of its ability to shift the world around it. I think we can use the quantum principle of consciousness affecting our personal reality – the law of attraction – to create better personal lives. Believe it enough, experience what it is you desire as already real for you – complete with the emotional experience of having whatever that item or situation is – and you may be able to magnetize it into your life. But more often the unconscious material we carry around that we have not yet touched upon keeps what we consciously desire out of reach. This underscores the importance of making our unconscious material conscious.

The shadow material we carry in the unconscious exerts a powerful effect from that place in the psyche. If we can learn to see the things around us in the world that we revile or fear as messages about what we may be holding in our unconscious, then we have a tool before us to learn about what it is we do carry in the unconscious. We just have to realize that the feared and reviled are as much parts of us as the things we love and enjoy. This principle is in action in the human collective in a far more powerful way than it is in individuals. It is all of us together that collectively create the world we see around us.

This explains the recurring motifs and archetypes universal to all human beings that Carl Jung attempted to explain through a postulation of a collective human unconscious. The things that go on in our world that we fear and dislike are the collective human Id presenting itself. With the things that have gone on in the last several decades increasingly disturbing to us, I have come to feel that this is an evolutionary process happening now, as we move through and beyond the 2012 portal. The collective shadow is more and more revealed. As it is revealed, the old thought and consciousness structures that once supported it are collapsing. It's a chaotic time as the collapse of old paradigms makes way for the new. If humanity truly awakens, "the new" can be as we desire and dream into being. Through unity, it can be a design that is mutually beneficial to all life. This process of breakdown and chaos is occurring for humanity's healing and integration, through which we can embrace a new era and become a more spiritually-evolved species.

Avatar

Who knows but that our world full of technology and gadgets is evidence of a devolution of humanity rather than an evolution? That forgotten, deeper longing for a world where we live in harmony with all life found open expression in the millions of people who saw *Avatar* – and went to see it multiple times.

The parallel between the Na'vi people and the indigenous cultures that have been destroyed or subverted on Earth is very clear. If people on Earth once lived in harmony with the land and all life that lived here, then it appears that we as human beings have lost something vital and life-giving. It has taken us hundreds of years down the trek of materialism to realize it, but in the face of our current environmental destruction, we finally are. Whether it is too late for us or not rests in our own hands.

The Na'vi lived happy, vital lives in harmony with and enjoying a tangible connection to their world, their ancestors and all life there. Human beings were the invaders on Pandora. Destroying their own world's ecosystem, they now turned to exploit and destroy other worlds, perpetuating the invasive rape of natural resources on Pandora. Eywa, the mother-goddess, conscious life-energy network embodied in Pandora herself, chose Jake Sully, a human soldier occupying his human-Na'vi hybrid form, to teach about the Na'vi way of life. As he came to understand it fully, he found it precious beyond measure and rose to the task of rallying all the Na'vi clans, and all other life on the planet to defend it. In the end, the Na'vi and Pandora herself evicted the occupying humans.

I'm not anti-technology. I think that we are ingenious enough to create technology that exists in harmony with the world around it. Yet, if there truly is nothing a machine or electronic device can do that we cannot do from within, from our own directed consciousness, is there a reason to have technology?

Perhaps. As fully-conscious beings, the possible purpose for technology, perhaps even living technology someday, could be to free our bodies, minds and spirits from the mundane concerns of life.

With more spiritual evolution, we could discover that we can create through consciousness. Our bodies themselves, understood fully as bio-technology, could become focusing points that channel whatever we need or want into being from the quantum field through our own directed desire, thought and intention.

To make this possible, we would have to recognize our subconscious shadow material and consciously weave it into the totality of who we are – integrated consciousness rather than compartmentalized consciousness. We would have to become self-realized to the degree that we *know* we are more than our bodies. Then the exercise of directed desire, thought and intention would bear the manifest fruit it's meant to, likely very quickly. As fully-conscious beings, through creating living technology to serve specific purposes and needs, we could be free to contemplate the Infinite; to experientially learn, evolve and explore ever further.

Thrive: What On Earth Will It Take?

This book was three-quarters of the way written when I saw this film, released to the public on 11/11/2011, also my birthday. *Thrive: What On Earth Will It Take?* is an important, landmark film that reveals just what kinds of agendas are going on behind the scenes. The world's population is primed for such information, seeking to understand all the disturbing to insane-appearing acts and policy-making by so-called leaders in government and corporations. By "following the money," *Thrive* reveals what is behind the alarming world-wide consolidation of power into the hands of an extremely elite .001% of the population bent on controlling literally every aspect of our lives. Foster Gamble and his wife, Kimberly Carter Gamble, spent decades researching the information in this film and eight years working on *Thrive* directly. Well-known scientists, thinkers, activists are interviewed in this film, including Deepak Chopra, Barbara Marx Hubbard, Nassim Haramein, Catherine Austin Fitts, Daniel Sheehan, Steven Greer, David Icke and many more. With wealthy family ties to Procter and Gamble corporation, Foster spent huge amounts of his own money, with the help of some other donors, to make the film and launch a solution-based website. Since its release, *Thrive* has been seen by over 8 million people and has been translated into 20 languages. It is now available to watch for free online at the *Thrive* website: www.thrivemovement.com.

While the Gambles and their movement have come under some criticism, I choose to support them, their film and website. At their website is also a "Solutions Hub" of 12 interconnected sectors that touch on all aspects of life on Earth. There are actions that we can all take in a whole variety of areas depending on what our particular passion is, from economics and the environment to science and spirituality. Solution-based offerings are a refreshing change to what has previously been a wasteland of complaints and impotent anger for those people who know what is going on behind the scenes, but have no real solutions to offer. I strongly suspect that many of the attacks are fronts for those in that elite .001% who are feeling exposed for what they are. Rather than go after the Gambles directly, they are launching many campaigns attempting to destroy their credibility. People deeply invested in conspiracy theories can be suspicious of everything and everyone and that suspicion can play right into the hands of those who would like to undermine and destroy a project like the *Thrive* movement. People who lump "conspiracy theories" into absurd fantasy too fantastic to believe – who have not taken the time to examine the sources of information, connecting the dots of much of the material presented in *Thrive*

– continue a pervasive policy of indoctrinated denial that plays right into the hands of that elite .001%.

Like all human beings, Foster and Kimberly Gamble and their staff are not perfect. Yet they had the resources and the will to produce *Thrive* and start a movement that has great potential to bring people together – unity – for a common and very necessary cause.

I would issue a challenge to those critics of *Thrive*: if you have answers or solutions of your own to the challenges that face humanity today, please offer them. If you don't then cease your attacks on a movement that offers a people's united front for creating positive shifts in a world that needs it so very badly. Any powerful movement such as *Thrive* could be targeted for subversion by the rich and powerful. It will take some very conscious and devoted attention from the Gambles to be sure their movement stays healthy and worthwhile for the common people.

Chapter 21: Consciousness

Primal Rhythm, Dance of Duality

Create... Destroy...

Darkness... Light...
Void... Form
Stillness... Action

EverNow fracturing
        into infinitesimal splinters
                of mirror brightness
                        to learn...

Original Abandonment...
        Original Grief...
                Original Rage...
                        To Re-union...
                        To Joy...

Separation... Oneness...
Fear... Love...
Hatred... Compassion...
War... Peace...

Destroy... Create...

Transcend.

~ Niara Terela Isley

What is Consciousness?

We live out our human lifetimes in bodies that operate at an individuated level of consciousness. As individuals within an entire human collective, we are all touched by every kind of experience that life on Earth has to offer.

The deeper layer of understanding is realizing that Oneness is the true reality. It is a field that underlies every reality paradigm in our universe. We are actually connected by the very space that seems to separate us. From galaxies, stars and planets to all the life forms that inhabit them, all energy fields overlap and intermingle. Differentiated in energy and vibrational rates by our own desire to investigate life as individual facets of the One, we *experience*. We *learn*. At higher celestial dimensions, these octaves of energy and vibration connect seamlessly, blending into the One Consciousness.

This One Consciousness permeates everything and everywhere. It occupies the same space we inhabit. All the existing dimensions also permeate throughout the same space. The quantum wave of pure potential likely originates with this original, primal One Consciousness. Sent out to the farthest reaches of space-time, resounding through every vibrational octave of time-space, it moves in an eternal rhythm like the inflow and outflow of our breath, like ripples in a pond. Consciousness sends out the original ripple, like the Big Bang that is thought to have created our universe. It travels outwards, reaches a boundary of sorts – a kind of zero dimensional point. Then it bounces back to the One Consciousness Source. As the outbound waves meet the inbound waves, intersecting, they may create interference patterns like those in a holographic plate. These intersecting waves, these interference patterns, could be seen as all the points of spin in the universe, from the spinning of galaxies to the orbits of electrons in atoms, even the whirling of chakras in our bodies. These interference patterns, these various vortexes of spinning energy may be the mechanisms that create the holograms making up our reality – the world we see around us and other, higher dimensions that still operate within form and substance – and throughout all the vibrational octaves of dimensions and the alternate universes they could contain.

As the poem at the beginning of this chapter suggests, we are a result of some action that took place in consciousness which then brought into expression what we experience as ourselves, our planet and all life on it. We extend our definitions and descriptions now, through science, to include the physical universe we observe through our telescopes.

We see a world around us that looks solid, feels solid. It's made up of various parts and pieces. We can take things apart to find out what they're made of and how they work. Yet as science kept disassembling the world down further and further to the molecular, atomic and subatomic, trying to better understand the structure of the universe, they discovered when they reached the quantum level that Newtonian physics no longer applied. At the level of energy, the basis of matter, they detected the mysterious action of quantum waves and particles. They identified the principle of non-local interconnectedness. And they also discovered that the act of "observing" brings our solid-seeming "real" world into existence. It is living beings imbued with consciousness that provide the meaningful, contextual observation for the quantum waves of potential to arrange themselves into the reality we see around us. We have a collective human "agreement" about the reality of our world and everything in it.

What are Dimensions and Densities?

In science and mathematics, dimensions are described as the minimum number of coordinates needed to specify each point within it. Diagrams can be shown to demonstrate up to four dimensions. Density refers to something's mass in a particular volume of measurement.

From a spiritual and energetic perspective, for me, dimensions are realms of varying vibrational frequencies that all exist in the same, so-called, space. I say "so-called" because it's possible that space does not exist apart from a construct we bring into being by our consciousness observing it as part of our "reality." If we disappeared as a species, as a planet, from this universe, and the universe continued to exist, it would be because something else, some other consciousness collective would still be observing it and acting in relationship to it.

As consciousness steps down, so to speak, from its original undifferentiated source to its individual elements – some of which are us – it *decreases* in vibrational frequency. There is also a corresponding *increase* in density that would appear to correlate to the formation of matter from the action of consciousness in relationship with the quantum field.

So, like a few handfuls of dirt and sand thrown into a jar of water, shaken, then allowed to settle, the "lower" levels are the heaviest and densest. The strata that arrange themselves in the ascending layers are lighter and finer with every upward increment. There is an area of overlap as each layer transitions to the next. Finally at the top of the jar is the standing water, still fluid, sensitive and responsive to the slightest vibrational action going on around it. The difference between this example and the realms of varying dimensions and densities is that they all occupy the same "space;" all the layers interwoven.

The realms of different dimensions and densities are made possible by the vibrational strata that make up various dimensions, from Source – undifferentiated consciousness – down to our third dimension. Moving to musical metaphor, in music we have single notes and octaves of notes. Sound and music are vibrations that we can hear, acting on the hearing mechanisms – our eardrums – our bodies designed; the evolutionary process reaching for and building any means for greater freedom of expression. Our eardrums take that vibrational information and allow our brain to instantly translate it into any number of sounds we share in our collective consensus reality; sounds that constitute language, music or noise – harmony or discord.

Single notes are in themselves pure and simple. In combination with other notes, they create melody, a progression of notes that forms a tune or movement. With other notes providing second, third or fourth "melodies" that intertwine with the first in the same tune or movement, a harmony is created between all of them that feels good vibrationally to hear. The arrangement can be beautiful, etheric, inspiring, stirring or exciting. Octaves are a family of notes that belong in a particular group, like the key of A, or the key of E. These octaves or groups also overlap. As you progress up the scales of notes and octaves, the frequencies increase.

It is this way also with the vibrational notes, octaves and their frequencies as they move back towards Source Consciousness. One octave of vibration, or "key" is our third dimensional physical universe. Just as there are 7 notes that belong to any key of music, so are there a specific spectrum of vibrations that form the density of the third dimension. Then there is the fourth dimension, the fifth, sixth and so on. How many dimensions are there? Scientists working with superstring theory posit at least 10 and concede that the number of dimensions could be infinite.

All kinds of sounds and music can occupy the same space also, just like dimensions. The way that dimensions occupy the same "space" is through the vibrational nature of each octave or family of frequencies. And they all overlap as they ascend or descend. So people with a heightened sensitivity to vibratory frequencies are sometimes able to perceive phenomenon or beings that occupy other dimensional realms. Some do it through clairvoyance, some through clairaudience, some tap into other areas like precognition.

The increase in people with heightened sensitivity in the world today suggests at least a couple of possibilities. More people are being born predisposed to heightened sensitivity, such as indigo, crystal and star children. Dolores Cannon finds this in the people she works with who discover they are volunteer souls, coming to help Earth "ascend." This could convey that while Earth's frequency may be increasing, at least some elements of the human population must also consciously raise their vibratory frequency to meet it, forming an energetic bridge for the possible dimensional shift. If there truly is a shift in progress on Earth to a higher dimension as so much 2012 literature proposes, then as the frequencies increase on our world, we move into the area of overlap between our third dimension and the fourth. Since retired Sergeant Major Robert O. Dean reports from his reading of The Assessment that some UFOs are inter-dimensional in their origin, then the increase in UFO sightings on our world in recent years could also be a symptom of a rise in the vibrational frequency of our world and ourselves. The orb phenomenon is also likely a sign of dimensional overlap as frequencies increase on our world.

I feel both possibilities are occurring. We have more evolved and sensitive souls incarnate on Earth than ever before. And as frequencies increase, more people are able to perceive phenomenon through the overlapping dimensions from an expanding awareness actually brought about by the raising of frequencies.

Since a shift to, and an understanding of, an expanded reality with a fuller comprehension of the relationship between consciousness, thought and intention could create a population capable of shifting reality, the reason for a covert war on consciousness and awareness expansion becomes clear.

Those who have operated the constructs of religion, nationalism and economics down through the centuries fear this change. They fear an end to their power. So they work to instill fear to keep people from raising their vibrational frequency. Multitudes of people weary of war, environmental destruction, strife and chaos could, through coming to know the true underlying nature of all reality, make institutions such as organized religion, nationalism, economics and corporate control unnecessary and obsolete.

These constructs are even now in collapse. Why? Because they have betrayed the trust people put in them on every level. They have mismanaged politics, human rights, the environment, the economy, greedily selling out to corporate interests. Corporations have been allowed exploit every area of life imaginable at the expense of the common people on this planet. Since most scientific research depends on funding, and funding is parceled out in ways deemed "appropriate" by the people with the money and power, we can't really even trust science completely anymore. Scientists in many venues have become puppets manipulated by corporate wealth. And if boards of directors or CEOs don't like the results that show up in the lab, they cover them up or twist them into something else.

Growing numbers of people don't believe in these structures and institutions any longer. They don't trust them. The very withdrawal of belief in them (consciousness acting on the quantum field) is likely the foundational cause of the present chaos and instability in our world on so many levels. If it is true, as some say, that the ruling elite of this planet have engineered current instabilities for their own purposes to institute a "new world order," then they are playing a very dangerous game where the stakes for them are very high. The more people awaken, the more probable it becomes that such a ploy could blow up in their faces. Consciousness expressing itself in form – human beings, all life – has the innate urge and drive to be free, to have full freedom of expression. The more the shadow elements of this world reveal themselves through overt acts, the more people get wise. The withdrawal of people's belief in the power structures of the elite undermines the stability of those structures themselves.

Elite empires are crumbling as a result. What we need is a change in focus from the fear of watching the structures we have depended on for so long collapsing, to a cultivated sense of peace and wonder. While acknowledging the collapse and dealing productively with our fear, we could consciously choose to spend some time each day contemplating the kind of reality we would like to design from our love for ourselves, each other and our world. And always realize that what we can imagine may have an even more grand and wonderful expression than we can conceive from where we stand now on Earth. Perhaps our star families will supply an additional element of consciousness, dreaming a new Earth into full expression.

The Game of Life on Earth Means 100% Commitment

If we could return to Source, we, as the unified whole observing humans on

Earth, might ask questions like: How could they be so lost? How can they twist simple truth into something so unrecognizable? How can they be so cut off as to not perceive their unity with each other?

Actually, as unified, undifferentiated consciousness, no questions would be asked at all. Perhaps there would be simply an experience of fascination as the whole learns from the countless facets of itself what it is to live in apparent separation and limitation. It knows that separation and limitation is just a product of differentiated consciousness. Separation and limitation are experienced in degrees within the various energetic octaves of vibration. The parts of Source that have chosen to immerse themselves in third dimensional reality however, have a radically different perspective.

On Captain Picard's ship, the Enterprise, in *Star Trek: The Next Generation* there are holodecks for the crew's recreational enjoyment during off-duty hours. Crew members can select a story from a novel, visit other worlds, experience historical events or create something from pure imagination. They know they are never in any real danger on the holodeck, since safety mechanisms are programmed in. While enjoying their experience on the holodeck, they know it's not real. They can end the fantasy with a word anytime they choose. They are not 100% committed to the fabricated reality in which they are playing.

Here on Earth, our consciousness creates the holodeck in which we live out our lives, but we are 100% committed to this reality we've collectively created. Whether we forget who and what we truly are when we come here on purpose or not, I'm not sure. I tend to feel it's a bit of both. The process of moving from a more formless or higher vibrational state into the denser vibrational state of 3D human life could be like the shock of being thrown into an ice cold pool of water. Everything is blanked out as you struggle to get your breath, and become acclimated to the temperature of the water. Once you adjust, you may retain a whisper of memory of where you came from, but in learning to navigate your new human life, just learning to make your hands, arms, feet and legs do what you want them to takes a great deal of your attention. From there, as you grow, all kinds of other things take up your attention. You become a human being. You know you will forget who you truly are and where you came from. You may even program yourself to forget so you can more be completely invested in living and learning from your human life viewpoint.

From the moment we choose birth on this world and come into a human form, we have made a decision to be 100% committed to playing the game full out, and that means forgetting we chose to come so we can be fully engrossed in the game. It makes no difference whether you are an adventurer or a couch potato. If you spend your life making choices to go here or do this, you navigate your life through those choices. If you spend your life avoiding making choices because you agonize over possible consequences, then you get a set of indirect choices by default. One way or another, by living on Earth in a body, we committed ourselves totally and utterly to the game.

Because we forget we did this on purpose and with a purpose, we often complain about it. We fall into victim and blame. We can't "see" with our physical eyes that we are connected to everything, so we fall into living in a reality of me and you, us and them. Human existence kind of degenerates from there. But that may have been part of the plan too, to provide us with the evolutionary pressure to find our way back to unity consciousness. Even though we can't physically see the interconnectedness of all life, we can observe the ripples in our reality that point to it. We learn that our actions have consequences. These become the clues that, if we pay attention and follow them, lead us back to a knowing of who we are and where we came from. This is the ultimate challenge of living in a world of such contrasts and freeing ourselves from becoming caught or trapped within them; finding that place within where we are all connected to the Infinite and each other. To learn *that* while living within the bubble world of our human-on-Earth-reality-paradigm is a pearl beyond price.

* * *

Reality is Relative

We don't exist separately or outside of the reality paradigm we like to think we objectively observe. And just our act of observing "reality" influences it.

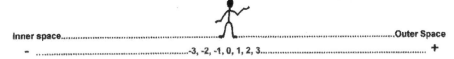

Inner space..Outer Space

- ....-3, -2, -1, 0, 1, 2, 3.. +

A zero point – focal point for consciousness created by Consciousness:
Human Consciousness

Implicate Order	Explicate Order
(Implied Order)	(Expressed order or "reality")
Wave Field of Pure Potentiality	Consciousness as Creator expressing
Inner realm of spiritual practice	itself
	Outer realm of empirical science

If, at the quantum level, we see our reality break down into energy waves – of which our reality is formed by our very thoughts, or by our consciousness in concert with the Primary Intent of Source Creator – then how can there be anything as purely "objective" observation, research or study? Everything is affected by how we think and feel about it. Even objectivity, as it turns out, is subjective.

The relationship between objectivity and subjectivity is an important one we need to at least begin to consider. We need to at least muse over the conceptual model provided by quantum physics that can begin to explain things like psychic phenomenon. Possible charlatans and hoaxers aside, we need to take a new look at channeled messages that come through human instruments where individuals allow their own personalities to step aside and go quiet, allowing some other intelligence to speak through them. These phenomena and possibilities exist, and are demonstrated time and again in our world. They provide valuable clues to the expanded nature of true reality beyond our myopic little third-dimensional world. As such, a whole new area of insight could emerge for serious study of other ways we could be experiencing contact, with extraterrestrial intelligences existing in our own dimension and higher ones.

In *The Thirteenth Floor*, when the main character, whose only known existence was circumscribed by his limited virtual reality, reached the boundaries of this virtual "world," he saw it dissolve into an energy matrix of glowing green grid lines. There was no where else to go. In the same way, quantum science is showing us that we as human beings are bumping up against the boundaries of our physical universe. Is it the end of our journey?

No. It's a whole new beginning. But we have to be willing to take a leap into learning to feel our way through an inner world of intuition. We have to expand our understanding of energy and "inner space" to begin the next stage of our journey to more knowledge.

Consciousness: The Origin of Spin in the Universe?

What if it's Consciousness that initiated all spin into form? What if form is revealed to be the intimate dance of energy between what consciousness dreams into being (observed particles) and the field of potentiality from which it springs (unobserved waves of potential)?

If the human body – all forms of physical matter, in fact – are focal points created by consciousness, brought into being through spin, consciousness could be the force that creates spin in our universe, from galaxies to chakras to atoms. If we are here to gain experience and learn through it, then we are also organizing that experience and learning in ways that have meaning for us. Our focal points of existence – our bodies – may also be two-way access ports both for ourselves and the greater Source Consciousness. Moving in both directions between the individual to the unified whole, there is access to other dimensions and levels of being, all in varying states of "apparent" separateness.

It is consciousness, desire and intention that spins human and other life forms into being from the greater Unified Field of Consciousness Itself, creating the "ports" and the levels of separation – the vibrational dimensions and densities to learn about Itself from infinite points of perspective. We already know that spin is a primal and elementary force in the physical universe and that it must extend into the other dimensional realms as well. Inherent in the Fibonnacci number sequence, in the magnetic fields of heavenly bodies, and observed by sensitives in the living auras and energy fields of other living beings, spin is a continual movement of energy in a completely interconnected universe.

Consciousness, Quantum Mechanics and Extraterrestrial Contact

We are learning new scientific models that show us how multi-dimensional realities can exist and how multi-dimensional life may inhabit those realms. Those of us who have, for years, been scrutinizing and trying to understand the extraterrestrial intelligences that have been engaging our planet and its people in various ways, have a new way of looking at how such contact could be occurring.

Craft show up in our skies, defying the laws of Newtonian physics, moving toward or away at speeds that are impossible by human calculations. They further confound us by morphing and changing shape, splitting into multiple craft or joining together into one.

There is the whole field of extraterrestrial abduction, experiencers and contactees. Such people report phenomenon in their contact that can only begin to be explained through a practical application of quantum principles of energy to matter and back again.

Crop circles of increasingly intricate design and beauty mysteriously form in farm fields, mirroring back to us pictorial metaphors and representations of what groups of human beings are considering in their own thoughts and studies. One of the most dramatic examples of this was the crop circle showing the huge Mandelbrot set glyph that showed up in an English farm field on August 11, 1991. Whomever is making the crop circles, "they" drop new designs into the mix for us to ponder on a regular basis.

Some human beings channel extra-dimensional beings or collective intelligences, providing us with communication and insight about ourselves and our own evolutionary process here on Earth.

In light of new discoveries in the fields of consciousness research and quantum mechanics and the undeniable connections emerging between the two, we must expand our contextual landscape to include all the various aspects of the UFO and extraterrestrial phenomenon to reach the fullest understanding possible, leaving nothing out. The context in which things occur, the expanding knowledge available to us in our own world – all the correlations, all the corroborating information we uncover, even when it comes from apparently disconnected and widely divergent sources, must be factored in. Once all the data is compiled, I would advise keeping a real or mental file labeled "Unknown" or "I Don't Know" for the information that doesn't fit in anywhere – yet. I would not consign it to any mental garbage can. Too many times I've done this and had to go fishing back through my own mind for things I discarded that fit into the picture later on.

I'm not saying to naively swallow as truth every bit of data that emerges. All I'm saying is to gather data as widely as possible. Look for any correlations. Look at what corroborates with other data, even from vastly different sources. And for sure, pay attention to what *resonates* for you. I don't think any one studying this field can do it effectively, or honestly, by trying to study one parcel of it in their own little vacuum, independent of the other aspects of what encompasses the study of the extraterrestrial phenomenon.

Chapter 22: Anatomy of the Human Psyche: Spirit, Mind, Emotions

Spirit and Super-Conscious Mind

As stated previously, Spirit, and soul – that ghost-like form of consciousness and energy inhabiting/animating our bodies – is the part of ourselves we are most out of touch with. Yet Spirit permeates our entire existence. Whether we are conscious or unconscious of it, spirit sits both within and without us, at the very core of our being and filling the space around and between us. For me, soul is the component of spirit that embodies the individual facet of consciousness experiencing life in form. It is the silent observer and witness of everything we experience in our lives, recording every experience in some cosmic record that exists as a field of pure energy. So even when the body dies and over time turns to dust, there is still an energetic record of all the experience that came through it.

This is an important point, because even if the neurological pathways in the brain – our biological hardware – are damaged in some way by accident or design, as multi-dimensional beings with layers of ourselves that exist at higher dimensions, we can still access our memories through other means. In alternative energy medicine, there is a growing understanding that the brain is not the repository of the mind, but that the mind exists in a field around the body, as part of its aura. This points even more strongly to the fact that the human brain is a piece of biological hardware through which we access mind, and memory. It is our biological hardware that forms the focal point of individuated consciousness expressed through our human forms. It is the desire and choice of consciousness to experience form that sets up the energetic template upon which our bodies are based. Consciousness then spins our bodies into form along the energetic lines of that template from the universal energy field. The procreative process of all organisms is the vehicle for that creation. Parents are carefully selected before birth – from the soul level – who will bring the best combination of elements to the process for that soul's optimal growth opportunities in that lifetime.

Drawings of the human auric field done by clairvoyants bear a striking resemblance to representations of the Van Allen belts and magnetic energy field around the Earth. It's one more point of truth in the theory of a holographic universe, in its infinite fractal expressions. The whole is contained and reflected in each part.

Some systems of spirituality have degraded over time, turning into religions. Self-appointed intermediaries have insinuated themselves between us and Spirit, claiming to speak "God's truth." When we have lost touch with our own access to Spirit, yet desire spiritual guidance in our lives, we are vulnerable to turning to such intermediaries to guide us. Then we can only hope that the intermediaries are operating with honor and integrity.

Other systems of spirituality have sets of practices and disciplines that, if followed, lead to one's own inner enlightenment, a clearing away of the veils of illusion that cloud this world. The inner observing witness becomes known, as well as the relationship that defines it, connecting to the limitless ocean of consciousness of which everything is a part.

It's possible that discoveries being made in quantum science are part of collective humanity's awakening process, that collective part of us reaching for insights about ourselves by another road than the path of the yogi, sage or mystic. If science and spirituality at their most highly evolved levels are truly one discipline and philosophy, then this discovery was, and is, inevitable.

When some ask questions about "good" and "bad" extraterrestrials, I tell them that the keys to knowing the kinds of extraterrestrials that have been interacting with humanity down through the ages are in our systems of religion or spirituality. The purveyors of doctrines that control their followers, ostensibly for their own good, through a twisted combination of fear of punishment and the bliss of reward are suspect to me as being something less than "pure." Those systems of spiritual practice that give us the keys to spiritual liberation of consciousness may very well have been taught to us in the beginning by those extraterrestrial cultures that desired us to realize our highest and best potential.

Spirit is connected to that part of the human psyche that we could call the super-conscious mind. It could also be said to be connected to the "right brain" functions, including the realm of inspiration, vision – the faculty of direct perception that makes the intuitive leaps beyond logic and analysis. It is that place in the psyche, joined to Spirit, where art, music, poetry and the birth of inspired ideas comes from.

The Conscious Mind

Our conscious minds – what most of us would identify as simply our "minds" – are the busiest parts of our psyches. Like a computer that is always on and always receiving some kind of input, millions of thoughts pass through our minds each day. We capture only the ones attached to subjects we are primarily focused on, and then likely not all of the thoughts that attach to each subject, just the ones most pertinent. Analysis, deductive and inductive reasoning and logic are part of the functioning of our conscious minds. The demands put on our conscious minds by the society and culture into which we've been indoctrinated are enormous, so they are generally functioning in overdrive much of the time. This is also due in part to a general societal conditioning to mistrust intuition and other super-conscious gifts of insight with a put-down of "that's just your imagination," or other disparaging remarks from outside voices of authority. Many of us have psychologically ingested an inner critic in our own minds from being subjected to such conditioning.

This is likely at the root of chronic stress that so many people are suffering from – the mind was never meant to do ALL the work. It was originally meant to function in a balanced way with the super-conscious and our emotional natures, most of which operate now from the subconscious.

Our minds have been doing a great deal of work through the ages that they are ill-equipped to do on their own. It is the job of our ego to make sure we and our bodies survive, as intact as possible. Why? Why have an ego that works for our survival, sometimes at any cost? I think its because we know at our deepest unconscious level that life is a sacred gift through which we learn and experience, and our life experience informs and enriches ourselves and the Unified Source Consciousness. If it was not somehow vital, none of us would be here doing any of this at all.

The mind is ego's instrument. Since we have been indoctrinated into believing we are just physical beings who may, or may not, have a soul that survives after death, we have come to rely on our minds to spin out endless strategies for survival, thinking and trying to out-think every possibility. The job of the mind is analysis, logic and trying to create meaningful comprehension. Allowed to reign (or appearing to reign) supreme, it weaves elaborate and endless thought-constructs. Without the balancing forces of consciously perceived and understood emotions in their proper expression, or a conscious connecting link to our spiritual intuitive gifts, the forces of Mind lumber through the world divorced from compassion, vision or insight. We see the results of this all around us today.

The other components of mind actually connect to our emotional and spiritual natures, because nothing is truly separate, for all our mind's compartmentalizations. Our super-conscious is that part of ourselves that is connected to Spirit and the Universal Consciousness; and depending on our proclivities and inclinations, we do have those flashes of vision and insight in our lives. Whether the mind lets us act on them or not is up to our holistic trust in ourselves as beings who are more than flesh, blood and bone.

Our subconscious or unconscious relate to our very powerful, and often disowned, emotional lives. Our limbic systems and emotional natures were well-formed and well-established long before the cerebral cortex processing unit was added to our biological tool kit. They exert a powerful influence from our subconscious, particularly when unacknowledged consciously.

Emotions are far more powerful than the mind, and far less understood. Yet it would seem that someone or some group understands them quite well enough to use them against a human population that generally feels that they are at the mercy of their emotions much of the time.

Emotions and the Realm of the Subconscious

Not all emotions are expressed through the subconscious, but like an iceburg, where so much is submerged and out of sight, much of our emotional nature is relegated to the subconscious. What emotions we are aware of are often just the tip of the subconscious iceburg.

What are emotions and just what are they for? To jerk us around through life? To bounce us like a ping-pong ball between pleasure and pain?

Emotions are a component of human beings that are hardwired into us by either evolution or intelligent design, or more likely a combination of both. When I speak of intelligent design, I mean extraterrestrial intelligence that has been here, on Earth, creating, guiding and watching since the dawning of any primate we could call human.

Each emotion, with all its various shades, serves a specific purpose.

Fear is part of all creatures' emotional make-up for survival. In a primeval world, fear caused our bodies to instantly be prepped for flight or fight upon the appearance of a predator or other dangerous situation. In its lesser-understood forms, it also causes freezing or fainting in the face of danger. This was also a good strategy, as many predators' eyes were keyed to spot movement. Some words that describe intensities and shades of fear: terror, horror, panic, dread, afraid, scared, trepidation, apprehension, aversion, revulsion, dismay, fretful, anxious, nervous, tense, concerned.

Anger is a small and near step down from fear. Anger is about the violation of one's personal safety boundaries, whether physical, mental or emotional. Anger says, "You may not do that to me and if you persist, I will protect myself!" Some words that describe intensities and shades of anger: rage, fury, outrage, indignant, surly, frustration, irritation, annoyance. Some of the less-exalted states of sexual expression and lust are related to anger, causing one person to take from another, in a sense, stealing sacred life energy from their victim.

Grief is a purgative emotion meant to resolve loss. Our ability to grieve any kind of loss we suffer, determines our future mental, emotional and physical health. Some words that describe intensities and shades of grief: anguish, heartache, despair, desolation, depression, sadness, sorrow, misery, despondency, melancholy.

Joy is an emotional state that flows essentially from a sense of connection and harmony. It is both a precursor and result of love, inseparable from it. At the most fundamental level, joy is experienced in connection with that sense of

Oneness that hums and vibrates within us and all around us, especially when we are consciously tuned into it. We feel the joy of connection and union in family, in friendship, in community and especially in the special and intimate connection of romantic love. It is difficult to even discuss joy and love separately. Words that describe intensities and shades of joy are: ecstasy, bliss, elation, delight, light-heartedness, cheerfulness, happiness, gladness, contentment.

Love is one of the most mysterious emotions we as humans experience, yet it's one of the most potent. When we have love we experience joy; we fear losing love; we suffer without some expression of love in our lives. In looking up the synonyms for love, I found them less clear than synonyms for the other emotions. Some that made sense to me were words like adoration, adulation, devotion, fondness, affection, enjoyment, like, respect and regard. Many words that relate to love also circle back to describing joy.

There were a few words that describe qualities that partake of illusion or delusion, like enchantment, infatuation and rapture. There were words equating love with the physical act of procreation. Lust was listed, though lust can often and quite easily operate separately from love, to the detriment and exploitation of others. Yearning – a desire or need for love in experiencing its absence – was also there.

And, rather ominously, "weakness" was also listed as a synonym for love. While one could make an argument that love makes us vulnerable, the meaning of love is separate and distinct from both vulnerability and weakness. If there was no love, there would likely be no sense of loss, hence no grief. But would you trade love out of your life to make sure you never experienced grief? To equate love with weakness is to make our own heart our enemy. When we do that, we murder a part of the world.

Apparently the English language is not fully capable of coming up with a description of love that covers all of its expressions. No wonder people are so confused about love.

The Greeks have more descriptive words for the various kinds of love we as human beings experience. There is "eros," the root of the word erotica. Eros is most often identified as intense and passionate physical love. It also means having a powerful adulation of beauty in all forms. There is "storge" which refers to the love between family members, parents and children, brothers and sisters. "Philia" describes love of friends, community and society, a kind of love that rests in familiarity and equality.

"Agape" is the highest form of love, pure and unconditional, a kind of divine love. The gentle commandments of the master teacher Yeshua ben Josef, known to Christianity as Jesus, "Do unto others as you would have others do unto you," and "Love your neighbor as yourself," pointed people in a direction where they could begin to embody agape. How tragic that a man whose whole life was an example of expressing and teaching an agape kind of love, should, after his execution, have his message twisted into more "us versus them" ideologies. Such ideologies have been used to justify bloody wars and persecutions of the worst kind down through history.

Even these greek words for "love" have various interpretations, but in general, the above descriptions are accurate.

So, is Love an Emotion?

In a sense yes. Love is something we feel inside in a multitude of different ways. Love inspires incredible works of writing, poetry, art and music, exalting all of love's many expressions. In its more selfish forms, love also drives people to commit terrible acts against each other in fear of the loss of it. In a society where our ability to love ourselves is so very diminished through centuries of religious and political indoctrination, where we have allowed that indoctrination to cut us off from our own inner knowledge of, and connection to the universal source of Love, we know we need love and feel we must have it from other people. If we get it, we fear the loss of it. If we don't get it, we live half-lives where we harden our hearts against our own need for love. From such hardened hearts, more misery leaks into the world.

The energy of love is so very vital to all of us. We know that babies fail to thrive and even die without the loving energy of nurturing touch. This is most certainly at the core of why so many ET abductees and experiencers are shown their own, or other, babies during their experiences aboard ships, and asked to hold them and feed them. The Zetas have learned that their hybrids need that vital connection and love in order to survive. In blending themselves with us, then this is something they will have to incorporate – or reincorporate if they truly once were as we are now – into their new hybridized species. Their union with humanity will forever shift who and what they are as a culture and as a civilization. Apparently it's a shift they are very willing to make.

Yet love, as I am learning about it, is more than an emotion.

Love is a profound and essential energy that permeates every level of every dimension and density throughout the multiverse. It is the primal Sound, or "Word" (vibration) that emanates from the Source of all creation. The sound is also the Light, one indistinguishable from the other. Quantum physics has broken down our world into its tiniest components and found pure energy and vibrating superstrings. It has found that particles act like waves when not observed by a consciousness contained in a focal point of form. It has found that what is done to one particle apparently alone and separate in one container has an identical effect on another particle in a distant container.

Everything is interconnected. Our very existence finds its expression through the dance of Consciousness with the sound and the light of this Univeral Source Energy. Ultimately creative through the flow of its waves of sound and light, that Energy is expressed as Love in infinite expressions of life everywhere, and in infinite combinations. Love in its highest expression – agape – seeks to live in harmony with the flow of those waves of light and sound.

Non-love goes against the flow, seeks to block the flow. Flow is the essence of truth. When a person, group or organization seeks to block truth in any form, it sets up blocks, resistances to the beauty, balance and harmony inherent in the flow from Source. But this flow will not be forever blocked or diverted. Placed under pressure from blocks and resistances, it will find its way free, at first through tiny spaces, later cascading around or breaking through obstacles.

Do we not observe that process of "breaking free" in our world today, as truthsayers come forward with pieces of truth that have long been withheld from the public? And like a great dam breaking, are not more and more whistleblowers finding their way through the increasing number of cracks in that dam? The structure of the dam of secrecy in this world is so undermined at this point, I don't think anything can really save it.

Everything, every person, every part of all creation throughout the entire multiverse is part of the all encompassing Oneness of All-That-Is. Even that which so many of us would like to name as "other," or "not-us." Even that which many of us name as "evil."

In the movie *Time Bandits* I was both amused and surprised by an insightful line spoken by "The Supreme Being" (God), played by Sir Ralph Richardson, near the end of the film. He had just swooped in to save his troupe of dwarfs who had stolen his map of the Universe and were using it to loot the greatest treasures known to man throughout history. The nemesis, "Evil" who had stolen the map from the dwarfs had just been exploded into what looked like chunks of volcanic, glowing rock. The Supreme Being said: "I had to have some way of testing my handiwork. I think he [Evil] turned out rather well!" When Kevin, the little boy who had been dragged into the adventure, asked why we had to have Evil, The Supreme Being answered that it had something to do with "free will."

How much does love mean if it is forced into expression? If people don't have a choice whether to love or serve or not? To force love where it is not freely given is to make of a person or population nothing but a group of mindless automatons. Yet to live in harmony with and in service to all life and the flow of energy in all life is to inspire and call forth love in others. Every person who chooses a life of love and service in harmony to all life creates yet another great wave of positive energy. This new wave is self-sustaining and self-perpetuating through its movement in harmony with the flow of sound and light emanating from Source.

The energy of fear, disharmony and discord is NOT self-sustaining or self-perpetuating. It can only be re-stimulated over and over again by the minions who wish to control others through it. Fear is an aberration that is like a jolt of electric shock. Apply it too much or too long, you kill the organism – or person – to which it is applied. Then that person is beyond the reach of the minions to keep stealing his or her energy. Between jolts of fear, every organism will calm down and return to a more natural state of relaxed balance. So the shocks can be randomly applied in devious ways to keep full relaxation from occurring. The organisms, or people, end up living on adrenalin, wondering when the next shock will come. It is my intention that by coming to understand this, and many other things shared in this book, people will gain the knowledge and inner resources to overcome this kind of manipulation, and pave the way for their own awakening.

Love is the energy and essence of what will ultimately shift and remake our world, especially if as many of us as possible align ourselves with it.

Original Purpose of Emotions in Natural Expression

Emotions enhance our survival and help us to thrive. At least, that was their original purpose. Fear is to preserve life through a strategy of running away, fighting or even standing stock still. Anger, close to fear – perhaps a less vulnerable-feeling expression of fear – is about defending our personal boundaries, tangible and intangible, that keep us feeling safe and able to function. Grief is for helping us to move through losses of all varieties, from the small to the profound. Joy and love are about connection – romantic, family, clan, tribe, community. Love of mothers for their offspring is the most powerful form of love on the planet. It causes the mother rabbit to attack the fox, the doe to attack the wolf without a thought of being over-matched. How could the young be assured of growing into adulthood without mother love? In ancient times, people thrived when they came together in community, sharing work, food gathering and trading with each other. Sharing in all ways inspires love, bonding and unity.

Imagine life in a small village. (No television.) Days are filled with the gathering and preparation of food, sharing the work with maybe laughter and songs. At night, meals are shared and the people come together to hear stories told around the fire. Stories that illustrate learning about love, heart, courage and honor. Everyone is strengthened and renewed in the listening. Lovers slip away after to find a quiet and private place to be together. Sleeping children are carried off in the arms of loving parents to be put to bed. The elders stay around the fire to warm their old bodies a bit longer before turning in. Companionship in all forms is comfort and quiet joy.

The next day is more challenging. An afternoon game being played turns to an angry confrontation as one young player, in his zeal, pushes another down harder than he meant to and that other gets up and cuffs him soundly for it. His boundaries are violated and he reacts. Some adults step in to resolve the conflict and restore understanding and harmony between the two youths.

The women gathering food return to the village and discover one of them is missing. They and the men go to search for her. Her body is found at the foot of a cliff where she fell, trying to reach a particular branch laden with berries. She is carried back to the village.

The whole village grieves. There is weeping. Keening and wailing fill the air. They prepare their friend for her burial and the ritual gives their grief focus and expression. They speak of her loves and dreams. The people comfort her husband and the children she left behind. He and his children walk at the front of her procession to the burial ground. Once there, each of them touch her in farewell, understanding they will see her again when they make their own journey into the world of spirit. They acknowledge how much they will miss her until then.

These two days described for this fictional village show a full range of emotions expressed in ways that are completely normal and natural. They were natural responses and reactions to various kinds of companionship and to conflict and loss – life and emotions in natural and healthy expression.

Love is hardwired into us, as all of our emotions are, because on so many levels emotions enhance our survivability as individuals and as a species. The difficult emotions of fear, anger and grief may stir us, but if expressed in healthy, productive ways, they soon discharge themselves and and we return to a balanced, relaxed state of peacefulness, living in the incremental levels of joy, from contentment to celebration.

At least this is how emotions were intended to be, and likely were long ago when our lives were much, much simpler.

Emotions: Overstimulated and Out of Balance

I got rid of television in my own home. I no longer trust the information being presented because of endless "spin" and outright lies. In addition, television is filled with excessive, mind-numbing commercial interruptions that are obviously trying to manufacture "problems" and "needs" I didn't even know I had in order to seduce or coerce me into buying something to take care of them. They do this by then trying to stimulate an emotion of fear or anxiety due to "the problem," with the promise of a rewarding emotion of relief or happiness if I bought and used the product.

This is just speaking of commercial product advertisements. Nearly all of the programming (a revealing word in itself) is continually trying to sell us something – ideology and rhetoric of one kind or another through religion, political party affiliation, or some other "us-versus-them" drama, real or fictional.

I was paying close to $50 dollars a month for for this TV mind-control feed into my own home, to the detriment of my own health and piece of mind. I got rid of it and have never looked back. Netflix was far less expensive and allowed me to see the movies or TV shows I wanted, when I wanted, with no commercial interruptions and lots of peace and quiet in between. Peace and quiet for my own expanded senses to relax, breathe, stretch and have a chance to be "heard."

Much televised sensory input is specially designed to keep us mentally and emotionally off-balance, right down to the electronic cycles per second flickering hypnotically on the screen. Today, our mental and emotional lives are a tangled up morass dealing with far too much contrived visual and auditory stimulus of all kinds. If we could develop the ability to rise up and take an eagle's eye view of this, see where the masses of incoming data are coming from and where the threads of that data attach to their sources, I don't think we can fail to miss that there is a covertly deliberate campaign going on to keep the mass of humanity's emotions tweaked to a pitch of intensity to whatever flavor of emotion groups of individuals have gotten hooked on.

And we do indeed get hooked on adrenalin and emotions, all kinds of them, expressed in all kinds of different dramas, on and off the tube. As illustrated by Candace Pert[1] and others in *What the Bleep Do We Know?* the neurological pathways in our brains become accustomed – even addicted – to certain kinds of experiences because of the emotions and sensations generated by them. Every time we create a familiar experience charged with the kind of emotional drama we unconsciously crave, those neurological pathways are strengthened again. Even though we consciously complain that we hate the things that are happening in our lives, unconsciously we seek out or create the same dramas over and over again because we have become hooked on the emotions they generate.

Before I got rid of television it was easy to spot the various different emotional manipulations there, served up 24 hours a day, seven days a week. If you liked tear jerkers, there was the Hallmark Channel. If the emotional tweak you were looking for was anger, you could get it from the perpetual news and political-spin programming. Sports channels, history channels, science channels, kids' channels, all kinds of channels. If you had some perverse need to be scared, you could find plenty of horror. I once suggested to the SciFi channel that they change their name to the Horror Channel as almost all of their material had shifted away from anything visionary or inspiring. If you wanted bliss, you could find it in religious channels. Charismatically and eloquently playing on a lifetime of their viewers' religious indoctrination, evangelists could toss you between the agony of being a miserable sinner and the bliss of glorious redemption – just accept in your heart that Jesus died for YOU and your sins on the cross. Never mind that his primary message was that we love one another.

The thread running through all of it, especially in the last few decades, is the stimulation of emotional intensity and excess adrenalin in television watchers. Some boardroom of elites, somewhere in a lofty skyscraper with a view, who know exactly what they are doing with such emotional tweaking, are most likely snickering with gloating glee. Because we ourselves pay them our own hard-earned cash to pipe a mind-control feed into our homes – a form of control

---

[1] One of the scientists of *What the Bleep Do We Know?* author of *The Molecules of Emotion: The Science Behind Mind-Body Medicine*, Dr. Candace Pert is known for her research on how emotions register in the body through neuropeptides and receptor sites on cells, and how we re-stimulate them by unconsciously attracting requisite situations. Her website: http://candacepert.com

they then use to manipulate us.

They know that negative emotional energy keeps our bodies stressed out, at the borderline of exhaustion and in a chronically-susceptible state to illness. And for people so affected, it's extremely difficult to climb out of such a rut and recover enough to begin to discover who they truly are, or to find ways to nurture any newly-surfacing inner knowing.

Overstimulated minds and extreme emotional states jam our intuitional radar. "They" have to keep jamming that intuitive radar for their own protection and continuity.

It all comes back to the expansion of conscious awareness in humanity and the "Game Over" reality and paradigm shift it represents that threaten the power structures and organizational controllers of the world.

Whomever "they" have been down through the ages – this elite .001%, or whatever name you give "them" – "they" built this world to suit themselves by seducing, convincing, coercing or threatening us – the human collective and its creative quantum energy of directed, focused thought and attention – into acceptance of their ideologies and rhetoric. Movies, television, news – all kinds of material that passes for "entertainment" keeps our attention and thought, charged with our emotional energy, on what they want us to keep spinning out for them from our consciousness, imprisoned in their cages of various types of indoctrination. They want to stay at the top of humanity's pyramid. As the rich and powerful who have been in control for so long, they fear not having a population of people whose energy they can steal anymore. They'd be reduced to nothing without it. People's energy is stolen in many ways – in the loss of health and well-being (a form of life energy) from environmental damage and emotional manipulation that causes us to spend money (another form of our energy) on trying to regain our health, while corporate interests lobby our policy-makers with mega-bucks to restrict our health care choices to what they have to offer – drugs and other medical interventions that suppress symptoms without addressing the root causes of illness or infirmity.

When we are indoctrinated to let our minds rule over our hearts; when we confine our spirituality to a seat in a church pew on Sundays; when we disown our emotions and our disowned and out-of-control Ids individually and collectively rampage through our world, laying it waste; the expansion of our consciousness languishes. Unawakened, unrealized, unfulfilled.

I have come to feel that this is the crux of the matter. The only real war going on on this world is the war on human consciousness by those who fear its awakening.

Dealing with Emotions, Distinguishing Them from Intuition

Dealing positively and productively with emotions begins with being able to recognize them in ourselves, hopefully before we take an action we might regret.

Because life is such a precious gift – an opportunity for learning and expanding awareness through the interplay of contrasts in third-dimensional duality – fear is part of us to preserve our lives by bringing about an immediate reaction to threats. Fear comes upon all of us now and again, but we don't have to have a knee-jerk reaction to it every time, though PTSD can cause this and be difficult to defuse. Unlike living in a wilderness with honest, straight-forward predators when an immediate launch into fight or flight is often both appropriate and necessary, in our modern world the threats we are exposed to are not immediate threats to life and limb. They are often phantom threats without real substance. Unfortunately they generate the same fight-or-flight adrenalin response. We can learn about fear and recognize it when it comes. We can then see it for what it is. We can breathe and move our way through it. The fear need no longer have us in its grip. We can choose what relationship we will have to our fear and how to deal with it constructively. We can put strategies in place to work with fear and calm it when it arises.

This is also true of our other emotions. We feel fear, anger and grief in the body mainly in our stomachs, our chests, our necks and shoulders and throats. By learning to feel the racy flutters and stomach constrictions of fear; the heaviness in our chest of sadness; and the neck and shoulder tension that often goes with anger; we can take steps through breathing and relaxation to regain our calm center and consider what is going on around us and what to do about it from a more enlightened perspective. Each of us may experience our emotions a little differently in the body. Start with identifying your body sensations, particularly in the torso.

Our emotions come from our thoughts; from words and images we are exposed to. They arise so swiftly that we often don't distinguish that they are a reaction to these forms of stimuli. They have an effect on our body-mind, which is the lens through which consciousness is filtered on this world. This is why staying positive is so important.

Being blissed-out feels wonderful. But be cautious of this too. Pause and check what is going on in your environment that is bringing on the feeling of bliss. Bliss is at the far end of the spectrum from fear, but it is still an extreme, and it can still jam your intuitional radar. There are times and places for bliss. There is the manipulative kind of bliss you get from a born-again evangelist under a revival tent playing on your religious beliefs, or watching a spectacular sunset in the western sky over the Grand Canyon. One is contrived, the other simply "is." Choose the settings or venues for your bliss carefully.

There is nothing wrong with emotions, or feeling them. However, human emotions have been grossly manipulated on this world until they have eclipsed the still, small voice of intuition, insight and inspiration within. Some people learn to fear emotional excess through the pain it brings, retreating into the world of the mind-ego, which is equally restricting from a different basis. But actually, the two are far more linked than we like to admit. One operates from the place of the conscious mind, the other pulls our strings like a puppet master from the subconscious, through emotions we dare not admit to ourselves that we are experiencing. Like the animal frozen in the forest at the pass of a predator, we don't want to look at those deep dark fears or violent impulses. If we don't look at them, maybe they won't "get us." We refuse to acknowledge them and make them "real."

We often mistake an emotional reaction with intuition. It's important to understand that our emotional responses are conditioned. They are conditioned through upbringing and the skewed and incomplete versions of science and history taught us in school; through indoctrination by organized religion and particular socio-political orientations and ideologic constructs.

When we are in the grip of emotions, they can be a true and proper response if they are brought about by real life events in our relationships and our communities. If they are brought about through the mind's observing of material on the television or read in the news somewhere, then they may be a manipulation. The more intense the emotions we are feeling, the more completely they can eclipse our guiding intuition. Feeling emotions is unavoidable. It is going to happen in response to various kinds of stimuli. Learning to recognize the process of this can free you to extract yourself and back off "within" to a calmer state and gauge what is going on around you and within you from a place of more reliable perception.

There is a saying that came out the last several years as we transitioned from the Bush to the Obama administration: "Regime Change Starts at Home." Truer than many might realize at first glance.

I would reframe it this way; "Consciousness Change starts from Within." It starts in each of our hearts, by seeking truth, by freeing and reuniting spirit, mind and emotions within these vehicles we call bodies.

Chapter 23: Resonance, Dissonance and Discernment

Consider that with our expanded abilities turned off, unacknowledged or not perceivable, we are in many ways equivalent to someone blind, deaf and dumb on our own world. Without our intuition, minds and emotions working together, we run the risk of being completely suggestible and gullible to every story that crosses our paths even when there is inherent danger in such blind acceptance, or we lose all ability to trust and become suspicious to paranoid – wary or afraid of any source of information.

Not having access to our expanded senses, such as telepathy, tel-empathy, clairvoyance, clairaudience, teleportation, psycho-kinesis, and more, we are very vulnerable. We don't have the ability to fully sense what is going on around us, to feel the motivations of those interacting with us. If we aren't one of the suggestible, accepting types, this can cause us to adopt an overarching sense of caution about everything. We've been forced to pass things through the rational mind, governed by an ego conditioned by past experiences to look for threats to our existence. We often react to new information with suspicion, perhaps even some degree of paranoia. This has been played upon by those in power who know this and wish to keep us blind, deaf and dumb; anchored in an ego-paranoid state. They know that keeping the human ego enslaved by fear will prevent the expansion of awareness necessary to activate the latent, star-ancestor parts of our DNA that will give us back our expanded senses and abilities.

I have found through personal experience that the energy of fear in the body inhibits the expansion of extra-dimensional awareness. The more I moved beyond my fear, the more my consciousness began to light up. Gregg Braden[1] shares scientific findings that the energy of fear causes our very strands of DNA to wind up tightly, restricting any access to the parts of it that could hold the keys to our spiritual evolution. Cultivating the love, compassion and joy inherent in understanding the very essence of who we truly are allows that DNA to unwind and relax. In this relaxed state, the energy waveforms of these positive, expansive emotions move through it, turning more and more of it on for our spiritual unfoldment, giving us access to greater realms of awareness.

[1] Gregg Braden is described by Deepak Chopra as "a rare blend of scientist, visionary and scholar with the ability to speak to our minds while touching the wisdom of our hearts." An accurate description for a man who has been working for decades to bridge the gulf between science and spirituality. Author of many books, most recently *Deep Truth: Igniting the Memory of Our Origin, History, Destiny, and Fate*, his website can be found at www.greggbraden.com.

Why do you suppose so much fear is dished up each day in print or televised media about terrorism, war, swine flu and more? They want to keep us energetically blind, deaf and dumb.

We need to work our way back to a consciousness of unity, wholeness, and awareness of the interconnectivity of us all, of the Oneness of the Universe. We must learn to navigate the difficult task of maintaining our open sensitivity in a world where current chaos can feel as if we are weathering an energetic hurricane.

What is Resonance? Dissonance?

As far back as the 1960s or earlier, people have talked of picking up good vibes or bad vibes. The hit single "Good Vibrations" by the Beach Boys signaled an entry into popular culture of peoples' early sense of picking up vibrational energy.

"That really resonates with me," is an expression we hear quite often in our society today, especially within the growing population of people whose sensitivity to the energetic and vibrational world around them is increasing.

There are many definitions of resonance relating to various disciplinary studies; however this one, from the *World English Dictionary* online, relates best to the word as it is falling into more common language usage: "sound produced by a body vibrating in sympathy with a neighboring source of sound."

In the chapter on Consciousness, I used musical metaphor to describe the vibratory properties of various dimensions and their densities as single notes and octaves or families of notes. To vibrate in sympathy with a neighboring source of sound, or energy, is to be in resonance with it in a melodic or harmonious way.

In contrast, dissonance is the opposite of resonance. Dissonance is produced when sounds – or energies – played together or in simultaneous proximity to each other produce disharmony, discord, cacophony. Unpleasant, even intolerable "noise." This can be subtle and experienced in the vibratory energy system of a person as an irritation. Or it can be so pronounced and blatant as to cause people to do all they can to get away from that noise – both auditory and/or vibratory.

I know that when I lived in larger urban areas of dense population, I often felt I needed to shut down energetically just to be able to exist there. To open to my sensitivity was to open to a bombardment of psychic noise from thousands of minds in proximity, many of which were vibrating at frequencies dissonant to my own. So, like a hermit crab, I pulled into my shell. I needed to learn how to open to my sensitivity and screen or reflect back the energies I didn't want to affect me. Moving to Durango, Colorado with a lower population density helped with this, providing a better place for learning how to be open, yet develop the necessary energy shielding.

I use a visualization of my auric field being encased in an egg-shaped reflective glass shield that allows me to interact with others around me, but reflects any unwanted energies coming in back to the sender. Within this shield I "see," with the inner eye, a brilliant white light shot through with rays of golden iridescence. When I had my session with Mary Rodwell where I visited my people, it was quite a confirmation that the reason I see this white light with rays of golden iridescence is because my people live in such light and energy on their ship, or perhaps I'm sensing higher dimensional energies that are around many people, with or without their knowledge.

The shielding works well with one caveat. If we have a marked adversarial relationship with someone who has dissonant energy from our own, then a relationship of sorts exists – there is an energy cord between that person and ourselves that will bypass our shielding and still directly affect us. In such cases, we need to do all we can to heal, forgive and let go of the adversarial relationship.

For those of us with a higher inherent sensitivity that is expressing itself in us, I think staying in our "shells" is a protective strategy that many of us employ to survive in an overwhelmingly high-intensity environment of increasing extremes – to the degree we can be completely out of touch with even realizing we have expanded abilities at all. The question to wonder about is, "How can I remain open in my sensitivity and still protect my energy system?" Watch what answers come and how they may shift and change with time as your energetic unfoldment proceeds.

How does Discernment Differ from Judgment?

Dictionary definitions of discernment are often related back to judgment, but I choose to opt for a new definition here, one that is shared in the communities of higher consciousness individuals. We need a term that applies to how we use the information we gather from our experiences of resonance and dissonance.

So, discernment to me has come to mean developing the ability to feel and sense in an ever-deeper way the energies around us emanating from people, places, things and situations. We may experience these as resonant, dissonant or neutral. Such sensory information, run through our feeling filters, can inform us in a way that helps us to assess the benefits or risks of a particular course of action. Rather than proceeding from sets of structured beliefs or ideologies drilled into us by rote, processed through the mind, we become receptive and responsive to the dance of energies swirling about us in our world. By their feel to us, we move closer to what we harmonize with, and away from that which jangles in our energy system as discord.

Judgment, from where I stand today, is an extract, often emotionally-charged, that comes from indoctrination to rigid sets of belief systems when people encounter something that runs contrary to their particular ideologies. If the belief systems are not open, fluid and responsive to change and new information, creating an evolving process of reformulation as new data comes to light, then judgment is the result – rigid, unyielding, resolute. An adversarial stance of "don't try to confuse me with the facts, my mind is made up," refuses to even try to think outside of its paradigm-box. From a black and white mindset, we could say that "bad judgment" is the product of a closed mind, while "good judgment" flows from a more open mind, a willingness to hear and to see, though the outcome may still be influenced by indoctrinated belief systems. The term "cognitive dissonance" has been coined to describe the internal conflict that arises within individuals who encounter information that challenges their cherished beliefs. The energy and vibration of truth is incompatible (dissonant) with ideologies based in indoctrination through institutional structures with agendas of control.

As we continue to consciously choose harmony and create harmony in our lives and environments, our bodies and therefore our consciousness can begin to unwind and expand. This is one more reason why, when I look at the sheer scope of corporate exploitation and invasion into every area of our lives for power and financial gain, I have to conclude that the most hidden and covert reason for it is to stop or slow the expansion of human consciousness. Understanding this is the key to overcoming it and choosing to take whatever steps we can to expand our consciousness and multi-dimensional awareness regardless of what "they" are doing. Not understanding what's going on carries the risk of being caught up in a whirlwind of negative emotional states about widespread destruction going on all around us, on multiple levels. This is why balancing every angering or depressing event going on in the world with five positive, joy-inspiring personal actions is so important. I don't believe in sticking our heads in the sand and ignoring what problems are going on in the world. I feel if we do this, we do it at our own peril. But in observing it all, then mindfully and positively dealing with it, finding a way to rise above it, the chaotic situations of the world truly lose their power over us. When negative people or situations lose their power over us, they stop restricting our spiritual evolution.

And our spiritual evolution may be the only way to truly correct the problems we see around us.

Mustering up local militias and creating civil wars to try and wrest power from the elite groups of this world is not the answer. If we have not learned by now that war and terror only perpetuates more of the same, then there is little hope left for us as a species. It's time for a new strategy, one based in spiritual evolution and understanding of the power of our own consciousness, especially as a unified collective. Love is the unifying energy that can bring us together. It must also be a conscious choice made day by day, and as time moves on and accelerates, it may even need to be made moment by moment.

I'm not talking about cloying, sentimental love. I'm talking about looking at the situations around us and assessing the simple difference between those things we can do nothing about and moving quickly to seeing what we can make better in some way for all concerned. When we ask ourselves, or a person or group who needs assistance, "How can I help?" we are exercising the power of unifying love. Relief, appreciation and gratitude of such actions leads to moments of quiet joy and peace, even celebration. *Bonding. Unity.* There is nothing so moving in movies – movies being the storytelling vehicles of our age – as when two adversaries suddenly discover a common ground between them that inspires them to lay down their arms and join together in common cause. This creates fertile ground for the expansion of human awareness.

Beauty, balance and harmony are natural states of being, both energizing and relaxing. To be attracted to them and to create them not only makes us feel good, it also attracts like energies to us – including the more spiritually-evolved and benevolent extraterrestrial races. Most such beings likely have far more finely developed extra-sensory abilities that operate at far greater ranges than we are currently aware of in ourselves. As humanity's spiritual evolution expands, they are aware of it, and they are attracted to it. They are likely even helping it along and crop circles appear to be one manifestation of this help.

Multi-dimensional awareness is part of us. It's interwoven into the very fabric of who we are as whole human beings. We've just been well-conditioned down through the ages to shut it out of our conscious awareness. Our emotions, our minds and our spirits are the parts of us that extend into dimensions beyond this 3D one that we have allowed to take up most of our attention. They are meant to work holistically, together in concert. Yet we have split ourselves into pieces. We exalt the mind and mental abilities in this world. We love our emotions when they bring us pleasure, revile them and learn not to trust them when they bring us pain, grief and suffering. We don't understand them and for many of us they are states that seem to happen to us willy-nilly, out of our control. We treat them like second-class parts of ourselves while we strive to be mentally smart and sharp in a world where the person with the most clever mind appears to win. The spirit part of us, our soul, we have made so conceptually intangible that many people even doubt its existence at all. Most traditional, structured religions have exploited people's need to reach "beyond" into the realm of spirit. They have managed and manipulated this spiritual need with sets of beliefs that keep real knowledge of the spiritual realms out of reach. People fear death out of a complete lack of experiential understanding of who and what they really are. And people who fear death are far easier to control, to frighten into compliance.

Yet if we undertake a study of what the pioneers of consciousness are discovering, we learn that death is an illusion. And if we just spend some time practicing with the requisite desire and intent to learn, we can experience the truth of this for ourselves. Today, many people are turning to psychoactive plants for a more swift opening to extra-dimensional knowing. I feel this is in itself a sign of the process of awakening accelerating on Earth. Spending twenty years meditating in a cave in the Himalayas to find the answers we all seek to the mystery of our existence is a luxury of time most of us cannot afford. The "Shift of the Ages" is upon us.

A Human Being is a Community of Many Voices

There are many voices that speak in our minds, telling us to do this and avoid that. How do we pick out "the still, small voice" of our intuitive expanded awareness from this inner chorus?

In the previous chapter, I discussed spirit, mind and emotions. Spirit corresponds to the super-conscious, our realm of expanded awareness, the part of us that knows our interconnectedness with All-That-Is or Source Creator. From it flows those flashes of insight and inspiration that we perceive directly and spontaneously without analysis or logic. Mind is the computer-like processing unit that interfaces with our biological hardware, the brain. It is constantly applying analysis, logic and solutions to our lives through the conscious mind. Then we have our emotions, the tip of a huge iceberg we see and acknowledge, while so much more remains hidden and out of sight in our subconscious.

The first step in picking out the still, small voice of our expanded intuitive sense within is to learn to, at any given time, identify what emotions we are feeling. Emotions are a wonderful gift. Essentially they are the part of us that helps us survive and thrive as human beings. But when they are in full expression from small or large life events, or artificially stimulated by whatever means to extremes – again and again – confusing us mentally and exhausting our adrenals, they jam our intuitive radar. If you can begin to identify what emotions you are experiencing at a given time and what stimulated them, then you can take steps to shift your emotional energy to a quieter, calmer state that gives insight and inspiration a chance to surface – including the insight you need at that particular moment to navigate the next steps you need to take, especially in that present moment.

Incoming stimulus immediately generates thoughts in the mind, and at the speed of those thoughts, emotions are generated in the body through the release of neuropeptides. We experience this instantaneously. The mind could yell "THREAT!" from something it sees, and our body is immediately poised for fight or flight. Yet if it was something we saw on TV, then there is no immediate threat. The living room is still as it was before we turned on the TV. But our ancient biological mechanisms are activated anyway. You might feel tension in your solar plexus, your breathing may have gotten shallow. You might feel a tightening along your spine, maybe in the neck and shoulders. Your throat might feel tight. This is just one example.

The sensations your body feels are the keys to identifying the emotion, or the layers of emotions you are feeling. If you can't quite identify and name an emotion, don't concern yourself about it. Just notice what sensations you feel in your body and notice the quality of your breathing. Observe your immediate environment and assess it. If there is no call to immediate action, then sit gently straight in a kitchen chair and begin to breathe, gently and deeply taking in as much air as possible all the way into your lungs. Let your chest and belly expand, let your spine gently undulate with each breath. Keep it up until you feel *calm* begin to come in again. This is a proven method of pranayama or yogic breathing.

Another pranayama breathing technique is alternate nostril breathing. Closing or covering one nostril using your fingers, breathe deeply into the open one. At the top of the inhale, close the open nostril and exhale through the other. Then inhale through that nostril as well, close it, and exhale through the opposite one. The rhythm is: one nostril closed, inhale through the other, close that one, exhale, inhale, close the opposite, exhale, inhale, and so forth. Continue for at least ten cycles or until you feel more peaceful again.

Being able to identify what you're feeling in your body can also help you to identify what voice you may be hearing in your mind. Each emotion has a voice of aversion or desire. We are pain-avoiding, pleasure and comfort-seeking beings. Fear, anger, grief will be voices of aversion. Our pleasure and comfort-seeking natures will whisper in our ear with voices of desire. These often combine to our detriment or real threat if the incoming information has been designed to produce a particular outcome in us. We have to be careful that those voices are not activated and our actions taken as a knee-jerk reaction to data that was contrived to push us in a "planned" direction.

Example: Fear of swine flu virus, H1N1, spurred many people to get vaccinations – they were listening to the voice of fear in themselves, generated by the voices of authorities they trusted. The vaccinations often turned out to be worse than the flu, causing deaths in some children and crippling health complications in other young people and adults. There was a huge increase in miscarriages for pregnant women who received the vaccine. This is yet another example of betrayal of peoples' trust by authorities that are supposed to be in charge of the public welfare. This betrayal has led to even more people getting wise to the fact that the very officials positioned in such agencies are failing in their mandates. Following the money reveals that there is far less concern about public safety than there is about safeguarding the profits corporations wished to gain from the sales of their vaccine, which cost them plenty to develop.

Where did the H1N1 virus come from? Was it a randomly mutated flu virus or something else? What was the true agenda of the H1N1 vaccine? A great deal of reliable and well-researched information flooded the internet about its flaws and consequences, as well as possible agendas. People need to look at and assess such data for themselves, both through educating themselves and paying attention to the energetic, rather than emotional, feel of such information.

Through a combination of education and intuition, I've come to feel that viruses are not the problem. Stress from living in a chaotic society, environmental toxins and additives in food, water and air that undermine our immune system are the problems. Make a commitment to consuming clean foods and water and you will learn that these choices are also under pressure to be taken away from us. Follow the money, look at what corporations and individuals stand to profit from taking away our freedom to live as we choose for ourselves. Keep peeling away the layers and looking deeper. Stopping or slowing the expansion of human awareness seems to be at the deepest core of it all.

The purpose of this chapter is to help you learn to expand your abilities through your intuitional radar, using it to assess and find your way through these times. It will not be foolproof in the beginning. It still is not completely foolproof for me, though it is improving greatly. No human being can claim absolute infallibility. The final assessment of resonance, dissonance and discernment, as well as the final choice, is always up to the individual. No other person can choose for us. We learn through trial and error, as with any new skill and ability. All we can do is learn to watch those flashes of insight and then choose to act on them or not. Start your practice with easy choices, like asking yourself which will be the fastest, smoothest route to drive to the grocery store. As the flash of spontaneous insight appears at the forefront of your mind, act on it. You'll come to discern when you are picking up correctly on intuition and when you second-guess yourself with analysis and logic by the results you get.

If you are in an emotional state when you are trying to make a choice, bouncing back and forth between your emotions and your analytical mind, you are generally caught in the pain-avoiding, pleasure or comfort-seeking tug-of-war. In the absence of intuition, calming yourself and educating yourself is the next best thing.

Perceiving and Recognizing Resonance and Dissonance and Using them for Discernment

There are ways we can tangibly see and feel the effects of vibrations. Then we take the known facts and understandings of our bodies and move forward from there.

If you set a clear glass of water on the table and drum next to it with your fingers, you'll see the vibrations of your drumming picked up by the sensitive medium of the water. If you sing a few notes over the water, also watching it carefully, you will also see the water's response to the vibration of your voice. Know that the water is picking up vibrations from the entire environment around you, though the effects may be so subtle, your eyes don't pick up any disturbance of the water.

Our bodies are around 70% water, always registering incoming vibrations of all kinds, and sending out others to the world around us. Most of it takes place on an unconscious level. But through the body, tuning in more and more attentively to every sensation it feels at subtler and subtler levels, we can train ourselves to pick up on the vibrational energy interaction that is always going on. The sensations we feel in our bodies are the movements of energy and vibration through it. There is usually so much various sensation going on that we tune most of it out. We use the faculty of our conscious minds and their focus on the abstractions of thoughts to screen out the background hum of body sensations and feelings. It's when something more profound – resonant or dissonant – enters the energy system of our body that it commands our attention. Yet we can train ourselves to pay attention to the finer sensations in the body, to notice the movement of vibratory energy as sensation, like the sound of a soft voice.

It's also worth noting here that our bodies also have a crystalline aspect to them in the very matrices of how our molecules are arranged, including our DNA. Crystalline structures are also very sensitive to frequencies and vibratory energy. When subjected to the movement of energy, such as emotion, they emit very subtle biological piezoelectric energy. I feel there is a high likelihood that our DNA as a crystalline structure functions as a transmitter-receiver between our dimensional realities and Source Consciousness – with Source Consciousness actively learning about Itself through our experience and the life-sustaining energy of Source being transmitted back to us through this holographic, circuit-like energy network. How much more vital it becomes with such knowledge to keep moving beyond constrictions that fear has over our lives, on our very vibrational and biological systems! When our DNA is constricted, how well can it function as the transmitter-receiver it is designed to be?

We can learn to tune into and discern a great deal about the resonance or dissonance of vibrational energy by just paying attention to the nature and quality of the incoming vibrations of various types of data by how they feel in our bodies and register on our psyches.

How does it feel to be in resonance with something? What does dissonance feel like?

Again, the best way is to return to a musical metaphor. If you have or can find a piano or keyboard, you can find out how resonance and dissonance feels through sound and hearing. A single note has a "true" quality to it. It simply is. A harmonious chord played on the same keyboard is composed of two or more true notes in vibrational resonance, generally a full note apart from each other. Notice how it feels in your body, how your body responds to single true notes and harmonious chords.

Now take a single key and play it together with the key immediately preceding or after your chosen note. The two played together have a sour, discordant quality. Notice your body's reaction to these dissonant sounds.

Now you know how it feels in your body to play a resonant, harmonious chord of music, and in contrast how it feels to strike two or more notes that are discordant – a "true" note, and one just close enough, yet "off" enough to create a third, bad-feeling tone that is dissonant. Playing around with harmony and discord on a keyboard can teach us a lot about information that we see or hear that has a particular feel to it in our bodies.

One you learn to recognize this process at a deeper level for yourself, you might be surprised to realize just how much the energy of resonance and dissonance may have been affecting how you've been responding to the world around you from an unconscious level. It functions in us at the unconscious levels all the time, and we respond to it at unconscious levels. We can learn, through using our bodies as the wonderful sensory instruments they are, how to bring that awareness to the conscious level.

Accessing Our Intuition

Just as I was told by my guides that I had to learn this process on my own, so must you. As they said, we have too many outer voices of authority on this world. We listen to these outer voices at the possible risk of losing touch with our own inner ability to assess the world around us. This process of awakening will be personal to each of you and perhaps slightly differently perceived and understood according to your individual life experience. It is my hope that you will develop the capacity to add your intuitive gifts to your set of assessment tools for navigating life on Earth. Understanding each of these facets of ourselves, allowing them to work in balance with each other, – our intuition, our minds and our emotions can be assets rather than liabilities.

Intuition may be a doorway we open to a whole new human adventure. A rediscovery of abilities locked away in our consciousness that we currently think are possible only through exterior mechanisms or technology.

I am sharing with you my process and discoveries as a map to inner discoveries of your own. This map is for your own personal empowerment. Because in this world, without our expanded abilities to perceive and discern, we are walking targets for every kind of information or disinformation out there – increasingly huge volumes of it – with various agendas to exact upon us. Trying to process it all with logic and analysis through the mind, our emotions reacting to it as well, is becoming overwhelming and exhausting.

We need to find a better way. We need to tune our personal intuitional radar.

In order to access intuition, we need to be in a calm and centered state. Emotions need to be quieted, and the mind's continual spin of thoughts must also be calmed.

In the chapter "Reclaiming Freedom" I discussed meditation as a strategy for opening to a new identity of who we really are by developing an awareness of, and relationship with the essence of ourselves that is the inner witness – consciousness observing our lives happening around us. The process of bringing ourselves into a centered stillpoint, where emotions and the mind are at peace, or where our awareness can move beyond them, is key to developing the ability to sift through the various voices of the inner chorus inside us. Getting in touch with that still, small voice connected to our super-consciousness can bring those flashes of insight and intuition that can help us to navigate our lives.

We navigate in these bodies within the space and time created through the third dimension. The super-consciousness operates both within and outside of 3D in a realm of no-time and no-space. The quantum principle of super-positioning, where all possibilities exist at once until consciousness selects one to focus upon and actualizes it, could be the model for how this works. Our super-consciousness may have the ability to instantly access the possibilities and bring us the intuitive flash that indicates what direction to move in. It can guide us from a holistic perspective not available to us when we are operating in a linear, 3D manner.

Intuitive Emotional Resonance

Emotions will be generated from flashes of insight and intuition just as they are from the thoughts and input of external information to the conscious mind. They are usually deeply moving and profound. It is through our own inner inquiry process that we learn to distinguish between our emotional resonance with spontaneous insight and intuition, and the emotional knee-jerk reactions to outer world stimulus and thoughts.

Emotions that are generated from incoming information playing on the mind are very different from intuitive emotional resonance. The progressions from one state to another are very different, once you learn to distinguish one from another. It's all in how incoming information "lands" in your body rather than how it is received and processed by the mind. All information has specific energy signatures that are, like musical notes, "true"/resonant or "off"/ dissonant. The progression is as follows:

> **Emotional fear-or-desire reactions:** Incoming information received by the mind >> mind makes associations that play on our fears (aversions) or our desires (things we want to be true) >> emotions, either fear-anger-loss-based or hopeful-pleasurable-happiness-based result almost simultaneously. There is no body-based perception of the energy of the information "landing" in the body with a corresponding resonance or dissonance.

> **Emotional resonance:** Incoming information "lands" in the body of a person who is in a neutral state, or state of inner quiet or stillness >> resonance or dissonance from the information simultaneously creates an emotional response that is felt at a cellular level throughout the body. Such perceptions allow this experiential information to become part of that person >> resonance causing them to simply perceive and feel, or take appropriate action; dissonance causing that person to discard the information or otherwise remove themselves from the source of the dissonance.

This explanation is barely adequate to communicate the full feeling of intuitive emotional resonance. Intuitive emotional resonance is often accompanied by goosebumps – in a good way; a flush or some other full-body sense of receiving the energy of whatever information has been perceived in some way, whether visual, auditory or energetic, or even multi-dimensional. Intuitive emotional resonance is felt in the body rather than mentally processed through the mind.

Developing an experiential understanding of intuitive emotional resonance is necessary in sorting out truth from half-truths and outright lies.

Frequencies of Truth and Disinformation

From what I've come to understand about the energetic nature of everything in the universe, truth stands in direct melodic or harmonic vibration to its causative vibratory source.

Let's examine truth and lies for a moment. What exactly are they?

Like a single "true" note from a musical instrument, truth has a resonant clear, clean vibration. Truth simply is.

If truths about any act or occurrence would bring consequences down on someone's head if they were known, and this person or group fears those consequences, then out of that fear, they lie. There are various ways to lie. There are direct lies and denial. There are half-lies and lies of withholding. All these varieties of lying are kith and kin to each other.

All seek to hide or obfuscate the truth. But it's like trying to hide a light under a blanket – the least little wrinkle, minute hole, or the folds of the blanket bunching up in a particular way, little rays of the light shine forth, calling attention to the hidden light of the truth.

Direct lies seldom hold up because the truth of a thing simply is. When such a lie is invented, the person fabricating it has to remember it precisely. Because it is a fabrication to hide a truth, often something can be missed in fabricating a complete lie. Someone can point out an inconsistency in the "story." At that point the lying person can either opt to tell the truth or tell yet another lie to cover the hole they left in their original lie. If they are afraid enough of consequences, they will tell another lie. Sir Walter Scott's words, "Oh what a tangled web we weave, when first we practice to deceive" end up being spot on.

Withholds are non-disclosures that hold back the truth of what exists or what has been brought into being behind barriers of secrecy. These types of lies can be very dangerous. UFO secrecy is effectively free energy secrecy and the resulting environmental damage affecting life on this planet has been and continues to be very real. If technology that has been discussed in conspiracy circles on the web has even a shred of truth to it, then things like Project Bluebeam, scalar weather-earthquake-volcano control technologies like

HAARP and chemtrails are a real threat to unsuspecting populations around the world. Because most people cannot conceive of the kind of psychopathic inhumanity that some powerful individuals are capable of in their quest for power and control, they will not comprehend or accept such inhumanity is real fact. They also will shun the thought that such exotic technologies could exist or be used against them.

Denial when one knows the truth is another kind of direct lie. It can only be perpetuated successfully by authority figures who engender a general public trust. There is a counter-attack of ridicule on those people that the purveyors of denial fear might expose the truth. "People who see UFOs or claim abductions are crazy or drunk" is an example of this. Since people generally trust the source of such denial, they fall in line with the denial, make it part of their belief system. The real tragedy here is for those who have experienced an undeniable sighting or some kind of contact experience; they know the denial is a lie. But out of the fear of ridicule placed on them or direct threats to their lives, they keep quiet about it. Denial only works as long as people are convinced to fall in line with it by trust in authority or fear of consequences to themselves if they tell their truth. Denial by trust in authority, over many years, makes such denial a solid thought structure within a society. It is one of those things that people come to accept by rote as "just the way it is" with little to no questioning. It is the breakdown in trust of authority figures, especially during and since the Bush-Cheney years, that has caused more and more people to question. And more people are risking their personal well-being to come forward with their experiences, and finding strength in numbers. Today UFO and ET experiencers number in the thousands to millions world-wide.

Half-lies can be some of the most insidious. Liars have learned that direct lies are often flawed from their inception, especially from an energetic and vibrational sense. What's more, I suspect those with access to secret knowledge and research regarding what truly constitutes a human being – or a spiritual being having a human experience – know that humanity has a latent sixth sense. Sayings like, "I have a hunch" or "I have a gut feeling" illustrate this. Unfortunately, when people are so conditioned and indoctrinated to a bubble-world reality, they can mistake hunches or gut feelings for emotionally-based cognitive dissonance – their conditioned and indoctrinated paradigm coming into conflict with a very real truth that they may not want to accept. Mental and emotional chaos can result. It can be resolved in a couple of ways. One is by resolutely returning to denial of the truth they've uncovered, no matter how stark and obvious its veracity is. The other is to become passably comfortable with the discomfort of the cognitive dissonance and to begin to examine where the particular truth you stumbled upon takes you – having the courage to follow its various threads and paths and stay open to where they lead. Finally, cognitive dissonance fades away and a new appreciation of truth and pursuing truth emerges.

Because of humanity's latent sixth sense or intuition, liars and obfuscators of truth in our society have learned that a lie needs to be linked to a truth in some way. The crux of obfuscation is to confuse, to evade, to be unclear... to "darken." The truth they try to link to their lie, denial or withhold has a clear, clean vibration. It becomes like a sugar coating for the dissonant energy of the lie to make it more palatable, more acceptable to those hearing it. Such obfuscators also can use the standard, bubble-reality rhetoric that people have learned over time to not even question, seducing them into believing such half-truths.

The blanket of secrecy over the light of truth is getting old and threadbare. It's unraveling. Some of the people that once held it together are now pulling it apart. More and more truth is coming to light.

Back to Us, Ourselves

We also need, as individuals, to tune our personal intuitional radar by looking at the belief sets we have developed over time and exposure to so much information about the institutional structures that are failing humanity today. For those who have been into "conspiracy theories" for a long time, the danger is in falling into having your personal radar scope select only those things that appear on your screen that confirm and justify your beliefs about shadow governments and Illuminati elites. Just be careful that all that is good and beautiful does not also escape your notice; all the ways in which people are doing amazing acts of kindness and compassion. Remember the formula of looking at five uplifting positives for every fearful negative. If the sun is still shining, if the birds are still singing, if your dog still wants to go for a walk and chase the stick you toss into the river, then get out and revel in that as well. Looking at the dark too long and too intently can become a habit, one that feeds all that is dark in the world with your vital life force energy. Back off to keeping a weather eye on it and expand the sweep of your personal radar to include all of what is going on in the world, the beauty and inspiration as well as the things going wrong. Otherwise you may find yourself indeed living exclusively in a world of "Abandon Hope All Ye Who Enter Here."

The other end of the extreme is not productive either. Like it or not we all live on a world that is made up of positive and negative elements. By trying to shun the negative completely, it's possible that you could be hiding your fears in your subconscious where they will sit and pull your strings. To open to them is the first step in freeing yourself from them. Individual by individual, such subconscious material varies by degree and content specific to their own experiences. The best way to assess what you carry in your own subconscious is to look at how the world around you appears to you and what your complaints about it might be.

If we distill everything down to love or fear, we have two different vibrations. One, love, is resonant, self-creative, self-sustaining and ever-expansive. Through kindness, joy, sharing, bonding and unity which inspires more of the same, love has the capacity to build upon itself continually and exponentially.

The other, fear, is dissonant, parasitic, entropic. It takes the love vibration and twists it into fear of loss, fear of destruction, fear of, fear of, fear of – fill in the blank. It is love perverted. It has to keep twisting love inside-out, continuing to apply the off-note "fear of" to the original true vibration of love to keep itself alive. So even again in this way, we have the true vibrational beauty of love, and the dissonance of what fear would twist love into for it's own ends, out of it's own fear of ceasing to exist.   Years ago, when I worked with people helping them to clear fear, anger and grief through dance and drumming, I discovered that, once these emotions were drummed or danced to completion and release, an energy and rhythm of joy would flood into them, energizing them. The rhythms and energy of fear, anger and grief would spend themselves in about three to seven minutes of moving expression. The rhythms, movements and energy of joy outlasted the negative emotional states by up to five times that three to seven minutes' length of time, sometimes even longer. This was yet one more way in which I learned the power of love and all its associated states over those of fear. This puts into words what I do my best to distinguish for myself on a vibrational level. I know I'm not foolproof. But in learning this and paying attention to my intuitive feelings, I'm doing much better than I used to, trying to navigate only on mind and emotions.

Some people tell me that the shadow government, the Illuminati, or whatever you want to call them are so good they can fake and fool even this kind of discernment.

Everything I've learned my whole life in the hard-won realm of experience and opening to my expanded awareness, including the quantum models for it that now also inform us, tells me this is another lie trying to trap me in a net of fear. I'm willing to bet my life on the truths I've discovered. I know I am more than my body. I know that the more I develop the ability to listen to my intuition, the better I navigate through life. I continue to encounter random synchronicities that amazingly confirm my insights and intuitions.

I can only do the best I know how – simply feel the vibes and take appropriate action on what I sense. It's working for me.

Chapter 24: Energy and Vibration, Flow and Healing

In "Chapter One: The Shadow and The Light" I shared the following:

> For all living beings, at the deepest core, their nature
> is wholeness, a seamless, flowing wholeness of being,
> interconnected with all life everywhere. Like a splinter of glass
> or wood buried deep in living tissue, that is worked to the
> surface to be expelled, the body works energetic blocks to the
> surface for release also. Living beings cannot live or function
> well in any kind of fractured state, physically, mentally,
> emotionally or spiritually. The drive towards wholeness is
> always there. Dis-ease of the body, disquiet of the mind and
> emotional distress are interventions from the body-mind-
> spirit, this inner chorus working to bring back into being the
> seamless integrated wholeness of body, mind, heart and
> spirit.

The essential flow of energy in the universe that we are part of is always seeking wholeness, unity, balance and harmony – from the individual to the whole human collective. Obstacles to this flow of energy – injury, trauma, abuse – will always create the synchronicities in our lives with people, places and circumstances guiding us to healing, wholeness, unity, balance and harmony with ourselves. When we consciously commit to and participate in our healing process, the synchronicities accelerate. It is almost as if the Conscious Living, Loving Universe tries to be gentle with us in coaxing us to heal; urging us to open our inner eye and gaze upon ourselves in deeply honest ways. In so doing, we open to the insights that can guide us back into balance and harmony. It is not that the Conscious Loving Universe "does anything" to us. It is more a result of the dance of energy between the inner blocks, those frozen places within ourselves and the Universal Flow that attract the circumstances, people and places that will give our body-minds an opportunity to remember, or "re-member" – to think of it in a shamanic healing sense. Injury, trauma, abuse – hurts of all kinds – from the tiny to the profound, split away pieces of ourselves, fragmenting our wholeness. Re-membering is, in a very real sense, spirit and soul retrieval work, no matter what therapeutic process or shamanic ritual facilitates it.

There are actual clues to this in the terminology applied to people who have suffered severe trauma. Multiple personality disorder inherently suggests a fragmentation of a single individual's psyche. Now called "dissociative identity disorder," this is an even more accurate description for the splitting away process that happens in situations of severe trauma – to dissociate or "go away" in the psyche from an incident of severe trauma.

But even the less-traumatic or smaller hurts of our lives can fragment us at less obvious levels. If not understood and processed in conscious, mindful and loving ways, these hurts result in the development of "personas" or masks that we adopt to deal with the world around us. The belief systems about the world that various personas formulate from the hurts that forged them shape the way in which the individual operating within the persona views the world, i.e., other people or organizational structures, with whom they interact.

Personas are personality defense mechanisms we develop as a result of finding that parts of ourselves are not "okay" with parents or others. Examples of personas, usually born of hurts or traumas; a child in a troubled home finds they can ease family members upsets by taking care of them in some way, forming a "caretaker" persona. Another child in a similar situation could adopt using humor to diffuse tensions, forming a "joker" persona. One of my personas is a "warrior" persona, a part of me that can always be on alert, even hypervigilant. Created in my childhood defending my mother from my violent, alcoholic father, this persona was reinforced by the risk and trauma of my military experiences. Personas end up negatively impacting us by preventing us from being able to connect authentically with other people due to the beliefs that run them. When in the grip of a persona that operates out of a particular belief set, especially the belief that the world is a dangerous place, adrenal exhaustion and a compromised immune system is often the result over time, leading to poor health. We don't need to get rid of personas, but we do need to understand them, their beliefs and motivations. I still keep my warrior persona around in case I need her, but I no longer let her run my life.

In my body-centered coaching training, I was taught about three areas of knowing. First are the things we know that we know, such as knowing how to cook an omelet or drive a car. Then there are the things we know that we don't know, like if we know we don't know how to fly a commercial jet or do deep sea diving.

The third and most vast realm is the realm of what we don't know that we don't know. This is the realm of the unconscious; the realm of our programming, our conditioning to accept "that's just the way the world is" without questioning it too much. We learn "that's just the way the world is" from our families, from school, from life. How? Our conditioning set us up to selectively choose and interpret our experiences in ways that justify and reinforce our inculcated beliefs.

Changing unconscious beliefs is one of the main themes of manifestation and law of attraction teachings, in alignment with quantum principles. Yet how do we discover what they are, from the vast realm of "what we don't know that we don't know?" With some careful attention to what the world around us mirrors back to us and by telling the truth about how we feel about it within and to ourselves as a simple observation of our experience – without wandering into blame, judgment or other kinds of mental spin – we will bump up against our unconscious beliefs through our interactions with the world around us. We can then discover and correct them. This is essentially the same insight my guides whispered in my thoughts that day in the Unity Church bookstore, years before my life experience and professional trainings refined this process for me. Simply live life consciously, with awareness, and life will teach you about your beliefs and what in them needs to change.

This is one of the fundamental principles of both manifestation and healing, and both terms are synonymous with each other in every case. It is through the conditioning of unconscious beliefs that we are taken out of flow with the Universal dance of energy between ourselves and the Divine. But the Divine wants us to remember our wholeness. It is a function of the Divine energy flowing through us for that energy and its expression to flow freely. It wants us to remember that we are seamlessly connected to It, to each other, to all Creation. So when we begin to notice that our belief systems are clamping off our energy flow in ways that inhibit and limit our full life's expression, it is right and natural to begin to question and observe how our beliefs are in conflict with the deeper essence of who we truly are, as energy and vibration, as light and love. We learn it is our belief systems that limit our freedom of expression.

I have come to regard manifestation like building a circuit board, since once upon a time I was a radar electronics technician. First, you decide what you want the circuit board to do. Then you design it with the proper component parts; resistors, capacitors and transistors. You solder them together in the proper sequence on the board. Then you apply the energy waves of alternating electric current to it. It turns on and does what it was designed to do.

Manifestation is approached by deciding what kind of life experience you would like to enjoy. You visualize an inner, energetic template for this new state of being. You create it with data from mindful observations of where your beliefs are inhibiting your full life expression. You accept and own the unconscious beliefs you've discovered, claiming responsibility for them in a consciously co-creative way, between you and the universal quantum field. This is not about burdening yourself with any blame or guilt for carrying around such beliefs for so long, nor is it about figuring them all out in specific detail. It is about simply acknowledging that some part of you was clinging to them for whatever reason and continuing to manifest your life experience from that unconscious place. Now that is going to change. You are choosing to create a new version of yourself with a more free and unlimited expression.

The last step is charging your new envisioned template-circuit board with your personal electricity – your *emotional energy*. You imagine what life is like in the new, desired state, aligning yourself with a new superposition, a new reality in the quantum field of all possibilities. You feel the feelings, sensations and emotions you will feel in this new reality as part of the actualization process. In this way, you energize the inner template-circuit board you created from your discovery process and mindful insights.

Now, on a collective level, consider how operating through various indoctrinated belief systems shapes humanity's consensus reality as expressed all around us. Begin to understand how the majority of humanity's thoughts and beliefs are manipulated to serve the interests of "The State." Conceptualize the unconscious action of millions to billions of people's attention captured through media by politics, by religion, by propagandized material of all kinds, reinforcing and justifying all kinds of engineered beliefs. Imagine all this exponential attention, thought and belief charged with purposely contrived, intense, out-of-balance emotional energy, and the kind of reality it creates and makes "solid" from the quantum field. When most of humanity is still mired in a Newtonian viewpoint of a material universe with mechanical causes and effects, is it any wonder we are confronted with so many issues dealing with our very survival as a species?

Do you begin to get an idea of how we might collectively, albeit subconsciously, be shaping the quantum reality in which we all find ourselves?

Belief systems build a personal radar within each individual, and within the human collective as well – a selective radar tuned to pick up and interpret all incoming data through the lens of those indoctrinated belief systems, seizing upon that which appears to confirm the beliefs and dismissing all other incoming data. Whether formulated by individuals who have suffered emotional or physical hurt or injury or whether the belief systems indoctrinate whole populations through religious, political or other ideologies with covert agendas of control, they take us individually and collectively out of touch with our authentic selves, with who we are in our essence – spirit taking human form to experience through contrast, to learn and enrich the understanding of the Whole of which we are all a part. The bliss and peace of existence within the One Consciousness cannot be fully understood or appreciated without a departure from that grace, without an experience of contrast to that bliss and peace. This is why life itself, as a human being or other conscious entity birthing itself into sentience is such a precious and sacred opportunity, and gift.

This is also why it is so vitally important that exponentially large numbers of people undertake the process of healing and manifestation today, person by person. As each healing human soul touches the hearts of others who come into their orbit, they inspire through example a necessary shift in consciousness and awareness, spreading it further still. Love is the energy, the language of the heart through which this message and energy is transmitted. How each of us individually choose to express our love is our own unique gift to the world. It can be grand and far-reaching, or quiet and subtle. No one can do it quite the way you yourself can, as a unique individual facet of the Conscious, Loving Universe, learning about contrast and freedom of expression in your own special way.

Through collective healed awareness and positive action in the world demonstrating real and practical shifts in understanding and consciousness, we can make a difference. We can turn the tide of affairs on our world. And we can proclaim our successful birth into full sentience as a species, sending a powerful message to the star nations who watch and wait in space above us. They shepherd us as they can, without direct interference in our free will, waiting for us to become conscious, empowered partners in the process of healing our world.

Practical Application of Quantum Principles

In applying what I've shared here to the chapter on Consciousness, what we are learning of the quantum unified field and the nature of our reality at more and more fundamental levels, i.e., the observer effect, the principle of non-locality and the law of attraction. We can begin to see just how the reality we live in here on Earth is governed by how our thoughts and beliefs line up, and how they are directed through institutional and organizational ideologies.

It is crucial to shake ourselves awake. To observe our relationship to and interaction with the world around us and understand the data it provides to us in a new way. To begin peeling away the layers of our belief systems and reclaim our true essence and authenticity. To re-tune our personal radar to take in and process, in a conscious and mindful way, ALL the data it receives. Disempowered by belief systems that cause us to see ourselves as single ineffectual and frail human beings, we fall into victimhood and blaming. Human relationships of all kinds and even the legal systems reflect this. When we only pay attention to that which seems to confirm and justify our belief systems, individual or collectively indoctrinated, we continue to make solid and keep intact a reality that does not serve us.

Years ago, listening with a group of friends, I heard a statement in a recording from Osho, or Bhagwan Shree Rajneesh, that struck a profound chord within me years ago. While I was never a follower of this man, and I am well aware of the storm of criticism and controversy surrounding him and his followers, his statement, paraphrased here, I found unequivocally true – that religions, governments and other organizational structures do not want us to love ourselves because we are so much easier to control when we do not. If they can make us believe we are not worthy of love unless we do as they tell us, they have the perfect mechanism of control. Love is a vital necessity to every living being and many of us will go to varying lengths to get it in one way or another.

401

Yet what is love worth when it is contrived and rooted in meeting various conditions? Not much. It is a poor counterfeit of a deeper unconditional love that we long for. A kind of love that, if awakened in every human heart, could sweep over this planet, healing it and all of us.

Herein lies the trouble in the unfolding human drama on Planet Earth; conditional "love," better known as codependency. Codependency is rampant in our societies today. Out of it, addictions of every variety are born as people search for some counterfeit of "love" to fill the emptiness inside them that hollow belief systems create. This aching human need to fill an emptiness within could be healed, beginning with an inspired whole-body insight of reconnection with our essential, authentic selves. From there we can expand to recognizing our connection to and existence within Source Consciousness.

I remember such a moment of profound connection for myself. The gentlest, most loving tel-empathic message flowed into my despondent thoughts one day, years ago. I was still adrift in my life, rudderless, without conscious purpose or direction, just trying to make it from day to day, from paycheck to paycheck.

> *Don't you realize that you are beloved of the Creator simply by virtue of your existence? You could sit like a bump on a log the rest of your life, never do a single worthwhile thing, and you would still be as beloved by the Creator as anyone who goes out and does great things in the world.*

This communication, the caress of its vibration in my body turning to the most loving of words in my mind, swept through me like a gentle tsunami, touching, resonating in every cell. I hung my head and wept tears of revelation and relief, feeling the power of "emotional resonance" long before I put a name to such experiences. Still, the life-long habit of feeling inadequate and "less than" took years of work to reverse to the point that I could step up to the plate and start expressing my reason for being here on this planet, and in doing so, begin to remember who I am.

Whether by accident or design, the contrivances of belief systems that convince us we are wanting in character and personhood have given rise to ways of relating and interacting with each other and our world that reinforce those beliefs of inadequacy. Human misery of all kinds issues forth from there. And unfortunately for us, it plays right into the hands of those who would control us for their own ends. People who desperately need some form of love, who feel bereft of it, will do all kinds of unfortunate things to get some semblance of it, from buying products that promise them some payoff they desire, to playing their own codependent games of manipulation and control of others.

We are individuals, and a species, in need of healing. Our planet needs healing, and may be reflecting her current state of chaos tectonically and environmentally as a mirror to us of our own need to step forward and commit to fully healing. In order for healing to be fully complete, we must work it all the way through; body, mind, heart and soul. Fortunately, this is a process that is built into us as living systems in connection with Source Consciousness.

Unconscious Pushes Towards Healing

We are inculcated with limiting beliefs about who and what we are from almost the first moment of our arrival at birth. We are taught to identify ourselves as our bodies, rather than as consciousness inhabiting our bodies. The body is a third-dimensional anchor and lens through which we perceive this wonderful, terrible, beautiful and troubling new world we've entered. It feels all kinds of sensations and emotions we have to learn to cope with, as well as learning how to use our hands and feet to move it around. It consumes our full attention, and before we know it, we are human beings. It can take time to rediscover that we are spiritual beings having a human experience, though many of the special children born on Planet Earth in the past few decades remember this far more naturally and quickly.

It is part of the cosmic plan coming in that we have predestined experiences we agreed to before birth. These are like forks in the road with multiple paths where we can choose to go one of several directions. Much of our lives we make up as we go through our free will. Our choices depend on our connection to the still, small voice within or how much we allow that voice to be obscured by our minds and emotions, and how much we listen to the others directing our choices when we don't feel confident in making them for ourselves.

As babies, our chakra vortexes pull in the energy from the unified field to keep our pattern integrity intact and functioning in a healthy manner. For many children however, trouble starts at an early age, even in those tender baby years. Dysfunction in families begins to affect them, beliefs start to form about "the way life is" that affect the flow of incoming energy from the unified field. Symptoms begin to manifest as warning signs of energy flowing out of balance, or shutting down entirely in certain areas. The bundles of nerves and glandular systems near the affected chakras begin to send erratic or incomplete information to the rest of the body, and the body's systems stop functioning in an optimal manner.

This is where the flow of energy from the Universal, unified field comes into play as a healing guide. If persons are sensitive enough, they begin to feel "off" in their energy. If they ignore it and keep on with their activities – particularly activities that reinforce any toxic belief systems they've picked up – that off-energy will become a symptom. These people might go to a doctor and get a pill to relieve the symptom, or start using drugs, alcohol or other strategies to squelch it. Not all drug or alcohol use is an escape. However, society is filled with examples of serious substance abuse problems and other activities taken to addictive extremes. As one of my earlier mentors once remarked, we cannot silence our bodies, but we can kill them off slowly or quickly with addictions while trying to silence them.

Just how hooked into an addictive behavior can people be? If you are wondering about yourself, ask yourself some quiet questions within. Could you stop it today? How hard or easy would that be? Do you hide the behavior from others? Do you compromise your values to do it? Does the behavior have you or do you have it?

In addition to other addictions I had to face and work on, I was also addicted to fear for a good many years. Yet there came a day when I could not allow fear to have or control me any more. The personal cost became too high. I was avoiding who I came to Earth to be and my life was not working on many levels. It put a tight clamp in my energy flow and freedom of expression. So today I now experience more inner peace and far less fear. I have not totally banished fear from my life, but I have developed a conscious relationship with it. I have the fear – the fear does not have me. With sex addiction, the moment of profound healing was the discovery of the truth that what I truly wanted to experience was love. My sex addiction behavior became a barrier to ever being able to experience love in any way that would have any depth or meaning for me. Thank the stars and my unseen family of guides that I was able to see and learn this truth before my behavior had severe consequences in my life.

That off-energy that people may notice and dismiss is the first whisper from the Conscious Loving Universe and its sustaining flow of energy that "something" needs to change. Somewhere in their thoughts and beliefs they swapped an essential truth of their inherent nature for a lie; and that lie, lodged in their auric energy field at or near a particular chakra, is costing them. They may have encountered a person, been in a place or situation that somehow made them notice that something was off. This is that flow of energy, conscious, seeking freedom of flow again through their chakras restored to full open functioning.

The river of Universal Energy we depend upon for life itself in the body guides us through our higher mind-super-consciousness into some confrontation with ourselves.

Many people do not get that first message. So the dance of energy goes on between you and the Conscious Loving Universe. It continues to guide you from the connection between It and your own higher self into instances where you will have further opportunities to face up to the ways in which you have swapped truth for the lies of indoctrinated beliefs, judgments, opinions and attitudes. If at first we don't listen to the little messages, then the Universe gets a bigger hammer. Yet it is not the Conscious Loving Universe that would ever bludgeon us with a hammer. It is our own proclivity to stubbornly stay on a self-destructive path. The Universal Energy trying to flow freely within us, in concert with our higher self, lines up the synchronicities to bring us into confrontation with ourselves in ways that will get our attention. Life-threatening illness or accidents are extreme ways that this confrontation can occur when we have missed perhaps hundreds of subtler messages along the way.

Applying this to humanity as a collective, we see the evidence all around us in the current chaos of the world. This is a result of the indoctrination, manipulation and control by organizational structures and the people who run them, and our own unconscious acquiescence through seductions and promises or threats and fear. We trade the challenges of sensing, feeling and thinking for ourselves and being 100% free and responsible for our own lives to complacently allowing ourselves to be led around like herds of sheep or cattle. After all, they convinced us that they know best, not us. We have become diminished into feeling we are unequal and inadequate. Thinking and being responsible for our own lives has become too much trouble; we are way out of practice.

Yet what are most herds bred, groomed and prepared for, in the end? We all know the answer to that question. It's time to awaken from the herd mentality.

What those secret societies that manipulate from the shadows most fear as the ultimate threat to their power is us – loving ourselves and each other enough to join together. Expanding our consciousness and multi-dimensional awareness as a unified collective would cut them off from stealing our energy, energy that they have been addictively glutting themselves on in endless ways down through history.

The crucible our world has become of political, economic, societal and environmental chaos is presenting collective humanity with a deep and urgent need to awaken. It has become a thunder in our ears and an assault on our eyes with every new environmental disaster. It is underscored by every certifiably-insane decision made by the political leadership on this planet to continue exploiting an ecosystem already pushed beyond to breaking point.

The drilling and use of oil and nuclear weapons and power plants risk ever more toxic and lethal damage to our environment. When alternative energy sources are available – have been available for decades – this is absolutely unconscionable. No wonder some extraterrestrial groups orbiting Earth, observing humanity, likely see us as not being a fully-sentient species. But today I would hazard an intuitive guess that those who are telepathic or tel-empathic sense the struggle within us as a species to become sentient now, on the proving ground of so many huge challenges before us.

The challenge to us as a human collective is this: can we learn to see this maelstrom of the world around us today as that now-thundering voice of the Conscious Loving Universe calling us all to awaken? For our own and our planetary healing? We missed or ignored the subtler clues in decades past. Apparently we need the sledgehammer of extreme challenge to hear the clarion call to our own awakening and healing as a species.

No one on this planet can truly hide from the global state of affairs confronting us today. Trying to plaster over our current challenges with positive affirmations alone will not suffice. Such strategies do contain keys to healing within them, if used from a place of full awareness and willingness to view the whole "catastrophe" in an honest way. We must face the maelstrom around us and claim responsibility for creating it through the avoidance of our collective human shadow. For not reading the writing on the wall long ago; for meekly joining the managed human herd because it was just too much trouble to truly educate ourselves. For drowning out the still, small voice within us all by allowing ourselves to be distracted by trivia. For ignoring decades of warning signs all around us.

We all did this, some more than others, but we must all reclaim responsibility. The sword of Truth has two edges, one is Freedom, the other is Responsibility. To be truly free demands accepting responsibility for all choices we have made and will make. We sense that, and this is why we acquiesce, give away our freedom – and our power. We didn't want to be responsible. It was too much damn trouble. It was easier to sit back and blame those we gave our freedom and responsibility to in the first place. Trouble is, we don't have the luxury of doing that any more. Not unless we want to blame "them" with our last gasp of air on our way into humanity's mass grave.

There is no time to waste vilifying ourselves for the messages we missed or abdicating our freedom and responsibility. We know why we did it. We know the day-to-day life pressures we have lived under – jobs, family and financial obligations. Treat that knowledge of yourselves with heart and compassion. Now is the time to forgive ourselves with love and move straight into action.

No more time to leave the world's challenges to any governing groups or individuals. We must take action, ourselves. Through one of the only true means left to us – our unified consciousness.

Engaging the Path of Conscious Healing

The first step in walking the path of conscious healing is reclaiming our freedom and accepting full responsibility for taking the mindful, loving and positive actions that go with it. This is as true for humanity as a collective as it is for each individual person. No more acquiescence, no more complacency. We must undertake educating ourselves, to join together in grassroots groups in our own communities.

Our political leadership may be selling us and our future down the river to corporate interests that mask the secret societies of this world; and while we can bring political pressure to bear on such matters, it cannot be our only means of action. We are flatly out-bid by the special interests lobbying our congressional and judicial representatives as well as presidents and vice-presidents. Without taking other action, we will only find ourselves locked in a struggle of We the People against the government-military-corporate complex in what could ultimately be a long-term, fruitless effort and waste of valuable time. It is still a divide-and-conquer, force-opposing-force struggle, rather than a unified joining together. It squanders our energy. Best to find like minds, kindred spirits and join directed consciousness and energy together with focused intent in a way that combines well-considered action right alongside inner visualization and manifestation techniques. I speak as a warrior who still likes to fight the good fight and defend the underdog with liberty and justice for all. I still hold to those ideals. But I have had to become a spiritual warrior where the challenges are less to do with what's out there in the world than what I confront within myself, and where I put my energy, attention and intention.

Consciously-directed intention is a powerful tool. It grows exponentially more powerful as increasing numbers of individuals join ranks for a common cause. I am very moved to see the evidence of directed group consciousness moving in such directions through mass joint efforts such as healing the ocean waters in the Gulf of Mexico. These are the very signs of shift happening on Planet Earth, through the expanding numbers of people of heart and conscience.

Eclipsing the Gulf disaster, the earthquake and tsunami that rocked Japan in March of 2011 caused severe damage to their Fukushima nuclear power plant. There is a likelihood of radiation leakage that could potentially spread across the Pacific to the Americas, contaminating everything in its path. The radiation has poisoned the sea water around the plant. A message went out from Dr. Masaru Emoto, whose work with water was featured in "What the Bleep Do We Know?" and as author of *The Hidden Messages in Water*. His heartfelt request was sent to thousands, perhaps millions of people around the world via email asking that, at noon on March 31, 2011, in whatever time zone around the world, each person speak aloud three times a simple prayer to the waters:

> [To] The water of the Fukushima Nuclear Plant;
> We are sorry to make you suffer.
> Please forgive us.
> We thank you, and we love you.

Those familiar with the Hawaiian healing technique of Ho'Oponopono will recognize these words as those used in healing and shifting perspective and frequency from a state of malady to one of health. Ho'Oponopono works from a position of taking 100% responsibility for how you are experiencing the world as it is, and using the statements, "I'm sorry. Please forgive me. I love you. Thank you" to realign yourself to Spirit/Creator/inspiration, rather than endlessly replaying problems in the mind. "I'm sorry" and "Please forgive me" are not aimed at the offending person, illness or situation you wish to heal, but to the part of you that is vibrating in sympathy with it, thereby anchoring it in the world. The statements are a way of clearing and cleaning your own vibration, bringing it into alignment with the quantum superposition of the alternate reality in which complete healing and wholeness also exist, healing the illness, person or situation.

407

When one looks at the work and implications of researchers like Dean Radin, Lynne McTaggart[1], Fred Alan Wolf[2], and other visionaries who express their emerging understandings of the actions of consciousness on the unified quantum field, a picture begins to emerge of humanity creating our Earth reality from our collective field of consciousness. This collective field of human consciousness is still largely working from the unconscious realms. Healing ourselves, our ecosystem and our planet will depend on successfully navigating the awakening process as a collective.

No one need feel overwhelmed about trying to awaken the whole human collective. If you feel like a tiny "awake" voice in this field of human unconsciousness, all you need do is continue to develop and awaken yourself. Keep on becoming. Teach not by words, but by example and loving positive action. Be willing at each moment to let go of who you are for the better self you can become. Continue to open your understanding ever-deeper into what that is, into who you truly are. You only need to shine your light into the world from your facet of this reality. Trust the process. Trust that your light will be noticed by people ready to begin their own journey of awakening. Just as each of us has that still, small voice within us, each of us who begin to awaken become – as a group – the still, small voice of the whole human collective, urging it to awaken as well. The process happens through one human soul, one human heart at a time. Know deep within yourself that no such heart opening, no such reach for the very best expression of yourself, is ever undertaken in vain. Our life experience and how we integrate it is the only thing we ever take with us into the Great Beyond after our bodies die.

Death: the Ultimate Release, the Ultimate Healing

If there truly is no death, then death as oblivion, or ceasing to be that so many people fear doesn't really exist. Death could be thought of as an ultimate form of healing, particularly from lives totally mired down in dysfunctions of various kinds. Our minds can resolutely hang on to false beliefs that take a toll on the body over time. Beliefs we formulate as protection from future hurt out of emotional injuries or beliefs indoctrinated into us are often the stuff of future illness, or dis-ease. Suppressing our essential nature and aliveness through clinging to beliefs that don't serve us is eventually fatal if we cannot grow, expand and shift into newer and freer modes of self expression.

If we could all live from a fully vibrant essential nature and the conscious truth that we are one with all that is, the flow of energy coming in from the

---

[1] Lynne McTaggart is a best-selling author, investigative journalist and researcher into consciousness and the quantum field. Her books include *The Field: The Quest for the Secret Force of the Universe*, *The Intention Experiment: Using Your Thoughts to Change Your Life and the World* and more. Her website: http://www.lynnemctaggart.com.

[2] Dr. Fred Alan Wolf is a theoretical physicist, author and lecturer who earned his PhD at UCLA in 1963. He conducts research into the relationship between quantum physics and consciousness. He has authored many books including *Taking the Quantum Leap: The New Physics for Non-Scientists*, *The Spiritual Universe: How Quantum Physics Proves the Existence of the Soul*, *The Eagle's Quest: A Physicist Finds the Scientific Truth at the Heart of the Shamanic World*, and many more. His website: http://www.fredalanwolf.com/.

universal energy field would be balanced, harmonious and unobstructed. However, when we come to Earth, we start to be indoctrinated with various sets of beliefs that do not line up with such essential truth. When we are young and fresh to this life, they are not so troublesome for us physically in most cases. But over time they can become serious health risks – especially if we keep our personal radar tuned to only select those experiences that seem to confirm our conditioned generalities about "how life is" or about "how people are" or any number of rote verbal resignations of how our lives play out. These globalized generalizations or rationalizations relieve us of having to feel into our direct experience fully or wonder creatively about it and how it might have come to us. When we lack self-love, this can be the root cause around which other layers of beliefs form. Admitting that we don't believe we are worthy of love can be very painful. We most often emotionally veer away from acknowledging it. Yet such an admission is very often the first crucial step to healing and change.

At or near every major chakra center in our bodies also reside ganglia of nerves and a specific endocrine gland center. The nerves can be thought of as the fiber-optic wiring that sends signals to these glandular centers to regulate their various functions. The chakra centers are those vortexes that spin energy in from the universal energy field. The dance of energy from the universal field and our consciousness then lines up into grid lines created in part by our desire to experience life in the 3D world, along which our bodies are formed. Our consciousness in a sense is a zero-point in the universal field that initiates the intricacies of the spin of the chakras that create our bodies, starting in the womb. In Barbara Brennan's book, *Hands of Light,* she worked with artists to illustrate the detailed auric layers that she observes energetically of how the human energy field is constructed. Each layer of the human energy field corresponds to a particular chakra. Hence there is an emotional body layer, a mental body layer and so on.

On the physical level, the chakras corresponding to the major nerve ganglia and endocrine glands regulate the energetic health of our bodies. Our health or lack of health is an indication of how these chakras are open and flowing or are skewed, blocked or closed down completely. The longer they remain out of sync and the more we hold onto the limiting beliefs that keep them out of sync, the more the body runs down.

Our super-conscious higher self, together with the Conscious Loving Universe, is always creating synchronicities, seeking ways to guide us back to wholeness and essential truth. If people truly desire to live in a state of optimal health, they will learn to see and make use of these opportunities to heal their lives and bodies. But sometimes people are so completely indoctrinated that they cannot bring themselves to give up dysfunctional beliefs about themselves, others or the world around them. When this happens, degenerative disease can take over as their lives progress. Stress created by the friction or impact of such beliefs also takes its toll over time through adrenal-physical exhaustion. The body becomes less and less able to recover. When the beliefs of the mind and the distorted emotional states they engender cannot be changed or overcome, then the only avenue of healing for such a soul is death of the body. The release of the soul into the Great Beyond allows review of the path of that just-previous lifetime. A plan might be devised for perhaps coming back and doing it again, setting up a soul contract that will provide even better circumstances for that soul's spiritual unfoldment and awakening.

These are not the only reasons a soul chooses a life that ends by terminal illness or accident. The lives of families, friends or enemies are all entwined together. When one of such a group exits through death of the body, all the others are affected. The event itself becomes an opportunity for each to reflect and make new choices. When mass exits of many souls occur, as in war or natural disasters, the collective lives of those left behind in the world are impacted. In many cases, millions of hearts are opened to compassion for the departed and the survivors as they contemplate how easily it could have been them or one of their loved ones whose life was lost, had they lived in the place of the war or catastrophe.

How long might we live if we lived in a state of essential truth? In a full expression of vibrant aliveness from our minds right down into the cells of our bodies? It would be interesting and fun to find out if we can manage such a shift as a whole human collective. It would be far easier for everyone to explore such life experience if it became an actual part of the human paradigm on Earth. If we awakened to our full awareness potential, feeling and sensing our interconnectivity, there would be psychic support all around each of us, created by us all. We could be tel-empathically lifted back into harmony with the whole if we slipped individually into feeling less-than or diminished.

Through the experiences of many, and research into out-of-body and near-death experiences, we are learning that we do not really "die." Our bodies die. We move on to another state of being. Many of us jump right back into the game of life on Earth, or life elsewhere in the multiverse. This learning is catching hold of the collective human imagination.

Trauma and the Individual and Alternate Views on "False Memory Syndrome"

The film *The Secret* touched on ideas to create a better world through focusing on what we desire to create. There was perhaps some implication of shunning what we don't want to be part of our reality. Many people living sunlit lives, unknowing and untouched by dark trauma, recoil from even hearing about it if they inadvertently stumble upon such a tale. They fear that to allow such thoughts to invade the inner sanctum of their carefully-constructed reality could bring it crashing down. Such fears reveal that a reality-construct of choosing only to include what is desired and enjoyed can be as fragile as a house of cards. Apparently, it cannot withstand any kind of honest look at a darker reality. I don't mean to pick on such people or chide them for maintaining a positive outlook – I feel this is incredibly very important myself. But there is another side of this to consider.

What about when bad things happen to good people? What about trauma so severe, that a person's mind splinters it away to the subconscious where it sits, festers and pulls the strings on that person's life from the shadows? Are such people to be forever-lost souls, condemned to stand in the shadows, looking in at the sunny world of people living, laughing and loving? Those people whose lives are untouched by severe trauma and terror?

This is like telling a child who has been traumatically sexually molested that they need to stay locked away in a closet out of sight so they don't remind anyone of the terrible things that happened to them. So they don't cast a shadow over anyone else's positive mood.

How can one heal locked away in a closet, either real or virtual? Those of us who have had to deal with such trauma, whether in childhood or as adults, have to find some positive way to deal with what happened to us or forever cower and huddle throughout our own lives. Often our friends are all we have since it's very hard to find a therapist or counselor we can trust to work with around such issues. Trust issues for those who have experienced extraordinary or severe trauma are huge and people who experience such trauma often have difficulty trusting anyone completely, even "friends."

Living in such a way becomes intolerably stressful over time. Ours becomes a greater challenge: to heal and not only survive, but thrive. Ours is the task to look straight into the darkest nightmares that humanity at its worst inflicts on their own kind. We must stand up to such realities. We must move through our fear and become that conscious part of the human collective that tells the rest that fear is a lie, told by self-appointed authority figures who are determined to keep human energy tied up in divide-and-conquer, war-and-conflict beliefs with ideologies that keep spinning out a matrix-like fabric of a humanity perpetually unawakened and unaware of the magnificent beings they truly are.

How do people heal from the trauma of mind-control abuse at all? I'm sure this thorny dilemma has mind-control perpetrators and experts scratching their heads. If they understood the true nature of the Universe as a unified and interconnected whole of consciousness and love, they would understand why at least some of their victims escape their programming. Our connection to the larger universe is one that guides everyone always towards healing and greater and greater freedom of expression. Mind control is the very antithesis of freedom of expression.

Still, as certain individuals do escape the webs that mind control weaves around them and speak out, those in the deep and shadowy bowels of such covert organizations surely became alarmed at the prospect of being exposed to public scrutiny and outrage. So it is entirely within the realm of probability that they sat down and cooked up a scheme to protect themselves by finding a way to discredit people who retrieve memories of horrific abuse. After all, horrific abuse is unthinkable and unspeakable to most people, especially if revered public figures are the ones accused.

This may be how "false memory syndrome" was concocted, complete with an organization and a board of directors to lend it weight and authority. Information being sifted to the surface shows an ugly trail between the False Memory Syndrome Foundation and the CIA by mind control researchers who want to see such heinous abuse exposed and ended. These researchers include Colin A. Ross, MD, author of *Bluebird: Deliberate Creation of Multiple Personality by Psychiatrists*, Armen Victorian, author of *Mind Controllers* and mind control survivor Carol Rutz, author of *A Nation Betrayed: The Chilling True Story of Secret Cold War Experiments Performed on Our Children and Other Innocent People*. There are many more researchers and whistleblowers drawing attention to these issues. Organizations now exist that offer support to survivors of mind control and ritual abuse victims.

Ross, Victorian and other researchers have uncovered that CIA operatives had a hand in forming the False Memory Syndrome Foundation and have served on its board of directors. The CIA is an agency with a lot to hide. They wish to avoid as much public scrutiny as possible, so much of what they do they execute through "front" organizations – organizations set up to perform functions that are very difficult to track back to the parent organization – in this case, the CIA. Memories retrieved from hypnosis raise ever more serious questions about extraterrestrial experiences and abductions, especially with so much commonality of experience reported across thousands of cases. With a growing number of people coming out and reporting sexual and other forms of abuse in mind control programs deep within the military and other government agencies – notably the CIA – there is even further risk of public exposure.

The CIA today is implicated in much covert criminal activity of various kinds. There is a gross conflict of interest with the CIA having anything to do with an organization such as the False Memory Syndrome Foundation or sitting on its governing board. Names of former or founding board members are: Martin T. Orne, psychiatrist and CIA researcher involved in mind control projects such as Project Monarch/MKULTRA and original board member Harold Lief, psychiatrist and CIA researcher.

When one takes the time to look into the sheer breadth and scope of information already in the public domain on mind control programs, one can quickly surmise who better than these nefarious individuals, with government financial and technical resources undreamed of by the general public, to be able to manipulate people's minds? From hypnosis and brainwashing during purposefully-induced brainwave states to the deliberate application of severe trauma and other techniques, these people know their craft. There are reports of false memories being introduced into unconscious subjects. Virtual reality simulations might be used also. Virtual reality has been explored in movies and television in its myriad good and evil applications. It is almost certainly a very real and very sophisticated technology being applied in various ways in government-military-corporate projects behind National Security Act of 1947 secrecy. By such manipulations, many incriminating memories victims might retrieve could be called into question.

Yet whether abuse is real or virtual, what is the real difference? Abuse is abuse, and people doing actual physical abuse or with their hands working the controls of a device to abuse people in virtual reality simulations is no less culpable either way.

Healing from mind control abuse, as other forms of healing, is a function of that flow of energy from the unified field and consciousness in which we have our very existence. If one survives mind control abuse and is also cut loose for whatever reason from continued manipulation and programming, the flow of energy in the affected person begins to reassert itself. As stated before, this flow of energy between the Universal Loving Consciousness and the super-consciousness of the person starts to set up and attract the people, places and situations that can provide opportunities for healing to begin. In all cases of healing from all kinds of illness and abuse – physical, mental, emotional or even spiritual – a wiser, more insightful being emerges, one more impervious to falling into situations of such abuse in the future. As philosopher Friedrich Nietzche stated: "That which does not kill us makes us stronger." While not always true in the strictest sense, the wisdom and insight gained from healing becomes a gift to that person and all whose lives are touched and informed by their process of recovery.

Memory and the Body, Mind and Brain

> Memories are not only stored in the brain, but also in the psychosomatic network extending throughout the body, along the connections between organs and even in our skin surface.
>
> ~ Candace B. Pert, author, *Molecules of Emotion: The Science Behind Mind-Body Medicine*

As we emerge into a world where research in quantum science provides working theories that support parallel findings in energy and mind-body medicine, we learn that it is the power of our consciousness that shapes and influences our reality for good or ill. Our psyche impacted in this way also affects our physical biology.

The brain and its neurons are not the sole repository of memory, if at all. Memory has been shown to be accessed throughout our bodies as cellular information and recall. The body is the focal point for our third dimensional experience. While memory can be stored in each cell of our bodies, it is not restricted to 3D physical matter alone. It is also possible that various specialized cells of the body may be more memory-accessing hardware to the mind-body energy field than repositories of memory in and of themselves. Memory also has

413

energetic field components that extend beyond the 3D body. The 3D body itself is based on energy flow from the universal field. If gathering life experience is one of the reasons we take form in the third dimension, it would stand to reason that this experience is necessary and must be saved and archived in some way so that it can be accessed as a holographic knowledge base of all experience across dimensions.

The following passages are quoted from an article, *Myofascial Release for the Whole Person*, by John F. Barnes, creator of the Myofascial Release Approach:

Therefore, mind/body awareness are two sides of the same coin, different aspects of the same spectrum, immutably joined, inseparable, connected, influencing and communicating constantly. Myofascial release techniques and myofascial unwinding allow for the complete communication necessary for healing and true growth. I believe that the body remembers everything that ever happened to it.

Studies have shown that during periods of trauma, people make indelible imprints of experience that have high levels of emotional content. The body can hold information below the conscious level, as a protective mechanism, so that memories tend to become dissociated or a reversible amnesia. The memories are state-or position-dependent and can therefore be retrieved when the person is in a particular state or position. The information is not available in the normal conscious state, and the body's protective mechanisms keep us away from the positions that our mind-body awareness construes as painful or traumatic.

It has been demonstrated consistently that when a myofascial release technique takes the tissue to a significant position, or when myofascial unwinding allows a body part to assume a significant position three dimensionally in space, the tissue not only changes and improves, but memories, associated emotional states and belief systems also rise to the conscious level. This awareness allows the individual to grasp the previously hidden information that may be creating or maintaining symptoms of behavior which deter improvement. With the information now at the conscious level, the individual is in a position to learn what holding or bracing patterns have been impeding progress. This release of the tissue, emotions and hidden information create an environment for change that is both conscious and effective.

~ Reprinted with permission from Rehabilitation Services Inc. T/A John F. Barnes, PT

This was also demonstrated in a different way in the Rolf Study done by researchers and volunteer subjects under the direction of Valerie Hunt – subjects remembering and/or having experiences of resolving trauma while being rolfed – a form of body work involving structural integration that works to place the client's body back into healthy alignment after the impact of injury or trauma. This study made observations on all the subjects through a variety of differing means, covering brain hemisphere functioning, energy field or Kirlian photography, EMG frequencies, neuro-muscular energy patterning, electronic auric field study and more. Significant and strong pattern correlations were found between each set of measurements in reviewing the study's data.

If our minds don't remember a trauma, that trauma is still imprinted in some way in the body's tissues and can be accessed from them. Memory is also stirred to recall by association, just as the flow of thoughts shared in a conversation branch out by association to various related subjects according to each person's experience and insight. This is what I mean by the energy flow between our higher selves and the Conscious Loving Universe setting up the places, meeting the people and providing the circumstances for memory through association to emerge, creating opportunities for healing. Having painful or frightening associations reemerge is certainly not comfortable. But when the cellular memory is activated by such associations, setting up a vibrational resonance in the present with past events, not only can memories reemerge, but also the opportunity to release and clear them becomes possible. The whole body can be engaged in the release. In talk therapy alone, exploration and discussion of issues is often just an intellectual exercise that skims only the surface of the emotions and can only reach what resides in the realm of the conscious mind.

In the course of writing this book, new associations have been made to physical phenomenon I have felt down through the years that link directly back to my trauma. At the close of Chapter 7, I spoke of intense heart palpitations I remembered having in the late 1980s, which I had checked out by a doctor. In Chapter 11, I mentioned a flashback about having someone rest their hands around my neck during a massage and a memory springing forth of being strangled until I lost consciousness, allowed to revive, then having this strangulation done multiple times. These two experiences of physical phenomenon match up quite precisely. While being strangled – suffocated – my heart would beat wildly in fear. The two sensations had always happened together. The trigger for these physical episodes occurred during my employment at EG&G – working again in a company dominated by men – as in the military – and subjected to more unwelcome sexual harassment, though no sexual assault occurred. The associations and similarities are quite clear and certainly enough to trigger the anxiety and arrhythmia I experienced.

Memory has energetic and vibrational components that are multi-dimensional, existing in the human energy field or aura, not just in the body's physiology. Since the atoms, molecules and cells of the body are formed from the universal energy field through the chakra system, then memory is also a component of the auric field and its connection to the unified field of the multiverse. The human body is not a purely physical mechanism that can be tinkered with and altered at whim. It is an energy system, based on an energetic template. It is linked to a larger universal energy field that steps the energy down through multiple dimensions that culminate in, but are not restricted to, the physical body. It is the experiential memory information stored in this field, as well as throughout the body's cells, that can be accessed in hypnosis or through skilled intuitive readings from our current lifetime or even past lives.

Blocking memory in the physiology of the neurons in the brain obstructs only a physical part of an entire energy network of information that constitutes memory. Just as the circuits in a computer electrically access memory stored in a hard drive, neurons and other cells may access memory stored in the auric and unified fields. How? By our consciousness directing through association what we are involved with, day-to-day, moment-to-moment in our lives. The habitual neurological pathways to particular areas of memory can be altered electrically or chemically in a way that may prevent the access to those areas of memory. But the memories of experiences still exist in the mind-body field, or aura, even if the hardware-neurological linkages have been disrupted in some way. And if the memory is retrieved in some other way, i.e., hypnosis, intuitive reading or flashes of insight through direct association that stirs memory through body phenomenon, then new neurological pathways can be built into those areas of field memory. This is true of both individual and universal fields, which are not separate in any case, as shown by the quantum principle of non-local phenomena.

It is entirely possible that everyone has an eidetic, or photographic, memory. It is just that certain people have a better, more holistic way to access it than most. I have come to feel that no experience, no information or knowledge ever conceived of or created is ever lost, even if all physical repositories of knowledge are destroyed. It is just a case of developing the expanded sense perception in such a way that one can retrieve it directly from the unified field.

My conscious awareness expansion began to blossom as fear lost its grip on me. My years of meditation and my training as a body-centered life coach have been very useful in helping me to realize just what I needed to pay attention to that expanded my awareness further. Almost all of it was rooted in the experience of the subtle movements and flows of energy in my body. Learning skills like whole-body perceptive listening and sensing opens up communication on multiple levels and dimensions, as well as with other people. Body sensations, thoughts and images that spring spontaneously to mind, and the emotions they generate are all forms of information and communication between elements of ourselves, such as our higher selves, and the larger universe. These are not arrived at by a logical deductive or inductive mental process, but through the experience of direct perception. Such an experience of direct perception carries its own resonance that can be felt in the body and assessed and discerned by the individual experiencing it.

These paragraphs illustrate a process that has been experiential for me in working with my own memory, aided by knowledge from researchers in consciousness and energy healing.

Healing in general, and healing from trauma and its shackles of fear specifically, frees and empowers us individually. Such healing also permeates the collective human field and subtly raises its vibration. With enough healed, empowered people working from within humanity as a whole, everyone could someday raise their heads and look upon the world around them with more love, more clarity and ever-expanding awareness.

Trauma and Whole Populations

It is extremely likely that the attack on the World Trade Center on September 11, 2001 was a premeditated and deliberately executed mind control trauma on the minds, hearts and emotions of the American people from inside the United States government. A demoralized and grieving nation turned to its government for answers and protection against further attacks. A suspiciously-quick draft containing hundreds of pages of Patriot Act legislation was speedily ready to be presented to Congress. Many congressmen voted it in without even troubling to read it through.

The applied formula for manipulating and controlling populations as stated by David Icke in his books and lectures is one of "problem-reaction-solution." If you and your constituents are in power and you have an agenda of more control, but the freedoms and protections outlined in the U.S. Constitution are getting in your way, then use the formula of problem-reaction-solution. Design the kind of "problem" needed to produce a particular "reaction" in the populace, then present to them your already secretly-conceived and designed "solution." They will almost certainly embrace it and thank you for it, thank you for keeping them "safe."

Unfortunately, the American public was not quite dumbed-down enough to swallow this plot whole. After a stolen election that put the Bush-Cheney administration in the White House, and with many intelligent people watching the towers fall just like controlled demolitions – no plane at all crashing into Building 7 that also fell in the same manner – it did not take long for nagging questions and doubts to creep into the minds of many people. The deterioration of constitutional rights under the Patriot Act further raised suspicions.

The timing of the event was spectacular. It came just after an announcement on 9/10/2011 by Secretary of Defense Donald Rumsfeld that 2.3 trillion dollars could not be accounted for in the Department of Defense budget. The Pentagon was also hit on 9/11 – by "something" – though it remains vague as to what that "something" was. The part of the Pentagon that was destroyed? The part containing the budget records that would have been under investigation to try to discover where the 2.3 trillion dollars might have been "mislaid."

Still, it was an effective way to use the trauma of shock and awe on the American people, on our own soil. An effective way to try and seize control of the huge military arsenal of a world super-power while at the same time trying to silence – and brand as aiding and abetting terrorists – any citizens who might raise public outcry against such a governmental "inside job." But many brave souls raised outcry a-plenty anyway, though their contentions have yet to be officially addressed now, over ten years after 9/11.

This is the very real danger of hiding, as a people and as a nation, behind terminology like "unthinkable" and "unspeakable." This is the risk of blindly accepting what authority figures in high public office tell you to accept. It allows incredible criminal acts to go unchallenged and unpunished. To have the opportunity to strike again or wreak other kinds of havoc.

The only way out of the mass mind control trap is to begin to look, so see, to *question*. "Follow the money" is becoming a cliché of our modern times, but a very apt one. For a powerful lesson in "problem-reaction-solution," including trauma wielded by the powerful for specific purpose, no matter how many innocents it harms, see the movie *V for Vendetta*.

Until we open our eyes as a people and look, see and question, we will remain targets of trauma-based mass mind control by the few and powerful with the resources to deliver their own brands of shock and awe at their discretion.

And they may be continuing to do so for their own purposes. More and more information is coming into the public domain about HAARP as a weather, earthquake and volcano control technology. In light of recent events of earthquakes and intense hurricane and tornado activity, it bears looking at that this technology could be being used to create the shock and awe of natural-seeming disasters. If it comes out that certain "people" under a cloak of secrecy have been creating "natural catastrophes" that are responsible for killing or injuring thousands to millions of people, there may be no hiding place for them.

Forgiveness as Healing

> Forgive others. Forgiveness is the only way to heal your emotional wounds. Forgive those who hurt you no matter what they've done because you don't want to hurt yourself every time you remember what they did. When you can touch a wound and it doesn't hurt, then you know you have truly forgiven.
>
> ~ Don Miguel Ruiz

It might seem like a very strange place to put a section on forgiveness as healing just after a section on trauma perpetrated on individuals and populations. Deliberate and cruelly-inflicted trauma seems to be about the most unforgivable crime on the planet. Yet that is what makes forgiveness so very necessary.

Forgiveness is as much – if not more – about helping ourselves release and transform the past as it is about forgiving the person or persons who have harmed us, whether they did it intentionally or not. It is like draining infection from a wound slowly poisoning us from within so it can heal cleanly. Forgiveness can help bring us peace where there was once the turmoil of hurt, betrayal and rage.

As long as we do not forgive, we remain in an energetic entanglement with those who have hurt us. Anger and pain is periodically re-stimulated and re-justified through remembrance. Justifiable anger is some of the hardest to let go of as there is a clear reason for it. The anger is valid regarding how we were violated. We know we were clearly harmed. Depending on how badly we were harmed, we can even justify never forgiving.

Yet, if we never forgive, we condemn ourselves to a lifetime of entanglement with the offender. The malignancy of the animosity and bitterness we carry around inside toward them continues to fester. Even worse, if someone new shows up in our present who reminds us of the past offender in some way, in action or demeanor, we often mentally and emotionally time-warp into our past, reacting sharply to the new person from the old wounds, even though the new person may actually have done very little to deserve such a reaction.

When we forgive, we also open a space for change and transformation in the person being forgiven. If they are no longer in an energy entanglement with us, then they could be presented with an opportunity to gaze more honestly upon themselves. A possibility for change could open up in them.

I find forgiveness to be an ongoing process. It is not something I can say I've done and am finished with. I forgive my parents for their human failings and the ways they affected me. But today, years later, I still find ways in which their dysfunctional upbringing affects me. So, like that metaphor of peeling away the layers of an onion in our process of healing, each layer making way for a deeper one, I find I must recognize the deeper levels in which the problems within my family impacted my life and forgive again, and yet again. And forgive myself for not seeing the deeper patterns earlier.

This is also true of the trauma I experienced while in the military. I sometimes still experience an inner shudder at a new piece of connecting information or testimony from another that directly touches my experiences – that old sinking-in-quicksand or someone-walking-over-my grave feeling still rumbles up from the depths.

Forgiving those who abused me while I was in the Air Force is ongoing. I feel an increasing level of peace around those experiences, yet sometimes I am still triggered by them. I still feel frustrated about all kinds of abuse caused by secrecy that still is going on in our world. I feel angered that abuse of others, of whole populations, still goes on. Does this mean I still have more forgiveness to do? Of course it does. It may be a lifelong process and I've come to accept that – and that it is also very necessary. Those who hurt me are responsible for what they have done, and in the fullness of time, they won't escape that responsibility. But it is also my responsibility – the responsibility of any who are injured or abused in any ways – to do all I can to heal and take care of my well-being in as many ways as I can. That includes forgiveness as a path to inner peace.

On a more positive side, I do try to take the abundant energy that anger provides and channel it productively into actions I can do to make a difference in this world. There is a difference in the energy of anger wielded in a mindful manner and rage that is destructive and out of control. In my recent studies about links between bodily pain and repressed rage, I'm learning that living in this world with all its problems and pressures on individuals – from day-to-day living to coping with global issues of politics, environment and economy – create inner rage, all the more potent when people don't know how to strike back or at whom. If we are nice loving spiritual people, we find that rage intolerable and psychically stuff it somewhere. It winds up lodged in our body as an energy block. Then it causes us other problems, usually with our health. The ways in which we have been hurt and betrayed by people often winds little vine-like tendrils throughout various areas of our life, like an insidious creeping vine. If we undertake the process of forgiveness with a willingness to discover and forgive each time we find a tendril of anger or rage that affects a particular part of our lives, we are doing well. We can release ourselves from any pressure to get all forgiveness over and done with in one fell swoop. We come to a place of peace, knowing we have the strength of heart to look, to see, to forgive and to release at each new discovery. Each time, whether we see the results or not, we can rest in knowing we have introduced a new, more loving energy into the world. It is best to cultivate a peaceful allowing of all our feelings. We can use the energies they provide to us mindfully, guided by our hearts.

As much as possible, forgive consciously with the other person involved. If living, you may, or may not, get an acknowledging response from the other person. But don't let your forgiveness become conditional on whether the other person accepts or rejects it. Create what closure you can for yourself. Remember it's even more for yourself than for them. They may just need a span of time with the new energy you've initiated. If they were psychopaths, they may never come around, but it's we, the traumatized, that need the closure and peace. We also need to remember to forgive ourselves for our own thoughtlessness and dysfunctions that have affected others. Understanding and love apply to ourselves as much to others. The light of understanding what we have done and why is a gift that invites transformation in ourselves. Insight without mindful, heart-centered action renders any real learning null and void. If you don't learn from your mistakes, you waste them. Later on bigger lesson-hammers may show up to command your attention.

I think we are seeing such lesson-hammers on a collective human level now with the huge tangle of problems woven throughout our world coming home to roost. While I hold the shadow governments of the world accountable for their wrongdoing, we as collective humanity must also hold ourselves accountable; for our complacency, our desire to be led and taken care of, our lack of responsibility to learn, question, investigate – to know what is really going on in our world so we can truly exercise our free will. It is like we handed our leaders absolute power in our desire for them to take care of us, and that absolute power corrupted absolutely. Now we must take back that power – and freedom and responsibility – and they do not want to surrender it. The one thing we can do is question, investigate and learn... seek the truth always. And forgive both them and ourselves as we heal and our capacity to forgive expands.

***

It's said that the Truth will set you free, but that's only the beginning.

If we think of truth as a sword with two edges, freedom and responsibility, the symbolism also shows these two attributes to be inseparable. No one can have complete freedom without also taking complete conscious and co-creative responsibility. Through conscious commitment, the quantum wave will manifest into form from our loving and mindful actions. Individual and collective choice through action will create the world we desire to live in. Once we have truth, freedom and responsibility are in our hands. This is true for our individual selves in healing from dis-ease, and from hurt, pain and trauma. It can also be true in healing human systems of governance, commerce and the Earth's ecosystem.

We can become truly sentient as a species. Do we have the love and courage in our hearts and minds to choose our values and convictions and live from them, even if some government agency says we can't?

This is the real challenge. One that can further force the huge shadow spider into the light that can kill it once and for all. We reclaim the freedom that is ours by virtue of our very existence. From that freedom, we do as we see fit in caring for ourselves and our planet. We force the shadow spider into the light where it must take overt and drastic action, rather than all its hidden, covert ways of undermining freedom, health and well-being, from individuals to entire living systems. Then everyone can see it for what it is.

The shadow spider won't survive such exposure. It might take some with it as it goes down. But if it did not have a secret knowledge, entangled with shame, that what it is doing is wrong, it would not do its work in secret, from the shadows. If its purpose was not to steal energy from living beings, it could have, and would have wiped all life that got in its way out of existence. This huge spider – the shadow government-military-corporate complex – has the means to do this. If it has not done so by now, then we must look at the other reasons it doesn't obliterate all people or life from the face of the planet. I intuit that they want or need a subordinate population. Parasites are dependent on a host organism to feed upon. The various programs from chemtrails and control of food and water supplies to the eugenics programs shown in the film *Thrive: What On Earth Will It Take?* are chilling to contemplate – a culling of the human herd to what the .001% elites consider a "manageable" number – small enough so as not to be a threat to them, but large enough to be a sufficient host to feed upon.

Claiming freedom and exercising conscious choice is where the rubber meets the road. And where the path forks in at least two directions.

One direction leads to a world of so much manipulation, monitoring and control as to create the living hell of an Orwellian *1984* reality, or a religious right's nightmare society similar to the one described in Margaret Atwood's 1985 book, *The Handmaid's Tale.*

The other path leads to our full expression of freedom, choice, and the ability to heal our world and each other. We do not have to mount a civil war. Just claim the freedom to care for ourselves, create sustainable communities, grow our gardens and honor all life. If that brings us into conflict with governments or corporations, then men like Mahatma Gandhi showed us the way – peaceful, non-violent resistance. It must be well-planned and very, very public. The more people see and understand, the more they will awaken and join in.

And there is deep, multi-dimensional healing to be found in Truth.

One of the most important parts of my story is about the personal empowerment we gain by facing our fears and moving through them. Freeing ourselves from any grip fear has on us can allow our consciousness to expand in ways that have the capacity to transform this planet. The essential flow of energy in the Universe in and through us – wonderfully-symbolized by the torus shown in *Thrive* – is always seeking wholeness, unity, balance and harmony – from the individual to the whole human collective. Obstacles to this flow of energy – trauma, abuse, and hurt – will also create the synchronicities in our lives – encounters with people, places and circumstances – to lead us to healing and wholeness.

Whether as a single person or an entire species, to heal is to restore the free flow of energy, creating beauty, balance and harmony through conscious unity with the Living, Loving Universe Itself.

Chapter 25: Spiritual Evolution Through the The Quantum Mirror

And is it not a dream which none of you remember having dreamt, that builded your city and fashioned all there is in it?

~ Khalil Gibran, *The Prophet*

Is it a dream that none of us remember having dreamt that created our world? And was it the now-unconscious desire of all of us to experience the limiting belief structures of this planet and dimension to teach us about breaking through them, about reaching for the stars? To reach within ourselves and discover the true nature of consciousness and energy, thought and matter?

The collective unconscious holds us in a powerful trance to participate in this reality. But throughout our lives, like little diamonds glittering along our path, are also the hints of something beyond, if we tune in and pay attention. We gather these little diamonds of insight, of synchronicity, until they begin to form an image of what lies beyond. They begin to apply pressure to the belief systems that keep us locked in this 3rd dimension of Holodeck Earth.

Manifestation is a function of desire, attention, intention and belief. It involves changing the internal belief structures in our minds to believe in the desired state of being. So while we are able to desire, dream, set intentions and place our attention on what we want to manifest, the toughest part of this equation is supplying the necessary belief. We can believe, work to convince ourselves with our conscious minds, but if the powerful subconscious does not respond and fall in line with the conscious mind, little to nothing happens.

Perhaps it is a necessary function of the collective unconscious and superconscious mind to create Holodeck Earth for our own individual and collective souls' growth. Is this a creation of just we human beings, or does the consciousness of all life contribute to the collective dream? Indigenous people of the Earth consider all parts of creation to have a living spirit. So consciousness inherent in every part of our world – animal, plant and mineral – may also enrich the vision of reality we see around us each day. It may also play a role in how life and events unfold on our world.

What forms of life, especially intelligent life, dwell out in the stars? How might their consciousness contribute to what we experience here? The existence of other intelligent life out in the Universe would certainly be part of the whole field of consciousness of the cosmos. While their existence or influence is not yet openly acknowledged here on Earth, that does not mean that extraterrestrial consciousness is not affecting us, our reality, or what happens on our world.

Is Our Ability to Manifest through Consciousness in a Maturation Process?

We play at directing our thoughts and our consciousness as we awaken by learning to manifest in a trial-and-error manner. For those of us with a strong desire to manifest wealth, we manage to achieve it with our own formulas for changing beliefs and applying the necessary intention and attention. Or we create healing, relationships, or other things that we desire. But this type of manifestation-play may simply be a maturation process of the human species re-discovering a new ability of consciousness and experimenting with it in the delight of that discovery.

Experiments by Dr. Dean Radin show that the collective human consciousness may exert a powerful influence over each individual within the collective. People working in groups are evidence of this, in the groups of meditators who bring down crime levels in cities, in mastermind manifestation groups, or groups like Intenders of the Highest Good.[1]

The essence of a spiritual path is to know one's self deeply and completely. Individuals have achieved this here and there down through the ages on Earth. Spiritual adepts, gurus and saints, no longer bound by the collective belief systems that keep us in limitation, are able to do all manner of seemingly miraculous things. Such abilities flow from the absolute, experiential knowledge of the Unity of Everything in the entire Living Universe and the ability to apply this knowledge in a practical manner. As scientists in quantum mechanics have discovered, everything is fundamentally interconnected, and fluidly responsive to thought and belief. Non-local phenomena observed in quantum labs show us these properties when an apparently separate particle in a distant container "magically" responds to what is being done to its fellow particle in another location. When we observe reality, it arranges itself according to what we expect to see, what we believe in. When we are not observing it, it exists as a quantum wave of possibility. Every possible reality, every possible alternative exists in superposition within the wave. It requires an observing consciousness – or collective consciousness – for this wave to arrange itself into the reality we see and experience all around us.

Where could this ability to manifest truly take us if we harnessed the energy of our consciousness as a collective? What could happen when humanity grows up, harnessing this collective energy of desire, attention, and intention? When

---

[1] Intenders of the Highest Good offers a structure and group direction, inspiration and intention for those desiring positive changes of all kinds in their lives, and for the whole planet and all people as well. Website: http://www.intenders.com.

we begin to apply powerful new knowledge gained from our journey through this reality? A new world could be birthed.

What kind of world could we envision and bring into form? Can we give up our belief in and attachment to the old forms? Some of us become quite adept at manifesting within the structures of the existing paradigms. What about creating an entire new order of things? Could those who have been successful at manifesting great wealth, even in enlightened ways, release operating within a currency paradigm to embrace a new order of life on Planet Earth where money is no longer necessary?

Could we be seeing a deconstruction of old paradigms all around us today? Could the very chaos swirling around us be evidence of old belief structures breaking down? If so, then the time is ripe for us to collectively dream into being a new paradigm, one that we design and choose with our hearts; new structures of thought and energy, more fluid, more responsive to the entire field of aware, integrated and unified consciousness – and far less compartmentalized into the conscious, subconscious and super-conscious realms of mind.

How do wizards or magicians fight a foe, or each other? Whomever resolutely maintains the strongest vision of what they want to happen, prevails. Illusions and psycho-kinesthetic tricks are attempts to distract and undermine the strength of vision in one's opponent. Much like the continual spin broadcasting across the various forms of media, directed by those desperate to remain in control. As in the film *The Matrix*, we are the ones powering our own "virtual" or thought-belief-emotion created reality. To understand the allegory further, replace the cables attached to the human body in *The Matrix* with the multi-sensory input of mainstream television, radio, newspapers and magazines. Are we now participating in and witnessing our own collective process of awakening, of the human collective achieving at least a first-stage enlightenment that will create a new Earth? Will those of us who successfully navigate our awakening find ourselves living on a healed and restored Terra?

And will those of us who do not, who cannot, break the hold fear and anger has on us continue to live out our lives on a sick planet with a failing ecosystem, and an ever-more fascist and controlling governing body?

Will reality itself split into two or more superpositioned versions guided by the consciousness, intention and belief of differing groups? Only the time we are now passing through will tell for sure.

What is a Quantum Mirror?

Aware or unaware, we are all conducting experiments in consciousness in the laboratories of ourselves, all the time.

~ Niara Terela Isley

If everything we see around us is a reality generated by the collective human consciousness, largely at the unconscious level, then what we see reflected in reality all around us can be a marvelous feedback device, once we accept responsibility for our role in its creation. The holographic nature of the Universe, each part containing the whole as much as the whole containing every part, instructs us in the principles of as above, so below – an entire energy spectrum flowing endlessly between microcosm and macrocosm, throughout all dimensions. Ever-expanding fractal iterations abound all around us, kindred, yet unique through the countless facets of consciousness and their expression.

We as individuals can create ripples of shift and change in our personal paradigms according to the strength of our own beliefs and our faith in our ability to shift reality in ways specific to ourselves. However, we still all wake up to the same world of earth and sky, cities or landscapes, trees, plants, animals – all the things that make up reality here for all of us, including our current environmental, social and political challenges. These are part of the reality paradigm of the collective human reality, or quantum mirror, on Planet Earth.

Individually and collectively, consciously and unconsciously, the world we see around us is an accurate representation of what we hold in our consciousness – every part and parcel of it – containing all we love, all we hate and everything inbetween. The parts we love, that bring us joy, usually reflect what we are conscious of. What we fear, hate and revile are those parts we have disowned. They lurk in the subconscious of the individual, in the unconscious of the entire collective. Such parts still manifest from those realms of the human shadow, mirroring to our conscious minds our more challenging collective selves.

And we can only work on shifting such a collectively-generated paradigm in the solitude of our own individual human hearts and minds. Only by shifting ourselves and our own perspectives, intentions and beliefs – only by being the change we wish to see in the world – can we hope to reach out to the people around us. Yet, by shifting ourselves individually, we strengthen the whole human morphic field[2] for true change. The morphic field is created by all human beings, and I would extend that to include all life, even that which many think to be inanimate and lifeless. Each human being has an energy field, an aura that extends out touching and interacting with all other life. This creates the morphic field, and is also a contributing basis for Jung's theory of the collective unconscious. The morphic field also relates to Teilhard De Chardin's "noosphere," a postulated stage or "sphere" of evolutionary process delineated by consciousness, mind, and interpersonal relationships.

The more individuals that join this field in kindred thought, desire and intention, the closer it moves into "morphic resonance." Rather than a chaotic

[2] Morphic field and morphic resonance are concepts devised by Rupert Sheldrake, English biochemist and was a former natural sciences research fellow at Cambridge University. He has authored such books as *Seven Experiments that Could Change the World* and *Dogs That Know When Their Owners are Coming Home*. His website can be found at: www.sheldrake.org.

cacophony of energetic noise, people pick up the sympathetic vibration of those around them through attraction to similar hearts and minds, embracing similar values and principles. Morphic resonance is a stabilization of the morphic field, birthing an actual state of consciousness and knowledge far easier for more and more people to tune into.

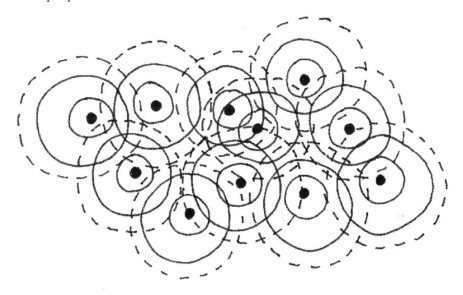

Black dots represent people as viewed from above;
circles represent their auric fields touching and interacting;
dotted circles represent the auric fields extending out to infinity

As individuals join in a field of endeavor to consciously shift the world in a positive direction, each individual contributes to reaching a collective critical mass of awakening consciousness. Once the tipping point is reached, morphic resonance in the consciousness field could be the process that takes over, cascading our world's reality into a new, visionary direction – if we can all become the shamans, wizards and enchantresses who have the strength to hold that vision truly and steadfastly. Holding that vision with heart, strength and determination will be essential as our collective shadow writhes, flails and strikes out on its way to conscious integration.

Using the Quantum Mirror: The Microcosm of the Individual

Change begins as a seed in each individual's heart, mind and soul. In using the principle of a quantum mirror as a teacher about what we carry inside of us, we need to look at what is occurring in our own lives, and especially the recurring themes that run through them. It is as though the very lessons we most need to learn are coded within each of us at the moment of our birth. If at first we don't get the lesson, it is repeated, giving us as many opportunities to learn and move beyond the lesson as we need. The lesson can become magnified as it repeats, our superconscious mind in concert with the Conscious Living Universe hoping that perhaps *this time*, we will not fail to grasp the lesson, and make the necessary changes to our consciousness and how we walk through our lives.

I cannot tell how many times, throughout my life, I have had to repeat "lessons" until I opened to finding a deeper inner path and mentors who provided the keys to understanding my deeper self. The moments of revelation where I could see and understand in the deep cellular knowing of my body were each opportunities to make new and different choices. In those moments, inspired by those insights, I did my best to make the choices that would alter my outcomes; changing the people, places and circumstances I was attracting, allowing me to live in the world in a new way. Yet I found that old habits die hard, even in the face of insight and inspiration. Even armed with powerful new understandings, I have found myself falling into old patterns in clever new ways, time after time in my life. It takes commitment and practice to make true changes permanent.

I am grateful for the words of the mystic poet Jalaladdin Rumi:

> Come, come, whoever you are.
> Wanderer, worshipper, lover of living, it doesn't matter,
> Ours is not a caravan of despair.
> Come even if you have broken your vow a thousand times,
> Come, yet again, come, come.

I am one of countless people in this world, people doing their best, their best varying with circumstances of the moment. Yet as long as I aspire to express the very best that is in me, even when I fall down, I can always return to the principles I aspire to. I can make fresh attempts to meet the world reflected around me in new ways that can create shift and change.

We are a process, a work of art in creation by our own hands. When we, through action or inaction, repeat a "mistake," it is best to allow all the feelings about it to unwind while we, as our own inner witness, take a step back and observe this process of unwinding, watching for the moment when we can release and let go. Sometimes we stubbornly hang on to our pain, justifying it, reinforcing it over time. Then it can become habitual and chronic, and as such, even harder to break out of, but not impossible. This is when the Universe appears to get the "bigger hammer" necessary to get our attention, and give us yet another opportunity for fresh insights and new, changed actions.

Such insights must be followed immediately by new actions to anchor and make real the changes in consciousness. If not, insights become a less-than-halfway measure; a seed planted, sprouted, then withering on the soil of old entrenched chronic ways of thinking and behaving.

Each of us as individuals can change only our own consciousness. How we choose to undertake our individual life journey is the only thing within our control. When we do so consciously, we are choosing to look at what "is" and meet it anchored in our chosen purpose in life, the calling of our heart and spirit. If we are unconscious, we are tossed around by the events unfolding around us in a way that feels random and accidental. We feel like victims.

All of us have times when we fall asleep at the wheel of our lives. We find ourselves feeling at the mercy of situations unfolding around us. We fall into feeling a victim of various people, places and situations. If we can turn the pain of feeling victimized into a call to wake back up and take up the reins of our lives again, then you snatch success from the jaws of defeat.

It can be exhilarating to have such an awakening, and we like to share it with the world. However, the best way to inspire others to join in the conscious co-creation of the reality we all share is by loving example. When you have a lapse that brings you a new lesson or, more difficult, comes up to reinforce an earlier lesson, own it. Look at the new or old place where you stumbled into the same circumstance again. Do your course corrections. And know that there are no mistakes, not really. Our deepest and oldest patterns are the ones that bring us the oft-repeated opportunities to examine them, from a multitude of vantage points.

The quantum mirror of the reality we create around ourselves, reflecting both our conscious and unconscious material, has much to teach us, individually and collectively, if we can learn to pay attention. If we can learn to grasp the lessons, even when the unconscious material we are shown is absolutely unpalatable to us, we stand the best chance to shift future outcomes through our insights, our deepened understandings, then choosing new directions and new actions.

The Macrocosmic Quantum Mirror of the Human Collective

Like cells in an individual human body being restored to health one by one, each having a healing effect on the cells around it, when we awaken our consciousness and express the best we are capable of we can stir the awakening of those around us through our example. Just as we experience and follow that still, small voice of our own inner guidance to learn, to expand, to evolve into the next best version of ourselves moment by moment, our energy in the human collective also joins with others who are actively evolving. We become the still, small, but growing voice of the larger human collective self.

Scientific research has recently produced models that illustrate how a tipping point is reached in human consensus beliefs and opinions. A minority holding a particular viewpoint, coming to consensus in 10% of a population, can rapidly spread that viewpoint to the remaining 90%. This model runs parallel to Sheldrake's theories of morphic resonance, adding a more material, structured concept to the body of ideas on fields of energy, consciousness and thought.

Those who do not respond to compassionate, evolving example, but seem to go the other way, are experiencing the opposite polarization of our current chaotic times. If the world is shifting dimensionally, there are some who, through their own free will, may choose to hang onto fear and anger. This choice is generally not conscious. It can be experienced as a default, hidden choice for those who don't undertake their own evolutionary process. Living out their lives at the effect of things they see transpiring around them, unaware of the concept that their own unconscious material is mirroring to them what they could be learning about themselves, they feel out of control, disempowered. They are unable to believe they are more than helpless pawns in the grip of external forces larger than themselves. Because they believe this, they make it true for themselves.

One of the persistent images my guides seemed to place in my mind for a time, was the vision of cell mitosis, or division. Under a high-powered microscope, observing a cell about to divide, the chromosomes in the cell containing the genes become active and visible. The chromosomes replicate, then polarize, one group being pulled in one direction, the other group pulled in the opposite direction. The process looks chaotic, yet a new order and stasis of the two daughter cells emerges from that chaos.

Since microcosmic and macrocosmic processes tend to holographically mirror each other, the analogy as I understood it is that we are undergoing this process on a global, human collective level. This includes the polarization. Our human societies are becoming very polarized. Those of us who are expanding our consciousness and evolving would love to see all humanity join us in that evolutionary leap. Perhaps with enough morphic resonance throughout the human collective, this can be achieved. Otherwise individual people's free will, exercised however unconsciously, may take them in a different direction.

Tuning Our Personal Radar

Since my time in the Air Force, I find myself using radar metaphors for how I look at life. Radars were used to look at the sky in a particular way, looking for certain kinds of aircraft, then identifying it as friend or foe. There are radars that look at the weather, those that can get you a speeding ticket, and still more varieties.

I have found that when I have a set of beliefs about the world, people, 2012, anything at all, I unconsciously set my personal radar to pick up from my environment only those things that can be interpreted in such a way as to confirm my belief set.

I've had to consciously widen my personal radar parameters to a much larger scale. I know it is vital to take in the beauty and wonder around me in this world to balance all the chaos and the suffering. Not hide from the chaos, but balance it – with the places where I can rest in peace and serenity, most often in silent communion with nature.

Is your personal radar stuck on selectivity of only negative events that fulfill your current belief systems? Or is it seeing a more balanced picture?

Facing what is going on in our world today is a first and necessary step to changing it. It can be seen as a collective creation, from humanity's collective and disowned shadow. However, don't get caught in a vortex of negativity with it all. Calmly look at it as a mirror of something you may still hold within at some level. Don't over-analyze either, scouring your psyche for where the specific "dark seed" could be hiding. Reflect on what it could be if necessary, to satisfy your analytical mind's need to work on the problem without allowing analysis to become a frantic dig through your psyche. This is one more trap of the mind that always leads back into fear. Whatever shadows may be in there, they don't need to be exorcised. They need to be lovingly integrated into the whole of who you are.

Simply accept that what is before you has something to teach you. Acknowledge that perhaps some part of you contributed to the current collective maelstrom from an unknown place deep inside, and now choose to send that part loving acceptance. Know that the loving acceptance will alchemically transmute whatever it is into integrated wholeness. Return your attention to what you love and what you consciously intend. If you are walking a consciously spiritual path in life, your share in the collective shadows of humanity are likely already in a process of transmutation. The only thing you may need to do is to bring more conscious awareness to the process.

Cultivating calm grows out of the acceptance of all the possibilities of what "could" happen. Make peace with your own mortality. Inner calm is necessary for insight, inspiration and intuition to enter into us. In calmly facing what is, we can consider how we would like our reality to be. We build the new, desired reality there in our imagination. We hold the desired reality in our consciousness. Then we ask ourselves what mindful, positive, well-considered action we can take to begin to shift into it. Positive action is a demonstration to our powerful subconscious of our consciously changing beliefs. This is similar to the old saying of, "Put your money where your mouth is."

Keep your personal radar consciously and positively tuned. We can all become the eye of the hurricane, that calm and beautiful center at the heart of a ferocious storm. When enough of us become such "eyes," what will be left of the hurricane?

Chapter 26: The Many Facets of Extraterrestrial Contact

… the truth apparently is simply this; that we're not alone, we've never been alone. We are apparently part of an infinite universe filled with intelligent life. I find that exciting. That doesn't frighten me. If they were malevolent or hostile, they could have taken this planet and cleaned it up, eliminated us, turned us into dog food or whatever, a long, long time ago. … the historical evidence indicates that they've been with us a long time… I believe that this reality, once we have accepted it – and understood it – and gone beyond the fear, will bring about an expansion of consciousness in the human race that will truly help us and prepare us to go out there and take our rightful place in that infinite community of life.

~ Retired Sergeant Major Robert O. Dean

Robert O. Dean held a cosmic top secret security clearance while serving in the U.S. Army, still the highest security classification known. Such a security classification was required to work at SHAPE (Supreme Headquarters Allied Powers, Europe) headquarters as part of NATO (North Atlantic Treaty Association). While working in SHOC (Supreme Headquarters Operation Center) in the war room, he read a report called *An Assessment*, published in 1964. It was a study the military had done on extraterrestrials visiting Earth, reported to be about twelve inches thick.

This study was initiated because of a 1961 UFO incident that could have started a nuclear war between the United States and the former Soviet Union. Three UFOs were tracked on radar appearing to come out of Soviet airspace. Fortunately, reason prevailed over paranoia and it was determined that they were true unidentified flying objects and were not of Soviet origin. To prevent such an incident from occurring again, the study that culminated in *An Assessment* was done.

Four groups of extraterrestrials were identified in that report, including a group that looked so much like human beings as to be nearly indistinguishable from us. Other types were added in the following years. Retired Army sergeant Clifford Stone – a UFO crash retrieval specialist – reported at the May 2001

Disclosure Project event at the National Press Club in Washington D.C. that fifty-seven varieties of extraterrestrials had been cataloged by the military by 1989. It is fascinating to note the number of different types of ETs spoken of by Stone, and then compare that figure with information from a completely different source – experiencers of extraterrestrial contact. The drawings of different types of ETs done by experiencers easily encompass and perhaps surpass that number. Even accounting for differences of age and genetic type within species that we see right here with humanity and other life forms on Earth, it would seem that our "visitors" are of many different species and types within species.

Holistic UFOlogy, Holistic Exopolitics

One of my primary ways to look at this vast topic of the UFO and ET phenomenon is to examine similarities of information, common threads from many differing and often widely divergent sources. I would call this a holistic approach, where no part of the phenomenon is disregarded for any reason and all information is comparatively laid out and correlations sought out or ruled out between all varieties of data.

I am continually astonished, and disappointed, at why there is not a huge annual summit where researchers of all kinds – suspending any judgments or criticisms of each others' work for the duration of such a summit – do not sit down and compare notes on their past and current findings. But in this very complex field of ufology, there are many niches. There are researchers who focus primarily on the government-military cover-up, gleaning what pieces of information they can pry out of secret places, including interviewing whistleblowers who come forward. There are researchers who focus on crop circles. There are researchers who focus on experiencers of extraterrestrial contact of one form or another. Many need hypnosis to recover memories, prompted by "missing time" or strange marks that appear on their bodies, but there is also a significant portion of those who remember experiences without hypnosis as well. The high similarity of their experiences to those who need hypnosis for recall provides a necessary counterpoint to critics of hypnosis. There are niches within the niches as well. Some researchers within their own niches don't want to approach or acknowledge the other branches of study within the UFO/ET phenomenon.

Ufology has spawned another discipline of study, called exopolitics. The following is a definition of exopolitics:

> Exopolitics is an interdisciplinary scientific field, with its roots in the political sciences , that focuses on research, education and public policy with regard to the individuals, institutions and processes, associated with extraterrestrial life, as well as the wide range of implications this entails through public advocacy and newly emerging paradigms.[1]

434

Since exopolitical proponents feel that extraterrestrial reality is well-established from the huge volumes of data gathered in all niches of research, they wish to next examine the more interesting sets of political, social and philosophical questions of extraterrestrial contact.

Add to this diverse mix all the players and personalities within these fields, including their social and/or religious conditioning and how aware or not they may be of it. How does it affect their beliefs, opinions, judgments and mindsets? Ufology can look like an overwhelming and confusing morass of juxtaposing information laced with personal, societal and cultural biases. There are evangelicals within the UFO field, vehemently insisting that they, or the person they revere, have the one and only true story of what is happening on Earth between humans and ETs. I have observed people within ufology and exopolitics ridicule and debunk each other, using the same tactics they decry in how the mainsteam media and traditional scientific communities debunk them. At times there seems no capacity to simply agree to disagree and acknowledge a different viewpoint in an amicable or dispassionate manner. The real truth, and the messages for humanity it contains, can get lost in personalities, egos and disagreements. It's enough to send any beginner trying to understand the human dramas and complexities that weave through the phenomenon back into denial, refusing to look at what is really there.

Yet the complexities of this tangle must be approached and unraveled when faced with one of the most profound realities of human history. Even more profound in its implications is how it will impact humanity, how it will affect who we are, who we have thought ourselves to be, and our true history and heritage on this planet. It is going to take a very broad, multidisciplinary approach to look at all the data available and theorize in an intelligent and comprehensive way what might be going on. Military personnel trained for threat assessment cannot be allowed to dominate such postulations. They should have a voice at such a gathering, but it must be tempered with other knowledge, philosophies and worldviews.

Extraterrestrials are real. They are here, and have been here for a very, very long time. Trying to achieve a rudimentary understanding of what is going on requires at least a look at the entire scope of the phenomenon. The full spectrum encompasses the government-military-corporate cover-up around UFOs and ETs, from how it occurred and where it has taken us as a society, to looking at the profoundly consciousness-altering implications of what contact with telepathic extraterrestrial beings of vastly different cultures might mean: beings with a mastery of the quantum sciences and both a spiritual and practical working understanding of the interconnectedness of everything, beings who can travel the vast parsecs of space through other dimensions at the speed of light, by folding space or even through a shift of consciousness, moving from

[1] This definition of exopolitics was arrived at through a consensus collaboration of members of the Exopolitics Institute founded by Dr. Michael Salla. The definition of exopolitics will continue to evolve as new aspects of the UFO and extraterrestrial phenomenon emerge, especially actual open, public contact some day. For more on exopolitics, see website: http://exopoliticsinstitute.org/?page_id=1043.

one physical location to another.

Cover-up research has indicated that covert contact has already taken place between military and government officials and a particular group of ETs well back in the last century. There are reports that a deal was cut involving getting advanced technology from that group of ETs – in exchange for permission granted to those same ETs to run a limited abduction program among humans. William Cooper's book, *Behold A Pale Horse* goes into this, as well as a more recent book by Dr. Michael Salla,[2] *Exposing U.S. Government Policies in Extraterrestrial Life: The Challenge of Exopolitics*. More recently, retiring New Hampshire state representative Henry W. McElroy[3] stated in a video released online in 2010 that he knew former President Eisenhower was briefed on extraterrestrials and that he also saw a document referring to Eisenhower's opportunity to meet these off-world "visitors." In McElroy's blog online, he also concedes:

> All in all, after much consideration, I have to concede that this theory, that the human race was created by another race of individuals who were much more advanced than our own, is quite probable.

Because the subject of this contact event – or events – has already been extensively written about and testified to concerning meetings between government and military officials and extraterrestrials, I will not reiterate it here. I will only say that it bears paying attention to, along with considering all other data available, cross-checking and referencing across all the related fields touching upon ufology and exopolitics.

Sanctioned by the Pope, the Catholic Church has admitted that extraterrestrials could exist, that they would be our brothers, and perhaps even without original sin. The Catholic Church is a very powerful ecclesiastical force in the world and has been so for centuries. That includes the power to be included in the councils of government secrets. In the event of open contact, I am sure that they do not want to "lose face," or their considerable power, in the eyes of their billions of followers. They can read the writing on the wall, and understand that the next major players on Earth may be extraterrestrials in an open, public contact event.

With the reality of extraterrestrials becoming harder and harder to ignore and deny, someday, perhaps soon, open public contact is going to happen. This is not a question of "if" but of "when." Humanity must prepare itself for this day, and begin to face the overwhelming amount of evidence before us of the extraterrestrial reality engaging Earth.

The sheer scope of excellent documentation and information necessary to

---

[2] Dr. Michael Salla's book *Exposing U.S. Government Policies on Extraterrestrial Life: The Challenge of Exopolitics* researches an alleged meeting between government officials, including former President Dwight Eisenhower and extraterrestrials.

[3] Retired New Hampshire state representative Henry W. McElroy also placed his statements on President Eisenhower and his meeting with extraterrestrials on his personal blog online here: http://henrymcelroy.wordpress.com/.

begin understanding the various aspects of the extraterrestrial phenomenon could fill a huge library, and therefore is beyond any realistic scope of this book. But I can touch on the various aspects of this subject as I have come to understand it and perhaps inspire readers to look deeper on their own.

Extraterrestrial Contact in the Past: Prehistory and Antiquity

Extraterrestrials may have once walked more openly among the earlier people of Earth. This has sparked my curiosity since my father handed me Erich Von Daniken's book, *Chariots of the Gods*. Also available on this subject is the program series *Ancient Aliens*, one of the History Channel's most popular programs.

There is a wealth of evidence in archeological records that defies placement into traditional theories of evolution and ancient civilizations. Non-traditional archeologist Michael Cremo discovered human footprints next to those of dinosaurs in the mud of the ancient past, metamorphosed into solid rock – very difficult evidence to "erase." There's the riddle of how early geographer and cartographer Piri Reis managed to come by such an amazingly accurate map of the western coastline of Africa, the eastern coastline of South America, and the northern coastline of Antarctica in 1513. Antarctica was ice-locked in 1513 as it is today. So how did Reis obtain such a map, when the last researched time that Antarctica was not covered in ice is estimated to be between 13,000 to 6,000 years *before Jesus Christ,* (B.C.)? Christ's birth and life mark the zero point from which time is measured forwards and backwards on our current calendar. No currently recorded ancient human civilization had the technology, that we know of, to create such an accurate map. Could it have been created by extraterrestrials and given to human beings? There are the plains of Nazca in southern Peru, with their huge etchings in the flat stony ground of a humanoid figure, various birds, a monkey and other glyphs. They have been dated from 300 B.C. to 700 A.D. Viewed from the ground, they look like sets of lines with no particular form or purpose. It is only when they are viewed from the air that their true forms are revealed. Yet where were the flying vehicles to view them at the dates they are estimated to have been created?

There are volumes of data now questioning the construction method of Great Pyramid at Giza, in Egypt. It is specious to consider that it was built by slaves over the incredible amount of time, decades, if not hundreds of years, it would have taken to align the structure with true north, and then to quarry the stone, transport it and build the pyramid by the means proposed by traditional thinkers. How might it truly have been built?

Such data is confusing, considering current popular theories of ancient human cultures and civilizations. What do we do with it? Where do we place it in our intellect? The very existence of these strange artifacts begs more investigation and research precisely because of the questions they raise. Yet often such evidence is filed under "Anomalies" – those troubling items that stand outside the neatly-packaged postulations into which most "accepted" evidence in the ancient or prehistoric record is placed. There these anomalies sit, ignored by mainstream science as contradictions to their pet theories.

How much ancient knowledge vital to understanding our past and mapping our future was lost in the burning of the great library at Alexandria so long ago? And how much easier it has been in the following centuries to keep humanity ignorant of its true origins by those who hold the power and control over true history and knowledge?

There is now so much in prehistoric and archeological artifacts and evidence to cast doubt on popular theories of the origins and evolution of humanity that it has moved beyond the scope of control of those who would like to destroy or hide all such information. Instead they dumb down the human population with substandard education, religious indoctrination, drugs, unhealthy food and water, and a continual stream of media propaganda and distraction to keep people from truly "seeing" and questioning.

Add to such "anomalies" the information channeled through Edgar Cayce on Atlantis, and thousands, if not millions of people around the world having conscious recall at this time – so very much of it eerily similar – about lifetimes in Atlantis and Lemuria. If human collective memory is as associative as individual human memory is; and if a great energetic record of all human memory, both individual and collective, does exist as akashic or soul records that are energetically accessible; and if this particular time in human history is so similar to the state of Atlantis just before its destruction – then the recall of so many people today of Atlantean lifetimes could be being sparked by the relationship of circumstances of "then" to "now." Are such "memories" emerging to guide the remembering souls through current chaotic times? Are they coming to light in these latter days in time to avert another major disaster?

Our Own ET Origins

Expanding the above section into a different branch of science, we come to evidence far closer to home and much more intimate; our human genetics.

Years ago, on the recommendation of a friend, I read Barbara Marciniak's[4] *Bringers of the Dawn*. Channelling information Marciniak said came from the Pleiadians, one of the things she wrote of was that humanity's genetics were a composite of twenty-two different extraterrestrial races. Andromedan contactee Alexander Collier[5] has also reported that he was taught that humanity is

[4] Barbara Marciniak channels a group known as Pleiadians and has several books published with this material, one of the most popular being *Bringers of the Dawn: Teachings from the Pleiadians*. Her website: www.pleiadians.com.

[5] Alexander Collier is a well-known contactee by a race known as the Andomedans. His sharings are available here http://www.alexcollier.org/ and at http://www.bibliotecapleyades.net/andromeda/lfa/lfa.html.

considered genetic royalty by his Andomedan ET contacts, Vasais and Moraney due to humanity containing this blend of twenty-two other extraterrestrial species. Similar information has surfaced in other places as well.

While one could make an argument that these individuals somehow got together in secret, concocted this story and agreed on the somewhat mystical number of twenty-two races contributing to the creation of human beings on Earth, there is other parallel information from an entirely different source – one with a very traditional scientific and scholarly background. With no relationship to ufology, channeled material or information from extraterrestrial contactees – belief or disbelief in either being immaterial here – information about extraterrestrial origins of the human race found a toehold in modern science in a discovery by Francis Crick[6].

Crick and co-researcher James Watson won the Nobel Prize in 1962 for discovery of the double helix structure of DNA, also explaining its replication process. Crick continued his DNA research with fellow researcher chemist Leslie Orgel, and found it dubious that theories of a haphazard "passive panspermia" (i.e., a random meteor strike with "microbes") could have been responsible for the advancement of life such as exists on Earth today. He and Orgel proposed a theory of "directed panspermia" initiated by an advanced intelligent extraterrestrial civilization. *Astrobiology Magazine* commented on the theory in a 2004 homage to Crick:

> It now seems unlikely that extraterrestrial living organisms could have reached the earth either as spores driven by the radiation pressure from another star or as living organisms imbedded in a meteorite. As an alternative to these nineteenth-century mechanisms, we have considered Directed Panspermia, the theory that organisms were deliberately transmitted to the earth by intelligent beings on another planet. We conclude that it is possible that life reached the earth in this way, but that the scientific evidence is inadequate at the present time to say anything about the probability. We draw attention to the kinds of evidence that might throw additional light on the topic.

Like the good mainstream scientists of their day, Crick and Orgel accepted that travel by faster-than-light means or folding space to be an impossibility. However in the recorded, testified behavior of UFOs, or extraterrestrial space or scout craft, is the ability to move with unimaginable speed, to disappear in a microsecond and reappear just as quickly in another part of the sky. So why could extraterrestrials not have just traveled here on ships with means of travel unimaginable by many scientists today? Why could they not have come here, directed and overseen the project of initiating life on Earth in person, taking

---

[6] From "Francis Crick Remembered" in *Astrobiology Magazine*, 7-30-2004; http://www.astrobio.net/index. php?option=com_retrospection&task=detail&id=1107.

all necessary care to see that it flourished? And why would they not have a continuing interest in how that life matures and grows into a civilization of its own?

Of course, this does not address the question of how life, as defined here on Earth, arose in the first place, be it on Earth or elsewhere. But since we now know through quantum science that our collective human consciousness is a major player in how physical reality shows up, Teilhard de Chardin's postulation of consciousness itself directing the tiniest building blocks of matter and life towards a form with greater and greater freedom of expression comes into focus as a distinct probability. With the coming into form of matter itself – then continually improving upon the form, reaching for greater and greater freedom of expression – sentient life, no matter where it sprang from in our universe, may have found its way step by step into more complex, increasingly sentient and self-aware forms. Whatever form it takes, life is itself an expression of consciousness, either one vast consciousness or many integrated and working together – and the one or the many are most likely a paradox of both combined.

In looking at the threads of information that intersect and connect across disciplines – here archeology, anthropology, genetics and other scientific disciplines, and there the psychic readings of Edgar Cayce and others, channeled material and contactee information – we find interesting corollaries.

The Human Genome Project completed the initial assessment of the number of genes in the human species in 2001. The late Zecharia Sitchen[7] devoted extensive years of his life to archeological research including deciphering ancient texts, hieroglyphs, and pictoral records. He wrote of his findings in books such as *The Twelfth Planet: Book I of the Earth Chronicles.* The following paragraphs are summarized from Sitchen's webpage titled "Adam."

> The scientists of the Human Genome Project expected to find that human beings had 100,000 to 140,000 genes. However, they found that we had only about 30,000 genes, a little over double the genes of a fruit fly. Neither were they unique. Human genes were identical to those of other mammals, reptiles, insects and even plants. This comprehensive study allowed scientists to confirm that there was a single source of DNA for all life on Earth and allowed them to trace how simpler life evolved into more complex life. This is referred to as an upward, vertical process.
>
> Reading through human genetics in this vertical manner, there was an unexpected discovery. Human beings have

[7] Zecharia Sitchen, 1920 – 2010, was a prolific researcher, authoring many books about his findings through the study of ancient texts and other archeological artifacts that extraterrestrials both created modern man through genetic manipulation and were a major influence in ancient Sumerian culture. For more information, visit his website at http://www.sitchin.com. The selection above was taken from this webpage: http://www.sitchen.com/adam.htm.

223 "extra" genes that do not show the prerequisite upward genetic process scientists could now read in the evolutionary tree of genetics on Earth. These "extra" genes were added in somehow horizontally – through a sidewise insertion into the human gene pool. Imagine a flowing double helix ribbon of human DNA, then a patch of 223 extra genes spliced in – from somewhere. How could this happen? Where did they come from? Who put them there?

It is surmised that they came somehow from bacteria, but that theory is not well supported by existing evidence, including the mitochondrial DNA tracking back to a single female human ancestor, popularly called "Eve." The addition of the genes resulting in an evolutionary leap forward is also not supported by current evolutionary theories according to Steven Scherer, previously director of the Mapping the Human Genome Sequencing Center at the Baylor College of Medicine, Houston, Texas.

Ninety-nine percent of our human genes are comparable to the genes of chimpanzees, less than 1% difference, genetically. Those extra 223 genes make up two-thirds of that 1% difference.

The 223 extra genes appear relatively recently in evolutionary time. Sitchen's educated estimate is at about 300,000 years ago, according to his studies of ancient records of the Annunaki. "Annunaki" translates as "Those Who from Heaven to Earth Came."

If the origin of humanity on Earth is an extraterrestrial creation, then the search for a "missing link" between humans and apes is a futile search. No defined precursor between apes and man exists.

***

On another front, Edgar Cayce speaks of sub-human, animal-like "things" of lower intelligence that existed in Atlantis. Some in Atlantis wanted to assist in their development, some wanted to use them as slave labor. Cayce called these two factions the "Children of the Law of One," (those who honored and supported all life) and the "Sons of Belial" (those who favored subjugation and exploitation.) Atlantis may have existed 40,000 to 50,000 years ago. According to Cayce, Atlantis went through three destructions, one of which was said to be a great flood, the last and final one said to be a terrific explosion caused by over-charging a great crystal. Were these sub-human beings early experimental attempts at genetic engineering by humans of the distant past?

In recent years, new discoveries in science around genetics and consciousness have come forth. Dr. Bruce Lipton's[8] research shows that it is our thoughts and consciousness that influence our cells, our biology and turn our genes on or off. He says our genes have very little to do with who we create ourselves to be moment by moment from our thoughts and beliefs. What treasures of expanded abilities might lie within that DNA previously thought of as "junk DNA?" How might the conscious application of thought and intention awaken abilities within us that we believed were simply beyond us as the "mere humans" we've been conditioned to believe we are?

I do not suggest here that anyone make any "leaps of faith" or swallow whole anything I share. I only suggest that people educate themselves as broadly as possible, keep an open mind, and note where common threads cross and join. Do not ignore or neglect a study of spirituality and the subtle energetic arts of psychic ability or channeling. Just use discernment in how such information lands in your being, in how it feels, noting any cognitive dissonance with established orders of "knowledge." Consider, especially in today's world, that we have power-hungry people who have seized control of corporations, governments and military forces, people who have a well-documented interest in withholding truth from the public on many fronts. They have the power to seize control of new discoveries in all branches of science, history or other related disciplines and control or suppress that information for their own purposes.

As long as people care about discovering the "really real truth" for themselves and continue to question more and more deeply, the truth will attend to itself in the unfolding of time.

Crop Circles

In crop circles, we have a current, continually recurring phenomenon that defies human reason or explanation. Their forms of intricacy and beauty often only truly appreciated from the air, crop circles are an enigma of our times that also track back hundreds, perhaps thousands, of years.

Over 10,000 crop circles have been recorded worldwide. Since 1980, over 6,000 of these complex glyphs have been observed and investigated. Some empirical data gathered about crop circles:

> Crop circles are usually not round, but slightly elliptical. In a
> real crop circle the plant's shafts/stalks (mostly wheat, but
> also grass, barley, canola, buckwheat, linseed, rice paddies,

---

[8] Bruce Lipton is a researcher and author of the ground-breaking book, *The Biology of Belief: Unleashing the Power of Consciousness, Matter and Miracles*. His website: www.brucelipton.com.

corn, sunflowers, blueberry bushes, trees, etc.) are bent around an inch above soil (corn stalks are bent a couple of inches above the soil) and the plants are laid in precise geometric swirl patterns with little signs of physical damage. There may be light burn marks at the base of stems, altered cellular structure and soil chemistry, increased magnetic particle deposits, discrepancies in background radiation, alteration of the local electromagnetic field, depletion of the local watershed, along with long-lasting energy patterns. Some analyzed crop circles have shown higher radiation levels. Crop circles range in size from a few inches to hundreds of feet across and have been as large as 200,000 sq. ft.

In real crop circle formations the stems are not broken but bent at 90° angles about an inch off the ground, at the plant's first node. The plants are subjected to a short and intense burst of heat or energy that softens the stems or stalks allowing them to be folded over onto the ground at a 90° angle. When the stems or stalks re-harden into their new position, the plants and crop are not damaged and continue to grow. This is the method used to identify a real crop circle formation (agriglyph). The canola oil plant has a structure like celery. If the stalk is bent more than about 45°, the stalk will break. When crop circles are found in canola fields, the stalks are bent 90°. Research and laboratory tests suggest that microwave or ultrasound may be the only method capable of producing this effect, but plant biologists are still baffled by this phenomenon.[9]

~ from the website *Crop Circle Facts*, www.cropcirclefacts.com

One of the interesting things I heard about crop circles in a presentation by Freddy Silva[10] was that they are quite often laid down over places with large natural underground aquifers or water tables. Silva and a number of other well-known crop circle researchers, such as Colin Andrews, are on the right track in looking at crop circles not just scientifically, but also from the mystic angles, as only a true synthesis of both science and spirituality will really approach an understanding of what is truly happening. Also, having seen the film *What the Bleep Do We Know?* and having that introduction to how water is influenced in beakers by words or phrases taped to the beaker, I have

[9] From website: www.cropcirclefacts.com.

[10] Freddy Silva, a researcher looking at both science and spirituality around crop circles, is author of *Secrets in the Fields: The Science and Mysticism of Crop Circles*. His website: www.cropcirclesecrets.org.

to wonder if this is one way that some intelligence is gently working to nudge humanity towards a greater expansion of consciousness. By imprinting the water supplies of our planet, which all interconnect in some way within Earth's ecosphere, could these graceful designs that inspire so much awe and study be specific glyphs with a message for us at some higher, superconscious level? The makers of true crop circles (disregarding "Doug and Dave" and others, and their crop-circle-hoaxing foot-planks that break the plant stalks) have shown themselves through the years of crop circle research as very responsive to what is currently happening for humanity on Earth. The shape of the Mandelbrot fractal appearing in a crop circle at the same time the Mandelbrot set was being developed and used as a fractal model is just one of many examples of this responsiveness.

My own spirit guides will place a recurring word or image in my mind, gently but insistently, until I pay attention to it and explore it. Perhaps the makers of crop circles wish us to know when we human beings stumble onto something of significant importance to us by reinforcing the discovery with a mirroring crop circle.

There is a wealth of research going on around crop circles alone by many fine researchers, exploring many fundamental questions. The most interesting of course is, who or what intelligence is making them? Are they moving humanity towards "something?" Evolution? Higher consciousness? Contact?

***

I started this chapter with the quote from Robert Dean. I end it with the same assessment, from all my years of trying to understand what has happened to me, who I truly am, and what might be occurring to all of us on Planet Earth at this time. The full import of understanding that we are not alone in this Universe, have never been alone, will bring about an expansion of human consciousness. It could usher in a new and golden age of collective human enlightenment, an age of multidimensional understanding, and truly beginning to apply that understanding to every area of our lives on this planet.

If starfaring, other-world civilizations are real and visiting our planet, then full, open public contact is inevitable. The only question is when.

How might extraterrestrials prepare this world for contact?

One strategy would be to make tentative, experimental contact in some way with the general population. Thousands, if not millions, of people are already having contact. Whether they call themselves abductees, contactees, wanderers, walk-ins or starseeds, for such experiencers, contact already is a reality.

444

Chapter 27: Experiencers of Extraterrestrial Contact

I was then faced with the choice of either trying to fit these individuals' reports into a framework that fit my worldview – they were having fantasies, strange dreams, delusions, or some other distortion of reality – or of modifying my worldview to include the possibility that entities, beings, energies – *something* – could be reaching my clients from another realm. The first choice was compatible with my worldview but did not fit the clinical data. The second was inconsistent with my philosophical grounding, and with conventional assumptions about reality, but appeared to fit better what I was finding. It seemed to me to be more logical, and intellectually more honest, to modify my cosmology than to continue trying to force my clients into molds that clearly did not suit them.

~ *Passport to the Cosmos: Human Transformation and Alien Encounters* by Dr. John E. Mack, 2000, reprinted with permission of the John E. Mack Institute.

I so very much wish I'd had the opportunity to know and talk with Dr. John E. Mack[1]. I look forward to undertaking a much deeper study of the research and materials he left behind as I move beyond writing down my own chronicle here. He was a man who understood the value of a transpersonal approach to this phenomenon. "Transpersonal" is defined as "relating to, or being psychology or psychotherapy concerned especially with esoteric mental experience [as mysticism and altered states of consciousness] beyond the usual limits of ego and personality."

As a person who has come to know the deeper healing power of the transpersonal approach, understanding so well that we human beings are so much more than what we appear to be on a solely physical level, the loss of a man of John Mack's stature to this field of research has been a serious loss indeed. In Mack's 2002 International UFO Congress presentation, *Transcending the Dualistic Mind*, he asked provocative questions such as:

[1] Dr. John E. Mack brought considerable academic credentials and a valuable expanded transpersonal method of observation to the field of abduction research before his untimely death in 2004. His books, *Abduction: Human Encounters with Aliens* and *Passport to the Cosmos: Human Transformation and Alien Encounters* are available with a great deal of other material relating to his work at his website: http://johnemackinstitute.org.

- What kinds of shifts in our philosophical framework or worldview do we need to make to grasp this phenomenon more fully?
- What sort of multidisciplinary collaboration would advance our exploration?
- How can we be more effective in establishing the power of this phenomenon (positive or negative) and knowledge about it, to effect constructive change?

He went on to list some of his own thoughts:

- Become more sophisticated in understanding physical evidence and physical laws.
- Learn more about worldviews, scientific and political, and how these shape what we and others can take in.
- Develop an understanding of subtle energy phenomena.
- Expand our epistemology, placing more emphasis upon intuitive, holistic and traditional ways of knowing.

Unfortunately, Dr. Mack's call for a multidisciplinary collaboration to explore the UFO and extraterrestrial phenomenon remains largely unanswered. Among the various scientific areas of study and research he mentioned as important were:

- Quantum mechanics
- Quantum holography
- Zero-point energy
- Chaos theory
- String theory
- Non-locality
- Possibilities of interdimensional travel

As spiritual beings having a human experience on Planet Earth, the transpersonal approach to the study and healing of people who are having extraterrestrial experiences that result in non-ordinary states of consciousness is both incredibly important and holds keys for going all the way in healing not as accessible in traditional psychotherapy and impossible in any type of drug-based interventions.

Extraterrestrial experiences and non-ordinary states of consciousness are traumatic in and of themselves when experienced by an individual who previously understood their life only from within specific Earth-based socially-indoctrinated paradigms. Indoctrination, denial, fear – and modes of therapeutic or psychiatric treatment designed to rearrange the mental and emotional furniture in the indoctrinated prison cell of the human mind – are the means by which the dominant reality paradigm is patched, oiled and kept clunkily creaking onwards. Such treatment makes oddities of those individuals with personal experiential truths that do not happen to fit within the indoctrinated paradigm.

As Shunryu Suzuki's zen proverb teaches us, "In the beginner's mind, there are many possibilities. In the expert's mind, there are few." Those upon whom academia and modern society confer the degrees and credentials that set them up as "experts" need to cultivate more of a beginner's mind when working with extraterrestrial experiencers.

I honor all the people who are working in this field to the best of their abilities today and are doing all they can from within their specific areas of expertise and knowledge. But I also call upon others from more mainstream areas of study to have the intellectual courage and sense of adventure exemplified by the late Dr. John E. Mack to join this field. And to proceed from the simplest, open beginner's mind: *I know nothing about this. Therefore it is my intention from a clear heart to truly look, truly see, dropping biases, judgments and conditioning to discover what might truly be occurring.*

From Abductee to Experiencer: A Process

Like the other branches of study that encompass the UFO and exopolitics fields, there are volumes upon volumes written by pioneers in the field of ET experiencer research. There is no way to cover it all here. I can only speak most authentically from my own experience.

For myself, I feel all the terms around how people are "taken" by extraterrestrial beings have a personal evolutionary progression. When I first discovered that I'd had experiences, starting in childhood, I remembered feeling afraid of such strange-looking beings – these Greys or Zetas with their large black eyes and thin bodies. I was also very angry about it. I was an *abductee*, being taken against my will.

As the experiences continued, I realized that I was not being physically harmed, so the fear relaxed its grip. Anger was slower to go. A feeling of invasiveness, discomfort and just strange other-worldlyness prevailed. I did not like what was happening. I had no guidelines or help on how to deal with the experiences until long after it was needed.

From a human perspective, the first knee-jerk response can be, "How dare they do such a thing?" This was my initial reaction. Yet no matter how I felt about it, it continued to happen. When I came to a place of wanting to heal my own feelings about it and try to see the bigger picture, I searched out all kinds of data to try to understand what was happening. These beings resembled humans in some ways – they had a head, eyes, a torso, two legs, two arms, etc. The conclusions of many researchers are, based on similarities of stories across thousands of abductees, that there is some kind of hybridization program underway, mixing our species with theirs. The next obvious question is "Why?"

One of the most prominent reasons for this hybridization program according to ET experiencer research and other congruent material channeled by Lyssa Royal, and from Darryl Anka who channels an extraterrestrial being called Bashar, is that the Greys have lost their ability to sexually reproduce. Their current method of reproduction seems to be through cloning. Cloning individuals over time has produced an instability in their species due to a loss of biodiversity. Generations of cloned copies of copies of copies could be resulting in genetic degradation over time. In order for their species to survive in some form, they must create a hybrid race. Reintroducing new genetic material and the recombining of genetic material through sexual reproduction in a manner that keeps a species fresh and strong – given a large enough population to insure biodiversity – is a means to preserve something of their own species and culture, if the children of such a hybridization program are raised by them. There are reports of other extraterrestrial species producing hybrid offspring with humans as well, though the primary agenda may not be the creation of a hybrid race.

Moral and ethical questions arise here, at least from the standpoint of our human sensibilities. Does any species have the right to create a hybrid race from themselves and another species if they have the scientific capability of doing so, AND if they are facing extinction if they take no action? If their need is great enough, should they proceed without the permission of the individuals or species they have chosen for their hybridization program?

If faced with extinction from a loss of biodiversity and such a hybridization option was available to Earth humanity, what kind of action might human beings, through their sciences, technologies and military force, take? What does our history tell us? Human history is filled with ideologies manufactured to create an "us versus them" schism; of making enemies of those who have something you desire so you can justify taking it by any means necessary.

The contrast of feelings between what happened to me with the Zetas and what happened to me at the hands of other human beings is very clear in my emotional landscape. The Zetas did what they felt was needed in a cool, clinical fashion without inflicting true physical harm, nor did I ever perceive from them any intent to harm me. Emotional turmoil, feelings of violation and loss of personal control are a form of harm, but often these are based in our perceptions of what is happening, and from a lack of understanding.

The same could not be remotely applied to what happened to me at the hands of others of "my own kind." There was specific intention to do harm. And since most human beings are repulsed by doing this kind of harm to another, individuals were employed to do it who lacked any feelings of empathy, compassion or capacity for remorse – people who were in fact gratified by having power and control over another and inflicting harm.

It is this contrasting comprehension, stamped in both body and energetic memory, that calmed and finally canceled out my anger at the Zetas, and I transitioned from the victim position of abductee to ET experiencer. And if they truly are trying to save their species, do they have a right to do so? How could they ask for permission from a species still in evolutionary infancy? A species not quite fully sentient, still hiding much of who they are from themselves in their subconscious and superconscious minds? A species conditioned to fear, that acts out out of intolerance, paranoia and violence against that which is different from themselves?

If the stories being pieced together of at least one group of Greys having a meeting with high-ranking government and military officials is true, then some kind of "permission" to interact with the human population was asked for and granted, most likely in exchange for advanced extraterrestrial technology. Extraterrestrial "consultants" were also allegedly provided to help in understanding the technology, per the testimony of the late Bill Uhouse.[2] Another interesting story came forth directly relating to the contact and collaboration of extraterrestrials and the military in the book, *Above Black: Project Preserve Destiny* by former USAF serviceman, Dan Sherman. As with much of this material from various individuals, if you take it by itself, it seems utterly fantastic fiction. Cross-checked and correlated with all the other data available about government and military UFO cover-ups, particularly about an advanced technology-human abduction program exchange between our military and the Greys and stories from ET experiencers, it deserves some serious attention as yet another revealing facet of this phenomenon.

Close Encounters of the Intimate Kind

One of the theories floating around out there that I've come to feel has some intellectual merit is that the Greys-Zetas are nearly identical genetically to us and that they could be us from an alternate timeline. They were once much like us, and out of their own ill-governed passions, they destroyed their world in something identical to or akin to a nuclear holocaust. Moving underground and seeking to never again be subject to the emotional excesses that nearly destroyed them, they bred emotions out of their species, including sexuality. They relegated their procreation to the process of cloning. By removing emotions and sexuality, they felt their species would be safe from the internal forces that almost led to their annihilation. In hindsight they discovered that they had

---

[2] Bill Uhouse, Captain, USMC retired (1924-2009) was a fighter pilot, serving in the U.S. Marine Corps for 10 years. As a mechanical avionics aerospace engineer, he testified for Dr. Steven Greer's *Disclosure Project* about his work at Area 51 designing a flying disc simulator. He also mentioned an extraterrestrial being he called "J-Rod," that he had contact with as a technical advisor in his work there. A video of his testimony appears here: https://www.youtube.com/watch?v=VzGYNJEA4Ag.

lost something else essential to their survival – cloning, over the ages, caused genetic degradation, putting their species in a slow decline to oblivion rather than the rapid one they feared happening again in a planetary destruction. From a position of superior understanding and knowledge of time, space and alternate realities, they found a way into our timeline to collect genetic material from us to restore qualities they found were vital to the survival of their species after all.

It seems that the challenge of emotions is not to breed them out of a species, but to learn what they have to teach us about ourselves and actively apply that knowledge out of the best angels of our nature. It is necessary to understand the two-edged sword that emotions can be – one edge leading to certain death and destruction through fear, hatred and continuing retaliation of injury upon injury – the other guarding and honoring all life from within our chastened and experientally-enlightened hearts.

Just how kindred enough are we to another species of similar form – head, torso, arms, legs, grasping digits – to be combined in the first place? Though I no longer in any way believe this to be the case, if we were to suppose Earth to be a closed evolutionary system, pure and pristine from off-planet influences, we at least know from our current understanding of genetics that we cannot breed two genetically-different species together and expect offspring. We may be able to force some kind of hybridization between two entirely different species in a test tube, but even then the process is dubious to risky or toxic as to what it may produce, as we are learning from genetically-modified organisms (GMOs) as foods. If two species are similar enough to mate, such as horses and donkeys, offspring can be produced, but such offspring are generally sterile. What kind of scientifically-directed nudging might push such a "mule" into being able to successfully procreate?

What might be involved in a hybridization program by a team of advanced and competent geneticists, such as the Zetas seem to be? In combining genetics from two different species, yet apparently kindred enough for their genetics to be successfully combined, extensive study is required. Here are my thoughts on the forms the Zeta's study seemed to take from my perspective.

If you want to restore sexuality to your species, you need to undertake an in-depth study of it. You need research subjects. You want to know every what, why and how of sexuality. That also means an in-depth study of human emotions. You choose your subjects carefully, examining their various genetic lineages. You measure their responses. You might even put implants in them, not just to keep track of where they are, but to measure the hormone and neuropeptide levels associated with emotions and sexuality. You want the hybrids you create to feel all the "right stuff" to motivate them to sexually procreate, because let's face facts – if sex didn't feel pretty powerfully good, who would do it, procreation or no procreation?

This has been my understanding of what happened to me as a research subject and unaware ovum donor during the years of my childhood, adolescence and young adulthood. It all started at far too young an age according to western human societal standards. I was scared and I was angry. Once the fear and anger wore off, I was still haunted by the high strangeness of it all. How easy to relegate any remaining shreds of memory that might have been there to "bad dreams." I had so many dreams of flying also throughout those years. I now feel they may have been due to the actual sensation of being lifted up out of bed, through roofs or walls into off-planet vehicles.

Having hypnosis finally shed light on so many strange memories and body sensations I had experienced down through the years, including the actual scarring inside my abdominal cavity. From within my earlier indoctrinated paradigm of Darwinian evolution, I thought, "How dare these invading creatures come along and meddle with people this way?" Yet overshadowing my experiences with the Zetas were the military experiences. Nothing happened to me with the Zetas that compared to the brutality of other humans. My sexual experiences with the hybrid male were gentle, even mildly kind in contrast. He did not have the depth of emotions of a human being, but he did sense my discomfort and was responsive to my distress at times.

Again, my experiences as I recall them fall within an entire collection of such stories of sexual and reproductive experimentation from many, many other people – experiences with Grey beings having large, wraparound black eyes, as well as hybrid beings who clearly look like a cross between them and us. There are many other types of extraterrestrials that humans have reported in their experiences as well, and drawings experiencers have done of the various varieties attest to this. Regarding the Zetas, I have come to feel that there are different groups of them. Other experiencers report this as well. There are reptilian beings often reported, and these reports are often – though not always – more frightening. They were for me, especially in connection with the military experiences. However, there are many people today coming forward with positive stories of reptilian contact. Just as there are good and bad individuals within any collective, this is very likely true of the various ET species as well.

Experiencers as Casualties

One has to wonder, just what the hell is going on with our government or military or whatever human group that is involved with such beings? People often report human military officers present on ET craft during abductions. What is up with that? We can only surmise. A huge body of questions from all of us who have had these types of experiences are waiting for some real answers. If the stories of advanced technology given in exchange for running a hybridization program in the general population are true, with our memories of ET experiences suppressed – for the most part – to protect such a deep dark secret, then extraterrestrial experiencers are, in part, casualties of this arrangement. The personal, emotional cost for us has been very high. People discover missing time, strange marks on their bodies, evidence of procedures they don't remember having. To risk talking about it is to risk appearing crazy

451

to an entire culture conditioned to dismiss extraterrestrials as nonsense and UFOs as something reported by the unsophisticated, the crazy, the uneducated or the intoxicated. People have had to go on with their lives, covertly living with ongoing experiences with little to no support, trying to cope with fear, post-traumatic stress and loss of personal control over their own lives. While there are other possible reasons such experiences of contact are not remembered, this is one that cannot be ignored or discounted.

In recent decades, fear of speaking out has decreased as people in serious need of healing and understanding have risked reporting their experiences despite fear of censure, of losing a job or career, or being labeled as disturbed or crazy. The reward for taking the risk to share our experiences is in beginning to find out how many others share similar experiences. When one of us risks speaking out, we begin to build a safe space for others to do the same. With every voice activated and freed, that safe space expands. Whether by accident or design, forcing conformity among people so that they fear to appear different or defective shuts them all down and isolates them from each other. By having the courage to risk saying what is happening to you, what you're experiencing, you give others the safety to open up and share their experiences. You feel the deep relief of no longer being isolated and alone. Dr. John Mack, with his stature in the academic and professional world, gave us all a great gift by investigating this phenomenon with true intellectual courage and an open mind. Through all those who were touched by his investigations, by his honesty, care and concern for what they were experiencing, the legacy of his gift to us lives on.

Sowing Life Throughout the Universe

In all my years of studying this phenomenon and the various, emerging contextual pieces of this huge puzzle – ranging from the archeological to the genetic to the experiential – I feel I can make an educated and confident assertion that the general population have not been told the truth about who we really are and what humanity's true origins are. Volumes of real knowledge about our human origins and evolution have been withheld from us, very likely as part of indoctrination programs to manage us. Those with the power to control information and regulate knowledge and research in ways that suit them dictate what the rest of humanity will be taught or informed of. Cross-disciplinary studies of human origins need not even look at the ET experiencer phenomenon to draw preliminary conclusions about who we humans really are and where we may have really come from. However, if the ET experiencer phenomenon becomes more widely accepted and studied in depth, placing the results of such studies alongside other evolutionary and genetic evidence, the true origins of our human species may become increasingly more clear. I have come to feel that this is the way that life is propagated throughout the universe; by the intelligent design of extraterrestrials.

As to origins of how life originated in the very beginning, into whatever form on whatever world or dimension, I find the work of Teilhard de Chardin to be a seminal philosophy. Put with the newer quantum knowledge that consciousness is a major player in how our reality shapes itself, including our bodies themselves, I feel de Chardin intuitively hit upon how it is the spark of consciousness in all matter – down to the tiniest particles – guides the evolution of lifeforms into greater and greater freedom of expression, physically, emotionally and mentally. Consciousness may have initiated the "Big Bang" – a popular theory of the creation of the universe – consciousness fracturing Itself into infinite individuated and living shards. Every curious, questing infinitesimal particle contains its internal spark of consciousness, reaching for some kind of expression in relationship to and with the other particles around it. Once the form allowing the greatest freedom of expression is attained, the next evolutionary leap to be made could be one of consciousness expansion itself. The expression of life may be a great circle of both devolution and evolution, the Conscious Living Universe itself learning from every great and small cycle that takes place within infinity.

If we are designed or assisted in our evolution and development by extraterrestrials, then the idea that Earth is a pure and virgin planet where life simply arose in a random or haphazard manner or was brought into being by an omnipotent elderly gray-bearded "God" is an idea perpetuated in error at the very least. Believing such myths, we are outraged at extraterrestrial interlopers who appear and meddle with God's creation. If these religious indoctrinated beliefs are in error, then our outrage is a product of that error.

I am not trying to take away anyone's anger or fear at anything that has happened to them. Our emotions about what happens to us are valid. However, through resolving our emotions, we can also pave the way to a newer and more expanded sense of who we truly are and what is really happening at a deeper level.

It is essential for all people who truly wish to heal that have been harmed in any way, physical or otherwise, by human or ET, to move beyond the role of victim. To remain a victim is to allow one's personal power taken away by fear; fear of speaking or acting on one's own behalf, fear of drawing a line in the proverbial sand that sets a boundary against harm. At the time such abductions or encounters happen, our powerlessness is a fact of the experience, enforced upon us. A part of us is fractured away from the wholeness of our being, a part we must then later go in search of and retrieve to be our full selves again. Yet in the journey of spirit or soul retrieval, we often encounter ourselves in such a way as to understand that, at a much deeper level of consciousness, we may indeed have been somehow complicit in our encounter or abduction experiences. We may discover things about ourselves that would have lain forever dormant, forever unconscious, had the encounters we perhaps chose at a soul level before birth not occurred. Such experiences and the drive to heal and understand them present those precious opportunities to awaken to a greater reality.

Alien abductee. For me, not very good words. Abductee is a word that implies victimization. Alien means other, different, strange, unlike oneself, even hostile. It is one of the words in language that we use to separate ourselves from others too different to even be tolerated. As I moved towards healing and integration, from research as well as from my own spiritual understanding of the oneness of everything that exists, the more neutral word, "experiencer" took the place of abductee. This is so for many, many others that have also taken a similar journey of healing.

Moving beyond the neutrality of the term experiencer is "contactee," which suggests a cooperative relationship between those chosen for contact and the extraterrestrials themselves. In coming to feel one is a contactee, there is a sense of learning things from the ETs. Many contactees, including myself, are shown the horror of nuclear holocaust. We learn about stewarding our environment instead of destroying it. We learn through having healings or telepathic abilities awakened within us through our minds being touched and opened. I have come to call this type of contact attending the "cosmic university" – while our bodies sleep, we travel to lightships for instruction or to be given what I call "seed knowledge." Like a computer zip or compressed file, it opens or unwinds over time and we find knowledge coming into our minds that we simply "know." Some of us are chosen to pass messages on to Earth humanity from the extraterrestrials themselves.

Wanderers, Walk-ins and Starseeds

> I just want to go 'Home.' I'm not sure where home is, but I know it's not here.
>
> ~ A very common yearning and expression of those who feel or know they are not from "here."

Whether one comes into human life, as I did, feeling like a stranger in a strange land from their earliest childhood, or whether awakening occurs later on through the impact unusual experiences have on us, feeling the keenness of separation from a sense of "home" we don't feel here on Earth in our human families is a common experience of those who identify themselves as wanderers, walk-ins or starseeds.

A wanderer to Planet Earth is one who comes in at birth – an extraterrestrial or celestial higher-dimensional soul born to human parents. Possibly one of these human parents can also be a wanderer or walk-in, so the newly-born wanderer has some connective resonance to assist them in acclimating to life on Earth, even if only at a subconscious level.

The purpose of such an incarnation is to in some way work to raise and awaken consciousness on this world. In the first book of the *Law of One* series, *The Ra Material: An Ancient Astronaut Speaks*, Ra, a higher-dimensional "social memory complex" stated that there were 65 million wanderers currently on

Earth. (I feel this number is likely much higher today.) Ra was channeled through Carla L. Rueckert and documented by Don Elkins and James McCarty in the Law of One books, published from 1984 to 1991.[3]

When such a soul chooses to be born as a Wanderer on Earth, it understands that it will forget its origins when it incarnates. The dangers of such a choice are that, while under the inevitable amnesia that occurs to souls incarnating on Earth that they could be caught up in earthly political or social chaos and unconsciously generate karma that could trap them here. It is a huge challenge to incarnate on Earth, especially at this time. Somehow wandering through life, the true higher self and likely unseen others from the higher densities or dimensions guide this individual from within to regain an understanding of who they truly are, where they really come from and why they chose to come to Earth in the first place.

If or when wanderers can peel away the layers of their human selves in true self-discovery, they have the gifts of being able to help consciousness to awaken and expand more rapidly and exponentially for those whose lives they touch. Wanderers who haven't awakened to their true selves usually feel alienated from other people and the world around them. They often have allergies – this has certainly been true of myself. Other health issues wanderers may suffer from include chronic fatigue syndrome, fibromyalgia, Epstein-Barr to name a few.

An added dimension of what it is to be a wanderer comes from the L/L Research website, dedicated to the Law of One materials and principles:

> What is a wanderer? Some wanderers are ETs who have come from elsewhere to planet Earth for this incarnation or at this time. Many other wanderers are earth natives who have matured spiritually to the point of awakening to their metaphysical identity, thereby making the worldly identity less real, and creating the sense of being a stranger in a strange land. Both types of wanderers are in the same situation here on Earth now, in that they often don't fit in well here, for their inner universe has shifted, and the "real" world for them has shifted from the earthly world to the aesthetic and ethical innerness of the metaphysical world.
>
> Wanderers are each unique and come in all shapes and sizes, but their likeliest common characteristics are a sense of alienation and isolation as they make choices of how to live and be, and cope with a strong and increasing inner knowing that they are here to serve. The lesson and mission that all wanderers have in common is to give and receive love. Their

[3] *The Ra Material: An Ancient Astronaut Speaks* and the *Law of One* series are deeply insightful books channeled through Carla L. Rueckert as part of a team also consisting of James Allen McCarty and Don Elkins. In addition to much esoteric material, an alternate history of the galaxy and universe is presented. Their website: http://www.llresearch.org/. A companion searchable website of the Law of One material can be found here: http://www.lawofone.info/.

common service is to be themselves, in as true and deep a
way possible in each moment, as they are working on this
life lesson. The main mission is a ministry of being, of living
in the open heart that is the deepest self of all beings within
incarnation here. They are light anchorers, bringing light
through into the earth planes as they breathe in and breathe
out with an open and loving heart.

~ from http://www.llresearch.org/wanderer.aspx

So we find that a wanderer is not always a celestial, higher-dimensional
entity or extraterrestrial taking on an Earth incarnation, but can also be one
who has awakened within the paradigm or matrix of a human lifetime, or serial
lifetimes as part of this collective Earth human experience.

A walk-in can be very similar, the difference being that walk-ins do not come
in at birth. A human being can have a close brush with death or near-death-
experience (NDE), and at a soul level an agreement is made between the walk-
in soul and the original incarnated soul. The original soul voluntarily chooses
to move on and the walk-in comes into that body and assumes that lifetime and
identity. The new walk-in soul may remake that identity, sometimes radically,
from what the person seemed to be before their brush with death. Walk-in
personality shifts are different from the changed consciousness that usually
occurs through near-death experiences in the originally-incarnating souls,
who return to life changed by what they discovered in their time outside their
bodies. In this case, the original soul continues in that same body, but bringing
new depths of insight to their post-NDE lives.

Starseeds is a newer term that describes the more recent influx of souls from
"elsewhere."

Common characteristics of Starseeds:

- A deep interest in spirituality.
- The ability to spiritually grow rapidly when needed as if they
  have done this before.
- A realization that earth is not their true home.
- They feel drawn to outer space, the stars and science fiction.
- Personal qualities such as being artistic, being sensitive and
  possessing higher consciousness.
- Star Seeds can have difficult and challenging lives.
- They sometimes have dreams or memories of places not on
  earth.
- They sometimes have experiences of physical and non-
  physical encounters with star guides and UFOs.

⅄ They often have noticeable gifts in the areas of healing, channelling and psychic sensitivities.

~ From the Paul McCarthy, starseed, channeler and author on his website: www.siriusascension.com from the webpage, *What Are Starseeds?*[4]

Dolores Cannon[5] sees thousands of people in her hypnotherapy practice which allows her to get pieces of information from many sources; pieces that fit together in ways that greatly support the information about wanderers that came through Carla Rueckert from the collective known as Ra. Because of the large numbers of people she has regressed, Cannon has found consistent threads in stories that show how various souls, extraterrestrial and celestial, "heard the call" and volunteered to come to Earth. She has identified three waves of volunteer souls because of the different general characteristics demonstrated by those born in particular decades.

Cannon discovered in her work that a much larger influx of other-dimensional souls began when human beings detonated the first nuclear bombs in 1945. When this occurred, UFO activity increased, especially in the areas that stored nuclear weapons. Roswell Army Air Field's 509th Bombardment squadrons were the units responsible for the bombing of Nagasaki and Hiroshima in Japan at the end of World War II. The USAF personnel involved in the Rendlesham Forest Incident that occurred near Royal Air Force Bentwaters in late December 1980 reported that one of the extraterrestrial craft involved hovered over a bunker containing nuclear weapons. At that time, authorities denied that any nuclear weapons were being stored there as it was a violation of terms between the U.S.A. and the United Kingdom (UK). Over ten years later, it was admitted that nuclear weapons had indeed been stored there during the 1980 incident. Through the ensuing years, UFOs, i.e., extraterrestrial space craft, have demonstrated on multiple occasions their complete proficiency at shutting down nuclear missile silos, down to the back-up generators and batteries and scrambling launch codes. Once more, from across a full spectrum of different varieties of information, I would urge interested and open-minded people to research, cross-check, cross-check and cross-check some more, and correlate the data.

Also, according to Cannon's research, extraterrestrials have watched over humanity from the very beginning of our species here on Earth. Human beings were seen as too spiritually and morally immature to handle such destructive devices. We could blow up the planet and that would affect life on other worlds

[4] From Paul McCarthy's webpage: http://siriusascension.com/what%20is.htm. Paul McCarthy is a starseed and spiritual channel. He is author of *Star Seeds and Star Masters*, a detailed guide to helping star seeds understand who they are and why they are on Earth, especially today; also *Ascension: Becoming An Ascended Master* and *Light Ships and Star Families*.

[5] Dolores Cannon, from her work with thousands of people, has written many books, notably her *Convoluted Universe* series and a more recent book called *The Three Waves of Volunteers and the New Earth*. Her website: http://wwwdolorescannon.com/index.html

as well as space-faring civilizations. Ecology is not a concept that begins and ends with Earth and her outer layers of atmosphere. To have any real meaning, the term ecology applies across the universe and throughout all dimensions. Energy fields extend from all forms of matter, overlapping and intermingling. The impact of nuclear detonations shakes this interconnected energy network in a destructive way that reaches far beyond the physical boundaries of our planet.

The call for volunteers to come to Earth went out as a way to intervene here without violating the sovereignty of human civilization. The only exceptions to the law of non-interference is if we do things where we could destroy ourselves and the planet, or negatively affect things out in the universe. The reason for the assistance here at this time in history is so we don't have to start the human process over again from the very beginning. This intervention is being undertaken by the volunteer souls coming here, being born as human beings, forgetting their origins so they can be a true part of humanity. Yet they bring the special vibration of where they come from – the transformative higher frequencies of their realms – within the Earth's 3D energy matrix. The three waves of volunteer souls, though they definitely overlap, are identified by Cannon as the 1st wave coming in from approximately 1945 to the 1960s. They have had the hardest time acclimating to Earth, being the trailblazers for the following waves. The 2nd wave began to enter from around 1970s to 1980s and Cannon describes them as antennas, generators, channelers of energy. The 3rd wave has been coming in from the 1990s to the present. Cannon calls them "gifts to the world," the special children coming in, inherently knowing so much more than their chronological ages would suggest, their DNA already upgraded at the time of their births.

Hate, fear and anger are emotions that are frightening and very difficult for wanderers or starseeds to deal with or get used to on this planet. Yet we did come here. And yes, I definitely feel I am one of these in a most profound way. The lists of issues that wanderers or starseeds have to cope with here on Earth are intimately my own issues.

Per my own understanding, expressed in this book, and as Dolores Cannon has also discovered in her work with people, frequencies of vibration shifting into another dimension is happening in a gradual way. All at once would be too difficult and devastating. From a place of awakening consciousness and an understanding of how our thoughts, emotions and feelings shape the reality we see around us, it's up to us to take full responsibility to keep those thoughts and feelings in alignment with what we want to create. This is also why there is such a movement in government to take away individuals' personal responsibility for health, education and much more, and why they serve up so much material designed to create fear, anger and hatred – to keep our vibrational state at a lower point where we cannot make the shift at this optimal point in human history. These times we are living through are a major completion of a 75,000 year cycle – this "Shift of the Ages." Government and corporate leeches – and the .001% self-styled "elite" parasites who control them – don't want to lose the host population they feed upon.

According to Cannon's research, an entire planet has never moved into a new dimension before in the universe. In order to go with Earth into this new dimension, we must get rid of old karma. My understanding of this is to take every opportunity to break out of old patterns of behavior. Every time a familiar fear or reaction to life around you comes up, question it. What would be a new and positive way of responding, rather than giving in to the knee jerk reaction you've done a thousand times or more? Forgive, release, let go of fear. Realize that Love is the only reality that leads to freedom, an abundant life and an entire multiverse of possibilities to explore on the inner and outer planes of existence.

Much of Dolores Cannon's work is mirrored and explored in new ways in the research of Mary Rodwell of Australia. In a presentation Rodwell calls *The New Human*, her work with over 1,600 cases shows that in the last 60 to 80 years, human beings are being born with special abilities, including healing abilities and speaking and writing in extraterrestrial, non-human language. Such people often have diagnoses of attention-deficit-hyperactivity disorder (ADHD), and children, especially in the U.S., are often medicated as a form of treatment. Yet what if this is simply a manifestation of new abilities and knowledge inherent in such children, many of whom are now adults, leading to high levels of boredom with traditional education? Such boredom could easily lead to behaviors that could be labeled "hyperactive." One hypothesis suggested by Rodwell, and another exopolitical researcher, Neil Gould[6], is that having ADHD somehow protects star kids from being fully indoctrinated into the "matrix" by flawed human educational systems, and may actually be a quality that will help to advance the consciousness evolution of the human race. Gould wrote a book about his personal experiences with this aspect of ET contact called *Close Encounters of the ADHD Kind*. Hearing this ADHD hypothesis completely floored me when I heard it, as I have jokingly tossed a similar remark off to friends in conversations many times through the years that my "woolgathering" or chronic daydreaming in school protected me from being fully indoctrinated. And I too am an experiencer of ET contact.

Earlier abduction or experiencer cases seemed to have been adjusted in their DNA by extraterrestrials, sometimes while in their mothers' wombs. Recall my earlier reference to Dan Sherman (author of *Above Black: Project Preserve Destiny*) being told this by a superior officer while in the military, thus causing him to be selected for training as an "intuitive communicator" by virtue of a special talent this adjustment gave him. The children born in more recent years are coming in with their new DNA already in place.

---

[6] Neil Gould is director of the Exopolitics Institute founded by Dr. Michael Salla. With his son Jake Gould, they produce films and videos that chronicle the UFO/exopolitics movement and document many of the important ET contact cases, such as the 1950s George Adamski and Howard Menger "space brother" years. His book *Close Encounters of the ADHD Kind* is an account of his own life with ADD/ADHD and his experiences with extraterrestrials. His website: http://exopoliticshongkong.com.

I remember how I anchored myself down in childhood to third-dimensional science and how left-brained I once was, yet always struggling to reconcile a part of me that seemed to hear whispers from within, instructing and guiding. I sensed I could trust this faculty, but the outer world did not seem to acknowledge the existence of this part of me. Learning to trust it came through haphazard trial and error over half a lifetime. Coming to recognize and understand these qualities in myself and embrace them – not just as concepts but experientially – seems a miracle. Today I know it as a miracle that was meant to be.

As wanderers, walk-ins or starseeds, we generate an energy from within the Earth matrix, like human crop circles. We are earth humans, but we also bring the energy from where we come from into the Earth matrix for human evolution and transformation.

Chapter 28: Planet Earth:
A Multidimensional World in
a Multidimensional Universe

Extraterrestrial Contact or Alien Invasion?

> When recalling the heady events of the late 1950s working day and night with [Otis] Carr, Ring again and again stressed that the key was working with nature. "Resonance," he would emphasize repeatedly. "You have to work with nature, not against her." He described how when the model disks were powered up and reached a particular rotational speed, "...the metal turned to Jell-o. You could push your finger right into it. It ceased to be solid. It turned into another form of matter, which was as if it was not entirely here in this reality. That's the only way I can attempt to describe it. It was uncanny, one of the weirdest sensations I've ever felt.
>
> ~ Ralph Ring, from Project Camelot's 2006 interview with him entitled *Aquamarine Dreams*.

I put Ralph Ring's quote here to illustrate the deeper understanding that he, Otis Carr and their team had for the underlying reality of the physical universe they were working with, right here on Earth. They demonstrated their depth of comprehension of the fundamental oneness in nature by taking it into practical application. They were able to translate that understanding into nuts and bolts; to build, and take for one single test flight, a terrestrial, man-made flying saucer. Swiftly, after that one flight, covert agencies within the government speedily shut them down and permanently disbanded their group. I have heard similar stories several times over the years; someone conceives of and builds a zero-point energy device only to have their work immediately seized or destroyed, the inventors themselves discredited or even dying under suspicious circumstances. I can only conclude from this that somewhere deep in the secret programs hidden from view, such agencies have devices that can detect the operation of free energy devices and triangulate their locations.

The vast parsecs of outer space become insignificant barriers when travel becomes a process of folding space or using some means of exceeding the speed of light. Because to travel faster than light also has a time dilation effect, faster than light travel also moves the traveler significantly forward in time, as time is measured at the traveler's point of origin. Consciousness would have to be a major factor in such travel, or origin and destination would become meaningless concepts for travel at such "velocities." For any linear continuity of "time" to continue to have meaning, one must be able to grok,[1] in the Heinleinian sense, not only factors of time and space, but the layering of dimensions and densities, and "vibrational coordinates" existing at particular points in time, space and dimensions. The concept of vibrational coordinates was explored in a program I listened to with Bashar,[2] the extraterrestrial being channeled through Darryl Anka, where he discussed UFOs and extraterrestrials. It was a remarkable program to listen to, all the more so because so much of the information matched up with some of my own realizations and insights from years earlier.

With a complete grasp of such knowledge, travel and return to specific points in space-time in a way as to continue the meaningful linearity of one's experiences in a particular place and time could become possible. If we can accept that human beings can learn to do this as demonstrated by the spiritual adepts of India and the Far East, then any sufficiently-evolved being of sentient consciousness could have such abilities. They could also construct craft that could do the same. In fact, craft designed for such inter-dimensional travel would free up the consciousness of the beings traveling aboard that craft for attending to other types of work or study while travel is attended to by pilots, or even artificial or organic intelligence of the craft itself.

For starfaring civilizations to have a comprehension of the entire fabric of space, time and dimensions that are inherent in the level of mastery that extraterrestrial space craft demonstrate to countless witnesses is also, in most cases, to have a deep appreciation of the unity of all life. I feel that this is the norm, through perhaps not the rule.

A full review of spiritual (not religious) teachings by masters of India and the Far East would be necessary to understand these references, as well as a personal practice of various meditative techniques. Concurrently with such spiritual study, it would also be necessary to familiarize one's self with quantum mechanics and new physics. Quantum observations are showing us how our third-dimensional physical reality is truly structured, not only materially, but energetically; and that it exists and takes form through the action of an observing consciousness, i.e., we humans, and all other forms of life, including extraterrestrial life.

---

[1] Grok is a word created by Robert A. Heinlein in his novel *Stranger in a Strange Land* that passes simple understanding or comprehending in human terms. Heinlein's definition: *"Grok means to understand so thoroughly that the observer becomes a part of the observed—to merge, blend, intermarry, lose identity in group experience. It means almost everything that we mean by religion, philosophy, and science—and it means as little to us (because of our Earthling assumptions) as color means to a blind man."*

[2] "Bashar" is an extraterrestrial being channeled through Darryl Anka. His teachings are widely popular. Bashar's website is www.bashar.org.

If the underlying reality is that consciousness is the instrument that orchestrates how matter comes into form and arranges itself, then extraterrestrials with the ability to travel here to Earth must understand this and much more. They would also understand that such fundamental scientific-spiritual principles can be put to work within their own organic forms through consciousness as well as in their technology. Reports of spiritual masters and adepts from India and the Far East being able to bi-locate, appearing in their bodies vast distances from their known locations is evidence of spiritual practice and discipline leading to enough consciousness expansion to understand this mode of "travel." So if one can at least consider the reality of such accounts of consciousness travel documented right here on Earth, it is not quite such a far stretch to understand that this and much more may be an actualized fact for extraterrestrial civilizations.

It is extremely short-sighted to think that this reality-creation-process of an observing consciousness, single and/or collective, stops at the boundary of Earth's outermost exosphere. We are not alone in the universe, nor are we the only form of sentient, intelligent life. And I apply the term *sentient* loosely to humanity – I believe we are only just now grasping the opportunity to birth ourselves into a truly meaningful level of sentience.

Quantum models are beginning to explain spiritual and psychic phenomenon and the quantum energetic network that makes such abilities possible. Such spiritual and quantum investigations must not be absent from the study of any branch of the extraterrestrial or UFO phenomenon. It is clear that UFOs, i.e., extraterrestrial space craft, show that spacefaring extraterrestrials have a mastery of quantum physics far exceeding an understanding only in its infancy here on Earth.

One of the fundamental understandings of both the deepest spiritual principles AND quantum physics, is the underlying truth that everything across the universe, at every level, density and dimension, is all ONE - a Oneness encompassing both the scientific and the spiritual, which we human beings traditionally regard as two separate areas of study. I have come to feel that for *most* extraterrestrial races, these are one seamlessly-combined discipline-philosophy, no division between the two. When a full comprehension of this Oneness is attained, spiritually-scientifically, the corresponding understanding is that ALL LIFE IS SACRED. All life has the right to exist, to develop, to evolve; and beyond naturally-occurring cataclysms, should remain as free from any outside interference as possible.

This is because to interfere is to become responsible for the results of what you interfere with. Such responsibility links you with the beings and/or system you have interfered with and this creates an energy debt you owe to those you have impacted in some way. In spiritual teachings, this is called karma, which is simply the energetic way in which the oneness principle of the Living Universe demonstrates its oneness; what someone does to another is the same as doing it to themselves because all is interconnected across space and time. Such actions taken, whether benevolent or malevolent, can have unforeseen consequences of varying degree and intensity over time, as we learn from chaos theory here on Earth. Learning through experience, it's clear that spacefaring species with advanced technologies have to very carefully consider when and how to intervene in the affairs of other species, or even stars or solar systems. When dealing with a world where malevolent extraterrestrials have meddled or invaded, then this becomes an even more delicate and sensitive business for benevolent ETs. It is not possible at such a juncture to restore the previous evolutionary process to it's natural course, so other means that don't further violate the sovereignty of the developing species need to be studied and implemented with care. The "Prime Directive" of Star Trek is not just a nice-sounding idea developed for a science fiction TV series. It is an important philosophy that we should be learning right here on Earth from the countless blundering ways more advanced cultures have either helped or harmed less advanced cultures down through our history here on Earth.

I would estimate that 70 to 80% of all life in the universe, especially at higher densities and dimensions, would implicitly understand this and be both spiritually-evolved and benevolent. The other 30 to 20% may indeed be opportunistic, predatory and malevolent. Some may be completely neutral. Some are very likely not even "humanoid," i.e., having bodies or forms like our own.

Observing what's happening on Earth could be a case-in-point of what may have happened to technologically-advanced extraterrestrial civilizations who did not simultaneously achieve the spiritual philosophy such technology is based on. Since human beings are allegedly obtaining, back-engineering and learning to use extraterrestrial technologies without having the spiritual evolution to understand the underlying unity or oneness principles they may operate on, I must also conclude that some other extraterrestrial races may have also managed to pilfer or somehow obtain advanced technologies without comprehending the underlying principles of how they were developed. Perhaps other civilizations had visionaries like Nikola Tesla, who were enlightened beyond the general capacity of their society. Perhaps their achievements were seized and misused by those of less-evolved sensibilities, just as has happened here on our world. Perhaps contact with an enlightened ET civilization brought the technology as a well-meaning gift given to those not spiritually or morally mature enough to truly understand its underlying philosophy. Such technologies in the hands of the less-evolved could be adapted over time to be more mechanical and less energetically advanced to serve the needs the less-evolved species. Unfortunately, human beings are on a dangerous path to becoming one of these technologically-advanced but spiritually-underdeveloped races, at least in part. There are other niches in human societies that are evolving their consciousness to the spiritual comprehension necessary to be technologically, spiritually and ethically advanced. A race of sorts between these two factions is being run on our world even now.

How wonderful it would be if those spiritually evolving on Earth right now could become the heart and conscience of those developing the technologies of the future, metamorphosing humanity into the best of both. I feel we need to hang on to such a dream and such a vision for our future.

To the question of extraterrestrial contact or alien invasion, I would just ask people to look at the maelstrom of energies in the world we live in; the chaotic tension between sinking into the darkness of totalitarian fascism or choosing to evolve into a fully-sentient human species, actualizing our fullest consciousness potential between the intellect of science and the heart of spirituality.

In a country where media is controlled and funded with no-longer-quite-so-hidden agendas, alien invasion movies would seem to be conceived and produced from a will to continue perpetuating fear by those who understand only fear as a means of control. A true study of the scope of the UFO-extraterrestrial phenomenon from antiquity to the present would suggest that we have already had contact with various extraterrestrial groups who may have had a negative agenda of control, or perhaps a well-intentioned one of control "for our own good" that was subverted later on under the principle that "power corrupts, and absolute power corrupts absolutely." The current chaos in our world could very likely be the result of not-so-enlightened ET tampering with humanity and our social and political structures. Those wanting to maintain control would intensely fear the coming of spiritually-enlightened and benevolent extraterrestrials who would bring with them the knowledge of true multidimensionality for humanity – a new collective Prometheus bringing an entirely new kind of Light and fire to humanity.

I feel that most alien invasion scenarios spun out in films and television may be made more from monsters lurking in our own ids or subconscious. If ETs have been visiting us from prehistory on, and their purpose was to conquer us or wipe us out, they would not have waited until we developed nuclear weapons of mass destruction to do it. The very fact that they have stood back and watched from the skies, or even by walking among us as the human-looking ones could do, attests to the fact that they do not mean us harm. Though they watch, they allow us full latitude to do as we will on our world, though they do stop us from exercising the full use of our nukes, perhaps out of their regard for the sacredness of all life, and perhaps also because splitting the atom impacts the larger ecosystem of the solar system or galaxy in an adverse way, affecting life or systems far beyond our world.

Freeing human consciousness to expand, however it happens, means game-over for those in power. Alien invasion scenarios are their attempt to induce fear in people of extraterrestrial contact. Fear as a powerful emotion shuts down intuition. Awakened intuition is the means by which we might be able to read the vibration and intent of such visitors to our world. And if the accounts about ET contacts of the 1950s era of George Adamski, Howard Menger, George Van Tassel and others are true, then ET contact can truly usher in a new and enlightened age on our beleagered and weary world today. Such contact would end draconian control, power and war-mongering according to the dictates of government officials and corporate owners who think only of themselves rather than the people they are supposed to represent and serve. I can't help but think that such people have a vested interest in creating fear of extraterrestrials so that the general population would fight them or flee from them when they do arrive, fear effectively jamming any intuitive ability to discern who these ETs really are and what their intentions might truly be.

Birthing Sentience: Glimpses of a New Underlying Reality

What might an opening in consciousness and a basic understanding of a multidimensional universe mean for human civilization on Planet Earth?

We could make a good argument today that humanity as a collective species is only just now beginning to pass into a meaningful version of sentience. It is not demonstrating sentience for a species to have such lack of vision – with little to no regard for the future – as to continue gross exploitation and destruction of non-renewable natural resources without properly managing those resources to provide for future generations.

The first line of text in the Wikipedia definition of sentience reads; "The ability to feel or perceive subjectively." Yet we are just now emerging from a reductionist world-view where everything is "objectively" studied as so many discrete parts that incidentally may happen to construct a larger mechanism or organism. Questions of soul or consciousness were shrugged off as improbable or unknowable. This mechanized view of the universe was devoid of any acknowledgment of the underlying energy make-up, perhaps because if people can be induced to believe that all they're made of are skin, meat and fluids wrapped around a skeletal structure, they can be frightened into compliance with any number of institutional agendas. Those who can control our perceptions, beliefs and emotions thereby control us.

The new underlying reality coming into view through quantum physics is one that is demonstrating conclusively that consciousness directs how reality shows up.

There is a conundrum in quantum science called "the measurement problem." This refers to the fact that the tiniest units of matter – atoms or subatomic particles – only appear in a particular place and time when a person – a window for consciousness – identifies them for taking some form of measurement. Unobserved, these same tiny units of matter appear spread throughout all space and time. They only appear, or particle-ize, when a human unit of consciousness tries to quantify them in some way. The more we break matter down to its tiniest components, the more reality dissolves. We find there are no objects, no locations and even time is illusory – there exist only relationships between an observing consciousness and what it is bringing into being by observing it.

What we as units of consciousness observe is governed by our beliefs, our opinions, our judgments – what we hold to be "true." We believe what we are indoctrinated to believe by all the structures of society and culture we dwell within. We are the authors of the reality we see around us, built by us out of an entire network of inter-relationships with ourselves, each other and the cosmos.

In light of this evidence, if we can shift our conscious paradigm enough, and do it as a collective, we have the power to change the reality we experience. Could this be at the heart of discussions in spiritual circles of a "new Earth" emerging as we pass through the portal of 2012? Could collective human consciousness be reaching that tipping point that will cascade us into a new, golden age?

If so, then the Controllers of this world, who have enjoyed age after age of power over human populations, fear any disruption of their parasitic feeding off the energy of humanity. Their dark wizards spin mind game after mind game out through the media to keep inciting fear and anger, which keeps the expansion of consciousness in check. The only true war going on on Planet Earth is a war against the awakening of consciousness. All the chaotic events spinning around us are just the various symptoms of that real battle for our energy.

It seems that the native, indigenous people's world view has been correct all along; that there is an underlying "spirit" to the entire world we see around us, a dreamtime world as the aboriginals of Australia believe. De Chardin's postulation – that a spark of consciousness within the tiniest bits of matter guided the evolutionary process into forms of increasingly greater freedom of expression – gains real meaning. His inspired ideas regarding matter and consciousness, in harmony with indigenous cultures' philosophies of a world of spirit underlying the material world, supply a congruent piece of the puzzle in the design of intelligent life, whether it began here on Earth, or originated elsewhere in the cosmos and came to this planet to direct the evolutionary process of humanity.

Even greater implications of quantum discoveries indicate that there may be no such thing as "objective, empirical observation" in the purest sense. When a true scientist formulates a hypothesis of what he thinks may be true, then tests that hypothesis in the laboratory, he does his very best to devise controls on his experiments that will yield impartial results. In the reductionist world of 3D Newtonian physics, we can rely on such results, at least up to a point. But if the quantum energy reality underlies it all, then any objective empirical study cannot ever be truly impartial. We must begin to accept that our beliefs, perceptions and feelings about the world we see through our own eyes shape the very world we observe. De Chardin's noosphere and Carl Jung's collective unconscious, which attempted to explain similarities cross-culturally around the world from population to population, may be the method by which we all make manifest – and participate in – a world that is familiar to us all.

The Extraterrestrial Factor

So what do extraterrestrials have to do with any of this? Because by so very many accounts today, UFOs, or extraterrestrial craft, seem to exhibit a mastery of quantum science and multidimensionality inherent in these newly emerging sciences on Earth. Even abductees and contactees talk of telepathy, astral or other-dimensional travel. What might contact mean with beings who have a mastery of multi-dimensional abilities? Could they awaken those possibly now-dormant abilities within us? What if opening to, and developing even just a beginner's understanding of quantum mechanics and the reality of multiple dimensions is a criteria for contact? What if initial glimpses of the underlying interconnectedness of the multiverse itself opens the door to beings that inhabit these other realms?

If these beings know how to apply quantum mechanics in a technological way, then they may also know how to apply this knowledge consciously and biologically. As written about in *Autobiography of a Yogi* by Paramahansa Yogananda,[3] spiritual adepts can bi-locate and perform other seemingly miraculous feats through a practiced understanding of quantum reality as a form of spiritual practice or discipline. Spiritually advanced extraterrestrial beings could also travel by the power of thought alone, but may use space craft for traveling to free their mental energy for other tasks.

Beyond any concerns about ET craft, their builders or their propulsion systems, the fact that extraterrestrials exist as attested to in volumes of testimony and other evidence, adds another vast array of players to games of consciousness and "reality." In dimensions from the third up to perhaps the sixth or seventh – where individual forms are still part of the paradigms and their various modes of expression intersect and interact physically, astrally or at some other energetic level – their tapestries of consciousness enrich the playing field within which we all find ourselves living out our lives.

Life on a Post-Extraterrestrial Contact Earth

There are a couple of scenarios that could be playing out right now on our world.

The term, "New World Order" is one that many of us have come to regard with wary caution, if not complete outrage, at the steps seeming to march on and on towards a fascist, totalitarian "big brother" world government. The current economic crisis could signal this. Crossing all the usual boundaries of political

---

[3] Paramahansa Yogananda is a spiritual teacher from India credited with bringing much of India's ancient spiritual teachings to the western world through his widely read book *Autobiography of a Yogi*. He founded the Self Realization Fellowship in 1920. More information about him can be found here: http://www.yogananda-srf.org.

parties, race, class (except for the extremely rich) or other seeming differences, the economic structures of this world appear to be crumbling. While the law of attraction folks keep hawking their systems of magnetizing abundant inflows of money, and while I do believe that they can have a measure of success on a universal abundance principle no matter what the state of the economy actually is, the entire system within which they are operating was ill-conceived from its inception. The current money structure is a fractional currency system set up to be debt-based. If you are going to practice principles of attracting abundance, I think that understanding this fact while still using the universal abundance principle to manifest more money is better than operating in the dark about what the current money structure was conceived to be from the start. Since the current structure of finance is in such disarray now, with home foreclosures, Wall Street bailouts and massive unemployment – connected to and underlying all other hierarchical power institutions of this world – it appears that society and politics are both crumbling at their foundations. The appearances are still there, but hollowed out from within by massive graft and corruption that has become blaringly obvious.

We have a unique choice point before us as a people right now. On one hand, a "collapse" of civilization as we've known it could very well be planned; another of the "problem-reaction-solution" scenarios detailed by David Icke. Problem: economic chaos threatening collapse (designed by those in power). Reaction: Distress, fear, anger, movements like Occupy Wall Street. Solution: Instituting a new global economic system, replacing the old, in a way that *appears* to alleviate all distress, fear and worry... until the manipulation starts all over again.

If the majority of the population is sufficiently dumbed down, feels helpless and powerless enough, a valiant-seeming rescue by those holding the power would be welcomed feverishly by those in travail. Then – ouch! This new "abundance" turns out to accompanied by more and more severe curtailments of personal freedoms and human rights.

On the other hand, it could be that the old structures have let people down so much for so long, that they as a group are withdrawing their longstanding beliefs in these structures as solid and absolute, resulting in the chaos and instability economic systems are exhibiting today.

It could be a combination of both: problem-reaction-solution, and the fact that billions of disillusioned people are withdrawing the energy of their beliefs from the age-old hierarchies of this world they've depended upon for so long.

If both are true, then the most wealthy and powerful on this world, who have manipulated the common people for so very long, are gambling hugely on just how successful they have been in their agendas to subvert, to control, to dumb down and to repress expanding consciousness in humanity.

The next truly interesting questions we have to ask ourselves are: How successful do WE think they have been? Can we wake up and smell the coffee here? Can we start reading between the lines?

The evidence is all around us. It's in an ecosystem continually assaulted by exploitation for obsolete forms of energy that fuel the debt-based economic system. Traditional "health" care does little to nothing to support true health and even destroying people's health by pursuing forms of "medicine" that increasingly do more harm than good. We no longer have true education in schools, colleges and universities, we have programs of indoctrination. The debt-based economic system keeps working class people on a treadmill – student loans insure that young people newly graduating from their indoctrination programs have a heavy load of debt to pay back, making certain they go out and find themselves a spot on the treadmill and become a cog in the "Great Machine." Hopefully they won't look up from working too often to really "see" what is going on.

But what if we could, what if we are waking up and seeing what has been going on? What if we choose a new way of being in the world? There are billions more of "us" than "them." It is our collective consciousness in one form or another that "they" have been using and harnessing to create their empires. Therefore, it is within our power to take back our freedom and the power to exercise intention and positive action, arising out of the exercise of consciousness and intelligence inherent within us. We can stop allowing the rich and powerful to divide and conquer us, and it is imperative that we do so, and without delay.

I was very excited to see the documentary I wrote about in Chapter 20, *Thrive:What On Earth Will It Take?* It shows a synthesis now occurring between groups that have been previously separate, that I have felt for years had to come together – someday.

On one hand, we have had a group of grim conspiracy theorists, who see the dark in the world, who glimpse the ugly forces trying to control from the shadows, yet have been fairly powerless to really get people to pay attention to them. The very term, "conspiracy theory" has been a prelude to blanket dismissal and denial. Their problem has been their lack of ability in many cases to also see the underlying energetics of a Conscious Living Universe. A Unified Consciousness of which we are all a part with only one agenda, the expansion and awakening of consciousness. Such people must come to an understanding of the the ebb and flow of awareness on a continuum of varying states of limitation to complete freedom.

On the other hand, we have had those who have at least a rudimentary understanding of consciousness, unity and energetic understanding. For a long time, such people refused to look at anything dark out of fear that it might engulf them, taking away their "Light" or destroying what they are trying to manifest through the law of attraction. But a fear of looking, of seeing the shadow, sits deep inside and festers. Spiritual adepts know that the shadow within must be faced and integrated fully for true enlightenment. What is true for the individual is also true, especially today, for the entire human collective. We cannot conquer, as lone individuals, the collective shadow that we are facing today. But we can do it if we unify and work together.

The *Thrive* documentary brought an incredible amount of speakers and information from both sides of the coin, beginning to bridge the gulf between the dark truths of "conspiracy theory" and the light truths of "unity consciousness" as well as a whole set of positive actions we can all take together to shift the course of human life on this planet in a positive direction for every single human being. A process called "F.A.C.T."[4] for positive change is at work in this film; Facing, Accepting, Communicating and Taking Action.

There are many important factors regarding what is going on in our world covered in *Thrive*. One of them is what I have known for many years; UFO secrecy is also free energy secrecy. I would go a step further and say that it is also secrecy about where liberated consciousness could take humanity as an entire species.

The multi-dimensional or extra-dimensional reality that would accompany extraterrestrial contact is a wild card that would likely throw the hierarchical power-based structures of this planet into collapse. The institutions of this world have been made real and solid for hundreds, if not thousands of years by those holding power, manipulating and coercing us to believe in and trust their voices of authority over our own innate feelings and intuitive perceptions. Keeping us off balance with emotionally-charged words and actions rooted in organizations that play upon carefully-constructed-over-the-ages consensus reality, these hierarchical systems have the power to push unaware populations this way and that through religious beliefs, misguided forms of patriotism and contrived societal-cultural ideas of right and wrong. These institutions have held power through being able to convince us to trust their versions of how the world should work – instead of us trusting our inner natures and feelings of resonance or dissonance of energy – our own sense of the underlying field of what makes up our material world.

Open public contact with extraterrestrials coming into the midst of such hierarchical power structures threatens those organizations with collapse, or at the very least, a complete restructuring. It is no wonder that the reality of an extraterrestrial presence and covert contact has been kept under wraps. However, today, our continued collective survival as a species may depend upon returning to an understanding of the energy or "spirit" inherent in all creation, animate and inanimate, supported by the new discoveries in quantum science. It may be this new way of looking at our world and how interconnected we are with every part of it that helps us to throw off the restrictions of the hierarchical power structures in our current 11th hour on this world to write a new story of life and living, one in which we develop the vision to see where we must put our energy and resources to thrive.

[4] F.A.C.T. is a process developed by Gay Hendricks, PhD and Kathlyn Hendricks, PhD, authors of many books about relationships and body-centered therapy. See their website for more information: www.hendricks.com/Trainings.

At such a point, two possible scenarios emerge. In the first, as we become collectively more aware of quantum realities and a living, conscious multi-dimensional Universe of which we are a part. We then act in accord with that new belief and begin building a new world through our conscious intention, withdrawing our thought, energy and attention from the old one. At that point we may become eligible for contact with evolved, benevolent extraterrestrials, having begun to demonstrate a satisfactory level of sentience. In the other, full open contact occurs and major change is a consequence of that contact – actually facilitating and hastening a new level of sentient collective consciousness in humanity as the veils are lifted on who we truly are in relation to other life in the cosmos.

All the words upon words that I, or others, use to try and describe the qualities and aspects of multidimensional experience could be grokked by experiencing a single nanosecond of our individual consciousness occupying one of the higher energetic realms. I say individual, but the awareness of oneself in connection to everyone and everything would also be simultaneously evident. Communication with others would be a matter of vibration and energy rather than speech and also very nearly instantaneous. You feel what everyone around you feels. The sense of "communion" is always around you, like a heavenly choir that you feel in the silence as a resonance rather than actual sound; though with more focus, the beauty of that resonance is heard, seen, tasted, smelled and tactilely felt in the energy network of the body. What we experience as five physical senses here in the third dimension, overlap and combine to become one greatly-expanded sense on the higher planes. In such a vibratory sea of full awareness, misunderstandings might not even be possible because the ambiguity of words is not needed. Grokking people, places and situations would be direct, transparent and instantaneous through the energetic medium of vibratory frequency.

Chapter 29: Disclosure and Amnesty

The denial of information, to most people, is a great crime against democratic rule, and against the traditional republican principles that the United States is based on. We need to understand what's actually going on. There's something serious, there's something big, and this is exactly what I'm trying to find out.

The day will come when the truth of this is out in the open. When that happens, I guarantee you there's gonna be some heads that roll. But the truth will also be a bright sunny day for many of us. There are very, very important practical reasons for getting this information out. We've got serious environmental problems in this world, we've got serious political problems in this world, and we cannot keep going on the way we are with this system. There's got to be something new and something better, and some of that answer lies in understanding the entire UFO phenomenon. It's a lot more important in other words, than just lights in the sky.

~ Richard M. Dolan[1], author of *UFOs and the National Security State, Volumes I and II* and *A.D. After Disclosure*, with Bryce Zabel

"Disclosure" sometimes seems as elusive a beast as the Loch Ness monster. It is sighted from time to time then apparently dives back into the watery depths. Water is a symbol of the unconscious. It would not be an idle endeavor to examine our collective human unconscious when it comes to disclosure of exotic ET technologies, how they're being used and how they could be used. The "need to know" compartmentalization in government and the world's elite rich looks more and more like a reflection of the parts of our collective Id, parts that we hide from ourselves.

---

[1] Richard M. Dolan, educated at Alfred University, Oxford University and completing graduate studies at the University of Rochester, is one of the most respected, credible and knowledgeable UFO researchers in the world today. He has authored several books, including the comprehensive tomes *UFOs and the National Security State*, (two volumes – the first covering 1941 to 1973, the second covering 1973 to 1991) and *A.D. After Disclosure: When the Government Finally Reveals the Truth about Alien Contact*, with Bryce Zabel and an upcoming new book, *UFOs for the 21st Century Mind*. His website: http://www.keyholepublishing.com/kp1.

Yet we live in times where more and more of the secret machinations of government and those ultra-wealthy shadow groups behind the curtains who buy and sell in government and military power are being increasingly exposed. At some level, humanity is doing its spiritual shadow work, or this kind of exposure would not be taking place.

Disclosure around extraterrestrial technology and contact is just one piece of a much larger world socio-political-economic pie. As I have known for years, and as has come out in the recent film *Thrive*, UFO secrecy is free energy secrecy. Free energy secrecy and suppression allows the unimaginable wealth accumulated and hoarded by less than one percent of the world's population to manage and control governments and corporations. This happens because oil has been extensively developed as the dominant form of energy to move people from place to place, to create and transport goods and services around the world. This wealth provided the power to buy politicians and influence and direct legislative processes. Any new scientific discoveries that might threaten a "new world order" paradigm, with big-brother types of control, are seized, sequestered and suppressed. Narcissistic and sociopathic leadership, driven to ever more grandiose and extreme agendas of control have worked to subvert and undermine constitutional systems of government that could be invoked to prevent their rise to ultimate power. The release and implementation of free energy technologies would break the corporate oil-economic monopoly and its stranglehold on this planet and bring down their whole house of cards.

We the People are getting fed up with business as usual in the U.S. government. We are tired of Wall Street bailouts, of losing our homes and jobs while tax breaks for the richest echelons of society continue and corporations gain ever more control over our political processes and our very lives. They do not care about us. They care about their profits and would take away our rights to every kind of choice we still have until we are left with no alternatives but to spend our hard-earned cash on what they have to offer. This, in part, has spawned the popular peoples' Occupy movements. Occupy Wall Street. Occupy the Fed. Occupy Washington D.C., and more. The Occupiers identify themselves as the 99% of the population and the echelons of the wealthy trying to control them as the 1%. We now have Julian Assange and Wikileaks. We have a group of unindentified cyber-hackers that call themselves "Anonymous." Their credo:

> We are Anonymous.
> We are Legion.
> United as ONE.
> Divided by zero.
> We do not forget.
> We do not forgive.
> Expect us!!

Such movements strike fear into the hearts of the so-named 1%. This is why we are now seeing a gutting of our United States Constitution, with the very recent passage of the National Defense Authorization Act in January of 2012 (NDAA). Without naming it specifically as such, this legislation, illegal in the face of the U.S. Constitution, is a soft declaration of martial law. The worst provisions:

- ⚔ American citizens suspected of terrorism to be indefinitely detained in military custody without charge or trial.
- ⚔ Allow the Armed Forces to engage in civilian law enforcement and to selectively suspend *due process and habeas corpus, as well as* other rights guaranteed by the fifth and sixth Amendments to the U.S. Constitution, for terror suspects apprehended on U.S. soil.

This is exacerbated by the Patriot Act. U.S. citizens who are investigated as suspected terrorists cannot let others know about such scrutiny without risking prosecution under Patriot Act provisions. The Patriot Act and NDAA together put a citizen suspected of terrorist activities (even if wrongly so) in the position where they could be held in military detention for months without trial. Should they be released they are then restricted from taking legal action against their captors if wrongly detained.

This could cause a return to the kind of blacklisting and prosecutions of the "McCarthyism" era of the late 1940s and 1950s, only worse. If one is suspected of sympathizing or providing any level of support to persons or organizations labeled "terrorist," one is subject to indefinite detention under the NDAA. And there are no time limits on such detention. The current "war on terror" is open-ended. How does one define when or how hostilities can be considered to be over? Especially when heavy-handed military tactics being used around the world, both known and covert, could continually create fresh crops of people who hate the United States of America and might attempt terrorist attacks to express that hatred?

By exercising our constitutional right to peaceful assembly and demonstration, U.S. citizens could be deemed as supporting terrorists. By what parameters will "supporting terrorists" be defined? Who will determine them and with what motives or biases? We clearly can see that the 1% are quite threatened by the 99% as is being defined in the Occupy movements in the U.S. and around the world. This drastically unconstitutional legislation enters the scene very conveniently, just as such movements are gaining momentum and support by people who have had it with an economy that panders to Wall Street and the rich while leaving them jobless and homeless.

The criminal elements – the parasites who self-style themselves as our betters and elites, who have seized control within the system – want to remove any and all chance that they could be held legally accountable through the U.S. Constitution for the crimes they know deep down inside themselves they are perpetrating against humanity. Free people are a huge threat. Armed with freedom as a divine right, enforceable under the supreme law of the land, they can go after you. So free people must be stripped of their freedoms, subjugated and controlled. These elite appear to be attempting this in increments rather than in one single coup d'état so people become acclimated to fewer and fewer freedoms over time. The Constitution must be undermined and eroded a chunk at a time until people don't understand what has happened until it is too late. Dumb them down, manipulate their minds and emotions, make them dependent and unable to make their own decisions, and then offer that you will "take care of them." All they need do is surrender their freedom to you.

I wonder what meaning "disclosure" can have in the social and political climate we are seeing in the U.S.A. today. Yet "government" is a huge, varied, compartmentalized and stratified collection of entities. This includes the Armed Forces. When a government, heavily infiltrated and controlled by corporate interests, rallies the Armed Forces to go to war for them under banners of spreading democracy throughout the world and liberating oppressed people from tyrants and dictators, they are playing a dangerous game. Just as do presidents, members of Congress and U.S. Supreme Court, members of the Armed Forces take that oath to defend and protect the U.S. and its Constitution against all enemies foreign and domestic. It does not take military service members too much deep thought to realize that a governing body that tries to make laws in violation of the Constitution that they also swore an oath to protect has become a domestic enemy of the United States, its Constitution and its people. This includes the mothers, fathers, sisters, brothers and children of such servicemen and women. With the open legislation out on the table today so destructive to the very Constitutional values that such servicemen and women took an oath to protect, just how much longer will such people continue to serve a democracy turned corporatocracy when the quality of life for themselves and their families hangs in the balance? Just how much longer will they stand for being propagandized and manipulated by a government so visibly selling out every freedom they hold dear and swore to protect?

Terms like "Operation Iraqi Freedom" and "Operation Enduring Freedom" (referencing the wars on Iraq and Afghanistan, respectively) are themselves propaganda words to persuade soldiers to go fight these wars. Freedom is the buzzword – freedom is what the American way of life has been based upon. Yet how hypocritical is it to make war on other countries in the name of setting them "free" from dictators when our own country is no longer a free country? Corporations in America have become the new tyrants, despots and dictators, continually using money to do away with our Constitution; to take away our freedom a piece at a time and force us to choose only from the limited choices they put before us.

It doesn't take soldiers possessed of any intelligence or conscience long to realize what is really going on with the wars they have been asked to fight. American rhetoric like "for the land of the free and the home of the brave," are used as banners for going war to protect "the American way of life." Pasting the word "freedom" into some "Operation" slogan is used to manipulate soldiers to go to war and for society to support that war. The general military, trained to follow orders, does as they are told, believing that it's for "Mom, baseball and apple pie."

And we must take that rhetoric back to fight fascism in our country today. The corporatocracy has abused symbols of American freedom to manipulate people into fighting/supporting wars of aggression. However, they may have painted themselves into a corner by doing so. They are teetering on the edge of a precipice where their agenda is becoming so transparent as to render any attempt to use U.S. symbols of freedom meaningless henceforth. The moment is upon us when We the People need to take up the flag of our country, take a stand for the Declaration of Independence, the Constitution and Bill of Rights, as the flag was intended, originally, to symbolize. We need to restore to such symbols the freedom and truth they were meant to represent. The corporatocracy has no right to such symbols. All they have done is exploit them and the people who revere them. They are all about controlling people, ostensibly "for the peoples' own good." In actual practice, they operate for how much profit they can squeeze from a population without killing them all outright.

The corporatocracy of the U.S. is the very antithesis of freedom. And the corporatocracy is just the visible layer of a deeper problem – a ruling Machiavellian aristocracy that never truly disappeared, but just went underground. There, through deception, duplicity and manipulation, they gathered money, power and influence towards a day when they could again rule and control.

The Rot Begins

Years ago the U.S.A. used technological superiority, intelligence gathering and military force to win World War II. Afterwards, our government and military deemed it necessary to bring the scientists and researchers of Hitler's Third Reich to the United States under Project Paperclip, scrubbing up their profiles, hiding many of them behind Americanized names and putting them to work for our government at some of the most secret, classified levels. The powers that be in our military-industrial complex wanted that terrible knowledge – from advanced technological expertise to refined trauma-based mind control techniques – purchased at a terrible price in human suffering and death, that the Nazi scientists had gleaned in their years serving under Hitler. With that knowledge came a comprehension of almost unlimited power – all the more potent because it was being wielded in secret, on a need-to-know basis with little to no Congressional oversight.

I am sure that, in the early days, those in charge convinced themselves that it was for the safety and security of U.S. citizens that such terrible knowledge was developed and refined, as well as keeping Nazi expertise out of the hands of the Soviet Union. Yet over time, with scientists who still held to Nazi ideologies of power and control whispering in their ears, many people within our military-industrial complex were subverted. With that sense of terrible power, shrouded in secrecy, came the corruption of the Constitutional values and principles upon which our country was founded. Over the decades, this rot within began to eat away at the very fabric of our free society.

This is a scenario that has played itself out countless times throughout the history of this planet: oppression and control breeding rebellion and war. Anger and rage turning otherwise good people into creatures who felt they had to use the same horror and demoralization tactics of their enemies to defeat those enemies. Whichever side won such nameless, meaningless conflicts was left with the same internal rot – a war won by force must also maintain the ensuing "peace" by force. Revolutionaries become administrators. Administrators get used to wielding control. They begin to fear the loss of it, begin to fear being controlled in their turn. How can it be otherwise? To use force and the threat of terror by whatever means is sure to awaken a terror within such administrators of the same tactics being turned back on them, should they fall from power. Fear becomes justification for more and more inhumane means to frighten enemies, to frighten even their own citizens into compliance with their policies, ostensibly for the citizens' own good, for their safety and security. Freedoms fought for begin to be sacrificed, a piece at a time.

In his 1961 "Military-Industrial Speech," former president Dwight D. Eisenhower gave us all a potent warning as he left the Oval Office at the end of his final term. A message that we as a people, in our innocent ignorance at that time, did not fully comprehend, nor did we take it nearly enough to heart. I give here a more complete quoting of his words than many do because this fuller text is so poignantly and imminently congruent with the times we find ourselves in today.

> Until the latest of our world conflicts, the United States had no armaments industry. American makers of plowshares could, with time and as required, make swords as well. But now we can no longer risk emergency improvisation of national defense; we have been compelled to create a permanent armaments industry of vast proportions. Added to this, three and a half million men and women are directly engaged in the defense establishment. We annually spend on military security more than the net income of all United States corporations.

> This conjunction of an immense military establishment and a large arms industry is new in the American experience. The total influence – economic, political, even spiritual – is felt in every city, every State house, every office of the Federal government. We recognize the imperative need for this development. Yet we must not fail to comprehend its grave implications. Our toil, resources and livelihood are all involved;

so is the very structure of our society.

In the councils of government, we must guard against the acquisition of unwarranted influence, whether sought or unsought, by the military-industrial complex. The potential for the disastrous rise of misplaced power exists, and will persist.

We must never let the weight of this combination endanger our liberties or democratic processes. We should take nothing for granted. Only an alert and knowledgeable citizenry can compel the proper meshing of the huge industrial and military machinery of defense with our peaceful methods and goals, so that security and liberty may prosper together.

Akin to, and largely responsible for the sweeping changes in our industrial-military posture, has been the technological revolution during recent decades.

In this revolution, research has become central; it also becomes more formalized, complex, and costly. A steadily increasing share is conducted for, by, or at the direction of, the Federal government.

Today, the solitary inventor, tinkering in his shop, has been overshadowed by task forces of scientists in laboratories and testing fields. In the same fashion, the free university, historically the fountainhead of free ideas and scientific discovery, has experienced a revolution in the conduct of research. Partly because of the huge costs involved, a government contract becomes virtually a substitute for intellectual curiosity. For every old blackboard there are now hundreds of new electronic computers.

The prospect of domination of the nation's scholars by Federal employment, project allocations, and the power of money is ever present and is gravely to be regarded.

Yet, in holding scientific research and discovery in respect, as we should, we must also be alert to the equal and opposite danger that public policy could itself become the captive of a scientific technological elite.

It is the task of statesmanship to mold, to balance, and to integrate these and other forces, new and old, within the principles of our democratic system – ever aiming toward the supreme goals of our free society.

479

It seems that narcissistic psychopaths have overrun our government and the top levels of corporations and other hierarchical institutions. Such individuals demand the public's attention to pander to their megalomaniacal egos. They crave being in the limelight. Yet it likely only seems this way. Others of good conscience, honor and strong principles of heart and compassion also walk the corridors of power. They have little need to demand such public attention. And it likely serves their purposes to move behind the scenes, doing what they can to restore our country to sane leadership and a return to the Bill of Rights and constitutional law upon which our country was founded. Perhaps with new amendments that will prevent corporate incursions into our political process and other inviolable areas of our personal lives in the future. Citizens of the U.S.A. will need to be accurately educated about their responsibility in the political process to prevent a relapse into the complacency that contributed to what has happened to our government in the last 60 to 100 years.

The Wild Card: Disclosure as a way "Out"

Within the various layers and departments of government and military, disclosure could be seen as a way to let not only the truth genie of the extraterrestrial phenomenon out of the bottle, but to let the free energy genie out as well. Truth be told, this related pair of genies are finding little escape routes into the public mainstream all the time, like water through the seriously-undermined structure of a dam. The more information that finds its way out about the reality of free zero-point energy, the more people are considering the possibilities of what a true free energy economy could mean.

One of the most recent and significant ways disclosure has popped up in the mainstream is with Foster and Kimberly Gamble's film, *Thrive*. Bringing together scientists, activists and other thinkers and researchers from previously widely divergent schools of thought, this film breaks new ground in both divulging free energy information, pointing out that UFO secrecy is in fact free energy secrecy and following the money from there. Interviews with such diverse individuals as Deepak Chopra, David Icke, Nassim Haramein, Catherine Austin-Fitts and many others help illustrate that there is far more standing in the way of UFO disclosure than blanket denial from presidential administrations or congressional ignorance.

Like the sporadic sightings of "Nessie," small signs surface that might be missed in mainstream media news. However they are not missed by those trolling the internet for signs that disclosure could be in the works.

For me, "official" disclosure began with the Disclosure Project's press conference at the National Press Club in Washington, D.C. in May of 2001. It was a people's movement, begun by people. Disclosure continues as a people's movement. Unfortunately any momentum the 2001 press conference created was dissolved by the attack on the World Trade Center on September 11, 2001. That day marked our country's descent into where we are today, poised on the brink of becoming an openly fascist regime.

There was a news flash tipped to Dr. Michael Salla of the Exopolitics Institute in February 2008 of secret meetings being held at the United Nations to discuss UFOs and extraterrestrials. Later in May that same year, the Vatican announced officially that extraterrestrial life could exist and if so, they would be our brothers, and that they could be more evolved than human beings. This statement came through Reverend Jose Gabriel Funes,[2] scientific advisor to Pope Benedict XVI and head of the Vatican Observatory.

A very notable event in January of 2011 was the Global Competitiveness Forum. Cutting edge business people from around the world gathered to hear a panel of speakers at this forum discuss UFOs and extraterrestrials. Sitting on the panel were well-known UFO researchers such as Stanton Friedman,[3] Nick Pope[4] and Jacques Vallee.[5] Theoretical physicist Dr. Michio Kaku[6] was also a guest speaker, offering his educated thoughts and opinions on contact with extraterrestrial life, categorizing them as Type 1, Type 2 and Type 3 civilizations.

According to Dr. Kaku, Type 1 civilizations control all forms of planetary energy, such as weather, volcanoes, earthquakes and would be perhaps 100 years ahead of us in energy and technology. Type 2 civilizations control the energy and output of suns and stars. They are immortal civilizations because they can deflect meteors and asteroids, and if for some reason they could not move their planet or re-ignite their own sun, they would be capable of simply moving their civilization to another world. Type 2 civilizations would be perhaps a few thousand years ahead of us. A type 3 civilization would be able to control the energy output of an entire galaxy. They can work with black holes and manipulate space and time with higher-dimensional physics. They would be many thousands of years ahead of us technologically.

At $5000 per plate for this corporate forum, the top people in attendance included former British and Canadian Prime Ministers Tony Blair and Jean Chretien, Boeing president and CEO Jim Albaugh, Walt Disney International chairman Andy Bird, and Google director of ideas, Jared Cohen, among many notable others. Not exactly your idea of the usual suspects for UFO conference attendees.

In August 2010 a well-researched book by Leslie Kean, *UFOs: Generals, Pilots and Government Officials Go on the Record* hit the New York Times bestseller list. Its forward was penned by John Podesta, former White House Chief of Staff under President Bill Clinton and co-chairman of the Obama-Biden Transition

---

[2] See article at this link: http://www.nytimes.com/2008/05/14/world/europe/14iht-vat.4.12885393.html.

[3] Stanton T. Friedman has been an established UFO researcher for many years, with many books and other published media. His website: http://www.stantonfriedman.com

[4] Nick Pope used to run the UFO program for the British government and today is one of the foremost researchers, authors and journalists in the UFO arena. He has been seen on many television documentaries. His website: http://www.nickpope.net.

5 Jacques Vallee, astrophysicist, author and researcher has had a varied career with many interests, including unidentified aerial phenomenon. His website: http://www.jacquesvallee.net.

[6] Dr. Michio Kaku is a physicist, a futurist and best-selling author with many television and radio appearances to his credit. His website: http://mkaku.org.

Project. Podesta has consistently supported the release of information on UFOs and worked to declassify 800 million pages of documentation while serving under Clinton.

On September 27, 2010, John Hastings[7], author and researcher, hosted the UFOs and Nukes Press Conference at the National Press Club in Washington, D.C. to affirm to the world that U.S. nuclear weapons have been compromised by unidentified aerial objects. Former military officers offered their first-hand testimony of UFOs hovering over nuclear weapons storage facilities, shutting down power and scrambling launch codes to nuclear missile silos and interfering with nuclear missile tests over bomb test ranges. Hastings has interviewed more than 120 veterans having personal experiences with this aspect of the UFO phenomenon. The following seven veterans spoke at the September 27 press conference: USAF Lt. Colonel Retired and communications center officer-in-charge Dwynne Arneson, former USAF nuclear missile launch officer Bruce Fenstermacher, USAF Colonel Retired and former deputy base commander Charles Halt; former USAF nuclear missile targeting officer Robert Jamison, former USAF nuclear missile site geodetic surveyor Patrick McDonough, former USAF nuclear missile launch officer Jerome Nelson, and former USAF nuclear missile launch officer Robert Salas.

Less than a month later, as if the ETs were underscoring the point of that conference, there was another nuclear missle incident involving a UFO on October 23, 2010 at Warren AFB at Cheyenne, Wyoming. A huge cigar-shaped craft hovered over the missile field as base personnel lost the ability to communicate with fifty of their Minuteman III nuclear missiles. This "malfunction" continued over several hours. One might wonder how much UFO occupants know of what goes on down on Earth regarding their presence in our skies. Perhaps they wanted to give the UFOs and Nukes press conference and its speakers their full support.

Also in October 2010, at a United Nations press conference, Mazlan Othman, Deputy Director-General, United Nations Office at Vienna (UNOV) and Director of the Office for Outer Space Affairs (OOSA), briefed journalists on the peaceful uses of outer space. As an incorrect rumor had been leaked before this press conference that Othman would be Earth's ambassador to extraterrestrial visitors should they appear, she had to answer many lively questions from the press about possible extraterrestrial contact scenarios. It was clear that UFOs are a subject that many of the journalists were very curious about. Again, this was not a crowd of avid UFO fans in tinfoil hats.

One wonders how such tidbits of news get out there if "someone" or some group of individuals do not want such news to get out. One could make an argument that with all the noise made by UFO groups over the years – which has swelled and grown rather than faded – such news bytes are tossed out to both placate and titilate the UFO and ET true believers. But what if something

---

[7] John Hastings is a researcher with a special interest in how UFOs have interfered with U.S. nuclear capabilities through the years. His website: http://www.ufohastings.com/.

else is going on? What if those "white hat" individuals that quietly and inobtrusively walk the corridors of power with the megalomaniacs would like to see, perhaps even direct or guide, positive world changes? What if they allow, instigate or even initiate such events happening, the news flashing out over the web at the speed of electrons?

On an entirely different level, UFO and extraterrestrial disclosure is happening all around us all the time. Disclosure has become far less an act that the UFO and exopolitics communities demand of government than it is a movement of the people, lead by those with direct experience who will no longer be intimidated into silence. Fear of ridicule and censure is less and less an obstacle to speaking out, especially for people who have had to carry the heavy weight of secrecy around for much of their lives. Nowhere is this more true than in the government and military. One might be convinced for decades by superiors that secrecy is in the public's best interest. But when individuals of honor, principles and conscience watch those decades march onwards and see the increasing level of government takeover by corporations; when they watch the U.S. flag held up for propaganda campaigns to get young people to go to war for ever more thinly-veiled corporate interests; then such people begin to speak out. More and more whistleblowers are stepping forward. Like a wave that gains both mass and momentum, the courage of those who do speak out give courage to yet more to do the same.

The dam of secrecy is cracking in thousands of places, every whistleblower a leak. The damage is rapidly outstripping the ability of any controlling elite to patch or control. The smart and savvy among them are jumping ship and getting out of the way of this dam before it breaks wide open and truth pours forth in a flood that no force can stop.

The Need for Amnesty

Let us consider that, in the near future, the peoples' disclosure movement is successful. UFO secrecy is swept away, free energy can no longer be suppressed or concealed; and visionary innovators, now knowing what is possible, begin to conceive and design zero-point or over-unity energy devices. People begin to put these devices to work. As more and more of the truth tumbles out into the mainstream with the flow of free energy, people begin to wake up to the massive amount of human and animal suffering and environmental exploitation and devastation that never, ever had to happen. A collective rage sets in as those who have lost homes, family and friends and who watched their communities ravaged by environmental disasters caused by oil or nuclear radiation begin to understand that it never had to happen... if those actively suppressing energy alternatives had been less greedy and more humanitarian.

In such an newly emergent social and political climate, many of the secret keepers might rush forward with what they know to join the side of the world now supporting and using free energy. Many others may try to maintain silence, hoping the public's rage will pass them by, unnoticed. After all, they were deep in secret black projects. No one would know their names or faces... except possibly other whistleblowers.

There will be large segments of the world community that will understandably be enraged at the sheer level of destruction and carnage that never had to happen. There will need to be tribunals set up to address crimes of secrecy, such as murder and illegal detention to keep secrets, mind control experiments and abuses, and especially free energy suppression, perpetrated against humans and the Earth's environment, causing widespread suffering and death by direct or indirect means.

Yet I have to believe that a world weary of war and exploitation – once the truth is out revealing the underlying manipulations of hundreds, likely even thousands of years – would be open to the incredible opportunity presented by a new world of free energy – to create a new, more unified and enlightened society. We have the thinkers, the visionaries, the futurists. It is certainly worth putting forward as a possibility.

So the next question, as an enlightened society, is: How will we deal with such criminals we will most certainly discover trying to slink away from responsibility for the devastation, suffering and death they caused?

Before dealing with such criminals, they must be positively identified and placed before the tribunals to determine their guilt and culpability as either initiators of or participants in programs that were criminal in nature, i.e., causing mental, emotional or physical harm to others against their will. In trying to decide what consequences should be meted out for criminal acts committed under secrecy and beyond the law for decades, there is the thorny issue of finding out the extent or degree of guilt of each individual. There would be those coming forward with their part of the truth and those who will try to stay hidden as long as they possibly can. Coming forward voluntarily would certainly count in one's favor.

Factors to consider would be initiation and instigation of programs requiring actions that would deprive others of life or liberty – including liberty of the mind – as a means of enforcing secrecy of black projects and covert operations. Next to be considered would be levels of guilt and culpability of participants in such programs: were they willing participants or were they coerced and threatened, either their own lives and/or the lives of their families? A scale would need to be established, from 1 to 10, with 10 being the highest level of culpability.

Multiple tribunal hearing panels would have to be set up with established questioning and testing criteria to insure fairness on each panel as every individual case is heard. The panels would be comprised of qualified *independent* forensic psychologists and psychiatrists, at least two for each panel, as well as independent attorneys with solid foundations in constitutional law. "Independent" means, as much as is possible, employing practicing professionals with as few connections to federal government as possible. And even screening such professionals to serve on panels should be done with care and thought to selection criteria, as well as reviewing resumes and references. Various forms of lie detection may have to be used and cross-checked, with, again, independent professionals administering such tests as peripheral members of each panel.

Each incriminated person would have to be assessed as to mental health and any psychological pathology that might have affected their behavior or decisions, not excusing such decisions or actions, but in understanding the degree of the pathology. Psychopaths such as sociopaths and narcissists are deemed intractable and incurable by mental health professionals for all intents and purposes. Because they are predisposed by their pathologies to manipulate, lie, cheat and control others, even sadistically if their pathologies are assessed to be severe enough, then they cannot be allowed enough freedom to continue perpetrating harm on others.

The network of secrecy is vast, and it could take time to catch up with everyone involved, if that is even possible. All we can do is the best we can.

Amnesty and Consequences for Criminal Behavior in an Enlightened Society

And if any of you would punish in the name of righteousness and lay the axe unto the evil tree, let him see to its roots; And verily he will find the roots of the good and the bad, the fruitful and the fruitless, all entwined together in the silent heart of the earth.

And you who would understand justice, how shall you unless you look upon all deeds in the fullness of light?

Only then shall you know that the erect and the fallen are but one man standing in twilight between the night of his pigmy-self and the day of his god-self, and that the cornerstone of the temple is not higher than the lowest stone in its foundation.

~ From *The Prophet*, by Kahlil Gibran, selection "On Crime and Punishment"

On a world in transition from the old to the new, amnesty programs of various levels need to be designed and offered as incentives for cooperation and truth from those who directed or served in programs or activities that caused great public harm, suffering or death.

485

Once guilt and culpability are established, then what consequences? The eye-for-an-eye and a tooth-for-a-tooth mentality gave us the old world we have been trudging through over the past two thousand years or more, a world of war and exploitation that led us to where we are today. We need a new paradigm, a more enlightened paradigm to work from today. We cannot hope to create a world in which we would want our children and grandchildren to happily live and thrive, free to explore their full potentials by using the old paradigm thinking that led to wars of aggression and conquest, empire and control at the whims of a tyrant or a ruling elite. We must rethink how to handle aggression and criminal behavior. We must sit down together and birth a new way of dealing with these traits and temperments and the acts they precipitate.

In his documentary, *Future by Design*, visionary and futurist Jacque Fresco[8] of the Venus Project stated that people are shaped by the environment they live in. Consider the world we have lived in for thousands of years and the paradigm for living and thinking in an environment of empires where groups of ruling elite own, control and parcel out resources, thereby controlling the people they wish to rule over. We have been living in a world, in a paradigm of scarcity and fear of lack. Once fear of lack takes hold of the mind, it creates a hunger and a thirst that is insatiable and unquenchable. The stronger, the more intelligent, the more technologically superior have consistently exploited the weaker or simpler folk on our world over the ages. Indigenous peoples living in a natural world of abundance all around them could not conceive of the mindsets of the conquerors that came to their lands – minds and personalities with an insatiable need to hoard resources and to exploit people out of an over-arching craving to control. The very need to hoard and control was alien to the native peoples. They could not comprehend it. Their cultures fell before the subtleties, manipulations and unthinkable savage violence of the invading conquerors.

Today, we are a product of that paradigm of scarcity and fear of lack. We have been conditioned into those modes of thought and action. We have been shaped by the environment that a group of ruling elites created from their own fear, and their need to control people and resources out of that fear.

Psychopathy of various varieties has likely been a product of living in such a paradigm. Compassion and empathy get in the way when one perceives that their survival is at stake. And what constitutes survival? Whatever such a mind dreams up that it needs. All beings need love. Yet that cycles back into compassion and empathy – a terrifyingly vulnerable state to a psychopath. So instead, such individuals settle for counterfeits of love. For narcissists, as much admiration and attention as they can manipulate others into giving them, considering those others merely objects to take from. For sociopaths, it

---

[8] Jacque Fresco is a visionary futurist whose lifework has been to bring together the best of science, technology and design, including architectural design to envison a new human society based on human and environmental concerns. He shares his vision in his documentary, Future by Design. Fresco's website: http://www.thevenusproject.com. Fresco and his work were also featured in the film, Zeitgueist Addendum, available for free viewing online at Youtube.com.

is cold iron control, the intimate fascination of a snake with terrified prey in its coils, slowly squeezing the life from it. But I have to wonder, have such individuals proliferated in our current society because of the entire cultural environment created by elite factions bent on control of all the Earth's resources and people?

How would a world of free and abundant energy, food and resources shape the people who lived and were born into such an ecosystem? No more lack, enough for everyone, time for people to relax, to learn, to explore, to expand their consciousness, to be creative in ways we might not be able to even imagine from where we are now. Time for love, with no fear of love's vulnerability. Open empathy and compassion for all life. Consciousness could open and blossom like a flower. Inner and inter-dimensional awareness could expand exponentially, no longer holding itself in unconsciousness out of fear of feeling all the suffering and pain that is rampant in today's world.

So what guidelines for consequences of identified and known criminal behavior in such a new world? By what means can we place criminals in a position to encounter themselves and face up to what they have done?

Some consequences need to be imposed to impress upon those individuals the true level of pain and suffering that was inflicted upon the people of the general population.

While those with psychopathic disorders may be incapable of any shame or remorse and will have to be dealt with differently, in more concrete, black and white terms – when most peoples' crimes are revealed and inescapably confirmed, many want nothing so much as to hide their faces. They don't want to face themselves, nor do they want to see the knowing eyes of others reflecting back to them what they have done. Though they may try to cover it with anger, they often feel deeply, perhaps even unbearably, ashamed. Shame is the built-in mechanism within almost all human beings that can correct their course in life when they have gone too far astray from their own humanity.

To that end, so that such criminals of greater or lesser degree experience themselves fully revealed as such to a knowing public, I would propose that they be mandated to face the populations they have harmed through their actions.

After they have been through the tribunal process, their criminality assessed and assigned a level of 5 or above on the culpability scale, they would then be detained in custody for a time to be transported from major city to major city in each state, perhaps even capitols of other countries. In each population center, they would be exhibited to the people there, behind heavy plexiglass shielding for their protection. Residents of those cities and states could file by and look upon those responsible for deaths and suffering of up to millions. People who lost loved ones, who were made ill, who had to live with environmental devastation and toxicity as in the Gulf oil spill would have the chance to at last see and understand the full responsibility resting on those individuals – individuals who continually made decisions over the years to suppress energy alternatives so that exploitation of the environment and the general population could continue filling their coffers with wealth. While this could be called turning such people into a circus side show, I know of no other way for people to be confronted in a way that would force them to see the depth of their past misdeeds.

After going through such a confrontation with themselves and society, they could earn amnesty of gradually-increasing freedom as they demonstrate over time their desires to be meaningful and caring members of society again. If the prospect of rejoining and facing the population is too daunting, they could be offered terms of detention in special facilities for their protection as a form of amnesty once their tour of major cities was concluded.

With the very worst of the psychopathic criminals, this strategy may make no difference at all. Psychopaths generally remain unrepentant and this produces the complex problem of what level of amnesty they can or cannot be granted. These people are consummate actors and superbly staged displays of remorse attempting to play on peoples' sympathies must be scrutinized with great care. Psychopaths are fully capable of exploiting the empathy and compassion of others while secretly despising them for such "weakness." They will require a lifelong probation at best, with the offer of carefully-monitored rehabilitation always available. Perhaps creating a kind of compound for them where they have only each other to interact with and where they could be allowed to keep some of the comforts they have gained through the years, with a strongly enforced understanding that no more can be gained at the expense of other people or exploitation of Earth's resources.

While some excellent arguments could be made that some of these people deserve capital punishment for all they've done, it becomes less an issue of what they deserve than whether people creating a new world based on values and principles of caring and cooperation can afford to build the foundation of such a world on the blood sacrifice of anyone. I for one do not feel we can afford to give in to such dark impulses of retribution, and I speak from having experienced some truly horrible abuse that could certainly justify the most severe criminal consequences on the perpetrators. Having angry and vengeful impulses and working positively with the energy of them to resolve them is one thing. Acting them out and depriving the offending person of life is quite another.

Just as we aspire to a principle of unconditional love at our best, we also need to build our new culture on a principle of unconditional forgiveness. We must remember that forgiveness is even more about healing our own hearts than it is about those we are forgiving. In those others, our forgiveness does create the possibilities for a change in consciousness. It's up to them to accept and embrace that change. And for those whose criminal behavior was coerced or did not arise out of true psychopathy, counseling must be provided for them so they can someday learn to forgive themselves.

In a post-extraterrestrial contact world, I would hope for humane ways we cannot yet conceive of that extraterrestrial knowledge and medicine might provide to rehabilitate such people.

Entr'acte VII
We are Waiting for You

Now I'm here on Terra again, living another human lifetime. It hasn't been easy. But my experiences here have helped my people, living out in their lightships beyond this planet, better understand all of you. Understand what you are up against here, the trials and challenges you deal with on a daily basis. Moving through my experiences led me to the calling of my heart – what has brought me back to Terra for every earthwalk with you; my love for all the beauty and life on this world, and especially the human beings we Lyrans seeded here so very long ago.

When I leave this lifetime, I will return to my now fully-restored homeworld, Lyra. I will walk through her once-again-primeval forests, swim in her sparkling seas with the cetacean people. My heart will be filled with a joy I can know only because of all the things I've learned since I left her. Things I've learned because of coming to Terra. Things I learned through helping humanity to be born here and how very much of my heart and love I poured into this world. How caught up I became in the story of humanity unfolding.

As Gibran, the wise poet wrote in his work, The Prophet:

> The deeper that sorrow carves into your
> being, the more joy you can contain.

How can I regret sorrow when it brings me the gift of such deep joy?

I am not the only Lyran, extraterrestrial or extra-dimensional being to be engaged in this unfolding human story. There are countless numbers of us, both out in ships in near to far Earth orbit and millions of us living out lifetimes on Earth as I am now. Consciously, or even all unknowing, we bring the energy of who we are into your midst. Like human crop circles, just being here as part of you and your culture, we radiate our love and energy to touch the hearts of those in our lives, subtly shifting the whole human collective towards awakening. It is our love for you that brings us here.

As for you, we are waiting for you to grow up. To realize your birthright: Freedom. It is not any birthright we granted you, but one that is a part of you simply by virtue of your existence, as individual expressions of Source Consciousness.

In a very real and intimate way, you are us and we are you.

And we are waiting for you to join us out in the stars.

Epilogue: Closing Thoughts on Writing this Book, 2012, Ascension

The story fire is now only glowing embers.
I cannot see all the faces of those
Who have joined this circle with me.

But no matter, that.
These words have been shared.
They have been heard.

What part can you play
In building a new world?

Where there is anger,
How to harness its energy for right action?

Where there is grief,
How can you bring comfort?

Where there are wounds,
What path will you choose to heal?

Where there is division,
How can you inspire unity?

For you who have listened,
How will you now choose to live?

Earthwalk for A New Terra
~ Niara Terela Isley

I did come back to Terra. As a Lyran wanderer, one of the many, many volunteer souls who, as Dolores Cannon has discovered in her work, "heard the call."

Writing this book has been over a four-year process. It is part chronicle, part healing catharsis for me personally, part expression of how my own spirituality has informed my process and perhaps even part political manifesto. Working on this book has felt like one of the twelve labors of Hercules. Chronic physical pain I deal with daily made sitting at the computer each day a race to see how much I could get done before my back forced me from the office chair. In dredging up all the past experiences to write about them, I felt the pain and fear, the anger and grief of them all over again, in some ways more sharply than ever. After years of feeling relatively happy and content, a resurgence of intense PTSD surfaced as I confronted the past again, listening to the audios of my hypnosis sessions and working with transcriptions for this book. I relived the pain of what it was like to wander through society as an isolated outsider, most people just not able to accept that the kinds of things that happened to me can happen at all. Just going to the grocery store was an ordeal through the seemingly endless months of work on parts one and two.

I wove all my emotions and feelings into my writing, in the hopes of giving you, my readers, a vicarious experience of what I went through. While I would never wish the terrible parts of my experiences on anyone, if people do not understand something of what it's like to go through them at a deeper level than a simply intellectual one, how will they be motivated to create positive change in our society, in our world?

There is a great deal of information packed into this book, some of it disturbing to downright frightening. I don't wish for anyone to give into fear, but to use the information and techniques I've tried to illustrate to move beyond fear – to make intelligent and informed choices about how you choose to live and take care of yourselves, your families and your communities. Stop looking to any authority figures – government, religious or others – to take care of you, especially in any exclusive manner. How best can you take care of yourselves? By doing your best to drink clean water and eat healthy, clean foods and standing up for your right to have them according to your own courage and conscience – in the face of whatever adversity presents itself. By developing your intuition and learning about how energy and information feels – is it resonant? Dissonant? And what do you discern from that resonance or dissonance? What is the first impulse, flash of insight, intuition or inspiration that jumps into your mind? If it feels right, if it resonates for you, can you find the courage and means to follow it?

My friend Mark Kimmel said to me recently, "Some day Niara, you're going to have to stop writing this book and publish it." How right he was! Yet it has been important for me to not only share my experiences, but who it really was that they happened to and where they have taken me. I have been encouraged to split this book into two volumes, but this book could not be truly complete without including the awakenings I've experienced as a result of it all. I have reached that transformational point where I would not trade any part of my life as it has been because of the gift of who I am becoming. The trauma is like a clinging vine with hundreds of tendrils that wrapped themselves throughout my life. I have untangled and unwound so many of them, freeing this part and that part of my life from their hold. As I bump into new ones, I work on untangling them and clearing them as well. It might take the rest of this lifetime to truly purge them all. If it does, then so be it. I am committed to the process and to accomplishing it with joy.

The awakenings I experience and have shared are a fulfillment of the journey I agreed to upon undertaking this lifetime. A fulfillment that continues to evolve and expand daily. I am very excited to finish this book, this process, and see where life takes me next.

It is up to my readers to decide what they think and how they feel about my story. I truly feel I am a wanderer – an ET soul who took on a human lifetime for a special purpose. It was a long time and a lot of peeling away of layers of experience, and opening to ever more of the multidimensional universe to get to that understanding, but my wanderer self feels as real to me today as any other memory or part of my life. I know some readers may think I have constructed an elaborate personal mythology here, and that is fine with me. If I'm in error, then it's an error that does no harm and has done me tremendous good.

I would much prefer that people do not simply believe all this at first glance. I would rather that they take what is in this book and do their own research. I would hope that they begin to apply some of the insights I share and see where this might take them in their own lives – become students of their own minds, emotions and intuition. Become sovereign individuals in their own right. Run everything through their feeling filters, including this book. Learn personal discernment, but not from the mind. Learn and feel the movements of energy in the body. Our bodies are living, bio-electric wonders, connected to an entire multidimensional and conscious Universe. They are sending and receiving antennae. This is only natural. If the Conscious Loving, Living Universe wanted to learn and set up the multiverse as a vehicle for learning, and we are all individuated units of consciousness within the multiverse, then sending and receiving information constantly is like being part of the nervous system of that Living Universe or Source Consciousness. As above, so below. We are a smaller model of a greater whole.

I do not feel I am anyone particularly special. If there truly are ET wanderers on Earth, as I have come to trust that there are, then I am just one of millions on this world today, each of them simply holding a loving space for humanity and doing their personal missions. I am an ordinary person who has had extraordinary experiences and has done her best to respond and evolve where they led me, without becoming mired in bitterness or despair, or going into denial. Each of us, whether public or private people, are doing our part in some way.

Many times while writing this book, I have been moved to tears as the understanding becomes inescapable, at least to me, that I am truly an ET soul who took on this human lifetime so my people would have a greater understanding of human beings, and perhaps, to pass on some of my knowledge and understanding to those I have lived among this whole lifetime. I have lived here as a human being for 58 years. There have been times in the writing of this book when what flowed onto the page has often caused me to get up, walk away from the computer and just spend time allowing the knowing to sink in. I have also become aware in recent years of other multidimensional contact with very loving benevolent beings who appear to me much more like other human beings, though more slender, luminescent and ethereal. This contact does not take place in the physical realm, but in a fourth or fifth dimensional realm. I hope to explore more of this contact once the task of finishing this book is complete.

My dream job would be to someday serve as a liaison between extraterrestrial civilizations and our military and government, mediating, creating connection and understanding, and helping to usher in a new age of egalitarian prosperity on this planet, with an ecosystem healed and restored by proper use and application of free energy technology.

Our Natural State of Being... Freedom

In the beginning of this book I talked of energy flow, and how energy wants to flow freely. When it hits blockages in our energy field, this conscious energy of the cosmos, embodied within us, begins to synchronistically attract the people, places and situations that can that can inform and inspire us to remove and heal the blockage, allowing energy to run free again. In the film *Thrive*, we were given the model of a torus of free-flowing energy and how that energy can be afflicted by a "tapeworm" – a parasite that wants to control or cut off that flow of energy. But it cannot be cut off or controlled indefinitely. This energy is far bigger than any control that can be put on it and it will break free. Each of us are that torus of free-flowing energy, and we are part of a larger network of the same energy. The more absolute the forms of control clamped around the energy trying to flow, the greater the pressure build-up is to break through the control. It cannot be otherwise. This is why I shared in the chapter on "Reclaiming Freedom" that freedom is who we are in our most essential state of being, and not a condition that can be granted to us or taken away from us.

Post-December 21, 2012... Still Here

From seconds to entire ages, time flows continuously and mysteriously forward, disappearing into eternity.

"Time" in these past few decades just happens to be a ticking countdown of passage through a portal we have all wondered about – December 21, 2012. This momentus date came and went with no apparent ascension, nor with any doomsday catastrophes.

How significant was the December 21, 2012 date, or the times and events swirling around it? I feel we are in a corridor of time symbolized by 12/21/2012. This corridor has extended out decades before that date and may extend for a decade or more after its passage. We are talking about vast stretches of galactic or cosmic time after all, not the seconds, minutes or hours that tick by on our earthly clocks.

There were many dire predictions about 12/21/2012 and many amazing "prophecies of light." Could these simply be humanity's insecurities, trying to somehow "know" or predict the future so that they can be "prepared" – whether for prophecies of light or for those of doom – or a little of both? For me, the truth is that none of us can truly know what is going to happen or how. At the cyclic turn of this major 24 to 26 thousand year galactic alignment, I feel intuitively that the energies upon which our world are formed are very fluid at this time, very responsive to our consciousness and almost impossible to predict. Humanity's collective consciousness creates the material world we live in from the quantum field and it also shapes how our future will unfold. As we move into this new great cycle, rather than a "lightning" strike effect of instantaneous change occurring on a single calendar date, it could be that a "lightening" effect will occur gradually for all humanity, our collective consciousness moving together in directions that mean more awareness and more awakening. However it occurs, circumstances on our world are contributing to that awakening as more and more secrets are revealed.

We have been in the vibration of "The Shift of the Ages" for some time, as early as the Harmonic Convergence back in 1987, over two decades ago, or perhaps even earlier, in the 1960s. Like countless others, I found it fascinating to take samplings of all the different perceptions and interpretations of what might happen. But I always remember the counsel of my own spirit guides for these times:

> *Stay very present, very centered in these times and then you will be able to respond to "the moment." As much as possible, simply be in the present and be like the Great Void, empty, waiting for the spark that will ignite you, that will illuminate your next steps on your path. As much as possible, keep yourself balanced, neutral, empty. Like a cup waiting to be filled with a nectar, you will know and choose in the moment it comes to you.*

> *If you must, go ahead and invest your energy in the best and most loving visions of the future you can imagine, while also understanding that the best and most loving vision of the*

494

future is still influenced by the limitations of living a lifetime on Earth in the third dimension, and perhaps limited by those experiences. Always add to your imaginings, "this, or something even better that I cannot imagine... yet."

Trying to predict the future can be a trap, trapping you into the future you are trying to predict, especially in light of recent research into quantum-observer-effect implications of thought, feeling and intention held in our conscious awareness. What thoughts, emotions and feelings move through you as you regard the future? What visions are you charging and energizing with your emotions? If you must attempt to plot your future through these extraordinary and uncertain times, do so from love and cultivating inner peace.

From conscious, loving action the future world will take shape, step by step. Something else I've done to the best of my ability – an absolute necessity as a whistleblower – is to make peace with my own mortality. I consider it vital to keep my heart-centered communications current – letting all the people in my life who are important to me know that I love them, that any and all disagreements are forgiven and to act with caring and compassion towards others. I accept that I "just don't know" how things are going to happen from 12/21/2012 onwards. But I can cultivate peace and responsiveness from within – even if it means I'm a casualty of these times.

I never really felt that there was going to be a huge ascension "event" on this date, though I confess, I hoped there would be. Who wouldn't want some relief and rescue from such an unstable maelstrom as Planet Earth seems today? What we *are* doing now is moving from the Piscean Age into the Age of Aquarius. I do feel Earth is traversing into a region of space and alignment with the galactic core which can bring positive changes that will expand over time. But I think it was a big set up for disappointment to hang so many hopes on a single date for some kind of "ascension" event – where none of us could possibly really know or envision how it was going to truly look or feel. We are also collectively caught up in the momentum of a world we've been part of our entire lives, with all its turmoil and foment distracting and diluting our attention.

Nothing can really absolve us of the responsibility we must take for our own lives and how we conduct ourselves in the world. With changes in energies and frequencies we all have *opportunities* to help create shift in this world by where we put our thoughts and intentions, and by the loving actions we take with those around us, even when it's difficult and challenging. So the old saying really applies – if we want a new world, each of us individually must be the change we wish to see in the world, especially when it is very difficult emotionally to accomplish. Positive actions speak to the Conscious Living Universe in the most powerful way and the more of us that stay that course of loving action, the more positive change we will see happening over time. It's time for lightworkers of all kinds to roll up their sleeves and get down to the real work of creating a better world. There are a million different ways we each feel called upon to offer loving service to our fellow humans and this world.

As time rolls onwards and consciousness continues to expand, catching hold more and more in the human collective, we may see some truly remarkable things unfold in the coming years. Pinning it to specific dates and times is fine. However, designated dates and times are in themselves nexus points – catalysts – for the initiation of a process whose real depth and meaning will manifest later, after the current birthing period. It may even only be fully realized in hindsight and reflection.

Ascension

What is ascension? When will it manifest? How? What will it feel like, look like, sound like? Many of us, like blind people feeling our way with new developing faculties, are getting some sense of this, even if still unformed and unarticulated deep within ourselves. Now is a time for paying attention to our intuitive impulses and following them whenever we possibly can.

Is ascension written into the very code of our DNA? Is it being catalyzed from without by photons, light energy from our overactive Sun, and also streaming to us from the galactic core? Is it being activated by patterns in crop circles that we study and try to understand, while the underground water tables they appear over are imprinted with an energy that makes its way into all the water on our planet, including that within our own bodies?

Is ascension being activated from within every time we choose a loving action or state of being over a fearful one? If, as discovered in laboratories, DNA is mutable and responsive to what we hold in our thoughts and feelings, can we learn to choose from the love and wisdom of our hearts and spirits? All we need do is look into the eyes of our children and begin to envision the world we want for them, one creatively-loving thought at a time. Like the indigenous people of the Earth, we become the present generation creating the world to come for the next seven generations.

Maybe ascension is simply awakening, at a full-body level, to who we really are and restoring our conscious ability to access other dimensions.

***

One historical and pivotal place humanity's awakening will take us is that expansion of consciousness that Bob Dean spoke of which could occur because of extraterrestrial contact. I wonder myself if this will happen because of extraterrestrial contact, or if contact will happen because humanity, pushed by the circumstances unfolding on the Earth right now, will evolve to the point that will create the energetic bridge or common ground upon which contact can finally take place. And by some accounts, an extraterrestrial "quarantine" imposed upon humanity on Planet Earth has been lifted as of 12/21/2012.

I feel strongly that contact with extraterrestrials will be about finding out who we humans really are, at last.

Extraterrestrials and their craft move in multidimensional ways and cannot be understood in only 3D empirical terms. If we want to understand ETs, we must understand ourselves better at the most fundamental levels of matter, energy and vibration. We are threads (superstrings?) within the infinite tapestry of this multidimensional cosmos throughout our very energetic structure. Whether aware of it or not, we exist on every vibrational density and dimension. We must continue to grow in our understanding of this infinite, conscious, multidimensional universe.

The expansion of consciousness is something the darker forces of this world fear like nothing else. The prospect of it has them resorting to the drastic and extreme measures we see around us. It means an end to their power, to their control. The chaos swirling about us at this time – wars, economic recession and so much more I've already shared – are all symptoms of the true and only war going on on this planet – a war on the awareness expansion of human consciousness.

Yet if we can learn to truly see and deeply listen on multiple levels; if we can learn to energetically discern, to come to truly understand ourselves, then all the chaos is simply the correct evolutionary pressure at the right fulcrum in Time to create the expansion of consciousness needed to free us. When consciousness quickens to a new level of sentient awareness, contact with spiritually evolved, benevolent extraterrestrials becomes possible and probable. We will have reached the point where we can begin to comprehend who they are and who we are in relationship to them. We will understand ourselves in a way that will open the door to meaningful contact and communication that can be heard, felt and appreciated for what it is. We need to remember we are dealing with perhaps several different extraterrestrial cultures. Spoken words alone, out of mental or egoic constructs limited by the narrow awareness of the conscious human mind, may not suffice to create understanding. Instead, resonant energies and vibrating in sensitivity and entrainment with each other can be understood in a multidimensional sense that could make misunderstanding impossible. The key is in discerning true intuition flowing from our calm, clear spirit center, and learning to distinguish intuition from a purely emotional reaction at either end of a spectrum, from fear to bliss. We must also learn to pinpoint and avoid getting caught in the webs of logic and analysis from the mind – this can only take us so far before it leads to a dead end. Identify, distinguish, discern and acknowledge – then breathe deeply and return to the calm center of your being.

As Ram Dass taught us, *Be Here Now*. The past is gone and the future is not here yet, though we can be paralyzed in the Now by ruminations of the past and dread or anticipation of the future. The present is the only true moment where positive action really counts.

The Really Real Truth

As in trying to know extraterrestrials and know ourselves, the really real truth of life and existence cannot be known by only 3D empirical standards. I have found that I have to reach beyond everything I have ever learned, everything I think I know. I have to be still and listen with my whole body, my entire energy system, for what the Cosmos might whisper there.

I cannot imagine ever ceasing to learn, grow and expand. To stop is to give in to entropy, to cease to be.

I've also had to unlearn so very much. I have thrown certain parcels of information into my mental trashcan only to go back and retrieve them later on, to reconsider them from a new place in myself. My mind, which I developed so well in the first half of my life, I have had to learn to quiet and still in the second half of my life to allow new insight and understanding to enter. And to open the doors and windows of my soul to what is "out there." As an adventurous youngster with the heart of an explorer, I once wanted to be an astronaut and go to Mars. Today, I intuitively find very little difference between the vastness of outer space and the equal vastness of inner space. Who knows but what we see through our telescopes is just what we expect to see? Who knows but that life on Earth is a collection of individuated units of consciousness, a noosphere creating our world from the movement of our own thought for our own play and learning? A collective consciousness that creates and makes "solid" the world under our feet and the society in which we move, breathe and love.

I poured heart, soul and love for this planet and all life into this book and still wonder, is it "enough?" Unknown. But this never was or could be a one-person effort. It is up to all of us to make shift happen. Each of us being the change we want to see in the world, teaching by loving example.

While dealing with the grief and rage of my traumas I thought any and all innocence I ever had was torn away and shredded, never to be part of me again. But in retrieving the lost parts of my spirit I discovered a new innocence, wonder and awe, a deeper understanding of the Universe that came through healing. I just now begin to understand all the differing elements and energies that make up the Conscious Living and Loving Universe. At the highest and broadest cosmic level, all of it exists for my soul's growth, for all of our souls' growth.

I pass to you these words in greeting, in blessing, and until we meet again in pages or in person: Mitakoye Oyasin... We are All Related. [Lakota]. In'lakesh... I am Another Yourself. [Mayan]. Namaste'... The Divine in Me Bows to the Divine in You. [Hindu].

Much Love,
Niara